GW00535727

Jane Ainsworth's Memorial Book tells the stories of the 76 Old Boys of Barnsley Holgate Grammar School who died as a result of their involvement in the First World War. It also includes a history of the grammar school, its headmaster and extracts from *Alumnus* magazine. Barnsley Holgate Grammar School was prestigious and its first headmaster, Reverend Charles Stokes Butler, was inspirational. The Old Boys felt a strong loyalty and affection for their school and this feeling was reciprocated by the teachers and other pupils. During the First World War, details of all those serving their country were recorded in the Old Boys' Association magazine *Alumnus*, which was sent to men fighting at the front along with copies of the *Barnsley Chronicle*. Many of the men in the forces visited their old school when home on their precious leave and some contributed articles and letters about their experiences, which have been reproduced in this book. Jane was determined to create a Memorial Book that was different from others and the breadth of her research clearly demonstrates how she has achieved this. She has told the men's life stories in as much detail as possible, concentrating on their family and personal development as well as experiences during the war. It is important to remember that 42 additional brothers served and five of these died, as did three brothers-in-law. The invaluable contributions from *Alumnus* and many obituaries from newspapers allow us to get to know these men as real people. Jane's aim is for these young men to be remembered as individuals, who could have achieved so much more if they had survived the sacrifice of their valuable lives for their country. Attending the Holgate encouraged the majority to go on to achieve their potential after school, with a lot becoming teachers. It instilled in them the values that led to early enlistment and rapid promotion in the forces. This is what united them – not the disparate "resting places" for their bodies, whether buried in a foreign grave or just a name on a War Memorial overseas. They were all much loved as sons, brothers, friends, colleagues, Old Boys of various educational establishments, husbands and fathers.

Jane Ainsworth was born in Hoyland in South Yorkshire, but spent most of her life living elsewhere until she and husband Paul decided to return to Barnsley for their (early) retirement. Jane was brought up in Chorley, Lancashire, then went to York University, where she obtained a BA degree in English and Related Literature. She then worked for many years in the Housing and Social Services Departments of Councils in the Cambridge area. Jane's passionate interest in family history research has developed over the last 13 years with a growing fascination for local history and the First World War. When Jane decided to research the Barnsley Holgate Grammar School War Memorial for the Centenary, she had no idea how difficult it would be to identify then research the lives of 76 strangers. However, she was determined to pay tribute to these brave young men by finding out as much as possible about them all. Although she has written a number of published articles on various subjects, this Memorial Book is Jane's first book and it is the result of more than two years' dedicated and almost all-consuming research. These men and their relations so far discovered now feel like Jane's own extended family.

Great Sacrifice

The Old Boys of Barnsley Holgate Grammar School in the First World War

Jane Ainsworth

Best Wishes

Jane Ainsworth

Helion & Company Limited

Helion & Company Limited
26 Willow Road
Solihull
West Midlands
B91 1UE
England
Tel. 0121 705 3393
Fax 0121 711 4075
Email: info@helion.co.uk
Website: www.helion.co.uk
Twitter: @helionbooks
Visit our blog http://blog.helion.co.uk/

Published by Helion & Company 2016
Designed and typeset by Mach 3 Solutions Ltd, Bussage, Gloucestershire
Cover designed by Paul Hewitt, Battlefield Design (www.battlefield-design.co.uk)
Printed by Hobbs The Printers Ltd, Totton, Hampshire

Text © Jane Ainsworth 2016
Images © as individually credited. Adverts, cartoons and several newspaper articles in *Barnsley Independent* and *Barnsley Chronicle* have been added by their kind permission.

Every reasonable effort has been made to trace copyright holders and to obtain their permission for the use of copyright material. The author and publisher apologise for any errors or omissions in this work, and would be grateful if notified of any corrections that should be incorporated in future reprints or editions of this book.

Front cover: Rev Charles Stokes Butler with a group of pupils c1905, photograph reproduced by kind permission of Memories of Barnsley; colour postcard of Barnsley Grammar School from the Author's collection. Rear cover: the Name Calling Ceremony for Remembrance Day 2014, photograph kindly provided by *Barnsley Chronicle* ©; Rev Butler with pupils c1905, photograph kindly provided by Barnsley Archives.

ISBN 978-1-911096-08-5

British Library Cataloguing-in-Publication Data.
A catalogue record for this book is available from the British Library.

All rights reserved. No part of this publication may be reproduced, stored in a retrieval system, or transmitted, in any form, or by any means, electronic, mechanical, photocopying, recording or otherwise, without the express written consent of Helion & Company Limited.

For details of other military history titles published by Helion & Company Limited contact the above address, or visit our website: http://www.helion.co.uk.

We always welcome receiving book proposals from prospective authors.

I dedicate this book to my parents: John Charles Hardy and Edith nee Firth. Dad was a Secondary School History Teacher and Priest, born in Elsecar to a family of Miners; mum was a Primary School Teacher, born to the younger son of C Firth & Sons Plumbers & Decorators of Hoyland. Thank you for supporting me to obtain a good education, for encouraging me to be 'my own person' and for inspiring in me a love of family, heritage and art.

My book is also in tribute to my two great uncles Bob and Sheriff, from Elsecar and Hoyland, who sacrificed their lives in the First World War, both aged only 20. Researching their much too short lives stimulated my interest in the Great War.

Lance Corporal Charles Robert Hardy served with the 2/5th Battalion of the York & Lancaster Regiment and was killed in action on 3 May 1917; his name is on the Arras Memorial.

Private George Sheriff Bailey served with the 41st Field Ambulance of the Royal Army Medical Corps in Mesopotamia; he died of an infection on 22 May 1918 and was buried in Baghdad War Cemetery.

I will remember you all with love and gratitude.
Jane

Contents

Forewords

G B (Barry) Jackson
Old Boy of BHGS, Retired History Teacher, President of Cawthorne Jubilee Museum

From 1946 to 1954 I was a pupil at the Barnsley and District Holgate Grammar School; a school which nurtured in generations of working class boys a love of scholarship and the pursuit of knowledge, and sent me and thirteen of my contemporaries to either Oxford or Cambridge University.

During those years I attended and listened to the reading out of the names of ex-pupils who had died in the two World Wars. For the last fifteen years of the building's existence as Holgate School, a mixed 11 to 16 comprehensive, I was privileged to represent Barnsley Grammar School Old Boys' Association at the Remembrance Service and read all seven verses of Laurence Binyon's poem "For the Fallen". Now, thanks to Jane Ainsworth's thorough and patient research, these boys are no longer merely names upon a board.

As Binyon's poem says:

They went with songs to the battle, they were young,
Straight of limb, true of eye, steady and aglow,
They were staunch to the end against odds uncounted,
They fell with their faces to the foe.

Thanks to Jane's work they now have personalities and, wherever possible, photographs. Of them it can quite truthfully be said: 'We will remember them'.

Nick Bowen
Principal of Horizon Community College

Horizon Community College is proud to continue the traditions established at Holgate Grammar School in honouring the brave young men who attended the grammar school and who fought and died for their country.

It is important that Barnsley, and in particular the young people of Barnsley, remember and pay tribute to the brave young men who were educated where the current generation are now educated, who lived where they now live and who fought for this to be possible.

Continuing the traditions of the name-calling ceremony along with the detailed story of each of the men outlined in this book, will help today's students to understand and appreciate the sacrifice they made. We are committed to keeping their memory alive, learning from the lessons of the past and helping our students today to understand that the casualties of war are real men and women, with names and families and with hopes and dreams unfulfilled.

Methodology

From early 2013, I spent many hours in Barnsley Archives exploring, photographing and transcribing records in the Holgate Collection and local newspapers, especially the digitized *Barnsley Chronicle* and *Barnsley Independent* on microfilm. I was fortunate that *Alumnus* magazines had photographs of 42 of the Old Boys and that quite a few were in old newspapers. None of these photographs are of high quality and they were difficult to reproduce, but I feel that any image of each individual is better than none. *Alumnus* and various newspapers also provided obituaries for most of the men but, unfortunately, I was unable to find photographs and obituaries for all of them

Even more hours have flown by while using my home computer to access resources available on the internet. I consulted the various informative free websites such as Commonwealth War Graves Commission, FreeBMD, the Long Long Trail, Wikipedia, the National Archives, several 'memorial' websites and Google search. My subscriptions to Ancestry, Find My Past and the Genealogist proved invaluable in fleshing out the Old Boys' stories, especially as a wide range of new First World War records continued to be added. I searched for births, marriages and deaths on FreeBMD and used details where I felt sure there was a suitable match. I tried to find the names of children who had died, as recorded on the 1911 Census, but on many occasions there were too many possibilities listed to use any of them.

I contacted any relatives I found, most via Ancestry, so that we could exchange information and photos; I have kept in touch with those who are interested to do so. I enjoy meeting them and I have been encouraged by their positive feedback on my work.

I also sent out a bombardment of emails to Archivists at Universities, Colleges, Schools, Banks and Local Archives around the country to help verify details and provide substance to the men's lives; the majority of them have done this for me with enthusiasm and without charge, for which I am very grateful.

I visited several churches, churchyards and cemeteries in the Barnsley area and beyond to photograph headstones and memorials related to my Old Boys and their families.

Officer Records are held in the National Archives at Kew and, unfortunately, they have not been digitized. As 27 Old Boys were officers, there were too many files for

At Wentworth Castle in 2014 with members of the Batley family. (© Jane Ainsworth)

Meeting Bob Hadfield, great nephew of Frank Hall, at Darfield Museum in 2015. (© Jane Ainsworth)

me to view at Kew or to buy copies of, but three relations obtained copies and kindly lent them to me.

There are many books and websites about the different Regiments, Royal Air Force and Royal Navy, the multifarious battles around the world and details of the War Cemeteries and Memorials. These have been compiled by people and organisations with far more expertise than I have so I have provided few such details in my book.

I take full responsibility for my research, which I have attempted to carry out as accurately as possible. If there are any errors I will be pleased to correct them if I am provided with supporting evidence.

Men Who Left Little Trace

I have made every effort to find out as much as possible about each Old Boy and I have been especially diligent in trying to find photographs and obituaries for the few whose stories seem rather scant. Frustrated by my lack of success with some men, I have had to accept that some people leave few records, particularly when they die young, and that different families dealt with their tragic loss in a variety of ways. I have drawn parallels with my own family to understand this better, but we can only guess 100 years later at the impact of this war on those left behind.

My great uncle George Sheriff Bailey's father lived all of his life in Hoyland, where all his 10 children were born; Edwin Hall and Julia Mary Bailey died in Hoyland and were buried in the Kirk Balk Cemetery. However, I have found no mention of their son's death in *Barnsley Chronicle* or other newspapers, who advertised that they would print details submitted. I have a copy of the photograph taken of Sheriff in uniform and must assume that his parents chose not to send it to *Barnsley Chronicle* for inclusion in May 1918. (During the main battles newspapers would have been inundated and probably would have been unable to publish all they were sent). I cannot believe that my great grandparents were unaware of the creation of the Hoyland War Memorial and yet Sheriff's name was not included on it, so I wonder if they found the prospect of seeing his name each time they walked past it too painful? Sheriff's name was added to their headstone as a memorial in the 1930s, a common custom since most families were unable to travel to France or Belgium to visit a grave, even if there was one, and visiting a cemetery in Mesopotamia (where Sheriff is buried) or other far flung Theatre of War would have been impossible. Two of his siblings named sons George Sheriff after their beloved brother, using the unusual 'Sheriff', and again this is a tribute that quite a lot of siblings adopted.

Photographs

Where these have not been attributed to anyone else they are my own. Almost all images of records in Barnsley Archives are from my own photographs, with the exception of photos from *Barnsley Chronicle* and *Barnsley Independent* plus the 1797 Enclosure Map, which are my scans of paper copies.

A few photographs are copyright but all others are used in my book by special permission of the owners. NO photographs or images are to be copied or reproduced without the specific consent of the originator.

New Information

I hope to find out more about some of the Old Boys whose life stories have seemed elusive and I am keen to have contact with more relations in future. If anyone is a relation or has any additional information or photographs of the Old Boys or their immediate family, I would be delighted if you could contact me me via Helion & Company or Barnsley Archives.

Acknowledgements

I am extremely grateful to a huge number of people, most of whom are acknowledged in relevant chapters for specific information, records or photographs. General thanks are due to the people listed below.

Paul Ainsworth, my husband, encouraged me when faced with unexpected difficulties; he was a sounding board, diligently proof-read several times and put up with my total preoccupation with this project for a period of nearly three years.

Amanda Stoner, Supervisor at the Cooper Art Gallery in 2013, showed me the Barnsley Holgate Grammar School First World War Memorial and was enthusiastic about my initiative from the start.

David Blunden, Gillian Nixon, Michael Hardy and Mark Levitt in Barnsley Archives and Local Studies Department gave me a lot of help with my searches. I am especially grateful to Archivist Paul Stebbing for his continuous support, answering specific enquiries, alerting me to new records and giving me permission to reproduce documents, mainly from the Barnsley Holgate Grammar School Collection, from my own photographs.

Barnsley Chronicle and *Barnsley Independent* newspaper archives have been invaluable for articles, obituaries and photographs; Jon Cooksey's *Barnsley Pals* provided a wealth of background information and I appreciate his generosity and that of his publishers Pen & Sword for allowing me to use some of his research and photographs.

The Tasker Trust kindly gave me permission to use photographs of the old Grammar School building and several business premises in Barnsley, for which they hold the copyright. Edward George Tasker (1910–1989, aged 78) was a Photographic Dealer in New Street, who had the vision in the 1960s of recording Barnsley's history. He took photographs of all the business premises in the town centre and wrote a fascinating series of books: *Barnsley Streets* (Pen and Sword). His collection forms the basis of the searchable website: taskertrust.co.uk.

In May 2015, after Paul and I did a Battlefield Tour to the Western Front, I contacted the Thiepval Memorial Project to offer to share some of my research with them. Pam and Ken Linge had some new information about four of my Old Boys on the Thiepval Memorial, which they have kindly allowed me to use in this book. I have another 13 Old Boys named on the Thiepval Memorial and I will share my detailed research with them; none of these men are included in their book *Missing But Not*

Forgotten published by Pen and Sword (September 2015), which tells the stories of 300 of the 12,000 men on their database.

For different reasons and at various stages of my project, I have appreciated the help of Jeff Chambers, Mike Cotton, Brian McArthur, John Puddephatt, Brian Sawyer, Peter Shields, Sue Smith and Barnsley MBC Bereavement Services.

I am very grateful to many University, Bank and Local Archivists for responding to my enquiries and for their generosity in searching records free of charge; they have allowed me to use material, photos and even art works in my Memorial Book. A lot of them sent me photographs of War Memorials showing the names of my Old Boys, which I have a personal interest in but not enough space here to include; I have listed all the ones I am aware of and I am glad that the men are remembered in so many different places.

Introduction

I was born in Hoyland, the fourth generation of families from Elsecar and Hoyland with most of my ancestral roots in the West Riding of Yorkshire. Although I had lived for 50 years elsewhere, the pull of Yorkshire was strong and my husband Paul and I decided to retire to Barnsley in November 2012.

By early 2013, I decided I wanted to carry out a project locally to commemorate the centenary of the outbreak of the First World War. Having a lifelong interest in art, the coincidence of the Cooper Art Gallery's 100th Anniversary of opening in the original Barnsley Grammar School building on 31 July 2014 resulted in my choice of researching in detail the 76 names of the Old Boys on the War Memorial displayed in the gallery.

I naively assumed that a Barnsley Roll of Honour would help me to identify the men so I was shocked to discover that there wasn't one. This led to my idea to create one and I began by finding out about war memorials in Barnsley, working entirely on my own for several months to locate, photograph and record names etc. I donated my files and photograph albums to Barnsley Archives on 11 November 2013 and sent copies on CD to the Imperial War Museum to update their records. I subsequently organized a meeting for all my contacts to find other volunteers interested to help me with this important research. I founded the Barnsley War Memorials Project at this meeting with the aim of eventually producing a fully searchable Roll of Honour for Barnsley; this work has continued since then with the input of many other people.

In the meantime, Paul Stebbing, Archives and Local Studies Officer, told me about the Holgate Records in Barnsley Archives and kindly allowed me access to them before they had been catalogued. The Admission Registers provided me with a wealth of information about the men's formative years, as did the Staff Registers when I discovered that two of the Old Boys had been teachers.

A former Librarian told me about the *Alumnus* magazines, which are an invaluable source of information for the period from 1914 to 1919. They contain photos, obituaries and fascinating letters and articles; I have transcribed those written by the Old Boys themselves and their brothers in this book but there is more treasure to mine from other members of staff and former pupils who survived. The content of *Alumnus* throughout the First World War stands as another Memorial to all of the students and teachers who served their King and Country. I was greatly moved at reading the words

Barnsley Pals marching in Barnsley, photograph kindly provided by the Tasker Trust (copyright).

of these intelligent, entertaining, brave men facing extremely difficult and uncomfortable challenges with such good grace – I wish I could have known them.

My parents taught me the value of a good education, having 'escaped' their respective family tradition of having to find employment after leaving school. They both won a scholarship to Ecclesfield Grammar School then continued their education to achieve qualifications to become teachers. (Dad's History degree studies at Sheffield University were interrupted by service in the Royal Navy in the Second World War). I attended Chorley Grammar School then York University and was fortunate to continue my professional development with a long career in local government in Cambridgeshire. I admire my Old Boys and their families for persisting with their further education at a time when boys often started work at the age of 12 and when many could only afford the school fees because they won a scholarship.

Barnsley Holgate Grammar School was prestigious and its first headmaster, Reverend Charles Stokes Butler, was inspirational. I have, therefore, included here a detailed history of the Grammar School and I have also told the story of its influential headmaster, whom the Old Boys respected.

I was inspired to tell the men's life stories concentrating on their family and personal development as well as experiences during the war. I want these young men to be remembered as individuals, who could have achieved so much more if they had survived serving their country. Attending the Holgate encouraged the majority to go on to achieve their potential after school and instilled in them the values that led to early enlistment and rapid promotion in the forces. Many of them appreciated their attendance at the grammar school and felt such a close bond with the staff that they visited them when home on their precious leave; they were sent copies of *Alumnus* overseas, as well as *Barnsley Chronicle*, and contributed to it. This is what united them – not the disparate 'resting places' for their bodies, whether buried in a foreign grave or lying unidentified in the fields around the Western Front with their name on a War Memorial overseas. They were all much loved as sons, brothers, friends, colleagues, Old Boys of various educational establishments, husbands and fathers.

As I delved into their family history, different sources highlighted that 42 brothers and four brothers-in-law served in the forces in the First World War, some of whom died; 32 brothers attended the Holgate and 20 of these were amongst those who also served. I have, therefore, included information about all of these men, along with details of other teachers at the Holgate who joined the Forces.

Some close relatives – such as fathers, a grandfather, a sister and an uncle – held significant roles in the public life of Barnsley so I researched them in greater detail. There were many connections between the Old Boys or other members of the different families and I have noted a lot of these.

Every Old Boy was an individual but I was interested to collate information about things they had in common as well as their differences. My main statistics are in the Appendices.

I am only too aware from researching my own family history that it is practically impossible to ever complete the stories of individuals. New information comes to light from a variety of sources, whether from discovering new family members, different recollections being shared, visits to relevant locations, finding more records in local archives or because of new records becoming available on the internet. I donated my original research in two display books to the Cooper Gallery at their centenary celebrations on 31 July 2014 then updated it before presenting my Memorial Book to Barnsley Archives on 2 December 2014. I subsequently added a lot more information from my continued research and contact with many other archives over the last year.

I am grateful to two relations, Deborah Toft and Adrienne McEnhill, who had just agreed to back me financially to get copies of my Memorial Book printed until serendipity intervened in August 2015. (Unfortunately, there are no sources of funding available to sole researchers like me for carrying out these projects and it is expensive to get copies made on your own).

Above all I am indebted to Duncan Rogers for his interest in my research and his keenness to publish it. His advice, flexibility and encouragement made my first experience as an author a very positive one. Thank you!

Jane Ainsworth
December 2015

Part 1

Barnsley Grammar School

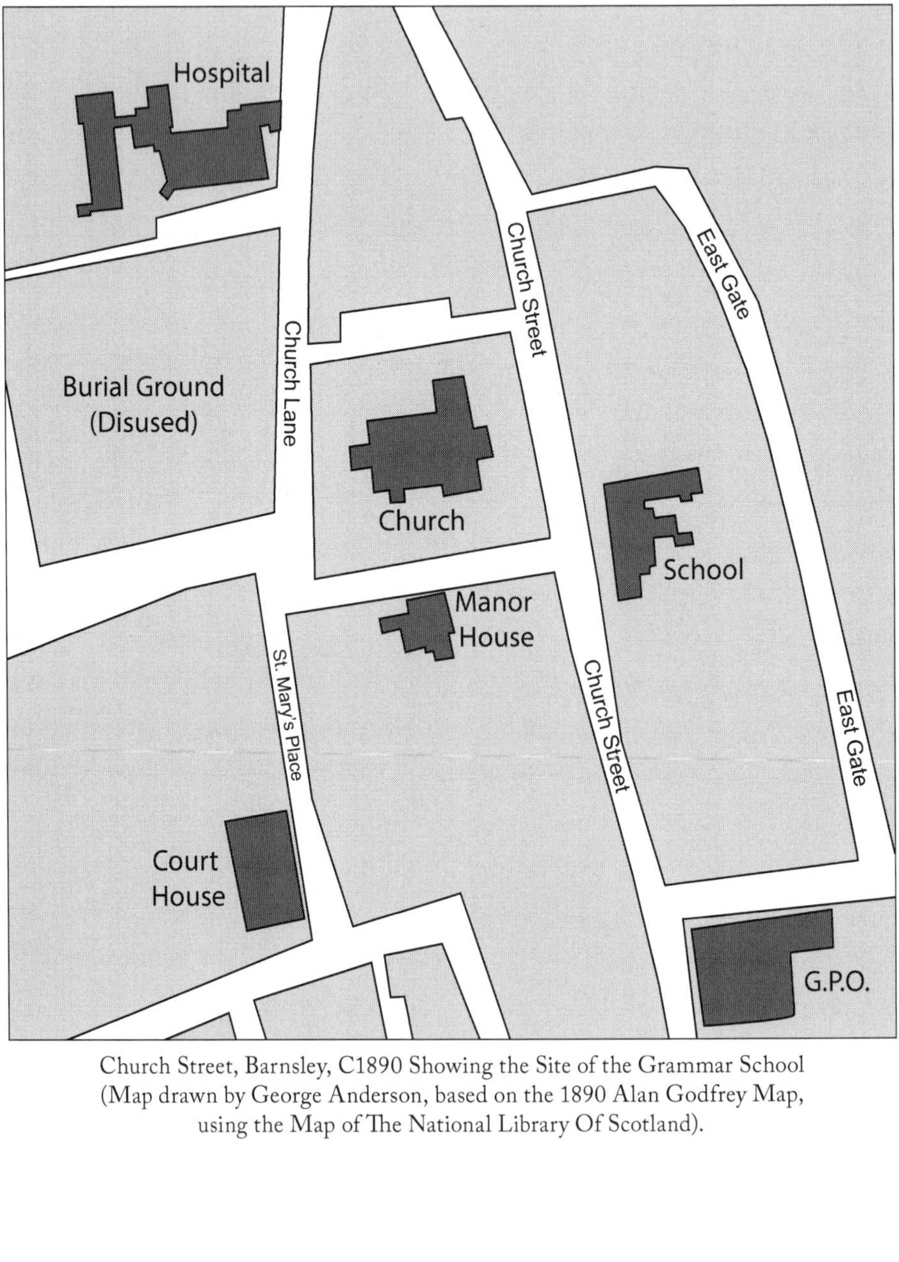

Church Street, Barnsley, C1890 Showing the Site of the Grammar School (Map drawn by George Anderson, based on the 1890 Alan Godfrey Map, using the Map of The National Library Of Scotland).

1

The History of Barnsley Grammar School

The lives of the 76 Old Boys on the First World War Memorial were influenced greatly by their time at Barnsley Holgate Grammar School (the Holgate) and, therefore, its history creates a significant context for my individual stories about them. Many of them knew each other; they were in the same Form or Class, they played in the same sports teams, took part in School Sports or Swimming Events and they participated together in Speech Days, whether providing the entertainment or winning prizes.

I have compiled my history of the school from many different sources, including the invaluable Holgate Collection in Barnsley Archives, various books, websites plus recollections and records from Old Boys alive today. I have concentrated on the period from its foundation as Barnsley Grammar School in 1660 until the retirement of the first Headmaster of the Holgate in 1919, but I have also added some key details until its 'absorption' into Horizon Community College in 2012.

The first Headmaster of the Holgate, Reverend Charles Stokes Butler, contributed a series of articles to the first *Alumnus* magazines in 1913 about the history of the Grammar School from its foundation in 1660 to 1865; an addenda was added to this by E G Bayford in 1930 (Part 1. Chapter 2). W Maudsley and Rev A Willan added their own reminiscences in later articles in *Alumnus* (Part 1. Chapters 3 and 4), and the magazine included other interesting snippets (Part 1. Chapter 5).

Reginald Harry Greenland, Careers and Mathematics Master at the Grammar School from 1924 to 1960, wrote a detailed history of Barnsley Grammar School. His comprehensive book also contains interesting background information about the history of grammar schools and chantry schools in England from the Middle Ages, including those in or near Barnsley, and also lists of Governors, other teachers of long service, benefactors etc.

Until the first Education Act in 1870, pupils had to pay fees to attend the Grammar School. Over the years, various Scholarships became available as a result of donations from local people, many of them Old Boys, or grants from the Council (Part 1. Chapter 6).

I decided to research some of the most important people involved with the founding, funding and management of Barnsley Grammar School and there are separate biographies of the following: Thomas Keresforth, Robert Holgate, the Lancaster Family, Samuel Joshua Cooper, the Newman and Bond Families and Rev Butler (Part 1. Chapters 11 to 16). I also researched a number of other people in less detail to explain who they were: William Cornelly, John Hargreave, Charles Harvey, Thomas Heelis, Dr John Fletcher Horne, Joseph Locke, Dr Michael Thomas Sadler, John William Sykes and Charles Froggatt Wike (Part 1. Chapter 17). Details about teachers who served in the First World War are in Part 1. Chapter 23.

Information about Keresforth House, the Headmaster's home adjacent to the school premises, is provided in Part 1. Chapter 9.

Key Dates

1660	Thomas Keresforth founded Barnsley Grammar School. The school was managed by the Master and the Trustees. (The Shaw Lands Trust had been set up earlier).
1726	A new house was built adjoining the school.
1769	The original school house was replaced by public subscription.
1848	The Church Institute was established and had its reading room over the Grammar School.
1887	Barnsley Grammar School and Holgate Grammar School in Hemsworth were amalgamated to form Barnsley Holgate Grammar School (the Holgate). An extension to the building was paid for by Edward Lancaster.
1888	The Holgate opened.
c1891	*The Holgate Journal* was introduced and circulated for a short period.
1897	The Old Boys Association was established; members held their first dinner on 13 January 1898.
1902	The Education Act transferred management of the Holgate to West Riding County Council.
1912	The Holgate moved into new premises in Shaw Lane; the building cost £15,000 and was on a site of more than eight acres. The original school building in Church Street was sold by auction to Samuel Joshua Cooper, who donated it to Barnsley as the Cooper Art Gallery.
1913	Management of the Holgate transferred from West Riding County Council to Barnsley County Borough Authority from 1 April. The school was renamed Barnsley and District Holgate Grammar School The Old Boys Association introduced *Alumnus,* a magazine produced three times a year at 6d per issue containing contributions from teachers, pupils and Old Boys.
1916	The first female teachers were appointed during the First World War.
1926	Rev Charles Stokes Butler moved out of Keresforth House, 35 Church Street. Newman & Bond Solicitors moved into the premises, after converting them to offices, and paid rent to the Cooper Trust.

1927–9	The Holgate was extended.
1974	The school became a comprehensive, still under the control of a voluntary board of trustees. It became the Holgate School.
1978	The school became co-educational as girls were admitted.
1990s	Honeywell School was amalgamated with the Holgate.
2012	The Holgate and Kingstone Secondary Schools merged to form Horizon Community College. Trustees continue to manage the Horizon Archbishop Holgate Foundation. The Shaw Lane premises were demolished amidst much controversy. The Shaw Lands Trust continues to operate separately with no benefit to Horizon.

Headmasters

1660 to 25 Jan 1721	unknown
26 Jan 1721 to 1743	James Tomlinson
1743 to c1770	unknown
c1770 to ?	Benjamin Whitley
c1800 to 1811	Rev John Pickles
11 Jan 1812 to Dec 1812	Rev J Milner
14 Dec 1812 to 3 Sept 1817 (died)	Rev Henry Sutcliffe
24 Dec 1817 to ?	Rev Thomas Westmoreland, MA
1818 to 1821	Rev Robert Willan
1821 to c1839	William Gilbanks
1839 to 1845	Rev Richard Boutein Howe
26 Sept 1845 to 1880	John Hargreave, BA Trinity College, Dublin
1880 to 1887	F R Hooper, MA
1887 to 1919	Rev Charles Stokes Butler, MA
1919 to 1939	Arthur John Schooling, MA
1939 to 1960	John Ward Roche, MA BSc
2012 ongoing	Nick Bowen, Principal of Horizon Community College

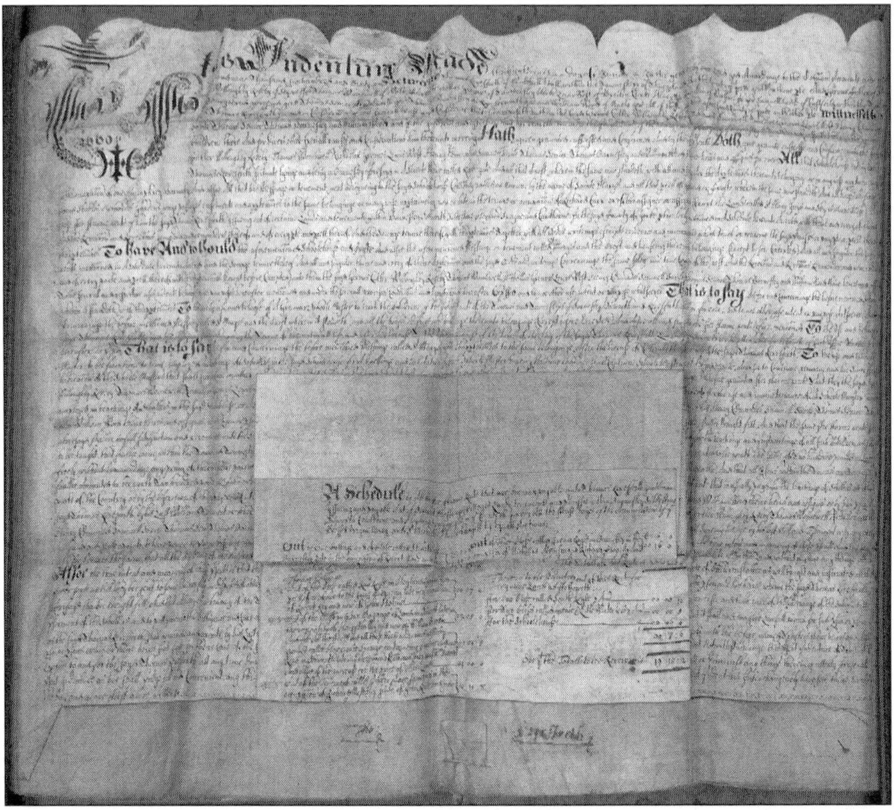

Thomas Keresforth's Deed of 1660 (with close up),
reproduced by kind permission of Barnsley Archives.

The Founding of Barnsley Grammar School, 1660

Thomas Keresforth, Gentleman, of Pule Hill Hall in the township of Thurgoland (biography in Part 1. Chapter 11) founded the Trust for a Grammar School in Barnsley by a Deed dated 18 June 1660. The original hand written Indenture, the first words on which were written in very large ornate script, is in Barnsley Archives, as well as an easier to read transcription of this lengthy document.

Thomas' ten Trustees were chosen because of his 'special trust and confidence in them' and 'their Heirs and Assigns forever'; they were (spelt as written):

Gervas Cutler of Stainesbrough, Esquire
Willoughby Rokeby of Skyers, Esquire
Thomas Wombwell of Wath, Clerk
Nichollas Greaves of Tankersley, Clerk
Lewis West of Bretton, Clerk
Henry Edmundes of Worsbrough, Gentleman
Samuell Savile of Eastfield, within the Township of Thurgoland, Gentleman
Thomas Senior of Dodworth, Gentleman
Thomas Barnesley of Kymberworth, Gentleman
William Wood of Nabb, Gentleman

Thomas set up the Trust because of 'the good will and affection that he beareth towards the Inhabitants of the Towns and Townships of Barnsley, Dodworth, Keresforth Hill and the poorer sort of children there'. He put into it his Schoolhouse in Kirkgate (now Church Street), Barnsley, the Croft occupied by Humphrey Barnaby, the Tenement and grounds adjoining the Schoolhouse called St Mary's, the land and buildings – ie houses, edifices, buildings, barns, stables, orchards, gardens, ways, passages, easements, appurtenances – in the tenure of Richard Carr, except for land at Mary Inge and Skyers Moore Close, plus the fee farm rents from land, 'messuages cottages and tenements' in Barnsley, Dodworth, Silkstone, Hoylandswaine and Cawthorne as listed in the Schedule.

The Trust was to pay 'for a Grammar School Master to teach the Children of the Inhabitants of the Town and Townships of Barnsley, Dodworth and Keresforth Hill in forever. And to no other Use Intent or Purpose whatsoever'. This would continue in the event of Thomas' death by any children or his wife Elizabeth. In addition to the School a dwelling was also to be provided for the School Master for the period of his employment as such and he was expected to instruct 'all such Children as shall come unto him to be taught' (born within the defined area). For those of parents not 'accounted to be worth £200 in land or debtless goods' their education would be provided 'freely without demanding any Penny of them or their Parents until such Time as such Children shall be made fit to be sent to some University or disposed of otherwise by their friends and parents in the Common Wealth'. Parents with land worth more than £200 would pay half the fees. The Trustees were to 'have a Care that the poorer sort of Children should be as well taught and instructed at the said School as the Richer Sort'. The Trustees had discretion to recruit and dismiss any School Master.

If any of the Trustees left or died, the others were to choose a replacement 'to the end that there may continually be a suply to oversee and take care of the well ordering of the School to the best advantage and preferment of the Schollers and to put forward the Dilligence and Care of the School Masters and ushers that shall from Time to Time be employed in teaching of Schollers in the said School' [sic].

The separate Schedule names the tenants and the amounts of rent payable for each property:

> BARNSLEY: Hewithirst, 7 Cottages (3 with land), 3 Closes called Brear Royds, Linge Crofts Close, 1 cottage 'lately built on the waste', 4 areas of land encroaching on the waste, 2 shops under the Moot Hall, The Heavenings Woods
> POGMOOR: 1 cottage
> DODWORTH: 7 messuages with land, Bottom Wood, Howbroade Springe Woods, Hugsett Spring Wood
> SILKSTONE: 1 messuage with land, other land
> HOYLANDSWAINE: Raw Royd Close
> Plus Lowden Springs and 1 tenement in Pinder Place; there are even three references to increases in the price of lambs.
> The total rent payable to Thomas Keresforth for the above was £20 2s 8d. From this he deducted the rents for his own lands: 10d for South Royd Close, 8d for 2 Closes called Great & Little Winterlees and 6s for the Schoolhouse, so that the total to be received was £19 15s 2d.

The Schoolhouse later became known as Keresforth School.

An Indenture dated 20 March 1676 between Thomas Keresforth's Executors, Nathaniel Bower (his first cousin) and Anne Keresforth (his widow), was for a lease of the manor or grange of Barnsley to Henry Wood and John Rooke.

Barnsley Archives have other original documents relating to 'the school in Kirkgate, Barnsley, erected by Thomas Keresforth', some with copies. They are difficult to read and to understand their purpose but they do not significantly affect the history of the Holgate. There are five short term leases – 'Release in Trust for a School in Barnsley' – dated 8 June 1682, 1 March 1722, 29 December 1758, 21 March 1797 and 28 October 1839.

Barnsley Grammar School from 1726 to 1887

In 1726, the Headmaster had a new house built adjacent to the school by voluntary contributions.

The original school house was replaced in 1769 by public subscription and a Latin inscription was added 'on the outside of the south wall of the School, just inside the Church Street entrance' (Rev Butler). There were two large rooms, one above the other, until 1887. The remaining premises in Kirkgate (now Church Street) consisted

The Earliest Photograph of the Grammar School,
kindly provided by the Tasker Trust (copyright).

Latin inscription 1769. (© Jane Ainsworth)

of a good dwelling house with ground behind (garden and playground) occupied by the Headmaster.

The Latin inscription is on the right side wall when facing the front of the Cooper Art Gallery: *DE PUBLICO REAEDFICATA / ANNO DOMINI / MDCCLXIX*

In 1784, brothers Godfrey and David Mason taught – for one shilling each – at the Sabbath School held in the upper rooms over the grammar school, 'which was then and till very recently approached by a stone staircase outside the building, recently removed' (Eli Hoyle).

The 1797 'Release in Trust for a School in Barnsley' is a wordy document but it essentially released the land and property, subject to the requirements of the Trust, from William Bosville Esquire to the Duke of Leeds. It was signed by 16 parties and has 16 seals – William Bosville, Francis Edmunds, Thomas Cotton, William Brooke, Thomas R Beaumont, Francis L Wood, Godfrey W Wentworth, W Spencer Stanhope, Joshua Dixon, Francis Offley Edmunds, Joseph Beckett and Henry Clarke. Thomas Heelis, Solicitor, who had lived in Grammar School Yard at some stage, signed the document as one of the witnesses (biography in Part 1. Chapter 17).

Rev J Milner was appointed as the new Headmaster in 1812 and he advertised in the *Sheffield Mercury* on 11 January that he could take a limited number of Boarders, who would pay 35 guineas per annum for 'board, washing and education, including the Latin, Greek and French languages etc etc' plus one guinea entrance; the fees for Day Scholars were: 15 shillings per quarter for English grammar, writing and accounts plus five shillings entrance; £1 5s per quarter for the Latin, Greek and French languages plus 10s 6d. Rev Milner, formerly Curate of Whiston, Rotherham, had been Assistant at Attercliffe Academy in Sheffield for five years, having taught Latin, Greek and French in the south of England for many years (John Hugh Burland. 1819–1888).

Rev Henry Sutcliffe of Darton became School Master on 14 December 1812 and the appointment letter from Trustees is in Barnsley Archives. The nine Trustees were: Francis L Wood, W Spencer Stanhope, Joseph Beckett, Henry Harker, Godfrey W Wentworth, Joshua Dixon, Thomas R Beaumont, Francis Edmunds and Francis Offley Edmunds.

A similar appointment letter survives for Rev Thomas Westmoreland, who became School Master on 24 December 1817.

Some information was provided about how the School was in 1839 in *The Schools' Enquiry Commissioners Report in October 1865*. William Gilbanks, Headmaster from 1821 to 1839, had taken sole control of the management of the school; 'he was also Postmaster for Barnsley, but being then a prisoner in York Castle at the suit of the Crown, the first act of the new Trustees was to displace him' (biography in Part 1. Chapter 17).

The Trustees appointed Rev Richard Boutein Howe as the next Headmaster and they determined that the School should be for boys only, agreeing a scale of fees for children with defined subjects being taught:

First Form (reading, writing, arithmetic)	one guinea per quarter
Second Form (geography, use of the globes, arithmetic)	one guinea and a half per quarter;
Third Form (Sciences, Latin and Greek Classics)	three guineas per quarter

A report in 1842 on Barnsley St Mary's Parish, Deanery of Doncaster, Diocese of York, stated:

> No scholars, at the time of the Report, had for many years been taught, or applied to be taught, gratuitously. There were then about 100 children of both sexes, who were instructed in English, reading, writing, and arithmetic, at the quarterly rate of 10s. for reading, 15s. for reading and writing, and 21s. for reading, writing, and accounts. An usher, and a female teacher for the girls, were employed by the master to assist him. The master professed his willingness to teach Latin to the scholars who might desire it, without additional charge.

John Hargreave (c1816–1880, aged 64) was Headmaster for 35 years, from 1845 until his death (biography in Part 1. Chapter 17, reminiscences about him in Part 1. Chapters 3 and 4). He was a teacher of considerable ability, especially in Latin and Mathematics, and determined to improve the reputation of the school. He wrote *A Manual for the Use of B. G. S.* (Extracts in Part 1. Chapter 7), a copy of which he presented to Mrs Phoebe Locke, widow of Joseph Locke, in whose name the Locke Scholarships were funded, in July 1861 (Part 1. Chapter 6).

Amanda Stoner told me about a stone with a Latin inscription dated 1852: '*EX DONO THOMAS KERESFORTH GENEROSI MDCLX*', which means 'the gift of Thomas Keresforth Gentleman 1660'. The reason for creating this tribute in 1852 is not known. This stone, the end of which is unfortunately broken, had been concealed in a flower bed behind the Cooper Art Gallery until the current building works for its extension. I was recently fortunate to be allowed access to take a photograph of it by John Bonner, Site Foreman for F Parkinson Ltd.

Photograph of stone dedicated to Thomas Keresforth in 1882. (© Jane Ainsworth)

GROUP OF LOCKE SCHOLARS, 1877.
S. Hudson, B. G. Senior, G. H. Danby, W. Taylor, A. G. Paterson, W. Rose, J. Hewitt, E. G. Rayford, A. Walker, and J. E. Jæger.
(For further particulars see our "Personal" Column, page 3, and for Report of Old Boys' Dinner, see page 8.)

Locke Scholars in 1877, *Barnsley Chronicle* cutting reproduced by kind permssion of Barnsley Archives.

In the report of the Commission of 1865, 22 boys attended the School in 1864. (Greenland stated that there were 27 with 2 boarders in the Headmaster's house). 'Dr' Hargreave received £159 per annum made up of £63 from endowments, £85 from school fees and £12 from other sources. The governing body was made up from 14 Trustees and that year some of those involved were: F W T Vernon Wentworth (of Wentworth Castle), The Right Honourable Viscount Halifax, John Spencer Stanhope (of Cannon Hall), John Staniforth Beckett (son of a Linen Manufacturer, and founder of Beckett Hospital and Dispensary in Barnsley in 1864) plus William Newman and Edward Newman (Part 1. Chapter 15).

In the late 1870s, the school was held in the downstairs room and the Conservative Reading Room was upstairs. The school room had a stove and was divided into forms with all boys seated facing the Headmaster's desk, being called up in turn while the others carried on with their tasks. An Usher had a desk behind the boys and the back of the room was empty except for a cupboard of books and some equipment. Locke Scholars paid 10 shillings each year for books and special art lessons were taken by them at the School of Art; there were strict rules of behaviour and they could be fined for disobedience.

Barnsley Grammar School, photographs kindly provided by the Tasker Trust (copyright).

Barnsley Holgate Grammar School, photographs kindly provided by Barnsley Archives.

Mr F R Hooper, Headmaster from 1880 to 1887, increased the number of pupils from 15 to more than 50. They took Holy Scripture, Latin, French, Maths, English and Bookkeeping. Fees were £4 10s per annum with books extra.

Barnsley Holgate Grammar School from 1887 to 1912

By the late 1880s, the Trustees of Hemsworth Holgate Grammar School wanted to expand and they originally considered amalgamating with Pontefract. However, the Mayor of Barnsley pointed out that they were closer, they already had a site and they were able to meet the cost of expansion as £2,015 had already been subscribed by Dr Michael Thomas Sadler and Mr Charles Harvey (Part 1. Chapter 17).

In 1887 Barnsley Holgate Grammar School was created, following an Act of Parliament, as Keresforth's School was amalgamated with the Hemsworth Grammar School, which had been founded by Archbishop Robert Holgate (biography in Part 1.

Chapter 12) in 1546. The Charity Commissioners were involved because of the Trust founded by Robert Holgate. Barnsley Archives have a copy in Latin with an English translation of the 'Letters Patent to the Archbishop Holgate for the Foundation of a Free Grammar School at York, Hemsworth and Old Malton' dated 24 October 1546 (38th Henry 8th). They also have a copy of Robert Holgate's Will dated 26 April 1555, 'Extracted from the Registry of the Prerogative Court of Canterbury' and other related documents in Latin.

In October 1887, *Barnsley Chronicle* reported two meetings of the new Governors – there were a total of 17 Governors with representatives from the Archbishop of York, Hemsworth Hospital and Barnsley Town Council. Mr W Spencer Stanhope, JP, CB, was elected as Chairman and other Governors named in the articles were:

W Aldam of Finchley Hall
John Dymond of Burntwood Hall
Charles Harvey, JP, of Park House
Rev J Hoyland of Brierley
C E Jones of Badsworth Hall
Rev W Knight, MA, Master of Hemsworth Hospital
C Leatham of Hemsworth
Lord St Oswald
Alderman H Pigott, JP
Dr Michael Thomas Sadler
Rev Thomas Thornely Taylor, MA of Dodworth
Rev C E Thomas, MA, Vicar of Hemsworth
Charles Joseph Tyas, MA
Captain Vincent, JP, of Hemsworth

The Governors agreed that Rev Charles Stokes Butler, Headmaster at Hemsworth Holgate Grammar School, would continue as Headmaster of the Holgate Grammar School in Barnsley. They set up a Sub Committee to consider alterations required to the house to make it fit for his occupation, with new bay windows, and the erection of dormitories to accommodate 25 boarders, in addition to a maximum of 100 day boys.

***Barnsley Chronicle* – 1 October 1887 Buildings, Garden & Playground**

> Together with certain buildings to the rear of Messrs Newman and Bond's offices, for the purpose of which provision was made under the scheme and which the late Mr Charles Newman had agreed to sell for £445. That was considerably under their value, Mr Newman's subscription being included. His successors, it was understood, felt themselves bound to carry out the arrangements and therefore there would be no difficulty on that score. …
>
> A rough statement was made showing the financial position of the trust and the opinion was expressed that they had a fair prospect of being able to make the school a thoroughly successful one.

Latin inscription 1887. (© Jane Ainsworth)

Thomas James Newman (Part 1. Chapter 15) was appointed as Clerk to the Management Committee, publicity was arranged for an examination to be held on 24 November 1887 for six Holgate and three Keresforth Scholarships and it was agreed that a 'Prospectus setting forth the general character of the school, the course of instruction and the fees payable should be forthwith printed and circulated'.

Newman and Bond advertised that the Barnsley Holgate Grammar School would open on 18 January 1888, 'under the scheme of the Charity Commissioners dated 12 July 1887', with Rev Butler as its Headmaster and other Assistant Masters. An examination was to be held in the school on 17 January for admission and fees per term were £2 for boys aged from 8 to 10, £2 13s 8d from 10 to 13 and £3 6s 8d for those over 13 years. A Wanted Notice asked people to submit details for a field within half a mile of the school premises for use as a cricket and [rugby] football ground.

A lintel above a window at the back of the old Grammar School building has an inscription: *IMPENSIS EDWARDI G LANCASTER / DE KERESFORTH GENEROSI / MDCCCXXCVII.* It means

Water pump next to rear extension. (© Jane Ainsworth)

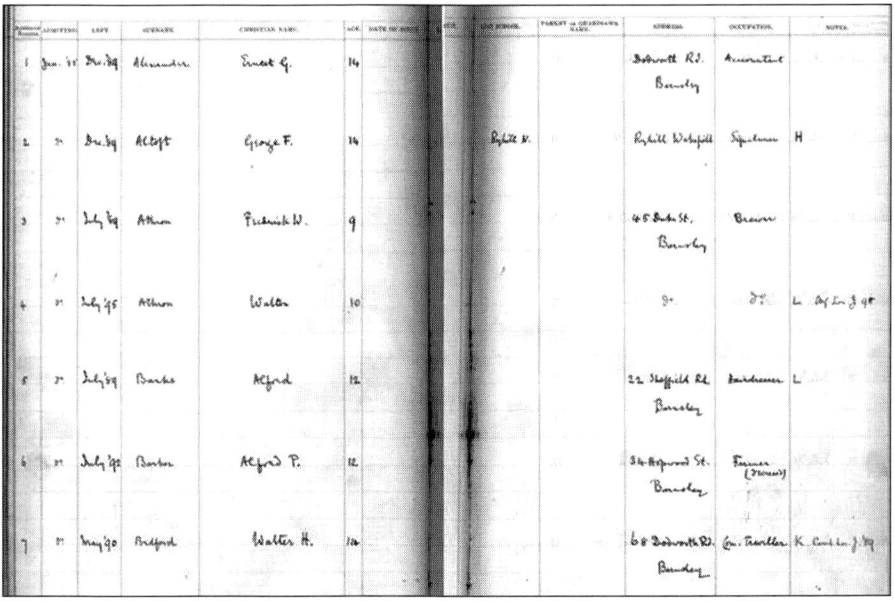

The first page of the Admission Register from 1888, used by kind permission of Barnsley Archives.

that Edward G Lancaster, Gentleman of Keresforth, paid for this in 1887. There is an old water pump adjacent to this 'extension', which I assume included the additional classrooms and extra rooms in the master's house. Edward George Lancaster also endowed a Scholarship (biography in Part 1. Chapter 13).

Barnsley Chronicle reported on 28 April 1888 that the Holgate Trustees had accepted various tenders for alterations to the school amounting to £1,780; Mr R Dixon (Part 2. Chapter 20) was the Architect. The Headmaster's house was to be extended to include a study, large dining hall, kitchen, scullery, pantry, attics and enlarged bedrooms; dormitories; Assistant Master's bedrooms and sickrooms were to be provided and the school premises would be improved by the addition of classrooms, dividing the school into two parts and using some of the Headmaster's house.

Reverend Charles Stokes Butler was appointed at a fixed annual stipend of £150 plus capitation payment of between £1–3 per boy; school age was from 8 to 17 and tuition fees were between £6–£10 pa. A new Admission Register was started from number 1: Ernest G Alexander (aged 14), whose father was an Accountant of Dodworth Road, Barnsley.

The new school was under the scrutiny of local people as there had been some controversy about the Hemsworth Holgate School transferring to Barnsley rather than Pontefract, but its progress in the first six months was deemed to be satisfactory. Their first Speech Day and Prize Distribution on 31 July 1888, reported in *Barnsley Chronicle* and *Barnsley Independent*, was attended by the Mayor Alderman Marsden, several Councillors, Governors, Samuel Joshua Cooper, Mr Dixon etc. The Mayor welcomed the large gathering and expressed the hope that those with different opinions about whether the grammar school ought to have been based in Hemsworth rather than Barnsley would set them aside. He pointed out that the new school was a success, it was being properly managed and it was fortunate in being supported by generous benefactors; he asked parents to ensure that their boys attended regularly and received 'home training', and he advised boys to be diligent in their studies in order to achieve future success.

Rev Butler stated that he was pleased so many independent people were present to see how well the school was performing as they wanted to be accountable to the public. He agreed with those who wanted pupils to receive training for commercial life but, as this ought to be in addition to a general education, parents would need to support their boys' education beyond the age of 14. Alderman Brady congratulated the Headmaster on his achievements so far and he hoped that 'the time would come when it would be considered an honour, as it is at Eton and Winchester and the Universities, for a student to say that his education had been grounded at the Barnsley Grammar School'.

Governors had invited an impartial and experienced examiner – Rev F Besant MA of Emmanuel College, Cambridge – to assess the boys and the school in 1888. Rev Besant wrote in his report that he had 'much pleasure in writing this favourable report of the school'. He had anticipated that exam results might be adversely affected by the newness of the school and the fact that almost half of the boys had only joined that year, more than half learning Latin, French and Science for the first time, but that they were better than expected. The premises were undergoing extension and 63 boys attended, although it could accommodate 100; the school was divided into six forms, working in three groups. Forms VI and V were assessed as fair to good in Scripture, very good in Latin Grammar but fair in Latin Exercises, very good in French, 'all well learnt' in English and satisfactory overall in Mathematics; the other forms achieved similar results. 'I may describe the work of all classes as real and thorough, and the order and discipline are excellent'.

Rev Butler emphasised that, although the school was open to all 'without distinction of class or creed', religious instruction would take place in the school while he was Headmaster; their daily routine began and ended with prayers according to 'the form prescribed by Archbishop Holgate himself'.

Prizes were awarded and the boys put on entertainment, including two scenes from William Shakespeare's *Henry V*. Details of these and the words of the School Song, composed by Rev Charles Stokes Butler (Part 1. Chapter 8), were provided in the Speech Day programme along with exam results, scholarships and sports teams (unfortunately the names listed are often just surnames). The text of an address delivered by H Fox in Latin, and its translation, were given in full; the following paragraph is interesting in its recognition of the issue of the naming of the school:

> Though it may be somewhat hazardous to conjecture what the feelings of Thomas Keresforth and Robert Holgate might be if the one should now see a school

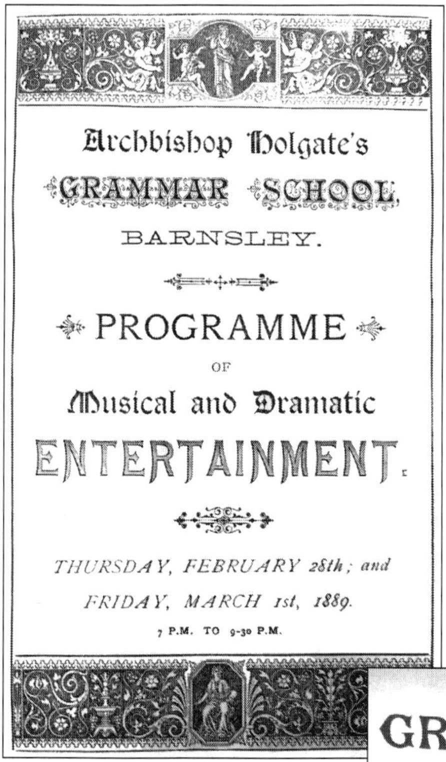
Archbishop Holgate's
GRAMMAR SCHOOL,
BARNSLEY.

PROGRAMME
OF
Musical and Dramatic
ENTERTAINMENT.

THURSDAY, FEBRUARY 28th; and
FRIDAY, MARCH 1st, 1889.
7 P.M. TO 9-30 P.M.

Programme of Entertainment 1889, reproduced by kind permission of Barnsley Archives.

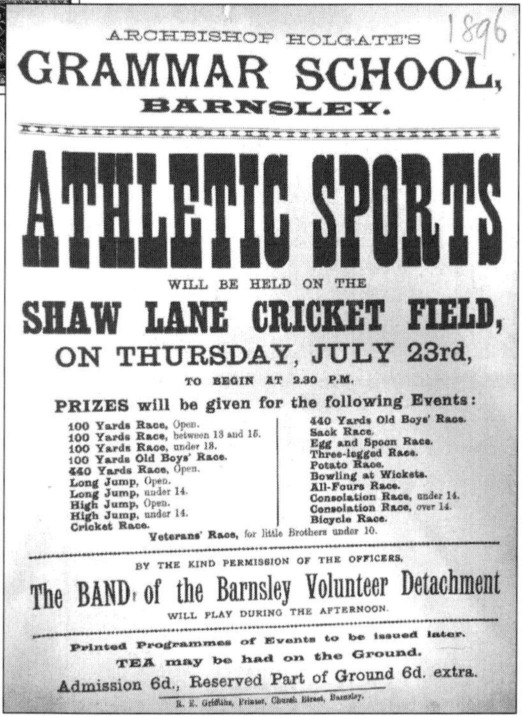
ARCHBISHOP HOLGATE'S 1896
GRAMMAR SCHOOL,
BARNSLEY.

ATHLETIC SPORTS
WILL BE HELD ON THE
SHAW LANE CRICKET FIELD,
ON THURSDAY, JULY 23rd,
TO BEGIN AT 2.30 P.M.

PRIZES will be given for the following Events:

100 Yards Race, Open.
100 Yards Race, between 13 and 15.
100 Yards Race, under 13.
100 Yards Old Boys' Race.
440 Yards Race, Open.
Long Jump, Open.
Long Jump, under 14.
High Jump, Open.
High Jump, under 14.
Cricket Race.
440 Yards Old Boys' Race.
Sack Race.
Egg and Spoon Race.
Three-legged Race.
Potato Race.
Bowling at Wickets.
All-Fours Race.
Consolation Race, under 14.
Consolation Race, over 14.
Bicycle Race.
Veterans' Race, for little Brothers under 10.

BY THE KIND PERMISSION OF THE OFFICERS,
The BAND of the Barnsley Volunteer Detachment
WILL PLAY DURING THE AFTERNOON.

Printed Programmes of Events to be issued later.
TEA may be had on the Ground.
Admission 6d., Reserved Part of Ground 6d. extra.
R. E. Griffiths, Printer, Church Street, Barnsley.

Athletic Sports on 23 July 1896 Programme, reproduced by kind permission of Barnsley Archives.

> founded by himself called by a name not his, and the other should see his name and benefaction used by a school that he did not found, yet perhaps we should not be far wrong in supposing that as men of large and enlightened mind they would rejoice to find that their laudable desire to promote education has been rendered more effectual after the lapse of centuries by modifications suited to the altered conditions of England in the present day.

When Rev Butler's wife died in 1893, the Governors decided that there would be no public distribution of prizes that year out of sympathy with the bereaved Headmaster.

Demonstrating the breadth of education that the pupils received at the Holgate, Programmes, newspaper articles and other records survive for entertainments and sports events amongst documents collected by the Headmaster and preserved in Barnsley Archives.

A Musical and Dramatic Entertainment was organised in 1889. Among the ten songs was one written by Rev Butler entitled *Some Folk Say That Barnsley's Black* (Part 3. Chapter 1), Altoft's *Old King Coal*, the School Song and *Rule Britannia*. The humorous drama was entitled *Guy Fawkes or Neglected Education, An Unhistorical Play*.

An Entertainment Event in 1890 raised funds for Beckett Hospital. No doubt inspired by all of this creativity, an unofficial magazine *Holgate Journal* was begun and circulated in 1891 (Part 1. Chapter 18).

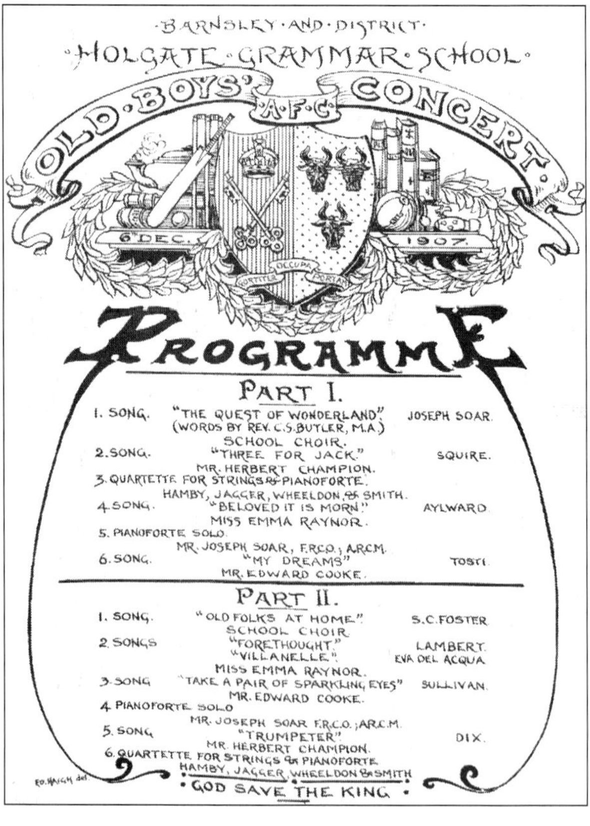

Poster for Old Boys Concert on 6 December 1907, reproduced by kind permission of Barnsley Archives.

A poster advertised the Athletics Sports Day on 23 July 1896 and there was also a detailed programme of events, listing participants, both current pupils and Old Boys, for the usual races plus 'Potato Race', 'All-Fours Race', 'Bicycle Race' and 'Consolation Race'.

Rev Butler with pupils c1905, photograph kindly provided by Memories of Barnsley.

Rev Butler with a large group of pupils c1905,
photograph kindly provided by Barnsley Archives.

The Old Boys Association was established in 1897 and their first annual dinner was held at the Queen's Hotel in Barnsley in January 1898. By 1903, the customary toasts were made after the meal to the Founders, Donors and Governors of Barnsley Holgate Grammar School, interspersed with songs and music and followed by speeches.

Fees were increased in 1899 to five guineas per annum for boys under the age of 13 and six guineas for boys over 13. In the ten years from 1889 pupils had achieved good results in examinations: Drawing – 201 Certificates; Science – 253 Certificates.

In 1903, Mr Buswell was engaged to teach boys how to swim. They held their first Swimming Sports Day that July; events included a race for novices and picking up the greatest number of plates from the floor of the pool.

In May 1904, a Notice was placed in *Barnsley Chronicle* stating that at 'Archbishop Holgate's Grammar School … a sound and liberal Education is given on modern lines. The Schoolrooms have recently been Refurnished, and are well supplied with Modern Apparatus. Fees: Boys under 13, £5 5s per annum; over 13, £6 6s per annum. Twenty four page illustrated prospectus sent on application to the Rev C S Butler, MA, Headmaster'. A Cricket Pavilion had also been provided by Charles F Wike, City Surveyor for Sheffield, who had been one of the first Locke Scholars and left a bequest for Scholarships (Part 1. Chapters 6 and 17).

A Notice for the new school year in 1908, pointed out that the fees were £6 6s a year for boys under 12 and £8 8s for boys over 12, 'fees inclusive of the use of Books and Stationery'.

Barnsley Holgate Grammar School in Shaw Lane,
photograph kindly provided by Barnsley Archives.

Barnsley & District Holgate Grammar School from 1908 to 2012

Barnsley Holgate Grammar School had outgrown the premises in Church Street by 1908 and it had been using two corrugated iron buildings to provide five additional classrooms. In early November 1908 a Notice in *Barnsley Chronicle* invited applications from qualified practising Architects to compete for the design and erection of new school premises in Shaw Lane to accommodate 300 pupils. In October 1909, tenders were sought for the erection of the new building 'according to the drawings, specifications and bills of quantities prepared by Messrs Crouch, Butler and Savage, Architects of Birmingham'. Many of the letters in the Manager's Letter Book for 1911 relate to the plans and contracts for building the new school in Shaw Lane, equipping various classrooms and laying out playing fields.

The new premises were formally opened on 23 January 1912 by the Archbishop of York and details were provided in *Barnsley Independent* and in *Barnsley Chronicle* under the heading: 'AN IMPRESSIVE CEREMONY / INTERESTING SPEECHES / HIS GRACE AT THE PUBLIC HALL / STIRRING ADDRESS TO MEN'. Numerous people attended the ceremony, including many Barnsley dignitaries, and took great interest in the building 'of commanding appearance' whose interior and exterior 'came in for much commendation' by both sexes.

The Archbishop of York, who was visiting Barnsley for the first time, was presented with a gold key to the main entrance. Charles Joseph Tyas, Chairman of the Governors, welcomed the Archbishop and reminded attendees of the history of the grammar school in Barnsley. He hoped that: 'When these new walls become grey, as the old school walls were that day, ... posterity would be able to say that the school had been a power for the spiritual, moral and educational life of all the boys who had passed through'.

The Archbishop responded that he was glad to have the opportunity to visit Barnsley and, despite misgivings about its reputation, he was pleased 'to feel himself in the centre of one of the great industrial districts of our strenuous Yorkshire'. He felt it was remarkable that the 89th Archbishop of York should 'open a new chapter in the buildings of a school partially founded by the 59th Archbishop of York, with whom he shared an intense interest and belief in the education of the people'.

The new premises cost about £15,000 and included: 'an assembly hall, twelve classrooms, science lecture room, laboratories for chemistry and physics, art room, woodwork room, gymnasium, dining room, sixth form common room, library, committee room, cloak rooms and sheds for cycles. The site comprises 8½ acres, a large portion of which is to be laid out as cricket and football fields'.

The original premises in Church Lane, which occupied about 2,500 square yards, were sold at auction by Messrs Lancaster and Sons, Auctioneers, on 18 September 1912 at the Royal Hotel in Barnsley. The Sale Particulars and Plan, drawn by R and W Dixon, are in Part 1. Chapter 10.

Samuel Joshua Cooper (Part 1. Chapter 14), who had attended the school for one term, been one of the Governors and made several endowments for Cooper

Chemistry Laboratory in 1934, reproduced by kind permission of Brian Sawyer.

Scholarships, purchased the premises for £3,419 2s 6d via Mr Pawsey of Newman and Bond Solicitors (Part 1. Chapter 15). He donated the original school building, a legacy plus his collection of paintings and statuary to the people of Barnsley for use as an art gallery. Newspaper articles about the Formal Opening of the Art Gallery in 1914 are transcribed in Part 1. Chapter 19.

A handwritten record by Rev Butler explains that after the school premises in Church Street had been sold to Mr Cooper (now deceased), the Governors had rented Keresforth House off him at £50 per annum so that it could remain the official residence of the Headmaster, but this arrangement ceased at the end of March 1914. Rev Butler was left to make his own arrangements and entered into a private agreement with the Cooper Trustees to become their tenant from 1 April 1914. Details of Keresforth House are in Part 1. Chapter 9.

The contents of the old building, which included school and laboratory furniture and fittings, were sold separately by auction by John Edward Jaeger, whose Auctioneer's offices were at 14 Regent Street, Barnsley (biography in Part 2. Chapter 45).

There were a number of new initiatives for the new school in Shaw Lane, which introduced school dinners. In April 1913, *Alumnus* was introduced by the Old Boys Association, who had formed in 1897, and they also founded an Old Boys Football Club. *Alumnus* cost sixpence per copy and Old Boys were encouraged to subscribe. The front cover was designed by the Art Teacher, Edwin Haigh. The new magazine was reported in *Barnsley Independent*, who explained the Latin name as 'a student, or one whose erudition had been acquired at some college or secondary school'; they reviewed its first contents and recommended it because 'any person who has the slightest interest in the school could not fail to derive infinite pleasure from a perusal of its pages', 'Mr E Davies is the able editor and he has a capable assistant in Mr J M Downend (Part 2. Chapter 22)'. *Alumnus* is an important source of information about Barnsley Grammar School (Part 1. Chapters 2 to 5, 18 etc) and an invaluable record

Holgate Coat of Arms on School Document, reproduced by kind permission of Barnsley Archives.

of the Old Boys who served in the First World War, who are the main subject of my memorial book.

Professor Kenny of Cambridge University, formerly MP for Barnsley Division from 1885 to 1889, addressed those present at the first Speech Day in the new premises; he reminded everyone of the history of Barnsley Grammar School and told the boys that they owed a debt to the founders and benefactors, as well as to their parents and teachers, to study diligently to justify the cost of their education and to be truthful.

Commemoration Day was introduced as a celebration of the fact that Barnsley had a grammar school, dating back to 1660, when Thomas Keresforth established his school in Barnsley. The first one was held on Saturday 11 October 1913 for current pupils and Old Boys. There was a football match in the afternoon followed by an evening entertainment – the programme included several speeches, songs and a performance of Act III from *Julius Caesar*. An article in *Alumnus* December 1913 explained that the date itself was not significant but its purpose was to 'celebrate all that the school stands for, all that it has achieved, rather than to make much of one particular event in the school's history'. 'It has always kept the lamp of knowledge burning'.

In July 1914, *The School List and Record* was produced and this lists the names of all current pupils by Form, noting Scholarships, and Old Boys attending Training Colleges and Universities.

The First World War had a major impact on the Holgate as recorded in *Alumnus* magazines (Part 1. Chapter 18). Details of Teachers who served and survived are in Part 1. Chapter 19, information about Memorials is in Part 1. Chapters 21 to 23 and the stories of the Old Boys who died are in Parts 2. and 3.

Female Teachers were appointed for the first time to cover for those in the forces; Ethel Rees replaced her husband from 1916 to 1919 and Dorothy Phyllis Roberts was Form Mistress, teaching History, from 1918 to about 1924.

Alumnus – December 1918:

> We view the approaching departure of Mr Evans with anxious foreboding as to the future of the school because of the practical impossibility of obtaining efficient teachers in these days. Since the outbreak of war, the school staff has undergone numerous changes:
>
> 2 former masters have been killed
> one has been wounded
> 4 are on active service
> one is in munition works
> 2 have become research chemists
>
> Two subjects of the curriculum have had to be abandoned on account of failure to obtain competent teachers. Moreover, of the 25 student teachers, who have

attended the school since the war and who in normal times would have entered colleges for teachers, 24 are now on active service.

Pupils at the Holgate were expected to behave properly at all times as a notice in 1917 made clear.

BARNSLEY GRAMMAR SCHOOL
Boys are not to stand or play about the School Entrance Gates,
or anywhere in front of the School.
No Boy may go outside the Playground Gates
during the Morning interval, 10.45 to 11am.
Boys are cautioned against Irregular or Disorderly Conduct
on their way to and from School, in the Street, or on Railway Journeys.

When Reverend Charles Stokes Butler resigned as Headmaster in 1919, after more than 30 years in Barnsley, an advert was placed in *The Times Educational Supplement* seeking applications for his replacement from September that year; the school had 300 pupils and the starting salary was £600. There were 106 applicants, from whom six were selected for interview and Arthur John Schooling was appointed (Part 1. Chapter 19).

Scholars were divided into four houses in 1919, each with its own colour, and these doubled to eight in 1925 as the school expanded with a different shade of the main colour for the new house.* There were 368 pupils in 1920, five of whom were Student Teachers, and the school was still growing.

1919		**1925**	
Keresforth	red	Lancaster	red
Holgate	green	Horne	green
Locke	blue	Sadler	blue
Cooper	yellow	Butler	yellow

I have been unable to ascertain when a uniform was first introduced at the Grammar School but the photographs taken with the Headmaster Rev. Butler about 1905 show pupils wearing standard jackets, trousers, white shirts with large collars, ties and caps with badges.

* Brian Sawyer, an Old Boy of the Holgate, kindly lent me his old records and photographs to use in my book. He kept in contact with his French Teacher, Dr Richard H Andrews, who had suggested simplifying the school badge for the blazer and cap but it was not introduced while he was still at the Holgate. Dr Andrews gave the artwork produced by the Art Teacher to Brian.

In 1922, a black school blazer was introduced with Archbishop Holgate's Coat of Arms on the pocket badge (image in Colour Section) and green caps, later replaced first with light blue ones then with black. However, not all pupils were able to wear a jacket during the Second World War because of clothing rationing. By the time that there were eight houses, the school tie was black and white stripes with a stripe of the relevant house colour. The school badge was changed to a simpler design c1950 and the original art work for the proposed change survives (see note page 49).

My uncle Arnold Firth attended the Holgate from September 1920 to July 1926. He won a County Minor Scholarship for his first four years. Arnold was awarded the School Certificate of the Joint Matriculation Board (Universities of Manchester, Liverpool, Leeds, Sheffield and Birmingham) in July 1925 after an examination in Group I. English Subjects (English, History, Geography, Scripture), Group II. Languages (French, Latin), Group III. Mathematics and Science (Maths, Physics, Chemistry) and Group IV (Art); he passed with Credit in Mathematics and Physics. Arnold worked as a Clerk in the Colliery Offices in Elsecar when he left the Holgate. Early 2016, his daughter Anne Owen lent me copies of various documents including Arnold's school reports.

In 1925, boys started to take the Northern Universities examination. A new wing opened in 1927 and on 16 December 1929, there was an opening ceremony for further extensions to the school buildings, reported in *Alumnus* April 1930.

From 1939 to 1945, the Holgate experienced disruption once more from the Second World War. The school played its part and former students once again served their country; 98 Old Boys lost their lives and were recorded on another War Memorial,

LIST OF SUBJECTS STUDIED AT SCHOOL.

Group I.	English, History, Geography, Scripture. (4)
Group II.	French, Latin. (2)
Group III.	Mathematics, Physics, Chemistry. (3)
Group IV.	Art. (1)

School Certificate A. 593

Universities of Manchester, Liverpool, Leeds, Sheffield, and Birmingham.

Joint Matriculation Board.

School Certificate.

This is to Certify that

ARNOLD FIRTH

born 12th June, 1909.

I. was awarded the **School Certificate** of the Joint Matriculation Board in **July, 1925,** after an examination in Group I. English Subjects, Group II. Languages, Group III. Mathematics and Science.

The candidate passed with **Credit** in the following two subjects:

Mathematics and Physics.

Signed on behalf of the Joint Matriculation Board.

Henry A Miers.

Chairman to the Joint Matriculation Board.

II. The candidate has attended at least three years continuous instruction at

Holgate Grammar School, Barnsley

and has pursued a course of study in the subjects enumerated on the back of this certificate.

A J Schooling *Head Master.*

III. **The Board of Education** have inspected the School and recognised it as an efficient Secondary School, and accept the examination as reaching the approved standard.

Signed on behalf of the Board of Education.

P. H. Pelham. *Assistant Secretary.*

[OVER

98085.7.25

School Certificate for Arthur Firth, reproduced by kind permission of his daughter Anne Owen.

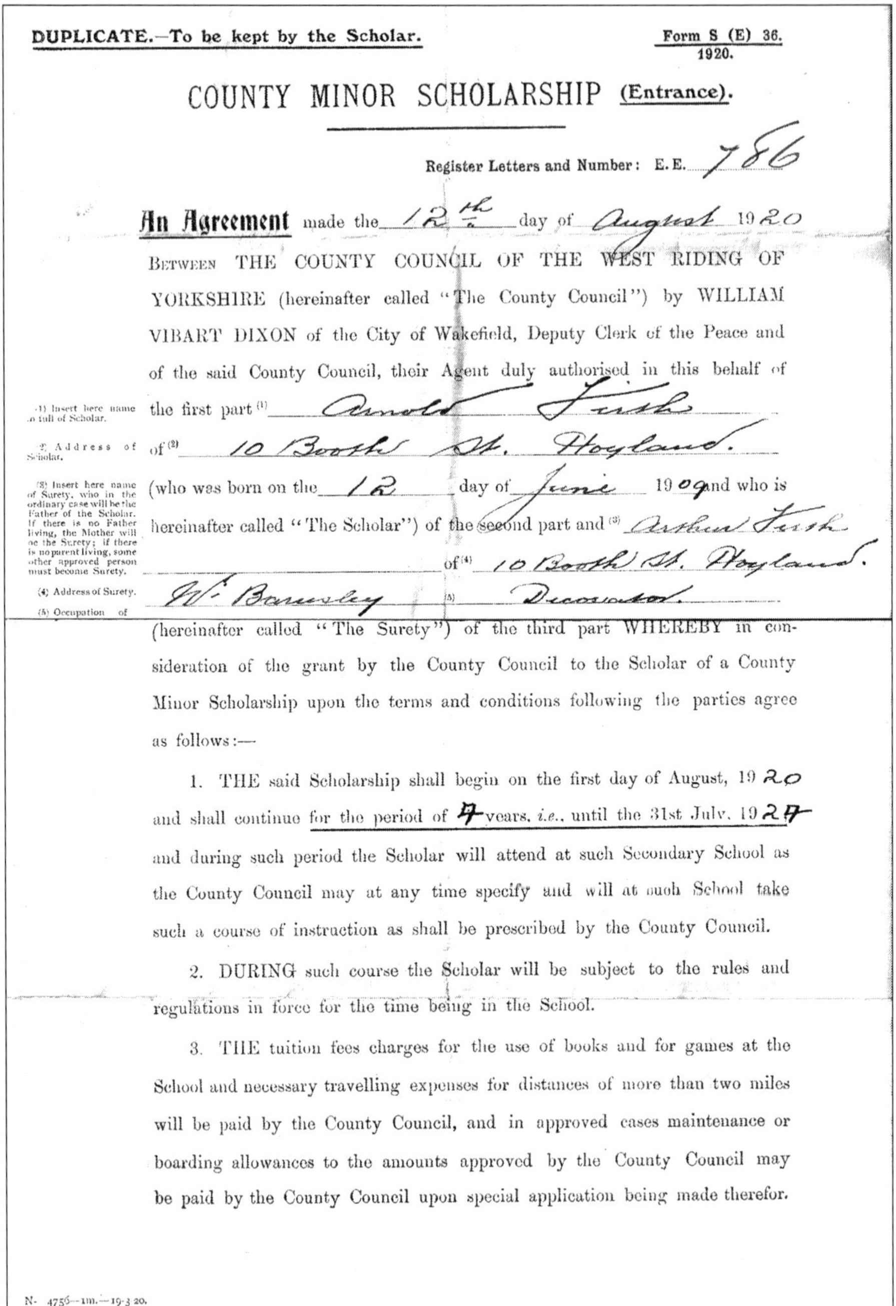

DUPLICATE.—To be kept by the Scholar.

Form S (E) 36.
1920.

COUNTY MINOR SCHOLARSHIP (Entrance).

Register Letters and Number: E. E. 786

An Agreement made the 12th day of August 1920

BETWEEN THE COUNTY COUNCIL OF THE WEST RIDING OF YORKSHIRE (hereinafter called "The County Council") by WILLIAM VIBART DIXON of the City of Wakefield, Deputy Clerk of the Peace and of the said County Council, their Agent duly authorised in this behalf of the first part (1) Arnold Firth

of (2) 10 Booth St. Hoyland.

(who was born on the 12 day of June 1909 and who is hereinafter called "The Scholar") of the second part and (3) Arthur Firth

of (4) 10 Booth St. Hoyland.

W. Barnsley (5) Decorator.

(hereinafter called "The Surety") of the third part WHEREBY in consideration of the grant by the County Council to the Scholar of a County Minor Scholarship upon the terms and conditions following the parties agree as follows:—

(1) Insert here name in full of Scholar.
(2) Address of Scholar.
(3) Insert here name of Surety, who in the ordinary case will be the Father of the Scholar. If there is no Father living, the Mother will be the Surety; if there is no parent living, some other approved person must become Surety.
(4) Address of Surety.
(5) Occupation of Surety.

1. THE said Scholarship shall begin on the first day of August, 1920 and shall continue for the period of 4 years, *i.e.*, until the 31st July, 1924 and during such period the Scholar will attend at such Secondary School as the County Council may at any time specify and will at such School take such a course of instruction as shall be prescribed by the County Council.

2. DURING such course the Scholar will be subject to the rules and regulations in force for the time being in the School.

3. THE tuition fees charges for the use of books and for games at the School and necessary travelling expenses for distances of more than two miles will be paid by the County Council, and in approved cases maintenance or boarding allowances to the amounts approved by the County Council may be paid by the County Council upon special application being made therefor.

N- 4756—1m.—19-3-20.

County Minor Scholarship document.

4. The County Council may on application renew the Scholarship from year to year when the period mentioned in Clause (1) hereof has expired, and during such extended period all the terms and conditions set forth in the foregoing clauses shall apply in the same manner as in the case of the original period of the Scholarship.

5. THE Scholarship shall be determinable by the County Council at any time if the attendance, diligence, progress or conduct of the Scholar is not satisfactory.

6. IF during the original period of the Scholarship or during any extended period thereof the Scholar shall unless owing to illness (certified by a Registered Medical Practitioner) or some other cause considered sufficient by the West Riding County Council cease to attend School, the Surety shall on demand refund to the County Council the sum of six guineas (£6 6s. 0d.) on account of payments made by the County Council in respect of the Scholar.

IN WITNESS whereof the parties hereto have set their hands the date first before written.

Signed by the Scholar in the presence of:— Arnold Firth.
(Signature of the Scholar).

(Witness's Signature) Arthur Firth.
(Address of Witness) 10 Booth Street, Hoyland
(Occupation of Witness) Decorator.

Signed by the Surety in the presence of:— Arthur Firth
(Signature of Surety).

(Witness's Signature) Edith L. Firth
(Address of Witness) 10 Booth Street Hoyland
(Occupation of Witness) Housekeeper

Blue Plaque for Joseph Locke.
(© Jane Ainsworth)

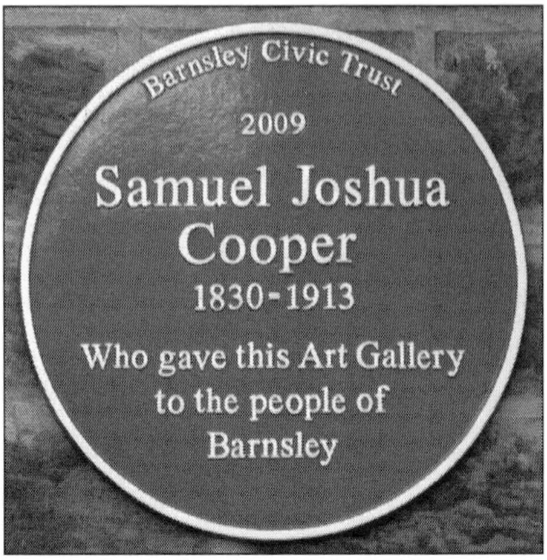

Blue Plaque for Samuel Joshua Cooper.
(© Jane Ainsworth)

The former school building in 2015 (front) – now the Cooper Art Gallery.
(© Jane Ainsworth)

The former Headmaster's House in 2015 (front) – now Newman & Bond Solicitors. (© Jane Ainsworth)

At the back of the school/gallery – left side. (© Jane Ainsworth)

At the back of the school/ gallery – centre and right. (© Jane Ainsworth)

which is currently in storage but ought to be put on public display, as was originally intended, when an appropriate location can be decided.

The School Badge Artwork, reproduced by kind permission of Brian Sawyer.

Two blue plaques were fixed onto the front wall of the Cooper Art Gallery in recognition of two Old Boys and benefactors of Barnsley Holgate Grammar School: Joseph Locke and Samuel Joshua Cooper.

The Current Situation

In 2012, Holgate School amalgamated with Kingstone School to form the new Horizon Community College, which opened in new premises in Dodworth Road, Barnsley, with Nick Bowen as Principal. The building in Shaw Lane was demolished and the records relating to the Holgate Grammar School were donated to Barnsley Archives, where they became available to the public early 2014.

Horizon Community College currently has about 2,000 students; it was the largest Secondary School in Western Europe when built and it achieves exam results consistently above the National average. The College is organised into separate 'schools' of 16 forms and whilst students have access to the outstanding facilities of the college as a whole, they actually attend the smallest secondary 'school' in the district. Horizon benefits from its large premises, having a theatre of 420 capacity (the largest theatre in the district), a canteen seating 300 and a Community Enterprise team, all of which led to the recent accolade by Theo Pathitis of the *Dragon's Den*: 'This is the most enterprising school in the UK'.*

* I am grateful to Nick Bowen, Principal, and members of his team for providing me with general information about Horizon Community College.

The Archbishop Holgate Foundation, established in 1888 when the grammar school in Hemsworth was amalgamated with the grammar school in Barnsley, transferred to Horizon Community College. This registered Charity was renamed the Horizon Archbishop Holgate Foundation and provides about £7,500 towards special projects each year. The aims stated on the Charity Commission website are:

1) to Permit the Use of Land and Buildings Belonging to the Trustees for the Purpose of a Voluntary Controlled School called 'Holgate School Sports College'.
2) to Provide Financial Assistance to the School for the Purposes Not Normally Provided by the LEA (Local Education Authority).
3) to Provide Financial Assistance to Promote the Education, Social and Physical Training of Pupils and Former Pupils.

The Shawlands Trust

This was established by a Deed dated 3 May 1568 (the 10th year of Queen Elizabeth's reign), after Ralph Bosville of London had originally conveyed lands to Robert Thwaites of Barnsley in 1558 for the benefit of local people. 'Robert Thwaites, in consideration of £20, paid by Thomas Keresforth [an ancestor of the founder of Barnsley Grammar School, who became one of the Trustees] and other inhabitants of Barnsley, and of the good will he bore to them, conveyed certain parcels of land, called The Shaws in Barnsley, to trustees for the general weal and benefit of all the inhabitants of the township of Barnsley, towards paying their common taxes, repairing their church and highways, making or amending their butts, stocks, pinfold and wells there, or in or about something pertaining to the whole common wealth of the said town or township'. 'The income consists of the rents of 48a. 3r. 12p. [ie 48 acres, 3 roods, 12 perches] and is applied towards repairing the church and the disbursements of the churchwardens, in paying the stipenda of the organist and sexton, occasionally repairing the highways, and in buying coffins for poor people'. The trust estate was let in 12 parcels at rents amounting to £179 17s 4d per annum.

The 1779 Enclosure Map shows the extent of Shaw Lands in Barnsley, which extend over a large area between Dodworth Road and Race Common Road, fairly close to Kerresforth [sic] Hall and Kerresforth [sic] Hill, where the family of that name lived.

In 1874, the Inspector of Charities reported that the income from 'Shawlands Trust' had been spent on the maintenance of the churches of Saints Mary, George and John in Barnsley until 1870, then nothing was spent except on management of the estate.

In 1877, 'the board of trustees consisted of the Mayor, chairman of the School Board in Barnsley and 30 non official Trustees'. Income was used as follows:

£50 on scholarships at university for BHGS
£30 for repair of the chancel of St Mary's
£25 maintenance of shooting ground and butts of Barnsley Volunteer Rifles
£25 to Beckett's Hospital
the residue on maintenance of fountains, drinking troughs, lighting and clocks in Barnsley, maintenance of Locke Park and other recreation grounds.

The Trustees agreed that £50 should be given each year to the Trustees of Barnsley Grammar School to augment the Endowment with the option of up to another £50.

In 1899, the gross annual income was £214 11s 9d, expenses were £34 9s 11d. Trustees met twice a year.

The Shaw Lands Trust continues to be managed by Trustees. It does not benefit Horizon Community College, but is used for educational grants for further education, which are means tested, and grants to local community groups that are registered Charities.

The original Drill Hall. (© Jane Ainsworth)

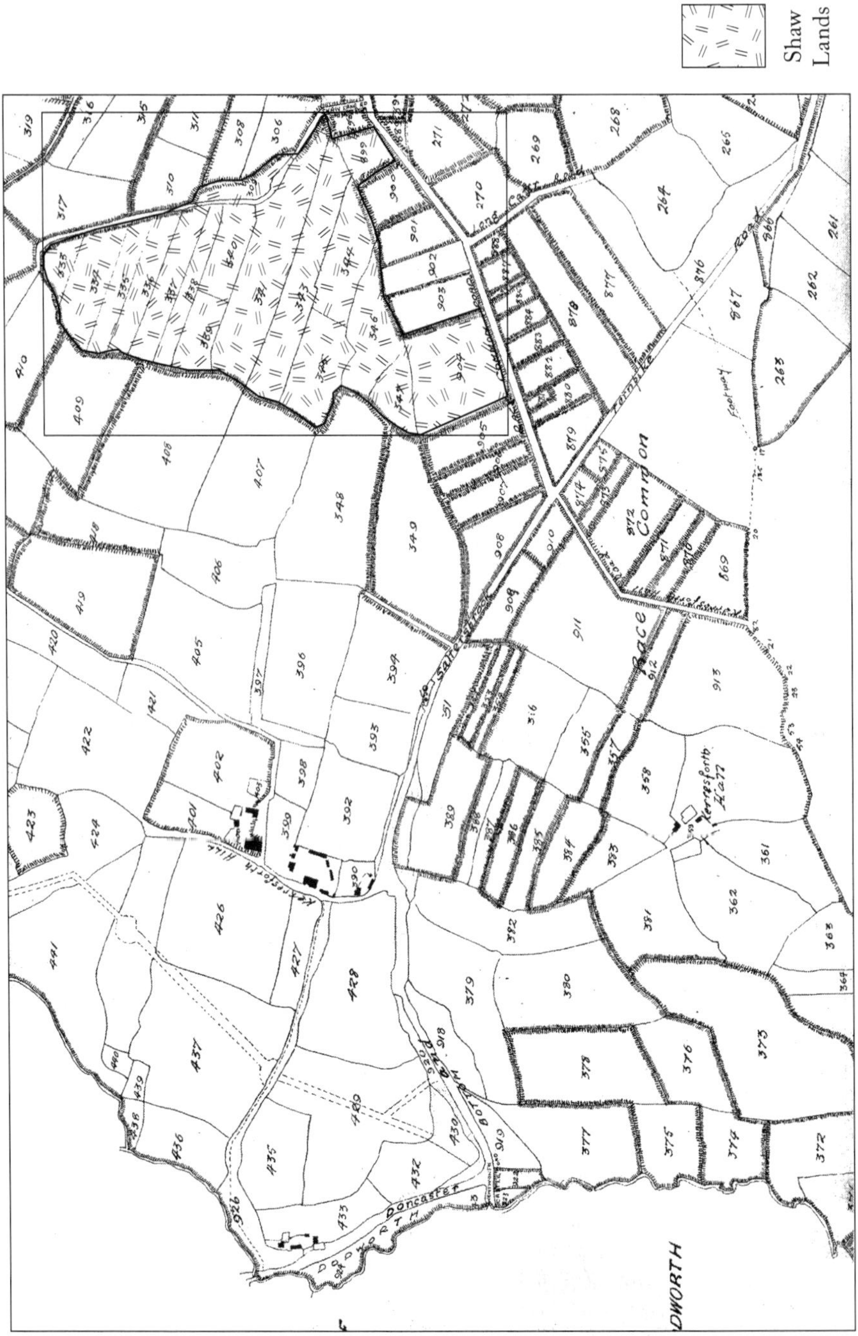

The 1779 Enclosure Map showing Shaw Lands, reproduced by kind permission of Barnsley Archives.

2

Rev Butler's History of Barnsley Grammar School

The Headmaster, Reverend Charles Stokes Butler, contributed a history of Barnsley Grammar School to the first three editions of *Alumnus* magazine. He wrote a lively account of its first 200 years, from its foundation in 1660 to 1865, in three parts in April, July and December 1913.

I have transcribed all of them in full because of their fascinating details about Barnsley Grammar School, but also because they highlight the qualities of the first Headmaster of the Holgate.

Foundation

We do not know what first suggested to Thomas Keresforth the idea of founding a Grammar School in Barnsley. But where facts fail us, fancy claims the privilege of roaming at will. Let us suppose then – nor is there anything improbable in the supposition – that on a fine summer morning in the year 1658, Thomas Keresforth mounted his horse and rode forth to take the air. He directed his course eastward, for to the west of his residence the country was too hilly and the tracks too rough for comfortable riding; and jogged along at a gentle pace as became an elderly gentleman, and as a careful rider had need to do, over roads that in any direction were bad enough. Open moorland, common and woodland extended on all sides close up to the village of Barnsley, where a few grey stone houses crowned the Hill at Old Town, and others clustered round the Church, and were scattered on the slopes south and east of it, with gardens and orchards among them. Passing over a grassy expanse on which a tall Maypole stood, now known as May-day Green, he took the lonely road towards Pomfret, through Shafton and so reached the hamlet of Hemsworth, where he turned south, intending to return over Ringstone Hill. From a long low building near the road on his left suddenly dashed out a score or two of boys, yelling and racing, and startled his horse. A grave person, evidently the schoolmaster, appeared at the door, looking upon the noisy throng, and seeming to contemplate their departure with feelings of relief. Getting into conversation with him, Thomas learnt to his surprise that this institution was a Grammar School, founded as long before as 1546 by Robert Holgate, Archbishop of York, not by his last will and testament, but by employing his wealth to such good purpose while he lived. When Thomas enquired why he chose so small and remote a spot for his benefaction, the Schoolmaster replied that it was the place of Holgate's birth, adding that he evidently followed the example of one of his most famous predecessors in the See, Cardinal Wolsey, who also, as Will Shakespeare had noted in his play called *King Henry VIII*, had founded a Grammar School some years before in his native town of Ipswich.

Thomas rode home that afternoon in a meditative mood. Naturally his thoughts turned to the neighbourhood where he himself had been born and brought up. He asked himself what opportunities of schooling it offered to boys, and how the poor scholar, the lad of parts and promise, could obtain help to make the most of his abilities to serve his country well in the offices of peace and war, perhaps even to rise in the world, and become distinguished in Church or State. He had to confess to himself that no such aids to learning and advancement existed in Barnsley.

But why should they not be provided there? The thought haunted him and the resolution gradually took shape in his mind to follow Holgate's example as Holgate had followed Wolsey's, and so take his place in the noble succession of lovers of their kind, who pass on from age to age the lamp of Knowledge, Truth and Life. Further he resolved not to put off this good dead till his death, but to give himself the pleasure of seeing it bear fruit while he lived.

The times, however, were very unsettled and no man knew what might happen next in England. Keresforth seems to have been a Royalist, for it is on record that on January 13th 1645 an ordinance of Parliament passed for pardoning his 'delinquency' on payment of a fine. Probably he thought it prudent not to proceed with his project till civil strife should cease and a better prospect of security and order appear. No sooner did the Restoration of Charles II, on May 29th 1660, seem to promise this than Keresforth promptly carried out his cherished plan. Only a fortnight later, on June 13th, he founded the Grammar School in Barnsley, conveying to Trustees by deed of gift about half an acre of land belonging to him on the East side of Church Street, with the house standing upon it then known as St Mary's House; and to this he afterwards added certain fee-farm rents. It is also stated that in 1665, he built a School-house; this probably means a Schoolroom on the site in addition to the dwelling house already there. 'Being old and the childless' [sic], as he recites in the Instrument of Foundation, he wished the school to be his child to perpetuate his name among posterity. As Thomas Keresforth survived till 1674, when he died at the age of 77, he had the satisfaction of being able to take for some years a fatherly interest in the growth and progress of his school.

During the 17th and 18th Centuries

> What see'st thou else in the dark backward and abysm of time.
>
> *The Tempest*

The original Deed by which Thomas Keresforth founded the School is still extant, in duplicate. It recites how the Donor gave for this purpose certain property to Trustees 'for and in consideration of the special trust and confidence that he reposeth in them: the said Gervas Cutler, Willoughby Rokeby, Nicholas Greaves, Lewis West, Henry Edmunds, Samuel Savile, Thomas Senior, Thomas Barnsley and William Wood; and of the goodwill and affection that he beareth towards the inhabitants of the Town and Townships of Barnsley, Dodworth and Keresforth Hill, and the poorer sort of children'.

The documents are in fair preservation and Thomas Keresforth's signature is legible, though much faded, and smeared before the ink was dry; the signatures of Samuel Savile, Henry Edmunds and Thomas Barnsley are also clear. New Trustees were appointed at long intervals, and Deeds of this nature exist, dated 1682, 1722, 1758, 1795 with others of later date. Evidently those chosen from time to time were men of position and influence in the neighbourhood, many of them bearing names still well known among Yorkshire families, such as Wentworth, Bosville, Francis Godolphin (Duke of Leeds), Sir F L Wood, Lane Fox, Armitage, Rooke, Wombwell and Strafford.

While the endowment of the Foundation was safeguarded from generation to generation, there appear to be no School records or registers to show names of successive Masters, numbers of pupils or the character of the education given during this period. Yet two pieces of evidence may be adduced which seem to indicate progress.

There is among the publications of the Surtees Society, in the Free Library, the Diary of John Hobson of Dodworth. An entry dated Oct 12th 1726 records that he gave a subscription of one guinea towards the building of a new house for 'Mr Tomlinson, the Schoolmaster at Barnsley'.

Then too every Old Boy will remember that on the outside of the south wall of the School, just inside the Church Street entrance, there is a Latin inscription (still to be seen) dated 1769 and commemorating the rebuilding of School by public subscription.

It would seem only reasonable to infer from this rebuilding of both the Master's House and School in the first century of the history of the Foundation that it was becoming increasingly useful to the inhabitants of the little Barnsley of the 18th century; and that the improvement and enlargement of its accommodation was an object which enlisted their sympathies, appealed to their interests and made them cheerful givers of guineas like John Hobson.

During the 19th Century

The *Sheffield Mercury* of Jan 11th 1812, contained the following advertisement:

> The Rev J Milner Curate of Whiston, near Rotherham, many years teacher of the Latin, Greek and French languages, at some of the very first literary Institutions in the South, and the last five years at the Academy, Attercliffe, near Sheffield, having been duly elected Master at the above School, eligibly situated in the most airy and central part of the Town, respectfully announces to the public his intention of opening it after the present recess on Monday January 20th, when he hopes to be enabled to accommodate a select limited number of Boarders, on such moderate but respectable terms as will secure a politer liberal and sedulous attention towards the cultivation of the juvenile mind ... Without literary ostentation Mr Milner can with strict justice affirm that few persons of his years ever came forward as instructors of youth in the literary pursuits of life, with greater experience or a more liberal Classical education ... Mr Milner begs leave to add that those gentlemen who may please to honour him with the tuition of their children may rest assured that the most unwearied efforts will be used towards instilling into their tender minds such precepts as when expanded and matured shall evince to the world the man of polished sense and confirmed virtue.

From whatever cause, Mr Milner's tenure of office was short. On Dec 14th 1812, the Rev Henry Sutcliffe of Darton was appointed Master of the Grammar School. His successor, appointed Dec 24th 1814, was Thomas Westmoreland, MA. It must have been under this Master and his predecessor that Joseph Locke (born 1805) was educated, as he is stated to have been in the School till he was 13 years of age, one of his sisters being in attendance at the same time. If we may trust the authority of Burland (Annals of Barnsley, Vol I) the pedagogues of this period 'conceived that nothing could be taught at all without supplementary kicks and cuffs'; 'they beat dull and quick alike' and 'Joseph Locke came in for his share of these brutal assaults'; nor did 'the concentrated determination with which he attacked, and the accurate rapidity with which he mastered his tasks, save him from having to endure them'.

The condition of the School in 1827 is thus described in the *Official Report of an Enquiry into the Charities of the Parish of Silkstone*:

> The School is conducted with utility to the inhabitants of the town and neighbourhood, and is at present attended by upwards of 100 children of both sexes, who are instructed in English, reading, writing and arithmetic at the quarterly rate of 10s for reading, 15s for reading and writing, and 21s for reading, writing and accounts: an usher, and a female teacher for the girls, being employed by the Master to assist him. The Master also takes a few Boarders as Latin scholars, and professes his willingness to teach Latin to the other scholars who may desire it, without charge.

The Master's name is not given in this Report, but apparently Mr Westmoreland was succeeded by the Rev Robert Willan, whose successor was Mr William Gilbanks, Master from about 1822 till 1839.

Among the answers given by the Trustees before the Schools' Enquiry Commissioners in October 1865, is to be found some information about the School as it was in 1839. After recording the fact that the last appointment of the Trustees had been made in that year, the Statement proceeds:

> Up to this period the revenues and management of the School had fallen wholly into the hands of the Master, who taught both boys and girls therein and charged for their education what he thought proper. He was also Postmaster for Barnsley, but being then a prisoner in York Castle at the suit of the Crown, the first act of the new Trustees was to displace him and to appoint as his successor the Rev Richard Boutein Howe, of Pembroke College, Cambridge, BA; to ordain that the School should be for boys only; and to sanction the following scale of fees: for children in the First Form, and who shall be taught reading, writing and the elements of arithmetic, one guinea per quarter; for children in the Second Form, and who shall be taught geography, thc use of the globes and the higher branches of arithmetic,including algebra, mensuration and Euclid, one guinea and a half per quarter; and for children of the Third Form, who shall be taught all or any of the above Sciences together with the Latin and Greek Classics, three guineas per quarter'.

At the date of the Commission of 1865, Mr John Hargreave, BA and subsequently LLD, of Trinity College, Dublin, had been the Master for 20 years, and continued in office until his death in 1880. The number of boys attending the School in 1864 was stated to be 22.

There is in existence a School Register of Admissions, Progress and Withdrawals. The entries extend from March 31st 1845 to September 1847; and from May 4th 1868 to October 25th 1880. There is also a list of Locke Scholars from July 1861 to October 1877. The few remarks appended to the Register mostly refer to difficult cases; for example: 'Very silent and obstinate, removed to business', 'Very little progress, not well cared for at home', 'Very erratic did not like close work', 'Withdrawn at my request, as he would not learn', 'Went home at 11 o'clock, would not learn anything'.

With the exception of this incomplete Register the present writer has not been able to trace any records kept by Masters of the School, or any Minute-books of the proceedings of the Trustees relating to the period under review.

It does not fall within the scope of this sketch to deal with the main events in the more recent history of the Grammar School, such as the foundation of the Locke Scholarships in 1861, the amalgamation in 1887 of the Holgate Grammar School Foundation at Hemsworth with the Foundation of Thomas Keresforth, the constitution of the School as the recognised Centre for Secondary Education in Barnsley and District by the West Riding County Council in the exercise of their authority under the Education Act of 1902, the establishment of the School in its new Buildings at Shaw Lane in 1912, its transfer to the jurisdiction of Barnsley County Borough Authority during the present year and the foundation of the four Cooper Scholarships. It may suffice to bring this retrospect to a close with the statement that the School now contains 207 boys with a Staff of 16 Masters; and that – thanks to the fostering care of public authorities and private benefactors – it is in a position to take an effective part in that wider diffusion and development of Secondary Education to which the signs of the times are pointing.

Addenda by E G Bayford, F E S in *Alumnus* 1930

In the first volume of *The Alumnus* the Rev C S Butler, MA, brought together all the facts he could glean concerning the history of the School from its foundation to 1887. Unfortunately, he failed to trace material that had at one time been accessible, in particular a minute book, which would have been of great service. Even if it had been found, it is doubtful whether or not he would have been able to compile a complete list of the Masters for the period in question. The following notes fill up some of the gaps, besides adding other particulars of interest, and the tabular arrangement will show at a glance 1) the extent of our knowledge and 2) what is yet wanted to make the list complete.

1) Mr Butler refers to a Master in 1726, whom he knew only in the reference to him in *The Journal of Mr John Hobson of Dodworth Green,* published by the Surtees Society in 1877.

   1726 – October 12th. At Barnsley. This year the schoolmaster there (Mr Tomlinson) had a new house builded by voluntary contributions, toward which I paid £1 1s, which I had formerly subscribed.

   To this I am now able to add considerably.

   When Bishop Thomas Herring was made Archbishop of York in 1743, he very soon began preparations for a visitation of his diocese.

   He prepared a list of questions, a copy of which was sent to each incumbent or vicar. Some returned very full answers, and some hardly answered at all. Amongst the latter was Barnsley Chapel in the Deanery of Doncaster. The Records of this Primary Visitation in his Register are now in the process of publication by the Yorks Archaeological Society in that Society's *Record Series*, with the title *Archbishop Herring's Visitation Returns 1743*. Two volumes have appeared, so far, the few details referring to Barnsley being found in Vol 1 published in 1928.

   The portion which immediately concerns us is as follows:

Grammar School Master
James Thomason. Licensed 26th January 1720. (ie 1721 as we should write it today; the year then began in March 25th).

The facts which emerge from this extract are:

His full and correct name, which was not "Tomlinson", but "James Thomason".
That he was Master for at least 23 years.

2) My next item is gleaned from *Memorials of Thomas Harvey*, printed for private circulation in 1886.

He was an elder brother of Henry and Charles Harvey (Part 1. Chapter 17), whose benefactions to our town are commemorated in the Harvey Institute. He says (p5):

> I went … to the Barnsley Grammar School. During part of my time there the mastership was vacant and the school was taught successively by two elderly clergymen. The former was, I think, kind, but severe on principle. I recollect being unable to learn my Latin lesson, and being sentenced to stripes, when, with tears, I begged for more time. This was granted; and after vainly puzzling over one of the conjugations, the bright thought occurred to me to go and ask the stern pedagogue to explain my difficulties. This he did at once, in the kindest way, and I soon learned my lesson. These good men were succeeded by one more liked in the town than respected. His defects in moral conduct had prevented his becoming a clergyman; but he was thought quite good enough for a Schoolmaster. He was a man of good abilities and attainment, but the errors that had spoilt his career at College clung to him for life. My brother William had been in due course sent to Ackworth School … I followed him in 1822 being not quite ten …

These are, I believe, the earliest reminiscences of an old boy which have come to light. Not only for their intrinsic interest, but equally for their author as an individual, and a member of a family Barnsley delights to honour, they deserve a place in our School Magazine.

3) List of Masters from 1660 to 1880:

1660	– 25 Jan 1721	???
26 Jan 1721	– 1743 x	James Thomason
1743 x	– 1811	???
11 Jan 1812	– Dec 1812	Rev J Miller
14 Dec 1812	– 3 Sept 1817 (died)	Rev Henry Sutcliffe
24 Dec 1817	– ???	Thomas Westmoreland, MA. (Vacancy temporarily filled by Rev Robert Willan)
? 1821	– 1839	William Gilbanks (Mr Butler says he was appointed about 1822 but Baines Directory pub. Jan 1 1822 gives him as Master so that he must have been appointed 1821 at the latest)
1839	– 1845	Rev Richard Boutein Howe
1845	– 1880	John Hargreave, BA LLD

3

Recollections of the Old School by W Maudsley

Alumnus – July 1913

First then as to the premises. The upper storey of the building being let as a reading room, our school-room consisted of the whole of the ground-floor only, a large room with whitewashed walls decorated only by a couple of long rolls on which were printed the objects and rules of the Locke benefaction. Cloakrooms being undreamt of, two rows of pegs at the far end of the room sufficed for our hats and coats. In mid winter artificial light was provided by one or two tallow candles, by whose feeble glimmer those boys who were kept late for any offence had to do their extra task. No wonder boys dreaded the sentence, 'Stay in half an hour this afternoon'. It was a cheerless and dismal experience.

In my time the number of pupils averaged from fifty to sixty, ten of these being 'Locke Scholars'. The latter were provided with college caps similar to those worn at Oxford and Cambridge, except that the tassels were blue. An examination was held every year and the head boy was styled Captain for that year and was distinguished by a gold tassel. The boys did not care much for their college caps as street lads used to follow them, shouting 'Lime board etc'.

The Locke Scholars were under stricter rules than the rest as regards attendance. They were fined 1d for being late and 3d for each half day absence, except when due to illness. It was the Captain's privilege to keep a small book, in which he entered the amount of the fine and the name. I wonder if any of these books are still in existence. At the end of a year, if there was sufficient money, it was used to provide prizes. There was no other prize fund, nor were there any Scholarships or Exhibitions or any means whatever of enabling a boy of ability to proceed to the University. There was in those days little or none of that interest in educational matters which we see today. ....

The education was sound and thorough, and included Commercial, Mathematical and Classical subjects, and French. These were taught by the Head Master Dr Hargreave and one Assistant. Drawing and Chemistry were taught by visiting Masters. While testifying to the thoroughness of the instruction, I must admit that the school books and teaching generally were somewhat dry and uninteresting. It might be said of most boys that

> They did their task because they must,
> Not gladly, truth to tell;
> For studies oft were dry as dust,
> Monotonous as well.

The Classics were a prominent feature of the school, but our editions of Caesar, Virgil etc had no notes explaining the difficult passages and no nice vocabularies giving the exact meaning of each word as used by the author. We had to hunt in the dictionary for the meaning most suitable. I am not sure this is not the better way. It throws a boy on his own resources, makes him think and find out both the primary and secondary meaning of words.

Then as to games we had no organized football or cricket; but we used to enter with some zest into our games at play time and after school hours. In winter sometimes we had snow-balling battles with the boys of St Mary's. They were the more numerous, but our boys were rather older, so we were fairly matched. While the battle was raging by the Town Hall and St Mary's Gate, we would send a detachment round by the Hospital to take them in the rear and so come off victorious.

The Head Master, Dr Hargreave [sic], was in more than one sense a 'striking' personality. Tall and strongly built with silvery hair and a long white beard, he had a patriarchal appearance. Latterly he took off his beard, a change not for the better to my mind. An austere man of the old school, his discipline was very strict, signs of approval being scarce while 'marks' of displeasure were plentiful. So much so that with many boys the unexpressed motto was 'Cave Canem', which might be interpreted as 'Beware of old Cane-em'. (I trust the Editor will forgive me this bit of *dog* Latin). [*Cave Canem* means literally "beware of the dog"].

The Doctor was a regular customer at the second-hand bookstall kept by 'Iron Joe', a character who will be remembered by many Old Boys. Here he purchased for a trifle many school books, more particularly Latin and Greek works, which were distributed to his pupils. The boys disliked these books, for they were often nearly a century old, with their long s's and generally antiquated appearance. No doubt his motive was to save expense to those boys whose parents were not over well-to-do, for these classical works would have cost to buy new as many shilling as he gave pence for them.

The Latin and Greek classes seemed to me to get into trouble more than any of the others. Woe to the lad who neglected his grammar or translation. I can see such a boy now stumbling through his lesson with the Doctor's stern eye on him. …

Altogether Dr Hargreave was a remarkable man, and if his rule was severe, still it cannot be denied that it produced manly boys, and a good number of his pupils have turned out successful men.

I personally have to acknowledge more than one instance of thoughtfulness and consideration on his part, which were all the more appreciated because unexpected …

4

Barnsley Grammar School by Rev A Willan

Alumnus – April 1914

It may be of some interest if I give a few of my recollections of my school days at the Barnsley Grammar School 60 years ago.

I was one of Dr Hargrave's [sic] pupils in the year 1851–2. The School was then managed by the Head Master and one assistant. Latin was taught in addition to the ordinary subjects of a commercial education. Great attention was given to penmanship and a good deal of our time was spent in writing copper-plate hand. Euclid was also taught to the older boys. The figure was drawn on the blackboard and the proposition was repeated in a loud voice by the master and boys standing round the easel.

Making maps was a pleasing relief from the ordinary lessons, which appeared to me to be dull and uninteresting. These maps were drawn on large sheets of paper, the latitude and longitude having been ruled in by the Doctor. Palestine was generally given as a commencement, being one of the easiest. Then would follow Africa and, as the greater part of the interior was then considered to be a desert, there was not much filling-in required.

Drawing was taught by the late Mr Abel Hold of Cawthorne, who was an artist of repute and an exhibitor at the Royal Academy. He was particularly skilful in the delineation of animal life,and his pictures adorn the walls of some of the older inhabitants of Barnsley.

I was one of the few weekly boarders and Mrs Hargrave, the Doctor's first wife, treated us with kindness and consideration. The food was plain but sufficient, as we were not allowed to leave any fat on our plates, but were required to eat it all up. Being unable to do this, I used to watch my opportunity and hide it in my pocket-handkerchief, to be thrown away when we regained the play-ground.

Dr Hargrave was a fine specimen of the old fashioned School Master and was painstaking and conscientious in the discharge of his duties. Corporal punishment was at that time the order of the day. It was expected by the boys and acquiesced in by the parents; but at the Barnsley Grammar School it was administered with what was considered, even in those days, unusual severity. At the commencement of every term or 'half' as it was then called, the rules of the school were read out to the assembled pupils and it was therein stated how various offences would be punished. The list was a long one and the writer can only now remember that the majority of offences were to be visited with corporal punishment.

It may be of interest if I describe how boys were sometimes punished 60 years ago. A blot in the copy book would be visited with a few cuts on the hand with the cane. If a boy at the other end of the school was seen to be talking, the Doctor would sometimes throw the ruler at him with the order to 'bring that here sir' and punishment would be inflicted on the outstretched hand with the ruler itself. In addition to the ordinary cane of long dimensions, the Doctor had a more formidable weapon in the shape of a long and thick piece of whalebone and a boy would sometimes receive a flogging laid face downwards across one of the desks.

One of the pupils was an orphan boy who came in for more than his share of punishment. He was not a bad lad, but was somewhat dull at his lessons. His name was Thomas Colley. One day we were standing round the Doctor's desk reading Latin and the proper name 'Scipio' was pronounced by Thomas as if it were spelt 'Skipio' (a pronunciation which is, by the way, now considered to be the proper one). The Doctor corrected him and allowed it to pass. When Tom's turn came round again, the same name unfortunately occurred and, no doubt through nervousness, was again mispronounced. The Doctor's wrath was now fully aroused and the boy received a punishment, which would now be considered to be out of all proportion to the offence.

I have sometimes wondered what has become of poor Tom Colley. Does he still live? and if so does he remember how he suffered for being in advance of his day in the matter of Latin pronunciation?

The younger brother of a respected inhabitant of Barnsley, only lately deceased, having been on one occasion severely flogged, the father requested to know the cause of this chastisement and the Doctor replied that it was for 'pretended ignorance'. I may add that it was a favourite idea that boys often pretended to be ignorant.

I never heard of opposition to the Doctor's severity going beyond a mild remonstrance on the part of the parents. The reader will already have come to the conclusion that Doctor Hargrave sometimes failed to control a naturally hasty temper, but he was not an unkind man, and reference has already been made in these pages to acts of kindness on his part. In justice to the memory of the Doctor it should be added that he possessed those sterling qualities of character which compelled the respect of both parents and pupils.

Previous to undertaking the head-mastership of the Barnsley Grammar School, Doctor Hargrave was assistant master to the late Rev W Sutherland [sic], Vicar of Penistone, whose sudden and lamented death was the result of a coach accident in the neighbourhood of Matlock.

Great changes have taken place during the past 60 years, both in regard to the way in which various subjects are taught in schools as well as in the administration of corporal punishment, which may now be said to be almost totally discontinued.

Grammar now takes a secondary place in the teaching of languages. In former years the Eton Latin Grammar, which was expected to be learnt off by heart, formed the ground work of the teaching of Latin. It is the opinion of many, and it is the opinion shared by the writer, that boys were more thoroughly grounded in the necessary elements of a commercial education fifty years ago than they are in the present day.

York and Lancaster Regiment Memorial in the Drill Hall
(now offices of *Barnsley Chronicle*). (© Jane Ainsworth)

5

Information about Barnsley Holgate Grammar School in *Alumnus*

Alumnus – April 1913 School Notes

THE OLD SCHOOL – the premises in Church Street, including both School and House, were sold by auction in September 1912, and are now the property of S J Cooper, Esq., of Mount Vernon. The House, now called Keresforth House, still remains by arrangement the residence of the Head-Master. Old Boys will be glad to know that the School Buildings are likely to be preserved almost unaltered in appearance.

THE COUNTY BOROUGH – on April 1st 1913, Barnsley became a County Borough. One effect of this is to constitute the Borough Council the Authority for Secondary Education within the Borough, instead of the West Riding County Council. A friendly arrangement has been entered into between the two Councils by which the School will continue to serve the District assigned to it within the W R Administrative area and the Borough will acquire the new School Buildings in Shaw Lane. The Governing Body of the School will continue to exercise its present functions.

PLAYING FIELDS – A plan and estimate have been approved for levelling and laying out as a Cricket-field the lower part of the ground at the back of the new School. It is hoped that the upper part may be dealt with at no distant date, so that the School may have, on the premises, its own ground for Football as well as Cricket. Until that is completed, games cannot take their legitimate place in the life of the School.

INSPECTION – The School was officially inspected in October 1912 by the Staff Inspectors of the Board of Education, the previous inspection having taken place in 1907. Their conclusions are summed up in the final paragraph of the Report as follows:

> Organization is systematic and works smoothly. School discipline is good without any undue punishment or severity. A School Dinner, recently provided at moderate cost, is a great boon to the large number who now come to School by train and cannot get home in the dinner hour. It should now be possible for the School to develop a rather more active Corporate life than could be expected in the old premises.

The School continues to do very valuable and creditable work.

Records of Old Boys

Four Old Boys are now Governors of the School:

Councillor W England, JP Alderman J S Rose, JP	} representing the Town Council
C F Wike, Esq., City Surveyor for Sheffield	representing Sheffield University
J E Jaeger, Esq.,	a Co-opted Governor

Among the oldest are
S J Cooper, Esq., of Mount Vernon, who entered in 1837
T J Newman, Esq., of Hamstead, 1832
the Rev T T Taylor, 1847

***Alumnus* – July 1913 School Sports**

The Annual Sports were held on Thursday, June 19th on Shaw Lane Cricket Ground. There was a splendid concourse of spectators, and the band of the 5th York and Lancaster Territorial regiment rendered a pleasing musical programme.

The racing was up to the usual standard, and was especially interesting this year owing to the close fight for the Old Boys' Challenge Cup. Great keenness was again shown amongst the Juniors and the winning of the mile by one of their fraternity was highly popular. The competition for the House Challenge Shield also helped to enliven the interest, particularly amongst the various house partisans.

The prizes were distributed by Miss Robinson, Head Mistress of the Girls' High School, and a pleasant afternoon ended with hearty cheers for Miss Robinson, the Headmaster, the Staff and the winner of the Cup.

Barnsley Old Grammarians Football Club

Since the appearance of the last number of *Alumnus*, the Old Boys' Football Club, which had its modest beginning in the Easter Term, has become a strong and thriving organization. Its first General Meeting has been held, a field has been secured and, last but not least, some very interesting games have been arranged, including matches with Leeds University, the Training Colleges of Leeds, Sheffield and York, Mirfield College and Sheffield Club. In addition the Club will take part in the Amateur Cup Competition of the Football Association.

OFFICERS

President	Rev C S Butler
Captain	F Ward, Esq
Vice-Captain	E Litherland, Esq

Committee: Messrs Berry, Litherland, Nicholson, Peddle and Sugden

Hon Secretary and Treasurer
A Fawley, Esq, 116 Park Road, Barnsley

Membership of the Old Grammarians is open to all Old Boys …

In conclusion, the Committee of the Old Grammarians wish to thank the Governors of the School for allowing the use of the School for meetings; E Riley, Esq, for his kind offer of a changing room free of charge; and E Haigh, Esq, for designing the badge of the Club.

Alumnus – December 1919

The school numbers have now reached a total of 342, which is nearly 30 higher than the previous record. The plan of erecting an Army Hut to house the overflow was abandoned, and we are carrying on, crowded but not downhearted. As a result of the high numbers, pressure on the dining-room accommodation became acute, and it was decided to have a small early dinner for the youngest boys. The average daily number of dinners served is now nearly 150.

Alumnus – December 1920

Ninety three new boys were admitted at the beginning of Term and the total number in the School (including five Student Teachers) was 368, this figure being 26 in advance of the previous highest.

The School is still growing fast and it seems that it will continue to grow. The idea of utilising the Army hut already on the premises had been revived and it is more than probable that this unfortunate structure will emerge from the obscurity in which it has languished for over a year and at last fulfil the purpose for which it was intended, thereby ceasing to provide the young with tempting ground for physical adventure.

To meet the extra numbers, although no additional classrooms were available, an extra Form had to be made. Certain changes have also taken place in connection with other Forms …

Alumnus – April 1930 The New Buildings Opening Ceremony by A Heathcote, Senior Prefect

On 16 December 1929, there was an opening ceremony for extensions to the school buildings of the Holgate. The Headmaster Dr J F Horne was absent because of illness, but Mr E G Lancaster, 'the oldest surviving Governor of the Trust and also the representative Governor appointed by the Archbishop of York', presided. The Archbishop of York, Dr Temple, opened the extensions and there was a large gathering of Governors, Masters, pupils and parents.

In the course of his speech, the Chairman said that he was present at the opening ceremony of the School in 1912 by the present Archbishop of Canterbury, who was then Archbishop of York. The School was now twice its original size; and as legacies, such as the one recently left by the late Mr C F Wike, continued to be bestowed upon it, we could look forward to the time when it would be the most richly endowed school in Yorkshire. Men would be proud to have got their first start in life at Barnsley Holgate Grammar School.

After a few introductory remarks, the Archbishop emphasised a promising feature of our national life: 'the perpetually increasing demand for a higher and deeper type of education' and 'a steadily growing concern of the masses of the people for education generally'. While he recognised the necessity for the propagation of scientific knowledge, His Grace warned us that, as a Grammar School, we had the special responsibility of preserving 'letters and literature, and the study of all things that are human'.

The main purpose of education was to stimulate and discipline the faculty of understanding, and in this the great human subjects were better instruments of education than anything else. As in all nourishment, the benefits of education came, not in amassing a large amount of information, which could be supplied on demand, but in assimilation.

The Archbishop struck a lighter vein in a short discourse on spelling, which, he said, was 'one of the minor decencies of life'. It was much more important to be able to punctuate. In concluding, His Grace addressed the parents and urged them to make a sacrifice in order to leave their boys at school so that they and their country might gain the full benefit of those last years at school, which were worth so much more than the early years.

Sir Percy Jackson proposed a vote of thanks to the Archbishop, in which he referred to the large number of West Riding boys in the School and declared that the future of the world must be in the hands of an educated democracy. In seconding, Lieut-Colonel W E Raley urged the necessity for preserving the home touch.

The Headmaster then presented the Archbishop with a silver salver, on behalf of the architects.

The proceedings were ended by a vote of thanks to the Chairman, which was proposed by the Bishop of Wakefield, who remarked on Mr Lancaster's generosity, and seconded by the Mayor (Councillor E Sheerien).

Barnsley Town Hall with main war memorial in front. (© Jane Ainsworth)

6

Scholarships

Keresforth Scholarships (3) were for pupils who had attended at least three years in elementary school in Barnsley or Dodworth. A notice in *Barnsley Chronicle* advertising an examination on 24 November 1887, stated that the scholarship entitled the holder to have tuition fees paid for at least two years. Thomas Keresforth had created a Trust to manage the Grammar School that he founded in 1660 (biography in Part 1. Chapter 11).

Holgate Scholarships (12) were for Hemsworth Parishes (also tenable at Wakefield, Pontefract and Doncaster Grammar Schools). An advert in *Barnsley Chronicle* for an examination on 24 November 1887 for six scholarships, stated that these entitled the holder to have tuition fees paid for at least two years plus £10 each year; they were open to boys from Hemsworth, Felkirk, South Kirkby, Ackworth, Royston (including Cudworth, Carlton, Monk Bretton, Woolley and Smithies) and Wragby. Archbishop Robert Holgate endowed his Foundation when he built the Grammar School in Hemsworth in 1546 and funding transferred to Barnsley when the schools amalgamated in 1887 (biography in Part 1. Chapter 12).

Locke Scholarships (10) were introduced in 1861 by Phoebe Locke, widow of Joseph Locke (biography in Part 1. Chapter 17), who donated £3,200 to create the Locke Fund; the Deed dated 20 July 1861 for this is in Barnsley Archives. There were Senior and Junior Locke Scholarships, which were paid for pupils aged 10 to 14 of parents residing in the townships of Barnsley, Dodworth and Keresforth Hill, 'without reference to religious tenets and with some peculiar aptitude for engineering, architecture, drawing, surveying etc but not limited to this'. The Head Locke Scholar (Captain) wore the college cap (called a Limeboard) with yellow tassels, whereas the other nine scholars had blue tassels. Locke Scholars could be fined 1d for lateness or 3d for each half day absence, except illness, and this money was put into a fund for prizes.

The School attracted other benefactions and endowments to enable boys to go to University:

The Cooper Exhibition was founded in 1893 by Samuel Joshua Cooper (1830–1913) to enable pupils of the Holgate, who lived within 10 miles of Barnsley and had been taught or wanted to learn Greek and Latin, to study Theology at Oxford or Cambridge. Mr Cooper made several donations to the school and he left money in his Will for three **Cooper Scholarships** for Oxford or Cambridge and a **Cooper Prize Fund** of £20 each year, which started in 1913 (biography in Part 1. Chapter 14).

The Edward George Lancaster Scholarship was endowed by him, as mentioned at the Old Boys' Association dinner in 1903; it is also referred to in his Obituary in *Yorkshire Post and Leeds Intelligencer* dated 1 November 1934 (details about the family in Part 1. Chapter 13).

William Carnelley left £3,000 in 1919 to fund three scholarships in his name, but the sum was subsequently found to be sufficient to only fund one. The examination for this in 1938 required pupils to write a composition on one of the following: All the Fun of the Fair, A Strange Dream, Wireless or What I do on a Saturday (biography in Part 1. Chapter 17).

Charles Froggatt Wike, one of the first ten Locke Scholars, bequeathed in 1929 a sum of £2,000 to fund Scholarships at Oxford or Cambridge (biography in Part 1. Chapter 17).

Dr John Fletcher Horne, MD and JP, was one of the benefactors listed in R H Greenland's book but I have been unable to find details for what he funded (biography in Part 1. Chapter 17).

County Major and County Minor Scholarships – Under the 1902 Education Act, Grammar Schools received help from local and central funds. From April 1913, Barnsley became a County Borough responsible for secondary education instead of the West Riding County Council. The County Minor Scholarship Class C was explained in 1902 as 'placed by the West Riding County Technical Instruction Committee at the disposal of the Governors for Boys attending the Grammar School'.

Bursary – There were two types of bursary: means-tested for students whose parents earn under a threshold value per annum and a scholarship or prize based on performance. The latter awards were generally given for good performance in the exams preceding university or college entrance in which the student achieved grades above the standard entry.

Exhibition – Under a new scheme introduced in 1888, Governors were empowered to spend £150 per annum in Exhibitions of a maximum value of £50 pa to boys who had been there at least three years for higher education. At certain Universities, such as Oxford and Cambridge, or other educational establishment, a financial award or grant could be made to a student on the grounds of merit.

Intending / Pupil or Student Teacher – students were required to pass the Board of Education Examination for Admission as Pupil Teachers. F Oliffe in *Alumnus* July 1913 explained this: 'one who, after attending a Secondary School for a period of about five years, is sent to an Elementary School for the purposes of learning how to teach'.

A number of people also contributed money to pay for prizes.

The J W Sykes Memorial Fund was established in 1904, when the Shaw Lands Trust made additional grants to the school; prizes were initially awarded to the two 'highest unsuccessful candidates in the Junior Locke Scholarship examination'. John William Sykes (c1850–1897) was Innkeeper at the Clarence Hotel in Sheffield Road, Barnsley, and Chair of the Barnsley and District Licensed Victuallers Association; he was also a Barnsley Councillor, held in high regard.

The following were introduced later:
- Pickles Geography Prize;
- John Bird Memorial Prize;
- The Duckett Memorial Prize;
- Pawsey Prize; and
- David Wade Prize.

Examinations

Barnsley Holgate Grammar School entered pupils into the Oxford Local Examinations at Junior and Senior level until about 1925 when they used the Northern Universities Examination. The subjects covered by each Examination in 1902 were:

Junior – Arithmetic, Religious Knowledge, English Grammar and History, A Play of Shakespeare, Latin, French, Mathematics and Theoretical & Practical Chemistry.

Senior – Arithmetic, Religious Knowledge, English Grammar and History, Two Plays of Shakespeare, Latin, French, Algebra and Theoretical & Practical Chemistry.

7

A Manual for the Use of B. G. S. by John Hargreave

July 1861
To Mrs Locke
Madam,

As a memento of grateful acknowledgement for your very liberal gift presented to Barnsley Grammar School, this Manual, which has been prepared for the use of the Pupils, and will be first used when the 'Locke Scholars' (through your munificence) are admitted to the School, is humbly dedicated by, Madam,

Your Grateful Servant
John Hargreave

Rules and Directions (extracts)

1) cleanliness before going to school detailing nails
4) never speak aloud unnecessarily
5) be kind to your school fellows
8) when speaking to a master bow and speak to him with modesty and respect
11) avoid pride and presumption – they are the marks of wickedness and folly
17) neither speak at home or elsewhere of what has been done in school; for nothing that passes there should be told out of it
18) choose for your companions the most decent and good-humoured of your school fellows and avoid such as are clownish, dirty, rude or cruel
27) do not reflect upon anyone's dress however mean it may be, not appear to notice, and never despise any personal deformity in anyone

[The actual list is not numbered]

Other headings include:

Reading – When you read, stand upright in a graceful position
Make A Quill Pen
Writing
Arithmetic [*this takes up most of the book*]

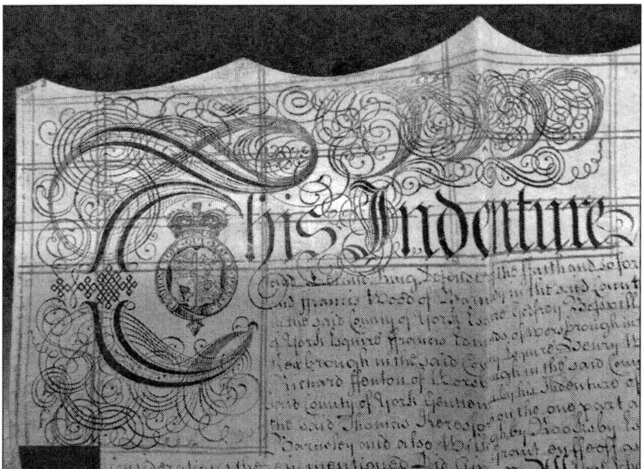

An old indenture relating to BHGS. (© Jane Ainsworth)

8

The School Song: *Carmen Holdgateianum*

Words by C S Butler, Music by Haydn Brear

FORTITER OCCUPA PORTAM
(The School Motto)

'Fortiter occupa portam', pray
What is the English of that?
'Ever be bold the gate to hold' –
There's the translation pat,
That Holgate with d you used to spell,
Archbishop, is clearly seen;
'Fortiter occupa portam' – say
What is the gate you mean?

Chorus
Whether young or old that gate we'll hold,
Whatever the gate may be,
Early or late we'll hold the gate,
Whatever the gate may be.

My sons, it is true I used to do
Precisely as you suggest:
And the sense of the Latin motto too
Right well you have expressed.
You may change the spelling of my name,
(Much else they have changed, I'm told!)
But never change this in woe or bliss
Boldly the gate to hold.

Chorus
Whether young or old that gate we'll hold,
Whatever the gate may be,
Early or late we'll hold the gate,
Whatever the gate may be.

'Tis the gate of Knowledge that opens wide
I call you to enter in:
Not the Scholar's name of a wreath of fame
But the joy of the light to win,
That gladdens the eyes of the seekers wise
As the great world's treasures unfold.
Up! Though the way may be toilsome, and say
Boldly the gate we'll hold.

Chorus
Whether young or old that gate we'll hold,
The gate of the Wise and Free
Early or late we'll hold the gate,
The gate of the Wise and Free

'Tis the gate of the heart I'd have you keep,
Against assaults of ill,
Then stand on guard, be the gate thrice-barred
With the might of a steadfast Will,
With a Conscience clear that knows no fear
And the faith of the men of old;
In the evil day of the tempter pray,
Boldly the gate to hold.

Chorus
Whether young or old that gate we'll hold,
The gate of the Pure and Free
Early or late we'll hold the gate,
The gate of the Pure and Free

'Tis the gate of Truth I would bid you seek,
Though the quest be long and far:
Nor listless dream of the things that seem,
But toil for the things that are;
With a high disdain for falsehood's gain

And the life enslaved to gold,
The love of the True shall strengthen you,
Boldly the gate to hold.

Chorus
Whether young or old that gate we'll hold,
The gate of the True and Free
Early or late we'll hold the gate,
The gate of the True and Free

There's a gate shall ope to a deathless hope,
In the realms beyond the sun,
And an entrance there through its portals fair
Shall be, when the world is done;
'Tis the gate of the True and of Wisdom too,
'Tis the gate of the Pure and Free;
O! ever be bold the gate to hold,
The gate of the World to be.

Chorus
May young and old that gate all hold,
The gate of The World to Be;
Early or late May we hold the gate,
The gate of The World To Be.

Reproduced from the First Speech Day Programme 31 July 1888.

9

Keresforth House – The Headmaster's House

KERESFORTH HOUSE, 35 CHURCH STREET, was occupied by the Headmaster of Barnsley Grammar School from 1830 to 1926. After Rev Charles Stokes Butler left in 1926, Newman & Bond Solicitors occupied it. According to E G Tasker, they shared it with *Barnsley Chronicle* from 1927 to 1994 and Nuttall, Yarwood & Partners Architects also moved in from 1970 to 1985. Newman and Bond Solicitors took over the whole premises in 1994 (details of Newman and Bond Families in Part 1. Chapter 15).

The Cooper Collection in Barnsley Archives contains details of this house from an Inspection.

LETTER DATED 7 MAY 1926 TO TRUSTEES FROM JOHN CLEGG OF NEWMAN AND BOND SOLICITORS: INSPECTION OF KERESFORTH HOUSE

The premises consist of the following:

tiled entrance
dining room with square bay (formerly 2 rooms)
study with small square bay
large room behind about 38' × 17'
staircase, which is not very good
large kitchen, well fitted up with cupboards and good kitchen range
second kitchen or scullery also with range
maid's wc out of scullery
back staircase out of kitchen
also small larder and back lobby with hanging space for coats etc

There are some good cellars, which do not appear to have been used for some years, also coal and coke cellar under scullery approached from the yard.

There are 5 bedrooms and a dressing room on the first floor, WC and bathroom on half space plus bedroom over study, divided by wood partition and approached through the back bedroom.

There are 3 attics or store rooms.

The back portion of the premises, which is not used by the Rev C S Butler, the tenant of Keresforth House, contains an entrance lobby with lavatory and store place, room on half space, bath room, WC, 2 rooms and store room on first floor.

The whole of the property is well and substantially built and structurally in a good state of repair.

The Keresforth House portion requires papering, painting and generally re-decorating.

The inside of the back portion of the premises is in a bad state of repair and requires thoroughly overhauling, cleaning, painting etc.

There is a small paved yard to the Keresforth House portion and also a good piece of garden with a frontage to Eastgate.

The site contains 970 'supl'. [supplementary] Yards or thereabouts.

Proposed usage – club, nursing home or private school – the back for warehouse or storage.

Rent – Rev Butler pays £50 pa which is very low – suggest £75–80 pa – the back portion about £30 pa.

If sold – value £2 000 – 'very considerably less than what the property originally cost'.

After Rev Butler gave up his tenancy in 1926, the house was let to Messrs Newman and Bond at £110 pa with the option to purchase within 10 years at £2 500. (Newman and Bond were Solicitors for Samuel Joshua Cooper and for the Trustees of the Art Gallery, two partners being Trustees). Newman and Bond Solicitors spent £1 200 converting Keresforth House into offices with a strong room for documents.

There is a First World War Memorial, made of brass with a thin wooden frame, inside these premises with details about the six 'gallant men, who in 1914, were assisting these offices' and who served in the Forces. 'Lest We Forget':

Alfred Dalton Bond, Second Lieutenant in the 5th Battalion (Territorial Force) of the York and Lancaster Regiment, who had been a Solicitor and Partner from August 1901 and enlisted in 1914, 'died serving' on 22 May 1916, aged 32.

Robert Arthur Abbs Simpson, Lieutenant in the Northumberland Fusiliers, who had been a Solicitor from January 1914 and enlisted in 1915, died of wounds on *30 October 1917, aged 38.*[*]

William Barraclough, Second Lieutenant in the 5th Battalion of the West Yorkshire Regiment, who had been a Surveyor from October 1912 and enlisted in 1914, was killed in action on 28 September 1916, *aged 30.*[†]

Walter George Burt, Second Lieutenant in the 14th Battalion (Second Barnsley Pals) of the York and Lancaster Regiment, who had been a Solicitor from September 1911 and enlisted in 1914, was wounded.

Francis John William Lyons, Second Lieutenant in the 13th Battalion, who had been a Clerk from August 1909 and enlisted in 1914, had been a prisoner.

Wilfrid Gray Bradley, Second Lieutenant in the Duke of Wellington's West Riding Regiment, who had been an Assistant Cashier from January 1914 and enlisted in 1914, was wounded.

* Commonwealth War Graves Commission website.
† Commonwealth War Graves Commission website.

10

Sale Particulars and Plan of Barnsley & District Holgate Grammar School on Wednesday 18 September 1912

VALUABLE FREEHOLD PROPERTY

IN

Church Street and Racecommon Road,

BARNSLEY.

Messrs. LANCASTER & SONS

WILL OFFER FOR SALE

At the Royal Hotel, in Barnsley,

On WEDNESDAY, the 18th day of September, 1912,

At 5 o'clock in the Afternoon precisely,

Subject to the General Conditions of Sale of the Sheffield and District Incorporated Law Society and to such Special Conditions as shall be then and there produced:

Lot 1.—The PREMISES known as

The OLD GRAMMAR SCHOOL

WITH THE

HEAD MASTER'S HOUSE

ADJOINING THERETO

The site has a frontage of 114 feet to **Church Street**, with a similar frontage to **Eastgate**, and contains an area of **2,530 square yards** or thereabouts.

The Premises are situate almost opposite the Parish Church.

The School Buildings themselves are of two storeys, and the numerous Class Rooms are conveniently arranged and have a modern Laboratory of recent erection.

In the Play-ground adjoining there is a covered Recreation Shed 110 feet by 19 feet.

The Head Master's House (now called "Keresforth House") is a dry, well-built, and commodious Residence, having an amount of accommodation such as few Houses in the town possess, viz., three Sitting-rooms, the largest 36 feet by 16 feet; nine Bed-rooms, Bath-room, Kitchen, Scullery, Pantry, Cellars, Out-offices, &c. In addition there are two large Rooms, each 36 feet by 17 feet; a Sitting-room lately used as an Assistant Masters' Room; two more Bed-rooms, and another Bath-room. This latter portion of the Building was erected in 1889, when the Premises were reconstructed.

The Buildings have a handsome and picturesque frontage to Church Street. They also have an historical interest to Barnsley, inasmuch as the Property forms part of the Foundation of Archbishop Holgate in 1546, and of Thomas Keresforth in 1660.

Lot 2.—ALL THAT VALUABLE

FREEHOLD GRASS FIELD,

Fronting to **Racecommon Road**, in Barnsley, and containing **4a. 0r. 21p.** or thereabouts, and now in the occupation of Mr Mark Oldham. The Field is situate opposite to Longcar Lane, and is one of the few remaining Properties available for building in the neighbourhood. It has a frontage of 380 feet 6 inches to Racecommon Road, and is admirably suited for immediate development. The back portion of the Field is intersected by a Footpath.

For further particulars and Plans application should be made to the Auctioneers; or to

NEWMAN & BOND,
Solicitors,
BARNSLEY.

31st August, 1912.

Description of property, image kindly provided by Ken Keen (his personal property).

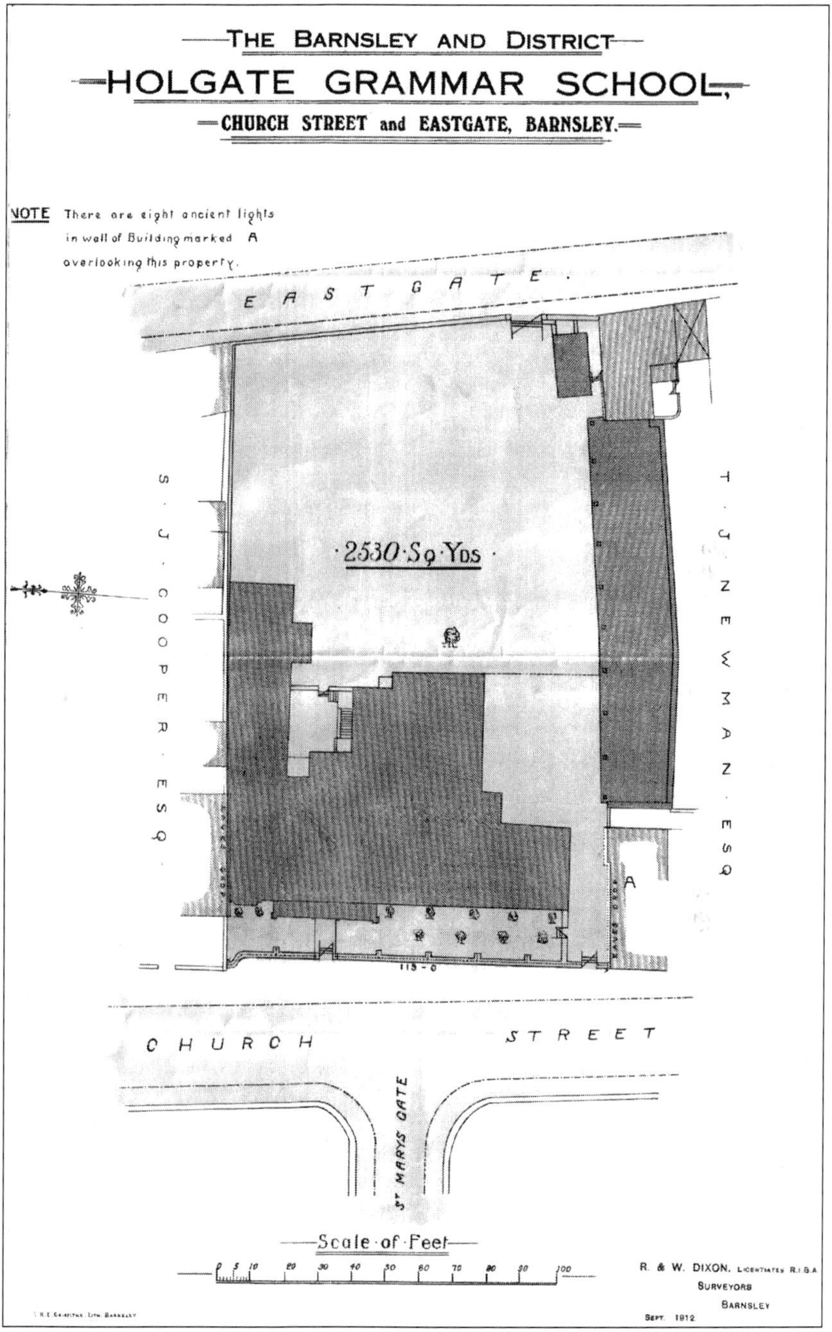

Plan of property, image kindly provided by Ken Keen (his personal property).

11

The Keresforth Family

Before the Conquest, Barnsley and Keresforth had formed one manor but they then became separated, with the land owned by the monks of Pontefract from c1150 until the Reformation. They appointed a steward, receiver and bailiff, which roles continued in the reign of Henry VIII. 'Creuesford, Beneslai' is in Doomsday Book.

In 1280, Thomas Keverosforth [sic] was one of the four witnesses when Alexander Portbref of Barnsley granted by deed a messuage (property with a dwelling house) near Westgate, 'towards the rivulet named Tunbruck', in Barnsley to Thomas, son of Robert del Rodis.

St Mary's chantry, sometimes called Lady Quire, was founded in 1461 by John de Keresforth and his son Richard. It was the burial place of the family for many generations. It was endowed with rents and farms in Barnsley to the annual value of £6 1s 5d, of which 18s½d went to the Prior of Pontefract.

In 1280, Roger de Keresforth, gentleman, attested a deed. In 1369 and 1417, Richard Keresforth was mentioned in records.

At some stage the Keresforth family acquired Keresforth Hill, which was also known as an ancient mansion, Toad Hole. In 1467, the prior of Pontefract granted to Richard Kerresforth [sic] and five others 'a parcel of the waste at the east end of Barnsley' at a rent of 2d.

The Keresforths were one of few local families with a right to bear arms; they had lived at Keresforth Hill since medieval times. 'Arms: Quarterly, 1st and 4th, Azure, two mill-rinds fesseways in pale argent; 2nd and 3rd, Argent, a fess embattled sable between three butterflies gules'. (This means that the shield was divided into four with the same design on opposite quarters. Backgrounds of top left and bottom right being blue, that of top right and bottom left silver. Mill-rind is an X shaped iron support, Fesse or fess is a bar or strip; embattled is square indentations on top, black. Gules is red.* A simplifed version of the Arms of Thomas Keresforth is at the bottom of the cover design of *Alumnus* (Part 1. Chapter 18).

The Keresforth family were connected to several Baronets: George Wombwell, Sir Francis Lindley Wood of Hemsworth and John Beckett of Leeds.

Rev Joseph Hunter provided a Keresforth Family Tree in his book and the earliest member was John Keresforth of Keresforth Hill, who married Elizabeth, daughter of Thomas Bosville of New Hall. They had two sons: (1) Richard and (2) John.

(1) Richard Keresforth married Isabel, daughter of Mr Normanvile of Billingley, and they had five children: Thomas and four daughters. (Mary married Richard Brome, Muriel married Richard Dyson, Ann married William Mindley and Elizabeth married William Ginger).

Thomas Keresforth (alive in 1585) married Alice, daughter of Matthew Wentworth of Bretton, and they had a son called Thomas. Thomas senior was involved in the establishment in 1568 of the Shaw Lands Trust to benefit the people of Barnsley (Part 1. Chapter 1).

Thomas Keresforth (c1552–buried 13.11.1598) got married twice, first on 18 November 1581 to Mary, daughter of Ralph Jenkinson, and second on 18 April 1593 to Elizabeth Lynsey. He had three children: John, Robert who had a son called Robert, and Elizabeth Agnes.

John Keresforth (16.11.1588–c1622) married on 2 June 1607 Margaret, daughter of Nicholas Cudworth of Westbrook, and they had two daughters. John sold Keresforth Hill.

(2) John Keresforth of Wombwell married the daughter of Mr Barker of Dore, Derbyshire, and had one son.

Robert Keresforth of Ardsley married the daughter of Mr Ward of Barnsley and they had four children: Gabriel and three daughters. (Jane married Edmund Barrowclough, Elizabeth married Thomas Browne and Grace married Robert Bower of Barnsley).

Gabriel Keresforth (?–1641) married Catherine, daughter of Mr Hall of Bolton on Dearne, and they had three sons: Thomas, Cotton and Robert. (Cotton was a student of Brasenose College, Oxford in 1623; Robert was baptised on 19 March 1599 in Barnsley).

Thomas Keresforth (1597–1674) of Pule Hill founded Barnsley Grammar School.

Thomas Keresforth (1597–1674, aged 77)

Thomas was born in Barnsley and his Baptism was on 23 October 1597 at St Mary's Church, Barnsley; he was the oldest son of Gabrill [sic] Keresforth and Katherine Hall.

* This explanation was provided by my nephew Gavin Hardy.

According to Rev Hunter, Thomas married Elizabeth, daughter of Mr Humphrey Clyncard of Abingdon. Whereas Elizabeth Keresforth is named in the 1660 Deed, later records give his wife's name as Ann.

Thomas, a Gentleman, lived with his wife Ann at Pule (also spelt Pewel and Pueil) Hill, Thurgoland, which he had acquired from John Bamford, a Royalist. He also owned St Mary's House in Barnsley, plus property and land in Silkstone, Dodworth, Cawthorne and Hoylandswaine.

Thomas was a Parliamentarian. In 1645 the Earl of Newcastle's army plundered his house and took all of his horses and hay to the value of £100 because he had sent arms and men to Lord Fairfax, in addition to being 'an assessor of money for Parliament'. Thomas was imprisoned but released when he agreed to act as 'collector for the King', although he never collected any money. Termed a 'Delinquent to the King's party', he then lost all of his cattle, worth £20, and fled to York to avoid imprisonment. He was fined £160 on 6 December 1645, at which time his property was valued:

His Estate: messuage and land in Dodworth	£44
2 messuages in Barnsley	£20
Fee farm rents in Dodworth, Barnsley and Silkstone	£18

Thomas paid the fine but the papers were mislaid. Fortunately for him, a report on 31 May 1649 confirmed that they had been found, with the outcome that 'Having paid his fine not to be molested'.

Thomas founded the Trust for a Grammar School in Barnsley on 18 June 1660; he may also have been a Trustee for the Shaw Lands Trust. (Part 1. Chapter 1).

There is no image of Thomas Keresforth but his signature is the closest connection we have to the man:

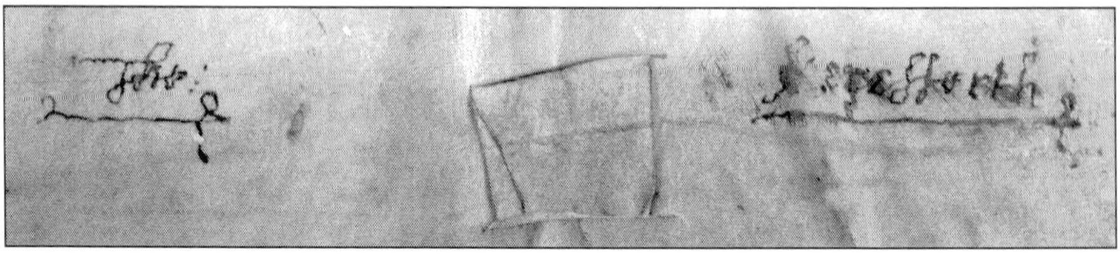

Signature of Thomas Keresforth from the 1660 Trust Deed, reproduced by kind permission of Barnsley Archives.

Thomas died in 1674, aged 77, and was buried in All Saints Church in Silkstone on 31 March 1674 (as Mr Thomas Kerrisforth). There is no evidence to confirm whether he was buried inside the church or in the churchyard but the former is more likely. His Will dated 22 October 1669 left to his wife Ann, 'providing she does not marry', his 'Capital Messuage' and cottage at Pule Hill, all the tithes of corn, wood, hay, wool and lamb, and the manor of Thurgoland. She remained a widow for almost 30 years before her death in May 1707, when she was also buried in Silkstone All Saints Church. The ownership of Pule Hill Hall then passed to Thomas' cousins with surname Bower in accordance with his Will; his aunt Grace Keresforth had married Robert Bower. Their son Nathaniel Bower, Solicitor, who was interested in local history and toured the area recording monumental inscriptions,* had already been living at Pule Hill, where he remained until his death in May 1694.

According to histories of Silkstone Parish, there was a Memorial Plaque in the Chancel of All Saints Church with a Latin inscription. Fortunately, this was transcribed but it was not described in detail and it no longer exists; it was most probably a wall plaque and at least one is missing without any record of the reason (TK*).

> *Spe certa resurgendi in Christo, hic situs est THOMAS KERRESFORTH de Pule-hill-hall, generosus; ejusdem tecum Catholicae ecclesiae membrum: sub eadem felicis resurrectionis spe, eandem Domini Jesu praestolans Epiphaniam. Hac positum in arena est corpus, olim animi domus. Animam Deo Servatori reddidit tricesimo primo die Martii, anno regni regis Caroli Iidi XXVI; aetatis suae LXXVII; Christi M. DC. LXXIIII. Hoc monumentum Nathaniel Bower, gen. et Anna Kerresforth uxor charissima, amoris et gratitudinis ergo, posuerunt.*

(Translation: In the certain hope of being raised up in Christ, here lies THOMAS KERRESFORTH of Pule Hill Hall, Gentleman; a member with you of the same Catholic church: with the same hope of happy resurrection, expecting the revelation of Lord Jesus. His body, once the home of his soul, was placed in this earth. He yielded his soul to God the saviour on the thirty first day of March, in the 26th year of the reign of King Charles II; 77th year of his age; in the year of Christ 1674. Nathaniel Bower, Gentleman, and Ann Kerresforth, his most beloved wife, placed this monument on account of love and gratitude.†

Thomas' Coat of Arms was at one time in the 'tower or bell house' of All Saints Church, Silkstone.

Thomas Keresforth's generous legacy lives on 355 years later.

* Information from Heritage Silkstone.

† Translation by Brooke Westcott.

12

Archbishop Robert Holgate (c1481–1555, aged 74)

Portrait of Archbishop Robert Holgate engraved from an original in the Hospital at Hemsworth, reproduced from *The History Of The Hospital in Hemsworth* by kind permission of the Master.

Robert Holgate, the youngest son of Thomas Holgate and Elizabeth Champernowne, was born c1481 in or near Vissett Manor in Hemsworth. He was educated in Cambridge and received a Bachelor of Divinity degree in 1524. In 1529, Robert became Prior of St Catherine's without Lincoln, part of the Gilbertine order. (St Gilbert founded the only English Order c1130 in Sempringham, near Grantham, Lincolnshire). He was also the Vicar of Cadney, Brigg, Lincolnshire, from where a lawsuit by Sir Francis Ayscough took him to London. He was noticed by King Henry VIII and became Chaplain to the court for a period, followed by a series of rapid promotions.

In 1534, Robert was the last Master of the Order of St Gilbert at Sempringham; the order had 26 houses, of which only four were deemed to be 'greater', ie with incomes over £200. Following the Dissolution of Lesser Monasteries Act of 1536, all of the Gilbertine houses surrendered 'of their own free will' to King Henry VIII with each Nun and Canon receiving a pension for life.

In 1536, he was Master of the Priory of Watton, where he was accused, without any evidence, of misappropriating funds, so he left quickly to be consecrated Bishop of Llandaff in 1537.

Considered to be a protégé of Thomas Cromwell, Robert was appointed President [ie the King's representative] of the Council in the North in 1538, a post he held for 11 years. He lived in the house of the former Abbot of St Mary's Abbey in York, which has survived as King's Manor.

Following the death of Archbishop Lee, Robert was named his successor and was consecrated as Archbishop of York at Lambeth in January 1544 (RH*), renouncing papal authority and accepting royal supremacy. His main tasks were to repress papalism and conspiracy, keep the Scots at bay and dispense impartial justice; during his time he suppressed two rebellions: the Wakefield Conspiracy and the Seamer Rebellion. The tenets of Protestant theology were regularly expounded in York Minster for the first time and organ music was abolished. He instructed that the Minster Library be furnished with new Protestant commentaries on the Bible by theologians like Calvin.

Robert Holgate obtained his first Coat of Arms in 1539. The shield is divided into two with, on the right, two black bulls separated by a black band on a gold background [based on the Holgate family Arms] beneath a section with alternate silver and red strips with 'crutched staff' from the Canons of St Gilbert. When he became Archbishop, the Arms assigned to him included these with the crossed keys of the See of York on the left half of the shield on a red backgound. The Armorial Bearings have the Archbishop's mitre above the shield. The Arms were used for the badge on the Barnsley Holgate Grammar School uniform (Colour Section).

Robert continued to flourish under King Edward VI until the Duke of Northumberland took precedence and made the Earl of Shrewsbury President of the North in 1550. Robert was required to surrender a substantial amount of property to the Crown as the King needed money to fund his wars.

Archbishop Holgate, who had acquired and retained much wealth, land and property, founded three grammar schools in 1546, endowed by his Will of 1555 and financed by tithes from his land. One was at his birthplace of Hemsworth in the West

Riding, one at Old Malton (in the cemetery of the former Gilbertine Priory) and one in York (in Lord Mayor's Walk, near to the Minster). Boys were expected to be able to read before being accepted and he required his Headmasters to be skilled in Hebrew, Greek and Latin and to take his pupils to the Minster on Sundays.

On 15 January 1550, aged 68, Archbishop Holgate got married in Bishopthorpe to Barbara Wentworth, daughter of Thomas of Hanthwaite and Adwick-le-Street, Doncaster. As this was a year after an Act of Parliament removed the duty of celibacy from the English clergy, it may have been to prove his Protestantism to the sceptical Duke of Northumberland. There was controversy around whether Barbara was already betrothed and the marriage displeased Queen Mary, who came to the throne in 1553 and returned England to Catholicism. Robert's wealth was seized from his houses at Cawood, Battersea and elsewhere, he was deprived of his Bishopric on 15 March 1554 and sent to the Tower of London for breaking his vow of celibacy.

Robert wrote a formal apology to Queen Mary and offered her £1,000 for his release, which was obtained on 18 January 1555. He recovered his properties, which enabled him to found a Hospital with 18 cottages for the poor in Hemsworth, the arrangements for which were made in his Will along with other bequests.

Archbishop Robert Holgate died on 15 November 1555, aged 74, in London and he was buried in the Church of St Sepulchre, Holborn, 'without worldlie pomp and vanity' in accordance with his wishes as detailed in his Will.

He is was a supporter of the poor and needy as well as someone willing to adapt to the changing circumstances of his times. This enabled him to accrue the great wealth from which his foundations have benefited – the Hospital Trust has substantial land holdings in Yorkshire and the Horizon Archbishop Holgate Foundation continues to thrive.

Archbishop Robert Holgate's legacy lives on after 460 years.

(Early 2015 I read Joseph Wilkinson's book, which provides a lot more details and a wealth of evidence with some speculation. There are some differences from the history I have used above but I made a decision to keep this history as simple and accurate as possible).

Armorial Bearings of Archbishop Robert Holgate, reproduced from *The History Of The Hospital in Hemsworth*, by kind permission of the Master.

Barnsley Chronicle – 5 November 1932

(This article about the death of Rev C S Butler (Part 1. Chapter 16) contains a biography of Archbishop Holgate).

It is said that Archbishop Holgate, who founded the Hemsworth Grammar School, now known by his name at Barnsley, on October 24th 1546, became personally the wealthiest prelate in England, having exchanged certain lands and manors belonging to his See for advowsons from the Crown, the latter being eventually more valuable. Three years after the foundation of the above – on 15th June, 1549 – the Archbishop married Barbara, daughter of Roger Wentworth, of an old Yorkshire family, having two children. He was deprived of his bishopric in 1554 by Queen Mary for being married. But in his will – he died November 15th, 1555 – no mention is made of wife or child, and he leaves all his lands for the erection and endowment of the famous hospital at Hemsworth – 'for a master and twenty brethren and sisters of the age of sixty, or blind or lame, belonging to that parish and three adjoining parishes'.

The Archbishop was born near Hemsworth 450 years ago and his bequests are still carried out. It is remembered, however, that the Roman Catholics in the reign of Queen Mary succeeded in alienating some of his personal properties, never refunded, and that the 'Holgate' charities would probably have been three times their present value had they been recovered.

The Hemsworth Holgate Grammar School was closed in 1881, when it amalgamated with Barnsley Grammar School, and it was subsequently demolished.

The original Holgate Hospital was replaced by another building in 1770 and the dedication stone survives at St Helen's Church. The second Hospital was demolished but the Trust built new premises in 1860, comprising 12 houses, eight cottages, boardroom, a chapel (dedicated as Holy Cross in 2000), a substantial house for the Master and a lodge for the porter and matron. Four cottages were added in 1914, making a total of 24 properties to let to older people from the local area and these remain in use today.

(RH*) date from the Catalogue of Archbishops of York with dates of their consecration in *Collectio Rerum Ecclesiasticarum de Dioecesi Eboracensi.*

Several original documents in Latin are in Barnsley Archives (Part 1. Chapter 1).

Archbishop Robert Holgate statue at Hemsworth Hospital. (© Jane Ainsworth)

13

Edward Lancaster & Sons

EDWARD GEORGE LANCASTER (1840–1934, aged 94)

Edward George was born in 1840 in Barnsley to Edward and Mary Ann Lancaster. He was a Valuer's Pupil in 1861 and became Auctioneer, Land Agent, Accountant, Tenant Right Valuer and Share Broker by 1881. On the 1911 Census, Edward (aged 70) Auctioneer and Land Agent, was living in 15 rooms at Keresforth Hall, where he had three domestic servants. Edward did not marry and he had no children; he was one of Barnsley's most generous benefactors and he played a number of roles in the public life of Barnsley.

Edward George Lancaster paid for Barnsley Grammar School to be extended in 1887. He was Governor of Barnsley Holgate Grammar School for many years, endowing a scholarship and paying for a chemical laboratory in 1901. He was also an agent to the Shaw Lands Trust. In 1912, Lancaster and Sons Auctioneers dealt with the sale by auction of the original grammar school building to Samuel Joshua Cooper (Part 1.Chapters 10 and 14).

He endowed St Edward's church and vicarage at a cost of £30,000 in 1902 and later paid for the parish hall to be built. The church is of neo gothic design with a square tower; it contains a fine font, reredos behind the altar and pulpit, all made of alabaster. During the First World War, St Edward's vicarage was used as a convalescent home for soldiers and Edward George bore the costs of this.

He was a longstanding JP, Chairman and longest serving Trustee of the Oaks Colliery Explosion Fund, Actuary of Barnsley Savings Bank, Trustee of the Beckett Hospital and other roles.

Edward George Lancaster died on 31 October 1934 (aged 94) at Keresforth Hall and he was buried by special arrangement in the grounds of St Edward's Church, beneath the East Window. The stained glass East and West windows were installed in 1936 in his memory; the East has a Crucifixion scene and the West a magnificent Ship of the Church. Probate was granted on 21 December 1934 at Wakefield to his nephew George Bingley Lancaster, Auctioneer, and James Gibson, Chartered Accountant. Edward left almost £250,000.

Yorkshire Post and *Leeds Intelligencer* – 1 November 1934

OBITUARY
MR EDWARD GEORGE LANCASTER
LARGE BENEFACTIONS TO THE TOWN
COMPANY CHAIRMAN AGED 94 YEARS

Mr Edward George Lancaster of Keresforth Hall, Barnsley, died yesterday, aged 94. He had remained physically and mentally active, and until ten days ago, was in daily attendance on the affairs of the many companies of which he was the head.

He was senior partner in the firm of Lancaster and Sons, auctioneers and valuers, had been chairman of Barnsley Gas Company since 1890, and chairman of Clarkson's Old Brewery Co. Ltd. For 24 years. His speeches at the annual meetings of these companies were models of lucidity.

His benefactions to Barnsley were considerable. He was patron of the living of St Edward's, Barnsley, which he built at the cost of over £30,000 in 1902, and it was through his gift of £1,000 that it was possible to erect a parish hall three years ago. During the war, St Edward's Vicarage was used as a convalescent home, the cost being borne by Mr Lancaster. There is no burial ground attached to the church but a faculty was obtained some years ago to enable Mr Lancaster to be buried in the grounds of the church, for which he has done so much.

He was a great supporter of Barnsley Beckett Hospital, and his interest in education is shown by the fact that he was the oldest Governor of Barnsley Holgate Grammar School, where he had endowed a scholarship. He was chair of the Oaks Colliery Explosion Fund, being the last survivor of the original trustees; for 40 years he had been an auditor of Barnsley Permanent Building Society; he was a trustee of Barnsley Beckett Hospital; agent to the Shaw Lands Trust; and for many years actuary of Barnsley Savings Bank, which was merged a few years ago in the York County Savings Bank. He was appointed to the West Riding Magistracy in 1899. …

Mr Lancaster's death snaps a link between Barnsley of the stage coach days and modern Barnsley, for he was alive before the first railway train entered the town. …

Mr Lancaster was Barnsley's oldest man and his death follows by a few days that of Barnsley's oldest woman, Mrs Margaret Parker of Albert Street, aged 94.

***Yorkshire Post* and *Leeds Intelligencer* – 5 January 1935**

£250,000 BARNSLEY WILL
LATE MR E G LANCASTER'S BEQUESTS TO SERVANTS

Many annuities for servants are contained in the Will of Mr Edward George Lancaster of Keresforth Hall, Barnsley, ... who died on October 31, aged 93 [sic]. He left an estate of £249,999 (net personalty £239,010) Mr Lancaster left, free from all duties:

£20,000 to Thomas Lancaster, brother
£10,000 to George Bingley Lancaster, nephew [etc]

To each of his indoor and outdoor servants at Keresforth Hall, in his employ at the time of his death, Mr Lancaster gave £20 and directed that each be provided with full mourning at the expense of the estate and provided that all servants be kept in their respective situations for 12 months after his death at their then rate of wage.

(Mr Lancaster left a trust fund to benefit friends, listed separately, and various annuities with the residue to Beckett Hospital).

EDWARD LANCASTER (1809–1897, aged 88)

Edward, the son of William and Mary Lancaster, was born on 3 March 1809 in Barnsley and his Baptism was on 11 March 1809 at St Mary's Church, Barnsley. Edward married Mary Ann Mawer on 27 September 1836 in Holton-le-Cley, Lincoln, and they had three children born in Barnsley: Edward George in Summer 1840, Thomas late 1842 and Fanny Jane late 1848.

Edward of Keresforth Hall was an Auctioneer, Valuer and Courier on the 1861 Census; by 1881 he was also Land Agent, Accountant and Share Broker; by 1891 he was JP West Riding and Retired Land Agent.

His son Edward George always lived at Keresforth Hall and continued to employ domestic servants.

Thomas Lancaster got married by licence on 23 April 1874 to Alice Halliday Milner (both of 'full age') at Holy Trinity Church in Wakefield; Alice's father William Milner was a Silk Manufacturer. They had five children and lived in 11 rooms at The Cliffe in Monk Bretton, where they employed domestic servants. Thomas died on 1 March 1930, aged 55, at Monk Bretton and Probate was granted to his brother Edward George, Land Agent, his surviving son George Bingley Lancaster, Auctioneer, and Edward Arthur Barker, Engineer; his effects were £60,481.

Fanny Lancaster (aged 24) married William Henry Shaw (aged 27) Mechanical Engineer of Droylsden, Manchester, whose father was Bentley Shaw, Brewer, on 11 September 1873 at St John's Church, Barnsley.

Edward died on 20 June 1897, aged 88, and Probate was granted to his two sons, both Estate Agents and Auctioneers; his effects were £50,460.

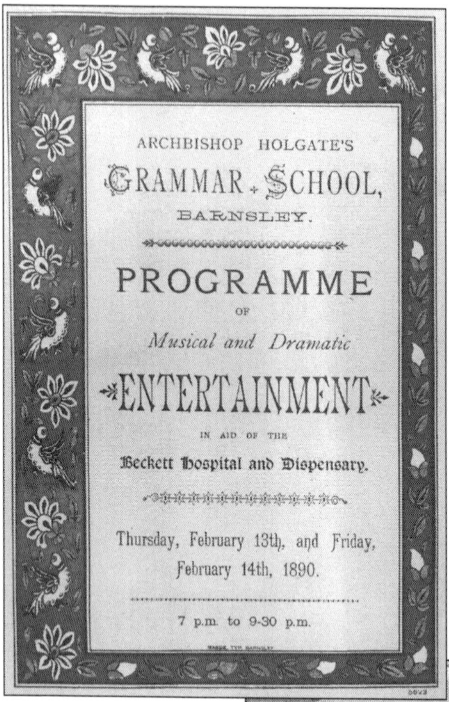

ARCHBISHOP HOLGATE'S
GRAMMAR SCHOOL,
BARNSLEY.

PROGRAMME
OF
Musical and Dramatic
ENTERTAINMENT
IN AID OF THE
Beckett Hospital and Dispensary.

Thursday, February 13th, and Friday, February 14th, 1890.

7 p.m. to 9-30 p.m.

Holgate Ephemera.
(© Jane Ainsworth)

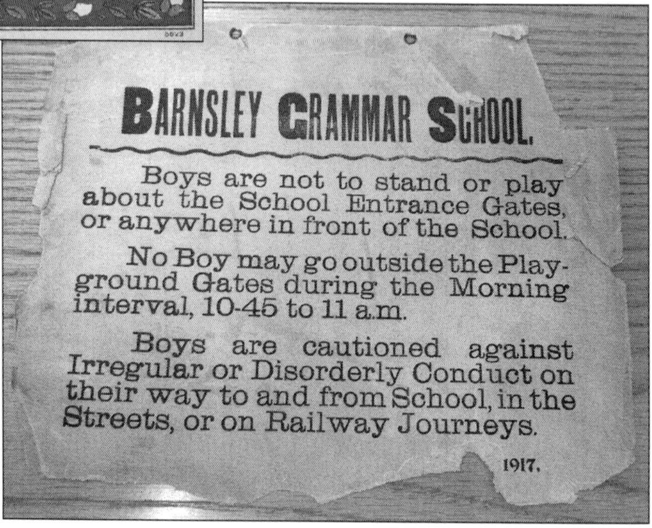

BARNSLEY GRAMMAR SCHOOL.

Boys are not to stand or play about the School Entrance Gates, or anywhere in front of the School.

No Boy may go outside the Playground Gates during the Morning interval, 10-45 to 11 a.m.

Boys are cautioned against Irregular or Disorderly Conduct on their way to and from School, in the Streets, or on Railway Journeys.

1917.

14

Samuel Joshua Cooper (1830–1913, aged 83)

Samuel Joshua Cooper, born in Worsbrough on 17 September 1830, was one of the five children of William Cooper and Harriet Mann, both of whose families made their wealth from iron and coal. Joshua was the only surviving son as his older brother George Thomas Mann Cooper died aged 34 and his younger brother William Alfred Cooper died aged 14. Maria Emily Cooper was the only sister to survive, but she spent most of her 63 years in York Asylum; Marianne had died aged 4 months. Joshua's parents and siblings who died young are buried in St Mary's Parish Churchyard in Worsbrough.

Photograph of Samuel Joshua Cooper, reproduced by kind permission of Barnsley Archives.

Joshua inherited the family businesses and lived at Mount Vernon in Worsbrough all of his life. He had attended Barnsley Grammar School for a short period and became a Governor as his father had been. Joshua married his first cousin Fanny Mann in 1859; they did not have any children but were extremely generous to Barnsley with their enormous wealth, especially to the churches in Worsbrough. Joshua contributed to the cost of St Luke's Church, which was built in 1874 with stained glass windows dedicated to his brother William Alfred; he paid for St James' Church to be built in 1907 and he provided much financial support to St Thomas' Church in addition to other Churches in Barnsley. Joshua also made substantial donations to the Beckett Hospital and paid for the adjacent nurses' home, he paid for the Oaks Colliery Disaster Memorial to the Rescuers who died and he bequeathed the Cooper Art Gallery to the people of Barnsley. (Newspaper articles about the Opening of the Art Gallery are in Part 1. Chapter 20)

Samuel Joshua Cooper died on 11 July 1913 and he was interred in St Thomas' Churchyard in Worsbrough with his wife Fanny and sister Maria Emily. He had made a number of bequests in his Will and left an enormous estate of £751,446.

Alumnus – December 1913

(This article acknowledged Samuel Joshua Cooper's generous contributions to Barnsley Grammar School. On Speech Day, the Headmaster had alluded to 'the extreme simplicity of life, loveable qualities and generous nature of Mr Cooper').

> In Memoriam: S J Cooper – We record with deep regret the passing away on July 11th 1913 of Samuel Joshua Cooper, Esq, of Mount Vernon, Barnsley. He was an Old Boy of the Grammar School, and there is in the possession of the Headmaster a small prize volume of Henry Kirke White's Poems, which he gained there in 1837 or 1838. For some years from 1888, Mr Cooper was a Governor of the School, as his father had also been. His benefactions to the School during his life included the Establishment of the Cooper Prize Fund, for providing special prizes to the amount of £20 annually, and the foundation of the Cooper Exhibition to Oxford or Cambridge, the value of which is about a £100 a year. By his Will he has bequeathed to Trustees the sum of £5,500, for the foundation of three additional Exhibitions or Scholarships, tenable at the same Universities by Grammar School Boys born in Barnsley. Through Mr Cooper's munificence the Grammar School is now unusually well provided with the means of giving liberal assistance to promising boys proceeding to the ancient Universities; and the name of Cooper will be forever gratefully remembered no less than those of Holgate, Keresforth and Locke.

S J Cooper Esquire of Mount Vernon had bought the Headmaster's house as well as the school building; now called Keresforth House it continued as the Head's house by arrangement. Mr Alfred G Bond disclosed the fact that Mr Cooper had bequeathed the old Grammar School building for use as an Art Gallery.

This Chapter is based on original research I carried out in 2014 and used in an article published in Memories of Barnsley *in December 2014.*

Peace tin (Barnsley British Cooperative Society). (© Jane Ainsworth)

15

The Newman and Bond Families

The Newmans of Newman and Bond Solicitors are not related to the Newman family of Worsbrough, Barnsley, although William Newman (1787–1870, aged 83), Solicitor and Land Agent of Darley (Cliffe) Hall in Worsbrough, was also a Grammar School Trustee c1865.

EDWARD NEWMAN JP (1798–1879, aged 81)

Edward was born in 1798 in Waterton, near Woburn, Bedfordshire. At the age of 25, he moved to Barnsley to practice as a Solicitor and lived in Church Street. (The numbering of this street changed over the years, but Newman and Sons Solicitors occupied the property on the right side, facing from the front, of Barnsley Grammar School from 1830 until 1897; this house no longer exists). He played an active part in public life in Barnsley being a Justice of the Peace, a supporter and Director of the Public Hall and Mechanics Institute, Chairman of the Board of Health from 1853, Magistrate until his retirement in 1862 and Trustee of Barnsley Grammar School c1865.

Edward married Mary Lister, the only daughter of James Lister, Merchant, and Frances Lister of Barnsley. They had five children: Thomas James, Charles, Frederick, Mary Helen and Emily. The two oldest sons were Solicitors; Frederick was a Linen Manufacturer, Mary Helen married Rev Alfred Gatty and Emily died aged 28 years. Edward died on 5 December 1879 (the same day as Henry Harvey (Part 1. Chapter 17)) and his three sons were Executors to his estate, valued at 'under £25,000'.

Edward had close connections with St George's Church in Barnsley, as did his wife's parents. He presented a new alabaster font on the occasion of the baptism of his granddaughter Dorothy Dalton Newman, daughter of Frederick and Garland Newman. Rev John Newman officiated at this first baptism on 18 March 1877. Edward was interred in the family vault at St George's Church, where there were separate tablets of marble, brass and alabaster on the north wall of the chancel to

Edward, his wife Mary and their two children Emily and Charles. As St George's Church was demolished in 1993, I do not know what happened to these tablets or those of James and Frances Lister, but fortunately details are recorded in Benjamin Turner's Retrospect 1821 to 1912.

THOMAS JAMES NEWMAN (1827–1915, aged 88)

Thomas was the oldest son of Edward Newman. A Gentleman, aged 38, Thomas got married in 1865 by Licence to Maria Walton, aged 28, at All Saints Church in Silkstone, where her father was the Vicar. They had seven children: Mary, Edward, Maximilian, Charles Arnold (Solicitor in Oundle in 1911), Dennis, Kingsley and Monica.

He entered into partnership with George Alfred Bond in 1881 and Newman & Bond Solicitors were based in Church Street from 1882 until 1910, when the firm relocated to Regent Street. Thomas was appointed as the first Clerk to the new Management Committee of Barnsley Holgate Grammar School in 1887, while living in Sackville Street, Barnsley. He retired to London as a widower and died on 10 December 1915 at Mayfield, Burgess Hill, Finchley Road, Middlesex; his estate was worth over £32,000.

CHARLES NEWMAN (1829 – 1886, aged 56)

Charles was a Solicitor; he did not marry but resided in Church Street, Barnsley, with his sister Mary and two domestic servants. He died on 11 March 1886 and was buried in St George's Church; he left over £25,000 and George Alfred Bond was one of his Executors. Samuel Joshua Cooper was a friend and client of Charles, who was a witness at his marriage.

GEORGE ALFRED BOND (1843–1927, aged 84)

George was born in Oxnead, Norfolk, where his father George was a Receiving Officer (Tax). He had moved to Barnsley by 1871 and married Anne Euphemia, daughter of Reverend Samuel Sunderland, at St Mary's Church in 1872. They had two children: Millicent Eleanor, who married Solicitor Ralph F Pawsey, and Alfred Dalton, who married Winifred Alderson. They lived at The Grove, Cockerham Lane, Barnsley, with Anne's widowed mother and three domestic servants.

In 1881, George formed Newman and Bond Solicitors and he became Honorary Secretary of the Beckett Hospital. George married again after his first wife died and retired to Devonshire, where he died on 20 December 1927; he left an estate worth about £5,000 with a fifth to his widow Louise Florence Bond and the remainder to his deceased son's two children.

George and the Headmaster John Hargreave were friends; John was a witness at George's marriage, George cared for Faith Lillian Stanley Hargreave in 1881 when she was orphaned at birth and George was an Executor for Faith Anna Hargreave, John's widow, who died in 1881.

RALPH FREDERICK PAWSEY (c1876–1953, aged 77)

Ralph was born in the Isle of Dogs, London, and he moved to Barnsley as a partner in Newman and Bond Solicitors. He was living at The Grove with George Alfred Bond, when he married George's daughter Millicent Eleanor Bond, on 7 April 1900 at St John's Church in Cheltenham, and they continued to reside at The Grove. Ralph was Executor and Beneficiary of Samuel Joshua Cooper's Will, Executor of the Wills of Charles Pigott Harvey and the widow of Headmaster John Hargreave as well as witnessing a number of significant documents related to Barnsley Holgate Grammar School. Ralph was Secretary of the Mineral Owners' Association, Clerk to Shaw Lands Trust and to the Governors of Barnsley Holgate Grammar School as well as Solicitor & Commissioner for Oaths for Newman & Bond. Millicent died on 30 June 1953 then Ralph, of The Grove, Barnsley, and Bursar's Cottage, Helmsley, died on 18 August 1953 in London; he left about £28,000.

16

The First Headmaster of Holgate Grammar School

Reverend Charles Stokes Butler (born in 1849 in Shepshed, Leicestershire, where he was Baptised on 16 April 1849) was the oldest of eight children of **Reverend Alfred Stokes Butler** (1824 Ireland – 1899, aged 75) and **Jane nee Underwood** (1826 Dublin – 1872, aged 46).

Charles attended King's School, Canterbury, for one year from 1858 then Repton School as a Foundation Scholar from 1860 to 1867. He went to Magdalen College, Oxford, from 1867 to 1870 to read Classics. He obtained a 1st Class Honours Degree then Masters in 1874.

Charles married **Harrietta Baker Carrick Rownsley** at St Mary's Church, Ealing on 4 March 1870; he was 21 and she was 20. They had no children and Harrietta died in Spring 1893, aged 42, in Barnsley.

Charles' first teaching post was at St Olave's, Southwark, from 1870 to 1878. He was then Headmaster until 1887 at Hemsworth Grammar School, where he and his wife had three Student Boarders (aged 10 to 18, from Yorkshire, Scotland and Ireland) plus three Servants (Housemaid, Cook and Page). Charles became Head of the new Holgate Grammar School in Barnsley in 1887; he and his wife occupied 12 rooms at 35 Church Street (Keresforth House), where they employed a couple of Domestic Servants.

Photograph of Rev Charles Stokes Butler, reproduced by kind permission of Barnsley Archives.

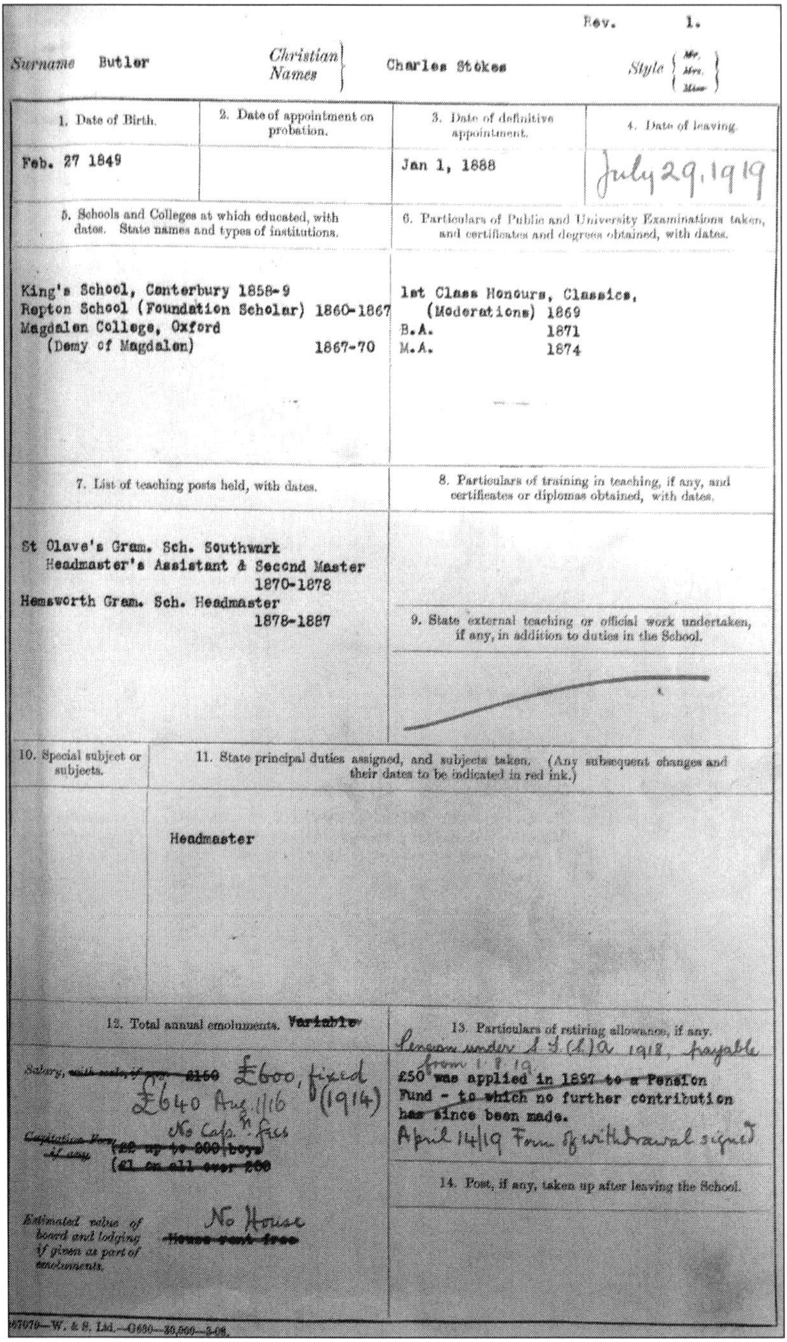

Rev. 1.

Surname Butler *Christian Names* Charles Stokes *Style* { *Mr.* *Mrs.* *Miss* }

1. Date of Birth.	2. Date of appointment on probation.	3. Date of definitive appointment.	4. Date of leaving.
Feb. 27 1849		Jan 1, 1888	July 29. 1919

5. Schools and Colleges at which educated, with dates. State names and types of institutions.	6. Particulars of Public and University Examinations taken, and certificates and degrees obtained, with dates.
King's School, Canterbury 1858-9 Repton School (Foundation Scholar) 1860-1867 Magdalen College, Oxford (Demy of Magdalen) 1867-70	1st Class Honours, Classics, (Moderations) 1869 B.A. 1871 M.A. 1874

7. List of teaching posts held, with dates.	8. Particulars of training in teaching, if any, and certificates or diplomas obtained, with dates.
St Olave's Gram. Sch. Southwark Headmaster's Assistant & Second Master 1870-1878 Hemsworth Gram. Sch. Headmaster 1878-1887	9. State external teaching or official work undertaken, if any, in addition to duties in the School.

10. Special subject or subjects.	11. State principal duties assigned, and subjects taken. (Any subsequent changes and their dates to be indicated in red ink.)
	Headmaster

12. Total annual emoluments. ~~Variable~~	13. Particulars of retiring allowance, if any.
Salary, ~~*with scale, if any*~~ ~~£150~~ £600, fixed (1914) £640 Aug. 1/16 No Capn. fees ~~*Capitation Fees, if any*~~ ~~(£2 up to 200 boys~~ ~~(£1 on all over 200~~	Pension under S. S. (S.) A. 1918, payable from 1.8.19. £50 was applied in ~~1897 to a Pension Fund - to which~~ no further contribution ~~has~~ since been made. April 14/19 Form of withdrawal signed
Estimated value of board and lodging if given as part of emoluments. No House ~~House rent free~~	14. Post, if any, taken up after leaving the School.

67070—W. & S. Ltd.—G630—30,000—3-08.

The first entry in the Staff List, reproduced by kind permission of Barnsley Archives.

On the following three Censuses, Charles had different members of his family staying with him. In 1891 his father Alfred (aged 67) Widower and Rector of Markfield, Leicestershire, was there until his death on 10 February 1899. Widowed in 1893, Charles' married brother Alfred Joshua (aged 50) Fellow and Bursar of Brasenose College, Oxford, was with him in 1901 and his unmarried sister Charlotte Louisa Anna (aged 55) resided there by 1911.

Charles devoted his life to education and he was an inspirational teacher. He encouraged pupils to be creative and he wrote many articles and poems, including composing the new School Song (Part 1. Chapter 8). Many examples survive with his poems being included in the Speech Day Programmes from 1888 and the annual Musical and Dramatic Entertainments from 1889. Charles was a great supporter of the Old Boys Association, which was established in 1897, believing that former pupils had much to contribute to as well as gain from such an organization. He wrote many contributions for their *Alumnus* magazines from its first edition in April 1913, continuing to send them poems after his retirement. Amongst his poems in the Holgate Collection in Barnsley Archives are: *Some Folks Say That Barnsley's Black, Football Song, The Quest of Wonderland.* I have transcribed those related to the First World War to give a flavour of this impressive man. (Part 3. Chapter 1).

Charles was an academic with a great sense of humour as the synopsis of his play about Guy Fawkes in 1889 testifies. He was President of the Barnsley Literary Society from its inaugural meeting in 1899.

Charles took a great interest in his Old Boys and he was especially concerned for their fates during the First World War. From 1914 to early 1919, *Alumnus* magazines provided details of all those who enlisted with updates about their progress and Obituaries for many of those who died. Charles recorded in red ink in the Admission Registers many of the deaths in action of the Old Boys and he meticulously added newspaper cuttings about them to his 'scrapbooks' (Programmes and Ephemera in Barnsley Archives).

***Barnsley Chronicle* – 29 July 1916**

BARNSLEY GRAMMAR SCHOOL
ANNUAL 'SPEECH-DAY'

> In conclusion the headmaster observed that he had not said anything about Barnsley Grammar School and that he did not intend to say much – only this, that they claimed for the young men, who had once been boys there, that they had been second to none in offering themselves for the Common Cause. They knew a large number who were serving in the forces of the Crown, many of them had come to visit them when on leave and some they would see no more. They reverenced their memory with mingled pride and regret and commended their example.

Charles retired in July 1919 after nearly 32 years as Headmaster of the Holgate Grammar School and 50 years as a teacher. He continued to rent Keresforth House, 35 Church Street, Barnsley until 1926, when he moved to Surrey. Charles' last duty to the Old Boys of Barnsley Holgate Grammar School was to dedicate the War Memorial on 28 October 1928, almost ten years after the First World War had ended.

Charles died suddenly on 30 October 1932, aged 83, at home in Upper Norwood, Surrey. Probate was granted for Reverend Charles Stokes Butler, Clerk of Glenthorne, 23 Hawkes Road, Upper Norwood, Surrey on 10 December 1932 in London to his nephews: Alfred Butler, Journalist, and Charles James Newcombe Butler, Accountant. Effects £3,838 9s 1d.

***Yorkshire Post* and *Leeds Intelligencer* – 4 November 1932**

FUNERAL OF FORMER BARNSLEY HEADMASTER (FROM OUR LONDON CORRESPONDENT) FLEET STREET, THURSDAY

Clergy from Yorkshire officiated at the funeral in London today at Elmer's End Cemetery, of the Reverend Charles Stokes Butler, who died on Sunday at Upper Norwood, at the age of 83. For many years he was Headmaster at Barnsley and District Holgate Grammar School until his retirement in 1919.

The service was conducted by the Rev. A G Shipley, Vicar of All Saints Pontefract, a brother in law of Mr Butler, assisted by the Rev. R H B Butler, Vicar of Sutton-in-Craven, Keighley, a nephew.

The family mourners were Miss Louisa Butler (sister), Mr Ormonde Butler, Mr Newcome Butler and Mr Shann Butler (nephews) and Miss Ailleen Butler (niece). Mr A J Schooling, Headmaster of Barnsley and District Holgate Grammar School, and Mr Miller, a master at the school, were also there.

***Barnsley Chronicle* – 5 November 1932**

DEATH OF REV C S BUTLER
FORMER HEAD OF BARNSLEY GRAMMAR SCHOOLDAYS

On Sunday night the death took place at Hawke Road, Upper Norwood, of the Rev Charles Stokes Butler, at the age of 83 years.

Mr Butler retired from the head mastership of Barnsley and District Holgate Grammar School in 1919. He had lived in Upper Norwood with his sister, Miss Louisa Butler, since leaving Yorkshire, was in his usual health at the weekend and died suddenly shortly before midnight on Sunday.

The son of the late Rev A S Butler, Rector of Markfield, Leicestershire, he was educated at King's School, Canterbury and at Repton, and he graduated at Magdalen College, Oxford. From 1871 to 1877 he was head master's assistant at

St Olave's Grammar School, Southwark, from 1872 to 1874 he was curate of St John's, Horsley-down, and from 1877 to 1878 curate of St Olave's, Southwark.

He was appointed head master of Archbishop Holgate's Grammar School, Hemsworth, in 1878 and remained there until 1887. That school was then merged under the Charity Commissioners' scheme with a school at Barnsley, which later became known as the Barnsley and District Holgate Grammar School.

His wife died at Barnsley many years ago, and he had no children. His brother, Dr A J Butler, was formerly Bursar of Brasenose College, Oxford, and is a noted Egyptologist. The funeral took place in London yesterday (Thursday).

The late Rev C S Butler's nephew, Mr Harold Beresford Butler, CB, now of Geneva, who entered the Civil Service (Local Government Board) in 1907, and was afterwards transferred to the Home Office, was private secretary to the Right Hon Ellis Griffith, KC, in 1913 (Mr Asquith's Ministry): Assistant Secretary, Ministry of Labour, 1917: and Secretary-General International Labour Conference, Washington, 1919.

He has published *Unemployment Problems in the United States* recently. His father, Mr Alfred J Butler, D Litt, of Brasenose College, Oxford, was tutor to the Khedive of Egypt, 1880, and has written important books on Egypt, including *Ancient Church Life, Monasteries, Ancient Coptic Churches etc, Verses from Greek Anthology, Islamic Pottery, Sports in Classic Times* and four very fine *Brasenose Quarter Centenary Monographs.*

He married fifty years ago Constance, daughter of Col Heywood, of Ocle, who is descended from the brother of the celebrated Rev Oliver Heywood, the doyen of Yorkshire Noncomformity in the 17th century. ....

A memorial service for the old headmaster of Barnsley Grammar School will be held at 12.15 today (Friday) at Barnsley Parish Church.

Charles Stokes Butler's Seven Younger Siblings

ALFRED JOSHUA BUTLER (1850–1936, aged 86)

Alfred married Constance Mary Heywood and they had four children. Alfred was a Historian and became Fellow and Bursar of Brasenose College, Oxford. He was known as 'the English friend of the Copts', and wrote *The Arab Conquest of Egypt; the Copts and Their Culture* in 1902.

HENRY ALEXANDER BUTLER (1852–1938, aged 86, in Canada)

Henry married Ann Maria Watts and they had five children. He was a Church of England Priest in Kent before they emigrated to Canada.

WILLIAM JOHN BUTLER (1853–1892, aged 39)
William was living with his sister Charlotte at The Rectory in Markfield in 1891.

CHARLOTTE LOUISA ANNA BUTLER (1855–1946, aged 90)
After the death of her parents, Louisa lived with different siblings: with her brother William in Markfield in 1891, living on her own means, with her sister Caroline and family in Sheffield in 1901 and with her brother Charles in Barnsley from 1911, relocating to Surrey with him until his death.

CAROLINE MARY ELLEN BUTLER (1858–1924, aged 66)
Caroline married Reverend Arthur Granville Shipley and they had one son. Arthur Hammond Butler Shipley was one of the 76 Old Boys killed in action in the First World War and more details are provided under his name.

FRANCIS NEWCOMBE BUTLER (1860–1904, aged 44)
Francis married Edith Mary Horseman and they had four children. Francis went to Oxford University then ran his own school in Minehead.

RICHARD PENN BUTLER (1862–1927, aged 65)
Richard, a Government Clerk aged 58, married Annie Hartley, aged 41, in 1921.

Mary Wortley, a distant relation of the Shipley and Butler families, provided me with background information about the family of Reverend Charles Stokes Butler and his nephew, an Old Boy who was killed in action in the First World War, Arthur Hammond Butler Shipley (Part 2. Chapter 58).

The Headmaster on his Retirement – Reverend Charles Stokes Butler

(*Alumnus* – July 1919)

One of Elia's Essays is called *The Superannuated Man*. Charles Lamb describes in it how the opportunity of retiring came to him and how that same day he 'went home – for ever'. Then he turns to his reflections on the past and a playful analysis of his feelings as he entered upon the unaccustomed leisure of seven days a week, every week as long as he should live. There was nothing playful about his retrospect of thirty-six years employment. He says it was 'irksome confinement', 'prison days', 'captivity', 'thraldom', 'servitude': and retirement from it was 'deliverance', 'emancipation', 'overwhelming felicity', 'giddy rapture'; he felt 'like a prisoner in the old Bastille let loose after forty years of confinement' and as if he had 'passed into another world'.

I have been reading this Essay once more, with renewed interest, because the title of it will soon apply to myself. Let me give the opening paragraph, only substituting 'A Schoolroom' for 'An Office': 'If peradventure, Reader, it has been thy lot to waste golden hours of thy youth, thy shining youth, in the irksome confinement of a Schoolroom, to have thy prison days prolonged through middle age to decrepitude and silver hairs, then and then only will you be able to appreciate my deliverance'.

For rather more than forty-eight years a Schoolroom has been my regular place of work; for forty-one of these I have been a Headmaster upon the Holgate Foundation and for more than thirty-one at the Barnsley and District Holgate Grammar School.

Am I then about to be released from Scholastic fetters, to look back on those years as prolonged drudgery and forward to what time may remain as a Schoolboy looks forward to his holidays?

Not so: I cannot share Lamb's feelings; he was so unfortunate as to spend the best years of his life in a task that he loathed, while I have given mine to work that I loved.

It is often supposed that the Schoolmaster's work must in time become to him a deadening monotony, like doing an everlasting sentry-go, pacing up and down the same narrow beat of dull routine every dreary day. His critics imagine him to be grinding out mechanically the same old range of stale and a thousand times repeated lessons, as a barrel-organ grinds out tunes. Look at the caged squirrel walking up his little revolving cylinder of wires and never getting any higher – there's the picture of your Schoolmaster! Or here is another; he is a man at the bottom of a deep muddy ditch on a hot day painfully digging out the accumulated rubbish with a tea-spoon; a swarm of flies buzzes round his head; a cloud of midges torments him; a passer by occasionally looks down and mutters 'Poor beggar'! And recommends him to hang a wreath of fly papers round his hat, or dry up the water with a sponge or hurry up his job with the aid of a steam navvy. I would not deny that there are some to be found in Schools who justify such ill-informed popular opinion and are even in their own estimation self-immolated victims of a lifeless routine, toilers in immeasurable sand, plodding along an uninteresting path that leads to nowhere or

> Dropping buckets into empty wells
> And growing old in drawing nothing up.

These look upon teaching as Lamb did upon his work. But they have failed to find the Philosopher's Stone that turns dull lead into fine gold.

This magic Talisman that banishes from the Schoolman the oppressive incubus of infinite boredom and exercises the evil spirit of irksome drudgery is drawn, as all best things are drawn, from the invisible world of Ideals. It is the conviction deep in the heart of the Teacher that his main business is with human lives, and incidentally with lessons, books, marks, examinations and all the other matters that make up the sum total that is called School, in short that he is not the keeper of a knowledge shop, but a *Pastor Agnorum* [literally a shepherd of sheep]. Here lies the perennial fountain flowing with the inspiration that sustains Duty, and invests the most common place and hackneyed features of School with the freshness of a new adventure. It is his privilege to deal with human nature in the making and where is there more infinite variety than in human nature? Every new boy is a new world to be explored or a new Garden of Eden to be cultivated and improved and the lurking snake to be scotched if possible. These young lives with whom our lives are in close contact for the brief period, usually too brief, of their Schooldays, whom human nature as yet but little spoiled and soiled by adverse influences and most easily moulded for good or ill, so that without an abiding sense of our Sacred trust and responsibility we shall not succeed in impressing upon this plastic material the outlines of Goodness, Truth and Beauty. '*Maxima debetur puero reverentia – ne tu pueri contempseris annos*' [we owe the greatest reverence to a child – do not despise the years of a boy].

I bid farewell to Barnsley Grammar School with its 300 boys and its many hundreds of Old Boys, of all of whom I shall ever think of with affection and interest, none of them bad, only some less good than others; to both sorts I apply the words used of its members by an American Society: 'The fruits of our brethren we write upon the sands, their goodness upon the imperishable tablets of Memory and Hope'.

To the loyal and devoted Staff of Assistant Masters many of whom have seen long service with me, I render my heartfelt thanks for the high sense of duty and the co-operation that have made the wheels of the School machinery work smoothly, and made their relations with myself so harmonious and happy.

Since I came to Barnsley Grammar School in January 1888, it has experienced many changes and varied times. I have known during those years times of anxiety and discouragement, downs as well as ups. But the difficulties which once seemed insuperable have been overcome. Progress and advance such as one dares scarcely to hope for or to dream of, have been made in all directions. Something has been achieved but there is no finality in the building up of a School and much more remains to be done. But coupled with the things that I cannot do it is a deep feeling for having had the happiness to see the School so far on its way to an assured future of prosperity and of constantly growing usefulness to the boys of Barnsley and the surrounding townships.

Alumnus – July 1919–29 July 1919

On the morning of July 29th, the Reverend C S Butler, MA, conducted the Service for the last time as Headmaster. When we consider that this was the last of many such occasions extending over a period of 31 years, the event assumes historic importance in the lifetime of the school. The service ended, a very pleasing function took place, that of presenting Mr Butler with tokens of our regard and esteem. From the Masters he received a solid silver tea service and from the scholars five volumes, beautifully bound in morocco, of Hastings' *Dictionary of the Bible*.* The senior member of the staff, in presenting the gift from the Masters, made a brief speech in which he aptly compared the sterling qualities of Mr Butler with the hall-marked qualities of the silver. Mr Butler most suitably replied, acknowledging the kindness of the Masters and boys and exhorting the latter to make the Bible their guide and comforter through life. All then sang heartily *For he's a jolly good fellow*, and one of the senior boys followed this up by calling for *Three Cheers*. The shout that followed from three-hundred boys and Masters was such that the flags of the Allies hanging round the walls seemed to flutter in acclamation.

Alumnus – July 1919 An Appreciation by Mr Evan Davies

After 32 years of faithful service as Headmaster of the Barnsley Grammar School and 50 years all told as teacher, the Rev C S Butler is now retiring from the profession, to the general regret of all those who know and appreciate the value of the ennobling and refining influence he has brought to bear upon the character and conduct of the boys in attendance at the school. The post of Headmaster he has held with honour and distinction. The successes at Universities and the professions on leaving school are sufficient evidence that the material interests of the scholars are well looked after. The progressive advance of the school in number, until the building is uncomfortably overcrowded, is further proof of its vitality and its high place in public estimation. These are rough tests of the school's efficiency. But there is no rule or plumbline to measure Mr Butler's own personal influence in the formation and development of character. His great intellectual gifts and his extensive knowledge of the teachings of master-minds have been excellently used in the training and guidance of youth.

But when the vacation comes along, in his quietness and obscurity, he escapes to the silence of the mountains or the loneliness of some remote valley, and there in the company of natural things and of his beloved books, he whiles away the golden time until the hour arrives for him to return once more to take up his life's work. As he finds his joy in the intellectual life and in the contemplation of nature and stands aside from the bustle and turmoil of life, the cries of "the market place" and the shouts of the political arena, his real character may be misapprehended by the public. His outward reserve of manner is nothing but a mask unconsciously worn, behind which is a heart beating with human kindliness and sensitive to a fault. His conversation with his few intimate friends is rich with the ore of the wisdom of the ages, veined with delicate humour and characterised by a wide and spacious tolerance. Those who know him best love and reverence him, for his character is built on moral foundations. In

* James Hastings published the original dictionary "A Dictionary of the Bible, dealing with the Language, Literature and Contents, including the Biblical Theology", between 1898–1904. It was in five volumes of about 900 pages each. A one-volume dictionary of 1,000 pages, with the same title, was published in 1909.

him there is no shadow of guile, no artifice or affectation. There is no jealousy, egotism or vanity in his nature. He is singularly free from all rancour of littleness of mind and whatever he does is from absolute purity of motive.

Therefore his personal influence over the boys is incalculably great. Discipline in school has been maintained by little or no punishment, never by loudly clamouring for it or by long and tedious homilies. Mr Butler shows no excesses of this kind. But it is brought about by direct appeal to the better nature of boys, and by their instinctive respect for nobility and grandeur of character, which are the best restraints upon tendencies to unruliness or dishonesty in conduct. Intellectually he knows there are tricks in the world but emotionally he does not. He himself treads the oath of duty fearlessly and conscientiously.

In his retirement we all hope that Mr Butler shall have many years in which to enjoy the leisure which is his recompense. May the evening of his life be long and unclouded by sorrow or sadness! May it be a source of comfort to him to know that he will be remembered by hundreds of Old Boys with a deep and abiding gratitude for all that he has done for them to fight bravely the battle of life and play their part in it with honour, courage and understanding.

C S B: An Inspiring Schoolmaster – R A H Goodyear

(*Alumnus* – April 1925)

He had a trick of placing his pen-holder across his mouth and raising his desk-lid to laugh behind it. The laugh was a noiseless one and it turned him red in the face, and I never doubted that he had found some quaint quip or quiddity in a dead-language book. I would have scoffed at any schoolmate who had suggested that such a learned Head as ours would laugh at anything he had read in *Punch* for instance.

He was not remarkably keen on games, and made no secret of the fact, but he was strong in the things I liked just as much – poetry and song, good English prose and amateur theatricals.

His Speech-day programmes were always a joy to me and to this day I can read them through with a reminiscent thrill. He once cast me for the role of Nicholas Nickleby in a duologue from that classic narrative, but I felt all the time, as I shivered and shook at the rehearsal, that the Fates would never allow me to inflict my rendering of it on the term-end audience. They didn't; I caught mumps and unlucky 'Piggy' Wadsworth went through the oratorical loop instead.

Mr and Mrs Butler, however, were determined that the dim star of the boy on the back row should have its chance to shine, so they rigged me up as Boaler, the page, in the Head's own dramatized version of F Anstey's *Vice Versa*. All I had to say was: 'Cab's at the door, sir, luggage all put in, sir', and I managed, by a process of pelmanism then unpatented to get it off my chest (at two performances, mind you!) without a mistake. I recollect seeing Mr Butler laugh as I collared young Bultitude and yoiked him off the stage – possibly I should have kept my hands off the boss' son, but it was as well to be firm. I thought: you never knew what a character in *Vice Versa* would be up to next.

I shall never forget the kind letter that C S B wrote to my parents when I had left school far too soon, begging them to let me return. It was a revelation to me as I had not dreamed that he took such a deeply personal interest in the welfare of his boys. My regrets were bitter that I had not chummed up to him more; others did it fearlessly, but I was too scared, worse luck. What lost opportunities I have to deplore because of my diffidence! I know now that he was almost as shy as I about it, and that his heart yearned towards my lonely awkwardness; but I did not even dare to show to him the first or any subsequent copy of my manuscript *Holgate Journal,* though his appreciation of its naïve contents and unconscious humour would have been intense, I am certain.

His school songs and his poems were, more than anything else, a guide and an inspiration to me. I took them home and studied them in the holidays, and by imitating the musical swing of them I succeeded in writing prize verses for the *Boy's Own Paper, The Golden Penny, Ching Ching's Own, Leeds Mercury Weekly Supplement*, and other papers which gave encouragement to young beginners. He thus helped, without knowing it, to prepare me for the profession of letters, from which I have drawn support (always irregular, but generally sufficient) since I was sixteen years old.

Even now I look to C S B at times for encouragement and assistance, and never in vain. I wish you could see the vigorous letters he sends me; you would believe him quite capable of starting afresh to make another big school out of a small one, as he splendidly succeeded in doing before he handed over the seals of office, in a manner of speaking, to your present excellent and most athletic Head.

(R A H Goodyear contributed an article to *Alumnus* in 1919 about the first unofficial magazine *Holgate Journal*, which he had jointly edited in 1891 (Part 1. Chapter 18)).

17

Other Significant People

WILLIAM CARNELLEY (1823–1919, aged 96)

William was born in Barnsley to Thomas Carnelley, Yeoman Farmer, and Ellen Pickard. He moved to Manchester and worked for Rylands & Sons Limited, a very successful Lancashire cotton manufacturer, for 78 years, starting at the bottom and working his way up to Chairman. William's first wife died young and he got married again in 1851 at Silkstone All Saints Church to Mary Sykes; he had five children. William died on 8 October 1919 in Manchester and he left about £36,000 in his Will; his four Executors were his son William Carnelley, Barrister, a Bank Manager, Wesleyan Minister and Secretary of Rylands and Sons. He was buried in Southern Cemetery in Manchester near to the Rylands monument.

Mr R F Pawsey wrote to the Editor of *Barnsley Chronicle* on 20 October 1919 to pubicise the generous bequests that William Carnelley had left to Barnsley: he left £2,000 to the Beckett Hospital to endow two beds in his name and £3,000 to Barnsley and District Holgate Grammar School to fund three scholarships in his name.

WILLIAM GILBANKS (c1793 to 1803–1869, aged 77)

There are few records for anyone in Yorkshire called William Gilbanks and some of these have discrepancies over his age. William married Ann Beevers of Bridgehouses in Sheffield Parish Church (the Cathedral) on 5 June 1824 by licence; the summary record has his age as 21, but she was only 15. They had ten children before Ann died in 1849, aged 40, soon after their tenth child was born. William had become Headmaster of Barnsley Grammar School in 1821 and also taken on the role of Postmaster for Barnsley; at the aged of 35, Schoolmaster. He was imprisoned in York Castle on the 1841 Census; he was one of 162 debtors from many different backgrounds and the prison, occupied by staff and their young children, also had 41 criminal prisoners.

Although he was dismissed in 1839, his mother-in-law Ann Beevers (aged 55) of independent means, was looking after his six youngest children and still occupying the Headmaster's house in Church Street on the 1841 Census, while his wife was probably in York to take care of her husband. In 1851, William (aged 58, born in Lanercost Priory, Northumberland) was a widower and Classical Teacher; he was living in Leeds with six of his youngest children and his widowed mother-in-law, Ann Beevers. William died on 28 December 1869 and was buried in the Beckett Cemetery in Leeds with his wife Ann and their daughter Margaret Ann (aged 10 weeks).

JOHN HARGREAVE (c1816–1880, aged 64)

John was born in Horsforth, Yorkshire, and he obtained his BA at Trinity College, Dublin. Reginald Greenland wrote that he was Assistant Master at Penistone Grammar School and married the sister of the Headmaster there, Rev Samuel Sunderland, and Rev Willan stated that she was his first wife. My research revealed that John Hargreave married Ann Sunderland on 11 September 1843 at St John's Church in Penistone. John, son of John Hargreave, was Schoolmaster living in Blackburn; Ann was daughter of William Sunderland, Grocer, of Penistone.

On the 1861 Census, John (45) Headmaster, and Ann (63 born Wakefield) lived in the Master's House, 16 Church Street, Barnsley, and they had one Boarder Scholar, Walter Tee (aged 12) and one domestic servant. In 1871, John (56) and Ann (71) lived in the Grammar School, 33 Church Street, where they had two Boarder Scholars: John Pallister (14) and Thomas Fox (11) plus two servants; Septimus Woodley, Assistant Master, also lived there. Ann Hargreave died in 1871 or 1872, aged 75.

John married Faith Anna Stanley, who was about 25 years younger than him, on 28 October 1873 in Braceborough, Lincoln.

The *Yorkshire Post* and *Leeds Intelligencer* reported on 12 January 1867 that John Hargreave, Schoolmaster of Barnsley, had been declared bankrupt in the Court of Bankruptcy for Leeds district. *Barnsley Chronicle* did not report this although they reported other bankrupts in the same period. [*I was extremely surprised to find this report while searching for an Obituary considering the position of trust that the Headmaster of Barnsley Grammar School was in and John Hargreave's good reputation according to others who knew him. I do not understand how he could have continued as Headmaster or kept this quiet*].

John died on 14 November 1880; he had not made a Will and his estate 'under £1,000' went to his widow, Faith Anna Hargreave, who died four months later on 15 March 1881 (aged 39), having given birth the previous day to Faith Lilian Stanley Hargreave. Mrs Hargreave left 'under £800' in her Will and her Executors were her brother William Edward Stainton Stanley, Surgeon, and George Alfred Bond, Solicitor and friend.

Baby Faith was baptised at St Mary's Church on the day her mother died and the fact that she was an orphan at one day old is recorded in the margin of the Parish Register. She was looked after by the Bond family initially then went to Lancaster to live with her aunt Catherine (aged 52), uncle Reverend Thomas Robinson (75) and their daughter Kate (27). Faith died in Bay View Hostel in Lancaster in 1952, leaving about £2,000 to one of her mother's relations.

CHARLES HARVEY JP (c1817–1898, aged 81)

Charles and his brother Henry were wealthy Linen Manufacturers and Quakers in Barnsley. According to E G Bayford (Part 1. Chapter 2) they had an older brother Thomas, who attended Barnsley Grammar School, and another called William. Henry died on 5 December 1879 (the same day as Edward Newman), aged 55, at his home in Pitt Street, Barnsley; he had never married. Charles lived at Park House in Ardsley, which had previously been the home of Samuel Joshua Cooper's uncle Samuel Cooper, Linen Manufacturer then Coal and Iron Master.

Charles married Lucy Pigott and they had three children; their daughter Mary Ann married Sir Michael Ernest Sadler. Charles died at Sudborough House near

The Harvey Institute, photograph kindly provided by the Tasker Trust (copyright).

Thrapston, the home of his only son Captain Charles Pigott Harvey, who was High Sheriff of Northamptonshire for six months in 1904, before his sudden death at the age of 44. Charles left an estate worth more than £70,000.

Charles was a generous benefactor to Barnsley, subscribing to an extension of Barnsley Grammar School in the 1880s, along with Dr Sadler, supporting the Beckett Hospital and, in 1877, donating the Harvey Institute. The Public Hall, with its Free Library, Technical School and Mechanics Institute plus shops and offices to generate income, had been supported by both Harvey brothers and Edward Newman (Part 1. Chapter 15), who were all Directors. A carved image of Charles forms the keystone in the arch over the main entrance. The building was used as Battalion Headquarters for the Barnsley Pals during the First World War, then became the Civic Theatre in 1962. The theatre is now accessed via a modern extension at the rear with modern art gallery and cafe while the entrance from Eldon Street provides access to a few offices for Barnsley Council.

THOMAS HEELIS (c1765–1802, aged 37)

Thomas was born in Skipton to John and Sarah Heelis; his grandfather was Edward Heelis, Yeoman Farmer and Steward of Skipton Castle. On 14 January 1784, Thomas was articled as a Clerk for five and a quarter years to John Field, Attorney; his father 'Yeoman of Gargrave' was a joint party to the Indenture. He married Hannah Watson in St Mary's Church, Barnsley, on 24 May 1796. In 1798, Thomas Heelis is listed in the West Yorkshire Land Tax Records for Staincross Division as occupying premises whose Proprietor was the 'Schoolmaster of Barnsley' and being liable for 'sums not exonerated' of two shillings and seven pence (Grammar School Yard). Thomas was a well known Solicitor and he witnessed an Indenture dated 21 March 1797, which was a Release in Trust for Barnsley Grammar School, his own signature being witnessed by his Clerk Wlliam Cookes Mence. Heelis Street in Barnsley was named after him. He died on 28 April 1802 and was buried in the Friends' Burying Ground in Burton according to Jonathan White, Grave-Maker, in the Quaker Registers on Ancestry.

Geoffrey Hutchinson checked Barnsley Quaker records in the Meeting House for me but Thomas was not mentioned; he may have attended meetings but was unlikely to have become a full member because of the nature of his occupation. Prior to 1830 Barnsley Quakers met and had their Meeting House & Burial Ground at Burton, Monk Bretton.

DR JOHN FLETCHER HORNE (c1849–1941, aged 93)

John was born in Barnsley and started work as a Chemist's Assistant to his uncle Alfred Badger Horne, Chemist and Town Councillor of Eldon Street, Barnsley. By 1881, John was a Surgeon, married to Emily and with two infants, Harold and Beatrice; they lived in Dodworth Road with a medical student and two nurses. He was a Councillor for 33 years, being Mayor twice, one of the first magistrates in Barnsley, a member of Barnsley School Board, Parishioners' Warden at St George's Church in Barnsley and author of a book about the buried cities of Vesuvius, Herculaneum and Pompeii. John retired to Shelley Hall in Huddersfield, where he died on 17 January 1941; he left an estate worth over £20,000.

JOSEPH LOCKE (1805–1860, aged 55)

Joseph was born in Attercliffe, near Sheffield, and moved to Barnsley by the age of five; he attended Barnsley Grammar School, aged 7, accompanied by his sister. He became a pupil of George Stephenson (1781–1848) at Newcastle on Tyne and qualified as an Engineer. He later succeeded George's son Robert (1803–1859) as President of the Institution of Civil Engineers and, alongside Isambard Kingdom Brunel (1806–1859), was considered to be one of the main pioneers of railway development, who all died young within months of each other. Joseph married Phoebe McCreery in 1834 and they had no children. He constructed the railway line from Warrington to Birmingham (Grand Junction), which opened in 1837, then went on to construct other lines in England, Scotland, France, Spain and The Netherlands entering into partnership with John Edward Errington; he was awarded the Legion d'Honneur for the Paris to Rouen line. Joseph was also a Liberal MP for Honiton and a Fellow of the Royal Society, living in Lowndes Square in Belgravia, London.

Joseph died suddenly of a seizure on 18 September 1860, while recruiting in Moffat, Dumfries, and enjoying the shooting in Annandale. He left a large estate 'under £350,000' in his Will, from which his widow Phoebe funded the Locke Scholarships at Barnsley Grammar School (Part 1. Chapter 6) and donated Locke Park to Barnsley in memory of her husband.

DR MICHAEL THOMAS SADLER (1834–1923, aged 89)

He was named after his father Dr Michael Thomas Sadler, GP; of Barnsley; he was himself a GP and Medical Officer for Barnsley for many years. Dr Michael lived in Church Street, Barnsley, and, although his house was demolished, Sadler Gate was named after him. He was a Governor of Barnsley Grammar School and subscribed to an extension in the 1880s, along with Charles Harvey. Dr Michael was influential in the opening in May 1915 of the Mount Vernon Sanatorium for people with Tuberculosis in the former home of his close friend Samuel Joshua Cooper.

Dr Michael married Anne Eliza Adams in 1860 and they had six children, two sons, three daughters and a child who died before 1911. His younger son Dr Francis Joseph Sadler took over as Medical Officer while Sir Michael Ernest Sadler, who married Mary Ann Harvey, became Master of Oxford University, was an avid collector of art and made several bequests to the Cooper Art Gallery.

Dr Michael retired to London in 1902 but was living in Rugby, Warwickshire, when he died on 11 October 1923; he left an estate worth about £20,160.

In Memoriam by Rev Butler (*Alumnus* December 1923)

> The death of Dr Sadler should not be allowed to pass without recalling the great services which he rendered to the Grammar School throughout the earlier stages of its development under the scheme of 1887. Under its first Chairman, the late Sir Walter Stanhope, he was for 14 years Vice-Chairman of the Governing Body, until his retirement from Barnsley in 1902. In that capacity he brought to bear upon the school business not only the resources of a highly trained mind and a knowledge of educational aims and ideals but also a warmth of enthusiasm for the cause of Higher Education, in marked contrast to the prevailing tone of public opinion at that time .... Through many difficult years his interest and support never waivered and for his counsels, full of understanding, sympathy and encouragement, a deep debt of gratitude is due to his memory. ....

CHARLES FROGGATT WIKE (c1848–1929, aged 81)

Charles was the only child of Charles Wike and Mary Froggatt. They had married in 1847 but his father died soon after he was born and his mother got married again to her first husband's younger brother George Wike. By the age of 12, Charles was a Scholar at Barnsley Grammar School, living with his grandfather William Wike, Pawnbroker at 106 New Street, Barnsley, and his half brothers William Robert (aged 6) and John Joseph (aged 5).

Charles married Elizabeth Mary Wilkinson in 1877 and they lived in 11 rooms at Collegiate Crescent in Eccleshall Bierlow, Sheffield, where they employed two servants; they had no children. He was the City Engineer and Surveyor for Sheffield Council for 32 years until his retirement in 1920.

Charles died on 14 August 1929 and was buried in Fulwood Churchyard in Sheffield. Auctioneer John Edward Jaeger (Part 2. Chapter 45), was one of his Executors and the bulk of his estate of £23,370 was left in trust to pay an income to his wife's siblings. When they died half the income was to be used to benefit one of several causes listed, including Barnsley's Beckett Hospital, and half to provide a recreation ground in Barnsley if certain conditions were met, otherwise to be used to endow Wike Beds at the Beckett. Charles, who had paid for a Cricket Pavilion at Barnsley Grammar School, left a bequest for Scholarships (Part 1. Chapter 6).

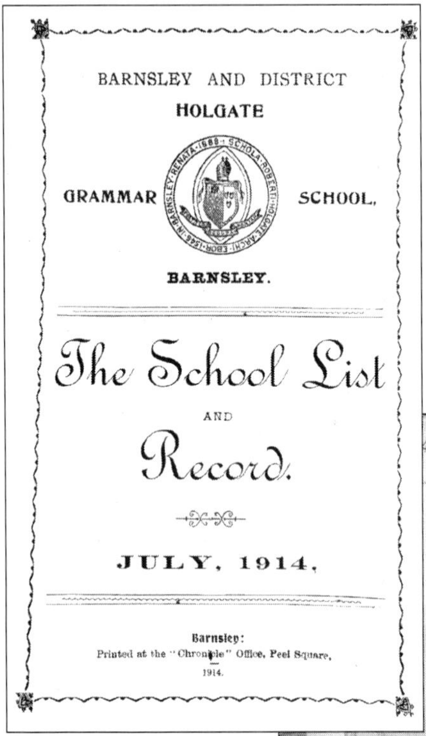

BARNSLEY AND DISTRICT
HOLGATE
GRAMMAR SCHOOL,
BARNSLEY.

The School List
AND
Record.

JULY, 1914.

Barnsley:
Printed at the "Chronicle" Office, Peel Square,
1914.

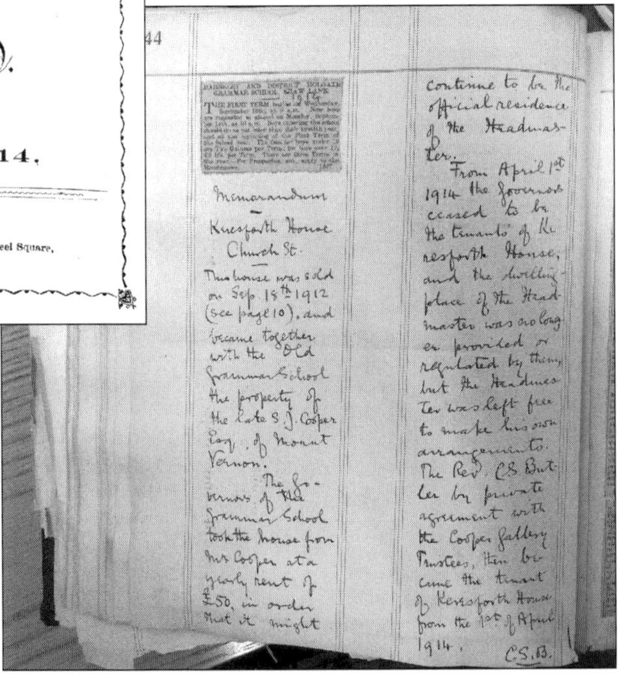

44

Memorandum
Keresforth House
Church St.
This house was sold on Sep. 18th 1912 (see page 10), and became together with the Old Grammar School the property of the late S. J. Cooper Esq. of Mount Vernon.
The Governors of the Grammar School took the house from Mr Cooper at a yearly rent of £50, in order that it might continue to be the official residence of the Headmaster.
From April 1st 1914 the Governors ceased to be the tenants of Keresforth House, and the dwelling place of the Headmaster was no longer provided or regulated by them, but the Headmaster was left free to make his own arrangements. The Rev. C.S. Butler by private agreement with the Cooper Gallery Trustees, then became the tenant of Keresforth House from the 1st of April 1914.
C.S.B.

Holgate Ephemera.
(© Jane Ainsworth)

18

Alumnus Magazine

The Barnsley Holgate Grammar School magazine *Alumnus* was introduced by the Old Boys Association from April 1913. There were three magazines each year in April, July & December and an annual subscription cost 1/6 (one shilling and six pence).

The Old Boys Association had formed in 1897 and its role was fully endorsed by the Headmaster, Reverend Charles Stokes Butler. An early issue of *Alumnus* contains a 'conversation' with a former pupil, who cannot understand the purpose of joining such an organization, and Rev Butler explains his support:

> The members of this body influence each other greatly, for good, and sometimes for evil. You have lived your life in this little world, and shared in its common studies and amusements and interests. You have passed here with many others some of those years when the lamp of life is burning most intensely and clearly. Whether you realise it or not, it has done something for you upon which, as upon unseen foundations, much of your future will be built. Would it not be somewhat ungrateful to forget that? The mere fact of having belonged to the same School is always a link between Schoolfellows, and has often formed the basis of friendship between men who met in after life though at School they were not specially intimate. This bond of sympathy between you and your companions, which will make you look back and remember with affection (I hope I am not too sanguine!) the days you passed here, is a right and healthy sentiment, which should not be lost or decried, but rather cherished and intensified, for your own sake and for the good of others.

The cover of the new magazine was designed by Edwin Haigh (born 30 March 1869) who was appointed to teach Art in 1899. He had attended Barnsley School of Art, completed courses at the Royal College of Art, London, and was qualified as FSAM (Fellow of the Society of Arts Masters) and Associate of the Society of Designs. He left in 1920 to become Headmaster of the Barnsley School of Art.

The cover design had four coats of arms with three mottos:

(Robert) Holgate 1546 at the top with an Archbishop's Mitre
Fortiter Occupa Portam = 'bravely hold the gate'
(a pun on the founder's name – Robert Holgate)

County Borough of Barnsley on the left
Spectemur Agendo = 'let us be judged by our acts'
(Ajax in Book XIII of Ovid's "Metamorphoses")

(Joseph) Locke 1861 on the right
Mente Non Marte = literally 'by mind not war'
(*mente* is mind, Mars was the god of war)

(Thomas) Keresforth 1660 at the bottom

Alumnus – April 1913

The first Committee comprised the following Old Boys:

President:	C F Wike Esq
Vice Presidents:	J A Jaeger Esq Councillor W G England Alderman J S Rose
Honorary Secretary and Treasurer:	C J Peddle Esq, MSc, FCS
Committee (in addition to the above) All 'Esquire':	E G Bayford; A Buckley; H Burton; G W Downend; J M Downend; A Fawley; J W Gantillon MA; H Horne MA MDC H Hutchinson; E Litherland; W A Littlewood; R E Mackridge; W Noble; J L Potts; G E Rushforth; D Shaw; F Ward
Editor:	E Davies Esq, BA (until December 1918)
Sub-Editor:	J M Downend
Entertainments Secretaries:	W Downend; W A Littlewood
Athletics Committee:	F Berry; E Litherland; A Fawley (Secretary); E Nicholson; R Sugden

(John Middleton Downend and Ernest William Litherland died serving in the First World War)

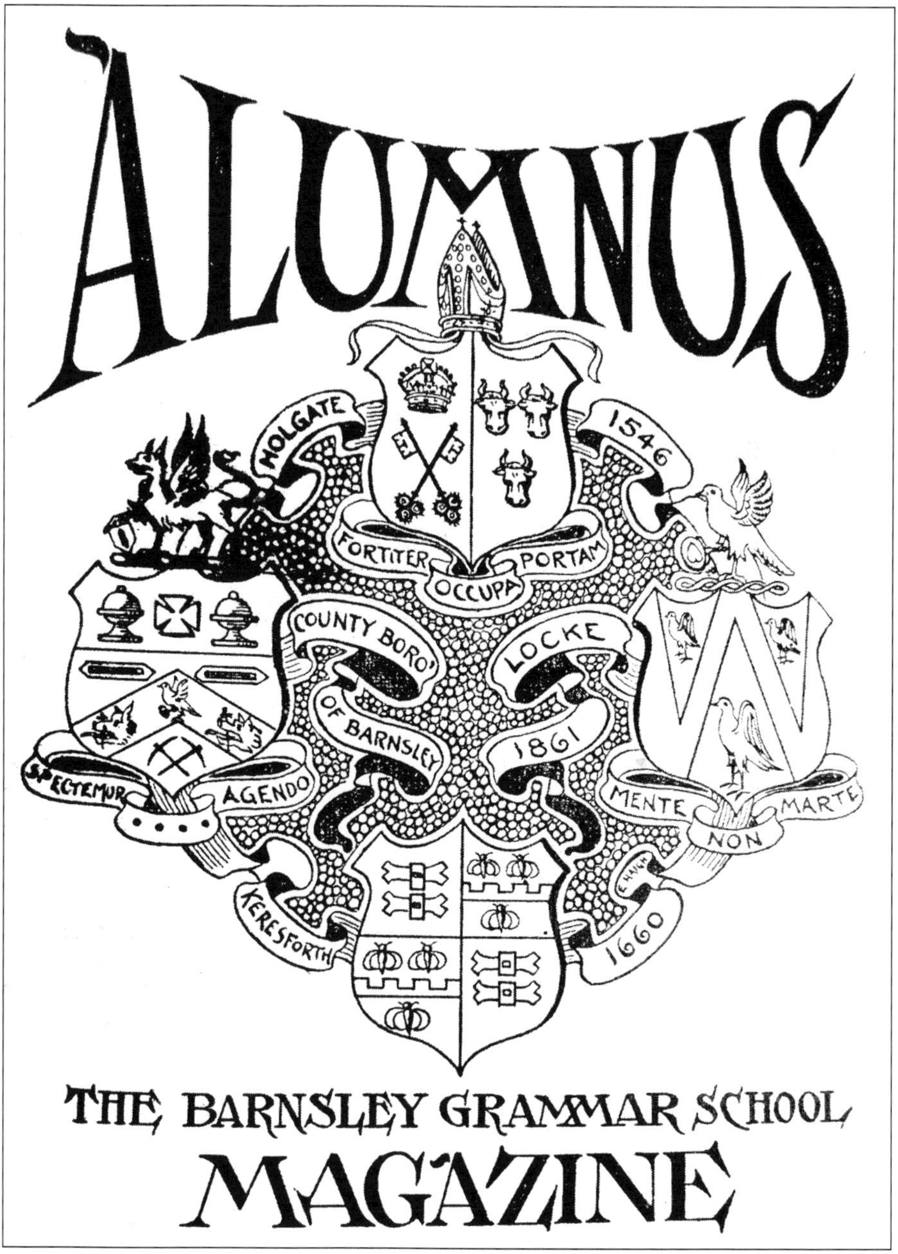

The front cover, reproduced by kind permission of Barnsley Archives.

The contents of the new magazine would develop over the years but they continued to include updates about the School and individual Old Boys, a wide range of articles and poems contributed by Old Boys, details of academic and athletic achievements, reports from sports teams, especially football and cricket, and social events organized by the Old Boys Association. There were also a few adverts.

Evan Davies (born on 6 March 1869) BA Leeds University, joined the Holgate as a Teacher on 11 October 1904. He was the first Editor of *Alumnus* and contributed many articles, demonstrating his imaginative literary skills, which were an impressive common feature of most of the contents of the magazines over the years.

The New Magazine – by the Editor (Evan Davies)

This, the youngest member of the magazine world, and one of the happy issues of the newly-revived Old Boys Association, is now about to risk its tender life in this world of rough and rude energies. Its title *Alumnus* includes alike 'Old Boys', whose education the school has fostered in the past, and those whom it nurtures within its walls today. If every *Alumnus* receives the young stranger and welcomes it as a guest by contributing towards its maintenance on its three periodic visits, one at the end of each term, during the year, its life is preserved and its continued existence assured.

In course of time, its arrival will come to be eagerly expected, for it will bring news of the achievements of boys, past and present, in their spheres of work and play; bring reports of the latest activities of the Association; comments on school life; recital of school doings, the after history of those who have left the school; and original contributions by Old Boys. The magazine has the strange potency of permanently retaining all impressions it receives and so conferring a sort of immortality upon men's thoughts and actions, which otherwise would be consigned to utter oblivion, with an attendant loss of recollected pleasure to the actors in many a vanished scene. In reviving past memories it will bring back a little of the gleam and glamour of boyhood's days and make one live over again the many glorious deeds and battles of long ago.

We express the hope that this publication will strengthen the corporate life of the school, stir up the sentiment of loyalty to it, increase the feeling of solidarity and promote social intercourse among the Old Boys, and keep alive with the passing of the years their sense of kinship with the old school.

The appearance of the magazine synchronizes with the creation of Barnsley as a County Borough. The concurrence of these two historic events augurs well, I hope, for the mutual good feeling that should exist between the town and the school: that the town give to the school its whole-hearted support and that the school become to the boys of Barnsley and District, even more than the past, a gateway – as its motto *Fortiter occupa Portam* implies – leading to vocations of every type and the training ground of the town's future citizens, providing it, as it should, with the brains and strength of character to influence and control its destiny in the years to come. I know of no school where individuality is more carefully fostered and developed, more enriched and ennobled with lofty ideals than at this school. Under the inspiring lead of the Headmaster, no boy feels crushed with the weight of inferiority, and although care is taken to train and discipline the boys in good and useful habits, no attempt is made to reduce personality and character to a dead uniformity by moulding and stamping them with one image. But each boy is made to rely on himself, to feel that his opinion is worth having, with the result – to take only the last three years – about 15 have been Captains and Prefects in their respective colleges, while many more have distinguished themselves in other noteworthy ways.

The pages of the Magazine will be open to contributions from Old Boys. There must be a profusion of good ideas scattered among them that only await this opportunity for them to become articulate. Many must have had romantic adventures, thrilling experiences, dramatic episodes. Others again must have full and intimate knowledge of special aspects of life. I strongly appeal to them all to share the treasures of their minds and the fruits of their ripe experience with their fellow alumni.

All Old Boys and others who have the welfare of the school at heart will be interested in the series of articles on the history of the school which the Rev. C S Butler, MA, is writing for the Magazine.

A special feature of the Magazine will be the personal paragraphs chronicling the doings of past students of the school. All items of news of this nature will be gladly received by the Sub-Editor J M Downend, Blythe House, Wombwell, to whom they should be sent.

All other communications should be addressed to the Editor, 11 Pollitt Street, Barnsley.

We are indebted to Mr E Haigh, FSAM, for the excellent and artistic design on the cover of the Magazine.

A Schoolmaster's Reminiscences – Evan Davies

In Sept 1905 the school considerably increased in numbers, so much so, that to provide rooms for the new boys we had to seek fresh quarters – the tin buildings had not then been constructed. For a term we wooed the muse of learning not by fountain or grove but in a dark low-roofed room overlooking George Yard, a receptacle for empty packing cases.

Once cold winter's morning there was heard a knock at the door and a lady was there enquiring if the latter-day saints were in that room. Now I saw no distinguishable signs of saintliness anywhere, although there was no incongruity in the room itself as an abode for saints. If P... and T... and all the others were saints, I thought, they would weigh every syllable they uttered, keep brooding over thoughts too deep for words, and for lengthened periods be plunged in deep seas of silence. But no, these boys had a passion for laughter; were inordinately fond of bad puns and poor jokes. At 12.30 when the morning's work was over, such was their urgent need for utterance, that all tongues were simultaneously loosened and of the twenty-four there was not a single listener. ...

But if these boys were not saints they were nevertheless an excellent set of boys, clean-minded, good-natured, full of generous impulses, irresponsible – and infallible.

When their time at the school ended, I felt it as a personal loss and greatly lamented their departure.

Alumnus – July 1913 Editorial Comments

The first number of the Magazine was received with a chorus of approval and the many congratulatory letters encourage us to persevere in our initial efforts.

Although we did not expect *Alumnus* to become a household word, or its fame to resound in many lands, we yet nourished a flickering hope that every Old Boy would welcome its appearance and acknowledge its arrival. The hope proved illusory. Yet we feel sure that the apparent neglect was merely due to the universal failure of human nature to realise at all times a good intention before it becomes enfeebled with age, and the resolution to act has grown cold. We hope that the cumulative effect of this further appeal will act as a stimulus to awaken the slumbering wills of all the Old Boys who have not yet subscribed. (Subscription 1/6 per annum or 6d per edition). …

In previous years we have deplored the withdrawal of many promising boys from school at the age of 14. It is the age when there is observed a marked increase in brain power and a genuine growth in appreciation of knowledge, attended with more determined efforts to get on. This year better council has prevailed and we rejoice to know that a majority of the boys will complete their four year's course.

It is a very short-sighted policy on the part of parents to apprentice their boys, before they have passed some qualifying examination, to professions where the long hours and arduous labout induce an aversion to study and militate against their chances of success at any examination.

Mainly about Barnsley – E G Bayford

If the average guidebook is to be believed there is little or nothing in or about Barnsley deserving of mention. Writers of guidebooks, however, are generally in too big a hurry to examine any town not in the front rank of show places, or else they are obsessed with the idea that objects of antiquarian interest must be ecclesiastical in origin … The residents in Barnsley know that we have frequently as clear a sky, as balmy an atmosphere as could be found in any other place in the United Kingdom; while the elevation of the town and its nearness to the moors give it a healthy braciness as is not usually enjoyed by other large towns with a similar population. On the more material side not so much can be said, yet the town and its immediate neighbourhood are not without buildings of considerable antiquity to interest the careful student. Such buildings as possess architectural merit are mainly of an unfashionable order which supplied severely plain erections and aimed at providing the maximum accommodation at the minimum of cost, while using the best materials. In this category may be placed the Town Hall, the 'Fenton' House in Church Street, the Market Hill Bank and Pitt Street Wesleyan Chapel.

Alumnus – December 1914

Articles included:

The School and the War
List of Old Boys on Active Service
An Old Boy at the Front
A Spoilt Holiday
Notes on the History of Germany.

From this issue until 1919, the contents were dominated by details of Old Boys, former pupils and teachers, who had enlisted (100 by April 1915). The Roll of Honour included their rank, regiment, promotions, wounds, missing or taken Prisoners of War, gallantry medals and deaths; there were letters, poems and articles written by those in the forces plus related ones by pupils and staff. Pupils were involved with fundraising to help soldiers, especially with cigarettes, and participated in 'War Work – a fair number of boys attending the school assisted in Garden or Farm Work or Munition Factories during the summer holidays.

> When the school first assembled at the beginning of term, the Headmaster gave a short address pointing out the reasons which justified our Country in going to war to maintain for our neighbours on the Continent and for our Empire a greater British interest than peace itself, namely Liberty and Right. A prayer for our Soldiers and Sailors was added to those used in opening School, and this is to continue to be said daily. At the close before the Forms dispersed to their classrooms *God Save the King* was sung.
>
> In order that all might be able to follow with intelligent interest the course of events, a course of special lessons has been given to every Form, dealing with the geography of the countries involved, and with general European history from the Napoleonic wars, particularly with the rise of Germany, and the more recent events which have led to the present conflict. War maps have been made accessible to all, and notice boards provided for newspaper cuttings, etc, containing accounts of important speeches, letters from the front, and descriptions of striking incidents and brave deeds.
>
> Contributions have also been sent from the School to the Belgian Refugees' Relief Fund and the Red Cross Society.
>
> Mr W E Evans, BA, our Senior French Master, has kindly volunteered to help a large class of men of the Barnsley Battalion, in gaining some acquaintance with the language of our Allies, which will be useful to them when they are ordered abroad.

By the December magazine 70 Old Boys had enlisted, including the following, whom I have researched in this book:

Armitage, Batleys AG & E, Braham, Cowburn, Dixon, Fitton, Hirst, Knowles H & E, Normansell, Potter FJ, Quest TP, Shipley, Speight, Thompson CC, Warr, Whitelock AT and Willott E.

FORM V
This form is very much given to puns, jokes and witty sayings. The following are above the average:

If the Kaiser and Lord Kitchener were locked up in a car, who would get out first? The answer is: Lord Kitchener as he has the Khaki (car key).

Tom: How long dost think t'war'll last?
Jack: I don't think it'll last long.
Tom: Haw's that?
Jack: Because it was made in Germany.

Alumnus – April 1915

Lieutenant C Thompson visited the school while home on four days' leave:

> The story of his experience in the trenches brought home to our minds with greater force than ever the horrors of this cruel and pitiless war. The brave men fighting and dying in the battlefield experience none of the illusions and glory of war. It is we, safe within the retreat of our island home, relying with complete confidence on the invincibility of our Boys, that feel the glow of exalted imagination and the thrill or awe and wonder, as we read accounts of brilliant achievements and sublime heroism. Ours is the glamour and romance; theirs is the grim and stern reality.

War Training and School Training – C S Butler, Headmaster

No, this article is not about a School Cadet Corps. Many Schools have them, all large Schools ought to have them, and we hope the time will come when Barnsley Grammar School will have its Cadet Corps and Miniature Rifle Range. But at present our subject is suggested by a little shilling book entitled *Quick Training for War,* published soon after the War broke out by the Chief Scout-Master, Lieut-General Sir R Baden-Powell. It was written for the instruction of the young Officers and men whose response to their Country's call has added to English History perhaps the most splendid instance of free-will offering of a free people to Freedom's cause. The style is clear, interesting and so free from technicalities as to be easily intelligible by any non-military reader. Now the aims and ideals of the good Officer have much in common with those of the good Schoolmaster; and the good soldier has many qualities which should be showing their flower-buds in the spring-time of the good Schoolboy. That is why B-Ps book can be recommended to Dominies and Disciples as suggestive and profitable reading.

Take for example the following remarks on DISCIPLINE:

> The men join the ranks full of goodwill and anxiety to acquit themselves well in performance of a duty demanded of them by the State. The Officers and non-commissioned officers are at least equally anxious to show them how best to achieve this national purpose. Gradually mutual esteem, and very probably affection, are evolved out of the relationship of eager master and willing pupil. The two are knit together more and more closely by the generous warmth of feeling consequent on working for a purely unselfish end. There is no money in it. If the Commander sweats the subordinate, that sort of sweat does not go to make the Commander fat.
>
> SUCCESS IN WAR … 'depends more on the moral than the physical qualities. Skill cannot compensate for want of courage, energy and determination, but even high moral quality may not avail without careful preparation and skilful direction. The development of moral qualities is therefore first of the objects to be attained'.
>
> THE FOUR C's OF SOLDIERING – These, as enumerated by B-P, are COURAGE, COMMONSENSE, CUNNING and CHEERFULNESS, to which he adds a fifth, which however is rather the sum total of all qualities, than a distinct quality, viz:
>
> CHARACTER – … 'the formation of character is the chief aim of the English Public School. But it needs to be insisted on no less strongly that the man or the boy can to a large extent train himself and by the exercise of his own will-power develop his own qualities, he is not merely a passive lump of clay to be moulded by the hands of the potter'. Of COURAGE B-P says 'some men are born brave and others require it to be thrust upon them. But in the large majority of cases it is a quality that can be cultivated'. ….
>
> CHEERFULNESS – 'WAR', B-P bids us remember, 'is not what the picture-books would have us believe, a continuous succession of glorious battles, but it is much more like … a dreary succession of days of hard and apparently aimless marching, dull dreary tramping in great herds, under heavy loads, utterly fagged and weary, without excitement, without hope … An army in this state is already halfway to defeat, were it not that its opponents are probably in much the same state. But here it is that a few cheery spirits exercise a vitalising influence …

Anyone who has played football or polo or cricket or indeed has taken part in any team work, knows well the value of a captain who can face the worst of games with a cheery smile, how it puts heart into all and inspires them to buck up and do their best even though things may be looking hopeless ... However sad a dog you may be you have got to cultivate a cheery spirit yourself, if you want others around you to have it also'. All reports from 'The Front' assure us that this is the spirit which in a remarkable degree animates both Officers and men at the present time. Nor are there any Kennels Scholastic where the 'sad dog's' drooping tail and weary whine, the cynic or the pessimist, ought to have any place among the pack. But if howling is banned, not so 'howlers'; without them the gaiety of the Muses would be eclipsed. Happy is the Form Master whose laborious days are refreshed with such delights! Happy is the School where the inscrutable smile never fades from the face of the Impenetrable Duffer, where the irrepressible spirit of the Immense Inane never suffers routine to become monotonous, and where learning's *Il Penseroso* goes hand in hand with the *L'Allegro* of perennial youth.

Alumnus – July 1915

I wonder if many of our young men, drawn in their thousands from school and university, and other professions, having known the pangs and wildness of life, will ever return to their sedentary lives again. One very much doubts it. Probably a good number will emigrate. But in any case those who return will have had their former values of things altered, and with their deepened consciousness and widened vision will influence profoundly the social and political life of the country.

It is worthy of note that out of 134 Old Boys who have become teachers since 1904, 56 have enlisted, many of whom are still in training but a few are out in France ....

Alumnus – April 1916

This is a righteous war. The Germans have been taught to believe that force is the ultimate principle and the only abiding reality in a universe of change and decay, while moral principles are foolish and meaningless, at the best ingenious contrivances for the protection of the weak against the strong, at the worst a superstition, or an accident in the evolutionary process, and therefore of no validity. Our brave soldiers are fighting not only to preserve for England her laws and priceless liberties, but for ideals which they believe in...

Alumnus – December 1916

The losses among teachers have been very great: **A E Armitage, J B Atha, E Batley, L Baylis, G Braham, N Bradbury, E Haigh, F Hall, G W Kellett, B Laycock, C W Wood** were all Certificated Teachers. On leaving the Grammar School most of these boys entered colleges for the training of teachers. Armitage went to Cheltenham College, Batley and Bradbury to York Training College, Bayliss, Hall and Kellett to Sheffield and Laycock to Southampton University College. All of them volunteered immediately war broke out. Nothing could be less to their taste and inclination than military life, and nothing less than duty impelled them to join the army. But they trod the path of honour wherever it led with fearless steps and indifferent to consequences. As I remember them they were full of the inextinguishable spirit of youth and laughter. They looked forward to a future bright with the promise of happiness of useful work, social service, home and love. The sacrifice of all these is not the least part of their tragedy.

The lot of **H Foxon, O Frost, A Hardcastle** and **H Loy** is greatly to be commiserated as they are unfortunately prisoners of war in Germany. A Hardcastle was the wireless operator on the SS Aaro, which was torpedoed and sunk by the Germans in the North Sea, the survivors being made prisoners. [SS Aaro was a British cargo ship that was torpedoed in the North Sea on 1 August 1916 and three crew members were killed].

Alumnus – April 1917

We lament the deaths of three more Old Boys who have laid down their lives for their country: **J Normansell, C E Savage** and **H Willott**. We can do little to mitigate the overwhelming sorrow that has fallen upon the bereaved parents, but offer our pity and sympathy, and express the hope that they will find the strength to suffer and support their grief and pain in the thought that their sons have won imperishable glory by the beauty and virtue of their lives, and the sublime heroism of their deaths. How heavily their loss must lie on the hearts of those who weep for them, our sympathy can faintly feel, and our imagination feebly realise, but their loss to the world cannot be measured or appraised. They had spent many years in serious preparation for their life's work, and were just about to reap the fruition of their labour, and enjoy the fulfilment of bright expectations when they died. Their personal attributes had gained for them the high respect and even the admiration of men; their sense of duty and right inspired trust and confidence; and their chivalrous & generous dispositions won for them strong affection and valued friendship. They died for freedom & conscience and the world today is richer by their sacrifice. Their lives were ennobled by learning, virtuous deeds and noble ideals, and the world is poorer today by the withdrawal of so much power for goodness.

Alumnus – July 1917

It is always a great pleasure to us all to see Old Boys when they come home on leave, and to hear them speak of their impressions at the Front. They have been thrown at so early an age into life's realities, experiencing all its pangs and wildness, when, in the natural order of growth, they should be enjoying its illusions. They have scaled the heights and plunged into depths of emotion beyond the reaches of our ordinary existence. But they make no virtue of their sufferings or of their surrender of personal aims. They utter no complaint or reproach. With one stride they have apparently attained such self mastery as to have steeled themselves to endure any blow of fate, and to nerve themselves into action during supreme crises of life.

Alumnus – April 1918

We deeply deplore the deaths of three more Old Boys who have fallen in action, and of one Old Boy who was accidentally killed when home on leave. For their parents we feel but the profoundest sympathy in the unutterable grief and pain that have suddenly overwhelmed them. Words of sympathy can soothe but cannot console for the loss of love, hope and ambition, which centred in and gathered round these boys. But comfort and strength are to be found in the thought that their sons gave up freely their lives for a noble ideal and a good cause, revealing thus invincible courage, endurance, and self-sacrifice, which are the proof and prophecy of the undying and eternal spirit of man.

Old Boys' visits to the school are much appreciated. Masters and old pupils meet on terms of equality and mutual friendship. The boys have lost their feelings of awe (if any!) and masters their sense of superiority (if any!) with the result that sympathetic understanding and pleasant companionship have succeeded the old relationship based on authority.

Alumnus – July 1918 Editorial

The last three months have been perhaps the most critical period the country has passed through since the outbreak of the war.

Dread and anxiety have often times possessed our hearts, but confidence in our ultimate triumph soon returns, as it springs from a rooted belief in the righteousness of our cause and in the victory of right over wrong.

All honour to the brave soldiers in their struggle to preserve for the world its priceless liberties and to protect our land from defilement by sacrilegious invaders. But we remain appalled at the awful spectacle of death, the unendurable personal suffering and the tremendous sacrifice of innocent lives.

Alumnus – December 1918 Editorial Notes – 11 November 1918

This is the day of deliverance, the day we have hoped for, longed for, prayed for. Words are ludicrously inadequate to express our thankfulness and joy that an end has come to the dreadful pain and slaughter. The doctrines of blood and iron, or force and fraud, are now discredited for ever. Tyranny and militarism are dead.

The defeat of the enemy came at last with surprising suddenness. In July there were no visible signs, no prophetic omens blazing forth the great victories to come. Then as if by the wand of a magician, the whole face of things was altered. Shattering blows were delivered against the enemy forces in France, Belgium, the Balkans and Palestine, and every day brought news of victories so great and overwhelming that imagination failed to rise to the height of these sublime achievements, and now, as a result of those victories, events are moving so swiftly that thrones are topping over, vast empires breaking up, revolutions shaking the whole fabric of society and republics rising daily from the dust of fallen kingdoms.

The war has revealed to us unsuspected possibilities and potentialities of human nature, which inspire us with hope and faith in the future destiny of mankind. For over four years millions of just ordinary men as we thought have shown such fortitude, such power of enduring the miseries and horrors of the battlefield – the rain, the mud, the frost and the exposure to frightful wounds and ever menacing death – that never in the history of the world has such a volume of heroism been shown.

This war has been fought and won by the masses of soldiers, sailors, airmen. It was their initiative, bravery, skill, resoluteness, alertness, the qualities belonging to free and democratic people, that gained the war in their desperate struggle with the forces of autocracy, the best trained and most wonderfully organised armies that the world had ever known.

The work of reconstruction is about to begin. The energy, determination, resourcefulness, power of organisation revealed in war should now be focussed on the problems of peace. If we choose, there is nothing in the way of reform that cannot be achieved. We can have beautiful and healthy towns, a liberal education within the reach of all and a total environment that will promote the happiness of the whole nation and build up noble and strong characters.

In the midst of our rejoicing there runs an undercurrent of sorrow and regret for the heroic dead, who have been cut off in the springtime of their lives. We sympathise with those who mourn for the loss of their dear ones, who were the pride and glory of their lives.

But as for the heroes, who have fallen –

They shall grow not old, as we that are left grow old,
Age shall not weary them, nor the years condemn.
But they shall remain
As the stars that shall be bright when we are dust.

Alumnus – December 1918 The Editor – Evan Davies Esquire BA

With this number my editorship of *Alumnus* Magazine comes to an end. I take this opportunity of thanking all, who, with their essays, donations and subscriptions, have done so much in helping to carry on the publication during the difficult years now happily over. I am also grateful to those who have cheered and encouraged us by kindly words of appreciation.

Our aims have ever been to promote and further the interests of the school and to keep a faithful and permanent record of the part that Old Boys have taken in the Great War. We believe that we have to a great extent realised these ideals. And now, with feelings of sadness, I resign my responsibility, but strongly hope and trust that the magazine will flourish for long years to come and that its success in the future will be even greater than it has been in the past.

But I feel leaving the school even more than the severance of my connection with the magazine. For 14 years I have trodden the stage of our little world with much happiness and few disappointments. It gives me much satisfaction to reflect that I have made many valued friends among the boys, who are now Old Boys; that my relations with my colleagues have been ever amicable; and that I have had, during this long period, the support, confidence and friendship of the Headmaster.

A Farewell to Mr Davies by C S Butler

I have required a reluctant Editor to put at my unconditional disposal a space in this number of *Alumnus* for a communication which is to be unedited and uncensored.

The resignation of Mr E Davies, BA, is to take effect at the end of this Term, upon his appointment by the Education Committee of the County Borough of Barnsley as Inspector of Primary Schools within the Borough.

I feel sure that I am expressing not only my own feelings but those of his Colleagues, the whole School and the Old Boys, in offering to him our sincere congratulations upon the honour, unsought but well merited, that has been conferred upon him by his selection for so important a position.

Since he joined the staff in October 1904, Mr Davies has had special charge of the Senior Boys, particularly in the English work of the two divisions of the Sixth Form and Form V. Moreover he has taken a leading part in the general life of the School and, not least, has been Editor of this School Magazine from its beginning.

He has brought to bear upon his teaching not only skill and a wide range of knowledge, but such a warmth of enthusiasm for his work and such individual interest in the progress of his pupils as never fails to elicit responsive effort from them, to stimulate mental activity and, more than that, to bind together teacher and pupils in bonds of affectionate regard which endure far beyond the brief life of schooldays.

I know this is high praise, but it is not the highest a Teacher can merit: and I should be stopping short of what is due to Mr Davies if I did not add that he has cared no less for the moral welfare of his pupils than for their intellectual training. This good influence which he has sought to exercise upon them has been gratefully acknowledged by many an Old Boy, who feels that he owes to his inspiring counsels and example much of those high ideals of duty and honour, of personal integrity and social responsibility, which are the moral foundations of the finest type of character.

Personally, as well as officially, I wish to place on record here my deep obligations to Mr Davies for his loyal co-operation, valuable counsels and friendly sympathy in the many changes that the School has passed through during these 14 years past. He leaves us with good wishes for his future from all of us: and it is some mitigation of the regret we feel at his departure that he will still reside in our midst as a neighbour and a friend.

Alumnus – April 1919 Editorial Notes

March 1st 1919 – These are days of transition: the old order is rapidly changing, yielding place to the new. We are advancing to the threshold of a new epoch not only in our own history, but in that of humanity at large. Never before, it would seem, throughout the ages of time, has there been such a period of critical days as those through which we are now passing, when political constitutions are found in the melting-pot, from which they are to be moulded and fashioned anew, when so many plans for restoration and reconstruction in every conceivable sphere of life, and not least in the sphere of Education and School, are elaborately outlined in such amazingly rapid succession. In these times of *sturm und drang* [storm and stress], a man must needs run very quickly if he wishes to remain in the same place.

And what is the cause of this state of critical tension? War! – hideous, barbaric war! which has visited mankind in the most inhuman, the most revolting, the most devilish of forms. He, foul fiend, has run his devastating course upon which he entered with his accustomed haste, and now humanity in nervous expectation of the advent of Peace complains at her slow-coming. She comes, however, as always, timidly and furtively, withholding her blessings until her coronation day is past. She shall reign when the necessary period of preparation is over. It was this period, this interregnum, this preliminary state of peace, to which Tacitus refers, when in narrating the ruthless depredations of the Romans, he makes the British Chief say: *Solitudinem faciunt, pacem appellant* [they make a desert, and call it peace]. And now the Huns of modern times, after creating a desert of the fair fields of N. France and Belgium, boldly insult the finer susceptibilities of other nations in speaking of 'an immediate peace'. One of the best of our own writers has succinctly expressed the same scene of utter desolation and abject misery which comes as an aftermath of war:

Wars with their noise affright us; when they cease,
We are worse in peace: -

But now Europe, stunned and bleeding from many wounds, is already beginning to open her eyes to the light of Day. Political surgeons and physicians are in conference over her mental and bodily condition and there are hopes and signs of returning strength. The future, in despite of its uncertainty and dangers, is one of hope and consolation for all nations, and particularly for our own, if she fail not to be true to herself. Therein lies the solution to all our national problems – 'Nought shall make us rue, if England to herself do rest but true': true to her wonderful past, true to her departed sons who gave their lives that she might live, true to her privileged heritage. If this condition of well-being were assured, we might confidently cease to harp upon the minor key and begin to strike the chords of joy and hope and strength. Then at last we might, with certainty, await the dawn of a heaven-born age which has been long-delayed but at last reached through great tribulation, an age when 'the wilderness, the solitary place shall be glad; and the desert shall rejoice and blossom as the rose. It shall blossom abundantly and rejoice even with joy and singing: the glory of Lebanon shall be given unto it'.

Alumnus – July 1919 The New Headmaster

The Governors at a Special Meeting held on July 11th elected as Mr Butler's successor Mr Arthur John Schooling BA, formerly scholar of Sidney Sussex College, Cambridge, who took First Class Honours in the Classical Tripos in 1903. Mr Schooling is at present Chief Classical Master at the Strand School, Brixton, and was formerly Assistant Master at Dean Close School, Cheltenham, and at the Liverpool Institute. He has also a good Athletic record and has held a Commission in the Army and been for three years on active service in the late War (Part 1. Chapter 19).

Alumnus – December 1919 That Other Barnsley Grammar School Magazine – R A H Goodyear

Your first School Magazine was born long before any of you were. I'm not certain of the exact year, blurred by the mists of time. We'll say 1891 and not be far out. It was called the *Holgate Journal* and occupied 16 unruled foolscap sheets, with an outside wrapper of brown paper. Edited by R A H Goodyear and S E Rushforth, it was set out in manuscript by the first-named and passed from desk to desk of the boys in Form V and VI. Some of them skimmed it in half-an-hour or so and were mildly approving or facetiously critical. Others took it home and were stimulated by its contents into sending contributions to subsequent issues.

Hirst, Major – 'Juddy' as we affectionately called him – was one of these, and Harry Dunk was another. These two were the head boys of the School, competing strenuously for the sparely-given and well-worth-winning commendation of the Headmaster (one of England's best) and I am convinced it came as a surprise to them that the shy boy on the back bench, whose absorbing desire was always to escape the Master's attention (particularly at *viva voce* time!) should be the first to give the old School a magazine of its own – for Sammy Rushforth will not mind me saying that he had little to do with it beyond writing its first serial, *Sequah the Medecine Man*, the plot of which became so weirdly involved that Sammy couldn't finish it 'in time for press', and I wrote the concluding instalment myself, throwing Sequah over a cliff, I remember, in a death grapple with one of his rejuvenated patients – thereby anticipating by some years the similar end of Sherlock Holmes.

'Juddy' Hirst brought to my home a bulging packet of delightful contributions.

I left the school at the far too early age of 14, so that the *Holgate Journal* ceased circulation with its eighth number. I hope it brought more smiles to the lips than tears to the eyes of its readers; you fellows of these stirring days are infinitely luckier in having a printed paper like *Alumnus* as your School Magazine; I give you my solemn word that I wish I were young enough to be back again at the grand old School, offering your Editor all the support that loyal contributors gave to me in those sunny summer days of yore.

ROBERT A H GOODYEAR was the 55th pupil to be admitted to the Holgate in May 1888, aged 11; he was the son of a Painter of 33 Tune Street, Barnsley, and left in July 1891.

Alumnus – July 1927 Old Boys' Association

It is gratifying to be able to record that during the last few months the Old Boys' Association has undoubtedly proved itself a more wide-awake organisation than has been the case for some years past. Let us hope that the present revival will lead to a permanent, active Association worthy of the Old School, which every Old Boy must remember with gratitude and affection.

OLD BOYS' REUNION DINNER

Over forty members of the Old Boys and Staff were present at this revival of 'Old Boys' activity and spent a very enjoyable evening at the Royal Hotel, Barnsley, on Friday May 6th. Mr B W Saville presided in an able way.

Mr Evan Davies, in proposing the toast of 'The School', recalled his early days on the Staff and delighted his listeners with anecdotes of the time when classes were held in a room in St George's Yard. Mr A J Schooling responded, referring to the relations that existed between the Governors and the triumvirate of aiding bodies and the Board of Education. The School ought to be, and is, grateful to its Governors for their helpful and considerate control. As Headmaster he could speak of the School's success in scholastics and sport, but not of its general character. He hoped that the School stood well in that respect, but he was sure that it did contain a set of sporting, happy-go-lucky and philosophical boys. Mr Schooling paid a tribute to the work of his predecessor, the Rev C S Butler, and announced that Mr Parkes, the oldest Master in service of the School, would shortly be retiring.

The toast of the 'Founders, Donors and Governors' was fittingly given by Mr C H Hutchinson, one of the first Locke Scholars of the School. He reminded those present of the munificent gifts, especially of Mrs Joseph Locke, Mr S J Cooper, Mr E G Lancaster and Mr W Carnelly.

His personal recollections of the School went back as far as 1859, when the establishment was much smaller than at present and the whole School could comfortably be taught in one room!

Mr J E Jaeger, an Old Boy and a Governor, replied. There were only about fifty boys in the School in his days; but he remembered that there were at least 120 present when the first Old Boys Dinner was held. It was the Old Boys' Association of those days, too, that took a great part in stimulating interest in the School; and as a result the OBA was asked to nominate a Governor, an honour bestowed on him. That was twenty-four years ago; since which time he had seen the School grow immensely, and since which several other Old Boys had joined the Governing Body.

Mr J Halmshaw, in moving the toast of the Association, referred to the number of Old Boys absent; and especially to more than seventy who fell in the Great War. He was sure that it was shyness rather than snobbery that holds back Old Boys from taking part in the Old Boys' activities.

Mr B B Smith proposed the health of the President, who suitably replied, and Captain Bizley, in a humorous speech, acknowledged the thanks of the diners to those who contributed to the musical side of the evening. Letters of apology for absence were read from the Rev C S Butler, Lt-Col Harold Horne and Mr R A H Goodyear.

19

Teachers at Barnsley Grammar School Who Served in the First World War

---

Staff Registers:

13. JOHN BRODERICK
15. JOSEPH SOAR
16. ARTHUR WHITTAKER
17. LEONARD ATKINSON
19. GEORGE HENRY REES
20. GEORGE EDGAR JOYCE DIED - ON THE MEMORIAL
22. WILLIAM EDWARD EVANS
23. HERBERT MARSHALL DIED - ON THE MEMORIAL
26. THOMAS SHAW
29. ARTHUR S MATTHEWS
30. HARRY CASMEY RANDS
35. JOHN ARCHIBALD GRAHAM GREENHALGH

The Headmaster Who Succeeded Rev C S Butler in 1919 (from *Alumnus*)

ARTHUR JOHN SCHOOLING

Teachers Who Joined the Staff after 1919 and Who Had Served*

J B BASFORD
CLIFFORD BURTON
JOHN COTTINGHAM
WILLIAM VERKEST

* Basic Information provided by Barry Jackson and Brian Sawyer

Details of Teachers Who Served and Survived

The Staff Registers in Barnsley Archives provide basic details for most of these teachers, with information about their education and appointment at the Holgate. I have told their stories in alphabetical order rather than date of appointment.

LEONARD ATKINSON (born 25 March 1877 in Barnsley) obtained City and Guilds qualifications and Board of Education. He was appointed on 28 January 1907 @ £40 then became full time from 1 September 1926. Leonard got married on 19 August 1909 in Wombwell to Lillie Britain (born c1883 in Wombwell). At April 1911, Leonard (34) was a Manual Instructor (for Governors of Barnsley, Doncaster and Normanton Grammar Schools), and they were living in five rooms at 164 Summer Lane, Barnsley. They had two daughters: Margaret Lenora (born 18 July 1911) and Gwendolin Mary (born 25 October 1913). Leonard was called up on 26 June 1916, aged 39 years and 3 months, to the Royal Flying Corps, renamed Royal Air Force (Service Number: 34538). Leonard served in France from 20 April 1918 to 11 January 1919 and was awarded two medals: British War and Victory. He was deemed discharged from 30 April 1920 but had returned to the Holgate as a Teacher on 16 January 1919. Leonard retired on 29 January 1943 (aged 66) after 36 years (including war service).

CAPTAIN JOHN BRODERICK (born 12 November 1861) was appointed as a Visiting Teacher on 15 September 1896 @ £18 (2/6 attendance), which increased to £40 in 1912. He taught Physical Exercises with all forms throughout the school. John left in July 1914 to train troops as a Sergeant Instructor with the York and Lancaster Regiment. There is a Medal Card for a Captain in the York and Lancaster Regiment with little information: 'Service Number: 44242/5, eligible 6.1.19'. His is a common name.

WILLIAM EDWARD EVANS (born 25 January 1881 in Wales) obtained a BA in History at the University of Wales. He was appointed on 14 January 1913 @ £170 to teach French and History then from 1920 he was Form Master and Senior French Master with special responsibility. Having been rejected for military service in 1916, William was called up on 14 September 1918. According to the Attestation Form, William was a Secondary School Master living at 191 Dodworth Road, Barnsley. He was 37 years and 8 months old, single, Non-Conformist and his mother was next of kin: Mrs Jane Evans of Buryport, Carnarvonshire. The Medical Form describes him as 5' 4 ¾ " tall, weight 113lbs, chest 35", dark hair, blue eyes, complexion pale, physical development fair, vision with glasses 6/6 both eyes, but 6/36 R and 6/60 L without. He had a medical condition and 'complains palpitations'. William committed an offence on 17 December 1918: 'Certified no entry' at Partrington, but no details are provided.

***Alumnus* – July 1918**

> Mr W E Evans BA is now at Partrington Camp near Hull. Although the training is hard and severe, he accepts the altered conditions of life with his usual philosophic temper, with good humoured serenity of mind. He has entered with zest into the work of learning bombing and bayonet fighting, although he does not quite see what use he is going to make of these highly skilled destructive acquirements'.
>
> William was transferred to the Army Reserve on 14 January 1919 for demobilization. He returned to the school on 16 January 1919 and retired on 31 July 1942 (aged 61) after 29 years.

JOHN ARCHIBALD GRAHAM GREENHALGH (born 24 August 1874 in Cambridge; Baptism 24 August 1876 at St Paul's Church, Nottingham, to parents Adam Gordon and Marianne Greenhalgh) was aged 32 and 'Student (for Oxford University)' on the 1911 Census. He was living with his widowed father Rev. Adam Gordon (63) Clergyman, and his sister Sissie Marianne (30) in 17 rooms at Loxley Vicarage, Warwick; they had a Cook/General Domestic Servant. John was appointed for one term only from May to December 1918. He was Second-Lieutenant in the 12th Battalion of the Worcestershire Regiment. John died early 1932 (aged 57) in Warwick.

ARTHUR STEPHEN MATTHEWS (born 24 February 1894 in Wiltshire) was one of five children of Henry and Rose Ellen Matthews. On the 1911 Census, he was a Student (aged 17) living in six rooms at Pepper Acre Cottage, Trowbridge with his parents – his father was Gardener Domestic – and three younger siblings, who were at school. Arthur attended Trowbridge High School then University College Reading in 1913/14 for his 1st year Diploma in Letters. He taught at Trowbridge High School for one year and obtained his Board of Education Teacher's Certificate. Arthur was appointed to the Holgate on 2 May 1916 as Teacher of Preparatory Form Subjects and Geography to the Lower School @ £130. He was called up in April 1918 and was subsequently reappointed on 16 January 1919. Arthur Matthews is a common name and I have been unable to find his military records. He died in summer 1968 (aged 74) in Hove, Sussex.

Brian Jackson and Barry Sawyer remember Mr Matthews, who taught Geography and was also Librarian until he retired in the early 1950s. He was wounded in the First World War and suffered from shell shock; this led to several disabilities, which some pupils took advantage of. He was deaf and wore an old fashioned hearing aid that had earphones and he could not work out from which direction sounds were coming; this either affected his speech or he had a speech impediment and he also had shaky handwriting.

HARRY CASMEY RANDS (born 15 April 1888 in Wombwell) obtained his BSc at London University in 1910; he did two years special post graduate study in Practical Physics at Sheffield University from 1909–1911. At April 1911, Harry (aged 22) Elementary Certificated School Teacher, was living with his parents – George Henry (51) Stone Worker in Coal Mine, and Charlotte Eliza (50) – in six rooms at 49 Cemetery Road, Wombwell. He had two siblings: Jane (25 born in Woolley) and George Edgar (5 born in Wombwell).

Harry was appointed on 14 September 1916 as Form Master and Teacher of Science and Maths Lower. He left on 4 April 1917 to become an Assistant for the Ministry of Munitions in the Labs Derby Crown Glassworks. Harry C Rands had married Gertrude H Bate late 1916 in Barnsley and they had four children between 1920 and 1930, Margaret, William and John in Derby plus George in Belper. Harry died on 7 October 1972 (aged 84) in Bushby, Leicestershire.

GEORGE HENRY REES (born 3 April 1883 in Swansea) attended Swansea Grammar School from 1895 to 1900 then went to University College of Wales at Aberystwyth from 1904 to 1907, obtaining his Teachers' Certificate and Second Class Honours BA. George obtained teaching experience at Manselton School, Swansea, and Chippenham County School before being appointed to the Holgate on 14 January 1908 @ £50. He was Form Master and taught various subjects: French, Latin, English, Mathematics and Scripture. George was called up on military service in July 1916 and returned to the school on 16 January 1919; his salary increased to £320 later that year.

According to the Royal Navy Register of Seamen's Services, George was a Schoolmaster when he was called up and his service began on 2 September 1916, when he joined HMS Victory (Service Number: M22531). He was 5' 7" with a 35½ " chest, brown hair, brown eyes and fresh complexion. George transferred to HMS Doris on 11 December 1916 and remained with her until 1 February 1918. George was paid a War Gratuity.

Alumnus – July 1918

> We were very glad to see Mr G E [sic] Rees MA, when he came here for 28 days' leave after his long absence in the East. Mr Rees, in the course of many voyages of the HMS Doris from port to port, had the rare opportunity of visiting many far distant towns and countries, including Malta, Lemnos, Salonica, Athens, Aden, Colombo, Australia, Mauritius, Somaliland, Bombay and Egypt'. [*HMS Doris* (built 1896) was serving with the 11th Cruiser Squadron of the Home Fleet when war broke out; she was classified as a depot ship in 1917 and sold for scrap in February 1919].
>
> Mrs Ethel Rees (born 7 March 1887, died early 1981 (aged 94) Barnsley) was appointed to cover for her husband from 1916 to 1919.

THOMAS SHAW (born 14 October 1891) obtained the Intermediate Exam in 1913 at London University. He was appointed on a temporary basis on 15 September 1915 to teach Elementary Subjects with Preparatory Form and Geography; this was to cover for Herbert Marshall, who was absent due to military service. Thomas was called up on 23 March 1916. His name is too common to search for records without more information.

JOSEPH SOAR (born 9 October 1878 in Derbyshire) went to Durham University, where he obtained a 1st Class Degree in Music; he was ARCM (Associate of the Royal College of Music) and FRCO (Fellow of the Royal College of Organists) and had Exhibitions at the Royal College of Music. Joseph was appointed on 1 May 1904 @ £25 to teach Music Theory to Pupil Teachers and Vocal Music to Lower Forms. On the 1911 Census, Joseph (aged 32) Professor of Music and Organist, was living in eight rooms at 8 Victoria Avenue, Barnsley, with his wife of one year Mary Dulcie (26); they had a visitor (5) and a Domestic Servant.

Joseph left on 4 February 1915 to join the Royal Army Medical Corps. There is a Medal Card for a Corporal in the RAMC (52873) whose first Theatre of War was Balkan on 7 May 1915. He was promoted to "A/WO C1 2" then transferred to the Indian Army Reserve of Officers, having received a Commission as Second-Lieutenant on 27 October 1918. The address on the card for Joseph was St David's, Pembrokeshire; he received four medals: Victory, British, 1914–15 Star and the Indian medal.

ARTHUR WHITTAKER (born 24 April 1882) had attended Barnsley School of Art and obtained Board of Education Certificates. He was appointed as a Visiting Teacher on 16 September 1905 @ £24. He left in July 1915 'on military service (munitions)'. Arthur may have married Elizabeth Good late 1913 in Barnsley but his is quite a common name.

The New Head in 1919

ARTHUR JOHN SCHOOLING (born 7 October 1881 in Tottenham, Middlesex; Baptism 13 November 1881 at Tottenham St Ann's Church) was the son of John Schooling, Clerk, and Sarah Ann of 2 Percy Villas, Tottenham. Arthur was educated privately until 1895, when he attended Merchant Taylor's School in London until 1900. He obtained a 1st class BA degree in Classics at Sidney Sussex College, Cambridge University, in 1903, followed by his MA in 1919. John's first teaching position ('scholarship work') was at Dean Close School in Cheltenham from 1905 to 1907. He became Assistant Master and Chief Classical Master at the Liverpool Institute from 1907 to 1912 then relocated to the Strand School in Brixton, London, as Chief Classical Master from 1913 to 1916. John married Eva Duprey in Edmonton in 1910 and they had two children: John D (Jack) in summer 1911 in West Derby and Molly W early 1914 in Wandsworth.

Arthur, who had a good athletic record, was called up in 1916 and given a Commission in the Army; according to *Alumnus* he 'spent three years on active service". An article in *Barnsley Chronicle* on 19 July 1919, about his appointment as Headmaster of Barnsley and District Holgate Grammar School, states that Arthur served for three years with the Artists' Rifles. (The only military information that I could find on Arthur John Schooling was a Medal Card for a Private (Service Number: 3769) in the Royal Army Medical Corps. However, Officers' Records are kept at the National Archives and have not yet been digitized).

Arthur was appointed as Headmaster, with the special subjects Latin and Greek, on 11 July 1919 at a salary of £600 per annum; his salary increased to £910 pa in 1925. Arthur died on 15 February 1971 (aged 89) while living at Powick, Worcester.

John Schooling taken in 1934, reproduced by kind permission of Brian Sawyer.

20

The Cooper Art Gallery in the Old Grammar School Building

An advert in *Barnsley Chronicle* on 25 July 1914 invited local people to apply to Newman and Bond Solicitors (Part 1. Chapter 15) for tickets to attend the Formal Opening by the Earl Fitzwilliam on Friday, the 31st July, 1914 at 3.30pm.

***Barnsley Independent* – 8 August 1914**

GIFT OF THE LATE MR S J COOPER
OPENED BY EARL FITZWILLIAM

> ... the fulfilment of another valuable acquisition to the town ... is one of the numerous benefactions of the late Mr Samuel Joshua Cooper (Part 1. Chapter 14) of Mount Vernon, who died in July last year. The new gallery is situate in the buildings formerly occupied by the Barnsley Grammar School, which on the transfer of that school to its new home in Shaw Lane was purchased by Mr Cooper with the scheme for providing Barnsley with an art gallery in view. Mr Cooper not only desired to provide Barnsley with an art gallery, but he possessed a large and valuable collection of pictures and these together with the building were to constitute another of his handsome gifts to the town.
>
> In accordance with the deceased philanthropist's known wishes, the trustees under Mr Cooper's will effected alterations to adapt the structure to the purpose of a gallery. This has been well done under the supervision of Mr R W Dixon (Part 2. Chapter 20). A stone porch has been erected, new oak floors and new fireplaces have been put in, and the lighting greatly improved, especially in the upper gallery. ... A sum of £3,300 was given for the buildings apart from the cost of alterations and the endowment amounted to £4,000.
>
> Mr Pawsey (Part 1. Chapter 15), in asking Earl Fitzwilliam to open the gallery on behalf of the trustees welcomed such a large attendance interested in the birth of the Cooper Art Gallery in Barnsley. He mentioned that that gallery stood on the site of the original school, founded by Thomas Keresforth in 1660, and that

school coupled with the one at Hemsworth, which was somewhat older, having been built in 1546, had been carried on there for a great number of years. For about three centuries it was the only centre for higher education in the district. Two years ago the population of Barnsley and the progressive nature of the town warranted an extension, which was found impracticable on that site and the new school was built in Shaw Lane. Mr Cooper, to whom Barnsley was particularly grateful, was at one time a pupil in that school, and he acquired it to be set aside as a gallery. By his will he left the pictures to be hung in the gallery and he personally took great interest in the alterations and superintended the planning...

***Sheffield Evening Telegraph* – 1 August 1914**

BARNSLEY CEREMONY
EARL FITZWILLIAM OPENS ART GALLERY
HISTORIC SITE

A fashionable and representative gathering took place yesterday at Barnsley when Earl Fitzwilliam opened the Cooper Art Gallery.

The buildings have a fine appearance and there is room for extensions. A caretaker's house is built at the rear and the grounds are tastefully laid out in accordance with the donor's instructions. The gallery is artistically arranged internally and contains a fine selection of art, chiefly the French school. Among the paintings is *In the Forest of Fountainebleau* (N Diaz) [Narcisse Virgilio Diaz], *The Wreck* (Eugene Isabey 1880), *The Entrance into Port* by the same painter, a landscape with two peasant women fishing in a lake in the foreground by J B C Corot [Jean Baptiste Camille Corot], and *Hurricane Before St Malo* by Eugene Isabey. Quite a little story surrounds picture No 140 J F Herring (1827) which at one time was not considered to be worth £5 but is now valued in the hundreds.

Lord Fitzwilliam expressed his pleasure at being present. 'When I was invited to open the gallery a few weeks ago', said his Lordship, 'I had to tell Mr Pawsey that I was very doubtful whether I could come. I said that nothing worse than a European war would stop me. That shows how lightly one can speak, how I treated it as a joke, and now we are about on the brink of it'. Continuing, his Lordship said it was interesting to open a building in commemoration of a gentleman, who spent his life in a way which politicians and soldiers did not, and that was in pursuit of peaceful industry. He paid a great tribute to the life and work of the late Mr Cooper and to the beneficiaries and trustees. He referred to the various endowments made by Mr Cooper... Speaking of the growth of Barnsley, his Lordship said when he was a lad before going to India, the population of Barnsley was about 36,000 and now it was over 50,000. He congratulated his fellow South Yorkshiremen on having achieved the dignity of being a County Borough. He remarked that the upkeep of the gallery was fully arranged for and that was a great point for there would be no tax on the local rates.

21

Barnsley Holgate Grammar School Memorials

Early volumes of *Alumnus* magazines were bound into a book, a copy of which was presented to the grammar school by the Headmaster, Reverend Charles Stokes Butler, and this is now in Barnsley Archives as part of the Holgate Collection.

Various different memorials were mentioned in *Alumnus* between 1914 and 1919, but I have been unable to find out what happened to some of them.

THE MEMORIAL CLOCK would have been in the Shaw Lane premises but does not appear to have been taken to Horizon Community School; I do not know whether the detailed ROLL OF HONOUR, kept up to date in the Assembly Hall, still exists and I have been unable to ascertain whether a MEMORIAL HALL was erected or a Sports Pavilion named this, but suspect neither happened since it took over 10 years after the war ended for the War Memorial to be completed.

When details of the dedication ceremony for the War Memorial 'Tablet' were provided in *Alumnus* December 1928, there was an added appeal for donations to a fund to establish 'OLD BOYS' MEMORIAL PRIZES' but I have not come across any other references to this.

There are a number of surviving memorials to the Old Boys.

THE FIRST WORLD WAR MEMORIAL, with list of 76 names, is on display in the Cooper Gallery (Part 1. Chapter 22 plus photographs in the Colour Section).

ALUMNUS MAGAZINES from 1914 to 1919 in Barnsley Archives provide details about the Old Boys who served and include many contributions from students and staff about their experiences.

HOLGATE EPHEMERA from 1888 to 1920 in Barnsley Archives contains many items, including newspaper cuttings with Obituaries etc, collected by the Headmaster Reverend Charles Stokes Butler.

'THE NAME CALLING CEREMONY' has been continued by Horizon Community College (Part 1. Chapter 22).

This book is a new memorial and tribute to the 76 Old Boys and their families.

Alumnus – April 1918

Lieutenant Colonel Hewitt donated £20, which was used for a Memorial Clock for the Assembly Hall. 'A handsome 14" Dial Clock, of the best workmanship, in an oak case' with the following inscription:

1917
Presented by Lt Col J Hewitt
Formerly Locke Scholar
in Memory of
Locke Scholars who have fallen in the War
Dulce et Decorum Est Pro Patria Mori.

Alumnus – July 1918

WAR MEMORIAL

At present the **Roll of Honour in the Assembly Hall** is the only way in which we can commemorate the part taken by hundreds of our Old Boys in the Great War. But it is rightly felt that the contribution of service to the National Cause, which the school has made, deserves a Memorial of a more substantial character, such as will provide on a generous scale some notable addition to the advantages or amenities of the School or School Premises to be associated for ever with the names of these Old Boys. The subject was discussed informally at the Governors' Meeting in April. A matter of such importance requires careful consideration and it is hoped that it may shortly be taken in hand by a Committee representing all parties interested, the Governing Body, the Old Boys Association, the Staff and present Boys of the School and the Parents and friends of Boys Past and Present.

Letter dated 4 October 1918

J Halmshaw LLB, Honorary Secretary of the Old Boys Association, sent letters out about a Barnsley Grammar School Old Boys' Memorial.

At an Informal Meeting of the Old Boys Association held at the Grammar School on July 25th last, it was decided this matter could no longer be left in abeyance, but that a movement should be instituted to the realisation of the Memorial so soon as convenient after the declaration of peace.

To this end it was agreed to call a General Meeting of all interested parties, namely the Governors, the Borough Council, Parents, the School Staff, the Senior School and this Association.

The meeting will be held on *Thursday evening October 17th 1918 in the general hall of the YMCA, Eldon Street, Barnsley, at 7.30pm.*

I sincerely hope you will make it convenient to attend.

Newspaper Cutting (Holgate Ephemera) – 17 October 1918

GRAMMAR SCHOOL OLD BOYS' MEMORIAL

A general meeting of the parties interested in the proposal for a memorial to the old boys of the Barnsley Grammar School who have served or are serving in the war was held last Thursday evening in the YMCA Buildings, Eldon Street, under the chairmanship of Dr J F Horne. Many letters of apology were read by the secretary from those regretting their inability to attend. Without discussion it was unanimously agreed that some fitting form of memorial to the old boys who have done so much for their country should be established and that now was the time to initiate the movement. Several suggestions as to the form the proposed memorial should take were put forward and thoroughly discussed but it was eventually decided that a general committee would more easily and definitely settle that question and should be formed immediately. Numerous offers to serve on this committee were forthcoming and accepted, many gentlemen being suggested as members and finally, on the motion of Mr Normansell, it was carried that the Secretary be asked to get into communication with the gentlemen mentioned with a view to their being placed on the committee. After further discussion and votes of thanks to the chairman and the YMCA (who gave the meeting the free use of their meeting hall) the proceedings closed. It is hoped that those interested in the movement who (unintentionally) were not notified of this meeting, will communicate with the hon. Secretary of the Old Boys Association, J Halmshaw LLB, Netherwood Hall, Wombwell.

Alumnus – December 1918

A Committee was formed under the chairmanship of Lt Col Hewitt, JP to make arrangements to erect a "Memorial Hall" to house the Old Boys Association.

Alumnus – July 1919

The Roll of Honour was completed by M E Haigh – four large frames with names, dates each left school, rank and regiment with marks to distinguish who was killed, wounded, missing or Prisoner of War.

420 Old Boys served plus some members of staff
80 held commissions ranks
68 lost their lives (plus 2 staff) [*list updated later to 76*]

Alumnus – July 1924

GRAMMAR SCHOOL WAR MEMORIAL FUND

Bernard Walter Saville, Honorary Secretary, provided a list of recent contributions that made the total fund to date £93 17s 6d.

Since the last issue of *Alumnus* there has been a steady flow of subscriptions towards the Memorial Fund, yet the amount received is still far below the objective – £250.

Mr Moxon has undertaken the duty of local secretary for Cawthorne. I should be pleased to hear from Old Boys from the outlying districts who would undertake to act in the same capacity.

Further subscriptions would be gratefully acknowledged by Mr G H Rees, at the Grammar School, or by myself at 209 Park Road, Barnsley.

Alumnus – April 1925

WAR MEMORIAL

Letter dated 21 March 1925 from Bernard Walter Saville, Honorary Secretary.

Sir, it is now over six years since the Great War ended, and those scholars and ex-scholars of our Grammar School, who so devotedly sacrificed their lives in it, still remain without any visible and grateful sign of remembrance.

That such an inexcusably long delay should occur before any fitting memorial has been erected or fixed must be clearly apparent to all well-wishers, and it is equally clear that it is full time that an ending of some kind should take place.

My present special appeal is therefore for aid in bringing this important matter to a satisfactory conclusion.

At least £250 is the estimated sum required, and that amount, surely, should be well within the calculation we are relying upon. Quite so, if we take into account that it is the inhabitants of the whole of Barnsley and District to whom we have a right of appeal, seeing that they all are more or less interested in the general welfare and reputation of what is in reality their special scholastic institution.

This being the case, an appeal on our behalf from the Editors of our three local papers would be of great value. This help, I am sure, they will readily give when fully acquainted with our needs, our aspirations and time-urgency.

Again I make a final and special appeal to those who would like to subscribe and have not yet had the opportunity. Subscriptions, no matter how small, will be gratefully received by Mr G H Rees, Grammar School, or by myself at 209 Park Road, Barnsley.

Yours faithfully
B W Saville, Hon Sec

[Bernard Walter Saville was the younger brother of Reginald John Saville, one of those who sacrificed their lives (Part 2. Chapter 57)].

***Barnsley Chronicle* – 15 January 1927**

OLD BOYS' MEMORIAL

The B G S is still without its Memorial to the Old Boys who fell in the War but the matter has not been entirely neglected (writes a correspondent). Up to the present a sum of over £91 is available (including promises amounting to about 17 guineas) but this is not sufficient. On Tuesday next (January 18th) a meeting of subscribers is to be held in room 5 of the YMCA Buildings in Eden Street, when suggestions will be welcomed. The small committee which has had the matter in hand, are agreed that a mural tablet, bearing the names of the fallen, should be placed in the school and, if funds permit, either a sports pavilion should be erected or a prize fund instituted. Nothing however has definitely been decided upon and it is desired that all Old Boys should express their feelings in the matter. It is hoped that Tuesday's meeting will hasten the accomplishment of the project.

***Barnsley Chronicle* – 15 October 1927**

BARNSLEY GRAMMAR SCHOOL
WAR MEMORIAL

To the Editor of the *Barnsley Chronicle*
Sir,
Now that the form which the School War Memorial is to take has been definitely decided upon, the Committee would appreciate the help of your valuable paper in order that the list of names to appear on the Memorial may be revised.

The list is appended and the Committee invite corrections and additions to be sent to the Secretary not later than Thursday October 20th.

A design to be executed in bronze, surmounted by the School Crest in coloured enamel and mounted on a plain polished oak base, submitted by Messrs E Pollard and Co Ltd, London, has been accepted at a cost of £95.

In addition to this it is hoped to establish a fund to provide an Annual Old Boys' Memorial Prize for which the sum of £60 is still required. Further subscriptions, no matter how small, would therefore be gratefully acknowledged by the Secretary or by G H Rees, Esq. The Grammar School, Barnsley.

B W Saville, Hon Sec

LIST OF 71 NAMES [H H J Mason's name was listed correctly]

***Barnsley Chronicle* – 3 November 1928**

B G S
UNVEILING OF MEMORIAL TABLET

In the presence of fully 300 persons, the ceremony of unveiling and dedicating the Memorial Tablet, erected in memory of the 76 Old Boys and two Masters who fell in the War, took place on Saturday afternoon at the B G S. The tablet was unveiled by Mr Charles H Hutchinson of Barnsley, who was one of the first 10 Locke scholars in 1861. The dedication ceremony was performed by the Rev C S Butler who was headmaster of the school from 1888 to 1919.

The tablet has an oak base which has been excellently decorated by the art master (Mr H Benson) and the names are inscribed in 3 columns on a bronze plate. The names inscribed are as follows:

LIST OF 76 NAMES [the Batley brothers' surname was spelt incorrectly as Battley and H H J Mason was now listed incorrectly as H H Jagger-Mason)

Messrs Joyce and Marshall are the two masters.

Prior to the unveiling Mr Hutchinson delivered a short address and expressed regret that one of the school's old boys Mr Whyke [sic], the Sheffield City Engineer, was unable to be present.

The Rev C S Butler expressed great pleasure at being back on the school platform, a spot on which he had never again expected to stand. He referred to the present boys at school and expressed the hope that they would not have a future such as the boys he taught. He mentioned that he taught boys in a classroom facing the tablet and he hoped that they would not have the same ending to life as the majority of those boys did.

Amongst those on the platform were Mr R F Pawsey (Clerk to the Governors), Canon H E Hone, the Headmaster (Mr A J Schooling) and Mr Berryman (first assistant master of the school). For the unveiling those on the platform passed into the corridor the remainder of the gathering staying in the hall. *The Last Post* was sounded by members of the 5th Batt Y and L Regt.

In addition to the erection of the tablet it is intended to establish Old Boys' Memorial prizes. A further sum of £85 together with the funds already in hand would make it possible to provide 5 annual prizes. Donations would be gratefully accepted by Mr B W Saville, the secretary.

Alumnus December 1928

THE WAR MEMORIAL (UNVEILING AND DEDICATION)

A touching and solemn ceremony took place at the School on Sunday October 28th 1928, when a Tablet was unveiled and dedicated to the memory of seventy six old members of the School who fell in the Great War.

The Headmaster's welcome to those present was brief but adequate and struck at once the note of simplicity and sincerity that marked the whole proceedings. He was particularly glad to welcome Mr C H Hutchinson, one of the first Locke Scholars of the School (1861), to unveil the Tablet, and to find the Rev C S Butler, MA, under whose headmastership the fallen old boys had been, able to come north once again and perform the dedication. With the Headmaster were Canon Hone (Rector of Barnsley and a School Governor), Messrs R F Pawsey (Clerk to the Governors), B W Saville (President of the Old Boys Association), and W J Berryman (Second Master). The congregation was mainly composed of relatives of the fallen.

Boys, the Staff and a specially selected Choir from the School [sic]. Among those present were Mrs Schooling, Mr E J F Rideal and Mr J Garbett (Governors) while apologies for their unavoidable absence were received from Mr J E Jaeger (Governor) and Mr C E Wike (the oldest "Old Boy").

The service began with the singing by the Choir and congregation of the hymn, *Oh God our help in ages past.* After the *Lord's Prayer* and special prayers for the occasion, Mr C H Hutchinson unveiled the Tablet and Rev C S Butler dedicated it.

To the honoured memory of the Seventy-six Old Boys of Barnsley Grammar School whose names are recorded on this Tablet, and who gave their lives in defence of their country's righteous cause, we do hereby dedicate this Tablet to be a perpetual witness to their spirit and courage and devotion, and a call to all who shall look upon this Memorial to follow their worthy example of service and self sacrifice.

As the congregation stood with bowed heads buglars sounded *The Last Post* very impressively.

After the congregation had sung J Russell Lowell's hymn, *Once to every man and nation*, the Rev C S Butler said that he wished to thank the Headmaster, the Memorial Committee and their Secretary, Mr Saville, for having done him the honour of inviting him to dedicate the War Memorial, and for the opportunity so given him of standing once more upon that platform, where he had never expected to stand and speak again. The occasion was one which must fill all present with mingled feelings and emotions, what life might have been, what life actually brought to the gallant lads who had fallen. He remembered that once in the classroom opposite to the Memorial Tablet he was taking the Form in their English Literature lesson; the poem for study happened to be Gray's *Ode on a Distant Prospect of Eton College*. Gray was of a melancholy temperament and his thoughts of the boys in the playing fields there led him to forecast with pity and lament all manner of troubles and suffering awaiting them in their manhood, of which they were blissfully ignorant in their happy school days. Among all the forms of human woe which his morbid imagination foreboded, there was one terrible experience and ordeal that the poet did not think of, and that was the supreme ordeal which those whose memory they were met to honour were suddenly called upon to undergo, those Old Boys and the two young Assistant Masters, Mr Marshall and Mr Joyce – the terrible experience of the unceasing strain and hardships and horrors of war, strife, bloodshed, wounds and death. These boys had no desire to be soldiers. Yet they went from the quiet occupations of civil life, in early manhood, and many of them straight from the schoolroom, to do and to suffer all that brave men could, in the training camp, the ranks, the battlefield, the trenches, the hospital. What is called militarism was not in them. Their country had need of them; they would not fail her. There was a stern duty to be done, that was it; they went and did it. Nor did he believe that there was any such alien spirit of militarism in the boys and young men of the present day. After all that the world went through in the Great War, there could be no more boasts of military glory and the romance of war; the only glory was in their noble British spirit of service and sacrifice. They were warned that any future war would be far more horrible than this last. All hoped it would never come. But if the wickedness and folly of any wanton aggression should ever assail the safety, honour and welfare of this nation, he felt assured that the young men of that generation – and might it be a far distant one – would come forward as readily and acquit themselves as manfully as those Old Boys whose loss they deplored and to whose memory they were that day doing reverence.

The proceedings concluded with the singing of the *National Anthem*.

(We should like to remind our readers that the Old Boys wish to establish a further memorial in the form of Old Boys' Memorial Prizes. A sum of £85, together with the funds already in hand, would make it possible to provide five annual prizes. Donations for this purpose would be gratefully received by B W Saville, 209 Park Road, Barnsley).

22

The Barnsley Holgate Grammar School War Memorial

The First World War Memorial is made of a bronze central panel with an oak wood surround. It was completed in 1928 and there was an unveiling and dedication on 28 October (Part 1. Chapter 21).

The bronze panel has the 76 names of the Old Boys (surnames with initials in alphabetical order) in raised lettering in three columns. The names are within a border design, which has enamel images in the four corners of the national emblems for England, Ireland, Scotland and Wales: rose, clover leaf, thistle and leek.

At the top of the oak frame are the words '1914–1918 TO THE MEMORY OF THE OLD BOYS OF THIS SCHOOL WHO FELL IN THE GREAT WAR', embellished with Archbishop Holgate's coat of arms and motto *FORTITER OCCUPA PORTAM.* On either side are decorative shields, one of a burning lamp for Knowledge, Truth and Life and the other a sword and laurel wreath for Honour and Victory. (My photographs of the Memorial with close ups of decorative details are in the Colour Section)

(© Jane Ainsworth)

Full Names of the Old Boys

PANEL ONE – 25 NAMES	PANEL TWO – 26 NAMES	PANEL THREE – 25 NAMES
ALLOTT, T R	GREEN, S	POTTER, F J
ARMITAGE, A E	GREGORY, G	POXON, E
ATHA, J B	HAIGH, E S H*	QUEST, H
BAKEL, F	HALL, F	ROYSTON, R
BAMBRIDGE, H L	HEATHCOTE, A	SAVAGE, C E
BANKS, A	HIRST, J	SAVILLE, R J
BARRACLOUGH, C	JONES, R	SHIPLEY, A H B
BATLEY, A G	JOYCE, G E	SKUES, C
BATLEY, E	JOYNER, B J	SMITH, G
BAYLIS, L	KELLETT, G W	SPEIGHT, J C
BOOKER, W R	KELSEY, W	STUART, C
BOYD, M B P	KILNER, J W	SWIFT, J S
BRADBURY, N	KNOWLES, H R	THOMPSON, A H
BRAHAM, G	LAYCOCK, B H R	THOMPSON, C C
CARTER, H	LAYCOCK, D S	THOMPSON, J E
CARTER, J R	LINDLEY, F	TIMSON, P E
CHOYCE, W H	LINDLEY, F M	UTLEY, A
CLARKE, J B	LITHERLAND, E W	WARR, G H G
COWBURN, G P	MARSHALL, H	WEMYSS, J A
DIXON, C B	MASON,** H H J	WESTBY, T
DOUGHTY, E M	McNAUGHTON, D	WHITELOCK, C R
DOWNEND, J M	MOORE, F H	WILBY, J T C
FAIRLEY, D	NICHOLSON, S	WILLIAMSON, M C
FEASBY, H	NORMANSELL, J	WILLOTT, H
GILL, S	PARKIN, H	WOOD, C W
	POTTER, E D	

* This H seems to be incorrect
** Incorrectly listed as MASON JAGGER

23

Name Calling Ceremony

Barnsley Holgate Grammar School introduced this ceremony for Remembrance Day in 1919 in the new school building in Shaw Lane. The Head Boy stood in the main hall and read out loud the names of the 76 men on the First World War Memorial one by one, each name being repeated by the Deputy Head Boy, who stood in the corridor outside the hall. (They subsequently added the names from the separate Second World War Memorial) This ceremony was memorable to those students who were present.*

At a later stage, a representative of the Old Boys Association attended the Remembrance Service and read all seven verses of the poem *For the Fallen* by Robert Laurence Binyon (1869–1943), first published in *The Times* newspaper on 21 September 1914:†

FOR THE FALLEN

With proud thanksgiving, a mother for her children,
England mourns for her dead across the sea.
Flesh of her flesh they were, spirit of her spirit,
Fallen in the cause of the free.

Solemn the drums thrill: Death august and royal
Sings sorrow up into immortal spheres.
There is music in the midst of desolation
And a glory that shines upon our tears.

* Brian Sawyer, Old Boy and retired Headmaster, explained the ceremony to me. He remembered watching through the school windows members of the public standing still in Shaw Lane at 11am when the ceremony took place on Remembrance Day itself.

† Barry Jackson, Old Boy and retired History Teacher, represented the Old Boys Association for many years at this ceremony.

They went with songs to the battle, they were young,
Straight of limb, true of eye, steady and aglow.
They were staunch to the end against odds uncounted,
They fell with their faces to the foe.

They shall grow not old, as we that are left grow old:
Age shall not weary them, nor the years condemn.
At the going down of the sun and in the morning
We will remember them.

They mingle not with their laughing comrades again;
They sit no more at familiar tables of home;
They have no lot in our labour of the day-time;
They sleep beyond England's foam.

But where our desires are and our hopes profound,
Felt as a well-spring that is hidden from sight,
To the innermost heart of their own land they are known
As the stars are known to the Night;

As the stars that shall be bright when we are dust,
Moving in marches upon the heavenly plain,
As the stars that are starry in the time of our darkness,
To the end, to the end, they remain.

When Horizon Community College (Horizon) opened in 2012, amalgamating the Holgate and Kingstone Schools, they decided to continue this tradition in the Sadler Room at the Cooper Gallery – in the original Barnsley Grammar School building, where most of the Old Boys had attended and where the First World War Memorial is on display. (The Second World War Memorial is currently in storage at Horizon until a suitable location can be found).

I had found it very moving to attend this simple ceremony for Remembrance Day 2013, when a group of students read out all 174 names on the First and Second World War Memorials (surnames with initials); a wreath was laid and *The Last Post* sounded before observing a two minute silence followed by *Reveille*.

However, the ceremony on Monday 10 November 2014 was made even more special for the Centenary of the outbreak of the First World War – and especially poignant for me after finding out so much about the 76 men – as for the first time ever the full names of all the Old Boys who died in that war were read out. I was delighted that the following relations were also able to attend, which was the first time that family have been present: John & Cath Batley (Arthur George & Edward Batley), Gay Yates (Walter Reginald Booker), Adrienne McEnhill (John Middleton Downend), Pam Kellett & Margaret Shepard (George William Kellett) and Paul Quest (Harold Quest).

We talked to the students afterwards and I was delighted that two of them subsequently sent me poems, included in this chapter (photograph in the Colour Section).

2014: YEAR 8 REMEMBERS

(Horizon Community College Website by Suzy Dix, Community Tutor)

This morning, four Y8 students were invited to the Cooper Art Gallery in Barnsley town centre for a very special Remembrance Service. Organised by our Chair of Governors, Mr John Bostwick, the service acknowledged and remembered the lives of those who were educated in the Cooper Art Gallery building and died during World War I. The service was short but very moving and included the reading of the full names of the 76 men who gave their lives between the 1914–1918 conflict.

The event marked the first time that the fallen soldiers' names had been read out loud in full, including middle names. Y10 student, **Aidan Stirk**, began the proceedings by playing the Last Post on his trumpet. This was followed by a 2 minute silence, before **Daniel Mara** (8K) and **Leah Hackleton** (8T) placed a wreath in specially marked space in the gallery. After this, Leah and Daniel, joined by **Mitchell Scott** (8N) and **Jack Walker** (8J), stood to read out the names of the fallen. The ceremony was made even more special by the attendance of some of the families of the soldiers.

Afterwards, our students were given the opportunity to speak to some of the other attendees, including Jane Ainsworth, who painstakingly researched and compiled the list of soldiers. It was a memorable, intimate and unique event.

We all felt very proud of our students for taking part and they in turn felt proud to be part of such an important occasion.

Poppies Grown by Leah Hackleton

Poppies grow to help you
Never doubt it's all we knew
Help them grow, so they can help you
For Remembrance Day is all for you
Poppies grow to be there for you
So this is for you too
Help them grow to help you
For Remembrance is on its way thanks to you.

The Battle by Ali Khosravi

My fellow being!
In battle of life!
By the weapon of pen!
Fight against violence!
Fight against ignorance!
Fight against darkness!
Fight against unfairness!
Fight against extremism!
Fight against racism!

My fellow being!
With intelligence!
Fight against negligence!
With rationality!
Fight against immorality!

My fellow being!
Fight for your right!

In 2015, Horizon decided to incorporate the history of the Holgate more meaningfully into their Remembrance Assemblies. They held special 30 minute Assemblies on 4 November in which the names of the Old Boys were read out for the first time, in addition to holding the Name Calling Ceremony in the Cooper Art Gallery on 11 November, which several relations attended, including Joan Hall (Jack Normansell). I donated an album of photographs of the 76 Old Boys with brief details to enable those participating in this ceremony in future to identify the names as real people.

24

The Holgate Second World War Memorial

Barnsley Grammar School in Honour of the Old Boys of this School Who Fell in the War 1939–1945

ADDY D
ATKINSON E
BAILES S N
BARRACLOUGH J
BELL H
BENSON A
BINGLEY S
BIRD J
BLUCK W
BOLSOVER A R
BOULTON G
BRAILSFORD H J
BROOKE A R
BROWN G
BROWN H
BRUCK R
BURDON S
BURNS A
BUTCHER J A
CLARKE H [# see end]
CLEGG H
COOKE A
COULSEY J R
COWARD J L
COWLEY R
CRASHAW L
CRASHAW M
CROSSLEY R
CUTHBERT G
DALTON D
DICKINSON R*
DICKINSON R*
DUNKLEY L
EATON E C M
FAWCETT J
FEATHERSTONE G
FLETCHER G F
FLETCHER L
FOX G
GOUGH M
GREEN G E
HAIGH R C
HALL S
HARDMAN C N
HARRIS P R
HAWKE G O
HEPWORTH F
HEWETSON H
HINCHCLIFFE E
HIRST B
HIRST T W
HOBSON A
HOLDSWORTH R W
HORSFALL A
HORSFALL D
HOWCROFT B W
HOWE A
HYDE B
HYDE N B
IVETT P F
JAMES W L
JONES D
KELL G W
KILNER J
LIVESEY M
MARSLAND J
MYERS D V
NORDON A A
OWEN W
PARKINSON F
PLATT G
PORTMAN J
POULTER J
RAYNER G
REYNOLDS J

RICHARDS J
RIDGE A
RIDGE F
RIDING B
ROBINSON G
ROWELL A W
SAGAR T
SHARLAND D
SIDDALL D
SMITH H S
SPARK G T
SPENCER W
STAFFORD W A
STEAR A T
STUBBS C J
TITLEY R
TURNER J
WAINWRIGHT G R
WARD L
WILBY R H
WORRALL F
WREAKES J
CLARKE E C#

E C Clarke was added to the end of the Memorial
* Ralph and Roger Dickinson

This War Memorial consists of an oak board with heading and three bronze plaques with 98 names listed as above. (I aim to work with Barnsley Archives to get the full names of all of these men).

When Holgate School in Shaw Lane closed in 2012 the building was demolished. Various items and archives were donated elsewhere, but Horizon Community College decided to keep the Second World War Memorial to display in the new premises when somewhere suitable could be agreed. (I will be liaising with Horizon to try to get the Memorial on display in 2016).

(© Jane Ainsworth)

Part 2

The 76 Old Boys

1

Thomas Richard Allott

Thomas Richard Allott
1888–1918 (aged 29)

THOMAS RICHARD ALLOTT was born in 1888 in Kexbrough to **Frederick Allott** (born c1865 in Kexbrough) and **Annie nee Smith** (born c1868 in Kexbrough). Frederick was the fourth of nine children; their father and grandfather, both called **Thomas Allott**, were Fancy Weavers (skilled workers who wove complex patterns on Jacquard looms). Thomas junior became a Coal Miner and this was the occupation that his son Frederick went into.

Thomas Richard was the oldest of six children: **Emma, James Henry**, a Solicitor's Clerk, **George Frederick** who died in 1909, aged 16, **Reginald Smith** (attended the Holgate) and another child who died before April 1911 (name unknown).

In April 1911, the Allott family lived in four rooms in School Street, Darton, having moved from Jacob's Yard in Kexbrough. At least four generations of Allotts had been born in Kexborough and continued to live in the area. **Emma Allott** got married on 29 March 1915 at Darton All Saints Church to **John Henry Wilkinson**, Mining Surveyor of Darton, whose father **James Richard Wilkinson** was Colliery Manager. **James Henry Allott** married **Edith Allemby** in summer 1937 and they were living at 34 Lake Avenue in Barnsley when James died in 1951.

Thomas went to Kexbrough school until the age of 12. He then attended the Holgate Grammar School in Church Street, Barnsley for about 18 months from 1901 to 1902. Thomas became a Solicitor's Clerk at Messrs Bury and Walkers Solicitors in Barnsley before he was called up. (*This firm is still around 100 years later, based in Regent St, Barnsley)*. He was the organist in Cawthorne Wesleyan Chapel (*now the Methodist Church*) and Westgate Primitive Chapel in Barnsley (*now the Lamproom Theatre)*.

Thomas married **Olive Charlesworth** in Cawthorne in summer 1912. Olive (born February 1886 in Cawthorne) was one of four children of **John and Elizabeth**

Thomas as a schoolboy, reproduced by kind permission of Sarah Greenwood.

Charlesworth, Farmers of Hill Top Farm, Taylor Hill, Cawthorne; in 1901 she was a Pupil Teacher and in 1911 she was an Assistant Teacher in the Elementary School.

Thomas and Olive on their Wedding Day, reproduced by kind permission of Sarah Greenwood.

Wedding group, reproduced by kind permission of Sarah Greenwood.

Thomas and Olive had a daughter, **Julia Katherine Allott,** who was born late 1916 in Cawthorne.

Julia married **Maurice Charles Dimond,** the son of a Vicar, in Exmoor, Somerset, in winter 1955; they did not have any children. Julia served in the ATS in the Second World War and she died in March 1978, aged 60. Maurice died in 1997, aged 78.

According to Barry Jackson's research, Olive's brother **Douglas Charlesworth** tried several times to enlist but was rejected on medical grounds. He kept a diary of events in Cawthorne during the war and donated several items to the Jubilee Museum there.

Thomas enlisted as a Private (Service Numbers: 202889 and 6355) in 1916 and was given a Commission on 29 January 1918 as Second Lieutenant with the 1st Battalion of the King's Own Yorkshire Light Infantry. He went out to France on 12 October 1918 and was killed in action three weeks later on 4 November 1918, aged 29 (only one week before the war ended). Thomas was buried in Romeries Communal Cemetery Extension, Nord, France (grave IV B 9).

Thomas was awarded two medals: Victory and British War. His widow Olive should have received the 'Dead Man's Penny' plaque and scroll from King George V.

Probate was granted for Thomas on 6 March 1920 at Wakefield to his widow. Effects: £206.

Olive with Julia, reproduced by kind permission of Sarah Greenwood.

Thomas in uniform, reproduced by kind permission of Sarah Greenwood.

Thomas' name is on the Holgate Grammar School Memorial, the Cawthorne Memorial outside the museum and the Memorial inside Cawthorne Methodist Church, where a tablet is inscribed:

IN LOVING MEMORY OF
SEC. LIEUT. THOMAS R. ALLOTT
KINGS OWN YORKSHIRE LIGHT INFANTRY
THE DEVOTED HUSBAND OF OLIVE ALLOTT
AND WHO DIED OF WOUNDS IN FRANCE
NOV. 4TH 1918 – AGED 30 YEARS
ORGANIST OF THIS CHURCH
FOR 9 YEARS.

Olive Allott got married again in Cawthorne in summer 1920 to **Joseph Barlow,** who worked for his parents **George and Sarah Barlow** at Hill Top Farm, North Lane, Cawthorne; he was the second of eight children. They subsequently moved to Somerset and did not have any children. Joseph died in 1962, aged 78, at Leighton House, The Parks, Minehead, and Probate was granted to Olive, who died in June 1972, aged 86.

Alumnus – December 1918

2nd Lieut T R Allott, KOYLI (1901–02) was killed in action on Nov 4th 1918. He was, before he enlisted, on the staff of Messrs Bury Walkers, Solicitors, Barnsley.

Barnsley Chronicle – 16 November 1918

VICTIMS IN WAR'S CLOSING STAGES
A CAWTHORNE LOSS
SECOND-LIEUTENANT T R ALLOTT

Monday's glad news of Peace was mingled with sorrow at Cawthorne by the sad news of the death of Second-Lieutenant T R Allott. He went out to France on October 12th 1918 and was killed in action near Le Inesnoy on November 4th. Mr Allott, who was in the King's Own Yorkshire Light Infantry, was educated at Barnsley Grammar School and prior to joining the Army two years ago, was on the staff of Messrs Bury and Walkers, solicitors. For several years he was the organist at Cawthorne Wesleyan Chapel and afterwards at Westgate Primitive Chapel. He leaves a widow and one little girl.

***Yorkshire Post* and *Leeds Intelligencer* – 16 November 1918 The Roll of Honour**

> SECOND-LIEUTENANT T R ALLOTT, KOYLI, of Cawthorne, near Barnsley, was killed in action on November 4 after being in France only a short time. He was an 'old boy' of the Barnsley Grammar School and prior to joining the Army two years ago was employed by Messrs Bury & Walker, Solicitors of Barnsley.

REGINALD SMITH ALLOTT (born on 13 June 1899; died summer 1980, aged 81) went to Darton Elementary School for four years until the age of 12, when he attended the Holgate for three years, from 1911 to 1914. He left to 'study mining surveying'.

Reggie married **Frances Mirfin Bennett** on 28 June 1921 at All Saints Church, Darton. He was a Mining Surveyor living in Church Street, Darton; Frances was living in her father George Thomas Bennett's Darton Hotel. Reggie's brother James Henry was one of the Witnesses. They had four children: **Kenneth** born 1920 in Dewsbury, **Geoffrey** born 1924 in Dewsbury, **David** born 1928 in Bradford and **Elizabeth** born 1931 in Bradford.

Reggie, reproduced by kind permission of Sarah Greenwood.

Sarah Greenwood, granddaughter of Douglas Charlesworth, generously lent me her family photographs and provided some information. I was able to share this and my research with Irene Hughes, a distant Allott relation.

The main photograph of Thomas is reproduced by kind permission of Sarah Greenwood.

2

Albert Edward Armitage

Albert Edward Armitage
1891–1915 (aged 24).

ALBERT EDWARD ARMITAGE was born on 22 April 1891 in Harley, Wentworth, to **William (Willey) Armitage** (born c1867 in Blacker Hill) and **Harriett (Lillie) nee Fox** (born c1866 in Mortomley). Willey was a Colliery Enginewright.

Albert had an older sister **Eveline**. His parents had two other children, who had died by April 1911 (names unknown).

By April 1911, the Armitage family had lived in six rooms at 63 Hoyland Road, Hoyland Common, for at least 10 years. Albert was a Student Boarder at the Church of England Teacher Training College in Swindon Road, Cheltenham. The family moved to 99 Carter Lane, Mansfield, in 1912; Willey was a Mechanic at Crown Farm Colliery and both Albert and Eveline were teachers at the same school in Mansfield.

Eveline Armitage (born in 1890 in Harley) School Teacher, married **Albert E De Barr** late 1916 in Mansfield. Albert De Barr (born c1889 in Hoyland) Coal Merchant's Clerk, was living in four rooms at 224 Sheffield Road, Birdwell, with his parents, four siblings and uncle on the 1911 Census. Eveline and Albert had moved to 48 Albert Avenue, Sedgely Park, Manchester, by 1919, but their two sons were born in Mansfield: **Albert Edward De Barr** in spring 1918 and **Jack De Barr** in summer 1921.

Albert went to Hoyland Common school until the age of 14. He then attended the Holgate Grammar School in Church Street, Barnsley for three years from 1905 to 1908; he was an Intending Pupil Teacher and Bursar. He passed the Oxford Junior exam in 1906 (3rd Class Honours), for which he won a Cooper Prize, and the Oxford Senior exam in 1907 (2nd Class Honours).

Cheltenham Training College c1910, photograph kindly provided by the Special Collections and Archives, University of Gloucestershire (copyright). Albert Armitage is the second young man seated from the left, on the second row.

Albert trained as a teacher at St Paul's College, Cheltenham from 1909 to 1911 (now part of the University of Gloucestershire). Two paintings by him are in the University of Gloucestershire Special Collections and Archives (reproduced in the Colour Section).

Albert was Assistant Schoolmaster at Hoyland Common Boys' School and had also taught at Worsbrough Dale for about a year, before he was appointed to York Street Council Schools in Mansfield Woodhouse from 1912, along with his sister. Albert was also a keen sportsman and played for both the Hockey Club and Tennis Club in Mansfield.

Albert enlisted in Mansfield on 21 September 1914, aged 23 years and 6 months, according to the Attestation form; he was an Assistant Schoolmaster. He was a Private (Service Number: 2585) in the 1/8th Battalion of the Sherwood Foresters (Nottinghamshire and Derby Regiment).

The Medical Form contains a personal description of Albert: Height 5' 6", Weight 9st 8lbs, Chest 34½" fully extended, Complexion: Fresh, Eyes: Grey, Hair: Light Brown.

Albert sailed from Southampton and arrived in France on 2 March 1915. He was 'killed in action on the field' either by a shell, while fetching more ammunition, or by the explosion of a mine in a trench captured from the Germans, 106 days later, after serving for 268 days. Albert died on 15 June 1915, aged 24. He was buried in the Kemmel Chateau Military Cemetery, West Vlaanderen, Belgium (D. 65)

Albert was the second Old Boy to die and one of only three who died in 1915.

He was awarded three medals: 1914–15 Star, Victory and British War. His parents should have received the 'Dead Man's Penny' plaque and scroll from King George V.

Probate was granted for Albert on 29 February 1916 at Nottingham to his father, Colliery Mechanic of 99 Carter Lane, Mansfield. Effects: £103.

Albert's name is on the Holgate Grammar School Memorial and three Memorials in Nottinghamshire: Mansfield St Lawrence's Church, Mansfield St Peter's Church and that for Nottinghamshire County Council Employees.

Connections

Albert was in the same Form as **John Bruce Atha, Frank Bakel, Ernest William Litherland** and **John Thomas Claude Westby;** they all won Cooper Prizes in 1907 for passing the Oxford Local Junior Exam.

Teacher's Last Letters (to his sister Eveline)

June 10th – We had a rather quiet time in the trenches. One day the Germans sent over a few shells, but not on our part. One trench about 300 yards away got a good number but beyond blowing up a few wire entanglements I don't think much damage was done. The last night we were in there was an exchange of trench mortars. These are most dreadful things – worse than shells – because they can with more accuracy be dropped into a trench. They didn't come our way, but just to the left, and they did a small amount of damage. Altogether we have had some bad luck this time, our casualties being rather heavier than usual. Of course, there is always the possibility that we have made the Germans suffer just as much, because we always return with profit whatever they send. I hadn't heard that Edmund Gill was anywhere out here at all. It is rather rough luck. Still, it's what will happen to a good many more yet, and we get paid occasionally, and I usually get a supply of stuff to take in the trenches, but things are very dear, about double the English price. The German snipers are really good shots. For instance, a periscope which exposes perhaps a surface of 2 inches by 3 inches above the parapet was shot clean through the other day. I am just going to have a sleep. It was 2.30 am when we got back from the trenches, and we were out last night until one o' clock, and I fancy we are out again tonight as our company is on duty.

June 11 – I expect you have got the Rosary I sent. We go into the trenches again tonight and are still at the same place, so I expect we shall get out for Wednesday. There is an exciting cricket match just being played on our field between our Company and 'A' Company, and I think we are winning. We find time occasionally for a few games like that.

Barnsley Chronicle – 3 July 1915

Nottingham Evening Post – 23 June 1915

ANOTHER MANSFIELD HOCKEY MAN KILLED / PRIVATE ALBERT E ARMITAGE

On Monday we had to record the fact that the Mansfield TBSOSA Hockey Club had lost their captain at the front and today news reached us that Private Albert E Armitage, 8th Sherwood Foresters, captain of the other hockey organisation in the town, the Mansfield HC, was killed last week by the explosion of a mine in a trench captured from the Germans.

Armitage was a thorough sportsman and well known and respected in the Mansfield district where in addition to playing a good game at hockey he also put in some valuable work as a member of the Forces Town and Colliery tennis clubs.

Mansfield and North Notts Advertiser – **Friday June 25, 1915**

PRIVATE ALBERT ARMITAGE
MANSFIELD WOODHOUSE TEACHER WHO DID HIS DUTY

Private Albert E Armitage, who was 24 years of age, was also with the 8th Battalion Sherwood Foresters, and was killed at the front on the evening of the same day as Private Hill was killed at dinner time.

He lived with his mother and father, Mr and Mrs William Armitage, at 99 Carter Lane, Mansfield, and prior to coming to Mansfield, three years ago, the deceased was formerly a teacher at the Hoyland Common School, near Barnsley. He first began teaching when only twelve years of age, and in 1903 he entered Barnsley Grammar School. In 1906 he was successful in obtaining third class honours, Oxford (junior), followed by second class honours, Oxford (senior) in 1909. He was trained at St Paul's College, Cheltenham from 1909 to 1911, coming out top of the certificate list. Private Armitage then became assistant master at Worsbrough Dale Schools, near Barnsley, a position which he held about a year. Exactly three years ago this month he came to Mansfield, where he accepted a position as teacher with his sister at the Yorke Street Council Schools, Mansfield Woodhouse, under Mr Stanley, headmaster.

Private Armitage enlisted on September 26th and after being trained at Newark, Braintree and Luton, he proceeded to the front on February 27th and was killed in action on June 15th.

He was the only son of Mr William Armitage, who is employed as a mechanic at the Crown Farm Colliery. The unfortunate young man was perhaps better known at Woodhouse than in Mansfield. He was very fond of sport and was an enthusiastic member of the Mansfield Hockey Club and the Forest Town Tennis Club.

The distressed parents and sister have been the recipients of many letters from the front, including those from Lieutenant Colonel Fowler and three of Private Armitage's chums in the firing line. The writer of one letter stated that Private Armitage was being buried next to Lieutenant Hollins, whilst another said the grave was well covered with flowers put on by his soldier comrades. One of deceased's chums writing on June 17th said: 'He was peacefully buried last night in our little cemetery not far from the firing line'.

The following letter, dated June 16th, was received from Lieutenant Handford:

> Dear Mrs Armitage, I am very sorry to have to tell you that your son was killed last night by a shell. He had been sent to fetch up some more ammunition, and died doing his duty, as he always did. He was Captain Wright's (Captain Wright was also killed in action) most valuable man. You have my most sincere sympathy in your loss, and I can assure you that the whole platoon will feel the loss of him. Your son is being buried tonight in the military cemetery here. Yours sincerely, Basil Handford.

The following letter was the last ever written by the deceased and was received by his sister only a few days before the news of his death came through.

> I expect you have got the rosary I sent. I got it from a small chapel right on top of the hill. There are quite a number of these chapels up and down, mostly at crossroads .... There is an exciting cricket match just being played on our field between our Company and A Company, and I think we're winning. We find time occasionally for a few games like that.
>
> I think I told you that Captain Wright was killed last Sunday, and I believe I'm to be the observer for the captain who has taken his place. I was recommended for a stripe about a week ago, but I'm not eager to have one as it only means more trouble.

It appears that Private Armitage had been acting as observer for Captain Wright on the Sunday previous to his writing his last letter and he had just left him when his Captain was killed. Private Armitage was of a very quiet disposition and was greatly liked, and he was a favourite teacher with the boys at the Woodhouse School.

The article from Mansfield & North Notts Advertiser *has been reproduced by the kind permission of Mansfield Library and local studies.*

***Barnsley Chronicle* – 3 July 1915**

PATRIOTIC PARS

> Two Hoyland Common men have fallen in the recent fighting. Private Albert Edward Armitage, 8th Sherwood Foresters, was killed by a shell while carrying ammunition to the forward trenches on June 15. He was a trained teacher (Cheltenham College), and a native of Hoyland Common, but prior to enlistment held a staff appointment at Mansfield Woodhouse.

(Also in *Yorkshire Post* and *Leeds Intelligencer* – 26 June 1915)

Louise Clough, Principal Library Adviser (Special Collections and Archives), University of Gloucestershire, generously sent me a copy of her information as part of her research on their 264 Old Boys, a scan of his signature, illustrations done by him and his year group photo, which are reproduced by kind permission of the University.

The main photograph of Albert is from Alumnus, *reproduced by kind permission of Barnsley Archives.*

WAR SUPPLEMENT FOR WEEK ENDING APRIL 20, 1918.

BACKING HIM UP.

MIDDLE-AGED WORKMAN: He didn't argle-bargle about joining up. Why should I?

[*"We at home must ensure that the man power is adequately maintained and that our workers, men and women, will continue nobly to meet the demands for all the necessities of the war."*

—THE KING TO SIR DOUGLAS HAIG.]

3

John Bruce Atha

John Bruce Atha
1890–1916 (aged 25)

JOHN BRUCE ATHA was born on 15 September 1890 in Liversedge to **Alfred Atha** (born c1863 in Leeds) and **Keziah nee Austin** (born c1863 in Wolverhampton). John's Baptism was on 15 January 1893 (aged 2) at St Bartholomew's Church in Armley, where they lived. Alfred was a Hotel Waiter in 1911, but had previously been Restaurant Manager at the Sailor Boy Inn, New Street, Barnsley (*this pub no longer exists*). **Alfred Atha** had also experienced military service. He had enlisted at Chelsea on 20 August 1884, aged 19; he was born in Leeds and his mother **Elizabeth Atha** continued to live in Leeds. He served 12 years as a Private then Driver for the Commissariat and Transport Corps; he was in Egypt for more than three years from 1 April 1885, for which he received medals, and earned a pension on discharge. Alfred suffered injuries to his left shoulder and back as a result of horse bites. (He was awarded 1d Good Conduct pay).

John was the oldest of five children with four sisters: **Mary Elizabeth, Mabel Agnes, Dorothy Miriam** and **Nellie Dora**.

In April 1911, the Atha family lived in four rooms at 10 Wall Street, Barnsley, but had moved several times in Barnsley after leaving Armley, Leeds. John's parents subsequently moved to Batley.

All of John's sister got married. Mary married **John O Sykes** in Spring 1926 in Dewsbury, Mabel married **Fred Schofield** in Spring 1927 in Oldham, Dorothy married **Wilfred Rhodes** in Spring 1935 in Bradford and Nellie married **John E W Sutton** early 1932 in Hatfield. Mabel had two sons in Oldham: **Ronald Sykes** in 1928 and **Joshua Sykes** in 1933. Dorothy had a daughter **Shirley Rhodes** born in 1935 in Leeds. Nellie had a son **Jack Sutton** born in 1932 in Dewsbury.

John attended the Holgate Grammar School in Church Street, Barnsley for four years, from 1904 to 1908. He was Intending Pupil Teacher and Bursar, passing the Oxford Local Junior exam (3rd Class Honours), for which he won a Cooper Prize in 1907, and the Oxford Local Senior exam. John trained to become a teacher and by 1911 he was an Elementary Teacher (aged 20). He was a Certificated Teacher at St John's Boys School, Barnsley, by 1915.

John enlisted in Barnsley on 16 January 1915, aged 24 years & 133 days, and he was a Schoolmaster living at 1 Nursery Street, Barnsley, at this time according to the Attestation form. He was posted as Private but promoted within three weeks to Corporal (Service Number: 14/331) in the 14th Battalion (Second Barnsley Pals) of the York and Lancaster Regiment. Duncan Fairley, Second Lieutenant and another Old Boy, signed the form for the Adjutant.

The Medical Form contains a personal description of John: Height: 5' 5 ¾ ", Weight: 116lbs, Chest: 34" fully extended, No Distinctive Marks, Physical Development: Good, No Defects. An Offence form stated that on 24 October 1915 John refused to comply with an Order while at Hudson Camp, for which he was 'severely reprimanded', but there are no details.

John embarked at Devonport at the end of December 1915 and arrived at Port Said a fortnight later. He served in the Mediterranean for two months before returning home to go out to France on 11 March 1916. John was killed in action on the first day of the Somme, 1 July 1916, aged 25, after serving for one year and 157 days. As his body was never found or identified, John's name is on the Thiepval Memorial, Somme, France (Pier and Face: 14A and 14B).

John was one of ten Old Boys to be killed in action on the first day of the Somme.

John had married **Constance Ena Hawley** from Masborough on 11 April 1916 at Rotherham Register Office, while he was home on leave, and they lived at 'Oaklea', Westville Rd, Barnsley. Ena received a Separation Allowance of 9/–, with 3/6 Allotment of Pay, while her husband was in the Army; they could only have spent a very little time together because of the circumstances.

Their son **John Philip Atha** was born on 11 January 1917. Tragically this was after John had died so their son never knew his father. Ena moved to Halifax at some stage and received a Widow's Pension from the War Office of 15/6* a week. *(* A Private's basic pay was 1/– per day plus 1d per day when in a war zone).*

John was awarded three medals: 1914–15 Star, Victory and British War. His widow should have received the 'Dead Man's Penny' plaque and scroll from King George V. A letter regarding John's personal items was stamped 'No Effects'.

John's name is on the Holgate Grammar School Memorial. His name was also on the War Memorial at St John's Church, Barebones in Barnsley, but this was lost when the church was demolished; at the end of 2015 a replacement oak plaque was created using a grant from Barnsley Central Ward and this will be displayed in St Peter the

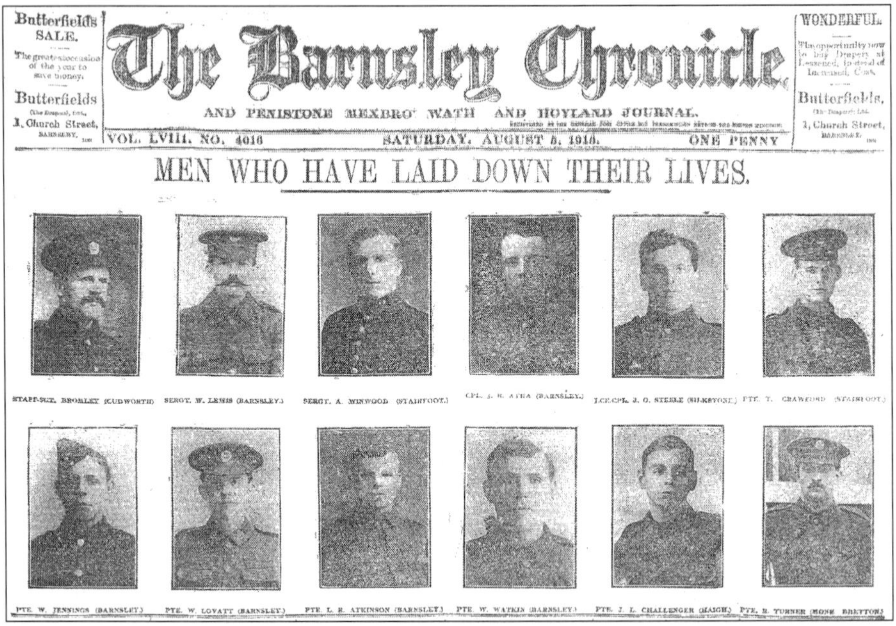

Butterfields SALE.

The greatest occasion of the year to save money.

Butterfields (The Drapers), Ltd., 1, Church Street, Barnsley.

The Barnsley Chronicle

AND PENISTONE MEXBRO' WATH AND HOYLAND JOURNAL.

WONDERFUL.

The opportunity now to buy Drapery at Lessened, instead of Increased, Cost.

Butterfields, (The Drapers) Ltd. 1, Church Street, Barnsley.

VOL. LVIII. NO. 4016 SATURDAY, AUGUST 5, 1916. ONE PENNY

MEN WHO HAVE LAID DOWN THEIR LIVES.

STAFF-SGT. BROMLEY (CUDWORTH) SERGT. W. LEWIS (BARNSLEY.) SERGT. A. WINWOOD (STAINFOOT.) CPL. J. H. ATHA (BARNSLEY.) LCE.-CPL. J. O. STEELE (SILKSTONE.) PTE. T. CRAWFORD (STAINFOOT.)

PTE. W. JENNINGS (BARNSLEY.) PTE. W. LOVATT (BARNSLEY.) PTE. L. R. ATKINSON (BARNSLEY.) PTE. W. WATKIN (BARNSLEY.) PTE. J. L. CHALLENGER (HAIGH.) PTE. R. TURNER (MONK BRETTON.)

Feature in *Barnsley Chronicle*, used by their kind permission.

Apostle and St John the Baptist's Church in Brinckman Street, off Doncaster Road, Barnsley.

Connections

John was in the same Form as **Albert Edward Armitage, Frank Bakel, Ernest William Litherland** and **John Thomas Claude Westby**; they all won Cooper Prizes in 1907 for passing the Oxford Local Junior Exam.

John served in the 14th Battalion (Second Barnsley Pals) of the York & Lancaster Regiment with **Frank Bakel, Duncan Fairley** and **Harold Quest**.

***Barnsley Chronicle* – 29 July 1916**

Corporal J B Atha, 2nd Barnsley Battalion, a teacher at St John's Boys' School, Barnsley, at the time of enlisting, was killed in action on the 1st inst. The deceased soldier was 25 years of age and had resided in apartments at 1 Nursery Street, Barnsley. His parents live at Batley. Corporal Atha came over on leave in April last and was married, returning to France the following day. His wife now resides at 128 Wortley Road, Rotherham. The news of Corporal Atha's death was received at St John's School with much regret, he having as a teacher gained the high esteem of his colleagues and the pupils alike. Mrs Atha would be pleased to hear from any comrade who saw her husband's end.

***Sheffield Evening Telegraph* – 28 July 1916**

AMONG THE FALLEN

The list of fallen in Barnsley and district continues to grow. Corporal J B Atha (25) a well-known school teacher.

***The Times* – 2 August 1916**

J B Atha was listed amongst those Killed in Action.

The main photograph of John is from Barnsley Chronicle, *used by their kind permission.*

4

Frank Bakel

Frank Bakel
1891–1917 (aged 25)

FRANK BAKEL was born on 18 November 1891 in Barnsley to **Robert Bakel** (born c1852 in Suffolk) and **Clara Ellen nee Worrall** (born 1860 in Hillsborough). Robert was a Fruit Dealer Employer.

Frank was the fourth of seven children: **Annie, Lily, Minnie, Walter** (attended the Holgate and served in the First World War)**, Nellie** and **Edward** (attended the Holgate). In 1911, the three older sisters were helping in the business or at home while the three younger brothers were at school..

In April 1911, the Bakel family lived in seven rooms at 71 Church Street, Barnsley, having previously lived at 65 Church Street (probably the same house renumbered). Their mother had died early in 1908, aged 48, and their father died late 1915, aged 65, leaving their youngest children, Nellie and Edward, as orphans at the ages of 15 and 12.

Annie Bakel married **George Owram** (1877–1967, aged 90) in Spring 1914 in Barnsley; he was a Pork Butcher as was his father Henry, who lived in 12 rooms at Melwood, Huddersfield Road, Barnsley. **Nellie Bakel** married **Frank R Clayton** in Summer 1922 in Barnsley; they had twin sons in Keighley in 1923: **Frank B Clayton** and **George W Clayton.**

Frank went to St Mary's Elementary School, Barnsley, until the age of 11. He attended the Holgate Grammar School in Church Street, Barnsley for five years, from 1903 to 1908. He won a Junior Locke Scholarship in July 1903 and passed the Oxford Local Junior and Senior exams.

Frank started work at the Union of London and Smith's Bank in the Barnsley branch on 6 May 1908. He became a Bank Clerk, passing the Institute of Bankers' examinations in 1910 (preliminary) and 1912 (final) as noted in the Journal of the Institute of Bankers, 1912.* *(The Union of London & Smiths Bank Ltd (1839–1918), established in London, was a past constituent of The Royal Bank of Scotland Group).*

Frank enlisted in Barnsley and, after a period in the Officers' Training Corps, he was promoted to Second Lieutenant in the 14th Battalion (Second Barnsley Pals) of the York and Lancaster Regiment. He served in other Battalions of this Regiment after the First Day of the Somme, 1 July 1916. Frank was killed in action on 20 May 1917, aged 25, and he was buried in Bailleul Road East Cemetery, St Laurent-Blangy, Pas de Calais, France.

Frank married **Constance Priscilla Thompson** on 27 April 1916 in St Mary's Parish Church, Barnsley; he was a Corporal in the York & Lancaster Regiment, residing at Princess Louise Schools, Blythe. Constance was the sister of **Captain C C Thompson** and **Private A H Thompson** (Part 2. Chapters 64 & 65). *Barnsley Chronicle* provided a description of the wedding.

* Ruth Reed, Archives Manager for the Royal Bank of Scotland, kindly provided details of Frank's career at the bank. Ruth is responsible for the RBS Remembers website providing details of 1,582 men, who worked for various banks amalgamated within RBS and died in the First World War.

Frank was awarded three medals: 1914–15 Star, Victory and British War. His widow should have received the 'Dead Man's Penny' plaque and scroll from King George V.

Probate was granted for Frank, Second-Lieutenant in the 3rd Battalion of the York & Lancaster Regiment, on 10 August 1917 at London to his widow Constance. Effects: £2,194 4s 7d.

Frank's name is on the Holgate Grammar School Memorial, the painted column in St Mary's Church, Barnsley, as 'Frank Bakell' on the Memorial List of names for Ebenezer Methodist Chapel, Barnsley (*now demolished*), War Memorials for Gibson Hall National Provincial and Union of London and Smiths Banks, the National Provincial Roll of Honour (as F Baker) and the RBS (Royal Bank of Scotland) Remembers 1914–1918 website.

Photograph of Frank in *Barnsley Chronicle*, used by their kind permission.

Connections

Frank was in the same Form as **Albert Edward Armitage, John Bruce Atha, Ernest William Litherland** and **John Thomas Claude Westby;** they all won Cooper Prizes in 1907 for passing the Oxford Local Junior Exam.

Frank started work as a Bank Clerk at the Union of London and Smith's Bank a few years after **Harry Liddall Bambridge, Ronald John Saville** and **Thomas Westby**.

Frank married Constance Thompson, sister of **Cecil Cuthbert** and **Arthur Henry Thompson**.

Frank served in the 14th Battalion (Second Barnsley Pals) of the York & Lancaster Regiment with **John Bruce Atha, Duncan Fairley** and **Harold Quest**.

Frank is on the Memorial List of names for Ebenezer Methodist Chapel, Barnsley, along with **Harry Bambridge** and **Sidney Nicholson**.

Barnsley Chronicle – 13 May 1916

A CORPORAL'S MARRIAGE

At the Barnsley Parish Church a pretty wedding was solemnized by the Rev, C A Howell between Corporal F Bakel, 15th York and Lancasters, eldest son of the late Mr R Bakel, of Barnsley, and Miss Constance P Thompson, only daughter of Mr and Mrs S Thompson, Outwood, near Wakefield. The bride, who was given away by her father, wore a pale cream gown of ninon and taffeta embroidered with silver, a veil of embroidered net caught round by a spray of orange blossoms, and she carried a shower bouquet of white carnations and white roses, the gift of the bridegroom. The bridesmaids were Miss Lily Bakel sister of the bridegroom and Miss Ethel N Davies, a college friend of the bride's. The former wore a dress of white net over silk, with a black picture hat while the latter wore a picture hat of black underlined with shell pink. Both carried shower bouquets of pink carnations, and each wore a pearl and aquamarine pendant, the gifts of the bridegroom. The bride's mother, who was attired in a gown of navy taffeta, also carried a shower bouquet of white carnations the gift of the bridegroom. Mr E S Knee acted as best man. The bride's brother, Captain C C Thompson, arrived from the trenches too late to act as groomsman. The reception was held at the Parish Room where Miss Nellie Bakel and Master Edward Bakel distributed white heather favours to the many friends of the bride and bridegroom. Later the guests dispersed round the Rectory Grounds which had been kindly lent by the Rev. Canon and Mrs Hervey. Subsequently the happy couple left by motor for Grassington, the bride's travelling costume being of covert cloth coating with a hat of crepe-de-chine to match. The bride's gift to the bridegroom was a smoking cabinet, while that of the bridegroom to the bride was a dress bracelet of pearls and sapphires. The presents received were both numerous and costly.

Alumnus – July 1917

2nd Lieut Frank Bakel was one of the most popular boys that have attended the Grammar School, distinguished as he was not only for the excellence of his intellectual qualities but also for the courtesy and gentlemanliness of his behaviour and the good humour and cheerfulness of his disposition. He was married to a sister of Captain C C Thompson and Private A H Thompson, both old boys who were killed in action during the Somme Battles of 1916.

The deceased officer was killed in the trenches on May 19th while in charge of a carrying party. His CO writes: 'We had been in a very hot part of the line and he had had many dangerous tasks, all of which he had performed cheerfully and thoroughly … He showed courage and a cheerful heart amid such great dangers and he was always to be depended upon whatever he had to do. We have lost a very gallant soldier and a thoroughly capable officer who was always cheerful and willing'.

Yorkshire Post and *Leeds Intelligencer* – 26 May 1917

THE ROLL OF HONOUR

Second-Lieutenant Frank Bakel, York and Lancaster Regiment, son of the late R Bakel of Barnsley, fell in action a few days ago. He was 29 [sic] years of age and had been for several years on the staff of the Barnsley branch of the Union of London and Smith's Bank.

Barnsley Chronicle – 2 June 1917 (Photo)

ANOTHER BARNSLEY OFFICER KILLED

The numerous friends of Second-Lieut Frank Bakel, Y and L Regiment, son of the late Mr and Mrs R Bakel of 2 Lingard Street (formerly Church Street) Barnsley, will learn with deep sorrow and regret that he was killed in the trenches on May 19th, whilst in charge of a 'carrying' party.

The late officer, who was 25 years of age, was educated at the Barnsley Grammar School, where he distinguished himself as a student and where his personal attributes won for him the high respect and affection of scholars and masters alike. On leaving the school he joined the staff of the Union of London and Smith's Bank. His cheerful and generous disposition and his gentlemanly and unassuming conduct and bearing made him *persona grata* everywhere. He will be sadly missed not only by his colleagues at the bank but also at Ebenezer United Methodist Church, where he was a faithful, loyal and helpful member from his boyhood upwards.

Sinking his personal aims and desires he was anxious at the outbreak of war to respond to the call of his country but was unable to do so for strong and sufficient reasons until about 14 months ago, when he was accepted for service in the Y and L Regiment. Subsequently he entered the Officers' Training Corps at Bristol and proceeded to France shortly after being gazetted.

His Company Commander writes *inter alia*: 'We had been in a very hot part of the line and he had had many dangerous tasks, all of which he had performed cheerfully and thoroughly … He showed courage and a cheerful heart amid such great dangers and he was always to be depended upon whatever he had to do … We have lost a very gallant soldier and a thoroughly capable officer, who was always cheerful and willing …'.

The deceased officer leaves a young widow, two brothers and five sisters to mourn his loss. His wife's parents, Mr and Mrs S Thompson, Outwood, Wakefield, have already sustained heavy bereavement by the death in action of their two and only sons: Captain C C Thompson and Private A H Thompson, who were both killed during the Somme battles of July and August 1916.

Barnsley Independent – 2 June 1917

BARNSLEY OFFICER FALLS
SEC-LIEUT. FRANK BAKEL

As briefly announced in last week's *Independent,* Second-Lieut Frank Bakel (Y and L) fell in action on May 19th. Further advices of the sad happening convey the information that he was killed whilst in charge of a carrying party.

The deceased officer was the son of the late Mr and Mrs R Bakel, of Lingard Street, and formerly of Church Street, Barnsley, and was 25 years of age. He was educated at the Barnsley Grammar School, where he distinguished himself, and on leaving school joined the staff of the Union of London and Smiths Bank, Church Street. He was closely identified with the Ebenezer United Methodist Church and his loss is greatly felt by relatives and a wide circle of friends by whom he was held in high esteem.

Second-Lieutenant Bakel enlisted about fourteen months ago, and subsequently obtained a commission and proceeded to France shortly after being gazetted.

The deceased officer leaves a young widow, whose parents, Mr and Mrs S Thompson, Outwood, Wakefield, have already sustained heavy bereavement by the death in action of their two and only sons, Captain C C Thompson and Private A H Thompson, who were both killed during the Somme battles of July and August 1916.

Walter Bakel, Seaforth Highlanders, brother of the late Second-Lieutenant, who has seen service in France for about eighteen months, is now on leave, prior to entering an Officers' Cadet Battalion.

WALTER BAKEL (born on 14 December 1894 in Barnsley) went to St Mary's school, Barnsley, until the age of 11. He then attended the Holgate for six years, from 1906 to 1912; he was a Junior and Senior Locke Scholar for six years and passed the Oxford Local Senior exam. He passed the Civil Service Exam and was Clerk to the Board of Agriculture in Edinburgh in 1913.

Walter enlisted as a Private in the 8h (Service) Battalion of the Seaforth Highlanders. He went to France on 6 October 1915 and was promoted to Lance Corporal in 1916. He was reported wounded in the Daily Casualty Lists on 17 February 1916, having suffered a gunshot injury to his right ear and undergoing medical treatment for about a week; he subsequently spent time in hospital following shrapnel wounds. Walter was given a Commission as Second Lieutenant on 25 September 1917; he served in the Rifle Brigade. He was reported missing on 21 March 1918 and became a Prisoner of War until repatriated on 18 December 1918. [I have been unable to find out any details for Walter as a PoW]. Walter was awarded three medals and the contact on his Medal Card was c/o the Board of Agriculture for Scotland, 29 St Andrew's Square, Edinburgh.

***Barnsley Chronicle* – 2 September 1916**

WOUNDED

> Lance Corporal W Bakel, 8th Seaforth Highlanders, is in hospital suffering from shrapnel wounds in the arm, neck and body. He has been at the front in France for nearly twelve months and has seen very hard fighting. He was previously wounded in the Battle of Loos and has sustained his present wounds in the Battle of the Somme. Lance-Corporal Bakel is well known in Barnsley and will be remembered by many of his Grammar School chums.

***Barnsley Chronicle* – 2 June 1917**
***Barnsley Independent* – 2 June 1917**

> Walter Bakel, Seaforth Highlanders, brother of the late Second-Lieut, who has seen service in France for about eighteen months is now home on leave, prior to entering an Officers' Cadet Battalion.

EDWARD BAKEL (born on 12 November 1903 in Barnsley) went to St Mary's School, Barnsley, for six years, then attended the Holgate for four years, from 1916 to 1920, having lost both of his parents by the age of 12 years. Edward was living at Rose Villa in Huddersfield Road, Barnsley, according to the Holgate Admission Register, under the guardianship of his oldest married sister **Mrs Annie Owram**. He became a Bank Clerk.

The main photograph of Frank is from Alumnus, *reproduced by kind permission of Barnsley Archives.*

5

Harry Liddall Bambridge

Harry Liddall Bambridge
1887–1918 (aged 30)

HARRY LIDDALL BAMBRIDGE was born 27 September 1887 in Barnsley to **Samuel Bambridge** (born c1853 in Wisbech, Cambridgeshire) and **Agnes nee Firth** (born c1853 in Barnsley). Harry's Baptism was at St Mary's Church, Barnsley, on 27 February 1890 (aged 2) – St Mary's was the family church for Baptisms and Marriages. Samuel had a well established Grocery in Shambles Street, Barnsley, and he had himself been a Volunteer in the Army and a 'crack shot', according to *Barnsley Independent.*

Harry was the fourth of five children: **Mary Ellen, Florence, George Frederick** and **Bertram Arthur** (attended the Holgate). All of them got married.

Mary Ellen Bambridge (aged 25), previously Postal Telegraph Clerk, married **Charles William Newton** (aged 24), Mechanical Engineer, on 2 January 1908 in in St Mary's Church. Charles' father Samuel Newton was Draper of Hope Street, Barnsley. They lived in Sheffield and lost their first child **Charles William Newton** late 1910, aged less than one year. They had another son **Frederick W Newton** early 1912.

Florence Bambridge married **Francis Pimblett Insley** (served in the First World War) on 22 July 1915 in St Mary's. They had a son, **John L Insley,** early 1921 in Christchurch, Hampshire.

George Frederick Bambridge (aged 31) Grocer in his father's business and living at 32 Victoria Road, Barnsley, married **Alice Sarah Clarke** (aged 24) on 7 April 1917 at St Mary's Church. Alice's father **James Clarke** was a Builder living at 36 Southwell Street, Barnsley. They had a son **John A Bambridge** early 1935 in Lexden, Essex.

Harry went to St Mary's Elementary School, Barnsley, until the age of 10. He attended the Holgate Grammar School in Church Street, Barnsley for five years, from 1898 to 1903. Harry won a Senior Locke Scholarship in July 1903 and passed the Oxford Local exams.

On 21 September 1903, aged 16, Harry went to work for London & Yorkshire Bank as an apprentice at its Barnsley branch; at around the same time, the bank was acquired by the larger Union of London & Smiths Bank. He passed the Institute of Bankers' preliminary examination in July 1908 and remained at Barnsley branch until 1 March 1913, when he was appointed agent in charge of its sub-branches at Hoyland Common and Royston. He later became cashier of the much larger Leeds Boar Lane branch, from where he enlisted.* *(The Union of London & Smiths Bank Ltd (1839–1918), established in London, was a past constituent of the Royal Bank of Scotland Group).*

In April 1911, the Bambridge family lived in ten rooms at 32 Victoria Road, Barnsley. By 1911 Harry, Bank Clerk, and his brother Bert, Analytical Chemist, had moved into six rooms at 32 Roach Road, Endcliffe, Sheffield, with their married

* Ruth Reed, Archives Manager for the Royal Bank of Scotland, provided details of Harry's career at the bank. She is responsible for the RBS Remembers website providing details of 1,582 men, who worked for various banks amalgamated within RBS and died in the First World War.

sister Mary. **Amy Norton**, Elementary School Teacher, aged 23, was also there as a visitor.

Harry married Amy Norton in December 1916 at Ebenezer Church, Barnsley. Amy was well known in Barnsley as a talented vocalist and Harry also seems to have been interested in musical entertainment. More details were reported in *Barnsley Chronicle*.

Photograph of Harry in *Barnsley Independent*, reproduced by kind permission of Barnsley Archives.

Harry enlisted in May 1916 as a Private (Service Number: 35814) in the West Yorkshire Regiment and was promoted to Second Lieutenant in the 7th Battalion of the East Yorkshire Regiment, after training with the Belfast Officers Training Corps.

Harry was awarded the Military Cross for conspicuous gallantry (*London Gazette* on 26 September 1917) listed as Temporary Second Lieutenant.

He was killed in action on 31 March 1918, aged 30, after being reported as missing for a long time 'since the early days of the German advance'. As his body was not found or identified, Harry's name is listed on the Arras Memorial, Pas de Calais, France (Bay 4 and 5).

Probate was granted for Harry on 12 February 1920 at London to his widow **Amy Bambridge** of 143 Park Grove, Barnsley. Effects: £436 14s. Amy did not marry again and she died at 143 Park Grove in 1956; she was buried with her parents in Barnsley Cemetery.

Harry was awarded two medals: Victory and British War, and his widow Amy should have received the 'Dead Man's Penny' plaque and scroll from King George V.

Harry's name is on the Holgate Grammar School Memorial, the Memorial List of names for Ebenezer Methodist Chapel, Barnsley (*now demolished*), War Memorials for Gibson Hall National Provincial and Union of London and Smiths Banks, the National Provincial Roll of Honour and on the RBS (Royal Bank of Scotland) Remembers 1914–1918 website.

He is remembered on his family's headstone in Barnsley Cemetery:

ALSO TO THE DEAR
MEMORY OF
2ND LIEUT HARRY LIDDALL BAMBRIDGE MC
EAST YORKS REGT – SON OF THE ABOVE
AND AMY'S DEARLY LOVED HUSBAND
WHO FELL IN FRANCE MARCH 31ST 1918
AGED 30 YEARS

Connections

Harry started work as a Cashier for the Union of London and Smith's Bank about the same time as **Ronald John Saville** and **Thomas Westby** – a few years before **Frank Bakel**.

Harry served in the 7th Battalion of the East Yorkshire Regiment along with **Foster Lindley**.

Harry's name is on the Memorial List of names for Ebenezer Methodist Chapel, Barnsley, along with **Frank Bakell** [sic] and **Sidney Nicholson**.

***Barnsley Chronicle* – 26 December 1914**

DODWORTH

Harry is probably the H Bainbridge [sic] referred to:
The pierrot troupe were highly successful, these comprising Mrs Peddle, Miss Amy Norton, Miss Ownsworth, Messrs H Bainbridge, **T Westby** (Part 2. Chapter 71), **Peddle, F H Westby, J Holland and W Norton.**

***Barnsley Chronicle* – 20 January 1917**

BARNSLEY

A PRETTY WEDDING was solemnized at Ebenezer Chruch by the Rev T M Rees. The contracting parties were Cadet Harry L Bambridge, son of Mr & Mrs Bambridge, Victoria Road, and Miss Amy Norton, only daughter of Mr & Mrs W Norton, Park Grove. The bride's dress was of white satin charmeuse & georgette with silver trimmings. She wore an embroidered tulle veil with wreath of silver leaves & jasmine and carried a bouquet of lillies and chrysanthemums, which together with a pearl & turquoise necklace were the gifts of the bridegroom. The bridesmaids were Miss Maggie Brown of Barnsley and Miss Helen Stuart (cousin of the bride), who wore dresses of blue silk, with hats of n--- brown. They wore pearl necklaces and carried bouquets of pink & white chrysanthemums, the gifts of the bridegroom. Two similar attendants were Master Denny (Frederick) Newton (nephew of the bridegroom) & Miss Mollie Baines, who looked very sweet, dressed in white satin and wore gold broaches, the bridegroom's gifts.

Both bride & bridegroom are well-known and greatly esteemed in Barnsley district and Leeds, and they were the recipients of many beautiful presents. A reception was held in the Lecture Hall after which Mr & Mrs Harry Bambridge left for London, where the honeymoon is being spent. The bridegroom was attended by his brother Mr Bert Bambridge as best man and Cadet Jackson P Heather of Halifax & Mr W Hilton Norton were groomsmen. (The marriage had been listed on 30 December 1916 as being on 28 December).

Barnsley Independent – 1 September 1917 (Photo)

M C FOR LOCAL OFFICER
SON OF A BARNSLEY TRADESMAN
SECOND-LIEUT H L BAMBRIDGE

Another name to be added to the long list of Barnsley soldiers who have gained honour by their bravery in the great war is that of Second-Lieutenant Henry Liddall Bambridge, of East Yorkshire Regiment, the second son of Mr and Mrs S Bambridge, Victoria Road, who has been awarded the Military Cross.

The gallant officer joined the Army in May 1916, and received his commission in December last, after training with the Belfast University O. T. C. He received his early scholastic tuition at the Barnsley Grammar School. Prior to taking to military life, he was one of the cashiers at the Union of London and Smiths Bank (Ltd), Boar Lane Branch, Leeds, but for many years was attached to the Barnsley Branch.

Lieutenant Bambridge was married on the 24th of December last to Miss Amy Norton, the only daughter of Mr and Mrs W Norton of Park Grove, Barnsley. Mrs H L Bambridge is well known in Barnsley and district as a talented vocalist.

The distinguished officer's father, who carries on an old-established grocery business in Shambles Street, is an old Volunteer, and was counted as one of the regimental crack shots. Two other members of Mr Bambridge's family – a son (Bert) and a son-in-law – are serving in the Army, both being in the Royal Garrison Artillery.

Newspaper Cutting (_Holgate Ephemera_) – September 1917 (Photo)

A BARNSLEY OFFICER'S GALLANTRY
AWARDED THE MILITARY CROSS

Second-Lieut Harry L Bambridge, son of Mr and Mrs Bambridge Victoria Road, Barnsley, has been awarded the Military Cross for conspicuous gallantry.

> Prior to joining the Forces 2nd Lieut Bambridge was on the staff of the Union of London and Smiths Bank Ltd, Barnsley, and latterly acted as cashier in the Boar Lane branch, Leeds, of the same bank. He received his commission in the East Yorks Regt in December 1916 and the news of his gaining the Military Cross has given much pleasure to his many Barnsley friends.

***Barnsley Independent* – 13 April 1918**

> BARNSLEY OFFICER MISSING (PHOTO)
>
> We regret to hear that Sec-Lieut H L Bambridge, M C East Yorks Regt, is reported 'missing March 31st no details known' and any information concerning him will be gratefully received by his anxious wife (formerly Miss Amy Norton) who resides at 143 Park Grove, Barnsley.
>
> Second-Lieutenant Bambridge joined the Army in May 1916, received his commission in December of the same year, and was awarded the Military Cross last August. He was home on leave a few weeks ago.

(The first paragraph was in *Barnsley Chronicle* on the same day)

BERTRAM ARTHUR BAMBRIDGE (born on 26 December 1889 in Barnsley; died in 1963, aged 73, in Scarborough) went to Worsbrough National school until the age of 12, when he attended the Holgate for five years from 1902 to 1907; he was a Locke Scholar and passed the Oxford Local Senior exam 3rd Class.

Bert was a Gunner (Service Number: 184316) in the Royal Garrison Artillery and he was awarded two medals: Victory and British War. (This is the only military record I have found).

Bert married **Muriel Hannah Lowrance** on 15 April 1925 at St Mary's Church in Barnsley. Bert (aged 35) was Works Manager of 32 Victoria Road; his father Samuel Bambridge had died early 1922, aged 69, and his mother Agnes was one of their Witnesses. Muriel (aged 36), daughter of **William James Lowrance**, Ironmonger, lived at Beech House, Huddersfield Road, Barnsley. They had a daughter **Honor E Bambridge** early 1926 in Hunslet.

***Barnsley Independent* – 1 September 1917**

> Two other members of Mr Bambridge's family – a son (Bert) and a son-in-law – are serving in the Army, both being in the Royal Garrison Artillery.

AMY NORTON (born 15 January 1888 in Barnsley) was the daughter of William Norton, Secretary to a Linen Manufacturer, and Annie Norton, who lived in Park Grove, Barnsley. There are several articles in *Barnsley Chronicle* about Amy's involvement in entertainments.

***Barnsley Independent* – 22 May 1915**

HELPING THE HOSPITAL

An interesting entertainment entitled Princess Ju-Ju was given in the Barnsley High School for Girls on Thursday evening in aid of the Beckett Hospital and The Motor Ambulance Fund. The principal characters were taken by ... and Amy Norton. Mr W Diggle made a very capable pianist and Miss Amy Norton was successful as the musical director ... (There had been an advert in the previous week publicizing this operetta on 20 May with tickets for sale at 1/6, 1/– and 6d).

***Barnsley Independent* – 22 April 1916**

BARNSLEY

THE UNION JACK CLUB FOR GIRLS held the closing social of the season in the Club Room, George Yard, on Thursday. The wounded soldiers from the Beckett Hospital and Lancaster Home were the guests of the evening. Miss Amy Norton's pupils entertained the company with a cantata entitled the Flags of All Nations which was much appreciated, the girls appearing in appropriate National costumes. Some members of the club also contributed songs.

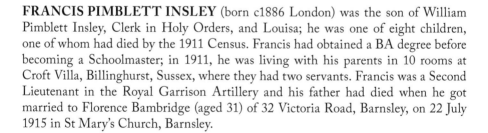

FRANCIS PIMBLETT INSLEY (born c1886 London) was the son of William Pimblett Insley, Clerk in Holy Orders, and Louisa; he was one of eight children, one of whom had died by the 1911 Census. Francis had obtained a BA degree before becoming a Schoolmaster; in 1911, he was living with his parents in 10 rooms at Croft Villa, Billinghurst, Sussex, where they had two servants. Francis was a Second Lieutenant in the Royal Garrison Artillery and his father had died when he got married to Florence Bambridge (aged 31) of 32 Victoria Road, Barnsley, on 22 July 1915 in St Mary's Church, Barnsley.

I have been unable to find any records for Francis' Army service but Officer Records are at the National Archives at Kew and have not yet been digitized.

Barnsley Independent – 1 September 1917

> *Two other members of Mr Bambridge's family – a son (Bert) and a son-in-law – are serving in the Army, both being in the Royal Garrison Artillery.*

The main photograph of Harry is from Barnsley Independent *in the Holgate Ephemera, reproduced by kind permission of Barnsley Archives.*

BEESON'S

Mourning Warehouse

We have always a Choice Stock of

Millinery, Costumes, Blouses, Coats, Skirts, and every requisite at Lowest Cash Prices.

Costumes ....from 21/-
Outsizes, 2/- extra.

Dress Skirts .... from 4/11.
Outsizes, 6/11.

Blouses.....................from 1/11½
Outsizes, 2/6.

Children's Millinery from 1/11½
Ladies' Millinery from 4/11.

Gloves, 1/2½. Ties, 11½d, Veilings. 1/6½.
Hosiery, 1/6½.

C. H. BEESON, Cheapside,

BARNSLEY.

6

Alfred Banks

Alfred Banks
1875–1918 (aged 42)

ALFRED BANKS was born on 10 November 1875 in Barnsley to **Alfred Banks** (born c1846 in Dodworth) and **Emma Mead** (born c1834–8 in Aylesbury, Buckinghamshire). Alfred's Baptism was at St Mary's Church, Barnsley, on 20 June 1879; he was 3 years old and his two older sisters were also Baptised at the same time, aged 9 and 7.

Alfred Banks senior was the oldest child of **William Banks**, Hand Loom Weaver of Dodworth, and **Sarah Banks** from Huddersfield. At the age of 15, Alfred was apprenticed to **George Harris** (23) Hairdresser at 53 Sheffield Road, Barnsley, and, by 25, he was a Hairdresser Employer at 22 Sheffield Road. Alfred Banks had married **Emma Mead** on 8 February 1869 at Westminster St James. Emma, who was much older than Alfred, was the youngest child of **Thomas Mead**, Baker of Aylesbury, and **Sarah Mead**, Shoebinder.

Alfred junior was the fourth of eight children. He had three older full sisters, **Laura Emma, Lucy**, and **Alice**, whom he had not known as she had died in 1872, aged 1. Their mother Emma died in 1879, aged 41, soon after her children had been Baptised.

Alfred's father married again early 1882 to **Ann Walker** (born c1850 in Barnsley) and they had five children, who all had Walker as their middle name. Alfred's half siblings were **Harry, Arnold** (served in the First World War), **Margaret, Helena** and **Dorothy**. Ann died in 1897, aged 47, leaving Alfred senior to raise the younger children with the help of his oldest daughters. Margaret died in 1903, aged 18.

In April 1911, the Banks family had lived in six rooms at 22 Sheffield Road, Barnsley, for at least 40 years, from where they ran their businesses, as Hairdressers and later Outfitters. (*The premises no longer exist*). Before 1891, Alfred senior had employed a domestic servant and an apprentice, but by 1911 he had help from his two sons, Alfred and Harry, Hairdresser Assistants, plus three unmarried daughters, Lucy, Helena and Dorothy. Laura Emma and Arnold had married and were living elsewhere.

Laura Emma Banks (born 27 November 1869 in Barnsley) was 30 when she married **Herbert Halton** (31) a Butcher from Barnsley, on 10 May 1900 at St Mary's Church, Barnsley; her father, brother Alfred and sister Lucy were Witnesses. Laura and Herbert, who had his own Butchery business, lived at 8 Shambles Street then in six rooms at 8 Swift Street in Barnsley. Laura had a daughter **Lucy Halton**, born in 1901, who was staying at 22 Sheffield Road with her grandfather on the 1911 Census; they had had another child, either Mary or John, who died in infancy in 1901 or 1902.

Alfred attended the Holgate Grammar School in Church Street, Barnsley for one year, from 1888 to 1889. He was a Locke Scholar and left school to become a Hairdresser's Apprentice then Men's Outfitter. Although he only attended the Holgate for one year, he kept in contact with the Old Boys and advertised in each edition of *Alumnus*; he also donated a prize for the Sack Race in the School Sports Day. Different adverts were put into the magazine until at least July 1932. (*According to E G Tasker's Barnsley Streets volume 1, the Banks family continued to use the premises, which were next door to the Alhambra Hotel, as Sports Outfitter's until 1929*).

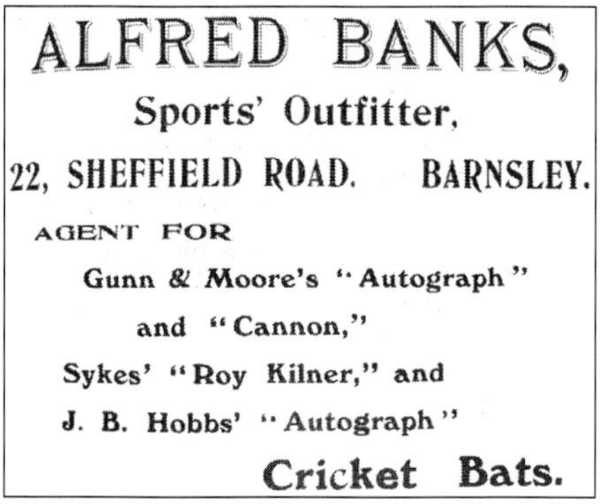
ALFRED BANKS,
Sports' Outfitter,
22, SHEFFIELD ROAD. BARNSLEY.
AGENT FOR
Gunn & Moore's "Autograph"
and "Cannon,"
Sykes' "Roy Kilner," and
J. B. Hobbs' "Autograph"
Cricket Bats.

FOR
CRICKET AND TENNIS
REQUISITES
ALFRED BANKS
22 Sheffield Road,
Barnsley . . .

Adverts in *Alumnus* between 1913 and 1923, reproduced by kind permission of Barnsley Archives.

Alfred was attested on 11 July 1918, aged 42 years and 243 days, as Private 2nd Class (Service Number: 267317) in the Royal Air Force, based at Blandford Camp. This was a month after his half brother Arnold was called up. *(The Military Service Act, which had introduced conscription in 1916, was extended in April 1918 to men aged 17 to 51, from 18 to 41).* Alfred was posted as an absentee soon after arriving at Blandford Camp in Dorset and his death was registered as on 20 July 1918, only nine days after arrival. The RAF Record tragically states: 'Found dead. Body disrobed in coppice at Blandford Camp. Suicide during temporary insanity'. An article in the local newspaper explained that his body was found on 31 July, badly decomposed and with his throat cut. An inquest was carried out.

Alfred was buried on 2 August 1918 in Blandford Cemetery, Salisbury Road, Blandford Forum, Dorset (Grave 1331). Alfred's is one of 50 British War Graves in this cemetery, where there is also a Memorial to 117 Blandford men who fell in the war.

Alfred was the oldest of the Old Boys to be called up and to die in service. He did not qualify for any medals.

Probate for Alfred was at London on 5 October 1918 to Herbert Halton butcher, his sister Laura's husband, and his unmarried sister Lucy. Effects: £1,326.

Alfred Banks senior died on 20 February 1919, aged 73, leaving £4,837 to his two spinster daughters, Lucy and Helena, and son in law Herbert Halton, Butcher.

Alfred's name is on the Holgate Grammar School Memorial.

Alumnus – December 1918

A Banks (1888–89) son of Mr Banks of Sheffield Road, died at Blandford Camp in August 1918. The deceased soldier was greatly interested in the Magazine and regularly advertised in its pages from the first to the last number issued.

Western Gazette – 2 August 1918

BLANDFORD
GRUESOME DISCOVERY
SOLDIER'S BODY FOUND IN A WOOD

On Wednesday morning a gruesome discovery was made in a wood adjoining the camp. It appears that a man was walking through the wood when he came upon the body of a man lying upon the ground. It was in an advanced state of decomposition and the deceased had apparently committed suicide, as it was seen that his throat was cut. A doctor was called and the remains were afterwards conveyed to the Blandford mortuary to await an inquest, which was fixed for yesterday (Thursday) afternoon. Deceased has been identified as Alfred Banks of the Royal Air Force, who came to the camp during July and had been posted as an absentee for some little time.

Barnsley Chronicle – 3 August 1918

DEATHS

BANKS At Blandford Camp, Dorset, Alfred, aged 42, eldest son of Alfred Banks, 22 Sheffield Road.

BLANDFORD CAMP *– In 1914 the camp was developed as a base depot and training camp for a Royal Naval Division. It also housed German prisoners of war, some of whom died of influenza in 1918. During 1918, the camp changed from being the depot for the Royal Naval Division to being an 'Intake Camp' for the Royal Flying Corps which was at that time being reformed as the Royal Air Force. At the end of 1919, the camp was closed and both the wooden huts built for the RN Division and the camp's railway line were removed. By the end of 1920 the site had been returned to agricultural use.*

ARNOLD WALKER BANKS (born c1883 in Barnsley) was 25 when he married Barbara Mary Peck (18) on 6 April 1908 at the Parish Church, Heeley, Sheffield. At April 1911, Arnold, aged 27, a 'Pork Butchering Worker', his wife Barbara (21) and two children were living in three rooms at Cedar Cottage, Hemsworth; Arnold's nephew **John Edward Barnes** (9) 'school', was with them. Arnold and Barbara had seven children: **Arnold, Dorothy, Mary, May, Constance Eveline, Lucy** and **Betty**.

Arnold had enlisted at Pontefract on 10 February 1906 as a Private (Service Number: 5520) in the Corps of the Dragoons of the Line, aged 21 years and 11 months. He was a Pork Butcher, weighed 133 lbs and had sallow complexion, brown eyes and dark brown hair; he had various scars. Arnold was discharged on 20 November 1906, after serving for 295 days, on payment of £18 – no other explanation is provided and when Arnold was called up on 12 June 1918 he stated that he had no previous service in any of the Forces.

Arnold enlisted at Sheffield, aged 34 years and 4 months, as a Private (Service Number: 66786) in the 3rd Battalion of the King's Own Yorkshire Light Infantry, then transferred to the 3rd Battalion of the Manchester Regiment (Service Number: 76062) on 22 June 1918. According to the Attestation form he was a 'Shell Forger'- elsewhere Journeyman Pork Butcher – at 2 Harold Place, Artisan View, Heeley, Sheffield. He was 5' 6⅜" tall with a 33½–37" chest and had several distinctive marks: scar to eyebrow, ring finger, arm, forehead, upper lip, shins. Arnold's youngest child Betty was only six weeks old when he left and she died at home on 7 September, aged 4 months, of 'Tubercular disease of mesentery (abdominal lining) and a convulsion' ; an Inquest was held. Arnold spent 151 days in Central Hospital Lichfield from 2 October 1918 to 29 February 1919 with Gonorrhoea. Arnold was discharged on 16 July 1919, having served 1 year 35 days.

PERSONAL COMMENTS

I was initially surprised that I was unable to find an Obituary for Alfred in *Barnsley Chronicle* and that his name only appears to be on the Holgate Memorial, despite his and his family's longstanding involvement with Barnsley and St Mary's Church. I was then stunned by what I discovered in July 2014, when the new RAF Records became available on FindMyPast, compounded by finding the report in the *Western Gazette*.

Being called up so late in the war and at an older age must have been a shock for anyone, but it turned Alfred's world upside down. He had always lived in the same house in Barnsley with his father and siblings; he had left school to work for his father, which he had done for nearly 30 years. Alfred must have been devastated by his removal from everything familiar to Dorset and by the dramatic change in his occupation and surroundings at Blandford Camp.

Alfred's desperate action and the impact this must have had on his family, who had already suffered so many tragedies, affected me greatly. Alfred's father would have been heart broken and this may have contributed to his death so soon afterwards.

He may well have wanted to keep the cause of his son's death quiet out of embarrassment; public attitudes at this time would have been most disapproving with no understanding of mental health problems.

I hope that one day I might be able to have contact with some of Alfred's relations to find out some more details and to see a photograph of him.

WAR SUPPLEMENT FOR WEEK ENDING APRIL 13, 1918.

"RATION"-AL FOOD FOR THOUGHT.

STOUT PARTY: These ration cards are a dashed nuisance.
THIN PARTY: Are they? We didn't have any where I've just come from.
STOUT PARTY: Please name that happy place, sir!
THIN PARTY: *Ruhleben*—a prison camp in Germany.

7

Crossland Barraclough

Crossland Barraclough
1894–1918 (aged 24)

CROSSLAND BARRACLOUGH was born on 27 April 1894 at Hoyland Common to **Oswald Barraclough** (born c1867 in Stainborough) and **Amelia nee Crossland** (born c1865 in Tankersley). Oswald was a Colliery Under-Viewer in Barnsley then Under-Manager at Willington-on-Tyne Collieries.

Crossland was nine years older than his sister **Constance Muriel**; their sister **Millicent Edna** had died in infancy in 1900.

In April 1911, the Barraclough family lived in six rooms at 16 Lingard Street, Barnsley, having previously lived in Cawthorne, Ardsley and Hoyland Common. They later moved to 31 Beech Grove, Wallsend on Tyne, where their father died in 1920.

Constance Barraclough married **Charles Davison** in Barnsley early 1921; they had one daughter **Greta Davison**, who was also born early 1921 in Barnsley.

Crossland went to Barnsley Elementary School until the age of 13. He attended the Holgate Grammar School in Church Street, Barnsley, for four years, from 1907 to 1911. Crossland was an Intending Pupil Teacher, Student Teacher and Bursar. Letters from the Holgate Management Committee confirm that Crossland, who had been a 'Borough Bursar', would continue as a private pupil for his last term and they agreed to accept half the usual fee, with £1 8s due. He passed the Oxford Local Senior exam and went on to York St John's Training College, from 1912 to 1914. Crossland was Assistant Master at Agnes Road Council School in Barnsley.

Crossland was living in Wallsend when he enlisted as a Private (Service Numbers: 512310/6093) in the 2 /14th Battalion of the London Regiment (London Scottish). He was reported as wounded in the Daily Casualty Lists on 22 August 1916. Crossland died of wounds in the Egyptian Theatre of War on 2 May 1918, aged 24, and was buried in Jerusalem War Cemetery, 4.5 kilometres north of the walled city, Israel and Palestine (Grave 0 55). Crossland's mother had the words 'AWAITING A HIGHER COMMAND' added to his War Grave headstone.

Crossland was the only Old Boy to die in the Egyptian Theatre of War.

Crossland was awarded two medals: Victory and British War, and his widowed mother should have received the 'Dead Man's Penny' plaque and scroll from King George V.

Crossland's name is on the Holgate Grammar School Memorial, the painted column in St Mary's Church, Barnsley, the Roll of Honour at St John's College in York, the oak wood Memorial in St Peter's Church in Wallsend plus in their Book of Remembrance/Roll of Honour, listed as the only man in the London Scottish Regiment, and his name is on the searchable North East Memorials Project website.

He is also remembered on his family's headstone in Barnsley Cemetery:

IN
LOVING MEMORY OF OSWALD
THE DEARLY BELOVED HUSBAND OF
AMELIA BARRACLOUGH
WHO DIED OCTR 16TH 1920
AGED 54 YEARS

ALSO CROSSLAND, THE ONLY
BELOVED SON OF THE ABOVE
WHO DIED FROM WOUNDS
RECEIVED IN ACTION IN PALESTINE
MAY 2ND 1918, AGED 24 YEARS

ALSO MILLICENT EDNA
THEIR DAUGHTER
WHO DIED IN INFANCY

"PEACE PERFECT PEACE"

Connections

Seven of the Old Boys qualified as Teachers after attending St John's College in York: **Crossland Barraclough** (B 1894), **Edward Batley** (B 1893), **Norman Bradley** (B 1891), **John Middleton Downend** (B 1888), **Arthur Heathcote** (B 1890), **Charles Edward Savage** (B 1893) and **Charles Waldegrave Wood** (B 1883). Several of them would have attended during the same period.

Crossland's death was reported to the same Education Sub-Committee meeting, as reported in *Barnsley Chronicle*, as **Melvin Clement Wiliamson**.

Alumnus – July 1918

Crossland Barraclough (1907–12) London Scottish Regiment, son of Mr and Mrs O Barraclough, late of Hoyland Common, now under-manager of Willington Collieries, Newcastle, fell in action in May 1918. On passing the Oxford Senior Local Exam he continued his studies at York Training College for two years, afterwards becoming assistant master at Barnsley.

Barnsley Chronicle – 18 May 1918

BARNSLEY & DISTRICT CASUALTIES
LOCAL HEROES OF THE WAR

Much regret is expressed at the death which took place in Palestine, from wounds received in action, of Crossland, the only son of Mr and Mrs Oswald Barraclough, late of Hoyland Common, now under-manager of the Willington-on-Tyne Collieries, near Newcastle. Crossland, who only last month entered his 25th year, was educated at St Mary's Boys School, Barnsley, and upon passing the examination of intending pupil teachers he pursued his studies at the Grammar School, followed by a two year training at St John's College, York, at the end of which he returned to Barnsley having been appointed assistant master at Agnes Road Council School. Fully realising his responsibility and duty he enlisted as a private in the London Scottish. He was held in great respect by all who knew him and his active figure and bright personality will be greatly missed by his many friends.

***Barnsley Independent* – 18 May 1918 (Photo)**

BARNSLEY SCHOOL TEACHER
DIES FROM WOUNDS IN PALESTINE
PTE CROSSLAND BARRACLOUGH

We record with regret, the death on May 2nd in Palestine, from wounds received in action of Crossland Barraclough, the only son of Mr and Mrs Oswald Barraclough, late of Hoyland Common and Barnsley,

The deceased hero, who was 24 years of age, was educated at St Mary's Boys' School, Barnsley, and being successful in the examination of intending pupil teachership, pursued his studies at the Barnsley Grammar School and St John's Training College at York. He returned to Barnsley, having been appointed assistant master at Agnes Road Council School, and later, feeling strongly his duty, enlisted in the London Scottish. He was held in great respect by all who knew him, and his active figure and bright personality will be greatly missed by his numerous friends. He was fond of music, and took a great interest in cricket, football and other sports.

His father, who formerly resided in Lingard Street, Barnsley, was undermanager at the Silkstone Fall Colliery, and is now under-manager at a colliery at Willington-on-Tyne, Newcastle.

***Barnsley Chronicle* – 1 June 1918**

BARNSLEY EDUCATION MATTERS

At a meeting of the Teachers' Salaries and School Staffing Sub-Committee … The Secretary reported the death in action of the following teachers: Mr Crossland Barraclough and Mr Melvin C Williamson (Part 2. Chapter 74), and was instructed to convey to the parents the Committee's deep sympathy with them in the sad loss they have sustained.

The photograph of Crossland is from Barnsley Independent, *used by kind permission of Barnsley Archives.*

8 and 9

Batley Brothers (Arthur George and Edward)

Arthur George Batley
1890–1918 (aged 28)

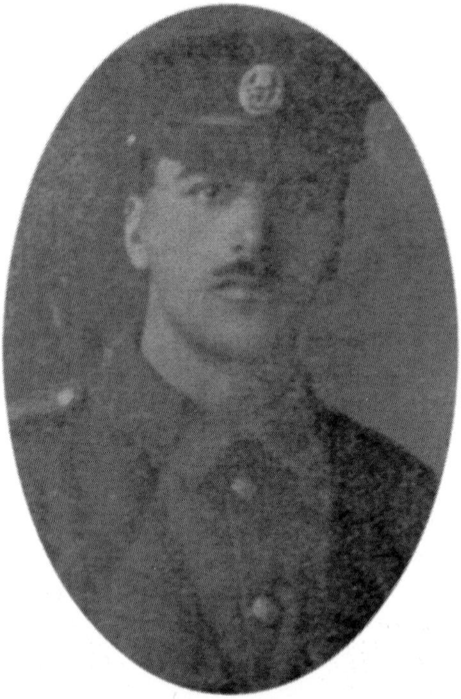

Edward Batley
1893–1916 (aged 23)

BATLEY BROTHERS

George Batley (born c1849 in Stainborough) and **Sarah Ann nee Beardshall** (born c1858 in Dodworth) had nine children: **Annie, James, Mary, Frederick** – Mechanical Engineer, **Edith** – Teacher, **ARTHUR GEORGE, EDWARD, John William** and **Grace**. (James, Arthur George, Edward and John William attended the Holgate and served in the First World War).

In April 1911, they lived in seven rooms at Nursery Cottage, The Garden, Stainborough Park. George Batley did a painting of Nursery Cottage and an image of this is in the Archives of Wentworth Castle Trust.

George was a Gardener at Wentworth Castle for more than 50 years and when he retired in 1914 this completed a Century of the Batley family's looking after the gardens there, for many years as Head Gardener. George's grandfather **William Batley** (born circa 1791 in Wakefield) was the first Batley to become a Gardener at Wentworth Castle and he is there when he married **Hannah Thorpe** at All Saints Church in Silkstone with Stainborough on 24 May 1813. William founded a dynasty of gardeners: of his three sons who survived to adulthood, the two oldest went to work in Warwickshire, while James worked at Wentworth Castle. (Records for William's parents and grandparents provide too limited information to know whether they were also gardeners).

The Batley Family c1897, photograph kindly provided by John and Cath Batley. Left to Right: Annie (18), Arthur (7), Edward (3), Grandfather James (77), James (16), Edith (9), Father George (48), John William (2), Mother Sarah (39), Frederick (10), Mary (12).

The Batley Family c1910, photograph kindly provided by John and Cath Batley.
Back Row, Left to Right: Frederick, James, Edith, Edward, Arthur.
Front Row, Left to Right: Annie, Grace, Father George, Mother Sarah, John, Mary.

George's father **James Batley** (born on 6 October 1820) married **Jane Eaton**, who had been his father's domestic servant, in 1843 at All Saints Church. James became Head Gardener at Wentworth Castle – probably when his father William died in 1852 – and lived in Garden House with his wife and three children. Frederick, the older son, was a Gardener in Halifax when he got married; he subsequently moved to Barnsley, where he owned his own business as Seedsman, Fruiterer and Florist in the town centre. George helped his father for many years, moving into Nursery Cottage next door when he married; George became Head Gardener when James eventually retired, aged 75.

***Barnsley Chronicle* – 6 February 1915**

(George Batley's retirement)

The subject of this notice has for a number of years taken a great interest in church work at Stainborough and was at one time a teacher in the Sunday School. He was an enthusiastic educationalist and for ten years occupied a seat on the Dodworth and Stainborough Education Committee, whilst he ever evinced a keen interest in the gardeners on his staff. Mr Batley is well known in Barnsley and throughout the district.

***Barnsley Chronicle* – 22 May 1915**

> As a mark of appreciation the under gardeners on the Wentworth Estate together with a few friends have presented a handsome silver-plated tea and coffee service and sugar sifter to Mr George Batley, head gardener, upon his retirement after 52 years service. The presentation was made privately by a chosen deputation consisting of Messrs C J Curtis, Robert Denton, A Goodall, R Hepworth and A Wigfield. Eulogistic speeches were made and Mr Batley suitably responded. The gifts were supplied by Messrs M Lowrance & Son, Barnsley.

I'm sure that the Wentworth family must have also showed their appreciation of the work of the Batley family over their 100 years of loyal service. The magnificent gardens and restored greenhouse today are a wonderful tribute to the devotion, skill and inspiration of the Batleys and other gardeners over many years.

Unfortunately, George's retirement would not be as relaxing as he hoped (and deserved) with the outbreak of war and the involvement of four of his sons.

***Barnsley Chronicle* – 15 July 1916**

LOCAL WAR CASUALTIES DODWORTH

> Dodworth, like other parts of the district has contributed its quota to the Colours and a number of the villagers' names appear in the casualty list. Mr George Batley, late head gardener at Stainborough Castle, has four sons in the Army, one of whom is missing and another wounded. …

According to a form dated 7 June 1919 in Edward's Service Records, requesting family details, George and Sarah Ann were living at Stainbrough with three daughters: Mary (34), Edith (30) and Grace (19). James (37) was at Brinkworth near Chippenham at the home of his brother Arthur and wife, Frederick (31) was at 588 Chesterfield Road, Woodseats, Sheffield, and Annie (40) (married surname Curtis) was at the Botanical Gardens, Clarkehouse Road, Sheffield. Other records have George's address as 1 Carrington Street, Barnsley, and 'Newlyn' Woodstock Road, Barnsley.

BATLEY FAMILY HEADSTONE AT ALL SAINTS CHURCHYARD WITH MEMORIALS TO ARTHUR GEORGE AND EDWARD

IN
LOVING MEMORY
OF
JANE, WIFE OF
JAMES BATLEY,
OF STAINBOROUGH
BORN SEPTEMBER 11TH 1814,
DIED NOVEMBER 24TH 1892

ALSO THE ABOVE NAMED
JAMES BATLEY
WHO DIED MAY 4TH 1902
AGED 81 YEARS

ALSO OF PTE EDWARD BATLEY
12TH Y & L REGT MISSING AT THE BATTLE OF THE SOMME,
JULY 1ST 1916
AGED 23 YEARS

ALSO OF ARTHUR G BATLEY
SEC LT 11TH MANCHESTER REGT
KILLED NEAR CAMBRAI, SEPT 27TH 1918,
BURIED AT MARQUION, AGED 28 YEARS

SONS OF GEORGE AND SARAH A BATLEY
OF STAINBOROUGH

ALSO OF THE ABOVE NAMED
SARAH ANN BATLEY
WHO DIED JANUARY 20TH 1923
AGED 64 YEARS

ALSO GEORGE BATLEY
DIED SEPT 26TH 1946, AGED 97 YEARS

Cath and John Batley generously shared with me family photos and information, including Arthur's Officer Records.

ARTHUR GEORGE BATLEY was born on 15 September 1890 in Stainborough. His Baptism was on 12 October 1890 at All Saints Church, Silkstone with Stainborough. Arthur went to Hood Green school until the age of 12 then attended the Holgate Grammar School in Church Street, Barnsley, for five years, from 1902 to 1907. He was a County Minor Scholar and passed the Oxford Local Junior exam and the Senior exam with 2nd Class Honours, winning a Cooper Prize in 1907 for the latter. 'On leaving school he entered the Civil Service'.

Arthur Batley enlisted at Dublin on 4 September 1914, aged almost 24, as a Private in the Reserve Regiment, 8th or 11th Hussars (Service Numbers: 1429 and 13700). He was a Clerk, Civil Servant in the 2nd Irish Land Commission but no records of his employment have survived.*

Arthur was promoted to unpaid Lance Corporal on 3 December but reverted to Private at his own request on 18 January 1915. He was transferred on 1 May 1915 as Private to the 12th Service Battalion (Sheffield City Battalion) of the York and Lancaster Regiment (Service Number: 1239) and saw action on the Somme, being slightly wounded on 1 July 1916. He then transferred again on 26 September 1916 as Lance Corporal to the East Yorkshire Regiment (Service Number: 31379). *(The Officer Records are difficult to follow to be certain of Arthur's army career).*

He was accepted for admission to No.1 Cavalry Cadet Squadron, joining at Netheravon, on 22 February 1917, but after a fortnight his assessment said: 'apparently this cadet has no mechanical knowledge and he is too young for HT or supply. Transfer to Infantry'. Arthur was discharged on 26 June 1917 on promotion to commissioned rank as temporary Second Lieutenant in the 4th Battalion (attached to 11th Battalion) of the Manchester Regiment; he was paid 7/6 per day for three months, then 10/6. *(A Private's basic pay was 1/– per day plus 1d per day when in a war zone).* He appears to have been in the No.19 Officer Cadet Battalion when confirmed as Second Lieutenant on 14 July 1917.

The Military History Sheet stated that Arthur had been training 'at Home' from 4 September 1914 to 19 December 1915. The Conduct Sheet detailed an offence committed by Arthur on 13 April 1915, when he was 'absent from midday stables', punishment for which was 4 days (not specified). *(Punishment could be extra fatigues or exercise, loss of pay or being confined to barracks).* Army Form B241 dated 17 April 1915 from the 12th Reserve Cavalry Regiment described his Character as Good but 'not likely to become an efficient cavalry soldier' and Arthur was transferred soon after. On 20 December 1915, he sailed from Devonport to Alexandria to serve in the Mediterranean until 9 March 1916, then transferred to France until 29 December 1916, when he returned home for six months after being wounded.

The Medical Form has a physical description of Arthur: Height: 5' 11½", Weight: 158 lbs, Chest: 38½", Fresh complexion, Brown eyes, Brown hair, Vision in both eyes

* The Land Commission in Ireland, now called the Department of Lands, checked their records but none have survived.

6/6, Physical Development: Good, Slight Defect: dental plate upper jaw. Assessed as fit to serve in the Corps of Hussars of the Line. Another form in 1917 stated that Arthur could ride, was a French Linguist, had passed matriculation, had knowledge of electricity and Morse code; he was 'desirous of serving' in the Army Service Corps.

Arthur was sick and admitted to General Hospital Wimereux twice while serving in France: on 7 January 1918 with an alveolar abscess, resulting in his return home to England as recommended, being 'unfit for any service for 14 days'; then on 28 February 1918 suffering from urethritis, being transferred to the 31st General Hospital in Etaples until May.

Arthur married **Winifred Welch** late 1917 in the Doncaster area.

Arthur was killed in action near Cambrai on 27 September 1918, aged 28, and was buried in Quarry Cemetery, Marquion, Pas de Calais, France (grave A 16) in a grave 'marked by a durable wooden cross bearing full particulars'. His widow Winifred, living in Brinkworth, Chippenham, received a telegram dated 1 October 1918: 'Deeply regret inform you that 2/Lieut A G Batley Manchester Regt was killed in action twenty seventh September the Army Council express sympathy'. Winifred had moved to Fulham, London, when she applied for a pension on 10 October. The Inventory of Arthur's items to be returned home listed: '1 AB 439, 1 Identity Disc and 1 Note Book'.

Arthur was awarded two medals: Victory and British War, and his widow Winifred should have also received the 'Dead Man's Penny' plaque and scroll from King George V.

Winifred married again in the summer of 1919 in Samford, Suffolk, to **William S Alden**, who had stated in a letter to the War Office that he was one of Arthur's friends. They had a daughter **Mavis Alden** early 1920 and a son **John Alden** in Spring 1928, but William died in June 1932, aged 32.

Probate was granted for Arthur at Wakefield on 28 April 1919 to his father George Batley, Retired Gardener. Effects: £399 2s. An application was made for relief from payment of estate duty under the Death Duties (Killed in War) Act 1914. Arthur had made his Will on 28 October 1917 leaving everything to his wife, but the War Office searched for a Will for some time being unaware of its existence. The amount left included a Gratuity payment from the War Office of 186 days @ 10/6 = £97 13s and a credit of £41 'Outfit Allowance'.

Arthur's name, along with his younger brother Edward's, is on the Holgate Grammar School Memorial, the Memorial/Roll of Honour in St James' Hall at Wentworth Castle (listed as serving in Kitchener's Army), Hood Green War Memorial and the WW1 plaque in the Stainborough Chapel within Silkstone Church. He is also remembered on the family headstone in Silkstone with Stainborough Churchyard.

Connections

Arthur was in the same form as **Duncan Fairley**, **Henry Ryland Knowles** and **Harold Willott**. They all won Cooper Prizes in 1907 for passing the Oxford Local Senior exam.

Alumnus – December 1918

2nd Lieut A G Batley (1902–07) son of Mr Batley, formerly Head Gardener, Wentworth Castle, died in action Sept 27th 1918. On leaving school he entered the Civil Service. In September 1914 he joined the forces and was wounded in July 1916. His brother E Batley, an Old Boy, has been missing since July 1916.

Barnsley Chronicle – 19 October 1918

LOCAL OFFICERS KILLED
SECOND-LIEUT A G BATLEY

The death in action on September 27th is reported of Second-Lieutenant Arthur G Batley, Manchester Regiment, son of Mr Batley, who for many years was the head gardener at Wentworth Castle, Stainborough. The deceased officer was educated at the Barnsley Grammar School and was in the Civil Service when war broke out. He joined the army along with his two brothers in September 1914 and was wounded in July 1916. In a letter received by the deceased's wife it appears that Lt Batley was shot through the head while leading his platoon against the enemy's position. Another brother has been missing for over two years and the third has been discharged after being wounded.

Barnsley Independent – 19 October 1918

STAINBOROUGH OFFICER FALLS

(A similar article to the above but states that Arthur George Batley was slightly wounded on 1 July 1916 and was granted a commission on 17 June).

Yorkshire Post – 19 October 1918

ROLL OF HONOUR

SEC-LIEUT A G BATLEY – Manchester Regt, who fell in action on September 27, was the son of Mr Batley, formerly head gardener at Wentworth Castle, Stainborough, near Barnsley. He was a Barnsley Grammar School 'old boy' and was in the Civil Service when he joined the Army in September 1914.

The main photograph of Arthur is from Alumnus, *used here by kind permission of Barnsley Archives.*

EDWARD BATLEY was born on 10 April 1893 in Stainborough. His Baptism was on Whit Sunday 21 May 1893 at All Saints Church, Silkstone with Stainborough. Edward attended the Holgate Grammar School in Church Street, Barnsley, for four years, from 1906 to 1910. He was Intending Pupil Teacher, Pupil Teacher and Bursar, passing the Oxford Local Senior exam with 3rd Class Honours. Edward went on to York St John's Training College, from 1911 to 1913, where he played in the cricket team; he became a Certificated Teacher at Askern School in Doncaster.

Edward enlisted in Sheffield on 11 September 1914, aged 21 years and 154 days, as a Private (Service Number: 12/294) in the 12th Battalion (Sheffield City Battalion) of the York and Lancaster Regiment. He was a Teacher. *Alumnus* stated: 'E Batley, Braham, Mountford, L W Smith, were left behind when Barnsley and Sheffield Battalions went to Egypt because of an outbreak of measles. Now attached to 15th (Reserve) Battalion of the York & Lancaster Regiment stationed at Colsterdale'. Edward went to France on 5 April 1916 as part of the British Expeditionary Force and rejoined the 12th Battalion on 23 April.

He was confirmed as killed in action on the first day of the Somme, 1 July 1916, aged 23, after being reported missing for more than two years. He had served for one year and 295 days. Edward was buried in the A. I. F. Burial Ground, Flers, Somme, France (grave VI L 7), having been reburied from the original place as 'Unknown British Soldier' identified by his khaki and boots. The only item sent to Base was 'Piece of w'proof "FF" Sheet:- E Batley 294'. An Imperial War Graves Commission Form relating to the headstone for Edward's War Grave shows that George Batley did not specify any personal message to be added to his son's headstone.

The Medical Form contains a personal description of Edward: Height: 5' 10½", Weight: 108½lbs, Chest: 38", Complexion Dark, Eyes Brown, Hair Dark Brown, Physical Development Good, Vision in both eyes 6/6, No Marks or Defects. A Company Conduct form stated that on 7 November 1915 Edward was absent from parade 'inlying licquer [sic] 9.45pm' and his punishment for this offence was for two days, with no further explanation. *(Punishment could be extra fatigues or exercise, loss of pay or being confined to barracks).*

Edward was awarded two medals: Victory and British War, and his parents should have received the 'Dead Man's Penny' plaque and scroll from King George V.

Edward was one of ten Old Boys who were killed in action on the first day of the Somme.

Probate was granted for Edward in London on 23 July 1917 to his father George Batley, 'out of business' (ie retired). Effects: £122 1s 4d.

Edward's name, along with that of his older brother Arthur George, is on the Holgate Grammar School Memorial, the Memorial/Roll of Honour in St James' Hall at Wentworth Castle (listed as serving in Kitchener's Army), Hood Green War Memorial and the WW1 plaque in the Stainborough Chapel within Silkstone Church. Edward's name is also on the Roll of Honour at St John's College in York and Sheffield Council's Official Roll of Honour. He is remembered on the family headstone in Silkstone with Stainborough Churchyard.

Connections

Edward played for the Second Eleven Cricket Team, which also comprised: **Ernest Litherland**, Captain (who won a cricket bat prize for bowling), **George Braham** and (probably) **Herbert Harry Jagger Mason**. The First Eleven Team included **George Percival Cowburn** (who won a cricket bat prize for bowling), **Cyril Burton Dixon** (who won a cricket bat prize for batting), **Duncan Fairley** plus **Harold Spencer** and his brother **Ernest Spencer Willott**.

The Service Numbers of Edward and his brother John William show how many men enlisted between one day and the next: ie 38 (John) and 294 (Edward). Edward's former classmate **Laurence Baylis** was number 296; **George Braham,** who was three years younger, was 307.

Edward served in the 12th Battalion (Sheffield Pals) of the York and Lancaster Regiment along with **Laurence Baylis, George Braham, Sidney Gill, James Stuart Swift** and **Arthur Henry Thompson**. They were all killed in action on 1 July 1916.

Seven of the Old Boys qualified as Teachers after attending St John's College in York: **Crossland Barraclough** (B 1894), **Edward Batley** (B 1893), **Norman Bradley** (B 1891), **John Middleton Downend** (B 1888), **Arthur Heathcote** (B 1890), **Charles Edward Savage** (B 1893) and **Charles Waldegrave Wood** (B 1883). Several of them would have attended during the same period.

Alumnus – December 1918

> 2nd Lieut A G Batley – His brother E Batley, an Old Boy, has been missing since July 1916.

The main photograph of Arthur is from Alumnus, *used here by kind permission of Barnsley Archives.*

JAMES BATLEY (born on 30 March 1882 in Stainborough; Baptism on 14 May 1882 at All Saints Church, Silkstone with Stainborough) went to Hood Green National School until the age of 13. He then attended the Holgate for two years from 1895 to 1897. He was a Pupil Teacher in April 1901. James married Gladys Elsie Minchin, who was seven years younger and from Hove in Sussex, on 28 December 1909 in Worcester. By April 1911, aged 29, he was an Elementary School Head Teacher living in six rooms at Ogbourne St George, Marlborough. They had two daughters: Gwendoline Mary Batley was born on 23 June 1912 in Marlborough and Ina Margaret Batley was born early 1920 in Malmesbury District.

According to the RAF Records, James was called up and attested on 31 August 1918, aged 36 years and 5 months, as a Private (Service Number: 290457) in the Royal Air Force; he was a Schoolmaster living at School House, Brinkworth, Malmesbury, Wiltshire. James was promoted to Corporal Mechanic on 9 November 1918 and discharged on 30 April 1920. James was 5' 9" tall with a 36" chest; his hair was dark brown, eyes blue and complexion fresh. He had a 'Right Inguinal Hernia, efficient teeth worn' and was assessed as Grade 2. (*Inguinal hernias are the most common and can appear suddenly due to strain on the abdomen, such as straining on the toilet or carrying and pushing heavy loads*). James' name is not on the Roll of Honour at Wentworth Castle because he was no longer living in Stainborough.

After the war ended, James returned to being a Teacher. Probate was granted on 4 July 1956 for James of 43 Scalby Road, Scarborough, who died on 28 April 1956, aged 74, at 172 Ombersley Road, Worcester, to his widow Gladys Elsie Batley. Effects: £2 909 18s 6d.

JOHN WILLIAM BATLEY (born 14 December 1894 in Stainborough; Baptism 30 March 1895 at All Saints Church, Silkstone with Stainborough) went to Hood Green school until the age of 11. He then attended the Holgate from 1906 to 1912 and was awarded a County Minor Scholarship for six years, passing the Oxford Local Senior exam. He became a Bank Clerk.

John enlisted in Sheffield on 10 September 1914 (the day before his older brother Edward), aged 19 years and 272 days, as a Private (Service Number: 12/38) in the 12th Battalion (Sheffield City Battalion) of the York and Lancaster Regiment. The Medical Form provides a personal description: Height: 5' 11 ¼", Weight: 134½ lbs, Chest: 35", Complexion Fair, Eyes Brown, Hair Brown, Assessed Fit for the Army Reserve.

John served in Egypt from 20 December 1915 until he was sent to France on 10 March 1916 for over two years; he was granted two weeks' leave early January 1918. John suffered a gun shot wound to his left leg on 14 April 1918 and was sent back to England 10 days later; he was discharged on medical grounds by an Invaliding Board on 9 October 1918, having served for 4 years and 30 days. John was awarded a weekly pension of 8/3* from 10 October subject to review in one year. (*A Private's basic pay was 1/– per day plus 1d per day when in a war zone*). He was awarded the Victory & British War Medals and the Silver Badge, c/o his sister Annie's address; he had previously been given a Good Conduct Badge and was described as 'Very Good'. John's name is on the Roll of Honour in St James' Hall, Wentworth Castle, serving in Kitchener's Army, along with his two brothers, and the Institute of Bankers Roll of Honour Sheffield.

John, Bank Clerk of 1 Carrington Street, Barnsley, married Doris Midgley on 26 February 1924 at St Edward the Confessor Church in Barnsley; his father George Batley was one of the Witnesses. They had two children in Barnsley: Dorothy M Batley early 1927 and John G Batley in Spring 1930.

10

Lawrence Baylis

Lawrence Baylis
1893–1916 (aged 23)

LAURENCE BAYLIS was born on 2 February 1893 in Selby to William Edward Baylis (born c1866 in Raglan, Monmouth, Wales) and Mary Ellen nee Tagg (born c1871 in Crookes, Sheffield). Laurence's Baptism was on 26 March 1893 in Selby. William was a Police Constable.

Laurence was the oldest of three surviving sons: **Raymond** (served and died in the First World War), and **William Stanley** (served in the First World War). Another child had died by April 1911 (name unknown).

In April 1911, the Baylis family lived in four rooms at 4 St Mary's Terrace, Stairfoot, Ardsley, having moved from Selby after April 1901. William and Mary subsequently moved to 58 Kingswood Street, Great Horton, Bradford.

Laurence went to Ardsley Elementary School Mixed until the age of 14. He attended the Holgate Grammar School in Church Street, Barnsley, for three years, from 1907 to 1910. He was an Intending Student Teacher, Student Teacher and Bursar, passing the Oxford Local Junior and Senior exams. Laurence went on to become a Certificated Teacher by 1911.

Different information is provided by Holgate records, which state that he attended Islington Training College and that he went to Sheffield Day Training College. Unfortunately, no records survive for either college; Islington College was part of the Church Missionary School and closed in 1915* whereas Sheffield College was formed from the merger of six Further Education Colleges in the 1980s, when old records were destroyed.†

Laurence enlisted in Sheffield while living at Stairfoot and was a Private (Service Number: 12/296) in the 12th Battalion (Sheffield City) of the York and Lancaster Regiment, the same as his younger brother. Laurence was killed in action on the first day of the Somme, 1 July 1916, aged 23, but his body was never found or identified so his name is on the Thiepval Memorial, Somme, France (Pier and Face: 14A and 14B).

Laurence was one of ten Old Boys who were killed in action on the first day of the Somme.

Laurence was awarded two medals: Victory and British War, and his parents should have received the 'Dead Man's Penny' plaque and scroll from King George V.

Laurence's name is on the Holgate Grammar School Memorial and Sheffield Council's Official Roll of Honour.

Connections

Laurence's Service Number was number 296, his former classmate **Edward Batley's** was 294 and **George Braham's**, who was three years younger, was 307.

* The Archivist at Islington Archives provided some details about the College and confirmed that Laurence is not listed on any Memorials in Islington.

† The Registrar at Sheffield College provided some general information and confirmed that no early records survive.

Laurence was a Teacher at Worsbrough Dale National School at the same time as **George Braham.**

Laurence served in the 12th Battalion (Sheffield Pals) of the York and Lancaster Regiment along with, **Edward Batley**, **George Braham**, **Sidney Gill**, **James Stuart Swift** and **Arthur Henry Thompson**. They were all killed in action on 1 July 1916.

***Sheffield Independent* – 27 September 1916**

TEACHERS IN THE FORCES

> Regret was expressed that eight teachers had been reported killed in action and two as missing. The latter were Lawrence Baylis and **George Braham**, Worsbrough Dale National … A letter of sympathy had been forwarded to the family in each case. It was decided that in the case of single men without dependents, one calendar month's salary be paid from the date of death …

RAYMOND BAYLIS (born 1895 in Selby) Baptism 3 March 1895 in Selby, was a Clerk at Glassworks in April 1911. He enlisted as a Private (Service Number: 12/1849) on 6 November 1915, aged 21, in Sheffield in the 15th Reserve Battalion; he was still a Clerk according to the Attestation form. Raymond was promoted to Lance Corporal on 7 May 1917 (unpaid for three months) then Corporal on 3 November 1917. He served in the 12th Battalion (Sheffield Pals) of the York and Lancaster Regiment, the same as his older brother, and qualified as a Bomber. The Medical Form provides a personal description: Height: 5' 6¾", Weight: 119 lbs, Chest: 34½", scar on back, Vision in both eyes 6/9, Physical Development good. Raymond suffered from Trench Foot which required hospital admission (in Liverpool) for nearly three months from 4 July 1916. The Conduct Sheet reveals that Raymond committed an offence on 26 December 1916 ; he overstayed his pass by one day 7 hours and 45 minutes and punishment awarded was the deduction of six days' pay, although remarks stated that three days' pay were forfeit. He enjoyed two weeks' leave from 6 January 1918.

Raymond died of wounds on 22 March 1918, aged 23, and he was buried in Dernancourt Communal Cemetery Extension, Somme, France (Plot III J 40). His personal possessions were sent to his parents, who were living in Great Horton, Bradford: pouch, pipe, pencil case, knife, two badges, nail scissors, watch, key, photos and letters, pencil, empty purse, dice and shoulder badges. The form to claim the 'Dead Man's Penny' stated that his brother William Stanley was in the Army.

Raymond's name is not on the Sheffield Roll of Honour website; he is mistakenly listed as 'one who returned' on the Hunningley Wesleyan Reform Church Roll of Honour.

WILLIAM STANLEY BAYLIS (born 1897 in Selby) Baptism 1 August 1897 in Selby, was a Draper's Errand Boy (aged 13) in April 1911. According to his brother Raymond's Service Records, William was a Gunner in the 42aa Section of the Royal Garrison Artillery based with the Army on the Rhine. (There is a Medal Card for a William Baylis, Gunner (Service Number: 135788) in the RGA but I have found no other information).

WAR SUPPLEMENT FOR WEEK ENDING AUGUST 10, 1918.

THE TEUTONIC THERMOMETER.

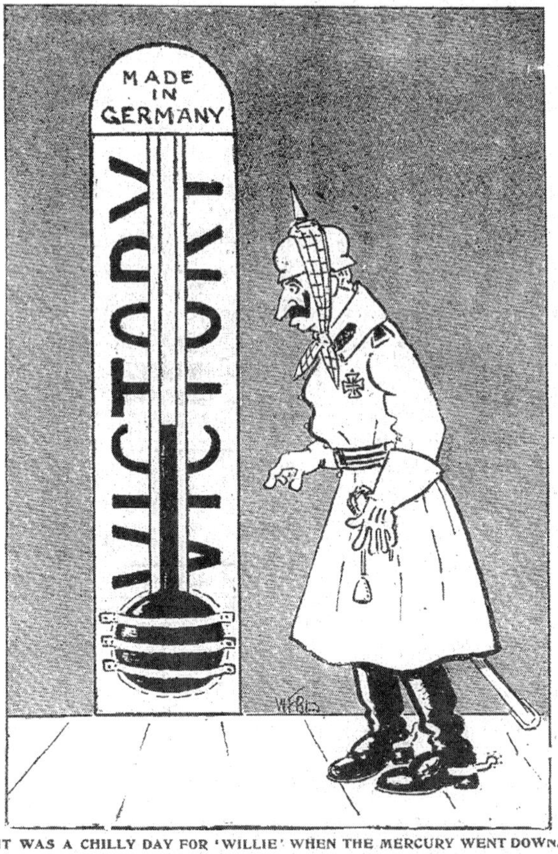

IT WAS A CHILLY DAY FOR 'WILLIE' WHEN THE MERCURY WENT DOWN.

11

Walter Reginald Booker

Walter Reginald Booker
1897–1918 (aged 20)

WALTER REGINALD BOOKER was born on 28 December 1897 in Barnsley to **Fred Booker** (born c1858 in South Elmshall or Doncaster) and **Margaret nee Giggal** (born c1859 in Higham or Silkstone). His Baptism was at St Mary's Church, Barnsley, on 23 January 1898. Fred was the son of John Booker, Cab Proprietor of Barugh Green, and Margaret was the daughter of William Giggal, Publican of Barugh Green, when they married in 1879. Fred worked as a Cab Proprietor, Linen Bleacher and Engine Tender before becoming a Baker and Confectioner Employer.

Walter was the youngest of seven surviving children: **Florence** – previously Confectioner's Assistant, **Arthur** (Served in the First World War), **Mary Gertrude, Edith Annie, Hilda May** and **Sarah Esther**. Another child had died by April 2011 (name unknown).

In April 1911, the Booker family had lived in seven rooms at 109 Barnsley Road, Wombwell, for more than 10 years, having previously lived in Barnsley. The three oldest daughters had left home.

Florence Booker (aged 22) married **Walter Ashton** (22) Journalist of 15 Somerset Street, Barnsley, on 27 August 1902 at St Mary's Church, Barnsley. On the 1911 Census, they were living in five rooms at 43 High Street Thurnscoe; Florence was an Assistant Confectioner and Walter was Newspaper Printing Works Manager for a weekly newspaper. Probate for Florence Ashton of Hill Crest, 153 Wombwell Lane, Stairfoot, who died on 9 September 1953, aged 73, stated that her husband was a Retired Newspaper Sub-Editor.

Mary Gertrude Booker (aged 19) married **Reginald Lambert** (aged 20) late 1908 in Barnsley District; they had three children: **Ronald Arthur Willey Lambert** in 1909, **Florence May Lambert** in 1910 and **Reginald Booker Lambert** in 1912. On the 1911 Census, they were living in seven rooms at 23 South Parade in Doncaster; Reginald was a Motor Engineer Employer and they had a domestic servant.

Edith Annie Booker (born c1890 in Redbrook) married **Bernard Washington Kilner** (served and died in the First World War) early 1910; by April 1911 they were living in four rooms at 96 Blythe Street, Wombwell, with their six month old son **Cyril Kilner**.

Hilda May Booker, who had been a Confectioner's Assistant, married **Ernest Weston** in Spring 1919 in Barnsley; they appear to have had four children, two in Barnsley then two in Surrey: **Walter R Weston** in 1920, **Pauline R Weston** in 1930, **Gordon R Weston** in 1932 and **Pamela J Weston** in 1935.

Sarah Esther Booker (aged 25) married **Richard Wylde** in Summer 1921 in Barnsley District; they had one daughter: **Margaret Doreen Wylde** in 1924.

Walter went to John Street Elementary School in King's Road, Wombwell, for six years until the age of 13. He attended the Holgate Grammar School in Church Street then Shaw Lane, Barnsley, for two years, from 1911 to 1913. 'He left to be a Confectioner'.

Walter enlisted at Barnsley on 6 June 1916 as a Private; he was a Baker of 109 Barnsley Road, Wombwell, aged 18 years and 6 months, at this time according to the Attestation form. He was mobilized on 9 October 1916 and posted as a Gunner

(Service Number: 123309) in the 293rd Siege Battery of the Royal Garrison Artillery, with his appointment confirmed at Clipstone Camp, Pontefract, on 13 October. Walter spent three days in Lydd Military Hospital with scabies from 22 February 1917. He sailed from Southampton to Le Havre on 30 March 1917 and was attached to Brigade Headquarters in the Field from 23 March 1918 until 17 May 1918, when he re-joined his unit.

The Medical Report contains a personal description of Walter: Height: 5' 7½", Weight: 130lbs, Chest: 36", Vision in both eyes 6/6.

Walter was the only Old Boy to serve and die in Italy. This little known campaign took place on the mountainous border between Italy and Austria-Hungary. The Battle of the Piave River – not far from Venice, Padua and Verona – took place from 15 to 23 June 1918 and resulted in defeat for the Austro-Hungarian Army, who suffered many casualties.

Walter was wounded in the hand on 15 June 1918, but continued to operate his gun for nine hours. He received another injury to his lower body and died the same day, aged 20; Walter was buried in Magnaboschi British Cemetery, Cesuna village, Vicenza province in Italy (Plot 1 Row B Grave 5). He had served for one year and 253 days. Walter's mother had the words DUTY NOBLY DONE added to his War Grave headstone.

According to a form requesting family details after his death, completed by his brother Arthur on 21 July 1919, Walter's parents were still at 109 Barnsley Road, Wombwell, with Arthur and two of their daughters: Hilda Weston and Sarah. Florence Ashton was still in Thurnscoe and Gertrude Mary [sic] Lambert was at South Road Garage, Doncaster. Edith, who had got married again early 1919 in Doncaster District to John Sanders and had another son, Fred, born late 1919, was at Marlborough Avenue, Thurnscoe. The Registers of Soldiers Effects show that £10 10s 4d was owed to Walter and this was paid to his mother; the form is stamped 'War Gratuity' with an additional amount of £7 10s entered in red.

Walter was awarded two medals: Victory and British War, and his parents should have received the 'Dead Man's Penny' plaque and scroll from King George V.

Walter's name is on the Holgate Grammar School Memorial and the Memorial outside St Mary's Church, Wombwell.

***Barnsley Chronicle* – 29 June 1918**

LOCAL CASUALTIES

> Profound sympathy has been expressed at the news of the death from wounds received in action on the Italian front of Gunner Walter R Booker of Clydesdale, Barnsley Road, Wombwell. Twenty and a half years old Gunner Booker had

been on active service fifteen months in France and latterly in Italy and up to June 15th had come through all operations unharmed.

On the date named, writes a colleague: 'we had been having a pretty rough time and he got his right hand slightly wounded, but stuck to his post. Later he got severely wounded in the lower part of his body. It was only a very small wound but, I am sorry to say, fatal'. This comrade then tells how Gunner Booker was carried to a place of safety but, despite all that could be done for him, he passed peacefully away 25 minutes later. 'We are all deeply grieved', adds the letter, 'to have lost so dear a chum, and one whom we all loved, and on behalf of the battery I tender all his relatives our deepest sympathy'. Another letter was received by the same post from the Battery Major confirming the sad news and also expressing sympathy with the parents and relatives, whilst a later message from the Battalion Lieutenant pays the following tribute to the dead gunner: 'You can indeed be proud of the work he has done in this battery. He was serving his gun for 9 hours before he was wounded'.

The deceased gunner was the younger of two soldier sons of Mr and Mrs Fred Booker, Wombwell, and formerly of Barnsley. An old boy of Barnsley Grammar School, he was with his parents in the confectionery business when he joined the Forces, and was a well-built and highly respected youth. Keen regret was felt at the news that the lad had fallen and much sympathy will be extended to the relatives in their bereavement following as it does the death in action of their son in law Fitter Staff Sergeant B Kilner, whilst the other son Private A Booker, DLI, is still in hospital badly wounded.

DEATHS: BOOKER In Italy on June 15th 1918, died of wounds received in action the same day. Walter R Booker (Gunner Royal Garrison Artillery) younger son of Fred and Margaret Booker, Clydesdale Barnsley Road, Wombwell, aged 20 years. 'Duty Nobly Done'. Mr and Mrs Booker and family thank all friends for the kind expressions of sympathy extended to them in their bereavement.

Barnsley Independent – 29 June 1918

ROLL OF HONOUR
THE GREAT SACRIFICE FELL IN ITALY
WOMBWELL GUNNER'S NOBLE END

News came to hand on Tuesday that Gunner Walter R Booker of Clydesdale, Barnsley Road, Wombwell, had died of wounds received in action on the Italian Front, and the gallant if tragic circumstances of his death furnishes another glowing example of the heroic part which local lads are playing in the war. (2nd and 3rd paragraphs the same as in *Barnsley Chronicle*).

The Photograph of Walter is from Barnsley Chronicle, *used by their kind permission*

ARTHUR BOOKER (born c1884 in Redbrook, Darton) was a Solicitor's Clerk in April 1911. Arthur served as a Private in either the Durham or Highland Light Infantry, according to the *Barnsley Chronicle* and *Independent*. He was badly wounded and in hospital when his younger brother William died of wounds received in action in June 1918. (I have been unable to find out any more details as Arthur Booker is a common name).

Arthur (aged 40) Solicitor's Clerk, was living with his parents at 109 Barnsley Road, Wombwell, when he got married to **Elizabeth Morton** (aged 40) Clerk of 33 Banstead Grove, Harehills, on 2 February 1924 at St Aidan's Church in Leeds.

Barnsley Independent – 24 November 1917

WAR BRIEFLETS
BARNSLEY CLERK WOUNDED

Official intimation is to hand that Private A Booker, Highland Light Infantry, eldest son of Mr & Mrs F Booker, confectioner, Wombwell, has been wounded in the left thigh in recent operations on the Western Front, and is in hospital in France. Prior to joining the Forces, Private Booker was on the clerical staff of Messrs E J F Rideal & Son, solicitors, Church Street.

BERNARD WASHINGTON KILNER (born c16 July 1889 in Wombwell) was the oldest child of Seth Kilner, Hotel Proprietor of the Half Way House in Wombwell, formerly a Colliery Deputy, and Mary Alice nee Washington. Bernard married Edith Annie Booker early 1910 in Wombwell Parish Church; their son **Cyril Kilner** was born on 5 September 1910. A Fitter at Treeton Colliery, Bernard enlisted at Woolwich, Kent, on 4 January 1915 and soon qualified for the rank of Fitter Staff Sergeant (Service Number: 52200) in the 51st Brigade of the Royal Field Artillery. He served with the Expeditionary Force from May 1915, fighting in Loos, on the Somme and at Ypres (Ieper); he was awarded the Meritorious Service Medal shortly before he died. Bernard died of wounds on 18 October 1917, aged 27, and was buried in the St Julien Dressing Station Cemetery, near Ieper in Belgium. He is listed in the UK De Ruvigny's Roll of Honour.

***Barnsley Independent* – 10 November 1917 Roll of Honour (Photo)**

WOMBWELL STAFF SERGEANT FALLS
MERITORIOUS SERVICE MEDALLIST
ELDEST OF FOUR SOLDIER BROTHERS
FITTER STAFF SERGEANT B KILNER

Official news came to hand on Wednesday of the death from wounds received in action in France of Fitter Staff Sergeant Bernard Kilner, the eldest of four soldier sons of Mr and Mrs S Kilner, Half Way House Hotel, Mitchell's Main, Wombwell. The sad news, which was the first intimation that anything untoward had happened, came as a painful blow to his relatives and friends, the deceased being well known and exceedingly popular. A fitter by trade, having served his apprenticeship at the Mitchell's Main Colliery, he latterly was employed at the Treeton Colliery, residing at Woodhouse Mill, and whilst there responded to the call in the New Year of 1915. He passed the necessary trade tests at Woolwich, qualifying straightaway for the rank of Fitter Staff Sergeant, went to France in May and had thus seen two and a half years of strenuous active service, taking part in almost all the big engagements. His able and devoted service, which has earned much commendation, was recognised a few months ago when he was awarded the Meritorious Service Medal, and up to the time of his death – October 18th – had come through it all without mishap. No other details beyond the official notice of his death are yet to hand.

Staff Sergeant Kilner was well known in cricketing circles having figured with the Mitchell's Main Club, and whilst at Woodhouse assisted the Fence C C. Like his brothers, he was a keen sportsman and held in the highest esteem by all with whom he came into contact. He married Miss E Booker, daughter of Mr and Mrs F Booker, confectioners, Wombwell, and with all the relatives the keenest sympathy is felt. He leaves a widow and one child.

The deceased's three soldier brothers are Roy, the County cricketer, who was wounded with the Leeds Pals, and is now with the RFA at Preston; Sergt Norman Kilner, KRR, who has been wounded three times and who set sail on Wednesday for foreign service again; and Corporal Collin Kilner, now with the Trench Mortar Batteries in France. All four joined up in the early days of the war.

12

Maurice Bradley Parker Boyd

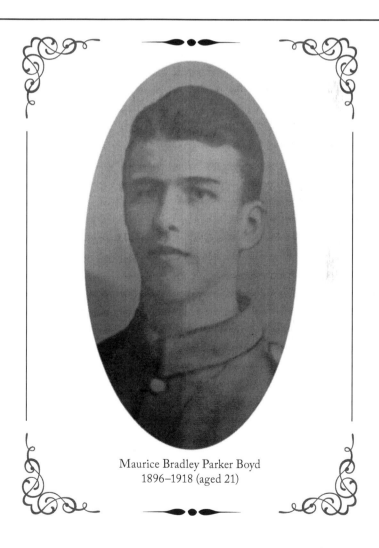

Maurice Bradley Parker Boyd
1896–1918 (aged 21)

MAURICE BRADLEY PARKER BOYD was born on 1 December 1896 in Royston to **William Boyd** (born 1870 in Kingston upon Hull) and **Mary nee Chapman** (born 1870 in Kirkstall, Leeds). Maurice's Baptism was at St John the Baptist Church, Royston, on 13 January 1897. William was Cashier for a Colliery Company in 1911 but then became an Estate Agent; his parents Hugh and Jane Boyd were both from Liverpool and his father had been a Schoolmaster and Assistant Overseer Poor in Hull.

Maurice had two sisters; **Dorothy Mary** and **Lorna Marian**.

Dorothy Boyd (aged 25) married **Harold Cecil Latham** (served in the First World War) on 18 November 1922 at Felkirk Parish Church.

Lorna Boyd married **George William Hoggan Gardner** in Spring 1932 in Hemsworth District; they had two daughters in Aldershot: **Judith M Gardner** in 1935 and **Lorna F Gardner** in 1937. George who became a Knight of the Realm, and they travelled to America and Indonesia*

In April 1911, the Boyd family lived in seven rooms at 162 Park Grove, Barnsley, having previously lived in Wellfield House, Church Hill, Royston; all three children were at school. They subsequently moved to Felkirk House in South Hiendley.

Maurice went to Royston Elementary School until he was 9. He then attended the Holgate Grammar School in Church Street then Shaw Lane, Barnsley, for nine years from 1906 to 1915. He was a Royston Grammar School Foundation Scholar for three years and a County Minor Scholar for seven years. Maurice passed the Oxford Local Senior exam in July 1913 (2rd Class Honours) and 1st division in the Northern Universities Matriculation in July 1914. The Governors of Barnsley Grammar School granted him £50 for three years. Maurice had been a member of the football team and in 1914 as 'Centre Forward has only recently stepped into his present position but adapts himself to it remarkably well. He holds his forward line well together and keeps the opposing goalers fairly busy'. Maurice 'joined the Military Service on leaving school'.

Maurice enlisted in Kingston upon Hull on 2 October 1915, aged 19 years and 2 months, and he was a Student living at The Mount, Woolley, at this time according to the Attestation form. He was a Gunner (Service Number: 290324/336) in the 11th Hull Heavy Battery of the Royal Garrison Artillery.

The Medical Form contains a personal description of Maurice: Height: 5' 6½", Weight: 133lbs, Chest: 33½", Physical Development Fair.

Maurice sailed from Devonport to Kilindini in Africa to join the East Africa Campaign; the journey took over five weeks. About a month after arrival on 16 March 1916, he was admitted to hospital for a fortnight with dysentery then about six weeks later he was admitted to hospital for over six weeks with malaria. After periods in hospital Maurice was invalided to South Africa, where he was 'employed in the

* Brian McArthur, who had carried out research for a distant relation of Maurice's, kindly shared some information about him and the North Africa Campaign.

Section Commander's office, Table Bay Defences, Cape Town'. After 22 months in Africa the Battery returned to England in January 1918. Maurice served for two years and 138 days.

Maurice was the only Old Boy to serve in East and South Africa.

Maurice kept in contact with the Grammar School and some of his letters home were printed in *Alumnus* (Part 3. Chapter 2). While home on leave, he visited his old school on 15 February 1918 and 'that evening (on bicycle) he collided with a pedestrian and died from the effects of the fall'. Maurice was admitted to the Beckett Hospital in Barnsley that night with a 'fracture at base of skull' but died the following morning, 16 February 1918, aged 21. Maurice was buried in St Peter's Churchyard, Felkirk, on 19 February 1918, in the Boyd family grave, close to the church building, with his parents and maternal grandmother.

Maurice was awarded two medals: Victory and British War, and his parents should have received the 'Dead Man's Penny' plaque and scroll from King George V.

Maurice's name is on the Holgate Grammar School Memorial and the Memorial on the lychgate of St Peter's Church, Felkirk, where inside the Church there is a Memorial Window on the east wall – next to a window dedicated to Ernest William Litherland.

The stained glass window has three panels depicting an angel with the ram about to be sacrificed instead of Isaac, Isaac and Abraham at the sacrificial altar and a group of servants. (My photograph of this window is in the Colour Section).

The dedication on the small glass panels underneath reads:

To the everlasting Glory of God
and in loving memory of Maurice Bradley Parker Boyd 1918

Beneath the stained glass window is a small brass plaque:

IN LOVING MEMORY
OF
WILLIAM BOYD
1870–1940
ALSO
MARY BOYD
1870–1956
AND
THEIR DAUGHTER
MARY WILSON

Connections

Maurice is commemorated at St Peter's Church, Felkirk, along with **Ernest William Litherland** and **Norman Bradbury** and at South Hiendley with **Norman Bradbury.**

Alumnus – April 1918

Most lamentable was the death by accident of MBP BOYD when home on leave after two years military service in East Africa, as Gunner in the RGA. He was the son of Mr and Mrs W Boyd of Felkirk. He had been a scholar at the Grammar School from 1906–1915, where he was highly popular and distinguished himself by the excellence of his work as a student, passing 2nd class Honours at the Oxford Senior Local Exam. and 1st division at the Northern Universities Matriculation Exam. Although he was awarded the Governors' Exhibition of £50 he was unable to utilise it, as immediately at the end of his school career, he joined the RGA. His battery was soon drafted out to East Africa, where he contracted malarial fever. He was invalided to Cape Town where he was put on garrison duty.

In Jan 1918, the battery returned to England. On Feb 15th he visited the Grammar school. The same evening when returning home on bicycle he collided with a pedestrian and died from the effects of the fall.

Barnsley Chronicle – 23 February 1918

FELKIRK SOLDIER'S TRAGIC DEATH
AFTER A VISIT TO BARNSLEY
CYCLING COLLISION WITH A PEDESTRIAN

Last Friday evening a sad cycling fatality occurred near Monk Bretton. The victim, Maurice Bradley Parker Boyd, collided with a pedestrian, being pitched into the roadway and died without recovering consciousness.

Mr P P Maitland, District Coroner, held an inquest on the body at the Town Hall on Monday morning.

William Boyd, secretary of the New Monckton Colliery, of Felkirk, said the deceased was his son and was 21 years of age. He was a gunner in the 11th Hull Battery, RGA, and had been out in East Africa two years being invalided to Cape Town with Malaria. A fortnight ago he came home, having recovered, though his heart was a bit weak from the effects of the fever. His leave was of 32 days' duration and during the period he was at home he seemed to be picking up nicely. On Friday afternoon at 2 o' clock he left Felkirk on his cycle with the intention of visiting the Barnsley Grammar School and Mr Butler, the Chief Constable. For a number of years he had been accustomed to riding a bicycle and his eyesight was all right. He was expected home about 10pm on Friday but witness heard nothing further of him until about 3 o' clock on Saturday morning when Mr and Mrs Butler came over and informed him of an accident having occurred. The young man had then died at the hospital.

Addressing Mr Boyd, the Coroner said he would like to express his sympathy with the unfortunate young man's parents. It was very sad indeed that a young man who had done his duty should have happened an accident like this. Mr Boyd briefly returned his thanks. His son, he said, had been very keen upon getting into the Army and abhorred the idea of being fetched.

George Henry Butler, son of the Chief Constable, said he met deceased at 4.15 on Friday afternoon on Market Hill. Deceased and witness' brother were school chums. Boyd seemed quite well and cheerful and stayed at witness' home to tea after which they strolled round the town. Deceased left for home at 9 o' clock on his cycle having both head and tail lights on. So far as witness knew the cycle was in good order having two brakes. The night was fine.

George Guest, dataller of 12 Pinfold Hill, Ardsley, said that on Friday night he was proceeding to his work at Monk Bretton and when a short distance past the Cundy Cross Bar, going down the hill, he heard a bell ringing and before he could get out of the way a cycle dashed into his back, throwing him forward on to the road. He was a few seconds before he came to his senses and when he got up he saw by the light from the cycle that the deceased was laid in the road with the machine on top of him. Deceased did not speak. A motor car came up and the young man was taken to hospital.

William Newton, a colliery packer, of 63 Shaftesbury Street, Stairfoot, deposed that on Friday night he was coming down the road when he saw deceased laying in the road unconscious. Witness turned him over onto his back but the young man did not speak. Deceased was put into a motor car by two soldiers and taken to the Lund Wood Hospital. Guest was present and he seemed dazed.

Detective Herbert explained to the Coroner that when the two soldiers got deceased to Lund Wood Hospital, the Matron at once saw that it was a case for Beckett Hospital and she immediately got into communication with the latter institution. The ambulance was procured and deceased removed to Beckett Hospital.

Dr Perry, house surgeon at the Beckett Hospital, said that Boyd was living when admitted but he was in a bad way, his skull being fractured. It was a hopeless case and death took place from coma.

The Coroner summing up said the evidence showed clearly that it was an accident. It was a dark night and the young man would seem to have got up close to Guest before he saw him – too late for him to pull up – and in the collision Boyd was thrown heavily on to the road, his skull being fractured at the base. Everything possible seemed to have been done for the poor lad and it was only natural that the two soldiers should take him to the military hospital.

The jury concurred and a verdict of 'Accidental death' was returned. A Juror said he and his colleagues would like to add an expression of sympathy with Mr Boyd in his sad loss. Mr Boyd was a gentleman well-known and highly respected in the district.

***Yorkshire Post* AND *Leeds Intelligencer* – 19 February 1918**

FATAL CYCLING ACCIDENT

An inquest was held at Barnsley yesterday on Maurice Boyd (21) RGA, son of Mr William Boyd of Felkirk. On Friday night the deceased was returning home from Barnsley, when, in descending the gradient from Cundy Crossbar towards Cudworth, he collided with a man walking in the road. He was thrown heavily and conveyed to the Beckett Hospital, Barnsley, but death occurred the following morning from fracture of the skull. The Coroner (Mr Maitland) and jury expressed sympathy with the deceased's family.

The photograph of Maurice is from Alumnus, *reproduced by kind permission of Barnsley Archives.*

HAROLD CECIL LATHAM (born in 1897 in Greenwich) was the son of Lovell Latham, Solicitor. There are two Medal Cards: Harold C Latham was a Private (1734 then 365172) in the 1/20th then 7th Battalion of the London Regiment; he served in France from 9 March 1915 and was awarded three medals. Harold Cecil Latham was a Second Lieutenant then Lieutenant in the 1/23rd Battalion of the London Regiment, serving in France from 26 May 1916, before being transferred as Captain to the 1/4th Battalion of the P Albert V Rajput Regiment of the Indian Army. When he got married in 1922 to Dorothy Mary Boyd, he was Army Captain living at 103 Boyne Road, Lewisham.

Harold continued his career in the Indian Army and was awarded an Officer of the British Empire, gazetted on 19 October 1944, for his work in Burma and the Eastern Frontier of India; he was Lieutenant Colonel, Temporary Brigadier (IA945), in the 7th Rajput Regiment.

Harold died on 5 October 1948, aged 51, at Lady Dudley Nursing Home in Johannesburg, South Africa although his usual residence was 26 Marlborough Road, Bournemouth.

13

Norman Bradbury

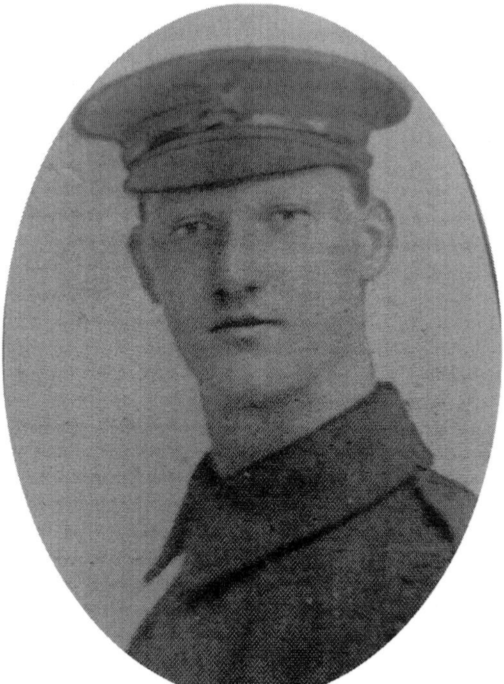

Norman Bradbury
1891–1916 (aged 25)

NORMAN BRADBURY was born on 12 July 1891 in Normanton to **Thomas Elijah Bradbury** (born c1858 in Staffordshire) and **Hannah nee Shepherd** (born c1862 in Staffordshire). Norman's Baptism was on 2 August 1891 at All Saints Church, Normanton. Thomas was a Police Constable in Leek, Staffordshire, in 1881 before moving to Yorkshire by April 1891, when he was a Coal Miner Hewer.

Norman was the fourth of six surviving children out of 10: **Maud Florence, Minnie Annie, Ernest, Doris** and **Cyril**. In April 1901, Minnie Annie (aged 16) was a Domestic Servant for a Widow living on her own means. Four children had died by April 1911 (names unknown).

In April 1911, the Bradbury family lived in five rooms in George Street, South Hiendley. The four oldest children were living elsewhere. Norman (aged 19) Elementary School Teacher, was a Boarder at Front St Martin, Gainsborough, with **Henry Gould**, Retired Butler, and his wife. Ernest (24) Filler Underground, was a Boarder with **Thomas Brown**, Bricky and Labourer, and family in Chilvers Coton, Warwickshire.

Maud Florence Bradbury (aged 24) of 47 Blenheim Road, Manningham, got married on 11 March 1906 at St Paul's Church in Manningham to **Arthur Garwell** (24) Butcher of Chelmsford Place, York. His father was **William Johnson Garwell**, Gas Stoker. They had six children: **Gladys Maud** was born in 1906 in Bradford and the others were in York: **Arthur** in 1907, **Doris** in 1909, **George** in 1911 and **Norman** in 1914 – **William** was born and died in the same quarter in 1910. In 1911, they were living in eight rooms in Fulford with Arthur's widowed mother **Emma Garwell**; **Ernest Bradbury** (24) Coal Miner, was visiting them.

Minnie Annie Bradbury (aged 20) married **Samuel Taylor** (22) Miner at Felkirk St Peter's Church on 24 April 1905; they were both of South Hiendley. His father was **George Hawkesley Taylor**, Engine Driver. Minnie's sister Maud and future husband Arthur were witnesses. In 1911 Samuel was a Colliery Pump Man and they were living in four rooms in South Hiendley with their four children: **William** (5), **Maud** (3), **Charles** (2) and **Mary** (1).

Norman went to Felkirk Parochial Elementary School until the age of 15. He then attended the Holgate Grammar School in Church Street, Barnsley, for two years, from 1907 to 1909. Norman was a Pupil Teacher at Felkirk C E School and passed the Preliminary Certificate parts I and II. 'He went into Teaching' and attended York St John's Training College, from 1914 to 1916.

Norman enlisted in Wakefield on 4 December 1915, aged 24 years and 4 months, as a Private (Service Number: C/12707) in the 21st Battalion of the King's Royal Rifle Corps and was promoted to Lance Corporal on 23 March 1916. He was a Schoolmaster living at home. Norman was killed in action on 17 September 1916, aged 25, after serving for 289 days; he was shot in the head while leading his unit after their officer fell. He was buried in Guard's Cemetery, Lesboeufs, Somme, France (grave IV F 3), having been reburied from the original grave where he was 'unknown'.

The Medical Form provides a limited physical description: Height: 5' 10½ ", Chest: 35", Weight: 135 lbs, No Distinctive Marks, Vision in both eyes 6/6.

Top: Lce.-Cpl. N. BRADBURY (South Hiendley, killed); Pte. H. T BRYCE (Royston, killed).

Photograph of feature in *Barnsley Chronicle*, used by their kind permission.

Norman's father received a letter about his son's property and this just listed '1 disc'. A form requesting family details in 1920 was completed by Thomas, who added when it came to Norman's nieces and nephews: '(Bunk um) Impossible to give these here if I could. (This you ought to know)'. Norman's parents and three children: Ernest, Cyril and Doris were living at George Street, South Hiendley. Maud Garwell was in Fulford, York, and Minnie Taylor was at Belmont, South Hiendley. Details of four grandparents were also given.

Norman was awarded two medals: Victory and British War, and his parents should have received the 'Dead Man's Penny' plaque and scroll from King George V. Both of Norman's parents died early 1922 and were buried in St Peter's Churchyard in Felkirk.

Norman's name is on the Holgate Grammar School Memorial, the Memorial on the lychgate of St Peter's Church, Falkirk, and the Roll of Honour at St John's College in York (as Bradley).

Connections

Seven of the Old Boys qualified as Teachers after attending St John's College in York: **Crossland Barraclough** (B 1894), **Edward Batley** (B 1893), **Norman Bradley** (B 1891), **John Middleton Downend** (B 1888), **Arthur Heathcote** (B 1890), **Charles Edward Savage** (B 1893) and **Charles Waldegrave Wood** (B 1883). Several of them would have attended during the same period.

Norman served in the 21st Battalion of the King's Royal Rifle Corps along with **Sidney Nicholson**.

Norman is commemorated at St Peter's Church, Felkirk, along with **Ernest William Litherland** and **Maurice Bradley Parker Boyd** and at South Hiendley with **M B P Boyd**.

***Barnsley Chronicle* – 28 October 1916**

A SOUTH HIENDLEY LOSS
PROMISING CAREER CUT SHORT

> News of the death in action of Lce-Cpl Norman Bradbury has caused widespread regret in South Hiendley, where his parents reside and are held in high esteem. The lad was educated at the village school where he won a pupil teachership. He went to Barnsley Grammar School and qualified as an uncertificated teacher. He acted as assistant master at a village in Lincolnshire, and from here he went to York Training College. He had just finished a year's training when he was called to arms. He joined the King's Royal Rifles under the Earl of Feversham. Deceased was liked by everybody he came into contact with and made many friends.
>
> He was in an advance on September 17 and took command after his leader fell. He, however, succeeded in getting over the first trench, but was shot through the head. Splendid letters have been received from officers of his regiment, testifying to the excellent soldier-abilities possessed by the deceased.

The main photograph of Norman is from Alumnus, *reproduced by kind permission of Barnsley Archives.*

14

George Braham

George Braham
1886–1916 (aged 29)

GEORGE BRAHAM was born 16 November 1886 in Hoyland to **Daniel Braham** (born c1852 in Garforth) and **Annie nee Goodall** (born c1856 in Barwick in Elmet). Daniel was a Stationary Engineman for a Colliery Company.

George was the fifth of nine surviving children: **William Henry** – Certificated Teacher, **Alice** – Assistant School Mistress, **Herbert** – Grocery Apprentice (in 1901), **Edith, Archibald, Ernest Goodall** (attended the Holgate and served in the First World War), **Lizzie** – Student Teacher, and **Arthur Goodall** (attended the Holgate and served in the First World War). Two children had died in infancy by April 1911: **Mary Harriet** in 1884 and **Edward Reginald** in 1901.

In April 1911, the Braham family lived in six rooms at The Briers, 185 Sheffield Road, Birdwell, having previously moved from Hoyland to Worsbrough.

George attended the Holgate Grammar School in Church Street, Barnsley, for two years, from 1904 to 1906. He was a Pupil Teacher and became a 'Certificated Master'. He was Assistant Schoolmaster at Worsbrough Dale National School by 1911.

George enlisted in Sheffield on 16 September 1914, aged 27 years and 10 months. He became a Corporal (Service Number: 12/307) in the 12th Battalion (Sheffield City) of the York and Lancaster Regiment. George was killed in action on the first day of the Somme, 1 July 1916, aged 29, and as his body was never found or identified his name is listed on the Thiepval Memorial, Somme, France (Pier and Face: 14A and 14B).

Alumnus: 'Braham, E Batley, Mountford, L W Smith, were left behind when Barnsley and Sheffield Battalions went to Egypt because of an outbreak of measles. Now attached to 15th (Res) Y & L stationed at Colsterdale'.

George was one of ten Old Boys who were killed in action on the first day of the Somme.

George was awarded three medals: 1914–15 Star, Victory and British War, and his parents should have received the 'Dead Man's Penny' plaque and scroll from King George V.

George's name is on the Holgate Grammar School Memorial, the Worsbrough Memorial inside St Mary's Church, Sheffield Council's Official Roll of Honour and Sheffield City Battalion Roll of Honour. Although George was born in Hoyland, his family moved elsewhere and his name was not originally inscribed on the Hoyland Memorial; however Peter Marsden included him in his memorial files in Barnsley Archives and Hoyland Library in addition to his website. George Braham's name was one of many names added to the Hoyland War Memorial in time for Remembrance Day 2014.

Connections

George played for the Second Eleven Cricket Team, which also comprised: **Ernest Litherland**, Captain (who won a cricket bat prize for bowling), **Edward Batley**, and (probably) **Herbert Harry Jagger Mason**. The First Eleven Team included **George Percival Cowburn** (who won a cricket bat prize for bowling), **Cyril Burton Dixon** (who won a cricket bat prize for batting), **Duncan Fairley** plus **Harold Willott** and his brother **Ernest Spencer Willott**.

George was a Teacher at Worsbrough Dale National School at the same time as **Laurence Baylis.**

George's Service Number was number 307 and two older Old Boys, who were classmates, had close numbers: **Edward Batley's** was 294 and **Laurence Baylis**' was 296

George served in the 12th Battalion (Sheffield City) of the York and Lancaster Regiment along with **Edward Batley, Laurence Baylis, Sidney Gill, James Stuart Swift** and **Arthur Henry Thompson**. They were all killed in action on 1 July 1916.

***Sheffield Independent* – 3 August 1916**

LOCAL CASUALTIES
GALLANT MEN FROM SHEFFIELD DISTRICT IN LISTS

> Corporal George Braham of the 'B' Company, Sheffield City Battalion, is unofficially reported missing since 1 July – the opening day of the great advance. Mr and Mrs Braham of 'The Briers', Birdwell, near Barnsley, are anxious to learn something of him and would be glad to hear from any of his comrades who were with him in the advance.

***Sheffield Independent* – 27 September 1916**

TEACHERS IN THE FORCES

> Regret was expressed that eight teachers had been reported killed in action and two as missing. The latter were Lawrence Baylis and George Braham, Worsbrough Dale National ... A letter of sympathy had been forwarded to the family in each case. It was decided that in the case of single men without dependents, one calendar month's salary be paid from the date of death ....

The photograph of George is from Alumnus, *used by kind permission of Barnsley Archives.*

ERNEST GOODALL BRAHAM (born 24 February 1891 in Barnsley) attended the Holgate from 1904 to 1908. He was an Intending Pupil Teacher and Bursar. In April 1911, Ernest was a Theological Student. According to the RAF records, Ernest enlisted on 2 July 1918, aged 27, as a Private (Service Number: 179603) in the Royal Air Force. He was a Wesleyan Minister and his next of kin was his father at The

Bryers, Birdwell. Ernest was 5' 9" tall with a 36" chest; his hair was brown, his eyes were blue and his complexion fresh. He was transferred to the RAF Reserve on 13 January 1919 and discharged on 30 April 1920.

Ernest got married on 1 July 1919 in Bristol District to **Ethel M Randall** and they had two children in Shepton Mallet, Somerset: **John R D Braham** in Spring 1920 and **Josephine I Braham** in Summer 1921.

***Western Daily Press* – 2 July 1919**

LOCAL WEDDING

> The wedding took place yesterday at Old King Street Wesleyan Church of the Rev Ernest G Braham ... and Miss Ethell May Randall, second daughter of Mr A G Randall of the firm of Randall and Co cycle agents and factors, 10 Newfoundland Street. The bridegroom is well known in Bristol having been attached to the Old King Street Circuit before he joined the RAF. .... The bride's dress was ivory satin veiled with Georgette wreath and veil of myrtle leaves ... breakfast at the Royal Hotel (with 50 guests) .... honeymoon (in the North of England).

ARTHUR GOODALL BRAHAM (born 5 July 1895) went to Hoyland Common Elementary School until the end of 1908, when he attended the Holgate from 1909 to July 1910. Arthur was a Lithographer's Apprentice by April 1911.

> *Alumnus*: 'A Braham – 5th Battalion of the York and Lancaster Regiment (Territorials)'. RAF records have A G Braham enlisting on 18 May 1918 in the King's Own Yorkshire Light Infantry (Service Number: 29810), then seconded to the Royal Air Force from 31 July. Arthur's promotion to Second Lieutenant "Obs O" was in the London Gazette on 2 August 1918. He was in the 110 Squadron, British Expeditionary Force, on 30 August then admitted to hospital on 15 October for about three weeks. Arthur was transferred to the unemployed list on 15 January 1919 and his service 'was considered for the grant of war medals'.

Arthur G Braham married **Olive Croxen** late 1917 in Wellingborough.

15 and 16

Carter Brothers (Henry and Joseph Robinson)

Henry Carter
1895–1916 (aged 20)

Joseph Robinson Carter
1896–1916 (aged 19)

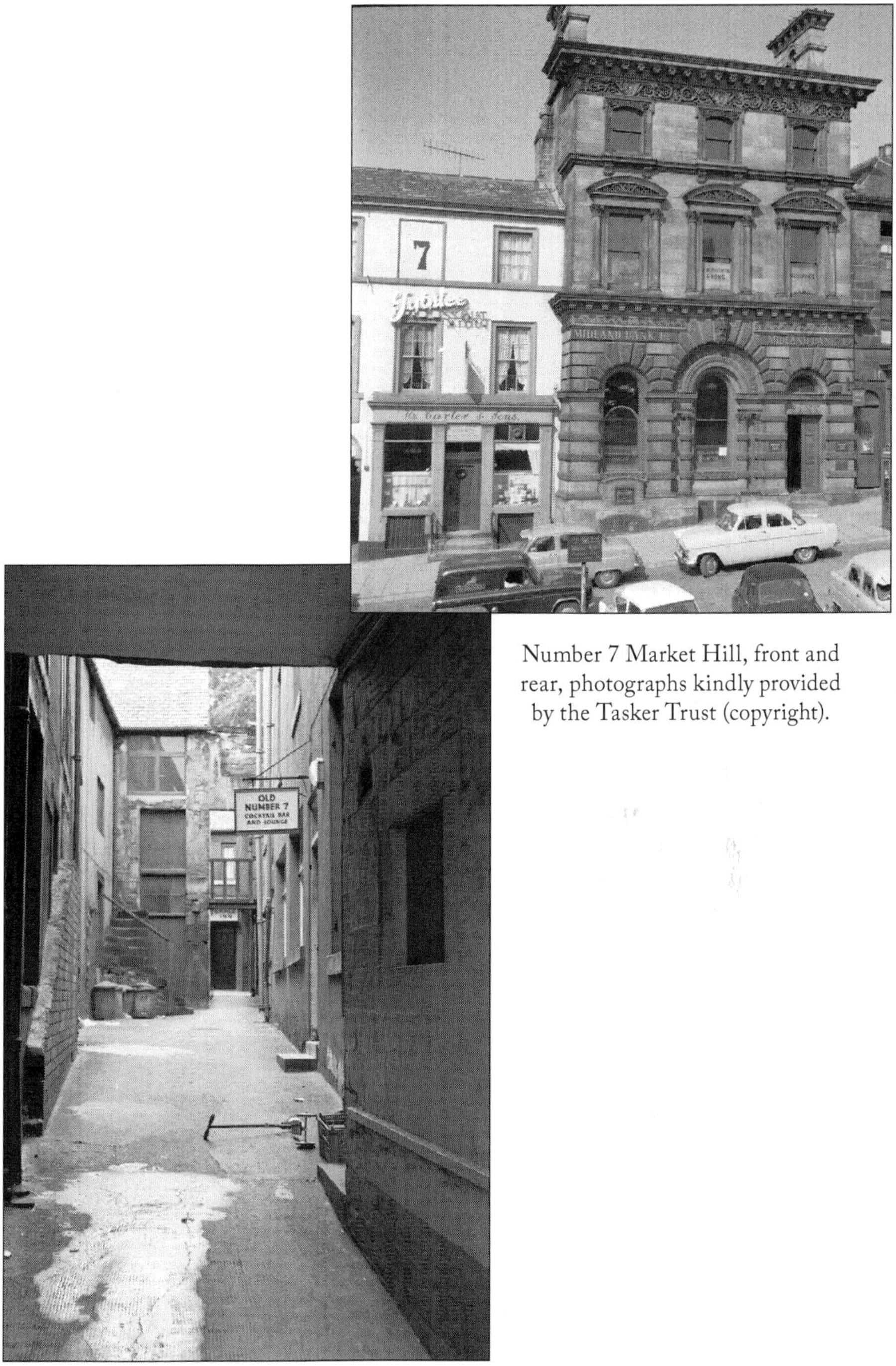

Number 7 Market Hill, front and rear, photographs kindly provided by the Tasker Trust (copyright).

Matthew Carter (born c1863 in Barnsley) and **Maude Mary nee Schofield** (born c1874 in Billingley) had six children: **HENRY, JOSEPH ROBINSON, Matthew Schofield, Mary, Maude** and **Marjorie**. The Baptisms of all their children were at St George's Church in Barnsley. Matthew senior was a Wine and Spirit Merchant 'on his own account' at 7 Market Hill, Barnsley, having taken over the family business from his father Henry Carter.

Philip Norman's article in 'Memories of Barnsley' Winter 2011 explains that the Carters had occupied the premises, now a pub now called Old No. 7, for almost 60 years from 1876 – 'under the shop was one of the largest and finest wine cellars to be found in Yorkshire'.

In April 1911 they had lived in seven rooms at Oxford Villa, 109 Dodworth Road, Barnsley for at least 10 years, having previously lived at number 52. They employed a Domestic Servant.

Matthew Schofield (born 12 November 1898) died on 6 October 1936, aged 37, at 154 Park Grove, Barnsley; Probate was granted on 14 December 1936 at London with Administration to his sister Mary; Effects: £855 15s 4d.

Mary Carter (aged 21) married **Herbert Snowden** in spring 1922 in Barnsley; they had one son **David C Snowden** early 1923. **Maude Carter** (aged 26) married **Harry Waite** late 1927 in Barnsley.

The parents of Henry and Joseph Robinson Carter lost their two oldest children, born just 16 months apart, in a period of about four months on the Somme in 1916.

HENRY CARTER was born on 30 August 1895 in Barnsley; his Baptism was on 19 October 1895 at St George's Church in Barnsley. He went to St Mary's Elementary School in Barnsley until the age of 11. Henry then attended the Holgate Grammar School in Church Street, Barnsley, for four years, from 1906 to 1910. He was an 'Inmate Student' at St Cuthbert's College, Sparken Hill, Worksop, after leaving.*

Henry was a chorister in the St George's Church choir with both brothers, Joseph and Matthew.

Henry enlisted at Grimsby on 21 September 1914, aged 19 years and 22 days; he was an Electrical Engineer at Taylor's Factory in Barnsley according to the Attestation form. (*Taylor's Mill was a steam-powered linen weaving mill opened in 1845 by Thomas Taylor, from a well-established family of linen manufacturers; it no longer exists*).

Henry joined the 10th Battalion of the Lincolnshire Regiment as a Private (Service Number: 418). He was killed in action on 30 May 1916 aged 20, having served for one year and 253 days; he was hit by shrapnel early morning while at his post and

* Worksop College have been unable to check their Archives as all records were packed up to relocate when I contacted them in December 2015.

died after being unconscious for half an hour. Henry was buried in Becourt Military Cemetery, Becordel-Becourt, Somme, France (grave I M 13).

Henry was awarded two medals: Victory and British War, and his parents should have received the 'Dead Man's Penny' plaque and scroll from King George V.

Henry's name is on the Holgate Grammar School Memorial; Barnsley Pace Street Swimming Club had an H Carter listed on its Memorial according to an article in *Barnsley Chronicle*.

Advert in *Barnsley Independent* 1916

ESTABLISHED 1836 NAT. TELEPHONE 450

HENRY CARTER & SONS

Wholesale Wine & Spirit Merchants

MARKET HILL, BARNSLEY

H, C & S have always the following Brands in Stock

PHONE 450

BLACK AND WHITE
BEGG'S LOCHNAGAR
HAIG'S GLENLEVEN
USHERS SPECIAL RESERVE
–"– C V G
JOHNNY WALKER
OLD SIMONS CHOICE
GREEN'S C V G
G I SPECIAL
OLD LIQUEUR SCOTCH
AINLEY'S ROYAL EDINBORO' WHISKY

OLD VINTAGE BRANDY, 1865
DUBOIS FRERES, 16 years old
OLD CHOICE BRANDY
MARTELLS –"–
TYRCONNELL –"–
JOHN JAMIESON WHISKY
BROWN CORBETT
SHAMROCK

ALL THE PRINCIPAL VINTAGE PORTS IN STOCK. PRICES ON APPLICATION

Connection

Henry served in the 10th Battalion of the Lincolnshire Regiment along with **George Percival Cowburn.**

***Sheffield Evening Telegraph* – 5 June 1916**

BARNSLEY SOLDIER KILLED

Private Henry Carter, son of Mr Matthew Carter, of the firm of Messrs H Carter and Sons, wine and spirit merchants, Barnsley, has been killed in action while serving with the Lincolnshire Regiment. Deceased was 20 years of age and an electrical student. He was a member of the Cadet Corps of St Cuthbert's College, Worksop, and enlisted on the outbreak of war.

***Barnsley Chronicle* – 10 June 1916**

A BARNSLEY TRADESMAN'S LOSS
MR M CARTER'S ELDEST SON KILLED
FINE TRIBUTES FROM COMRADES

Profound sorrow has this week been expressed by a wide circle of friends at the death in action on May 30th of Private Henry Carter, of the firm of Messrs H Carter and Sons, wine and spirits merchants, Market Hill, Barnsley. The deceased would have been 21 years of age next August. As a boy he attended St Mary's school and later the Grammar School, finally finishing his education at St Cuthbert's College, Worksop, and it was fitting indeed that when he decided to take his share in the great war he should join the Lincolnshire Regiment with the St Cuthbert's Squad in September 1914. It was in November last that he was drafted to France, and his parents and friends were eagerly looking forward to his shortly enjoying a furlough at home. This, however, was not to be, the information being received last Saturday that he had fallen a victim to the enemy. Mr and Mrs Carter have been inundated at their residence in Dodworth Road with letters and verbal expressions of sympathy, and all those kind friends they desire through these columns to sincerely thank.

Captain C Ferry wrote from France: – 'Dear Mrs Carter – It is my very painful duty as Officer Commanding B Co. to have to write this letter to you telling you the sad news that your son was killed in action about one o' clock in the early morning of May 30th. Your son always did his duty and did it well. He died at his post being hit by shrapnel. The Company have lost a good man, and I especially feel his death, as I am an old Worksop boy myself. It will be some small comfort to you to know that your son suffered no pain being unconscious from the time he was hit until he died half an hour afterwards. Everything that was possible was done for him but was of no avail. He was buried the next evening by the Chaplain in the English Cemetery here and carried to his last resting place by six friends from his own section. We all sympathise very deeply with you in your great trouble and if there is anything else I can tell you or do for you please let me know and I will do my best'.

Lance Sergeant J Turner in the course of a letter of sympathy said the deceased was on sentry duty in one of the bays along with his 'pal' Private Ivor Griffiths, when a whizz-bang burst close to him. 'Hearing him call I rushed and caught him in the act of falling and he was unconscious to the end. I know you will feel your great loss terribly and that the only consolation is the fact that he died fighting for home and country'.

Ivor Griffiths above referred to is a son of Mr R E Griffiths, printer, Church Street, Barnsley, and he enlisted in the same regiment along with Harry. Writing to Mr and Mrs Carter, Private Griffiths says: 'I have lost one of my best friends for since we enlisted we have slept together and shared our comforts. I feel his loss very much indeed, and all the boys in the section have asked me to express their sorrow'.

Second Lieutenant Jack Proctor, of the same regiment likewise forwarded a message of sympathy. 'Your dear boy was not in my platoon but he being a Yorkshireman – and I myself coming from Leeds – I took an interest in handing on to him any papers I received. He is buried in a lovely little spot surrounded by flowers and trees and near to where we are going when we leave the trenches tonight. It is no good me telling you how bravely he did his duty but I wish to say how deeply we feel the loss of such a fine member of our Company'.

***Barnsley Independent* – 11 November 1916**

(ARTICLE ABOUT PRIVATE J R CARTER)

It will be recalled that Mr Carter's eldest son, Private Henry Carter, Lincolnshire Regiment, fell in action on May 30th last. He was killed by a whizz-bang, a portion of which shell caught his comrade, Private Ivor Griffiths, son of Mr R E Griffiths, printer, but the latter had a miraculous escape, as it did not even break the skin. Deceased was an electrical student at Messrs Taylor and Sons, Barnsley, and would have been 21 years of age in August last.

The main photograph of Henry is from Barnsley Chronicle, *used by their kind permission.*

JOSEPH ROBINSON CARTER was born on 20 December 1896 in Barnsley; his Baptism was on 20 December 1897 at St George's Church in Barnsley. He went to Barnsley Elementary School for four years until the age of 12. Joseph attended the Holgate Grammar School in Church Street then Shaw Lane, Barnsley, for three years, from 1909 to 1912. He was a Junior Locke Scholar for three years and left to become a Draper's Assistant – he was an apprentice at Messrs James Massie and Sons, Drapers, in Church Street, Barnsley.

Joseph was a chorister in the St George's Church choir with both brothers, Henry and Matthew.

Joseph enlisted at Barnsley as a Private (Service Numbers: 6330 and 202976) in the 1/5th Battalion of the West Yorkshire Regiment (Prince of Wales' Own), which became part of the 49th (West Riding) Division. The Division participated in the Battle of the Somme and had been involved at Flers-Courcellette from 15 to 22 September 1916, when High Wood and Delville Wood were cleared – tanks were used for the first time here and the Canadian Corps joined the Somme fighting here. Joseph was reported as missing before being confirmed as killed in action on 28 September 1916, aged 19; he was buried in Connaught Cemetery, Thiepval, Somme, France (grave I D 19).

Joseph was one of the youngest of the Old Boys to die in the First World War – there were nine young men aged only 19 years of age.

Joseph was awarded two medals: Victory and British War, and his parents should have received the 'Dead Man's Penny' plaque and scroll from King George V.

Joseph's name is on the Holgate Grammar School Memorial; Barnsley Pace Street Swimming Club had a J Carter listed on its Memorial according to an article in *Barnsley Chronicle.*

***Barnsley Chronicle* – 4 November 1916**

PRIVATE J R CARTER OF BARNSLEY
TRADESMAN'S SON MISSING

We regret to hear that Pte J R Carter, York & Lancaster Regiment attached to the 14th West Yorkshire Regiment, No. 6330, is posted as missing. He is a son of Mr Matthew Carter, wine and spirit merchant, Market Hill, and any information concerning the missing soldier will be gladly welcomed at this address or at 109 Dodworth Road, Barnsley.

***Barnsley Independent* – 11 November 1916**

POSTED AS MISSING
BARNSLEY TRADESMAN'S ANXIETY
PRIVATE J R CARTER

Private Joseph Robinson Carter, West Yorkshire Regiment, son of Mr Matthew Carter, wine and spirit merchant, Market Hill, Barnsley, and of Dodworth Road, is posted as missing, and, up to the time of writing, no further tidings are forthcoming regarding him. Naturally, the intimation came as painful news to his parents who have already lost their eldest son in the war and the utmost sympathy is felt for them in their anxiety and suspense. In the absence of anything to the contrary, the hope that better news will come along, and they are making all possible enquiries with that end in view. It is quite probable that he may be a prisoner of war and, needless to say, any information concerning him would be most gratefully received.

Twenty years of age next month, the missing soldier joined the Forces early this year, previous to which he was an apprentice at Messrs James Massie and Sons, drapers, Church Street, with whom he had been about three years. He was an old St Mary's and Barnsley Grammar School boy and a winner of the Locke Scholarship. He was a member of the St George's choir for several years, his deceased soldier brother and a third brother all being choristers together. He is posted as missing from September 26th.

The main photograph of Joseph is from Barnsley Chronicle, *used by their kind permission.*

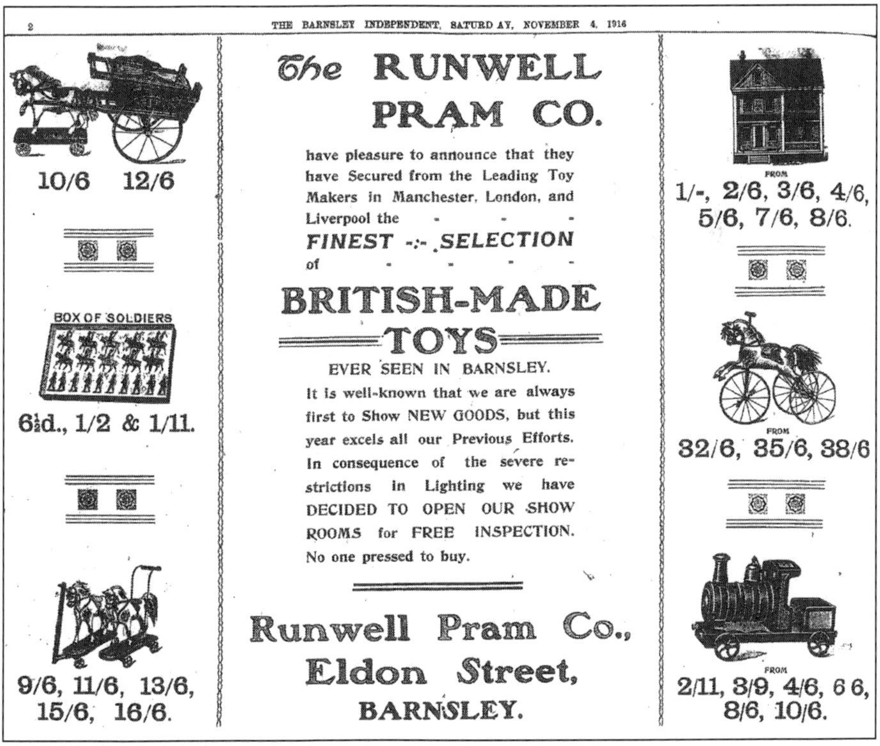

17

William Henry Choyce

William Henry Choyce
1880–1917 (aged 36)

WILLIAM HENRY CHOYCE was born in 1880 in Worsbrough Dale to **Thomas William Choyce** (born c1851 in Northamptonshire) and **Elizabeth nee Booker** (born c1853 in Minsthorpe). His Baptism was on 16 May 1880 at Worsbrough Church. Thomas was a Gardener (Domestic) having previously been a Coachman.

William was the oldest of five children, with three surviving sisters: **Sarah Lily, Edith Mary** and **Lucy Kathleen. Alethea Priscilla** had died in infancy in 1892.

In April 1911, the Choyce family lived in five rooms at 38 Western Street, Barnsley, where they had been for at least 20 years since moving from Worsbrough – their three oldest children had left home.

William – Groom (Domestic) aged 30 – was living in four rooms at 9 King Street, Salford, with his sister **Edith Mary** (26), her husband **Joseph William Sofe** (29) Police Constable, and their son **Clifford Harry Sofe** (2). Edith and Joseph had married on 10 October 1907 in St Mary's Church, Barnsley.

Sarah Lily (28) Milliner own account, was living in four rooms at 2 Plumber Street, Barnsley, with her husband **Ernest Harold Cooper** (27) Body Maker Coach Building. Sarah and Ernest had married on 16 February 1909 at St Mary's Church, Barnsley; they had a son **Donald Cooper** in summer 1916 in Barnsley.

William went to St Mary's Elementary School, Barnsley, until the age of 12. He then attended the Holgate Grammar School in Church Street, Barnsley, for three years, from 1892 to 1895; he had been a Keresforth Scholar.

William married **Florence Smith** in spring 1916 in Salford. He was a Driver for the *Manchester Evening News* and they lived at 19 Vincent Street, Higher Broughton. Florrie subsequently moved to 46 Mosley Street, Manchester.

William enlisted in Manchester early in the war and was a Private (Service Number: DM2/165797) in the 740th Mechanical Transport Company of the Royal Army Service Corps. He died of 'accidental injuries' (no details found) in the Balkans Theatre of War on 22 January 1917, aged 36, and was buried in Lahana Military Cemetery, Lachanas village, 56 kilometres north east of Thessaloniki in Greece (grave III A 1). His widow had the words LET PERPETUAL LIGHT SHINE UPON HIM – HIS DEVOTED WIFE FLORRIE added to his War Grave headstone.

William was the only Old Boy to serve and die in The Balkans Theatre of War. The Balkans comprised Greece, Serbia, Bulgaria, Macedonia and Bosnia and was strategically important being located between four seas: Black, Mediterranean, Asiatic and Aegean. There had been instability and conflict in the Balkans prior to the outbreak of the First World War and the assassination of Archduke Franz Ferdinand in Sarajevo in June 1914 was a catalyst for it.

William was awarded two medals: Victory and British War, and his widow should have received the 'Dead Man's Penny' plaque and scroll from King George V.

William's name is on the Holgate Grammar School Memorial, the painted column in St Mary's Church, Barnsley, and the Manchester Evening News Memorial. (The MEN plaque, dedicated to 161 workers who sacrificed their lives in the First World War, was restored and rededicated in November 2012).

***Barnsley Chronicle* – 17 February 1917**

ACCIDENTALLY KILLED
FATE OF FORMER BARNSLEY MAN

William H Choyce, whose death was announced in our last week's obituary column, was a Barnsley man, being the son of Mr and Mrs Choyce, of Hope Street. Thirty Six years of age, he joined the transport section of the ASC not long after war broke out and the sad feature of his demise is that it was caused accidentally while in the Army. At the time of his enlistment the deceased soldier was an employee of the proprietors of the *Manchester Evening News* and resided with his wife and family in Vincent Street, Higher Broughton, Manchester. (*No earlier listing found).*

***Manchester Evening News* – 1 February 1917**

FALLEN FIGHTERS

Private W H CHOYCE, Transport Section ASC, has been accidentally killed on active service. He lived at 19 Vincent Street, Higher Broughton, and was formerly employed as a driver by the 'Manchester Evening News'.

DISTRICT HEROES.

Top: Pte. W. H. CHOYCE (Barnsley, accidentally killed); Able Seaman D. MITCHELL (Barnsley, killed in action).

Photograph of feature in *Barnsley Chronicle*, used by their kind permission.

The main photograph of William is from Barnsley Chronicle, *used by their kind permission.*

18

James Burford Clarke

James Burford Clarke
1894–1918 (aged 24)

JAMES BURFORD CLARKE was born on 11 July 1894 in Bedford to **James Clarke** (born c1867 in St Albans, Hertfordshire) and **Alice Sophia M nee Foskett** (born 1870 in Dartford, Kent). James senior was a Builder 'on his own account', having moved to the Barnsley area from St Albans with his parents by 1881; he had previously been a Coal Pit Labourer in Worsbrough, aged 14, then a Bricklayer in Ardsley, aged 24.

James Burford's grandparents were **Michael Clarke**, a Bricklayer then Colliery Labourer, born in County Mayo, Ireland, and **Sarah Clarke**, born in St Albans.

James Burford was the second oldest of fivechildren, with three surviving sisters: **Alice** – Teacher, **Gladys** and **Stella**. Another child had died before April 1911 (name unknown).

In April 1911, the Clarke family lived in five rooms in Blackburn Lane, Barnsley. James' parents subsequently moved to 36 Southwell Street then 'Redwoods', Cockerham Lane, Barnsley.

Stella Clarke got married to **Thomas Snow** in Spring 1928 in Barnsley and they had a daughter **Stella T Snow** late 1932.

James went to Barnsley Higher Elementary School until the age of 12. He then attended the Holgate Grammar School in Church Street, Barnsley, for two years, from 1908 to 1910. 'He left to assist his father'.

James was one of the early committee members of the Old Boys Association, who produced the *Alumnus* magazine from April 1913.

James enlisted as a Private (Service Number: 24638) in the 10th Battalion of the Royal Regiment of Fusiliers. On 28 August 1918, he was given a Commission as Second Lieutenant in the 4th Battalion of the South Lancashire Regiment (Prince of Wales' Volunteers) attached to the 12th Battalion Somerset Light Infantry. They formed part of the 74th (Yeomanry) Division, who transferred from Palestine to France, arriving in Marseille on 7 May 1918. After travelling to the Western Front, the Battalions underwent training, including for gas defence. The Second Battle of Bapaume took place on the Somme from 31 August to 3 September 1918 and it was part of the 'Allies' 100 Days Offensive', the turning point of the war with the advance helped by air support and tanks.

James was killed in action on 2 September 1918, aged 24, and his death was reported in the Daily Casualty List in *The Times* on 20 September. He was buried in the Peronne Communal Cemetery Extension, Somme, France (grave III K 32), having been reburied from the original location. His father had the words OUR ONLY SON added to the War Grave headstone.

James was awarded two medals: Victory and British War, and his parents should have received the 'Dead Man's Penny' plaque and scroll from King George V.

James' name is on the Holgate Grammar School Memorial and on the painted column in St Mary's Church, Barnsley.

Alumnus – December 1918

Second Lieutenant J B Clarke Somerset Light Infantry (1908–10) was killed in August 1918. He joined the Egypt Expeditionary Force in January last and fought in Palestine. In July his battalion was sent to France where he fell in action.

An extract from one of James Burford Clarke's letters to the Editor was published in *Alumnus*:

The country in which our troops are fighting varies greatly, most of it being desert land. The natives travel about and dress just as they are supposed to have done 2,000 years ago. Shops are almost non-existent, and Bedouins generally live in caves and the Jews in stone hovels, which, whilst very picturesque looking with their arched windows and domed roofs, do not appeal to the Europeans, particularly the interiors. Mules, oxen and poultry all take their place with the occupants within. The willing natives, who are generally women, are found assisting our engineers in the construction of much needed roads. If only this country were developed like France, progress would be much more rapid, but you cannot rely on obtaining billets, food or transport, so that the army has to be self-supporting and make its own advances. Mules and camels are the chief means of transport as is shown by the numerous dead bodies of these beasts of burden on the steep hills in Palestine.

19

George Percival Cowburn

George Percival Cowburn
1890–1918 (aged 27)

GEORGE PERCIVAL COWBURN was born on 16 September 1890 at Littleworth in Gloucestershire, to **Charles Chapman Cowburn** (born c1865 in Chapeltown, Leeds) and **Clara nee Robinson** (born c1861 in Halifax). Charles was an Assistant Clerk, Local Taxation Licences, for the County Council, having previously been a Schoolmaster.

George was an only child.

The Cowburn family moved from Stroud, Gloucestershire, to Flanshaw Road in Wakefield by 1901, when Charles was a Schoolmaster. In April 1911, they lived in five rooms at 22 Silcoates Street, Wakefield, and Charles was working as a Clerk. Charles and Clara Cowburn subsequently moved to 93a Northgate, Wakefield, then 4 Green Lane, Holmfield, Halifax.

George went to West Bretton National School until the age of 12. He then attended the Holgate Grammar School in Church Street, Barnsley, for three years, from 1903 to 1906, and passed the Oxford Local Junior exam. George became a Clerk in the Accountants' Office at Wakefield City Council, where in 1914 he passed the Intermediate exam of the Society of Incorporated Accountants and Auditors, but no records survive to confirm this.*

George enlisted in Wakefield on 5 October 1914, aged 24 years and 19 days, as a Private (Service Number: 663) in the 10th Battalion (Grimsby Battalion) of the Lincolnshire Regiment. He was a Clerk born in Amberley, Stroud, according to the Attestation form. George was promoted Lance Corporal, Corporal, Lance Sergeant then Regimental Quarter-Master Sergeant within a short period of time. He reverted to Lance Sergeant for about nine months before becoming a Warrant Officer Class II (RQMS) on 28 June 1917.

George went out to France on 9 January 1916 and died in a Casualty Clearing Station of severe wounds received from a bomb the previous day on 29 January 1918, aged 27. He had served for three years and 117 days, with more than two years at the Western Front. He was buried in Achiet-le-Grand Communal Cemetery Extension, Pas de Calais, France (grave II E 16). His father had the words GRANT HIM HEAVENLY REST O LORD, LET LIGHT ETERNAL SHINE UPON HIM added to the War Grave headstone.

The Medical Form contains personal information about George: Height: 6'¾", Weight: 164 lbs, Chest: 39", Physical Development Good, Vision in both eyes 6/6, Complexion Sallow, Eyes Blue, Hair Light Brown.

George was awarded two medals: Victory and British War, and his parents received the 'Dead Man's Penny' plaque and scroll from King George V.

* Rosie Hall at Wakefield Archives searched for records about George but, unfortunately, none survive for his employment at the City Council.
Ben Brewster, ICAEW Library & Information Service, checked the records of The Institute of Chartered Accountants, but he was unable to verify details of George's professional qualification. They do not hold records of Articled Clerks and George only passed his Intermediate exams.

The following personal items were returned to George's parents: letters, photographs, pocket book, watch, cards, stamps value 9d registered receipt, silver cigarette case, knife, scissors, badge, buttons, two crowns, gold ring.

Probate was granted for George at Wakefield on 27 July 1918 to his father Charles Cowburn, County Council Clerk. Effects: £263 15s 9d.

George's name is on the Holgate Grammar School Memorial and the Wakefield Family History Society website's City of Wakefield Roll of Honour.

George has not been recognized on any War Memorials or Rolls of Honour for Wakefield City Council or the Institute of Chartered Accountants.

Photograph of *Wakefield Express* article in the Holgate Ephemera, reproduced by kind permission of Barnsley Archives.

Connection

George (who won a cricket bat prize for bowling) played for the The First Eleven Cricket Team, which included **Cyril Burton Dixon** (who won a cricket bat prize for batting), **Duncan Fairley** plus **Harold Willott** and his brother **Ernest Spencer Willott**. **Ernest Litherland** (who won a cricket bat prize for bowling) was Captain of the Second Eleven Cricket Team, which also comprised: **Edward Batley, George Braham** and (probably) **Herbert Harry Jagger Mason**.

George served in the 10th Battalion of the Lincolnshire Regiment along with **Henry Carter**.

Alumnus – April 1918

G P Cowburn (1903–06) RQMS, Lincolnshire Regt, died of wounds on Jan 29th. He was the only son of Mr and Mrs C Cowburn, 93a Northgate, Wakefield.

Newspaper Cutting (Holgate Ephemera) – February 1918

[*section missing*] Dr B M Chaplin, superintendent of Zion Sunday School, writes in a sympathetic and commisoratory way: 'I can imagine what this must mean to you as all who came in contact with him in the school were very fond of him; he had such a bright and happy disposition'.

Regimental QMS Cowburn, who was 27 years of age, was educated at the Wakefield [*crossed out and Barnsley added*] Grammar School where he passed the Oxford Local Examination. On coming to Wakefield he joined the staff of the City Accountant meanwhile continuing his studies and his work gave great promise of a bright and successful future. In 1913 he passed the Interim Examination of the Incorporated Society of Accountants and Auditors and when war broke out was preparing for the final examination of that Institution.

He joined the Lincolnshire Regiment as a private in October 1914 and soon received promotion, becoming sergeant in July 1915. He went to France early in January 1916 with his Battalion and was made Regimental Quarter-Master Sergeant about twelve months ago. He was a great favourite with all ranks and his death is a severe blow to the Battalion.

In a kind and sympathetic letter, the officer commanding the Battalion writes: 'It is with the deepest regret that I have to inform you that your son Quarter-master Sergeant Cowburn has been killed. He was severely wounded on the evening of the 28th and he died in hospital the following day. Both for myself and on behalf of the Battalion, I wish to convey my deepest sympathy in your great loss. Since your son became Quarter-master Sergeant just a year ago he has performed his duties with the most marked ability, often under very difficult and dangerous circumstances. His death will be greatly felt by all ranks in the Battalion'.

The Wakefield Express – 9 February 1918 (Holgate Ephemera)

WAKEFIELD AND DISTRICT WAR ITEMS (PHOTO)
WAKEFIELD REGIMENTAL QUARTER-MASTER
SERGEANT'S DEATH. WOUNDED BY A BOMB,
PERFORMED HIS DUTIES WITH MARKED ABILITY.
A PROMISING CIVIL CAREER CUT SHORT

Another promising citizen in the person of Regimental Quarter-master Sergeant George Percival Cowburn, only son of Mr and Mrs Charles Cowburn 93a Northgate, Wakefield, has paid the supreme sacrifice. He died in a Casualty Clearing Station in France on January 29th from wounds caused by a bomb the previous evening. It came as a great shock to his parents and many friends to hear of his untimely end, which was foreshadowed in a telegram stating that he was dangerously ill from wounds, followed later by a wire announcing his death and a letter from the Matron of the Casualty Clearing Station, where he died.

The Matron, writing to Mr Cowburn on the 29th ult. stated: 'It is my sad duty to write you the news of your dear son's death. He was brought in here last night very badly wounded by a bomb. From the first there was very little hope of his recovery. He died at mid day. It may be of some comfort to know that he had every care & attention and everything was done for his comfort. I feel for you very much in your sad loss. He will be buried in a burial ground near here'.

... [letter from Battalion CO]

In a sympathetic and appreciative letter, his Lieutenant Quarter-master writes that RQMS Cowburn was a very brave man and his death will be keenly felt in the Regiment as he was always so thorough in the performance of his duties and spared no effort to make everybody comfortable.

The Chaplain, who officiated at the graveside, in the course of a very kind letter, says: 'I buried your son today in a quiet little cemetery not far from the hospital. A good number of men were present at the ceremony and the *Last Post* was played by a buglar'.

Letters of sympathy and condolence have also come to hand from his late comrades and staff, sharing the esteem in which he was held in his Battalion and expressing the loss sustained by his death.

The Town Clerk (Mr A C Allibone) writes: 'I am sure every member of the Council will receive the news with unfeigned regret for, although your son died a hero's death for his country, he was that type of man whose loss is irreparable owing to his sterling character, his great ability and his amiable qualities. His character and service both as a private citizen and as a soldier have been of such outstanding excellence as, even in the midst of your sorrow, may well be a matter of pride, and I hope this will prove to be of no small solace to you'.

The main photograph of George is from Alumnus, *reproduced by kind permission of Barnsley Archives.*

20

Cyril Burton Dixon

Cyril Burton Dixon
1890–1918 (aged 28)

CYRIL BURTON DIXON was born on 24 April 1890 in Kexbrough to **Willie Dixon** (born c1863 in Kexbrough) and **Amelia Ann nee Burton** (born c1865 in Clayton West). Cyril's Baptism was on 13 July 1890 at Darton All Saints Church; his parents had married on 14 August 1888 in High Hoyland Parish Church, Amelia being a Farmer's daughter. Willie was an Architect and Surveyor (Licentiate RIBA) Employer, in partnership with his older brother Robert.

William Dixon (born c1829 in Kexbrough) Farmer, and Hannah had five children living with them at Cudworth Fold House in Kexbrough on the 1871 Census; Robert (19) was an Architect and the others were Scholars: Ann Elizabeth (15), George (12), Mary (10) and Willie (8). Both daughters died in their 20s.

Robert Dixon (c1852–1926, aged 74) married **Ann Paley Walker**, a Farmer's daughter, at Silkstone Parish Church in 1879 and they had seven children. On the 1911 Census, they were living in 10 rooms at 171 Park Grove Barnsley, where they remained until Robert died; one of their children had died and four were living at home: Alice Mary (29), William Herbert (25) Architectural Assistant, Emily (24) Domestic Science Teacher, Ethel Milnes (23) Architectural Student, and Robert Stanley (19), who also became an Architect. Robert Dixon was Architect for the alterations to the Holgate school premises and Headmaster's house in 1888 and his firm was involved in the conversion of the old Grammar School building into the Cooper Art Gallery in 1914.

Cyril had a younger sister **Mary Aline**, whose Baptism was on 26 July 1894 at Darton All Saints Church. **Mary Dixon** married **Robert Allatt Heptonstall** at Darton All Saints Church in 1922; they had a son **Cyril P Heptonstall**, born summer 1924 in Goole.

By April 1911, the family had lived in eight rooms at Jacob's Hall, Kexbrough, for at least 20 years. Mary Aline, aged 16, was staying with her uncle Robert Dixon, Architect and Surveyor, and his family.

Cyril went to Kexbrough National School until the age of 10. He then attended the Holgate Grammar School in Church Street, Barnsley, for six years, from 1901 to 1907. Cyril became an Architect and Surveyor in his father's and uncle's firm. (Messrs R & W Dixon contributed to the Barnsley Patriotic Fund).

Cyril enlisted in September 1914, aged 24, as a Private in the 13th Battalion (First Barnsley Pals) of the York and Lancaster Regiment. He was appointed as Temporary Second Lieutenant as listed in *Barnsley Chronicle* on 10 October 1914; he was promoted to Lieutenant on 1 February 1915 then Captain on 27 September 1918. Cyril went out to Egypt in December 1915 before being sent to France, where he was wounded several times. Some time after the Battle of the Somme on 1 July 1916, Cyril joined the 10th then 2nd Battalions before transferring to 2/4th Battalion of the York and Lancaster Regiment.

Cyril was shot in the chest on 4 November 1918 at Maubeuge and died of wounds in hospital on 14 November 1918, aged 28 (just three days after the war ended); he was buried in Awoingt British Cemetery, Nord, France (grave III D 25). His

Photograph from Jon Cooksey's *Barnsley Pals*, reproduced by kind permission of the author and Pen and Sword Publishers.

father had the words A NOBLE LIFE SACRIFICED FOR OTHERS added to the War Grave headstone.

Cyril served for about four years with three years overseas, one of the two Old Boys to have served longest.

Cyril was awarded two medals: Victory and British War. Although his father applied for the 1914–15 Star for Cyril, the word 'ineligible' was written on his Medal Card. His parents should have received the 'Dead Man's Penny' plaque and scroll from King George V.

Cyril was posthumously awarded the Military Cross for gallant and distinguished service in the field, the official record stating: 'On 27 Sept. 1918, in front of Ribecourt [south-west of Cambrai], he advanced his platoon under intense fire through the village, passing through troops who had been held up. He beat off a determined attack by the enemy, and captured 35 prisoners. On 28 Sept, after his Company Commander had been wounded, he reorganized his company under heavy shell fire, and held his position against another enemy counter-attack. He showed fine courage and leadership' (*London Gazette*, 18 Feb. 1919).

Cyril Burton Dixon.

Photograph reproduced from De Ruvigny's *Roll of Honour 1914–1918*.

Probate was granted for Cyril at Wakefield on 16 May 1919 to his father Willie Dixon, Architect. Effects: £360 0s 3d.

Cyril's name is on the Holgate Grammar School Memorial. He was listed on Darton Working Men's Club Memorial according to an article in *Barnsley Chronicle*. The War Memorial in Darton All Saints Churchyard does not have names listed.

Cyril's grandparents Willie and Hannah Dixon were buried in Darton All Saints Churchyard and have a headstone showing their details and those of their two daughters who died young.

Inside All Saints Church, Darton, are special Memorials to Cyril Burton Dixon: there is an ornate white marble plaque and a stained glass window with three panels showing King Solomon, Saint Wilfrid of York, Archbishop, and Saint Alban. (My photographs of this window and the plaque are in the Colour Section).

The plaque has the crest of the 13th Service Battalion of the York and Lancaster Regiment on top.

TO THE GLORY OF GOD AND IN LOVING MEMORY OF
CAPTAIN CYRIL BURTON DIXON MC Y&L REG'T,
BELOVED AND ONLY SON OF WILLIE AND AMELIA ANN
DIXON OF KEXBROUGH, WHO DIED NOVEMBER 14TH 1918,
FROM WOUNDS RECEIVED IN ACTION NOVEMBER 4TH 1918
AGED 28 YEARS.
AND WAS INTERRED IN AWOINGT BRITISH CEMETERY, FRANCE.
HE DIED THE NOBLEST DEATH A MAN MAY DIE
FIGHTING FOR GOD AND RIGHT AND LIBERTY
AND SUCH A DEATH IS – IMMORTALITY.

Small panels underneath the main figures in the stained glass window have dedications to Cyril and his father:

To the Glory of God and in loving memory of
Cyril Burton Dixon MC of Kexborough
Capt York and Lancaster Regiment
Died Nov 14 1918 May he rest in Peace

To the Glory of God and in loving memory of Willie Dixon of Kexborough
Died June 21 1923 [aged 60] May he rest in Peace

Connections

Cyril was Baptised on the same day as **Ernest William Litherland** at Darton All Saints Church.

Cyril (who won a cricket bat prize for batting) played for the The First Eleven Cricket Team, which included **George Percival Cowburn** (who won a cricket bat prize for bowling), **Duncan Fairley** plus **Harold Willott** and his brother **Ernest Spencer Willott. Ernest Litherland** (who won a cricket bat prize for bowling) was Captain of the Second Eleven Cricket Team, which also comprised: **Edward Batley, George Braham** and (probably) **Herbert Harry Jagger Mason.**

Cyril served with the 13th Battalion (First Barnsley Pals) along with **Jack Normansell**, Temp Second Lieut October 1914.

***Barnsley Chronicle* – 8 May 1915**

PATRIOTIC PARS
OFFICERS FOOTBALL MATCH

This article explained how teams were selected from the Commissioned Officers in the First and Second Barnsley Pals to play at Oakwell – the First won 1–0 (Lieutenant Dixon was captain). Second Lieutenant Quest was captain of the Second, which included Second Lieutenant Fitton.

***Barnsley Chronicle* – 20 April 1918**

THE TOLL OF WAR
A KEXBRO' OFFICER WOUNDED

Lieutenant Cyril Burton Dixon has been admitted into hospital in France suffering from a gun shot wound in the chest. He is the only son of Mr and Mrs W Dixon of Kexbro'. He received his commission in September 1914, and has also seen service in Egypt, he having been previously wounded in France. Lt C B Dixon was previous to the war an architect with the firm of Messrs R and W Dixon, Barnsley.

(The same article appeared in the *Barnsley Independent* – 13 April 1918 and the *Yorkshire Post* & *Leeds Intelligencer* – 16 April 1918)

***Barnsley Chronicle* – 16 November 1918**

LOCAL OFFICERS WOUNDED

Captain Cyril Burton Dixon, York and Lancaster Regiment, was dangerously wounded in the chest whilst leading his Company on November 4th. He is the only son of Mr and Mrs W Dixon of Kexbrough and is in hospital in France. Captain Dixon has held a commission since September 1914 and seen much fighting, being promoted Captain on the field. His Commanding Officer writes:

'Since your son has been with this Battalion he has commanded his Company with the greatest ability and his gallantry in action has gained the admiration of his men and brother officers'.

Alumnus – December 1918

Captain C B Dixon, Y & L Regiment (1901–07) … died from wounds November 14th 1918. The deceased officer who was an architect in civil life, received his commission in September 1914. He had seen service in Egypt, much fighting in France and had been wounded three times. The Military Cross had been awarded him for his action in repulsing an enemy counter-attack.

Alumnus – April 1919

The death of Captain C B Dixon, Military Cross, was announced in our December issue. His Commanding Officer Lieut-Col Hart writes thus of him: 'He was an exceptionally good fellow and a very efficient officer and was beloved by his men. He was a special favourite of mine and I promoted him to command "A" Company as I was certain he would do it very well; and very ably he carried out his duties and thoroughly justified and enhanced my already good opinion of him'.

Barnsley Chronicle – 23 November 1918

KEXBOROUGH OFFICER'S DEATH CAPTAIN C B DIXON

We deeply regret to announce the fact that Captain Cyril Burton Dixon, York and Lancaster Regiment, died from wounds on the 14th inst at a Casualty Clearing Station in France. The deceased officer was leading his Company in a most successful attack when he was mortally wounded. His Battalion was attached to the 62nd Division so often recently mentioned in despatches.

Captain Dixon … was then attached to the 13th Barnsley Battalion. He had seen service in Egypt and much fighting in France, having been twice wounded. His Commanding Officer writes that he had won the affection of all his brother officers and men by his gallantry and ability in leading his Company in action. He was a fine sport and an excellent cricketer and, just before going again to the font last September, he did some fine batting on the Kent County grounds against whom were some of the County players. The news of his death on Saturday afternoon caused widespread sorrow in his native village and the surroundings of Darton, where he was so well-known and respected for his cheery disposition.

Barnsley Chronicle – 30 November 1918

KEXBOROUGH OFFICER'S POSTHUMOUS HONOUR C B DIXON

Splendid tributes are paid to the sterling military abilities of the late Captain Cyril B Dixon of Kexborough in a letter just received by his esteemed father from Lieutenant-Colonel H P Hart, Commanding 2/4th York and Lancaster Regiment, and the information is conveyed that the gallant Captain has been awarded the Military Cross. After expressing his own personal sorrow, as well as the sympathy of the officers of the Battalion, in the loss of Captain Dixon, Lt-Col Hart proceeds: 'He was an exceptionally good fellow and a very efficient officer and was beloved by his men. His conduct in the field has been very gallant and he has just been awarded the Military Cross for his action on September 27th in front of Ribcourt in repulsing an enemy counter attack. He was of a particularly charming disposition, very popular with everyone, and we shall miss him very greatly. He was a special favourite of mine and I promoted him to command "A" Company as I was certain he would do it very well; and very ably he carried out his duties and thoroughly justified and enhanced my already good opinion of him. All the Battalion mourn with you on your great grief, it seems so particularly sad just when the war is over. Again I express my deepest and sincerest sympathy in your great loss and bereavement'.

De Ruvigny's Roll of Honour 1914–1918

DIXON CYRIL BURTON

... born 24 April, 1890; educ. Barnsley Grammar School ; was an Architect and Surveyor ; volunteered for active service on the outbreak of war, being gazetted 2nd Lieut. 13th York and Lancaster Regt. 19 Sept. 1914 ; promoted Lieut. 1 Feb. 1915, and Capt. 27 Sept. 1918; served in Egypt from Dec. 1915, and with the Expeditionary Force in France and Flanders from March, 1916, where he saw much fighting ; was twice wounded ; became attached to the 2/4th Battn. of his regiment in Sept. 1918, after having served with the 10th and 2nd Battns., and died at Awoingt 14 Nov. 1918, of wounds received in action at Maubeuge on the 4th. Buried in Awoingt British Military Cemetery, south-east of Cambrai. ... unmarried.

The main photograph of Cyril is from Alumnus, *reproduced by kind permission of Barnsley Archives.*

21

Edwin Mossforth Doughty

Edwin Mossforth Doughty
1895–1917 (aged 21)

EDWIN MOSSFORTH DOUGHTY was born on 27 April 1895 in Barnsley to **Job Doughty** (born c1847 in Nottinghamshire) and **Lucy Ellen Fletcher nee Neatby** (born c1864 in Barnsley). Job, who was a Machine Pattern Maker, aged 24, became a Minister 'with no denomination' (Plymouth Brethren) by the age of 34.

Edwin was the oldest of seven surviving children: **Andrew Fletcher** (attended the Holgate and served in the First World War), **Joseph Neatby** (attended the Holgate and served in the First World War), **Sarah Margaret, Eleanor Shaw, Madeline May** and **Samuel Clifford**. A child had died by April 1911 (name unknown).

None of Edwin's sisters married. Samuel Clifford (born 1907) emigrated; a Ship's Passenger List for the SS *Kano Maru* from Japan to London arriving on 26 April 1930 had his permanent address as Singapore, where he was a Civil Engineer; there is a US Naturalization Record dated 19 October 1935 for California.

In April 1911, the Doughty family lived in 14 rooms at The Hawthorns, Keresforth Hall Road, Barnsley, where they had four Domestic Servants. Lucy's widowed mother was living with them (Eliza Neatby nee Shaw). This house was originally the home for over 20 years of Lucy's parents: Joseph Neatby – a Timber and Slate Merchant – and Eliza. Job Doughty had moved from his parents' home in Sheffield to Barnsley by 1881 and he was a Visitor at The Hawthorns between then and 1891; he and Lucy got married in 1893. Job and Lucy moved to 33 Clarkehouse Road in Sheffield by 1915.

Edwin went to a Private School until the age of 10. He then attended the Holgate Grammar School in Church Street, Barnsley, for six years, from 1905 to 1911, before the family moved to Sheffield, where he continued his education at Central Secondary School (this boys' school was replaced by a new building renamed High Storrs Secondary School in 1933).

Edwin went on to Sheffield University, where he matriculated in June 1914, but there is no record of what he studied or any photograph of him.*

Edwin was called up and enlisted at London Whitehall on 20 November 1916, aged 21 years and seven months; he was a 'Processman TWD', which means that he was a chemical worker in the chemical industry, living at 24 Birch Street, London, according to the Attestation form. Edwin was a Pioneer (Service Number: 209630) in 'M' Company No. 3 Special Railway Battalion of the Royal Engineers; he had been a Chemist at the Royal Engineers Depot before going to France, awarded 1/8 per day. As Edwin's two brothers indicated a preference for serving in non-combatant roles, one specifying that he was Plymouth Brethren, it seems likely that Edwin chose to serve in the Royal Engineers rather than fighting in the Army. The railway was the main way of moving men, munitions and supplies to and around the Western Front; the work of the special battalions was invaluable if largely unrecognised and the men were at risk of injury and death when close to the front line.

* Matthew Zawadzki, Records Manager at Sheffield University, kindly checked their records and confirmed the date Edwin started at the University.

Edwin died of wounds received in service on 1 March 1917, aged 21, having served for 102 days, of which 50 were in France; his name was on the Daily Casualty List in *The Times* on 7 April 1917. Edwin was buried in Ecoivres Military Cemetery, Mont-St Eloi, Pas de Calais, France (grave IV E 6).

The Medical Form contains a limited readable personal description of Edwin: Height: 5' 7¼", Chest: 36".

The following items of Edwin's private property were signed for by his father on 13 June 1917: Disc, Wallet, Letters, Photos, Cards, Bible, Cigarette case, Holder, Pouch, Watch & chain, Penknife, Scissors, Hymn Book, Pipe, Diary, Note book, Book, Note case, Pencil, Registration card.

Edwin was awarded two medals: Victory and British War, and his parents should have received the 'Dead Man's Penny' plaque and scroll from King George V. His father, Job Doughty, died in 1922.

Edwin's name is on the Holgate Grammar School Memorial, Sheffield Council Official Roll of Honour, The University of Sheffield Roll of Honour, Central School Leopold Street Roll of Honour now in High Storrs School Library and listed on the Sheffield Soldiers of The Great War website.

***Alumnus* – December 1917**

> E M Doughty (1905–11) whose home was in Sheffield, was educated at this school and Sheffield University. He enlisted shortly after the out-break of war and was killed in action in June 1917.

ANDREW FLETCHER DOUGHTY (born on 2 July 1897 in Barnsley) went to private school until the age of 8, when he attended the Holgate for six years, from 1905 to 1911. This was the same period as his older brother Edwin as they left when the family moved to Sheffield. Andrew was a Locke Scholar for three years and became a pupil at Central Secondary School in Sheffield.

Andrew was called up on 10 May 1916, aged 18 years and 10 months, when he was a Student (Civil Service) living at 33 Clarkehouse Road, Sheffield. The Attestation Form dated 8 July 1916 at Pontefract, is stamped: 'No. 3 Northern Company Non Combatant Corps' (NCC*). He was a Private (Service Number: 1954). The Medical Form gives some personal details: Height: 5' 6¼", Chest: 36 ¼", 'small scar on left buttock'. There is no other information about his service.

Andrew got married in Autumn 1927 in West Derby to **Muriel Barker** or **Muriel Meyer**; two children are listed for each mother's surname on FreeBMD.

When his mother died in 1948, Probate was granted to Andrew, Schoolmaster, and **Henry Edward Cox,** Doctor of Science. Effects: £8 894 7s 6d. He died in Warrington aged 77.

JOSEPH NEATBY DOUGHTY (born on 14 May 1900 in Barnsley) went to private school until the age of 10, when he attended the Holgate for one year from 1910. He left in 1911 when the family moved to Sheffield and he went to Central Secondary School in Sheffield.

Joseph was called up in 1918 ; he was examined on 9 May 1918, just before his 18th birthday, and joined on 24 July 1918 at Sheffield, when he was posted as Private (Service Number: 106561) in the 5th (Reserve) Battalion of the Durham Light Infantry. He was a Student living at home and his religion was Plymouth Brethren. The recommendation was that Joseph should be in a non combatant role but a letter dated 23 August from the Posting Officer stated that this was not possible without a 'Certificate of Exemption from Combatant Service'.* The Medical Form provides a physical description: Height: 5' 8½", Weight: 138 lbs, Chest: 31–34½", Physical Development Good, Vision in both eyes 6/6, recent injury to left thumb and assessed as Grade A4. Joseph's hair was brown and eyes hazel.

Joseph married **Bertha Bound** in Eccleshall Bierlow in Autumn 1926; they had three children in the Sheffield area: **Ralph T M Doughty** in Autumn 1927, **Basil T L Doughty** in summer 1930 and **Barbara M Doughty** early 1932. Joseph died in Portsmouth aged 84.

Members of the Plymouth Brethren Christian Church served in the First World War but wanted to be recognised as non–combatants as distinct from conscientious objectors. They experienced disapproval for refusing to carry arms, but they demonstrated great courage in going unarmed to rescue the wounded.

* NON COMBATANT CORPS AND PLYMOUTH BRETHREN After the passing of the Military Service Act in early 1916 it was decided to form a Non-Combatant Corps (NCC) of conscientious objectors for work on roads, hutments, timber work, quarrying, sanitary duties and handling supplies. Eight NCC Companies existed by the middle of June 1916.

22

John Middleton Downend

John Middleton Downend
1888–1917 (aged 29)

JOHN MIDDLETON DOWNEND was born on 30 September 1888 in Wombwell to **Thomas Downend** (born c1850 in Worsbrough, Baptism on 7 April 1850 at Worsbrough St Mary's Church) and **Sarah Ann nee Ducker** (born in 1850 in Belton, Lincolnshire). Thomas was an Iron Founder Employer by 1911, having worked his way up in the iron industry.

Thomas was the youngest of eight children of **William Downend**, Horse Keeper, and **Ann nee Lockwood**, who lived in Worsbrough Bridge. On the 1871 Census, Thomas was living with his parents, for whom their widowed daughter Elizabeth (Lizzie) Wadsworth, aged 24, was General Servant, and his niece **Aurora Wadsworth** (3). By 1881, Thomas was living with his widowed mother (73), his sister Lizzie and her daughter Aurora at 5 Vernon Row in Worsbrough; this house was close to Mount Vernon, where **Samuel Joshua Cooper** lived *(Part 1. Chapter 14)*.

Sarah Ann Ducker was the daughter of **George Ducker**, Agricultural Labourer, and **Sarah Ducker**, Schoolmistress, who lived in Belton, Lincolnshire. In 1871, she was working as Housemaid for **George Griffiths Phillips**, Surgeon, and his family at North Gate, Tickhill; in 1881, she was Lady's Maid for **William Elmhirst**, Chaplain of Stainborough, and his family at Elmhirst, Worsbrough. Sarah and Thomas got married in Thorne in Spring 1882.

John was the youngest of three children: **George William** (attended the Holgate) and **Alice Ann**, Assistant Grocer, who died in Barnsley in 1961, aged 67.

In April 1911, the Downend family lived in six rooms at 145 Blythe Street, Wombwell, having moved to Wombwell by 1891; their son William continued to live with his aunt Lizzie in Worsbrough. Thomas Downend died on 28 January 1916, aged 66, at 145 Blythe Street and he was buried in Wombwell Cemetery. Probate was granted in Wakefield in May 1917 to his son William, Bank Manager. Effects £1 559 4s 1d.

John attended the Holgate Grammar School in Church Street, Barnsley, for three years, from 1904 to 1907; he was a Pupil Teacher at Wombwell Council School and passed the Preliminary Certificate Examination for Teachers in 1907. John went on to York St John's Training College, from 1907 to 1909, supported by his brother; he was College Monitor and an oarsman in the rowing team. John became a Certificated Teacher at King's Road School, Wombwell, before being promoted to Headmaster of Cross Hill Boys School in Hemsworth.

John was one of the founder members of the Old Boys Association and was Sub Editor of the new *Alumnus* magazine that started in April 1913: 'J M Downend is engaged in collecting interesting items of news relating to Old Boys and will be delighted to receive notes at Roslin Villas, Hemsworth, near Wakefield'. The programme of events to celebrate the Holgate's first Commemoration Day on 11 October 1913, included … John's 'stirring song'.

He wrote to the Editor about his experiences in France (Part 3. Chapter 3) and also confirmed in his letter a donation of 20/– which he had sent, 'with characteristic generosity', to the magazine fund.

Photograph of John in De Ruvigny's *Roll of Honour 1914–1918.*

John married **Jane (Jennie) Hiles** in Wombwell on 26 December 1913 and they lived at Roslin Villas, Hemsworth, near Wakefield. Jennie, one of seven children of **George Hiles**, Pawnbroker, and **Lucy Hiles**, was an Elementary School Teacher in Hemsworth. After John's death, Jennie moved back to 1 High Street, Wombwell with her parents. She got married again in Autumn 1919 to **David G Guest**; he may have been an Australian and they possibly emigrated to Australia.

John joined the Inns of Court Officers Training Corps in London on 26 August 1915, aged 26 years and 10 months, as a Private (Service Number: 5847) then Lance Corporal from 22 January 1916. After 242 days he was discharged to a Temporary Commission as Second Lieutenant (129234) with the 32nd Local Reserve Battalion of the Northumberland Fusiliers at Newcastle on Tyne; his character was 'very good'. John transferred to the 26th (Tyneside Irish) Battalion of the Northumberland Fusiliers.

The Attestation form, Medical Inspection Report and forms related to different promotions and Commission are in the Officer Records, held in the National Archives (JMD*). John was 6' 6" tall with chest 39", he had 6/6 vision in both eyes and good physical development. He was unable to ride a horse and applied for a Commission in the Infantry.

John went to France on 15 June 1916 and, as a new officer, had to lead a platoon in the action on 1 July at the Somme, where he was the only officer out of 20 to escape unharmed and one of 12 men out of 38 in his platoon. John was quickly promoted up to Captain but was killed in action on 24 November 1917, aged 29. John was buried in St Martin Calvaire British Cemetery, St Martin-sur-Cojeul near Arras, Pas de Calais, France (grave I D 15) and this was originally 'marked by a durable wooden cross with an inscription bearing full particulars'.*

* Adrienne McEnhill, whose mother was Cicely Frances Downend (1916–2010), kindly shared family information and photographs, including the one taken by Rev Dr Banham when he visited John's War Grave with Adrienne's mother and grandmother in the 1930s. Adrienne purchased John's Officer Records and generously allowed me to use them. Adrienne discovered in 2015 that a notebook of John's had survived and she hopes to collect it soon; I hope that one day I might be privileged to read it and I am sorry it will be too late for my Memorial Book.

John's original burial cross, photograph taken by Rev. Dr Banham of Worsbrough during the 1930's and used by kind permission of Adrienne McEnhill.

A Telegram from the War Office dated 29 November 1917 bluntly informed Jennie that her husband, whom she had last seen in early August when home on leave, had died: 'Deeply regret to inform you that Captain J M Downend 26/Royal Fusiliers was killed in action November twenty fourth The Army Council express their sympathy'. The error over the name of the Regiment was one of a series of no or incorrect information that newly widowed Jennie had to sort out with the War Office; she had to chase them for a Death Certificate to deal with Probate, to amend their records when she moved house – 'This request has already been made by wire, but yet Their Majesties' expression of sympathy was wired through to my former address in Hemsworth' – and to clarify John's rank at the time of his death. Eventually, in response to the latter, she was informed that he had been 'temporary Second Lieutenant granted acting rank of Captain from 20 July 1917 and subsequently promoted temporary Lieutenant with effect from 24 October 1917', 'I am to add that for all obituary purposes he may be described as Captain'.

A Gratuity of £125 11s was awarded for John being killed on active service and was granted relief from payment of Estate Duty under the Killed in War Act 1914. John had made his Will on 21 June 1916; Probate was granted at Wakefield on 18 March 1918 to Jane Downend: Effects: £291 1s 1d.

The following items belonging to John were sent to Jennie: watch (glass deficient), prayer book, cigarette case (damaged), sketch book, leather wallet, photo case & photos, cheque book, advance book, letters etc

John was awarded two medals: Victory and British War, and his widow should have received the 'Dead Man's Penny' plaque and scroll from King George V.

John's name is on the Holgate Grammar School Memorial, the Memorial outside St Mary's Church in Wombwell, the Wombwell Church of England Men's Society list of names inside St Mary's Church, Wombwell, the Roll of Honour at St John's College in York and the Memorial in St Helen's Church in Hemsworth.

Connections

Seven of the Old Boys qualified as Teachers after attending St John's College in York: **Crossland Barraclough** (B 1894), **Edward Batley** (B 1893), **Norman Bradley** (B 1891), **John Middleton Downend** (B 1888), **Arthur Heathcote** (B 1890), **Charles Edward Savage** (B 1893) and **Charles Waldegrave Wood** (B 1883). Several of them would have attended during the same period.

Alumnus – December 1917

> The above notes had already been sent to the press when we learnt with feelings of profound sorrow, and with a sense of personal loss, of the death in action of Captain J M Downend of the Northumberland Fusiliers. The reason for concealment of the writer of the letter which appears in the introductory notes no longer prevails. He had also confirmed in the letter a donation of 20/– which he had sent, with characteristic generosity, to the magazine fund.
>
> Captain Downend was one of the principal agents in the work of reorganization of the Old Boys Association and was the able sub editor from its inception to the outbreak of war.
>
> The deceased officer was educated at the Barnsley Grammar School (1904–07) and at York Training College, at which institution he had a successful and distinguished career, and at the latter was chief prefect of his year. He afterwards became Head of Hemsworth Cross Hill Boys School. In August 1915 after much anxious thought he resigned his position and entered the Inns of Court Officer Training Corps, when in due course he was gazetted to the Northumberland Fusiliers and arrived in France on the eve of the Somme Battles. He took part in these battles and also in most of the subsequent and severe engagements on the

Western Front. He was promoted to full Lieutenant and in August was raised to the rank of Captain. But the tragic end came on November 24th and we now mourn one who for his winning personality and noble character was loved and honoured by many friends.

I extract the following from a letter describing the manner of his death written by an officer who was 2nd to him in command: 'It is awfully difficult for me to write about the poor old 'Skipper' because I have known him so long. ... We were relieving another Battalion in the line having just come up from rest billets. We were all in the trenches when the shelling started and cleared the trenches at once. We were all together at the head of one of the dug outs when this shell burst right in the entrance. Some of us had remarkable escapes. My servant was killed at my side and also another man of the company and the men of other units. Just our rotten luck that that shell should pitch there ... It has deprived us of the best company commander any man could wish to serve under. He was popular wherever he went and was always the same, serene but exacting in the execution of any duties which he might be called upon to perform ... He was buried this morning November 26th at 10.30am in the little military cemetery near here – Each of the other companies sent an Officer. The ceremony was impressive to us all. So, we saluted him and left him'.

Barnsley Chronicle – 8 December 1917

HOW THE YORKSHIRE LADS FOUGHT & FELL SERRE BATTLE
DR C H CHANDLER WELL KNOWN LOCAL SCHOOLMASTER

The news of the death in action of Captain John Middleton Downend, of the Northumberland Fusiliers, on Nov 24th, has been received by his relatives and numerous friends with a shock of painful surprise, and with feelings of profound sorrow. As he had faced death on so numerous occasions and had passed unscathed through so many terrible conflicts, hope was cherished that he would live to see the end of the war. ...

In August 1915, Captain Downend joined the Inns of Court O. T. C. and left for France in June 1916, where he took part in the Somme battles and later in the fighting in Arras in 1917. He came home on leave in August 1917, was promoted full Lieutenant and later to the rank of Captain. With a winning personality and with a nobility of character inspired by high ideals, the deceased officer was loved and honoured by a great number of friends. England can ill afford to lose such noble sons as he was and although victory over the enemy will surely be hers, it will be victory won by the priceless blood of the best and bravest who would in time of peace be her light and her glory. Captain Downend leaves behind to mourn his loss his widow, mother, sister and brother.

The following is an extract from a letter written by Lieutenant Ruddock to Captain Downend's mother: 'The enemy commenced shelling so we cleared the trenches and were all standing together at the head of one of the dug-out shafts. A shell burst right in the entrance. Some of us had remarkable escapes but Captain Downend was killed instantaneously. We have been deprived of the best Company Commander any man could wish to serve under. He was popular wherever he went and was always the same, serene but exacting in the execution of any duties, which he might be called upon to perform. We miss him very much and I am asked by the officers and men to express their deepest sympathy with you. He was buried this morning (Nov 26th) at 10.30 in the little Military Cemetery near here. The whole Company wanted to attend the funeral, but as this was impossible, I took out 10 of the men who had been longest in the Company. The ceremony was very impressive to us all, so .... we saluted him and left him. A battalion cross is being made and as soon as completed will be fixed at the head of his grave'.

Newspaper Cutting (Holgate Ephemera) – 1917 (Photo)

J M DOWNEND KILLED WELL-KNOWN
LOCAL SCHOOLMASTER

(This article is the same as the one in Barnsley Chronicle with the following second paragraph).

Captain Downend was an old boy of the Barnsley Grammar School and after leaving York College became assistant master at the King's Road School, Wombwell. He was later appointed headmaster of the Cross Hill Boys' School, Hemsworth.

***Yorkshire Evening Post* – 7 December 1917**

THE YORKSHIRE ROLL OF HONOUR
LATEST CASUALTIES AMONG OFFICERS AND MEN

Captain J M DOWNEND, Northumberland Fusiliers, killed in action, was before enlistment headmaster of the Cross Hill Boys' School, Hemsworth.

UK De Ruvigny's Roll of Honour 1914–1918

DOWNEND JOHN MIDDLETON

Captain 26th (Service) Battalion The Northumberland Fusiliers ... He joined the Inns of Court OTC on 26 August 1915, gazetted 2nd Lieutenant 24 April 1916 ...

His Commanding Officer wrote: 'The loss to the Battalion both as a soldier and companion is irreparable. He knew no fear, he never failed in a single duty. He was with me for the great part of 1 July, the first time he had been under fire; he was splendid. His company had complete confidence in him, and they all loved him. Neither the battalion nor myself will ever forget him'. ...

The main photograph of John is from Alumnus, *used by kind permission of Barnsley Archives.*

GEORGE WILLIAM DOWNEND (born 31 March 1883 in Worsbrough) was Baptised on 10 June 1883 in Worsbrough St Mary's Church. William lived with his father's older widowed sister **Elizabeth (Lizzie) Wadsworth** from the age of eight and for more than 20 years. William's aunt's only daughter **Aurora Downend Wadsworth** also lived there with another aunt **Jane Downend**, who had her own means. They were in four rooms at 1 Mount Vernon Crescent in Worsbrough.

Photograph of William, reproduced by kind permission of Adrienne McEnhill.

Lizzie Downend had married **William Wadsworth** in Spring 1867 and their daughter Aurora was born early 1868; she was named by her father as she had arrived at dawn. William Wadsworth had been Bookkeeper for **Samuel Joshua Cooper** (Part 1. Chapter 14), who let Lizzie live in a small cottage, close to his own home at Mount Vernon, after her husband's premature death in summer 1868, aged 22, when their daughter was only a few months old.

William went to Worsbrough Dale school until the age of 12, then he attended the Holgate for three years, from 1896 to 1899. He was Entertainments Secretary for the Old Boys Association. William was a Bank Clerk by the age of 18 and a Bank Manager by 1916. William married **Frances Elizabeth Elvin** in Autumn 1915 and they had two children: **Cicely Frances Downend** in 1916 and **John Gorden Downend** in 1920. William died on 25 November 1927, aged 44, at Bank House in Wath-upon-Dearne.

WAR SUPPLEMENT FOR WEEK ENDING NOVEMBER 9, 1918.

OUT OF MISCHIEF.

Where he will be if we at home follow the example of the boys at the Front and relax no effort

23

Duncan Fairley

Duncan Fairley
1890–1916 (aged 26)

DUNCAN FAIRLEY was born on 30 June 1890 in Barnsley to **Barker Fairley** (born 1856 in Sunderland) and **Charlotte nee Rutter** (born 1857 in Sunderland). His Baptism was on 15 July 1890 at Barnsley St John the Baptist Church. Barker Fairley was from a family of Seamen and Shipowners for whom that first name had passed down the generations. He was a Teacher then relocated to Barnsley, where he became Headmaster at St John's Elementary School for many years from when it opened in 1882. Barker continued teaching when he moved back to Sunderland by c1907; he died in 1914 in Wallsend, Sunderland.

Duncan was the youngest of three surviving brothers: **Joseph** (attended the Holgate and served in the First World War) and **Barker**. Their sister **Jessie Charlotte** had died in infancy in 1886.

In April 1901, the family had lived in Park Road, Barnsley, for about 23 years – at numbers 129, 165 and 195, which was probably the same house renumbered as the road was developed. By April 1911, Duncan was a Student in Leeds; his parents had moved back to Sunderland, where they lived with Charlotte's brother, and Joseph was a Schoolmaster in Liverpool.

Barker Fairley (born in 1887 in Barnsley) emigrated c1910 to Canada, where he was a University Lecturer in German Literature and established a reputation as a Goethe scholar. He married Canadian **Margaret Adele Keeling** in 1914 and they had five children. Barker was very involved with the Group of Seven Artists, and late in life became a successful painter connected to this group. Barker was awarded an Honorary Doctorate of Letters from Leeds University in 1950 and, in 1978, he became an Officer of the Order of Canada for his 'unique contribution to Canadian Scholarship'. He died in Toronto in 1986, aged 99.

Duncan went to St John's National School in Barnsley until the age of 12. He then attended the Holgate Grammar School in Church Street, Barnsley, for six years, from 1902 to 1908. Duncan was both a County Minor Scholar and a County Major Scholar, and passed the Oxford Local Junior exam (1st Class) and the Oxford Local Senior exam (2nd Class Honours), winning a Cooper prize in 1907 for the latter. He went on to Leeds University for three years from 5 October 1908, where he obtained a first class BA Honours Degree in English in 1911. (DF*). He subsequently obtained a Teachers' Diploma in Secondary Education from Manchester University.

As an Old Boy, Duncan was one of the judges for the Athletic Sports in 1910 along with Henry Rylands Knowles; he contributed several poems to *Alumnus* (Part 3. Chapter 4).

Duncan became an Assistant English Master at Scarborough Municipal Secondary School by 1914 and he had a narrow escape during the bombardment. (*This school was taken over by Scarborough High School for Boys in 1922, then became Westwood County Modern before becoming Yorkshire Coast College).*

Early in the morning of Wednesday 16 December 1914, four German warships launched an attack on the East Coast, shelling Scarborough, Whitby and Hartlepool, their main target. They killed 137 people, most civilians, seriously injured nearly 600 and caused great destruction of property. This action was in breach of the Hague

Convention which required 24 hours' notice to be given of any such attack to enable civilians to evacuate the area. The German ships managed to carry out the raid and escape home unharmed as the British Navy failed to stop them. The raid on Scarborough took place from 8am for half an hour when more than 100 shells were launched from a distance of about 600 yards from the coast, hitting hotels, churches and many homes. Seventeen inhabitants were killed of whom eight were women and four were children, aged from 4 months to 15.

Duncan enlisted at Barnsley in September 1914 in the 14th Battalion (Second Barnsley Pals) of the York and Lancaster Regiment; he was promoted to temporary Second Lieutenant on 18 May 1915 and was subsequently promoted to Lieutenant. (He is listed in Jon Cooksey's *Barnsley Pals* as Assistant Adjutant in 'B' Company). Duncan was killed in action on the first day of the Somme, 1 July 1916, having celebrated his 26th birthday the day before, and was buried in the Euston Road Cemetery, Colincamps, Somme, France.

Duncan was one of ten Old Boys who were killed in action on the first day of the Somme.

Duncan should have been awarded two medals: Victory and British War but no details are provided on his Medal Card. His widowed mother should have also received the 'Dead Man's Penny' plaque and scroll from King George V.

Butterfields SALE.
Butterfields
1, Church Street,
The Barnsley Chronicle
AND PENISTONE MEXBRO' WATH AND HOYLAND JOURNAL.
VOL. LVIII. NO. 4014 SATURDAY, JULY 22, 1916. ONE PENNY
WONDERFUL.
Butterfields,
1, Church Street,
LOCAL OFFICERS AND MEN WHO HAVE FALLEN.
MAJOR T. H. GUEST. CAPTAIN DE VILLE SMITH. LIEUTENANT DART. SERGT. R. DUNK (BARNSLEY.) CPL. J. HARRIS (BARNSLEY.) PTE. H. MILLTHORPE (BARNSLEY.)
LIEUTENANT MALEHAM. LIEUTENANT S. O. SHARP. LIEUTENANT D. FAIRLEY. PTE. L. SMITH (BARNSLEY.) PTE. F. KNAPTON (BARNSLEY.) PTE. H. LOACH (BARNSLEY.)

Photograph of feature in *Barnsley Chronicle*, used by their kind permission.

Duncan's name is on the Holgate Grammar School Memorial, the painted column in St Mary's Church, Barnsley, and on the War Memorial on Olive's Mount in Scarborough incorrectly listed as 'FAIRLY D'. Duncan is mentioned in Leeds University's journal *The Gryphon*, which has been digitized, as 'Past Students' in the Roll of Honour for December 1914.*

Connections

Duncan was in the same form as **Arthur George Batley, Henry Ryland Knowles** and **Harold Willott**. They all won Cooper Prizes in 1907 for passing the Oxford Local Senior exam.

Duncan played for the the First Eleven Cricket Team, which included **George Percival Cowburn** (who won a cricket bat prize for bowling), **Cyril Burton Dixon** (who won a cricket bat prize for batting) plus **Harold Willott** and his brother **Ernest Spencer Willott**. **Ernest Litherland** (who won a cricket bat prize for bowling) was Captain of the Second Eleven Cricket Team, which also comprised: **Edward Batley**, **George Braham** and (probably) **Herbert Harry Jagger Mason**.

In April 1911, Duncan was a Student in the same Boarding House at Brudenell Avenue in Leeds as **Henry Rylands Knowles**, Medical Student, both aged 20. They both attended Leeds University.

Duncan served with the 14th Battalion (Second Barnsley Pals) along with **John Bruce Atha, Frank Bakel, Frank Potter** and **Harold Quest.** He was promoted to temporary Second Lieutenant, a week later than **Harold Quest** and their names appeared together in the London Gazette on 4 June 1915.

Alumnus – December 1916

> Duncan Fairley (1902–8) and Frank Potter (1902–8) 'have fallen on the battlefield, during the recent great advances made by the British'. Duncan Fairley was 'one of the most brilliant boys that have attended the grammar school'. He won a County Major Scholarship and entered Leeds university where he achieved BA 1st class honours. 'A most promising career has been suddenly cut short'.
>
> Duncan Fairley, BA, was Lieut in the Barnsley Battalion of the Y & L Regiment. He had repeatedly been rejected on account of defective eyesight, but undeterred by failure persisted in his attempts until he obtained admission, true to the inner appeals of patriotism and humanity. He was gentle, modest, loveable and deeply affectionate by nature, noble minded and highly intellectual. With

* Nick Brewster, Archive Assistant at Leeds University Special Collections Library, kindly checked records and confirmed the details of Duncan's attendance.

the soul of a youthful poet he was responsive to the glory of nature, delighting in her wonder and beauty.

By kind permission of his father we publish a poem written by the dead hero.

***Barnsley Independent* – 5 July 1916**

LIEUTENANT DUNCAN FAIRLEY To the list of Barnsley officers who have made the great sacrifice has to be added Lieutenant Duncan Fairley, the third son of Mr and Mrs Barker Fairley of Park Grove. Lieutenant Fairley received his early education at St John's School, of which his father is headmaster, and gained a Locke scholarship tenable at the Barnsley Grammar School. A County Major scholarship took him to Leeds University, where he obtained his BA degree with 1st class honours. Afterwards he took the Diploma of Education, with distinction in English, at Manchester University and subsequently was English master for nearly three years at the Scarborough Municipal Secondary School. He was at Scarborough during the bombardment in the early days of the war.

He endeavoured to join the Army on five or six occasions, but was rejected on account of eyesight, but in May last year he obtained a commission in the Second Barnsley Battalion. Lieutenant Fairley is officially reported 'missing believed killed', but a brother officer has written to Mr Fairley stating that he saw Lieutenant Fairley fall. The deceased officer was 26 years of age the day before he fell, and his death in the Country's cause has cut short a scholastic career of great promise. Mr Fairley's eldest son is at the Front with the Canadian Forces.

***Yorkshire Post* & *Leeds Intelligencer* – 8 July 1916**

THE STRICKEN BRAVE

LIEUT DUNCAN FAIRLEY York and Lancaster Regiment is reported 'missing, believed killed'. He was 26 years old ... He gained the Locke Scholarship and took his BA degree with first class honours at the Leeds University. Subsequently he became English master at the Scarborough Municipal School and had a narrow escape during the bombardment of that town.

***Barnsley Chronicle* – 15 July 1916**

LIEUTENANT D. FAIRLEY

Lieut Duncan Fairley, of the 14th Battalion York and Lancaster Regiment, was the youngest son of Mr Barker Fairley ... Although no official intimation has been received, letters from comrades have conveyed the sad news to Barnsley, and there is no doubt that Lieut Fairley has made the highest of all sacrifices. He was 26 years old and had a distinguished and promising scholastic career.

After receiving his early education at St John's School, he gained the Locke Scholarship and a County Minor Scholarship, and proceeding to the Barnsley Grammar School, he was successful in matriculating and securing a County Major Scholarship. Lieut Fairley took his BA degree with first class honours at the Leeds University, and subsequently became English master at the Scarborough Municipal Secondary School. He was in Scarborough at the time the town was bombarded and had a narrow escape, a piece of shell striking his bed whilst he was in the room.

Early last year Colonel Raley asked Lieut Fairley to accept a commission in the 14th Battalion York and Lancaster Regiment and this he accepted, joining on May 18th 1915. When the Battalion left for Egypt Lieut Fairley remained behind on Salisbury Plain in charge of a draft of men, and after a period of suspense, when he three times received orders to embark, to be cancelled at the last moment, he left for Egypt. After being only six days in Alexandria Lieut Fairley went with the Battalion straight to France, where he has been ever since. He had been looking forward to getting leave at Whitsuntide but this was stopped and the parents of the gallant officer have not seen him since Christmas Day.

The greatest sympathy is felt with Mr and Mrs Fairley in their irreparable loss, for their son was known to a very wide circle of friends and he was held by all in the highest esteem. An able scholar, he gave promise of having a distinguished career as a schoolmaster, and he proved himself during his short military life to be a capable and gallant officer. Mr and Mrs Fairley's eldest son is a Quartermaster-Sergeant with the Canadians and he has been with them in the trenches for many months.

Barnsley Chronicle – 22 July 1916

Mr and Mrs Fairley of Barnsley would gladly welcome any news from the comrades of their son Lt Duncan Fairley who took part in the action of July 1st. Will members of the 2nd Barnsley Battalion please note?

Manchester Evening News – 18 July 1916

LATEST CASUALTIES
MANCHESTER UNIVERSITY STUDENT

Lieutenant Duncan Fairley of the York and Lancaster Regiment is reported missing. He entered the University of Manchester in 1911 and obtained the teachers' diploma in 1912. He was a graduate of the University of Leeds.

The main photograph of Duncan is from Alumnus, *reproduced by kind permission of Barnsley Archives.*

JOSEPH FAIRLEY (born on 30 May 1884 in Barnsley) went to St John's National School until the age of 13 then the Holgate for two years from 1897 to 1899. He was a teacher in Liverpool by April 1911. In September 1912, as a Clerk aged 28, Joseph sailed on SS *Empress of Britain* to Quebec from Liverpool, with the intention of staying permanently in Canada. Joseph is on several Ships Passenger Lists early 1914, travelling from Peru to Liverpool, then Liverpool to New York, then to visit his brother Barker in Canada in March 1914, giving his occupation as Agent and Broker.

He enlisted in Edmonton on 25 November 1914, aged 30 years and 7 months, as a Quarter-master Sergeant (Service Number: 79833) in the Canadian Expeditionary Force. Personal details on the Attestation form: Schoolteacher, Height: 5' 7 ¼", Chest: 39", Complexion: Medium, Eyes: Green, Hair: Brown. Joseph remained in Canada until he died.

JACK AND TOMMY: "No, you don't!"

24

Harold Feasby

Harold Feasby
1892–1918 (aged 25)

HAROLD FEASBY was born on 25 November 1892 in Barnsley to **Henry Feasby** (born c1866 in Thornville) and **Florence Kate nee Mountain** (born c1866 in Chelsea). His Baptism was on 18 December 1902 (aged 9) at St Edward the Confessor Church, Barnsley. Henry was a Tailor Employer.

Harold was the oldest of six surviving children: **Cyril, Mabel Kathleen, Clifford, Douglas John** and **Jessie May. Madge** had died in infancy in 1896. Harold's three brothers served in the First World War.

In April 1911, the Feasby family lived in nine rooms at Longcar House, Barnsley, where they had two Boarders, who were relations: **Jessie Mary Mountain** (39) Manageress Lady's Outfitters, and **Arthur William Feasby** (41) Shop Assistant Drapery. They had previously lived at several different addresses in Barnsley. By December 1915 they had moved to 37 Park Grove, Barnsley.

Harold went to Central School until the age of 12. He then attended the Holgate Grammar School in Church Street, Barnsley, for one year, from 1905 to 1906. He worked in the office at Carlton Main Colliery before joining Newman and Bond Solicitors as a Solicitor's Clerk in 1911; he became a Clerk in Earl Fitzwilliam's Estate Office at Wentworth Woodhouse about 1913.*

Early in the war, Harold joined the York and Lancaster Regiment as a Private (Service Number: 14/142) with the 14th Battalion (Second Barnsley Pals) and was subsequently promoted to Quarter-master Sergeant and Acting Adjutant for the 1/5th Battalion. He entered the Mediterranean Theatre of War on 28 December 1915, where he served in Egypt before being transferred to France and the Western Front. Harold was promoted to Second Lieutenant and his name was listed in the Supplement to the *London Gazette* on 21 July 1917. Harold was killed in action, while leading his platoon in an attack with a Lewis machine gun, on 11 April 1918, aged 25. As his body was never found or identified, Harold's name is on the Tyne Cot Memorial, Zonnebeke, West-Vlanderen, Belgium (Panel 126 to 128).

Harold was awarded two medals: Victory and British War, and his widowed father, at 23 Eldon Street, Barnsley, should have received the 'Dead Man's Penny' plaque and scroll from King George V. His mother had died in 1920, aged 54

Harold's name is on the Holgate Grammar School Memorial, the painted column in St Mary's Church, Barnsley, and the list of names read out at the old St George's Church, Barnsley. His name is also on the Village War Memorial and on the plaque in the new Holy Trinity Church in Wentworth.

Connections

Harold served in the 1st/5th Battalion of the York and Lancaster Regiment along with **Arthur Heathcote** and **James Edward Thompson.**

* Sheffield Archives advised me that the survival of staff records was patchy and a lengthy search might result in no information so I did not pursue this.

Alumnus

Harold Feasby, Second Lieutenant Y & L Reg, son of Mr & Mrs H Feasby of Park Grove and Eldon Street, Barnsley, fell in action on April 11th. In the early days of the war he joined the Barnsley Battalion as a Private and was soon promoted to be Quarter-master Sergeant. He saw service in Egypt and France and was recommended for a commission. On being gazetted he made further progress as a Lewis Gun Officer and was acting as Assistant Adjutant at the time of his death. He was leading his platoon in a vigorous attack against a German position when he fell mortally wounded. Before he enlisted he was employed in Earl Fitzwilliam's Estate Office.

***Barnsley Chronicle* – 28 July 191**

PATRIOTIC PARS

The friends of Quarter-master Sergeant H Feasby, York and Lancaster, one of the sons of Mr Henry Feasby of Barnsley, will be pleased to hear that he has received his commission as Second-Lieutenant.

***Barnsley Chronicle* – 27 April 1918**

ANOTHER BARNSLEY OFFICER HERO
SEC-LIEUT HAROLD FEASBY KILLED

Profound sympathy has been expressed with Mr and Mrs H Feasby of Park Grove and Eldon Street, Barnsley, in the loss by death in action of their eldest son, Second-Lieutenant Harold Feasby, York and Lancaster Regiment, which event occurred on the 11th April. The deceased officer was exceedingly popular and his Regiment have lost a gallant and faithful member. Lieutenant Feasby, in civilian life, was a young man who by his amiability and kindly disposition won the affection of a wide circle of friends. As a boy he attended the Central and St Mary's Schools and later going to the Barnsley Grammar School, and for a period of time he was a member of St George's Church Choir. He was fond of sport and was an esteemed member of the tennis section of the Barnsley Cricket Club. After leaving school, he was for a short time in the office of Carlton Main Colliery, subsequently taking up a position in Messrs Newman and Bond's office, Barnsley, but for a year prior to enlisting he had been on the staff at the Estate Office at Wentworth Woodhouse. In the early days of the war, he joined the Barnsley Pals as a private and he rapidly gained promotion in the ranks, early becoming a Quarter-master Sergeant. He saw service in Egypt and France and was recommended for a commission, which he accepted. After a course of special training in Ireland, he was gazetted and returned to France, where he made further progress as a Lewis gun officer and was acting as Assistant Adjutant at the time of his death. Details as to how Lieutenant Feasby gave his life in the great cause have this week been received, and it appears that he was leading his Platoon in a vigorous attack against the Germans, who were holding a village very strongly and putting up a desperate resistance, aided by terrific machine gun fire. He was last seen rushing forward with a Lewis gun under his arm, the inference being that he had spotted a machine gun emplacement and intended to engage it with his Lewis gun when he fell mortally wounded. He was 25 years of age. Lieutenant Feasby has 2 other brothers with the Colours – Driver Cyril Feasby, Royal Engineers, who is in France, and Corporal Clifford Feasby, who is stationed at the Infantry Record Office, York.

***Barnsley Chronicle* – 29 June 1918**

PATRIOTIC PARS

A fine tribute to the noble character of the late Second-Lieutenant Harold Feasby, York and Lancaster, has this week been paid in a letter to his parents by Major-General Neville Cameron. 'Please accept (he writes) my very warm sympathy with you in the loss of your son Second-Lieutenant H Feasby, who was serving with the York and Lancaster Regiment when he lost his life in the service of his country in April. His Battalion Commander held a very high opinion of your son. He was understudying as Adjutant at the time of his death. He was a good leader of men and a very capable officer. I thought it might be of some consolation to you to know that his comrades out here recognized and appreciated your son's good qualities and that we share your sorrow here'. The late Lieutenant was a son of Mr and Mrs H Feasby of Barnsley and it is worthy of note that their remaining son, Douglas John Feasby, has just been accepted in the Royal Air Forces this week, making the fourth member of the family to join the colours.

***Yorkshire Post* & *Leeds Intelligencer* – 23 April 1918**

THE ROLL OF HONOUR

Second-Lieutenant Harold Feasby, York & Lancaster Regiment, eldest son of Mr H Feasby, Park Grove, Barnsley, was killed in action on April 11. He was 26 years of age. A Barnsley Grammar School 'old boy', he was on the staff at the estate office at Wentworth Woodhouse when he enlisted in the autumn of 1914 and he gained promotion from the ranks.

The photograph of Harold is from Alumnus, *reproduced by kind permission of Barnsley Archives.*

CYRIL FEASBY (born c1894 in Barnsley) was a Tailor's Assistant in April 1911. He enlisted on 7 December 1915, aged 21 years and 9 months, as a Driver (Service Number: 104617) in the 105th Field Company of the Royal Engineers. His parents, Harry and Kathleen Feasby, of 37 Park Grove, Barnsley, were his Next of Kin. Cyril was a Tailor living at 11 Longman Road, Barnsley, according to the Attestation form; the Medical Form contains limited personal information: Height: 5' 2", Chest: 35".

CLIFFORD FEASBY (born 1898 in Barnsley) enlisted as a Private (Service Numbers: 65553 and 38980) with the West Yorkshire Regiment on 21 October 1916, aged 17 years and 11 months. He was later transferred to the Yorkshire Regiment, having been promoted to Corporal, and was stationed at the Infantry Record Office in York. Clifford was a Bank Clerk living at 37 Park Grove, Barnsley, according to the Attestation form; personal information: Height: 5' 7 ¼", Chest: 33½", Weight: 122lbs with 6/6 Vision but he suffered from 'infantile paralysis' resulting in leg shortening and knock knees. Clifford served for three years and 40 days 'at home' then was transferred to the Reserve, but lost his certificate, which was required for employment with the GPO [General Post Office] in 1936. A letter from Clifford, who was living at 144 Welbourne Road, Leicester, in January 1936 states: 'I enlisted 1916–1918 and was attached the whole period to Infantry Records at York, my Regiment was Depot West Yorkshire Regiment and later transferred to Depot Yorkshire Regiment'.

Clfford A Feasby married **Margaret M Broadhead** early 1923 in Barnsley. They had two children in Barnsley: **John A Feasby** in 1924 and **Isobel M Feasby** in 1928.

DOUGLAS JOHN FEASBY (born 13 June 1900 in Barnsley) was called up on 21 June 1918, shortly after his 18th birthday, for the Royal Air Force, Reserve Class G (Service Number: 260921). Douglas was a Motor Mechanic Apprentice living at home.; he was 5' 6½" tall, had 31½" chest, dark hair, blue eyes and a fresh complexion.

Douglas married **Doris Brown** on 11 May 1931 at St Helen's Church in Sandal Magna; he was a Motor Mechanic living at 14 Hamilton Street, Wishaw, Scotland, and she was a Nurse, residing at Church View, Sandal, with her father Frank Ward Brown, Traveller.

25

Sidney Gill

Sidney Gill
1895–1916 (aged 21)

SIDNEY GILL was born on 10 February 1895 in Mosborough, Rotherham, to **Sidney Gill** (born c1870 in Worsbrough) and **Lois nee Peace** (born c1872 in Kilnhurst). Sidney senior was Manager of Carlton Main Colliery, as had been his father, Thomas Gill of Greasebrough.

Lois was one of four children of **John Peace** (born c1845 in Coalville, Leicestershire) and **Henrietta nee Jessop** (born c1848 in Swinton); her siblings were **Clara, Owen** and **Ira**. John Peace was a Labourer in Coal Mine and Local Preacher (Methodist) on the 1871 Census, when the family were living at 10 North Terrace, Thomas' Buildings, Swinton. By April 1881, John was a Missionary Preacher in Stockport and, subsequently, Town Missionary in Rochdale. Lois had been a Teacher at the old Belfield Board School, Rochdale, before she got married in 1894.

Sidney was the oldest of four children: **Nellie** and **Raymond** were full siblings whereas **Alice Undine** was their half sister. Sidney's mother died on 20 November 1899, aged 27, and his father got married again to **Maria Andrews Tomlinson** in 1904.

Sidney had an unsettled childhood. He was probably staying with his mother's family in Rochdale when his sister was born there in 1896 and returned there from the end of 1899, when his mother died. By April 1901, Sidney (aged 5), Nellie (4) and Raymond (2) were with their aunt **Clara nee Peace Crabtree** and uncle **Robert Crabree** in Rochdale, while their father was at Rob Royd House in Barnsley, staying with his married sister **Kellie (Ellen) Senior**, her husband **Fred Senior** and baby **Alice**.

It seems likely that the family were back together after his father remarried in 1904, as by April 1911, they were all living in eight rooms at Oak Tree House in Grimethorpe with their new stepmother and baby Alice.

Raymond Gill married **Kathleen Elsie Atkinson** in summer 1928 in Worksop; there are too many Gill/Atkinson children listed to know whether they had any. Gill is too common a surname to know whether Nellie and Alice got married.

Sidney went to Grimethorpe Elementary School for six years until the age of 13. He then attended the Holgate Grammar School in Church Street, Barnsley, for three years, from 1909 to 1912. 'He went into Surveying and Mining after leaving'.

Sidney enlisted as Private (Service Number: 12/114) in the 12th Battalion (Sheffield City) of the York and Lancaster Regiment. He was killed in action on the first day of the Somme, 1 July 1916, aged 21, and his name was included as one of almost 4,000 casualties on the Daily Casualty List in *The Times* on 17 August 1916. As his body was never found or identified his name is on the Thiepval Memorial, Somme, France (Pier and Face: 14A and 14B).

Sidney was one of ten Old Boys who were killed in action on the first day of the Somme.

Sidney was awarded two medals: Victory and British War, and his father, who had moved to The Grove, South Kirkby, Pontefract, should have received the 'Dead Man's Penny' plaque and scroll from King George V.

Sidney's name is on the Holgate Grammar School Memorial, the Grimethorpe Memorial, Sheffield Council's Official Roll of Honour and Sheffield City Battalion Roll of Honour.

He is remembered on the headstone on his mother's grave in Barnsley Cemetery, which is adjacent to the grave of his grandparents.

In Loving Memory of
LOIS
THE DEARLY BELOVED WIFE OF
SIDNEY GILL
WHO FELL ASLEEP IN JESUS
NOVEMBER 20TH 1899, AGED 27 YEARS

THERE IS SWEET REST IN HEAVEN

ALSO OF SIDNEY GILL
THE BELOVED SON OF THE ABOVE
BORN DECR 10TH 1895
AND FELL IN ACTION IN FRANCE,
JULY 1ST 1915

HE DIED THAT WE MIGHT LIVE

Connections

Sidney served in the 12th Battalion (Sheffield City) of the York and Lancaster Regiment along with **Edward Batley**, **Laurence Baylis**, **George Braham**, **James Stuart Swift** and **Arthur Henry Thompson**. They were all killed in action on 1 July 1916.

Barnsley Chronicle – 15 July 1916

LOCAL WAR CASUALTIES
DODWORTH

Dodworth, like other parts of the district has contributed its quota to the Colours and a number of the villagers' names appear in the casualty list … Sidney Gill.

ROCHDALE OBSERVER – 2 August 1916

PRIVATE SYDNEY GILL KILLED

Mr John Peace of 7 Fitton Street, Rochdale, has been informed that his grandson, Private Sydney [sic] Gill of the Sheffield City Battalion of the York and Lancaster Regiment, and son of Mr Sydney [sic] Gill, manager of the Carlton Main Collieries, Yorkshire, has been killed during the recent fighting. Private Gill was 21 years of age. He enlisted at the outbreak of war. Formerly his mother was a teacher at the old Belfield Board School.

I am grateful to Pam and Ken Linge of the Thiepval Memorial Project for letting me use the Obituary they found in the Rochdale Observer.

CHRISTMAS GIFT TO ARMY AND NAVY.

PRINCESS MARY OPENS A FUND.

The following appeal is issued by Princess Mary:—

"For many weeks we have all been greatly concerned for the welfare of the sailors and soldiers who are so gallantly fighting our battles by sea and land. Our first consideration has been to meet their more pressing needs, and I have delayed making known a wish that has long been in my heart for fear of encroaching on other funds, the claims of which have been more urgent. I want you all now to help me to send a Christmas present from the whole nation to every sailor afloat and every soldier at the front.

"On Christmas Eve when, like the shepherds of old, they keep their watch, doubtless their thoughts will turn to home and to loved ones left behind, and perhaps, too, they will recall days when, as children themselves, they were wont to hand out their stockings, wondering what the morrow had in store. I am sure that we should all be the happier to feel that we had helped to send our little token of love and sympathy on Christmas morning—something that would be useful and of permanent value, and the making of which may be the means of providing employment in trades adversely effected by the war. Could there be anything more likely to hearten them in their struggle than a present received straight from home on Christmas Day? Please will you help me?

(Signed) Mary.

It is hoped that a sum of £100,000 will be forthcoming. The gift will take the form of a bossed brass tobacco or cigarette box, pipe, and tinder lighter. In the case of the Indian troops sweets will be supplied, instead of tobacco or cigarettes.

26

Stewart Green

Stewart Green
1882–1917 (aged 35)

STEWART GREEN was born in 1882 in Ecclesfield to **Richard Green** (born c1853 in Thurgoland) and **Susan Tofield nee Hibbs** (born c1858 in Ecclesfield).

Richard was one of nine children of **William Green** and **Mary nee Rowland**, who had married on 23 May 1848 in Saxton, near Leeds. William (born c1823 in Darfield) who had been a Farmer of 180 acres at Stainborough Folds in 1861, was an Iron Founder employing 28 men and 12 boys at April 1871, when his oldest son, **John Green** (22), was Manager of the Works and Richard (18) was Ironmoulder. Richard became Master Ironfounder at his father's Company – William Green & Co, Norfolk Foundry, Ecclesfield – but he died on 20 November 1889, aged only 37, at Mostyn House, Ecclesfield. He left a personal estate worth about £2,400 to his widow Susan, who is shown as living on her own means on subsequent Censuses. (*The foundry continued until about 1970 and may have been on the site where Morrisons supermarket is now).*

Stewart had two younger brothers: **Maurice** and **Douglas** (both attended the Holgate and served in the First World War). The brothers may have got married but Green is a common surname.

Stewart and his brother Maurice were living with their mother at Mostyn House, Ecclesfield, at April 1901, but they were in different households at Shirbrook, Woodhouse, near Sheffield, by April 1911. Stewart was a visitor to his mother's cousin **Edwin Tofield**, Solicitor, his wife **Mabel Tofield** and daughter **Victoria Gwendoline Tofield**, who occupied ten rooms and had a Cook; his mother was living in seven rooms with her uncle **Frank Tofield,** Retired Saw Manufacturer, who had two General Domestic Servants. Maurice and Douglas were living elsewhere.

Stewart's mother Susan was the oldest of five children of **Susannah Tofield** and **Samuel Hibbs**, Accountant. Susannah and Frank Tofield were two of 12 children of **Thomas Tofield**, Farmer, and **Mary Tofield**. Edwin Tofield was one of Frank's six children, making him a first cousin of Susan Tofield Hibbs.

Stewart went to Private School until the age of 12. He then attended the Holgate Grammar School in Church Street, Barnsley, for three years, from 1895 to 1898.

Stewart was articled to Norris Henry Deakin of Sheffield and took his Preliminary examination in June 1899, Intermediate examination in June 1902 and Final examination in June 1904. He was admitted to membership of the Institute of Chartered Accountants in England & Wales on 3 August 1904. He became a partner in the firm of Green & Young, Chartered Accountants, Bank Street, Sheffield, who amalgamated with Beard, Bashforth & Co.*

Stewart enlisted twice at the Corn Exchange in Sheffield for the York and Lancaster Regiment. He was a Chartered Accountant, apprenticed to Lornes Deakin, Sheffield, for five years according to the Attestation form. The first enlistment: was on 10

* Jonathan Bushell at ICAEW Library & Information Service kindly provided details of Stewart's qualifications and employment and sent me a photograph of the Institute of Chartered Accountants' War Memorial.

September 1914 when, aged 32, he joined as Private (Service Number: 127/14007) 'A' Company in the 12th Battalion (Sheffield City) of the York and Lancaster Regiment. He was discharged after 42 days because of medical unfitness: 'poor physical development' and 'unable to undertake full training necessary to become an efficient soldier' but 'Character Very Good'.

Stewart's second enlistment was on 23 October 1914, just six weeks later, when he was accepted as Private (Service Number: 2579) in the 1/4th Battalion (Hallamshire Reserve) of the York and Lancaster Regiment, noting that he 'had been in Sheffield Battalion 42 days'. Stewart was subsequently promoted up to Company Quartermaster Sergeant (Service Number: 200777).

The Medical Form contains a personal description: Height: 5' 4", Weight: 116 lbs, Chest: 34", Complexion dark, Eyes brown, Hair darkest grey, Physical Development good, Distinguishing Mark: scar on right buttock.

Stewart served in France from 13 April 1915. He died of wounds on 17 December 1917, aged 35, after serving for three years and 56 days, of which two years and 250 days were at the Western Front, the longest period of all the Old Boys. His death was reported on the *War Office Weekly Casualty List* on 14 January 1918. Stewart was buried in the Lijssenthoek Military Cemetery, Poperinge, West Vlaanderen, Belgium (grave XXVII C I).

Stewart's brother Douglas acted as Executor and received Stewart's medals and personal possessions: disc, letter & photos, pipe, wristwatch & strap, fountain pen, pocket knife, nail clippers, tobacco pouch, lock of hair, packet of photos, notebook and plate of false teeth.

Probate was granted for Stewart of Mostyn House, Ecclesfield, on 2 March 1918 to 'Douglas Green a captain in the Royal Army Medical Corps'. Effects: £1,510 19s 11d.

Stewart was awarded three medals: 1914–15 Star, Victory and British War, and his widowed mother should have received the 'Dead Man's Penny' plaque and scroll from King George V. She was living at 2 Camping Lane, Woodseats, Sheffield.

Stewart's name is on the Holgate Grammar School Memorial, the Ecclesfield War Memorial, the alabaster, marble and bronze War Memorial at the entrance to Chartered Accountants' Hall – on the panel for Members opposite the panel for Articled Clerks – and he is listed in the publication called *With the Colours* (Roll of Honour for Chartered Accountants) as well as the website of Chartered Accountants who died in the First World War.

Connection

Stewart served in the 1st/4th Battalion of the York and Lancaster Regiment along with **John Thomas Claude Wilby.**

Alumnus – April 1918

STEWART GREEN (1895–98) Y & L Regt, died of wounds on 17th December 1917. He joined the Hallamshire Battalion in Sept 1914 and rose rapidly to the rank of CQMS.

His brother Captain D Green (left 1904) RAMC is at the Labour Headquarters, France.

The Accountant – 5 January 1918

The Roll of Honour News has been received of the death from wounds of Quartermaster-Sergeant Stewart Green, A.C.A., son of Mrs. S. T. Green, of Mostyn House, Ecclesfield, and the late Mr. Richard Green, of William Green & Co., Norfolk Foundry, Ecclesfield. Quartermaster-Sergeant Green enlisted in a Sheffield battalion and afterwards transferred to a Y. & L. battalion, proceeding to France in the spring of 1915. He was a partner in the firm of Green & Young, Chartered Accountants, Bank Street, Sheffield, recently amalgamated with Beard, Bashforth & Co., and was widely known in Ecclesfield and district and amongst business circles in Sheffield, and his loss will be keenly felt. He became an Associate of the Institute in August 1904.*

MAURICE GREEN (born in 1885) had private tuition until the age of 12, when he attended the Holgate for two years, from 1898 to 1900. By April 1911 Maurice, Ironmongery Secretary, was one of two Boarders with **John Cambridge**, Retired Engineer, and his wife in eight rooms at 6 Queen's Villas in Bath, where they employed a servant.

Maurice enlisted as a Private (Service Number: 57406) in the 6th Battalion of the Welsh Fusiliers then served with the Royal Army Service Corps (Service Number: S/442342). He was awarded the Victory and British War medals, issued in 1932.

DOUGLAS GREEN (born in 1887) had private tuition until the age of 11, when he attended the Holgate for six years, from 1898 to 1904. Douglas was granted a County Minor Scholarship and passed the Oxford Local Senior exam 2nd Class before gaining an Entrance Medical Scholarship for University College, Sheffield.

* Magazine published by Gee, copy obtained from ICAEW (Institute of Chartered Accountants) Library & Information Service and used by their kind permission.

He was a Visitor at the home of **Edward B Collings**, Physician and Surgeon, of 40 Church Street, Barnsley, at April 1901.

According to *Alumnus*: 'Captain D Green, Royal Army Medical Corps, is at the Labour Headquarters, France'. A Medal Card for Douglas Green lists promotions from Lieutenant to Captain to A/Major in the Royal Army Medical Corps; he served in the Mediterranean from 17 March 1915 and earned three medals: Victory, War and 1914–15 Star. At this time Douglas was living at 2 Camping Lane, Woodseats, Sheffield.

THE TURKEY:—"I wonder what Wilhelm said when he heard of this!"

27

George Gregory

George Gregory
1881–1917 (aged 36)

GEORGE GREGORY was born in 1881 in Hoyland Nether to **Henry Edward Gregory** (born c1850 in Sheffield) and **Jane nee Kenyon** (born c1849 in West Leigh, Lancashire). Henry, the son of William (born in Sheffield) and Martha (born in Blackburn), was a Mining Engineer, having previously been a Brass Moulder. He later became Manager of the Cortonwood Colliery until he died in 1906, aged 57.

George was the fourth of nine children: **James** – Mining Engineer Iron Ore, **Ethel, Henry** (attended the Holgate), **Ellen, Robert, Maud** – Literature Student, **Elsie May** – Domestic Economy Student, and **Irene Jane**. It is difficult to ascertain whether any of George's brothers served in the First World War because their names are common.

In April 1911, the Gregory family were living in ten rooms at Marrow House, Vernon Road, Worsbrough. They had previously lived in Glamorganshire, Wigan, Hoyland, Worsbrough and Brampton Bierlow according to where the children were born.

On the 1911 Census, Robert (24) Colliery Draftsman, was a Boarder in six rooms at 3 Oak Terrace, Llanbradnack, Glamorgan, with **John Bowen**, Mining Repairer, and his family. Ethel (34) was visiting her sister Irene Jane (19) Science Student Boarder, at Oak House Halls of Residence, Manchester, where there were 19 other female occupants: two Teachers, three University Student Boarders and 14 Domestic Staff.

Ethel Gregory married **George Lodge** in Summer 1913 in Barnsley; they had three children in Barnsley: **Muriel Lodge** in 1914, **Laurence Lodge** in 1917 and **Leonard Lodge** in 1919. **Irene J Gregory** married **Francis W Platts** late 1925 in Sheffield; they had one son **Arthur G Platts** in Summer 1922 in Prestwich, Lancashire.

George attended the Holgate Grammar School in Church Street, Barnsley, for nine years, from 1890, when he was only 8, to 1899. His guardian is described as Colliery Manager of West Melton. No other details are provided about his education despite the length of time he spent at the school – the longest of any of the Old Boys who died in the First World War.

HSBC Staff Registers confirm that George began his banking career with the York City & County Banking Company on 25 September 1899, at the age of 18. He started at the bank's Rotherham branch on a salary of £30 per annum. One year later, on 1 September 1900, he moved to the Sheffield branch and on 22 October 1900 he transferred again to the Wath branch, where he remained until he began his military service. By 1915 his salary had risen to a respectable £175 per annum (GG*). (*The York City & County Banking Company was acquired by the London Joint Stock Bank in 1909, which in turn became part of Midland Bank in 1918 and subsequently the HSBC*).

George enlisted as a Private in 1914 (Service Numbers: 381, 5/84125) before being promoted to Sergeant then Second Lieutenant in the 7th Battalion of the York and Lancaster Regiment. He served in the Mediterranean Expeditionary Force from 1 January 1916, aged 35, before being sent to France. George was wounded as a Private and this was reported in the *Daily Casualty Lists* on 17 August 1916.

George was killed in action in Belgium on 26 September 1917, aged 36, and was buried in Bleuet Farm Cemetery, West Vlaanderen, Belgium (grave I B 48). His mother had the words THE SOULS OF THE RIGHTEOUS ARE IN THE HANDS OF GOD added to the War Grave headstone.

Probate was granted at Wakefield for George Gregory of Marrow House, Worsbrough Bridge, 'who died in Belgium, on 23 February 1918' to Ethel Gregory spinster. Effects: £2,192 9s 7d.

George was awarded two medals: Victory and British War, and his widowed mother should have received the 'Dead Man's Penny' plaque and scroll from King George V.

George's name is on the Holgate Grammar School Memorial and the War Memorial in front of HSBC Group Head Office at 8 Canada Square, Canary Wharf, which lists the names of the 717 employees of the London Joint City & Midland Bank who lost their lives in the First World War.

*The HSBC Memorial was originally unveiled on Armistice Day in 1921 at the bank's Threadneedle Street branch, before moving to Leadenhall branch and then Canary Wharf in 2002, when a re-dedication service took place.**

Connection

George probably knew **James Stuart Swift**, who was four years younger, as they both worked for the London Joint Stock Bank prior to enlisting in the Army.

Alumnus – December 1917

G Gregory (1890–99) was killed in action August 1917. He was before he enlisted, Cashier in the London Joint Stock Bank at Wath.

Barnsley Chronicle – 13 October 1917

WATH BANK CASHIER KILLED

> Second-Lieutenant George Gregory Y & L is officially reported killed. At the time he joined up he was Cashier at the Counties Bank (Wath Branch). Lt Gregory was the second son of the late Henry Edward Gregory, Manager of Cortonwood Colliery. He joined the York and Lancasters directly after the outbreak of war and was wounded during his first year of service overseas.

* Gertrude Zimmerman at HSBC Archives confirmed details about George's career with the bank and the War Memorial; she generously allowed me to use their photograph of him. (Copyright)

***Yorkshire Post* & *Leeds Intelligencer* – 6 October 1917**

THE ROLL OF HONOUR

> SEC-LIEUT GEORGE GREGORY York and Lancaster Regiment, who was killed in action on September 26, was the second son of the late Mr H E Gregory, manager of the Cortonwood Colliery, West Melton near Rotherham, and before enlistment he was cashier in the Wath branch of the London Joint Stock Bank. He was wounded in July 1916 and upon recovering was granted a commission.

The main photograph of George is copyright HSBC Holdings PLC (HSBC Archives) and has been reproduced in this book by their kind permission.

HENRY GREGORY (born on 25 September 1879 in Wigan) was Baptised 'in its [sic] father's house' on 10 October 1878, entered in the records of the Wesleyan Methodist Chapel in Wigan. Henry attended the Holgate for six years, from 1890 to 1896. He passed the Oxford Local Junior exam and received an Exhibition of £30. Henry went on to work for Firth Cole of Sheffield before emigrating; he became 'Manager of the Mazapil Copper Mines in Mexico in 1907'. In April 1901, Henry was a Colliery Surveyor living with his parents and siblings in Brampton Bierlow. A Passenger List has Henry (29) departing on 5 November 1910 from Liverpool to Quebec and Montreal. Several Passenger Lists to and from Liverpool between 1919–1926 confirm that Henry, Mining Engineer, was married to **Ellen** (born c1879) and they had a son **Henry Edward Gregory** (born c1914); their permanent home was in Peru and on each occasion they came to England it was to stay at Morrow House in Worsbrough Bridge. (I have been unable to find details for the marriage or birth so these were probably in Peru).

28

Edward Sidney Haigh

Edward Sidney Haigh
1887–1916 (aged 28)

EDWARD SIDNEY HAIGH was born on 11 October 1887 in Worsbrough Common to **Walter Haigh** (born c1856 in Scisset) and **Sarah Ann nee Wiggins** (born c1855 in Leeds). Walter was a Headmaster and Sarah Ann was a Certificated Teacher.

Edward was the third of four children: **Walter Bertram**, **Joseph Reginald** and **Ida Muriel Mary**. Both of Edward's brothers served and died in the First World War. Their mother died in summer 1904, aged 50. Their father died in the summer of 1917, aged 63.

By April 1911, the Haigh family had lived in eight rooms in the School House, Highstone Road, Worsbrough Common, for at least 20 years. They had a General Domestic Servant. Joseph was living elsewhere. Edward's father, brother Walter and sister Ida subsequently moved to 131 Derby Road, Loughborough.

Edward attended the Holgate Grammar School in Church Street, Barnsley, for three years, from 1904 to 1907. He was a Pupil Teacher there and at Worsbrough Common Council School. He went on to become a Teacher, but I have found no more information about where he qualified or taught.

Edward enlisted at Loughborough on 1 September 1914, aged 26 years and 11 months, as a Private (Service Number: 12649) in the 8th Battalion of the Leicestershire Regiment. He was a Teacher and had previously served in the York Dragoons. Edward trained at Aldershot, Folkstone and Pelham Down; he was promoted to Lance Corporal on 1 February 1915, but reverted to Private on 17 May 1915 at his own request. Edward had suffered an injured hernia on 30 April 1915, when he was transferred from Thorncliffe to Deal for 31 days.

Edward went to France on 29 July 1915 and was killed in action on 15 July 1916, aged 28, having served for two years 139 days, 173 days of which were in France. He was reported missing until his death was confirmed on the Daily Casualty List in *The Times* on 26 March 1917. Edward was buried in Flatiron Copse Cemetery, Mametz, Somme, France (grave IV C 10).

The Medical Form contains a personal description: Height: 5' 7", Girth: 38", Complexion: fresh, Eyes: grey normal, Hair: dark brown, normal vision in both eyes.

The undated Military History Sheet, which is stamped with the medals Edward was eligible for, states his next of kin as his father, brother Walter and sister Ida with no mention of his brother Joseph. Later, when Ida signed for her brother's Memorial Scroll, she was living at 1 York Road, Harrogate.

Edward was engaged to be married to **Clara Edith Carter** of 301 or 501 Humberstone Road, Leicester. Edward made an Informal Will (undated): 'I bequeath my property and effects, to be equally divided, between my sister Ada Haigh and my intended wife Miss Clara Carter, who is residing at 131 Derby Rd L'boro'. According to the Register of Soldiers Effects, they were each given £2 10s 11d from money owed to Edward plus £4 5s each as War Gratuity. (I have been unable to find out more about Clara).

Edward was awarded three medals: 1914–15 Star, Victory and British War, and his sister Ida, who was living at 209 Park Road, Barnsley, received the 'Dead Man's

Penny' plaque and scroll from King George V as well as her brother's personal possessions. Ida subsequently moved to 'Clevelands', Westcliffe Road, Birkdale.

Edward's name is on the Holgate Grammar School Memorial, Carillon Tower Memorial in Loughborough, the War Memorial in St Peter's Church, Loughborough and on the Leicestershire and Rutland Soldiers Died Record on the internet.

Connection

Edward was in his second year as a Pupil Teacher at Worsbrough Common Council School at the same time as **Reginald Royston.**

WALTER BERTRAM HAIGH (born c27 December 1884 in Barnsley District) was an Assistant Teacher living at home on the 1911 Census. He enlisted in Loughborough on 17 November 1914, aged 29 years and 325 days, as Private (Service Number: 16059) in the 9th Battalion of the Leicestershire Regiment; he was appointed Lance Corporal on 26 September 1915. Walter was a Musician living at 131 Derby Road, Loughborough, according to the Attestation form. The Medical Form contains a personal description: Height: 5' 10", Weight: 180lbs, Chest: 40", Vision: normal in both eyes.

Walter was killed in action on 25 September 1916, aged 31, and his death was reported on the Daily Casualty List in *The Times* on 8 November 1916. As Walter's body was never found or identified, his name is on the Thiepval Memorial, Somme, France (Pier and Face 2C and 3A). In January 1917, his sister Ida signed for various articles received but the list is unreadable; she later signed for his three medals: 1914–15 Star, Victory and British War, and his 'Dead Man's Penny' plaque and scroll, the latter sent to her in March 1920 at 209 Park Road, Barnsley. Walter's name is on the Carillon Tower Memorial in Loughborough and in St Peter's Church, Loughborough.

JOSEPH REGINALD HAIGH (born 1886 in Worsbrough) Baptism on 4 February 1886 at Worsbrough St Mary's Church, was an Elementary School Teacher at April 1911, boarding with **Ernest Luck**, Insurance Agent, and family in six rooms in Lancaster Avenue, Hitchin. Joseph enlisted in Loughborough as a Private (Service Number: 23696) in the 7th Battalion of the Leicestershire Regiment. He died of wounds on 29 March 1918, aged 32, and was buried in St Sever Cemetery Extension, Rouen, France (Grave P VII L IIA). Joseph's name is on the Carillon Tower Memorial in Loughborough. In All Saints and St Peter's Churches, Loughborough.

Edward and his two older brothers, Walter and Joseph, enlisted in Loughborough in different Battalions of the Leicestershire Regiment; all of them died while serving in France. Edward and Walter were both killed in action in different battles about

10 weeks apart in 1916, although Edward's death was not confirmed for about eight months. Joseph died of his wounds about 18 months later. They were 'buried' in different places in France with Walter's body never being found. After their mother's early death, their sister Ida must have been devastated to lose all of her brothers and their father during the period of the war. She does not appear to have got married.

The three brothers would have shared similar involvement in the First World War because the 6th, 7th, 8th and 9th Service Battalions of the Leicestershire Regiment all formed at Leicester in September 1914 and became the 110th Infantry Brigade (known as 'The Leicester Tigers Brigade'). After a period of training, they crossed to France in summer 1915; lengthy forced marches led them to their first experience of fighting in the Battle of Loos, in which the 21st Division suffered over 3,800 casualties. In 1916, they participated in the Somme campaign as, from 7 July, part of 37th Division starting with the battles of Albert (1–13 July) then Bazentin Ridge (14–17 July), during which Edward was killed in action.

Heavy bombardment began at 3am on 14 July 1916 and, after suffering many casualties, they advanced over the 450 yards of no man's land to Bazentin le Petit Wood then village. By 8am the enemy, who had resisted strongly, retreated to the outskirts of the village, but fighting continued as the Leicestershire Regiment consolidated its position until reinforcements arrived. A party of Germans continued sniping overnight and the next day, as the Leicestershire Regiment withdrew to the rear of Mametz Wood before resuming positions in Bazentin le Petit Wood.

Walter and Joseph took part in the next battles at Flers-Courcelette (15–22 September) and Morval (25–28 September), during which Walter was killed in action. The afternoon advance on Gird Trench on 25 September 1916 took place under an extremely intense and deep barrage from the enemy; they sustained heavy casualties, there was a shortage of bombs and only two of the many reports sent to the Brigade HQ reached them as the orderlies were either killed or wounded.

Joseph continued to participate in battles in the Arras Offensive then Ypres during 1917 and probably received his fatal wounds at Passchendaele (12 October to 10 November 1917).

Details from the Long Long Trail, War Diaries and Leicestershire and Rutland Soldiers Died websites

I have tried to find Obituaries and photographs without success. Jenny Moran, Senior Archivist at Leicestershire Archives, kindly checked the Leicester newspapers for me but without success; they may be included in the Loughborough newspapers which have not been digitized.

29

Frank Hall

Frank Hall
1894–1916 (aged 22)

FRANK HALL was born on 15 May 1894 in Hoyland to **Charles Hall** (born c1854 in Chesterfield) and **Eliza Ann née Fox** (born c1853 in Scholes). Charles was an Engineer Traveller at April 1911, having previously been a Coal Miner and an Iron Founder.

Although born in Chesterfield, Charles' father, also called Charles Hall, was born in Thorpe Hesley and returned to live in Kimberworth, working as a Coal Miner, with his wife and 11 children after a short period in Derbyshire as a Colliery Agent.

Frank was the second youngest of nine surviving children: **Sevilla Fox, Clara Elizabeth** – Dressmaker, **Linda** – Dressmaker, **Arthur Edward, Lavinia, Marsenor** – Engineer Fitter, **Mary Ann** and **Elsie May**. Two children had died by April 1911, including **John Charles** early 1897, aged 7, and another (name unknown). Their mother died on 25 April 1914, aged 60.

It seems that Frank was the only brother to serve in the First World War, but their common surname makes this too difficult to verify.

In April 1911, the Hall family lived in seven rooms at 103 King Street, Hoyland, having previously been at 115 King Street. Sevilla and Arthur were elsewhere.

Sevilla Fox Hall married **Charles Ernest Clayton** in 1906 and they had a son **Leslie Stuart Clayton** early 1908 in Cheshire.

Arthur Edward Hall married **Ada Brearley** in 1906 and they had three sons in Barnsley District: **Sydney, Lewis** (1) and **Maurice**. In 1911, Arthur (28) Iron Founder General Engineer, was living in six rooms at 17 Gainsford Road, Darnall, Sheffield, with his wife and two oldest sons.

Mary Ann (Molly) Hall married **Herbert Kay** and had two children in Barnsley District: **Kathleen Margaret (Kitty) Kay** I 1921 and **Jeff Kay** in 1923.

Marsenor Hall (29) an Engineer at Wombwell Foundry, married **Mary Hannah Vaines** (29) Teacher at Elsecar National School, in Spring 1915 at St Peter's Church in Hoyland and their wedding was described in *Barnsley Chronicle*. They had two children in Barnsley District: **Doreen** in 1916 and **Donald** in 1923, then moved to Sheffield. Their children each married and had three children; **Doreen Hall** married **Leonard Hadfield** and she carefully stuck family photos into a

Photograph of Charles and Eliza Ann Hall, used by kind permission of Bob Hadfield.

Photograph of the Wedding of Marsenor Hall and Mary Hannah Vaines in 1915, used by kind permission of Bob Hadfield.

scrapbook and added names to many of them, with the result that her son Bob was able to let me view and copy these family photos.

Frank went to Hoyland Common Elementary School until the age of 14. He then attended the Holgate Grammar School in Church Street, Barnsley, for four years, from 1908 to 1912. Frank was a Pupil Teacher and passed the Oxford Local Senior exam. According to the Holgate Collection, he went on to Sheffield University to become a Certificated Teacher but they have no record of him.* He may have attended Sheffield Day Training College or the Teachers' Training College, which was requisitioned for use as a hospital in the First World War, but all records were destroyed when Sheffield College was formed from the merger of six Further Education Colleges in the 1980s.†

Frank enlisted at Sheffield on 12 December 1914, aged 21 years and 6 months, as a Private (Service Number: 1/16054) in the East Yorkshire Regiment; he joined at Beverley on 13 December 1914 and appears to have been based at the Company Depot. Frank was promoted to Lance Corporal on 21 April 1915, but was not paid in this rank until 13 July 1915. He was a School Teacher living at 103 King Street, Hoyland, according to the Attestation form in the Army Pension Records.

* Matthew Zawadzki, Records Manager at Sheffield University, kindly checked their records but Frank did not attend the University.

† The Registrar at Sheffield College provided some general information and confirmed that no early records survive.

The Medical Form contains a personal description: Height: 5' 5½ ", Girth: 35", scar on left knee. Frank was discharged on 2 February 1916, having served for 1 year and 57 days, as he was assessed as 'physically unfit for further war service'.

Full-length photo of Frank, used by kind permission of Bob Hadfield.

I have not been able to find any records to confirm to which Battalion Frank was attached or whether he served in any theatre of war overseas. However, he must have been assessed as fit enough for some level of service on enlistment and he served for over two years. The Medal Card for Frank states 'nil' but no reason is given for this. Frank may have been in the 3rd (Reserve) Battalion of the East Yorkshire Regiment, formed in Beverley in August 1914; this was a training unit, which remained in England throughout the war, moving to Hedon, east of Hull, within a few days of declaration of war for duty at the Humber Garrison. (It relocated to Withernsea in April 1916, after Frank's discharge and death)

Gateway of the East Riding Regiment's Depot at Beverley (my collection).

Frank had Tuberculosis (TB) and returned home to 103 King Street, Hoyland, where he died on 27 August 1916, aged 22; Charles Hall was present at his son's death and registered it the following day. The Death Certificate states that the causes of death were '(1) Tuberculosis of Spine, (2) Psoas Abscess Exhaustion'. He was buried two days later in St Peter's Cemetery, Hoyland, where his mother had been buried on 28 April 1914, aged 61. Frank's father would join them on 12 July 1921 (aged 66). Their names are on the kerbstones around the grave:

IN LOVING MEMORY OF
CHARLES HALL
WHO FELL ASLEEP JULY 9TH 1921,
AGED 67 YEARS.

ALSO ELIZA ANN,
THE BELOVED WIFE OF THE AFORESAID,
WHO FELL ASLEEP APRIL 25TH 1914,
AGED 60 YEARS.

ALSO FRANK, THEIR BELOVED SON,
WHO FELL ASLEEP AUGUST 27TH 1916,
AGED 22 YEARS

REST IN PEACE

Probate was granted at Wakefield on 29 September 1918 to Frank's sister Linda Hall. Effects: £45 5s 5d.

As Frank was discharged before he died, he is not recognized as a casualty by the Commonwealth War Graves Commission and, therefore, he is not included on their database.

Frank's name is on the Holgate Grammar School Memorial. He is listed as CORPL Fk HALL on the Roll of Honour in Hoyland Library, which only indicates whether a man was killed in action. Frank's name is not on the Hoyland War Memorial although I feel that there is a strong argument for adding him if criteria used are not as strict as for CWGC.

In Spring 2015, I searched for relations of Frank Hall to support my request for his name to be included on the Hoyland War Memorial. Articles in Barnsley Chronicle *and* Sheffield Star *led to my meeting Bob Hadfield, who by a strange quirk of fate turned out to be a distant relation of mine via his grandmother, Mary Hannah Vaines, who had married Frank's brother Marsenor. Bob did not know anything about Frank but agreed that the photograph of an unidentified young man in uniform (with no regimental badges) could only be of Frank. He generously lent me his family photographs to use.*

The main photograph of Frank is a family photograph, used by kind permission of Bob Hadfield.

Tuberculosis (TB) in WW1

TB is an infection with Mycobacterium Tuberculosis, which can occur in any organ of the body but is most well known and most common in the lung (Pulmonary Tuberculosis). It is one of the oldest diseases known and has been a major killer of mankind since Neolithic times. It has been given many names including: Pthisis, Consumption, the Great White Plague and the Graveyard Cough. It is infectious and spreads by prolonged contact with someone who has the disease; the body's ability to cope with the infection depends on the immune system, which is less effective with poverty, malnutrition and insanitary conditions.

TB of the spine is also known as Pott's Disease, after Sir Percival Pott, a British Surgeon who first described it in 1779, although it has been found in Egyptian mummies. Spinal TB can result from the spread of TB from other areas, such as the lungs, and often leads to a Psoas or Iliopsoas Abscess, ie a collection of pus on the muscle near the hip joint, abdominal aorta etc. It causes back pain as a result of damage to the vertebrae.

Approximately 50,000 people died of TB each year in the early 20th Century, but this number increased during the First World War by about 17%. Soldiers who were invalided out of the forces with TB only qualified for a pension if the Medical Board decided that their condition was due to military service – a disability pension could only be paid if a man's disability or injury had originated during their service. This made it difficult with diseases, whose cause and time of origin were hard to pinpoint, and particularly so with TB as it could lie dormant in the body for years before becoming active; sometimes taking effect because the body has become weakened in some way. Someone could be medically fit for active service on enlistment then develop TB during service.

During the First World War soldiers diagnosed with TB were discharged as unfit, which could cause great financial hardship as the Separation Allowance was stopped and they were not eligible for an Army Pension. Treatment was usually in a sanatorium and was optional, which meant that some men, who may have regained a reasonable level of health if treated, became chronic invalids or died; they could also be a source of wider infection.

For soldiers such as Frank Hall, the discharge and cause of death meant that their service was not recognized by the Commonwealth War Graves Commission and their grave is not designated as a War Grave; it also prevented their name being added to local War Memorials. The CWGC are willing to review their decision if there is sufficient evidence that the TB was as a result of service in the Forces, but this would appear to be unlikely in Frank's case.

30

Arthur Heathcote

Arthur Heathcote
1890–1917 (aged 26)

ARTHUR HEATHCOTE was born on 14 December 1890 in Ardsley to **Minnie Heathcote** (born in 1869 in Barnsley) and his Baptism was on 23 January 1891 at Ardsley Church. Minnie, daughter of Richard Heathcote, Gardener, and Ann of Sheffield Road, Barnsley, had been Baptised in 1869 at St John the Baptist Church.

Minnie was a single parent who was 20 when her only child Arthur was born. At April 1911, she lived with her widowed mother **Ann Heathcote** and some of her six siblings in five rooms at Bleach Croft, Church Street, Ardsley. They were Market Gardeners.

Arthur went to Ardsley Elementary School, where he was Monitor, until the age of 15. He then attended the Holgate Grammar School in Church Street, Barnsley, for three years, from 1906 to 1909. Arthur was a Pupil Teacher for two years and he passed the Preliminary Certificate Examination with a Distinction in History. He went on to York St John's Training College, from 1909 to 1911, with a History Scholarship. Arthur taught at Rawmarsh, Rosehill County School, then Ardsley Oaks Council School.

Arthur enlisted in 1915 under the Derby Scheme (AHDS) and, in February 1916, joined the 1/5th Battalion of the York and Lancaster Regiment as a Private (Service Number: 21978) and was promoted to Lance Corporal. On 14 November 1916, he obtained a Musketry Qualification 2nd Class at which time he was listed as being Acting Sergeant. Arthur was killed in action during the Third Battle of Ypres on 22 October 1917, aged 26, but because his body was never found or identified his name is listed on the Tyne Cot Memorial, Zonnebeke, West Vlaanderen, Belgium (Panel 125 to 128).

Arthur completed an Informal Will form on 19 August 1917: 'In the event of my death I give the whole of my property and effects to my mother Mrs Minnie Heathcote, Bleachcroft, Ardsley, Barnsley'.

Arthur's mother subsequently moved to 8 Littlehill, Ardsley, Barnsley, where she died on 6 May 1944, aged 74. Probate for Minnie Heathcote was granted on 5 July 1944 in Llandudno* to the Yorkshire Penny Bank Ltd. Effects: £549 11s 10d. (I have been unable to find out where Minnie was buried). The Obituaries in the newspapers for her son make no reference to her.

Arthur was awarded two medals: Victory and British War, and his mother should have received the 'Dead Man's Penny' plaque and scroll from King George V.

Arthur's name is on the Holgate Grammar School Memorial and the Roll of Honour at St John's College in York.

His name is included on a family headstone in St Thomas' and St James' Churchyard in Worsbrough, with his grandparents, Ann and Richard Heathcote plus three of their children who died young:

* The Probate Commissioner at London Probate Registry confirmed that Llandudno dealt with all Probate during the First World War.

NOT LOST BUT GONE HOME

ALSO ARTHUR HEATHCOTE, GRANDSON OF THE ABOVE ANN HEATHCOTE, KILLED IN FRANCE OCT 22ND 1917 AGED 25 YEARS.

Connections

Seven of the Old Boys qualified as Teachers after attending St John's College in York: **Crossland Barraclough** (B 1894), **Edward Batley** (B 1893), **Norman Bradley** (B 1891), **John Middleton Downend** (B 1888), **Arthur Heathcote** (B 1890), **Charles Edward Savage** (B 1893) and **Charles Waldegrave Wood** (B 1883). Several of them would have attended during the same period.

Arthur served in the 1st/5th Battalion of the York and Lancaster Regiment along with **Harold Feasby** and **James Edward Thompson.** Arthur and James were killed a fortnight apart.

Arthur was a teacher at Ardsley Council School along with **James Edward Thompson** and their deaths are included together in the article in Barnsley Independent.

Alumnus – December 1917

Lance-Corporal H (SIC) Heathcote, Y & L Regiment (1906–09) of Beachcroft, Ardsley, was killed in action October 1917. On leaving the school and passing the Preliminary Certificate Examination with distinction in History, he entered York Training College. Afterwards, he became Certificated Master at the Ardsley Oaks Council School.

Barnsley Independent – 10 November 1917

ROLL OF HONOUR
STAIRFOOT'S TOLL
TWO TEACHERS FALL

Sergeant Arthur Heathcote, Y and L Regiment, who was a certificated assistant master at the Ardsley Oaks Council School, has also fallen in action. Aged 26 years, he was one of the first to attest under the Derby scheme, and joined the Forces in February 1916. He was rapidly promoted to sergeant and acted as instructor until August 1917, when he went to France – in Barnsley Feast week.

***Barnsley Chronicle* – 17 November 1917**

AN ARDSLEY TEACHER KILLED
PROMISING CAREER CHECKED IN THE WAR

Much sorrow has been expressed at Ardsley on the death in action of Lance-Corporal Heathcote. He was an Ardsley lad, aged 26, being educated at Ardsley National School, Barnsley Grammar School and York Diocesan Training College, where he passed with much distinction. He was a keen student, a born naturalist and a most successful teacher. Lce-Corpl Heathcote was the third "Derby" recruit at Barnsley and was called to the colours in February 1916. Promotion was rapid and after passing various army examinations with much success he acted as Quarter-Master Sergeant and senior musketry instructor in the 3rd Y and L. After having previously volunteered for France he finally went at the end of August and was drafted to the Y and L (Territorials), where a career of much promise has been brought to an untimely end. His loss is felt very keenly by his Ardsley friends, who were many, and by none more than the staff at Ardsley Oaks Council School.

(AHDS) The Derby Scheme

The Derby Scheme (or The Group System) was introduced in 1915 by Edward Stanley, 17th Earl of Derby, Director-General of Recruiting. Its aim was to encourage men to enlist voluntarily as, unless they did, conscription would become necessary. However, the scheme was unsuccessful and it was abandoned in December 1915; the Military Service Act 1916 was passed and this introduced conscription.

Although 215,000 men enlisted under the Derby Scheme with another 2,185,000 added to the list for future enlistment, 38% of single men and 54% of married men (not in 'starred' or 'reserved, occupations) failed to come forward.

The photograph of Arthur is from Alumnus, *reproduced by kind permission of Barnsley Archives.*

31

James Hirst

James Hirst
1890–1918 (aged 28)

JAMES HIRST was born on 29 April 1890 in Hoyle Mill, Ardsley, to **James Hirst** (born c1852 in Doncaster) and **Harriet nee Jubb** (born c1851 in Monk Bretton). James Hirst senior was a Publican, having previously been an Inspector in the Pit.

James had a brother **Albert**, who was 13 years older and became a Butcher (attended the Holgate). Their mother died in August 1909, aged 58.

The family had lived in Wombwell before moving to Ardsley, where their father was Innkeeper at the Dearne Grove Inn for more than ten years. By April 1911, James Hirst senior, Retired Publican, was living in five rooms at 16 Oakwell Lane, Barnsley, with his son James (aged 20); 'Pork Butcher Apprentice', and a Servant Housekeeper. [*The Census appears to be incorrect as James' brother Albert was a Butcher whereas James was a Teacher*]. Albert was living elsewhere.

James went to Hoyle Mill School until the age of 14. He then attended the Holgate Grammar School in Church Street, Barnsley, for four years, from 1904 to 1908. He was a Pupil Teacher at Hoyle Mill Council School before attending Goldsmiths College from 1912 to 1914.* James became a Teacher at Brampton Bierlow School.

James was a member of the Territorial Army at the outbreak of war before becoming a Private (Service Number: 1184) in the 20th Battalion of the London Regiment. He saw action in France from 9 March 1915 and was promoted to Lance Corporal then Sergeant. He served in the Battle of Loos, in which he was wounded and invalided home until his recovery, and contributed an article to *Alumnus* on his experiences (Part 3. Chapter 5).

James, who received a Commission as Second Lieutenant on 30 October 1917, served in Palestine before returning to France, where he was killed in action a few months later on 14 September 1918, aged 28; he served for about four years with three years overseas, one of the two Old Boys to have served longest. James' body could not be retrieved at the time he was killed by a bullet during an early morning attack and it was later not found or identified; his name is listed on the Vis en Artois Memorial, Pas de Calais, France (Panel 10).

James was married at the time of his death to **Ethel Powell**, who had been the Hirst family's Housekeeper on the 1911 Census; they married in Summer 1916 and lived in Oakwell Lane, Barnsley. Ethel (born in 1891 in Wombwell) was one of seven children of William Powell (born in Sutton, Nottinghamshire), Coal Miner Hewer, and Martha (born in Manea, Cambridgeshire), who lived at 23 Mitchells Terrace, Wombwell.

James was awarded three medals: 1914–15 Star, Victory and British War, and his widow should have received the 'Dead Man's Penny' plaque and scroll from King George V.

He was awarded a Military Medal for his bravery in the Battle of Loos (*London Gazette* on 14 September 1916).

* The Students Services Archives Officer at Goldsmiths, University of London, kindly sent me a photograph and details of their Roll of Honour, which includes the years James was at Goldsmiths. Unfortunately, the University is undergoing a restructure so no other records could be checked at this time.

James' name is on the Holgate Grammar School Memorial, the Hoyle Mill Memorial to Past Scholars and on the Goldsmiths, University of London, Roll of Honour wooden plaque (altered after the Second World War to include men who died) located in their Main Reception area in the Richard Hoggart Building.

He is remembered on his parents' headstone in Wombwell Cemetery:

In Loving Memory
of
HARRIET
(and) .... JAMES HIRST

ALSO SEC LIEUT JAMES HIRST, MM
20TH BATT LONDON REGT
SON OF THE ABOVE
WHO WAS KILLED IN ACTION IN FRANCE SEPTEMBER 14TH 1918
AGED 28 YEARS.

PEACE, PERFECT PEACE

Connection

John William Kilner, who was two years younger than James, was killed in action on the opening day of the Battle of Loos.

***Alumnus* – December 1918**

Second-Lieutenant J Hirst MM London Regiment (1904–08)was killed in action on September 14th. During his last year at school he passed the Preliminary Certificate Examination and entered Goldsmiths College for training as a teacher. When war broke out he was a Certificated Teacher at Brompton Council School but soon joined up. He was at the Battle of Loos and for his bravery on that occasion, he was awarded the Military Medal.

***Barnsley Chronicle* – 28 September 1918**

THE TOLL OF BARNSLEY OFFICERS
LT J HIRST KILLED

The death in action in France of Lieutenant James Hirst, London Regiment, adds another to the growing list of Barnsley military officers, who have made the supreme sacrifice in the war. The deceased's home was at 16 Oakwell Lane, where his wife resides, and for whom much sympathy has been expressed in her sad bereavement. Lt Hirst fell in the early morning of September 14th and Lt-Colonel W Warde-Aldam in a letter to Mrs Hirst says: 'Your husband was leading his Platoon with great gallantry in a very successful attack. I understand he was killed by a bullet but I regret to say he had got on so far that we had been unable to recover his body before we came out of the line. I hope, however, that the line will soon be advanced further and I will make enquiries and hope to be able to tell you where he is buried. Your husband had done some most valuable reconnaissance work just previous to the attack, which contributed materially to its success. All the time he has been with this Battalion he has proved himself a most conscientious and capable Platoon Commander, and he has shown great gallantry in action. Will you please accept the deepest sympathy of myself and all ranks of the Battalion'.

Lieutenant Hirst was a member of the local Territorials at the outbreak of war and went to France in March 1915, being awarded the Military Medal when Sergeant in the London Regiment and recommended for a Commission. Later he was invalided home and upon recovery he took up his Commission and went to Palestine returning to France about three months ago. He was educated at Barnsley Grammar School and Goldsmiths College and when hostilities commenced was a teacher at the Brampton Bierlow School near Rotherham.

***Barnsley Independent* – 5 October 1918**

OTHER CASUALTIES

Second-Lieut James Hirst, London Regiment, of Oakwell Lane, Barnsley, was killed in action on September 14th. He was formerly a member of the local Territorials, went to France in March 1915, and was later awarded the Military Medal when Sergeant in the London Regiment. Subsequently he took up a commission, went to Palestine and returned to France a few months ago. He was 28 and married.

The main photograph of James is from Alumnus, *reproduced by kind permission of Barnsley Archives.*

ALBERT HIRST (born 1877 in Wombwell, died on 28 December 1939, aged 62, Barnsley) went to Mapplewell School until the age of 12, when he attended the Holgate for one year, from 1907 to 1908; he was a Beaumont Scholar. Albert became a Pork Butcher and his first shop was in Cheapside, Barnsley, in 1897. He married

Albert Hirst Butcher's Shop, photograph kindly provided by the Tasker Trust (copyright).

Rosetta Hirst in Rotherham District in Spring 1903 and they had three sons: **James** born 1906, **John** born 1907 and **Albert** born 1908. On the 1911 Census, Albert (33) was living in five rooms at 103 Pontefract Road, Barnsley, with his wife Rosetta (33) and their three sons: they employed a servant and had a boarder, who was also a Pork Butcher. When Albert died in 1939, his home was in Queens Road, Barnsley, and he left nearly £13,000.

His three sons James, John and Albert Hirst were all Butchers; they worked in the family business, which expanded to shops in Cheapside, Sheffield Road, Peel Square, Eldon Street, Eldon Street North and the corner of New Street in Barnsley. There were two shops in Eldon Street, one of which was a Confectioners.

Albert Hirst (1908–1982, aged 74) lived at 36 Queens Road, Barnsley. He married Dorothy Dickinson in 1952 in Blackpool and they had one son in 1953. When Albert died in 1982 he left £126,796. Barnsley chops – lamb chops weighing about 1lb 6ozs each – became well-known when Albert served them as a special dish for HRH Edward, Prince of Wales, who visited Barnsley to open the Town Hall in 1933.

Albert Dickinson Hirst (born 28 January 1953 in Barnsley; died on 13 December 2015, aged 62) became well known internationally for black puddings; he won three gold and other medals at Mortagne-au-Perche, Normandy, earned the title 'Black Pudding King' and created the longest black pudding in the world. (There is a sign in one of the glass cases in Experience Barnsley, donated by Jim Gosling, with the words in white on a red background: 'Albert Hirst's FAMOUS BLACK PUDDING') The Obituary for Albert in *Barnsley Chronicle* in December 2015 led to my being able to contact his long-term partner Marilyn to exchange information.

I am very grateful to Albert's partner Marilyn Plimmer for clarifying details about the three generations of Albert Hirsts.

32

Rowland Jones

Rowland Jones
1895–1918 (aged 23)

ROWLAND JONES was born on 4 October 1895 in Barnsley to **Samuel Jones** (born c1870 in Burslem, Staffordshire) and **Annie nee Swift** (born c1871 in Monk Bretton). Sam Jones was a Coal Miners' Checkweighman, who became an early Labour Councillor, Mayor and Justice of the Peace.

Rowland was the second oldest of seven surviving children: **Olive** – Draper's Shop Assistant, **Leah, Gladys, Sylvia, Violet** and **Trevor**. Their sister **Jessie** had died in infancy by April 1911.

In April 1911, the Jones family lived in seven rooms at Gilsland House, 36 Rockingham Street, Honeywell, Barnsley, where they would remain until after the death of Sam Jones in September 1935; they had previously lived at 58 Smithies Lane, which was how Sam met Annie, whose family lived in Smithies Green, Monk Bretton.

Olive Jones (aged 29) got married to **Walter Gunhouse** (aged 29) Coal Miner of Cudworth, in summer 1923; there are several family photographs of this occasion. Walter was one of nine children born in Wombwell to Tom and Mary. His family had moved to six rooms in Barnsley Road, Cudworth, by 1911, when Tom Gunhouse and three sons were Miner Hewers; three of Tom and Mary's children had died. Olive and Walter's daughter **Rhona J Gunhouse** was born late 1927.

Wedding photograph, used by kind permission of Tonia Devonport. The Jones family in front of Gilsland House in 1923, at the wedding of Olive and Walter Gunhouse. The Reception was held at the back of the house. Olive was 29, Leah 25, Gladys 23, Sylvia 19, Violet 18 and Trevor 15.

Invitation to the Mayor's Lunch, used by kind permission of Tonia Devonport. This embossed invitation to luncheon at the Arcadian Restaurant was sent to Walter in Doncaster in 1922 from his future father in law: The Mayor (Mr Alderman Jones, JP).

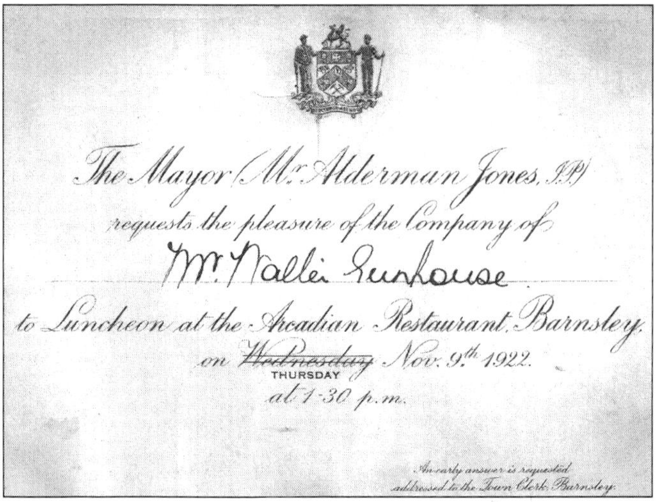

The Mayor (Mr. Alderman Jones, J.P.)
requests the pleasure of the Company of
Mr. Walter [illegible]
to Luncheon at the Arcadian Restaurant, Barnsley,
on ~~Wednesday~~ THURSDAY Nov: 9th 1922.
at 1-30 p.m.

An early answer is requested
addressed to the Town Clerk, Barnsley.

Gladys Jones married **Walter Whitfield** in Spring 1926. **Sylvia Jones** married **George H Wilkinson** late 1929. **Violet Jones** married **Frank Briggs** in Summer 1933 and they had three sons, all born in Barnsley: **Michael T** early 1935, **David N** early 1940 and **Robert I** late 1948. **Trevor Jones** married **Jessie Marshall** in summer 1934 in Barnsley and they had a daughter **Christine** born in 1938 Barnsley; they may also have had two children who died in infancy: **Eric** in 1937 and **Irene** in 1941. Trevor died late 1946, aged 39.

Rowland went to Barnsley Higher Elementary School for three years until the age of 13. He then attended the Holgate Grammar School in Church Street, Barnsley, for one year, from 1909 to 1910.

Rowland enlisted at Barnsley on 28 February 1916, aged 20 years and 4 months, as a Private (Service Number:

Photograph of Rowland (seated) and an unknown soldier, used by kind permission of Tonia Devonport.

40955) in the York and Lancaster Regiment; he was an Underground Haulage Hand living at Gilsland House according to the Attestation form. Rowland was transferred as a Private to the 85th Training Reserve Battalion on 12 June 1917 and promoted to Lance Corporal (unpaid) from 22 July 1917. On 26 June 1918, he was granted a Commission as Second Lieutenant in the 3rd Battalion then 1/2nd Battalion attached to the 9th Battalion of the Duke of Wellington's (West Riding Regiment).

He died of wounds in France – 'out but a fortnight' – on 13 October 1918, aged 23, just nine days after his birthday and less than a month before the war ended. Rowland had served for two years and 227 days. He was buried at Rocquigny – Equancourt Road British Cemetery, Somme, France. (grave XII B 14).

Rowland was awarded two medals: Victory and British War, and his parents should have received the 'Dead Man's Penny' plaque and scroll from King George V.

Rowland's name is on the Holgate Grammar School Memorial and on the painted column in the South Chapel of St Mary's Church in Barnsley.

Rowland is remembered on his parents' headstone in Monk Bretton Cemetery.

SEMPER FIDELIS
IN PROUD MEMORY OF
SAM JONES J. P.
ONE TIME MAYOR OF THIS TOWN
WHO DIED SEPT 1ST 1935, AGED 66 YEARS.
A GOOD NAME ENDURETH
BUT A GOOD LIFE ENDURETH FOR EVER

ALSO ROWLAND JONES
KILLED IN ACTION 1918

AND JESSIE, WHO DIED IN INFANCY.

ALSO ANNIE, BELOVED WIFE OF THE ABOVE
WHO DIED NOV. 15TH 1942, AGED 74 YEARS

***Alumnus* – December 1918**

Second-Lieutenant R Jones (1909–10) West Riding Regiment, son of Councillor S Jones JP of Gilsland House, Barnsley, was killed on October 14th 1918. He had been out in France but a fortnight when he made the great sacrifice.

***Barnsley Chronicle* – 19 October 1918**

LOCAL OFFICERS KILLED
SECOND-LIEUTENANT R JONES

Profound sympathy is felt for Councillor S Jones, JP, and Mrs Jones of Gilsland House, Barnsley, on the receipt this week of the official news of the death from wounds received in action of their only son Second-Lieutenant R Jones, West Riding Regiment, which occurred on the 14th inst. Lt Jones enlisted in February of last year and only as recently as the 1st of this month went to France.

DEATHS
Mr and Mrs Jones and family, whose son, Second-Lieut Rowland Jones, West Riding Regiment, died of wounds at the 18th CCS (Casualty Clearing Station), France, on October 4th 1918, desire all who have written letters of sympathy, to please accept their sincere thanks.

In this our greatest sorrow,
Our hearts are just broken.
Gilsland House, Barnsley

***Sheffield Evening Telegraph* – 26 October 1918 (Photo)**

BARNSLEY SOLDIER'S SACRIFICE

Second-Lieutenant Rowland Jones, West Riding Regiment, only son of Councillor Sam Jones JP and Mrs Jones of Gilsland House, Barnsley, died from wounds.

Photograph of Rowand from the notice of his death in *Sheffield Evening Telegraph.*

I had been finding it extremely difficult to find details because of Rowland's common surname of Jones and was delighted to make contact with relations, Anthony and Tonia Devonport, grand-daughter of Rowland's older sister Olive. They were able to provide some more information and some family photographs, including one of Rowland discovered in October 2015.

The main photograph of Rowland is a family one, used by kind permission of Tonia Devonport.

COUNCILLOR SAMUEL JONES (c1870–1 September 1935, aged 66) was born in Burslem to William Jones, a Coal Miner, and Sarah. He was the oldest of seven children, who were born in different places. William moved a number of times after Sam was born – to Worsley (Manchester) then Stanley cum Wrenthorpe, Wakefield, then by 1891 to Smithies Green in Monk Bretton.

Sam was a Labourer in a Brick Yard by the age of 14 before becoming a Miner; he was promoted from Miner to Checkweighman at Wharncliffe Wood Moor Colliery. Sam was living at 58 Smithies Lane in Barnsley when he got married to **Annie Swift** at St Paul's Church in Monk Bretton on Christmas Day 1891. Sam and Annie Jones had eight children.

Annie, who was one of six children of **Jeremiah** and **Martha Swift**, had always lived in Smithies Green, Monk Bretton, where her father was a Miner. Jeremiah Swift was born in Higham, Baptised at Darton All Saints Church and married at St Mary's Church in Barnsley. Neither parent was present at the wedding of Annie to Sam Jones as Martha had died in 1882, aged 52, and Jeremiah died, aged 63, less than 3 months before their big day.

Sam played a prominent role in public life in Barnsley for many years. He was the Labour nominee in North Ward in 1904. and was elected as one of the earliest Socialist Councillors in Barnsley, serving for over 20 years. In 1914, he became Chairman of the Hospitals Committee and the same year was lucky to escape unharmed from an accident, in which his taxi driver was thrown through the windscreen on crashing into a wall, while trying to avoid collision with a motor cyclist, who died.

Alderman Sam Jones was the first Socialist Mayor from 1920 to 1922 and his photograph is in the Mayors' Gallery in Barnsley Town Hall. Replying to congratulatory speeches in 1922, the Mayor expounded on several important issues for Barnsley. Sam believed that the proposed construction of the Scout Dyke reservoir would solve the water problem of Barnsley for the next few years. He described the housing problem as a tragedy as, although 473 houses had been provided, there still remained 1,300 families homeless. He pointed out that the Council had spent £19,000 in relief of unemployment during the last 15 months; the Government had contributed £6,000 while paying out £50,000 to the unemployed for walking about the streets, which was 'degrading and demoralising but men had become hardened in the process'. Sam suggested that the Labour Exchange should be handed over to the Corporation along with the £1,100 per

Photograph of Councillor Sam Jones, used by kind permission of Tonia Devonport.

week which was being paid so that they could get men back into employment - those who refused work would get no money. He was sure that on that basis '19 out of 20 of the men would embrace the offer and gladly erase the stigma which rested on them'. Sam was involved in the issue of providing a War Memorial in Barnsley to those who were killed in the First World War.

Elected onto the Board of Directors of the Barnsley British Cooperative Society (BBCS) in 1906, Sam Jones was President from 1933 until his death – his name is on some of the dedication stones at local Co-op branches and on a Jubilee tea caddy.

(The BBCS had started in August 1861 with nine men paying in one shilling a week; the first store opened in 1862 in Market Street and they moved to larger premises at the junction of Wellington & New Streets by the October. The Coronation History of BBCS 1862–1902 gives details of its rapid expansion with stores throughout the district, providing many goods, services and employment opportunities, investment, loans, relief and education, with reading rooms and evening classes. In 50 years, the membership increased from 178 to 20,781, capital from £335 to £501,687 and profits from £88 to £115,292).

Sam was made a JP for the West Riding in 1907, he was an official of the Yorkshire Miners' Association for 30 years, a member and President of both the Barnsley Trades & Labour Council and Barnsley Chamber of Commerce and he was a founder-member and President of the Barnsley Rotary Club.

Sam, who continued to carry out his duties diligently despite his health failing for some time, died at home at Gilsland House on 1 September 1935, aged 66. His funeral was a huge occasion in Barnsley and he was buried in Monk Bretton Cemetery, where Annie joined him seven years later, and their headstone is a memorial to baby Jessie and older son Rowland, who died serving his country. In the Death announcements, his sister Polly added: 'Always thoughtful and always kind, a beautiful memory left behind', while his wife wrote: 'Shadows deep have crossed our pathway. The eternal God is our refuge'.

An Obituary was in the Yorkshire Post & Leeds Intelligencer the following day; a very long one appeared in *Barnsley Chronicle* with photographs of his interment and extracts from this are provided below.

Daily Gazette for Middlesborough – 29 June 1914

DASHED INTO TAXI CYCLIST INSTANTLY KILLED
AND CAR WRECKED

Robert Radley (40) Piano Tuner, died after crashing his motor cycle into a taxi at Bretton Bar. The taxi crashed into a wall when the driver took evasive action and he was thrown through the windscreen with resulting cuts and bruises. Cllr Sam Jones of Barnsley was in the taxi and escaped with shock.

***Yorkshire Post & Leeds Intelligencer* – 10 November 1922**

BARNSLEY – SUGGESTED ALTERNATIVE FOR THE DOLE

Alderman Sam Jones was yesterday elected Mayor for the third year in succession. Replying to congratulatory speeches, the Mayor expressed the opinion that the proposed construction of the Scout Dyke reservoir would solve the water problem of Barnsley for the next few years. ... Describing the housing problem as a tragedy he said though 473 houses had been provided there still remained 1 300 families homeless. Speaking of unemployment he said the Council had spent £19 000 in relief during the last 15 months. Of that sum the Government contributed £6 000 whilst during the same period they had paid £50 000 to unemployed for walking about the streets. This was degrading and demoralising but men had become hardened in the process. He suggested the Labour Exchange should be handed over to the Corporation for the next six months. Give them £1 100 per week, which was being paid, and the Corporation supplement with this £200, and offer the men work at about 20 per cent over the present scale. The men who refused work would get no money. He was sure that on that basis 19 out of 20 of the men would embrace the offer and gladly erase the stigma which rested on them.

***Barnsley Chronicle* – 7 September 1935**

DEATH OF MR SAM JONES, JP (PHOTOS)
FIRST LABOUR MAYOR OF BARNSLEY
TOWN AND DISTRICT PAY LAST HOMAGE

... Mr Jones was one of the pioneers of the Labour movement in Barnsley and held a seat on the Town Council in the Labour interests for 23 years .... (and) was the chairman of many important committees and was a keen advocate of housing schemes and the welfare of local industries.

A founder and first president of the Barnsley Rotary Club, he was also a Freemason and the first president of the Barnsley Football Club's Supporters' League.

Always alive to the interests of Barnsley, Mr Jones was a member of the Chamber of Commerce, of which he was a past president. His year in the presidential chair was notable because of the persistent, though unavailing, efforts made to secure better railway facilities for Barnsley.

Mr Jones was created a Justice of the Peace in 1907 and almost invariably he presided over the Bench at the Monday morning sittings. In 1912 he was elected arbitrator to the West Riding Miners' Permanent Relief Society, an office he filled with considerable ability. ...

His connection with the Yorkshire Mine Workers' Association extended over a period of 30 years and for most of his lifetime he had been associated with the Smithies Wesleyan Reform Church, where he conducted a Men's Bible Class. ... Only last May Mr Jones was presented with a silver salver and tea service by the Society's departmental managers. ...

The flags on the Co-operative buildings and on the Town Hall were flown at half mast as a token of respect for Mr Jones. He leaves a widow, five daughters and one son.

THE FUNERAL

Rarely has public sympathy in Barnsley and district been so manifest as on the occasion of the funeral ... Almost every business, church and social organisation in the town was represented, in addition to which officials of the Co-operative Societies throughout the Midlands ... No fewer than a hundred motor cars comprised the funeral cortege, which extended for almost a mile. Dense crowds gathered at every vantage point along the route ...

The seating accommodation in the church proved totally inadequate and the service was relayed to the schoolroom, while the churchyard was crowded with people living in the vicinity, including a great many miners from Wharncliffe Woodmoor Pit ...

MINISTER'S TRIBUTE

(Rev W H Jones of the Wesleyan Reform Union Church) ... "He was a friend of all ... He was enthusiastic in matters which he believed to be right, yet generous enough to admit that others had a right to champion their cause also. A man of rare gift and quality, he was well fitted for leadership. ... His great work lay here. Smithies was written on his heart. Little children loved him ... The school behind this church is a memorial to his zeal of loving thought for children and worship."

There was then an extremely long list of mourners, including his family, the Mayor & many Councillors, the Town Clerk & Chief Officers, representatives of many different organisations & businesses and friends. This was followed by a very long list of floral tributes.

33

George Edgar Joyce

George Edgar Joyce
1887–1916 (aged 29)

GEORGE EDGAR JOYCE was born on 13 August 1887 in Leicester to **William Henry Joyce** (born c1863 in Tamworth) and **Mary nee Wass** (born c1864 in Leicester). William Henry was Secretary of the 'Lester' Coffee House Company Limited.

George had an older brother **John William Henry,** who was a Clerk in Holy Orders. Rev John Joyce married **Doris Alice Sermon** in 1929 in Bournemouth and they may have had a daughter **Mary**; they were still living there when John died in 1964.

In April 1911, George's parents and brother were living in eight rooms at The Quadrant, Billeston, Leicester, where they had a General Servant; George was in Barnsley. The Joyce family subsequently moved to 103 High Street, Leicester.

George attended Wyggeston Grammar School for Boys in Leicester for three years, from 1899 to 1902[*] then he was a Pupil Teacher until 1906. George matriculated at Queens' College, University of Cambridge, in 1906 and graduated Bachelor of Arts in 1909 (Geography).[†] He obtained a Teaching Diploma in 1910.

George was appointed Geography Teacher at Barnsley Holgate Grammar School – in charge of a Preparatory Form and teaching Geography with other forms – from 16 September 1909 at a starting salary of £140. His salary increased to £155 for the year 1911–12. George was elected Fellow of the Royal Geographical Society on 4 November 1912, while he was in post at the Holgate and living at 93 Dodworth Road in Barnsley; he remained FRGS until his death.[‡]

George obtained his MA from Cambridge University in 1913 then left the Holgate on 19 December 1913 to become a 'Gilchrist Student in Geography' – the Gilchrist Educational Trust have no records for George and are unable to explain what this was.[§] George registered at Wadham College, Oxford University, at Easter 1914 for 'some special study' until he left on 11 January 1915 – details are not known but the College did not have a presence in Geography then.[¶]

George enlisted in 1914 in the Cambridge Officers' Training Corps, having been appointed as Master of St Anne's School in Redhill, Surrey, in August. The Royal Asylum of St Anne's, founded in 1702, later became the St Anne's Society and was, essentially, an orphanage. It moved to the premises at Redstone Hill, Redhill, in 1884, where it remained until 1919. Few records survive for early 1900s so it is not possible to confirm how long George actually spent at the school.[**]

* Wyggeston & Queen Elizabeth 1 Sixth Form College, Leicester.

† The Rev Dr Jonathan Holmes, Life Fellow & Keeper of the Records at Queens' College, Cambridge.

‡ Joy Wheeler, Assistant Picture Librarian, at the Royal Geographical Society.

§ The Gilchrist Educational Trust were unable to find any records for George or mention of any award named 'Gilchrist Student in Geography'. However, the Trust has made various different awards over the years to individuals and small teams for expeditions.

¶ Cliff Davies, Keeper of the Archives, and Julia Banfield, Head of Website & Communications at Wadham College, Oxford – photographs of the War Memorial, list of names on the Roll of Service.

** Duncan Mirylees at Surrey History Centre for Information.

George was gazetted in January 1915 to the Leicestershire Regiment and was Musketry Officer for about a year. He was promoted to Lieutenant in February 1916 in the 10th Battalion attached to the 7th Battalion of the Leicestershire Regiment. George went out to France on 24 August 1916 and was reported missing less than a month later; his name was on the Daily Casualty List reported in *The Times* on 18 and 19 May 1917, which confirmed that he had been killed in action on 20 September 1916, aged 29. (Some records state that he was killed on 19 September but I have used the date provided by the Commonwealth War Graves Commission). As George's body was never found or identified his name is listed on the Thiepval Memorial, Somme, France (Pier and Face: 2C and 3A).

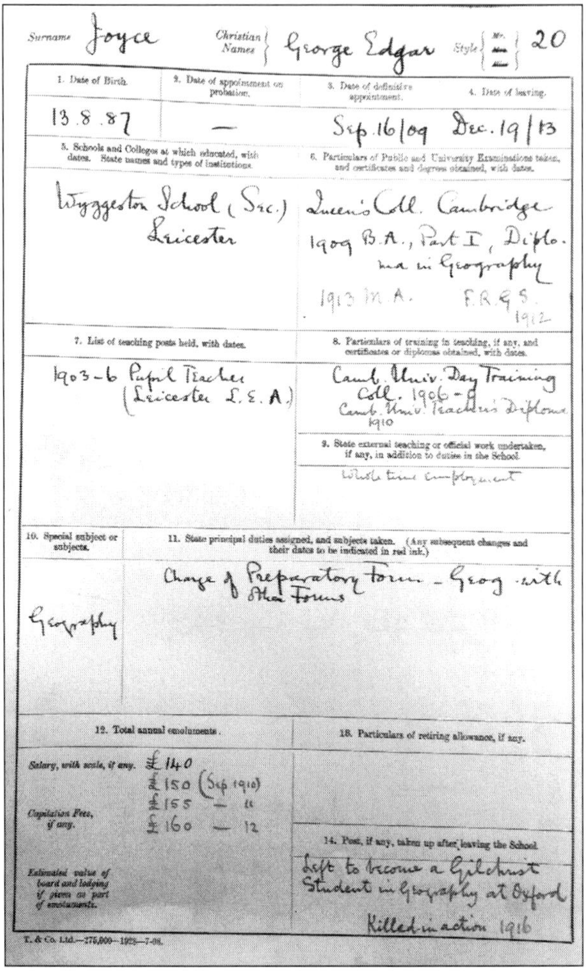

Surname: Joyce | Christian Names: George Edgar | Style: Mr. | 20

1. Date of Birth. 13.8.87
2. Date of appointment on probation. —
3. Date of definitive appointment. Sep. 16/09
4. Date of leaving. Dec. 19/13
5. Schools and Colleges at which educated, with dates. State names and types of institutions. Wyggeston School (Sec.) Leicester
6. Particulars of Public and University Examinations taken, and certificates and degrees obtained, with dates. Queen's Coll. Cambridge 1909 B.A., Part I, Diploma in Geography 1913 M.A. F.R.G.S. 1912
7. List of teaching posts held, with dates. 1903-6 Pupil Teacher (Leicester L.E.A.)
8. Particulars of training in teaching, if any, and certificates or diplomas obtained, with dates. Camb. Univ. Day Training Coll. 1906-9 Camb. Univ. Teacher's Diploma 1910
9. State external teaching or official work undertaken, if any, in addition to duties in the School. Whole time employment
10. Special subject or subjects. Geography
11. State principal duties assigned, and subjects taken. (Any subsequent changes and their dates to be indicated in red ink.) Charge of Preparatory Form – Geog. with other Forms
12. Total annual emoluments. Salary, with scale, if any. £140, £150 (Sep 1910), £155 — 11, £160 — 12. Capitation Fees, if any. Estimated value of board and lodging if given as part of emoluments.
13. Particulars of retiring allowance, if any.
14. Post, if any, taken up after leaving the School. Left to become a Gilchrist Student in Geography at Oxford. Killed in action 1916

T. & Co. Ltd.—275,000—1923—7—08.

Staff Register entry for George, reproduced by kind permission of Barnsley Archives.

George was awarded two medals: Victory and British War, and his parents should have received the 'Dead Man's Penny' plaque and scroll from King George V.

Probate was granted for George at Leicester on 28 July 1917 to his father. Effects: £185 11s 6d.

George's name is on the Holgate Grammar School Memorial, the Memorial in St Andrew's Churchyard in Kegworth, Leicestershire, and the Memorial and Roll of Honour at Wyggeston Grammar School for Boys in Leicester.

His name is on the War Memorial in the Chapel at Queens' College, University of Cambridge, where the 84 names of those killed in the First World War are read out at the Remembrance Day Service; he was reported in the College Magazine as 'missing' in the Michaelmas Term 1916 issue. His name is also on the Wadham College War Memorial, Oxford, at the entrance to the Goddard Building, plus the Oxford University Roll of Service.

The Royal Geographical Society did not have a Roll of Honour or War Memorial for its members, although many discussions took place and some names were recorded for the first two years of the War in their Journal, but George is not included as he died in 1916.

Connection

George was a Geography Teacher at Barnsley Holgate Grammar School as was **Herbert Marshall**, who had been appointed to replace George after he enlisted in 1914. Both were killed in action

Cambridge Daily News – 18 June 1917

UNIVERSITY LOSSES

Lieut George Edgar Joyce, Leicester Regiment, younger son of Mr & Mrs W H Joyce of Leicester, was aged 29 and was educated at the Wyggeston School, Leicester, and Queen's College, Cambridge, graduating BA in 1909 and MA in 1913. He was one of the first to obtain the degree in Geography. He also took the Diploma in Education and was elected a Fellow of the Royal Geographical Society in 1912. From 1909 to 1913 he was master at Barnsley Grammar School. In 1913, he was elected to the Gilchrist Studentship in Geography at Oxford University, and he joined Wadham College in 1914. In August 1914, he became a master of St Anne's School, Redhill, Surrey, and later in the year joined the Cambridge OTC. In January 1915, he was gazetted to the Leicester Regiment, and for some twelve months after his training became musketry officer. He was promoted lieutenant in February 1916 and sent to the front last August. On September 19th he was reported missing and is now reported killed.

Barnsley Chronicle – 23 June 1917

MISSING NOW REPORTED KILLED FORMER MASTER AT BARNSLEY GRAMMAR SCHOOL

A former master at Barnsley Grammar School has given his life in the great struggle for freedom; we refer to Lieutenant George Edgar Joyce, Leicester Regiment, younger son of Mr and Mrs W H Joyce of 13 Tennyson Street, Leicester. He was 29 years of age and was educated at Wyggeston School,

Leicester, and Queen's College, Cambridge, graduating BA in 1909 and MA in 1913. He was one of the fist to obtain the degree in Geography. He also took the Diploma in Education, was elected a Fellow of the Royal Geographical Society in 1912. From 1909 to 1913 he was a master at Barnsley Grammar School. In 1913 he was elected to the Gilchrist Studentship in Geography at Oxford University and joined Wadham College in 1914. In August 1914 he became master of St Anne's School, Redhill, Surrey, and later in the year joined the Cambridge OTC. In January 1915 he was gazetted to the Leicester Regiment and for some 12 months after his training became musketry officer. He was promoted Lieutenant in February 1916 and went out to the front last August. On September 19 he was reported missing and is now reported killed.

The deceased officer was, of course, well known to many "old boys" of the Barnsley Grammar School and by them held in the greatest esteem. News of his death has caused sincere sorrow.

***Yorkshire Post* & *Leeds Intelligencer* – 23 June 1917 (listed twice)**

HEAVY CASUALTIES TO YORKSHIRE UNITS
LONG LISTS ON TWO DAYS & THE ROLL OF HONOUR

LIEUT GEORGE EDGAR JOYCE Leicester Regiment, who for four years was a master at Barnsley Grammar School, is now reported to have been killed in action. He was reported missing in September last. He was 29 years of age.

34

Bernard Jaques Joyner

Bernard Jaques Joyner
1896–1916 (aged 19)

BERNARD JAQUES JOYNER was born on 17 November 1896 in Ardsley to **Henry Joyner** (born c1858 in Crigglestone) and **Eliza nee Jaques** (born c1860 in Worsbrough). Bernard's Baptism was on 20 December 1896 at Ardsley Church. Henry was a Coal Miner; Eliza had her own General Dealer Shop.

Bernard's grandfathers had the unusual names of **Septimus Joyner** and **Butterfield Jaques**, both Coal Miners.

Bernard was the youngest of five surviving children: **Amy Amelia**, **John Herbert** – Colliery Bricklayer, **Florence Annie** and **William Henry** (attended the Holgate and served in the First World War). Five children had died by 1900, including **Lewis Arthur** in 1894 (aged 5). (*The most likely other four were Ernest Septimus died in 1885, aged 1, plus three in infancy: Edith Alice in 1885, Alice Grace in 1888 and Albert Edward in 1890*). Their father died in the autumn of 1900, aged 42.

The Joyner family moved from several addresses in Barnsley to Hoyland and then Cudworth. By April 1911, Bernard and his two brothers were living with their widowed mother in five rooms at 114 Barnsley Road, Cudworth; they had two boarders who worked for the Railway. Bernard's two sisters had both married and were living elsewhere; William Henry was about to be married.

Florence Annie Joyner (born 18 November 1884 in Barnsley) married **Herbert Harry Brook** (26) Bricklayer of Cudworth, on 28 March 1910 at St John the Baptist Church in Cudworth. Herbert's father **Henry Brook** was a Labourer (Colliery Sawman) having previously been a Linen Bleacher; **Henry and Charlotte Brook**, who had married at St Paul's Church in Monk Bretton, lived in Cudworth and also had a daughter **Lily Brook.** At April 1911, Florence was living in four rooms at 88 Rock Cottages, Cudworth, with her husband Herbert, Colliery Bricklayer, and their son **Harry Brook**, aged two months.

John Herbert Joyner (born 1882 in Barnsley) married his sister in law **Lily Brook** on 19 April 1914 at St John the Baptist Church in Cudworth; John was a Bricklayer. In April 1911, Lily (aged 28) Music Teacher own account, was living with her parents in Cudworth. John and Lily had one son **Archibald Joyner,** who was born early 1915. John died in June 1948, aged 66, and was buried in the churchyard in Cudworth.

Bernard went to Cudworth Elementary School until the age of 12. He then attended the Holgate Grammar School in Church Street, Barnsley, for one year, from 1909 to 1910. He had a partial exemption of fees because of a grant of £7 10s for two years from Cudworth Educational Foundation. He became a Colliery Officer at Grimethorpe Colliery on leaving school and was training to become a professional organist.

Bernard was a Private (Service Number: 3667) in the 6th Battalion of the Black Watch (Royal Highlanders). He was killed in action on 30 July 1916, aged 19, but as no body was found or identified his name is listed on the Thiepval Memorial, Somme, France (Pier and Face: 10A).

Bernard was one of the youngest of the Old Boys to die in the First World War – there were nine young men, who were only 19 years of age.

Bernard was awarded two medals: Victory and British War, and his widowed mother should have received the 'Dead Man's Penny' plaque and scroll from King George V.

Bernard's name is on the Holgate Grammar School Memorial, the painted column in St Mary's Church, Barnsley, and the War Memorial at St John the Baptist's Church, Cudworth, where there is a Memorial Cross.

The wooden Memorial Cross with carved wood detailed figure of Jesus Christ is on a pillar facing the altar in the Lady Chapel of St John's Church, Cudworth; my photograph is reproduced in the Colour Section. It has this dedication on the base:

Photograph of Bernard in *Barnsley Chronicle*, reproduced by their kind permission.

IN LOVING MEMORY OF
BERNARD JAQUES JOYNER
WHO FELL IN ACTION IN FRANCE
30 JULY 1916
R. I. P.

He is also remembered on his parents' headstone in the Churchyard:

In
Loving
Memory Of
HENRY
THE BELOVED HUSBAND OF
ELIZA JOYNER OF CUDWORTH
WHO DIED SEPTEMBER 10TH 1900
AGED 42 YEARS

ALSO PTE BERNARD JAQUES JOYNER
1/6th BLACK WATCH
THE BELOVED SON OF THE ABOVE
WHO FELL IN ACTION IN FRANCE
JULY 30TH 1916 AGED 19 YEARS
THY WILL BE DONE

ALSO IN LOVING
MEMORY OF
ELIZA JOYNER
THE BELOVED WIFE OF
HENRY JOYNER
WHO FELL ASLEEP DEC 22ND 1924
AGED 64 YEARS

'I WILL LIFT UP MINE EYES UNTO THE HILLS'

***Barnsley Chronicle* – 12 August 1916**

Private Bernard Joyner, 1 6 Black Watch, was killed in action on July 30th during an attack on the German lines. He was only 19 years of age and joined the Forces 13 months ago, at which time he was a junior clerk at Grimethorpe Colliery and at the same time studying with Mr H N Horton at Barnsley for the professional career of organist. The deceased soldier was the youngest son of Mrs H Joyner of Cudworth and a brother of Madame Amy Joyner of Hopwood Street, Barnsley, the well known vocalist. Lieut R L West, commanding the 3rd Co. of the same regiment as Pte Joyner, has written Madame Joyner a letter which was received on

Tuesday: – 'Your brother was killed in action on July 30 while taking part in an attack on the German lines. I would like to convey to you and to all who are near and dear to him the very deep and sincere sympathy of all the officers and men who remain. We are proud to have had such a lad in our ranks. He died a noble death doing his duty bravely and well in face of the enemy, for the sake of those he loved and for the sake of his country'.

***Barnsley Independent* – 12 August 1916**

WITH THE BLACK WATCH
BARNSLEY AND CUDWORTH COMRADES FALL
PRIVATE BERNARD JOYNER

Quite a good number of lads from Barnsley and district joined the renowned Black Watch, and some have already fallen in the country's cause, and quite in accord with their regiment's reputation and fame. Private Bernard Joyner, brother of Madame Joyner, the talented Barnsley vocalist, Private John Betchetti of Belgrave Road, and Private Fred Walton, along with other Barnsley colleagues of the Black Watch, have been engaged in the big offensive, and news has arrived from Private Walton, also confirmed by other messages, that both Privates Joyner and Botchetti have been killed in action.

Lieutenant B L West, officer commanding the company in which these lads were members, in a letter conveying the sad news to Madame Joyner, wrote: 'The news I have to send will come as a great shock if it has not already reached you. Your brother was killed on the 30th July, while taking part in an action on the German lines. I would like to convey to you and to all who were near and dear to him the deep and sincere sympathy of all the officers and men who remain. We are proud to have had such a lad in our ranks. He died a noble death, doing his duty bravely and well, in face of the enemy for the sake of those he loved and for the sake of his Country'.

Private Joyner was 19 years of age, and the son of Mrs H Joyner of Barnsley Road, Cudworth. He enlisted thirteen months ago, when a clerk at Grimethorpe Colliery. A keen musician, he intended joining that profession, being a student under Mr Horton, organist at the Parish Church, Barnsley. He was formerly a member of the Cudworth Church Choir.

The main photograph of Bernard is from Alumnus, *reproduced by kind permission of Barnsley Archives.*

WILLIAM HENRY JOYNER (born in 1887 in Hoyland) went to Cudworth National School until the age of 13 then he attended the Holgate for one year from 1900; his father was a Sinking Contractor. William was a Colliery Clerk in April 1911 and was living at home. He married **Beatrice Mosley** on 17 April 1911 at St John the Baptist Church in Cudworth; William's brother John was a Witness and Beatrice's father **George Mosley** was a Railway Guard living in Cudworth. They had two daughters in West Ham: **Amy A** in 1912 and **Irene B** in 1918.

The Service Records for William were damaged and many documents are incomplete or difficult to read. He appears to have enlisted as a Private on 29 November 1915 and served in the Royal Army Veterinary Corps (Service Number: 23037) before being transferred as a Gunner in the 6th Reserve Brigade of the Royal Field Artillery (287380) in September 1918. William was a Clerk, living at 195 Leyton High Road, Stratford E15.

A letter dated 23 May 1916 from the RSPCA in Jermyn Street, London, stated: '[we are] the organisation approved by the Army Council in cooperation with the Army Veterinary Department in providing Vet. Hospitals etc for the British horses in the war. Under these circumstances I have appealed to the Westminster Tribunal for exemption for Mr Joyner on the ground that he is employed in this work for the Government'. Another letter dated 20 October 1916 to Colonel Aitken at Officer Records in Woolwich from the RSPCA stated: 'He is a first rate Clerk and Book keeper and I am sure he would do good service in your Record Office. He had been in our employ several years and we shall take him back in his old position when he is discharged from the Army'.

The Medical Form has a physical description: height: 5' 5", weight: 135 lbs, chest: 35", physical development good, vision 6/9 right eye, 6/6 left with 'defective teeth and suffers from bronchitis occasionally'. Correspondence between the Captain RAMC and a specialist at Cambridge Hospital in October 1918 related to a problem with his legs/knees – 'there is no cardiac lesion'. On the form transferring William to 'Class 'Z' Army Reserve on Demobilization' dated 14 February 1919, he was described: 'Character V Good. Is a well conducted man of very good character, honest, sober and reliable. He was an excellent Clerk".

William, of 80 Granville Street, Barnsley, died in 1941, aged 54, and was buried on 7 February in Cudworth Churchyard.

AMY AMELIA JOYNER (born 1880, died 18 February 1940, aged 59) was 'Professor of Singing' aged 20, when she was a boarder at 23 Hamilton Gardens, St Marylebone, London. Amy married **Archibald William Jarman**, Colliery Clerk, in 1906. They lived in eight rooms at 57 Hopwood Street, Barnsley at the 1911 Census, subsequently moving to Kirkhaven in Cawthorne. The family headstone in St John's Churchyard in Cudworth includes their only two children, who both died very young: **Irene Hope Jarman** died 10 October 1912, aged 4 years and 10 months, **Charles Jarman** was born and died on 21 August 1913.

Amy, a soprano vocalist and Associate of the Royal Academy of Music (ARAM), was known professionally as 'Madame Joyner'. She was very actively involved in entertaining and raising funds for men serving their country, at home and overseas, by organizing and participating in concerts throughout the war period and afterwards. There are a number of adverts and reports about these in *Barnsley Chronicle* and other local newspapers. The first concert in September 1914 raised £60 19s 10d for the main Barnsley Patriotic Fund; Amy went out to France in summer 1917 with a group of vocalists to entertain the men at the front and when war ended she started fundraising for St Dunstan's Home for Blind Soldiers. Amy and her husband were both involved with the Choral Society in Cawthorne.

Amy Amelia Jarman (Madame Joyner) was an invalid for some time before she died at home at Kirk Haven, Cawthorne, on 18 February 1940, aged 59. Her husband was Juvenile Employment Officer for Barnsley. The funeral service was held at All Saints Church in Cawthorne, conducted by Rev F B Greenwood with the assistance of three other Vicars; there was a lot of music and many floral tributes, as described in detail in an Obituary in *Barnsley Chronicle* on 24 February 1940.

Despite the number of references to Madame Joyner in the local newspapers I have not been able to find any photographs of her that are of good enough quality to use.

***Barnsley Chronicle* – 12 December 1914**

PATRIOTIC PARS

The second patriotic concert … was very successful. The chief attraction was the fact that Madame Amy Joyner, ARAM, was announced to sing and she received a very hearty appreciation of her beautiful rendering of 3 songs

***Barnsley Chronicle* – 26 May 1917**

LETTER FROM S A WOMBILL,
MATRON OF LUND WOOD HOSPITAL

I have this morning received a cheque from Madame Joyner for the handsome sum of £7, part proceeds of a concert given by her choir, a token of their great sympathies for our sick and wounded heroes. In addition to this magnificent gift our lads were the partakers of a sumptuous tea and supper and were delightfully entertained by Madame Joyner and her choir a few weeks ago …

***Barnsley Chronicle* – 4 August 1917**

A BARNSLEY VOCALIST IN FRANCE
AMY JOYNER'S ENTHUSIASTIC RECEPTION

I know you will be pleased to know I have been fortunate in coming across a few of our own Barnsley boys out here, writes Madame Amy Joyner from France. 'I cannot describe to you what it is like to be singing out here to the boys who are fighting to keep us safe in England. If you could hear the shout when I am announced and see even caps thrown up with intense delight; if you could see their faces light up with pleasure – but more than all if you could feel the hard strong grip of a hand thrust into yours as you pass through on your way to another camp – you would never forget it. One boy said to me: "You cannot understand, Madame, what it has meant to us to see you, hear you and really speak with you". I looked at his war-worn face and my heart simply went out to him and all of our brave boys. All are eager for us to see "Mother" when we return and I shall do my best you may guess!

I am having a very busy and harassing time and it is really a great strain but I am becoming daily more thankful and pleased that I stuck to my promise and came. I shall have a large diary and some wonderful scenes to describe; words cannot express them I am afraid. We are in the heart of things and can hear the constant thud of guns.

I have sung already to thousands and thousands of men, been miles out in a huge dark forest to camps where boys are resting from the line and where you would never think there was a living creature. Little do we know in England what these boys are enduring and their wonderful spirit! We take "Little Peter" with us (a small closed up piano) and we sometimes sing outside in a valley. The boys sat up the hill all around and we have an impromptu platform which wobbles about very ungraciously; always a camp dog and sometimes hundreds of frogs leaping about. I used to be afraid but I am now quite brave and don't mind the frogs at all. We travel about in a car that was a car once upon a time and we are often delayed on our way home when it refuses to go. We give three shows a day most days and we go anything from 10 to 40 miles out. We oftener than not dine at the Mess and arrive back about 2 or 3 o' clock in the morning and needless to say our mornings are spend in rest. I could write you pages of all I have done but that must be kept for another time. I am the only one from the North in this party except the entertainer who is a Lancashire man. The others are London artistes.

***Barnsley Chronicle* – 9 March 1918**

CONCERTS AT THE FRONT
MADAME AMY JOYNER'S EFFORTS

Amy 's latest fundraising venture 'for the concerts given during the war to the soldiers at the front by Miss Lena Ashwell and her enthusiastic band of vocalists & instrumentalists'. Lieutenant-Colonel J Hewitt presided and the programme included Amy's 'ever popular rendition of "Annie Laurie" plus her account of her experiences performing at the front'. Lt-Col Hewitt in his introductory speech asked the gathering to consider the situation of the lads at the front. 'At that very moment those gallant soldiers might be standing starved, war-worn and hungry looking across "No Man's Land" where perhaps death was awaiting them .... How these songs (of Amy and musical colleagues) rendered so sweetly on the battlefield must touch the hearts of lads just as water to the lips of men in the thirsty desert!'. Amy explained that despite some insinuations, she was not making money from these concerts but doing them 'to raise funds for the providing of musical treats for the soldiers'. 'I have the boys' interests at heart and I am doing this work absolutely for the love of it.

***Yorkshire Evening Post* – 14 February 1919**

MADAME JOYNER'S SUCCESS

Barnsley is making musical history in that it has produced the first lady conductor to take charge of a chorus on a large scale, namely Madame Amy Joyner, a Barnsley vocalist. Madame Joyner who, as a soprano, has appeared at leading concerts all over the country, organised a victory concert at the Public

Hall, Barnsley, last night in aid of St Dunstan's hostel for blind heroes. …. (She) studied at the Royal Academy of Music in London.

Barnsley Chronicle – 24 February 1940

BARNSLEY SINGER'S DEATH (PHOTO)
MADAME AMY JOYNER'S WORK IN LAST WAR
RAISED £3,000 FOR CHARITIES

Sincere regret has been occasioned in town and district by the death of Madame Amy Joyner, whose lovely soprano voice thrilled thousands of people in many parts of the country, and who will be particularly remembered for her work on behalf of the men who fought in the Great War. ….

During the last war, Madame Joyner raised no less than £3,000 for war charities. As a member of Miss Lena Ashwell's Concert Party, she went to France in 1917, and entertained the troops there for eight weeks. When she returned, she raised a further £800 by singing and lecturing, and this money was devoted to Miss Lena Ashwell's Concerts at the Front Fund.

A native of Cudworth, Madame Joyner studied for six years at the Royal Academy of Music, for which she won an open scholarship. Later she sang at important musical centres throughout the country and was particularly successful in oratorio work.

She did a great deal to encourage singing in the Barnsley district generally, forming a Ladies' Choir in Barnsley with a membership of about 120, and a male voice choir ('The Men's Musical Class') composed mainly of miners in the Old Town area. Along with her husband she founded the Cudworth Choral Society, of which she was conductor for 23 years. When the Barnsley Boys' Club was started she held a garden party at her home to raise funds for the boys.

… Madame Joyner had 'lived' music throughout her life … 'The possession of a glorious soprano voice, her cheerful and lovable disposition and her willingness at all times to help any good cause, made her a host of friends'. 'Her kind heart prompted her on many occasions to entertain the wounded soldiers. On the memorable night that the enemy Zeppelin came over Barnsley she was entertaining the wounded soldiers to tea followed by a musical evening in the Miners' Hall. Some of the fellows were so badly shell-shocked that they had to be assisted with their food and, just as the soldiers were leaving for their Convalescent Home, singing "Kind, kind and gentle is she" (a song which had been rendered by one of the artistes), over came the enemy with his cargo of destruction.'. …

Cawthorne Church Service

(Music included: two of Madame Joyner's best loved pieces from Handel's 'Messiah' ("I know that my Redeemer liveth") and from 'Elijah' ("Hear ye, Israel") on the organ, two favourite hymns 'I heard the Voice of Jesus say' and 'Abide with me'). ….

So many floral tributes were received that the pathway from the door of Kirk Haven to the garden gate was banked with flowers on each side. (There was a long list of donors)

(Mourners included her husband, her three siblings and their spouses, her in laws and many friends, amongst whom were two Misses Charlesworth, J C Wemyss, Mrs Laycock and Mr F Jagger.)

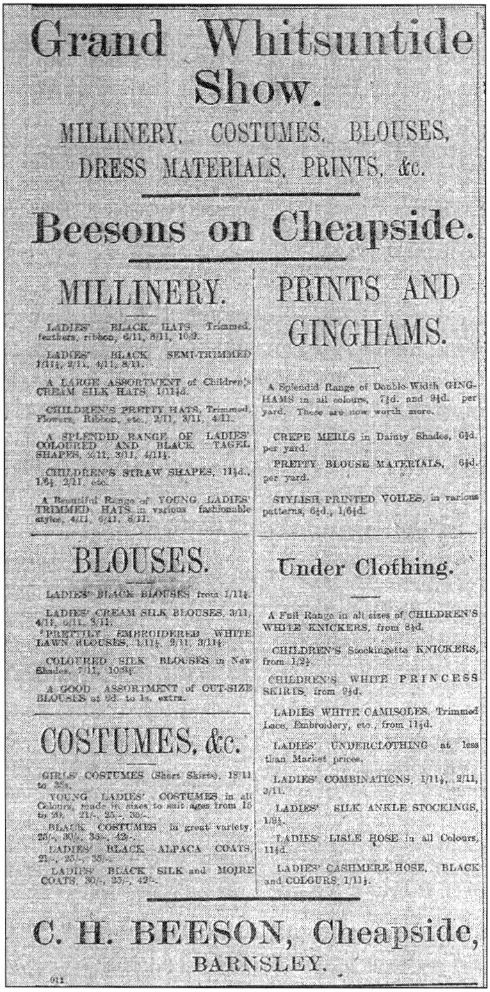

35

George William Kellett

George William Kellett
1892–1916 (aged 24)

GEORGE WILLIAM KELLETT was born on 19 August 1892 in Worsbrough to **John Kellett** (born c1868 in Worsbrough) and **Jane nee Matthewman** (born c1870 in Stainborough). George William's Baptism was on 2 October 1892 at St Mary's Church, Worsbrough. John was a Drayman then Confectioner's Traveller.

William was the second oldest of six surviving children: **Ethel, Raymond** (served in the First World War), **Colin, Clarice** and **Ralph**. **Henry** died in 1900, aged 3, and **Ida** died in infancy in 1907.

In April 1911, the Kellett family lived in five rooms at 63 The Walk, Birdwell, having previously lived at 13 Birdwell Common, Worsbrough. They were at 79 The Walk, Birdwell, in 1919.

Colin married **Elsie Blackledge** in Wortley late 1919 and they had two children: **John** in spring 1921 and **Betty** early 1925. Clarice married **George E Cunnington** in Barnsley in spring 1927 and they had one daughter **Brenda Cunnnington** in 1930.

William went to Birdwell Elementary School, where he was a Monitor, until the age of 15. He then attended the Holgate Grammar School in Church Street, Barnsley, for three years, from 1907 to 1910. William was a County Continuation Scholar for two years, Bursar and Student Teacher. He passed the Oxford Local Senior exam and went on to Sheffield Day Training College, which was requisitioned for use as a hospital in the First World War, to become a Certificated Teacher at Worsbrough Common School.

William enlisted at Easter 1915 in Sheffield as a Private (Service Number: 15913) in the 1st Battalion of the Coldstream Guards. He was reported missing before it was confirmed that he had been killed in action at Ginchy on 15 September 1916, aged 24. As William's body was never found or identified his name is listed on the Thiepval Memorial, Somme, France (Pier & Face: 7D and 8D).

William was awarded two medals: Victory and British War, and his parents should have received the 'Dead Man's Penny' plaque and scroll from King George V.

William's name is on the Holgate Grammar School Memorial and the Memorial at St Mary's Church in Worsbrough.

He is remembered on his parents' headstone in Worsbrough St Mary's Churchyard.

IN
LOVING MEMORY OF
JOHN
THE DEARLY LOVED HUSBAND OF
JANE KELLETT
WHO PASSED AWAY JAN 5TH 1925, AGED 67 YEARS
ALSO THE ABOVE NAMED
JANE KELLETT
WHO DIED MARCH 18TH 1966, AGED 85 YEARS

**ALSO GEORGE WILLIAM, THEIR SON,
WHO WAS KILLED IN ACTION IN FRANCE
SEPT 15TH 1916, AGED 24 YEARS**

AT REST

***Barnsley Chronicle* – 21 October 1916**

LOCAL CASUALTIES
MISSING

Notification was received on October 11th, that Private G Wm Kellett, No. 15913 No. 11 Platoon, No. 3 Company, 1st Battalion Coldstream Guards, is reported as missing after the engagement at Ginchy, September 15. Any news of him would be gratefully received by his parents at 79, The Walk, Birdwell, Barnsley. Before enlisting at Easter, 1915, Private Kellett was a certificated teacher at Worsbro' Common School.

***Barnsley Chronicle* – 28 October 1916**

WORSBRO' TEACHER MISSING

Mr and Mrs Kellett of The Walk, Birdwell, have been notified that their son, Private George William Kellett of the Coldstream Guards, has not been heard of since September 15. Prior to enlisting Private Kellett was a teacher at the Worsbro' Common School.

***Barnsley Chronicle* – 18 November 1916**

BIRDWELL LANCE-CORPORAL KILLED

Official Intimation has been received by Mr and Mrs Kellett of The Walk, Birdwell, of the death in action of their son Lance-Corporal G William Kellett of the Coldstream Guards. He had been missing since September 15th. Before enlisting he was a certified teacher at the Worsbro' Common school.

***Barnsley Chronicle* – 2 December 1916**

DEATHS

KELLETT In affectionate remembrance of George William Kellett, 1st Battalion Coldstream Guards, the beloved son of John & Jane Kellett, who was killed in action at Ginchy, France, September 15th 1916, aged 24 years. Mr &

Mrs Kellett and family desire to thank all friends for their sympathy in their bereavement.

The main photograph of William is from Alumnus, *reproduced by kind permission of Barnsley Archives.*

RAYMOND KELLETT (born in 1894 Worsbrough) was a Confectioner's Sugar Boiler in April 1911, living at home. Raymond enlisted on 4 February 1916, aged 21 years and 3 months, as a Private (Service Numbers: 15223 and 5395) in the 3/5th Battalion of the King's Own Yorkshire Light Infantry; he was a Sugar Boiler living at 79 The Walk, Birdwell, with his parents, according to the Attestation form. Raymond was promoted to Corporal in 1917 then to Sergeant on 11 February 1918. Records state that he was Home from 28 March 1916 until he went to France on 19 July 1916, where he was taken Prisoner of War on 28 March 1918. Raymond was released on 1 January 1919 and returned home via Leith the following day. He was discharged on 30 March 1919.

Raymond, Motor Driver of 79 The Walk, Birdwell, married Ada Sutcliffe of Kirkburton at All Hallows Church in Kirkburton on 5 February 1921. He died in June 1959, aged 64, at 60 Sheffield Road, Birdwell and Administration was granted to his widow.

Pam Kellett, whose father was George William's first cousin, sent me a photograph of the family headstone with memorial to their son. Another relation Margaret Shepard told me that Colin's wife had been William's fiancee.

36

William Kelsey

William Kelsey
1896–1916 (aged 20)

WILLIAM KELSEY was born on 15 April 1896 in Barnsley to **Albert Henry Kelsey** (born c1865 in Barnsley) and **Clara Jane nee Laycock** (born c1865 in Barnsley). William's Baptism was on 3 June 1896 at Barnsley St John the Baptist Church. Albert Kelsey was a Provision Merchant until he died on 8 June 1900, aged 36. Clara had to live on her own means when widowed and was a Shopkeeper residing at The Manse in Sheffield Road when William started at the Holgate.

Clara Jane was the oldest daughter of **Benjamin John Laycock**, Butcher of 179 Sheffield Road, Barnsley, and **Sarah Ann Rymer**. Clara had four siblings, two brothers and two sisters: **George Henry Laycock**, the father of Old Boys **Benjamin Holroyd Rymer and Donald Stanley Laycock** (Part 2. Chapters 39 and 40), then **Clifton Laycock**, a Butcher retired early because of ill health, who married and had four children, then **Verona Laycock** and then **Mary Ada Hinchcliffe Laycock**, who married **Benjamin James Jagger**, Estate Agent, and had two children.

William was one of two surviving children with a sister **Gladys Mary Kelsey**, who was eight years older. Three children had died by April 1911: **Dorothy** in 1881, aged 8 months, **Frances Ethel** in 1896, aged 6, and **Sarah Marion (known as Sally)**, in 1905, aged 10.

In April 1911, the Kelsey family lived in six rooms at 24 Bond Street, Barnsley, having previously moved from 17 Corporation Street, 199 Sheffield Road and 16 Beech Street in Barnsley. William was elsewhere, probably boarding at Rossall School, Fleetwood, Lancashire.

William went to Park Road School until the age of 11. He then attended the Holgate Grammar School in Church Street, Barnsley, for two years, from 1907 to 1909. He left to go to Rossall School, which had the oldest Combined Cadet Force and ran its own Officer Training Corps; he was a pupil in Rose House between 1909 and 1914.* William started at Clare College, Cambridge University, with a view to becoming an Electrical Engineer. Cambridge University had a ceremony at which new students were entered onto the register and the photograph of William from Clare College is from this 'matriculation' in Michaelmas term 1914.†

William enlisted in 1914 as a Driver (Service Number: 35) in the Royal Horse Artillery and the Royal Field Artillery; he was promoted to Second Lieutenant on his 19th birthday, then later to Lieutenant. He went out to France on 21 April 1915 and was wounded in the thigh and spine while on observation duty at the front on 14 July 1916, reported in the Daily Lists on 26 July. Left in the open until he could be rescued two days later, William was treated in the Royal Hospital before transferring to the

* Sharon Potts, Alumni Officer at Rossall School, provided details about William's education and a photograph of the Memorial.

† Various staff at Clare College, Cambridge University, very kindly sent me photographs of William Kelsey (CCPH/2/1/1/1914), his Death Plaque and their Memorial. They confirmed his matriculation and sent me a video link to the reading of names at the Tower of London on 3 November 2014 as well as details of their commemoration.

Empire Hospital, Vincent Square, Westminster, London, where his mother and sister visited him. He died there, after prolonged suffering, on 23 September 1916, aged 20, and was buried in Barnsley Cemetery (grave M 128).

William was awarded three medals: 1914–15 Star, Victory and British War, and his widowed mother should have received the 'Dead Man's Penny' plaque and scroll from King George V. William was recommended for a Military Cross but was not awarded one.

Probate was granted in London for William, whose home was at 13 Victoria Road, Barnsley, on 3 February 1917 to his sister Gladys Mary, spinster. Effects: £5,398 5s 11d.

William's name is on the Holgate Grammar School Memorial, the painted column in St Mary's Church, Barnsley, on the wooden plaque with three panels in the Chapel at Rossall School, Fleetwood, and on the metal plaque with three panels in Clare College Chapel, Cambridge.

Clare was the only College to honour its 198 war dead by having their names read out in the Roll of Honour Memorial at the Tower of London for the Centenary of the outbreak of the First World War; they were read on 3 November 2014. Each man is being commemorated on the centenary of his death by displaying a poppy plaque with brief details about the individual on the Clare College Chapel noticeboard. A total of 2,470 students and graduates of Cambridge University lost their lives in the First World War.

The family grave in Barnsley Cemetery has three plots with an obelisk; inscriptions round three sides of the four tiers also commemorate William's parents, Albert & Clara Jane Kelsey, his three sisters: Dorothy, Frances Ethel & Sarah Marion, and other relations: William & Mary Kelsey plus their sons Francis & William, Alfred Berry, Francis & Frances Kelsey plus their son William & his wife Mary. (There is no Commonwealth War Grave Commission headstone):

IN LOVING MEMORY OF
WILLIAM KELSEY
2ND LIEU ROYAL FIELD ARTILLERY SR
ONLY SON OF THE ABOVE ALBERT & CLARA KELSEY
WHO DIED IN THE EMPIRE HOSPITAL LONDON ON
SEPT 24TH 1916
OF WOUNDS RECEIVED IN FRANCE ON JULY 14TH 1916
AGED 20 YEARS

Connections

William was the first cousin of **Benjamin Holroyd Rymer Laycock** and **Donald Stanley Laycock**.

Extract Taken From *The Rossallian Magazine* – October 1916

William Kelsey (Rose 1909–1914) 2nd Lieutenant RAF:

He was always brightest when in the greatest danger, and his men would go anywhere with him and do anything for him'. These are the worlds of brother officers; and what finer epitaph could be written?

As a boy his simple character and sunny smile endeared him to everyone, masters and boys, who came into contact with him at Rossall. Nothing ruffled his serene temper, and he could always be relied upon to do his best contentedly in face of a difficult problem or a formidable 'forward' charging down upon him at half-back.

The same spirit characterised his all too brief career in the Service and his long illness after he had been badly hit. A plucky fight he made of it during many weeks of bitter pain, his one wish being that those dearest to him who sat by his bedside might not know how terribly he suffered.

His Commanding officer wrote of the glorious work he did at the front, and recommended him for the Military Cross 'which he had earned several times over'.

***Barnsley Chronicle* – 22 July 1916**

WOUNDED

Second-Lieutenant W Kelsey (20), Royal Field Artillery, the only son of Mrs Kelsey of Victoria Road, Barnsley, is at the base hospital suffering from severe wounds in the thigh and back. He was educated at Rossall School and Cambridge.

***Barnsley Chronicle* – 29 July 1916**

WOUNDED

Second-Lieut W Kelsey, RFA, Special Reserve, is still lying at the base hospital, Rouen, suffering from gunshot wounds in the back and thigh. The wounded officer's mother resides at Victoria Road, Barnsley.

***Barnsley Chronicle* – 30 September 1916**

FUNERAL OF A MILITARY OFFICER
SECOND LIEUT W KELSEY

The funeral took place at Barnsley Cemetery on Wednesday of Second Lieut William Kelsey, RFA, the only son of the late Mr Albert Kelsey and Mrs Kelsey of Victoria Road, Barnsley. The deceased officer who was only 20 years of age, was buried with military honours, a firing party from Silkstone Camp attending, together with a number of officers. An impressive service was held in St Mary's Church at 1 o' clock.

Second Lieut Kelsey was educated at Rossall and Clare College, Cambridge, and was preparing for the career of an electrical engineer. On his nineteenth birthday he obtained his commission and manifested a keen desire to get to the Front on active service. When engaged on observation work he was wounded in the thigh and spine, and at the same time two of his men were killed. After lying wounded and helpless for two days he was eventually rescued and treated at the Royal Hospital for five weeks. He was then removed to the Empire Hospital, London, where he died on Sunday. Whilst in hospital in England he was frequently visited by his mother and sister.

The service was taken by Canon Hervey (Rector) and Captain, the Rev R Huggard. A telegram of sympathy was received from the Secretary of State for War, and also from the Officers of Second Lieut Kelsey's battery. The mourners included Mrs Kelsey (mother), Miss G M Kelsey (sister), Mr and Mrs B J Jagger (aunt and uncle), Miss V Laycock (aunt), Miss E Laycock and Miss K Jagger (cousins), Mr Clifton Laycock (uncle), Mr and Mrs J Taylor, Mrs Stringer, Mr Herbert Rymer, Miss Moore, Mrs Joe Burnett, Miss Burnett, Mr Alfred Clegg, Mrs G H Hall, Miss Edith Hall and Miss May Hall.

Barnsley Chronicle – 7 October 1916

PATRIOTIC PARS

The late Second-Lieutenant William Kelsey, RFA, Special Reserve (whose death and interment at Barnsley we announced last week) was rescued on the battle-field after a considerable period, and conveyed to the No, 2 Red Cross Hospital at Rouen. His mother and sister were in attendance upon him the whole of the time he was a patient, both at Rouen and the Empire Hospital, London, in which latter institution he died. The deceased officer obtained his commission from Cambridge University where he was preparing for the mathematical tripos, having proceeded from Rossall College Officers' Training Corps. Amongst many beautiful floral tributes sent was a magnificent wreath from the House Master and school colleagues at Rossall where the deceased officer held the rank of sergeant.

***Sheffield Evening Telegraph* – 25 September 1916**

BARNSLEY OFFICER'S DEATH

Another young Barnsley officer has given his life in the active service of King and country. The deceased Second-Lieutenant William Kelsey, RFA, was 20 years of age and the only son of the late Mr Albert Kelsey and Mrs Kelsey of Victoria Road, Barnsley. He was educated at Rossall and Clare College, Cambridge, and was preparing for the career of electrical engineer. He obtained his commission on his 19th birthday and was very keen to get to the front on active service. He was wounded in the thigh and spine when engaged on observation work, at the same time as two of his men were killed. He was rescued after lying wounded and helpless for two days and was treated at the Royal Hospital for five weeks and then removed to the Empire Hospital, London, where he died yesterday. He was frequently visited by his mother and sister whilst in hospital in England.

***Yorkshire Post* and *Leeds Intelligencer* – 26 September 1916**

THE ROLL OF HONOUR

Second-Lieutenant William Kelsey, RFA (Special Reserve) of Barnsley, after a good deal of suffering from wounds received in action, died at the Empire Hospital, London, on Sunday. Aged 20 years, he was the only son of the late Mr Albert Kelsey and Mrs Kelsey of Victoria Road, Barnsley. He was educated at Rossall and Clare College Cambridge, preparing for the engineering profession. Early in the war he joined the ranks and got his commission on his 19th birthday. He had been at the Front for a considerable period and on July 14 he was wounded in the thigh and spine whilst on observation duty. Two of his men were killed at the same time. He lay in the open for two days before he could be rescued and after treatment in hospital he was transferred to London. His mother and sister have been able to remain with him during his long suffering.

The main photograph of William is reproduced by kind permission of the Master, Fellows and Scholars of Clare College, Cambridge (copyright CCPH/2/1/1/1914).

37

John William Kilner

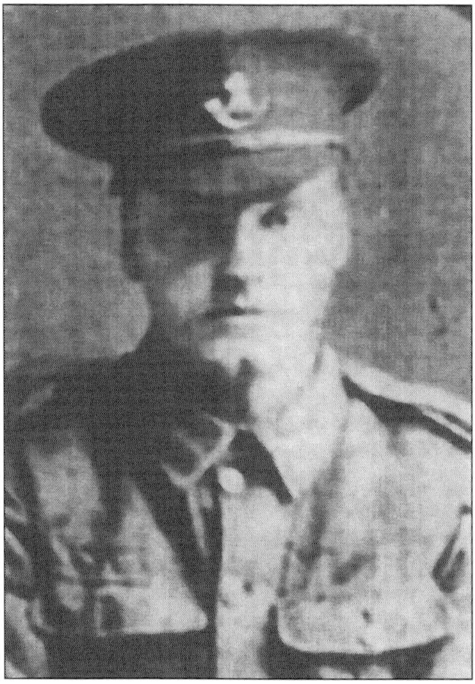

John William Kilner
1892–1915 (aged 23)

JOHN WILLIAM KILNER was born on 15 September 1892 at High Green, near Sheffield, to **William Kilner** (born c1870 in High Green) and **Mary nee Savage** (born c1869 in Barnsley). William was a Licensed Victualler in his own pub, having previously been a Butcher then a Publican.

John had two younger sisters: **Annie** and **Nellie**. A child had died before April 1911 (name unknown).

In April 1911, the Kilner family lived in seven rooms at the White Horse Hotel in Chapeltown, where they employed two Domestic Servants. They had previously lived in Market Place, Chapeltown, where they also had two servants.

John went to Thorpe Hesley National School until the age of 12. He then attended the Holgate Grammar School in Church Street, Barnsley, for five years, from 1904 to 1909. John became an Accountant's Clerk with Messrs J Gibson and Sons and later joined an Auctioneer's firm at Bromsgrove, near Birmingham.

John enlisted early 1915 in Birmingham as a Private (Service Number: 17865) in the 2nd Battalion of the Oxford and Buckinghamshire Light Infantry. He went out to France on 26 May 1915 and was killed in action on 25 September 1915, aged 23, just 10 days after his birthday and after four months in France. As his body was never found or identified John's name is listed on the Loos Memorial, Pas de Calais, France (Panel 83 to 85).

The Battle of Loos opened on 25th September with insufficient supplies of ammunition or heavy artillery and it was the first time that the British Army used poison gas. Chlorine was released at 5.50am but it formed a dense blanket over the British troops adding to the number of their casualties.

John was the third Old Boy to die and one of only three who died in 1915.

John was awarded three medals: 1914–15 Star, Victory and British War, and his parents should have received the 'Dead Man's Penny' plaque and scroll from King George V.

John's name is on the Holgate Grammar School Memorial, Chapeltown War Memorial and in the St John's Memorial Book at Chapeltown.

Connections

John's uncle **William Savage**, Sanitary Inspector, was the same age as and would have worked with **Edward Saville**, Assistant Sanitary Inspector, who was the father of **Ronald John Saville**.

James Hirst, who was two years older than John, also fought in the Battle of Loos but survived this to be killed in action later; he wrote an article about this battle for *Alumnus*.

***Barnsley Chronicle* – 23 October 1915**

PATRIOTIC PARS

Mr and Mrs William Kilner of Market Place, Chapeltown, have received notification that their only son has been killed. Pte John William Kilner, aged 23 years, was very well known and respected in the Chapeltown district, and had before him a promising career. He received his early education at Barnsley Grammar School, served in the office of Messrs J Gibson and Sons, Chartered Accountants, Barnsley, and was subsequently articled to an auctioneer at Bromsgrove. He enlisted at the beginning of this year in the 2nd Oxford and Bucks Regiment. He was a nephew of Mr William Savage, sanitary inspector, Barnsley.

***Sheffield Evening Telegraph* – 22 October 1915**

FOUGHT AND DIED
HEROES FROM BARNSLEY AND DISTRICT

Private John William Kilner (23) 2nd Oxford and Bucks Regiment, son of Mr and Mrs William Kilner of Market Place, Chapeltown, killed in action. Educated at the Barnsley Grammar School, he was articled to chartered accountants and an auctioneer in turn.

Birmingham Library and Archives were unable to carry out a free search for more details of John's employment, any local obituaries or his name on any local war memorials.

The photograph of John is from Barnsley Chronicle *and is used by their kind permission.*

John William Kilner's Uncle William Savage

WILLIAM SAVAGE (born c1860 Barnsley, died 21 June 1919, aged 59) was one of four children of **John Savage**, who was a Linen Warehouseman before working on Barnsley market, and **Margaret nee Johnson.** His three sisters were **Anne, Eliza** and **Mary,** who married **William Kilner**.

William became a Butcher and was living in Sheffield before he got married to **Selina Robinson Ostcliffe** on 10 May 1881 at Felkirk Parish Church of St Peter. Selina (also aged 21) was the daughter of **Charles Ostcliffe**, Labourer, and **Caroline**

nee Robinson of Shafton. They had four children: **Percival John Savage** (attended the Holgate from 1895 to 1899), **Ethel, Charles Vernon** and **Annie**.

By 1891, William was Assistant Sanitary Inspector and living with his family at 108 Pontefract Road in Barnsley. On the 1911 Census, William (51) Inspector of Nuisances, was living in eight rooms at 76 Pontefract Road, Barnsley, with his wife Selina and daughter Annie (9); he employed a servant. Their oldest son John had got married but Ethel and Charles Vernon had both died in 1909, in their twenties.

William held a position of great responsibility within Barnsley Council and appeared in *Barnsley Chronicle* on many occasions while carrying out his work. He was the same age as **Edward Saville**, Assistant Sanitary Inspector, who was the father of **Ronald John Saville** (Part2. Chapter 57).

William continued to work while suffering from ill health; he went into a Sheffield Nursing Home following an operation in Sheffield Hospital, but died there on 21 June 1919, aged 59. His funeral was held at St Peter's Church and he was interred in Barnsley Cemetery.

***Barnsley Chronicle* – 15 July 1916**

> COUNTY BOROUGH monthly meeting under Mayor Alderman Holden Reference to the Sanitary Inspector's report – 'nearly the whole of Mr Savage's work had a direct bearing on the public health of the town. Many of Mr Savage's observations were well worth their serious consideration. They were all founded on common sense and good judgement'. These included the cleanliness of milk and the use of tips.

***Barnsley Chronicle* – 22 September 1917**

> BARNSLEY SANITARY AFFAIRS
> INSPECTOR'S INTERESTING REPORT
> PUBLIC ABATTOIR ADVOCATED
>
> Mr William Savage, the Sanitary Inspector for the County Borough of Barnsley, has just issued his annual report dealing with work accomplished by the sanitary department. During the year inspections have been made of seven canal boats, all of which were found to be in satisfactory condition. …
>
> (Under the Factory and Workshops Act 1901) Mr Savage had made 33 inspections, which, on the whole, were of a fairly satisfactory character. … some of the chimneys (of manufactories) have emitted more smoke than is economical from the owners' standpoint and the atmospheric pollution by coal smoke, which is preventable, is a danger to the public health. …

THE MILK TRAFFIC
There are nine farmers within the borough who produce and sell milk from an average aggregate of 80 cows. The sanitary condition of the majority of the cowsheds leaves still room for improvement. There are 37 milk sellers bringing milk into the town from surrounding districts, 45 registered milk shops ... which have been inspected but not as frequently as they should be. .... there are about 1,320 gallons of new milk sold in the town daily or about one fifth of a pint per person.

BAD FRUIT AND FISH
Regular inspections have been made of the markets, warehouses and shops dealing with fruit and vegetables for the detection of unsound (produce) with the result that the following goods have been destroyed as unfit for human food: gooseberries: 27 baskets containing 704 lbs; cherries: 32 baskets, 675 lbs; black-currants: 13 baskets, 260 lbs; mushrooms 2 baskets, 34 lbs; gherkins: 1 barrel, 168 lbs; bananas: 16 lbs; figs: 2 boxes, 22 lbs; or a total of 1,879 lbs. ....

A COMPLIMENT TO BUTCHERS
The meat market and butchers' shops have ... been regularly inspected ... the great need still exists for a public abattoir ... we do not appear to have much dealing with inferior or "screw" meat ... every assistance rendered by the butchers when disease has been discovered ... 33 requests to have meat inspected. The following is a list of unsound and diseased meat found and destroyed: 4 beasts weighing 176 stones; 2 sheep 8½ stones; 30 pigs 300 stones; etc ...... slaughter houses ... 16 registered and six licenced annually ... inspected weekly ....

The report also dealt with housing and scavenging.

***Barnsley Chronicle* – 28 June 1919**

MR W SAVAGE, BARNSLEY

Barnsley has lost a valued and greatly respected townsman and official by the death of Mr William Savage, which occurred in a Sheffield nursing home on Saturday. We announced last week that Mr Savage was seriously ill and had undergone an operation. He never regained consciousness and it later became clear that he could not recover.

Mr Savage was 59 years of age and for seventeen years had held the posts of Sanitary Inspector and Markets Superintendent. A native of Barnsley, Mr Savage first served as Assistant Sanitary Inspector under the late Mr William Waterton. He then left the service of the Corporation and started in business in Cheapside as a fish and game merchant, but upon the death of Mr Winterton in November 1902 was appointed Markets and Sanitary Inspector. He was an associate of the Royal Sanitary Institute, and a member of the Institute of Cleansing Superintendents. Mr Savage was secretary of the Barnsley and District Sub Committee of the West Riding War Agricultural Committee, worked whole-heartedly in connection with the provision and laying out of a large number of allotments which have been established in the town in recent years. Since the inception of the Christmas Fat Stock Show he acted as hon treasurer, whilst he was also treasurer or the recently formed local branch of the National Association of Local Government Officers.

... He leaves a widow, a son and daughter.

The deceased gentleman was a most efficient servant of the Corporation and his place ... will be hard to fill. Keen and thorough in his work ... prompted by one motive – the health of the Borough. As Alderman Holden (Chairman of the Health Committee) said at last week's meeting of the Town Council: "a better official than Mr Savage the Corporation has not got and has never had" ...

THE FUNERAL

... The sad procession left deceased's residence, 76 Pontefract Road, and was preceded by members of the Corporation, workmenn of the Sanitary and Markets Departments etc. The family mourners (included: his wife and children), Mr and Mrs W Kilner, Chapeltown... Amongst others present were the Mayor (Colonel W F Raley), the Deputy Mayor (Alderman H Holden) (and seven Councillors), Mr W P Donald (Town Clerk) (plus other chief officers etc), Mr E Saville etc.

There were many beautiful floral tributes.

The Barnsley Chronicle.

WAR SUPPLEMENT

"Our first duty is to win the war."—*President Wilson.* FOR WEEK ENDING JUNE 1, 1918. "Our second duty is to win it worthily."—*President Wilson.*

AN OUTPOST NEAR YPRES.

The outposts in the Ypres salient are ever on the alert to hold up German patrols "feeling their way" against the British positions. Barbed wire entanglements are a precaution against rushes.

JOCKS IN ACTION.

British Official.

This picture taken under fire gives an idea of the desolation in a shell-shattered village. Notice how the Jocks take cover by sprawling flat amongst the *debris*.

38

Henry Rylands Knowles

Henry Rylands Knowles
1890–1916 (aged 26)

HENRY RYLANDS KNOWLES was born on 29 April 1890 in Barnsley to **Dr Henry Knowles** (born c1857 in Guiseley, Leeds) and **Malinda nee Rylands** (born c1866 in Swinton). Dr Knowles was a Surgeon and Physician in his own premises and a Consultant Surgeon at Bennett Hospital in Barnsley.

Dr Henry Knowles was one of six children of **Joseph Knowles** (born c1825 in Bingley; Baptism 9 March 1825 in Bingley) and **Mary Ann Ellis**. Joseph was a Farmer of 70 Acres then Stone Mason in Yeadon. In 1861 he employed farm servants and in 1871 he employed a 20 year old Domestic Servant, who had a ten day old daughter. I have been unable to find any military records for 'Captain [Joseph] Knowles of Guisley, Yorkshire'.

Henry Rylands was the second oldest of six children: **Eirene, Olwin** – Pharmacy Student at Leeds School, **Cyril Reginald**, **Ernest Arthur** and **Marjorie**. (Cyril and Ernest both attended the Holgate and served in the First World War)

In April 1911, the Knowles family were living in 34 and 36 Pitt Street, Barnsley, where they had been for at least 20 years. They occupied nine rooms – the other seven were either empty or used as a Surgery – and they had two Domestic Servants. Henry, Eirene and Ernest Arthur were living elsewhere. Henry (20) Medical Student, was one of three Boarders in nine rooms at Brudenell Avenue, Leeds, with a Boarding House Keeper and her two children. Eirene (22) School Teacher, was one of ten female Boarders, staff and pupils aged from 12 to 22, at 65 Boundary Road, St John's Wood, London, with the Boarding House Mistress for the Francis Holland School in Upper Baker Street. Ernest Arthur was probably at Agricultural College in Australia.

Henry's parents moved to Heysham, Lancashire, after April 1911 and were living at 23 Quay Road in Bridlington by March 1919. **Eirene Knowles** married **Reginald P Russell** late 1920 in Bridlington.

Henry went to New College in Harrogate, a Private School, until the age of 14. He then attended the Holgate Grammar School in Church Street, Barnsley, for four years, from 1904 to 1908. Henry was a Locke Scholar and he passed the Oxford Local Senior exam with 3rd Class Honours, winning a Cooper prize for this in 1907, and the Northern Matriculation exam.

As an Old Boy, Henry was one of the judges for the Athletic Sports in 1910 along with Duncan Fairley.

He was awarded the County Free Studentship and Medical College Entrance Scholarship for Leeds University. Henry qualified as MB Ch B (Bachelor of Medicine and Surgery) in 1914, after a 'brilliant career' at the University, where he had 'won the Mile Championship in splendid time' in the Inter Varsity Sports in 1913. He became FRCS (Fellow of the Royal College of Surgery) and was (Primary) House Surgeon at Leeds Infirmary.

'Henry R Knowles MB' joined the Royal Army Medical Corps (RAMC) in August 1914 and obtained a temporary commission as Lieutenant on 14 September. Henry served in different Military Hospitals in England until January 1915, then went out to France and was attached to the 7th Battalion of the King's Own (Royal Lancaster) Regiment. He was promoted and listed in the Supplement to the London Gazette on

14 January 1916 as Temporary Captain; he was subsequently confirmed as Captain and was gassed at some stage in 1916. Henry was killed by a shell while helping at the front near Bazentin-le-Petit, Somme, on 30 July 1916, aged 26. As Henry's body was never found or identified his name is listed on the Thiepval Memorial, Somme, France (Pier and Face: 4C).

Henry ought to have been awarded three medals: 1914–15 Star, Victory and British War, and his parents should have received the 'Dead Man's Penny' plaque and scroll from King George V.

Henry was Mentioned in Dispatches (*London Gazette* on 1 January 1916); he was given a Distinguished Conduct Medal (DCM) for his work among the wounded at Hill 60 and was also awarded the Military Cross for bravery in attending the wounded under fire (*London Gazette* on 14 January 1916). *Alumnus* April 1916: 'We heartily congratulate Captain H R Knowles, RAMC, on the honours that have come upon him. He has been twice mentioned in Lord French's Dispatches and has been recommended for the Military Cross for the splendid work he did amongst the wounded. He was badly gassed some weeks ago but has now recovered.

Henry's letters to his parents from France in February and March 1915 were included in *Alumnus* (Part 3. Chapter 6).

Henry's name is on the Holgate Grammar School Memorial, the Roll of Honour at Leeds University, which comprises 18 panels flanking the entrance to the Brotherton Library, and he is mentioned in Leeds University's journal *The Gryphon* as an 'Ex Cadet' and for receiving Military Distinction; both University Memorials have been digitized. He is not included on the Heysham War Memorial in St Peter's Churchyard but is listed on the Lancaster Roll of Honour and has been recognized on the Lancaster Military Heritage Group website.

Connections

Henry was in the same form as **Arthur George Batley**, **Duncan Fairley** and **Harold Willott**. They all won Cooper Prizes in 1907 for passing the Oxford Local Senior Exam.

In April 1911, Henry was a Medical Student in the same Boarding House at Brudenell Avenue in Leeds as **Duncan Fairley**, Student, both aged 20.

***Barnsley Chronicle* – 26 September 1914**

PATRIOTIC PARS

Lieutenant H R Knowles, MB CHP, has left the West Norfolk and Lynn Hospital to prepare for the front.

Alumnus – December 1916

H R Knowles, MB, Ch B, FRCS, held the rank of Captain in the Royal Lancs Regiment. He had been twice mentioned in Despatches from the Front and had been awarded the Military Cross for splendid work done among the wounded.

He was distinguished for his strength of character, for his humanity and integrity, and for great charm of personality. .... Letters from Dr Knowles have appeared in the Magazine.

Yorkshire Evening Post – 11 August 1916

YORKSHIRE CASUALTIES IN FRANCE
DEATH OF THE SON OF A FORMER BARNSLEY DOCTOR

Captain Henry Rylands Knowles, R.A.M.C., whose death in action is announced, was the eldest son of Dr H Knowles, who for many years was in practice in Barnsley, and now resides at Heysham Cottage, Heysham. Educated at Barnsley Grammar School and Leeds University, Captain Knowles secured his M.B. Degree and passed the Primary London F.R.C.S. Examination. He joined the R.A.M.C. in the month in which the war broke out, and went to France in January last year. For bravery in attending the wounded under fire he was awarded the Military Cross.

Sheffield Evening Telegraph – 11 August 1916

BARNSLEY OFFICER KILLED

The death in action of Captain Henry Rylands Knowles (26) RAMC ... is deeply regretted by his large circle of Barnsley friends... He went to France early in 1915 and was decorated with the Military Cross in April last.

Lancaster Observer and *Morecambe Chronicle* – 11 August 1916

CAPT. H R KNOWLES – KILLED

Capt. Henry Rylands Knowles, R.A.M.C. (attached to the Royal Lancaster Regiment) was killed in action on July 30th. A telegram to this effect was received by Dr and Mrs Knowles ... Capt Knowles was 26 years of age, and joined the R.A.M.C. in August 1914. He was educated at Barnsley Grammar School, and the Leeds University, where he gained several successes as an athlete, besides securing his M.B. Degree and passing the preliminary London F.R.C.S. Examination. He was a grandson of the late Captain Knowles of Guisley, Yorkshire. Capt Knowles went to France early in 1915 and received the

D.C.M. For his courageous work among the wounded at Hill 60, and was later (in April this year) awarded the Military Cross. He was badly 'gassed' and was in hospital for some weeks.

***Barnsley Independent* – 12 August 1916**

CAPTAIN HENRY RYLANDS KNOWLES

.... the sad news will cause much regret in Barnsley, for the young officer was extremely well known and held in great esteem. ...

Captain Knowles ... joined the RAMC in the month the war broke out, and after serving at different military hospitals in this country he went out to France in January 1915. For bravery in attending to the wounded under fire he was awarded the Military Cross, receiving the decoration from King George in April last. Captain Knowles gave every promise of becoming a prominent member of the medical profession, and the sympathy of Barnsley people will go out to the parents in their sad loss.

A younger son of Dr and Mrs Knowles, Ernest, went out to Australia after leaving school, went through the Gallipoli operations with the Anzacs, and is now in France. Another son, Cyril, after taking his final degree last month joined the RAMC.

***Barnsley Chronicle* – 12 August 1916**

KILLED, WOUNDED & MISSING
BARNSLEY AND DISTRICT HEROES
ANOTHER BIG CASUALTY LIST KILLED

Deep sorrow is felt in Barnsley at the death in action of Captain Henry Rylands Knowles, RAMC, son of Dr and Mrs Knowles, who were formerly highly esteemed residents of Barnsley ... Captain Knowles went to France early in 1915, and was decorated with the Military Cross in April 1916, this honour when reported in these columns causing intense pleasure to the many local friends of the family.

***Barnsley Chronicle* – 19 August 1916**

LATEST LOCAL CASUALTIES
THE LATE CAPTAIN KNOWLES

Dr Knowles of Heysham, formerly of Barnsley, has received from the Colonel of the 7th K O R Lancaster Regiment, a sympathetic letter relating to the death in action of Captain H R Knowles, an extract from which is given below: 'As usual, he was right up in the firing line dressing the wounded when a shell hit him and killed him instantly. He is a tremendous loss to this battalion and to myself, as all the officers and men believed and trusted in him so much: I have never in all the two years I have been out here seen a medical officer so popular with one and all – in fact we have lost a brave man ready to sacrifice himself for his duty and any man in trouble in the battalion'.

Dr Knowles has also received a telegram from the King and Queen expressing their sympathy. The deceased officer's younger brother, after serving through the Gallipoli campaign with the Australian Infantry, is at present in France, and his remaining brother has just been gazetted a lieutenant in the RAMC.

(Obituaries were also included in *The Times* – 11 August 1916, *Lancaster Guardian* – 12 August 1916, *Newcastle Journal* – 12 August 1916).

British Medical Journal – 19 August 1916

Captain Henry Rylands Knowles, R.A.M.C. was killed in action early in August, aged 26. He was the son of Dr Knowles of Heysham Cottage, Heysham, and was educated at Barnsley Grammar School and at Leeds University, where he graduated as M.B. and Ch.B. in 1914. He took a temporary commission as Lieutenant in the R.A.M.C. on September 14th and was promoted to Captain on completion of one year's service. He went to the front early in 1915 and was attached to the Royal York and Lancaster Regiment [sic].

Lancaster Roll of Honour

Knowles Henry Rylands Temporary Captain KIA 30 July 1916 (Royal Army Medical Corps attached 7 KO – in attack near Bazentin-le-Petit, the Somme).

The University of Leeds Roll of Honour Page of The Western Front Association Website

Captain Henry Rylands Knowles, R.A.M.C., attached to the King's Own Royal Lancaster Regiment, who was killed on 30 July, was formerly a student at the University of Leeds, where he gained several successes as an athlete, besides securing his M.B. degree and passing the primary London F.R.C.S. examination. His home was at Heysham.

Pam and Ken Linge of the Thiepval Memorial Project kindly allowed me to use Obituaries they found (in *The Times*, *Lancaster Observer* & *Morecambe Chronicle* and the *British Medical Journal*) and their better quality photograph of Henry from the Yorkshire Rugby Football Union's *In Memoriam 1914–1919*.

The main photograph of Henry is from the Yorkshire Rugby Football Union's In Memoriam 1914–1919 *via the Thiepval Memorial Project, reproduced by their kind permission.*

CYRIL REGINALD KNOWLES (born on 27 January 1893 in Harrogate) went to New College, Harrogate, until the age of 12, when he attended the Holgate Grammar School for six years, from 1905 to 1911. He was a Locke Scholar for three years and passed the Oxford Local Senior exam 3rd Class and the Northern Universities Matriculation 1st Class. Cyril went on to Leeds University and *Alumnus* July 1914 congratulated him on passing 'the Second MB, Ch B, Part II', at the same time as his brother Henry passed his Finals.

Cyril enlisted in the RAMC in July 1916, after completing his degree. The Medal Card for Cyril of 23 Quay Road, Bridlington, shows that he was a Captain in the RAMC and he was awarded the Victory and British War medals having entered into the theatre of war on 2 September 1916. He was also awarded a Military Cross.

Cyril's letter from the Mesopotamia Expeditionary Force in October 1918 was printed in *Alumnus* in April 1919 (Part 3. Chapter 6).

***Yorkshire Evening Post* – 11 August**

> (Captain Henry Rylands Knowles, R.A.M.C)
> .... another brother, after taking his final degree last month, joined the R.A.M.C. ...

(Also in *Barnsley Independent* – 12 August 1916)

***Barnsley Chronicle* – 14 October 1916**

PATRIOTIC PARS

> Lieut C R Knowles, MB, RAMC, eldest surviving son of Dr and Mrs Knowles, The Cottage, Heysham (Lancs) and formerly of Barnsley, has been gazetted Surgeon to the Hospital Ship 'Glenart Castle'.
>
> (HMHS Glenart, formerly called Galacian, was requisitioned during the First World War as a hospital ship; she was torpedoed by a German U-boat on 26 February 1918 and sunk. There were few survivors but 162 died, including 62 medical staff).

***Barnsley Chronicle* – 22 March 1919**

FORMER BARNSLEY DOCTOR'S SON
AWARDED MILITARY CROSS

Captain C R Knowles RAMC Mesopotamia Expeditionary Force, eldest surviving son of Dr and Mrs Knowles, 23 Quay Road, Bridlington (late of Barnsley and Heysham) and grandson of the late Captain Knowles of Guiseley, Yorkshire, has been awarded the Military Cross for valuable and distinguished services rendered in connection with medical and military operations in Mesopotamia during the last 2 years.

ERNEST ARTHUR KNOWLES (born on 17 January 1894 in Harrogate; died 22 August 1950 in Australia, aged 56) went to New College, Harrogate, until the age of 12, when he attended the Holgate Grammar School for four years, from 1906 to 1910. Ernest then went to 'Agricultural College in Dookie, Victoria, Australia'.

Ernest enlisted at Surrey Hills, Victoria, Australia, on 21 August 1914, aged 20 years and 6 months. He was a Farmer, according to the Attestation form, and his personal details were: Height: 5' 11", Weight: 10st 6lb, Chest: 37", Complexion: Fair, Eyes: Brown, Hair: Fair. Ernest was a Private in the 8th Battalion of the AIF, Australian Infantry, and was promoted to Lance Corporal in 1916 then Sergeant in 1917, serving in Gallipoli, Egypt and France. He suffered from several periods of illness. On 6 August 1918 he received a severe reprimand for going into town without a pass; Ernest was granted 75 days furlough in the United Kingdom from 3 October 1918 but was Absent Without Leave from 30 December until 4 January 1919, for which he had to forfeit five days pay. He returned to Australia and was discharged on 1 June 1919.

Ernest's letter to his parents from Cairo in February 1915 was printed in Alumnus *(Part 3. Chapter 6).*

***Barnsley Chronicle* – 10 October 1914**

PATRIOTIC PARS

Mr E A Knowles, son of Dr Knowles of Barnsley, has joined the Australian Expeditionary Force from Melbourne, which is now on the way to the front.

***Yorkshire Evening Post* – 11 August**

(Captain Henry Rylands Knowles, R.A.M.C)

… A younger brother went through the Gallipoli operations with the Anzacs and is now in France…

***Barnsley Independent* – 12 August 1916**

CAPTAIN HENRY RYLANDS KNOWLES

A younger son of Dr and Mrs Knowles, Ernest, went out to Australia after leaving school, went through the Gallipoli operations with the Anzacs, and is now in France.

WAR SUPPLEMENT FOR WEEK ENDING AUGUST 17, 1916.

THE PRUSSIAN SCORPION.

COMBINED EFFORTS WILL CRUSH IT.

39 and 40

Laycock Brothers (Benjamin Holroyd Rymer and Donald Stanley)

Benjamin Holroyd Rymer Laycock
1890–1916 (aged 25)

Donald Stanley Laycock
1897–1918 (aged 20)

LAYCOCK BROTHERS

George Henry Laycock (born c1862 in Barnsley) and **Annie Eliza nee Holroyd** (born c1871 in Crigglestone) had three children: **BENJAMIN HOLROYD RYMER**, **Mabel Elizabeth** and **DONALD STANLEY**.

George Henry was the oldest child of **Benjamin John Laycock**, Butcher of 179 Sheffield Road, Barnsley, and **Sarah Ann Rymer.** He had four siblings: **Clara Jane Laycock** married to **Albert Henry Kelsey**, whose son **William Kelsey** was an Old Boy (Part 2. Chapter 36), then **Clifton**, a Butcher retired early because of ill health, then **Verona** and then **Mary Ada Hinchcliffe Laycock**, who married **Benjamin James Jagger**. George's son Benjamin was given as middle names the surnames of his mother and paternal grandmother.

George was a Butcher, who appears to have been separated from his family after the 1891 Census, leaving his wife to bring up their family alone. His name is on the Baptism record for Mabel on 4 December 1892 and Annie's status remained 'married'. He seems to have emigrated and was living in New York in 1916. Passenger lists show that George (34) Butcher from Barnsley, was a passenger on the Cunard Line SS *Pavonia*, travelling alone from Liverpool on 17 December 1896 and arriving in Boston Massachusetts on 28 December 1896. He had previously been to Brooklyn. A George Laycock, aged 62, Baker of 26 Hollingroyd Yard, Dewsbury, was a passenger on the White Star Line SS *Doric* arriving in Liverpool on 15 June 1924 from Canada via Quebec.

Photograph of Benjamin and Donald in Cawthorne Museum, used by their kind permission.

The Laycock family stayed in Woolley with Annie's parents, James Holroyd, Farmer and Ironmonger, and his wife Sarah, for about 20 years. In April 1911, after James Holroyd had died, they lived in six rooms at Victoria Cottage in Cawthorne, except for Mabel.

Mabel Laycock (18) Nursery Governess, was one of three servants of Solicitor John Frederick Falwasser and family, who had 13 rooms in The Red House, Cawthorne. Mabel married **John W Towriss** in late 1920 in Tadcaster; they had five children in Tadcaster: **Joan Towriss** in 1912, **Sylvia** in 1926, **Irene** in 1928, **Douglas** in 1931 and **Maureen** in 1934.

BENJAMIN HOLROYD RYMER LAYCOCK was born on 20 November 1890 in Woolley; his Baptism was on 28 December 1890 at Chapelthorpe St James' Church – his middle names were the unmarried surnames of his mother and paternal grandmother. He went to Cawthorne National School until the age of 14 then attended the Holgate Grammar School in Church Street, Barnsley, for three years, from 1905 to 1908. Benjamin was an Intending Pupil Teacher. He went on to Southampton University College to become a Certificated Teacher.

Benjamin Laycock was from Cawthorne in Yorkshire where he had attended the Elementary School. He was a day training student at Southampton University for two years 1911–13 and he lived first on Graham Road and then Bellevue Terrace; he went aged 20 and, unusually, no father's name was recorded.*

Photograph of Benjamin in Cawthorne Museum, kindly provided by Barry Jackson.

Benjamin enlisted at Chesterfield as a Private (Service Number: B/20083) in the 26th Battalion (City of London Regiment) of the Royal Fusiliers. This unit was known as the Bankers' Battalion as it had been raised by the Lord Mayor of London from men who worked in the financial firms in the City. Men also joined from outside London and this profession because it was probably advertised in various newspapers. Benjamin was one of the original members of 26th Battalion and crossed to Le Havre on 5th May 1916.†

According to the *26th Battalion, Royal Fusiliers, Movement and Relief Tables* for late October 1916 the men marched from Connaught Camp to La Clytte, where they trained for about a week. They were inspected by General

* Stephen Bennett, Alumni Relations at Southampton University, sent me photographs of their War Memorial and suggestions for finding other records. John Rooney, Archivist at the Hartley Library, Archives & Manuscripts at Southampton University, provided details of Benjamin's attendance from their records: MS 1/3/476/2/5 Register of students of the day training department, 1899–1915 and MS 1/3/476/2/3 Registration book of day students for University College Southampton, 1912–24

† David Carter, Volunteer Research Assistant at the Royal Fusiliers Museum, provided information about the Battalion, including the operation that led to Benjamin's death.

Photograph of Benjamin's Display in Cawthorne Museum, used by their kind permission.

Plumer, Commander of the 2nd Army, who congratulated them on the work they had done fighting on the Somme. From 29 October to 2 November inclusive, they improved the trenches for the winter months, patrolled at night to ascertain the strength of the German line, did inspections then began repairing their wire. Some men were recorded as wounded but three of these died, including Benjamin. The 26th Battalion were relieved on 3 November and went into Support at Ridge Wood.

Benjamin is listed as killed in action, but may have died of wounds, on 2 November 1916, aged 25; he was shot by a sniper according to Barry Jackson's research. Benjamin was buried in Ridge Wood Military Cemetery, West Vlaanderen, Belgium, initially as an 'unknown British soldier' but identified later.

In his last letter to his mother, Benjamin wrote:

> I can only say as Arthur in Morte d'Arthur:
> I have played my part and that which I have done may He himself make pure.

Benjamin was awarded two medals: Victory and British War, and his mother received the 'Dead Man's Penny' plaque and scroll from King George V, which is on display in Cawthorne Museum.

Benjamin's name is on the Holgate Grammar School Memorial, the Cawthorne War Memorial and the Southampton University Memorial Plaque, located in the Hartley Library reception.

Connections

Benjamin and Donald were first cousins of **William Kelsey**.

Benjamin served in the 26th Battalion (City of London Regiment) of the Royal Fusiliers along with **Ronald John Saville**.

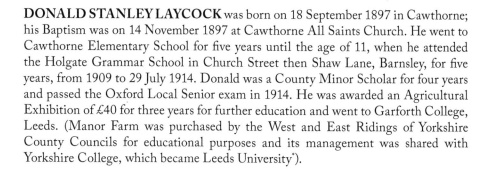

Barnsley Chronicle – 2 December 1916

DEATHS

> LAYCOCK November 2nd, Killed in action in France, in his 26th year, Benjamin H R Laycock, Royal Fusiliers (Bankers), dearly beloved elder son of Annie E Laycock, Cawthorne, Barnsley, and of George H Laycock, New York, USA. 'Until the day breaks and the shadows fly away'.

The main photograph of Benjamin is from Alumnus, *used by kind permission of Barnsley Archives.*

DONALD STANLEY LAYCOCK was born on 18 September 1897 in Cawthorne; his Baptism was on 14 November 1897 at Cawthorne All Saints Church. He went to Cawthorne Elementary School for five years until the age of 11, when he attended the Holgate Grammar School in Church Street then Shaw Lane, Barnsley, for five years, from 1909 to 29 July 1914. Donald was a County Minor Scholar for four years and passed the Oxford Local Senior exam in 1914. He was awarded an Agricultural Exhibition of £40 for three years for further education and went to Garforth College, Leeds. (Manor Farm was purchased by the West and East Ridings of Yorkshire County Councils for educational purposes and its management was shared with Yorkshire College, which became Leeds University*).

* Nick Brewster, Archive Assistant at Leeds University Special Collections Library, confirmed details of Donald's education and provided information about *The Gryphon* and the Farm, from Gosden & Taylor's *Studies in the History of a University*.

Donald enrolled at Leeds University on 12th October 1914 for his first year of a non-degree course in Agriculture in the Agriculture Department. Class fees were £10 and Union fees were £1 1s with funding from a West Riding Scholarship. (DSL*)

At the outbreak of war, Donald 'joined the Army Veterinary Corps, composed of about 200 men, from whom drafts were sent to France to attend wounded horses' as Private (Service Number: TT/0252). He was promoted to Second Lieutenant in the 70th Battalion 34th Brigade of the Royal Field Artillery (Territorial Force) in July 1917. Donald died on 24 March 1918, aged 20, after receiving a shell wound above the knee the previous day. Donald was buried in Beaulencourt British Cemetery, Ligny-Thilloy, Pas de Calais, France (grave IV G 23).

Photograph of Donald in Cawthorne Museum, used by their kind permission.

Photograph of Donald's Display in Cawthorne Museum, used by their kind permission.

Donald was awarded two medals: Victory and British War, and his mother received the 'Dead Man's Penny' plaque and scroll from King George V, which is on display in Cawthorne Museum.

Probate was granted in London on 13 August 1918 for Donald to Annie Eliza Laycock, 'wife of and Attorney for George Henry Laycock. Effects: £197 1s 2d.

Donald wrote an article for *Alumnus* (Part 3. Chapter 7).

Donald's name is on the Holgate Grammar School Memorial and the Cawthorne War Memorial in Barnsley district. He is listed on the Roll of Honour at Leeds University, which comprises 18 panels flanking the entrance to the Brotherton Library, and he is mentioned as 'Student' in Leeds University's journal *The Gryphon*, which listed students' army status in 1914 with a later Roll of Honour; both of these Memorials have been digitized.

Connections

Benjamin and Donald were first cousins of **William Kelsey**.

Donald Stanley Laycock was Baptised at All Saints Church, Cawthorne, 11 days before **James Alec Wemyss.**

Alumnus – July 1918

> Donald Laycock (1910–14) Second Lieutenant RFA, son of Mrs A Laycock of Cawthorne, died of wounds on March 24th 1918. After completing his education at the Grammar School and receiving a West Riding CC scholarship, he became a student at Garforth Agricultural College, Leeds. When war broke out he joined the RA Vet C and subsequently obtained a commission in the RFA.
>
> From a letter received by his mother, I quote the following: 'One of the drivers and I carried him to a hut close by when we found that he had been hit by a shell making a big gash just above the knee. Our medical officer dressed the wound and we carried him to a dressing station half a mile away. This was about 4.30pm on 23rd. We got him away on the first motor ambulance which arrived. He told me that he felt much better and was very pleased at the idea of getting away to a comfortable hospital. A week later I was shocked and surprised to hear he had died of his wound on the following day, as, although it was a bad wound, I hoped and believed he would recover. I am sorry about his death and he is a great loss to the battery, both to the men and us officers, who knew him so well. He had worked untiringly on the day he was wounded and had given me great help. Two of my brothers have been killed in this war but I feel somehow that I shall see them again some day'. (From Major F).

***Barnsley Chronicle* – 13 April 1918**

A CAWTHORNE OFFICER DIES OF WOUNDS FORMER BARNSLEY GRAMMAR SCHOOL LAD

Second Lieutenant Donald Stanley Laycock, RFA, the only surviving son of Mrs Annie E Laycock of Cawthorne, Barnsley, and of Mr George H Laycock, formerly of Barnsley, died of wounds received in action on March 24. He was educated at Holgate Grammar School, Barnsley, and was continuing his studies at the University of Leeds with a view to specializing in Agriculture. At the outbreak of war he enlisted in the Army Veterinary Corps. He received his commission in the RFA in July 1917. Mrs Laycock's other son was killed in action 18 months ago.

***Barnsley Independent* – 13 April 1918**

YOUNG BARNSLEY OFFICER DIES OF WOUNDS

Second Lieutenant Donald Stanley Laycock, RFA … died of wounds received in action on March 24th.

Second-Lieutenant Laycock, who was in his 21st year, was educated at Holgate Grammar School, Barnsley, and had been successful in obtaining several scholarships. He was continuing his studies at the University of Leeds with a view to specialising in agriculture. At the outbreak of war he enlisted in the Army Veterinary Corps, and received his commission in the RFA in July 1917. Mrs Laycock's other son was killed in action 18 months ago.

(The same article appeared in ***Yorkshire Post*** & ***Leeds Intelligencer*** – 9 April 1918, and The University of Leeds Roll of Honour Page of The Western Front Association Website).

The main photograph of Donald is from Alumnus, *used by kind permission of Barnsley Archives.*

41 and 42

Lindley Brothers (Foster and Frank Marcus)

Foster Lindley
1889–1918 (aged 29)

Frank Marcus Lindley
1898–1917 (aged 19)

LINDLEY BROTHERS

Thomas Lindley (born c1855 in Mapplewell) and **Alice nee Elvidge** (born c1862 in Barnsley) had 7 surviving children: **Thomas Harold**, **Sarah Elizabeth (Cissie)**, **Annie**, **FOSTER**, **Walter** (served in the First World War), **FRANK MARCUS** and **Marie Elvidge**. One of their children had died by April 1911 (name unknown).

Thomas was a Plasterer Employer and his oldest son Thomas Harold assisted in the family business; Walter was a Draughtsman in an Iron Foundry. In April 1911, the family lived in nine rooms at 144 Park Grove, Barnsley, having previously lived at 56 Princess Street and 97 Doncaster Road in Barnsley; they had a Domestic Servant. Thomas Harold and Sarah Elizabeth had left home by 1911.

Thomas Harold Lindley (born c1881 in Barnsley; died 11 January 1948, aged 67) Plasterer of 64 Park Grove, Barnsley, married **Helen Gelder** of 2 Shepherd Street, Barnsley, on 18 September 1905 at Barnsley St George's Church. Helen's father was **William Dryden Gelder,** Shoemaker. By April 1911 Thomas, Foreman Plasterer, had a daughter **Alison Mary Lindley** (aged 5) with his wife Ellen [sic], and they lived in four rooms at 7 Day Street, Barnsley.

Sarah Elizabeth (Cissie) Lindley (born c1883 in Barnsley) got married to **Claude Scott** in spring 1915 (served and died in the First World War); she was living with her parents in 144 Park Grove when her husband was killed in action.

Annie Lindley (born c1886 in Barnsley) married **George Henry Townend** early 1913; George (born c1887) was a Tailor and Draper in his widowed mother's business and was living at home in April 1911 with his three siblings in nine rooms at 13 Longman Road, Barnsley, where they had a Domestic Servant. They had a son **Allen Lindley Townend** early 1914, who died at the age of 3 years. George died in 1929, aged 42.

Marie Elvidge Lindley married **Benjamin Clegg** in spring 1936 but died on 17 November 1940, aged 32. They had a son **David B Clegg** in spring 1939.

Thomas and Alice Lindley were buried in a family grave in Barnsley Cemetery with two of their children, a son-in-law and grandson, whose names are inscribed on the tiered stones at the base of a stone Celtic cross. The names of their two sons and son-in-law killed in action in the First World War are also included as a Memorial:

Sacred to the Memory of

SGT CLAUDE SCOTT, 12TH BATT EAST YORKS REGT
DIED OF WOUNDS RECEIVED IN ACTION
IN FRANCE NOV 13TH 1916, AGED 34 YEARS

ALSO OF PTE FRANK MARCUS LINDLEY
5TH LANCS FUSILIERS
DIED OF WOUNDS RECEIVED IN ACTION
IN BELGIUM JULY 29TH 1917, AGED 19 YEARS

ALSO SEC LIEUT FOSTER LINDLEY 7TH BATT EAST YORKS REGT
DIED OF WOUNDS RECEIVED IN ACTION
IN FRANCE SEPT 5TH 19, AGED 29 YEARS

THE AFFECTIONATE SON-IN-LAW & SONS OF
THOMAS & ALICE LINDLEY

In October 1919, *Barnsley Chronicle* reported that Alice Lindley had Communion Chairs dedicated to her sons and son-in-law in the Blucher Street United Methodist Church (now Hope House Church and School) as a Memorial, but their whereabouts are now unknown:

To the Glory of God and in ever loving memory of
Foster Lindley, Frank Marcus Lindley, Claude Scott,
who fell in the Great War 1914–1918

FOSTER LINDLEY was born in 1889 in Barnsley. He went to Barnsley Higher Elementary School until the age of 12, when he attended the Holgate Grammar School in Church Street, Barnsley, for four years, from 1901 to 1905. Foster won a Junior Locke Scholarship in July 1901 and in July 1902, while in Form IV, he won the Chemistry (Elementary) prize. Foster passed the Oxford Local Junior exam in 1903, subjects: Religious Knowledge, English, French and Maths; he later passed the Senior exam with 3rd Class Honours.

He went on to 'Manchester College to qualify as a Pharmaceutical Chemist' in 1910. (I have been unable to find any records to confirm Foster's further education*). Foster was initially articled to Mr Rigby, Chemist, Barnsley, and, after periods working in Sheffield and Rushden, joined in partnership with Mr J C Hall, Lytham Street, Blackpool, in about 1912.

Foster had been involved with the Blucher Street United Methodist Church, Barnsley, for many years then, after moving to Blackpool, he became associated with the Adelaide Street United Methodist Church, where he was a member of the choir.

Foster enlisted in February 1917 as a Private (Service Number: 36321) in the Royal Lancashire Regiment and trained in Fermoy, Ireland, and Witherness. He went out

* I have been unable to locate any records for Foster Lindley at 'Manchester College' but I am grateful to Julia Carruthers, Will Spinks, Sue Killoran, David Seymour, Dr James Hopkins, Paula Dunn and Dr James Peters at Manchester College, Manchester University and Harris Manchester College Library, Oxford, for checking their records for me and providing general information.

to France in April 1918 and was promoted to Lieutenant in the 7th Battalion of the East Yorkshire Regiment. Foster died in No. 3 Canadian Casualty Clearing Station in France, of wounds to his right thigh received the previous day, on 5 September 1918, aged 29. He was buried in Varennes Military Cemetery, Somme, France (grave III F 25).

Foster was awarded two medals: Victory and British War, and his parents should have received the 'Dead Man's Penny' plaque and scroll from King George V.

Probate was granted at Wakefield on 18 January 1919 for Foster, of Lyndhurst, Park Grove, to Thomas Lindley, Plasterer, and George Henry Townend, Tailor. Effects: £752 19s.

Foster's name is on the Holgate Grammar School Memorial; he is also remembered on the family headstone in Barnsley Cemetery and he had a Communion Chair dedicated to him.

Connection

Foster served in the 7th Battalion of the East Yorkshire Regiment along with **Harry Liddall Bambridge**.

Alumnus – December 1918

> 2nd Lieut F Lindley, East Yorks Regt (1901–05) son of Mr and Mrs T Lindley, Park Grove, Barnsley, died of wounds Sept 5th 1918. After passing the Oxford Senior Local Exam he was articled to Mr Ribgy, Chemist, Barnsley. He afterwards joined in partnership with a Blackpool Chemist.

Barnsley Chronicle – 14 September 1918

A BARNSLEY OFFICER KILLED

> Second-Lieutenant Foster Lindley (29) East Yorks Regiment, second son of Mr and Mrs Thomas Lindley, Lyndhurst, Park Grove, Barnsley, died in France on September 5th from wounds received the previous day. Prior to joining the forces the deceased officer was in partnership with a Blackpool chemist, being articled in his youth with Mr Rigby, Barnsley. In July last year Mr and Mrs Lindley lost their youngest son and a son in law in 1916. Another son, Lieutenant Walter Lindley is at present in a London hospital suffering from shell shock.

***Yorkshire Post* & *Leeds Intelligencer* – 14 September 1918**

THE ROLL OF HONOUR

Second-Lieut Foster Lindley … has died of wounds received on September 5. In civil life he was a chemist at Blackpool. Mr and Mrs Lindley lost their youngest son in the war last June. …

***Barnsley Independent* – 18 September 1918**

ROLL of HONOUR (PHOTO)
FALLEN BARNSLEY OFFICER
FAMILY'S GREAT SACRIFICE
SEC-LIEUT FOSTER LINDLEY

Above we reproduce a photograph of Second-Lieut Foster Lindley, East Yorkshire Regiment, who, as previously announced in our columns, died in No. 3 Canadian Casualty Clearing Station in France on September 5th from wounds received in action the following day. Following a War Office telegram, the parents received a letter from a chaplain stating that the deceased officer was wounded in the right thigh, and was interred on the day of his death in Varennes Military Cemetery.

… As a boy he attended Park Road School and the Barnsley Grammar School, and was later articled to Mr W Rigby, chemist. Subsequently, he furthered his professional studies at the Manchester College, and afterwards was with Mr Medley, Sheffield, and Mr Smith, Rushden. About six years ago he entered into partnership with Mr J C Hall, Lytham Street, Blackpool, and became well known and highly respected in the Lancashire resort. From his youth he attended the Blucher Street U M Church, Barnsley, and, taking up his residence in Blackpool, he became associated with the Adelaide Street U M Church, being a member of the choir. He joined the Forces in February 1917, and after training at Fermoy, Ireland, and at Witherness, went out to France in April last.

Much sympathy is felt for Mr and Mrs Lindley, who lost their youngest son, Marcus, last year, and a son-in-law, Sergeant Claude Scott, the previous year, whilst their son, Lieut Walter Lindley, is in a London hospital suffering from shell shock.

The University of Manchester taught courses which led to the diploma of the Pharmaceutical Society, as well as a B.Sc. Degree. The Manchester College of Pharmacy was a private school, located close to the University, but independent of it, which had been established in 1882. It was probably the largest pharmacy school in the city at the time – Foster was not in any of their student registers.

The Manchester Municipal School of Technology (which later became UMIST) also apparently taught pharmaceutical courses, but only definitely from 1918 as no records could be found before that date. Foster Lindley is not recorded as a day student of the School before 1909, when the University's records end, and they do not have any records for the evening students.

There was also a Northern College of Pharmacy, again located in the vicinity of the University, but very little information is available about this institution, other than it taught part-timers. There are no known records surviving for this school.

The photograph of Foster is from Alumnus, *reproduced by kind permission of Barnsley Archives.*

FRANK MARCUS LINDLEY was born on 18 January 1898 in Barnsley. He went to Barnsley Elementary School in Racecommon Road for three years until the age of 11, when he attended the Holgate Grammar School in Church Street, Barnsley, for one year, from 1910 to 1911. According to the Holgate records, Marcus left school to assist his father in his Plastering business but *Barnsley Independent* states that he was a Student Farmer at the time he enlisted.

Marcus enlisted in Blackpool as a Private (Service Number: 204616) in the 3/5th Battalion of the Lancashire Fusiliers. He died of wounds on 30 July 1917, aged 19, and was buried in Coxyde Military Cemetery, Koksijde, West Vlaanderen, Belgium (grave I L 38).

Marcus was one of the youngest of the Old Boys to die in the First World War – there were nine young men aged only 19 years of age.

Marcus was awarded two medals: Victory and British War, and his parents should have received the 'Dead Man's Penny' plaque and scroll from King George V.

Marcus' name is on the Holgate Grammar School Memorial; he is also remembered on the family headstone in Barnsley Cemetery and he had a Communion Chair dedicated to him.

***Barnsley Independent* – 18 August 1917**

ROLL OF HONOUR
BARNSLEY TRADESMAN'S LOSS
PRIVATE F M LINDLEY DIES OF WOUNDS

On Tuesday morning, Mr & Mrs T Lindley of 'Lyndhurst' Park Grove, Barnsley, received official notification of the death from wounds received in action on July 30th, of their youngest son, Frank Marcus Lindley. Much sympathy will be extended to the bereaved family in their great loss.

The deceased hero, who was 19 years of age, was a student farmer and joined up in March last year. He was attached to the Trench Mortar Battery of the Lancashire Fusiliers. It will be re-called that Mr & Mrs Lindley lost a son-in-law in the war some time ago. (*Claude Scott)*

The photograph of Frank is from Alumnus, *reproduced by kind permission of Barnsley Archives.*

WALTER LINDLEY (born 1891 in Barnsley) was a Draughtsman in an Iron Foundry in 1911, living at home. He enlisted and was promoted to Lieutenant but his common name makes it difficult to find any military records. W Lindley (Service Number: 4983) Manchester Regiment, was reported on the Daily Casualty List for 7 August 1916 as 'Wounded Shock (Shell)' (WLSS).

***Barnsley Chronicle* – 14 September 1918**

… Another son, Lieutenant Walter Lindley is at present in a London hospital suffering from shell shock …

Shell Shock

British doctors working in military hospitals became aware of patients suffering from "shell shock" and some felt that the only cure was for soldiers to take a break from fighting. Where officers were likely to be sent home to recuperate, ordinary soldiers were treated less sympathetically and some senior officers thought they were cowards trying to avoid fighting. Although between 1914 and 1918 the British Army identified 80,000 men (2% of those on active service) as suffering from shell-shock, many more soldiers with similar symptoms were classified as 'malingerers' and sent back to the front-line. This resulted in some men committing suicide and others breaking down under the pressure and refusing to obey the orders or deserting, with the consequence of being shot. The official figures list 304 British soldiers who were court-martialled and executed or subjected to Field Punishment Number One, ie being attached to a fixed object for up to two hours a day and for a period up to three months, often within range of enemy shell-fire.

CLAUDE SCOTT (born c1881 in Wakefield) was the 4th of 6 children of George **Scott**, Bookbinder, and **Susannah**. At April 1901 Claude was a Bookbinder; he married Sarah Elizabeth (Cissie) Lindley in Spring 1915. Claude was living in Barnsley when he enlisted at Hull in the 12th Battalion of the East Yorkshire Regiment. He was a Sergeant (Service Number: 12/511) and was killed in action on 13 November 1916, aged 35. Claude was buried in the Euston Road Cemetery at Colincamps, near Albert, on the Somme. Claude is remembered alongside his two brothers-in-law on the Lindley family headstone and Memorial Communion Chairs. His widow received a War Gratuity of £12 according to the *Army Registers of Soldiers Effects.*

***Hull Daily Mail* – 11 December 1916**

ROLL OF HONOUR

> SCOTT – Killed in action on November 13th 1916, Claude Scott, East Yorkshire Regiment, the dearly-loved husband of Cissie Scott, 144 Park Grove, Barnsley, aged 35 years.

***Barnsley Chronicle* – 14 September 1918**

> … In July last year Mr and Mrs Lindley lost their youngest son and a son in law in 1916.

43

Ernest William Litherland

Ernest William Litherland
1890–1919 (aged 28)

ERNEST WILLIAM LITHERLAND was born on 11 May 1890 in Darton to **John Edward Litherland** (born c1864 in Darton) and **Edith Mary nee Braithwaite** (born c1871 in Bretton). Ernest's Baptism was on 13 July 1890 at Darton All Saints Church. John Edward was a Commercial Manager at a Colliery; he was the only son of **William Litherland**, Engine Worker at a Colliery, who died aged 33, and **Jane Litherland**.

Ernest was the oldest of six surviving children: **Muriel, Cyril**, Colliery Clerk (attended the Holgate and served in the First World War), **Frances Jane, George Thomas** (Served in the First World War) and **Richard Douglas. John** died late 1902, aged 1.

In April 1911, the Litherland family lived in 13 rooms at The Grange, Monckton, Havercroft with Cold Hiendley, and they employed a Domestic Servant. They had previously lived at Laburnum House, Darton, then 53 Huddersfield Road, Barnsley.

Ernest went to St Mary's School, Barnsley, until the age of 13; he later became a member of the St Mary's Church Choir. He attended the Holgate Grammar School in Church Street, Barnsley, for three years, from 1903 to 1906, and passed the Oxford Local Junior exam. He was Captain of Locke House and Captain of the Second Eleven Cricket Team. Ernest became an official at Monckton Collieries on leaving school.

Ernest was one of the founder members of the Old Boys' Association; he was on the Athletics Committee and was one of the main organizers of the first Old Boys' Dance, which was a great success. He was Captain of their football team and wrote an article on it for *Alumnus*: 'Litherland, owing to his smallness, is inclined to be timid, but nevertheless makes a good forward and can shoot well on occasions. He never loses heart, a feeling shared, though to a less degree perhaps, by the rest of the forwards'.

The RAF Record shows that Ernest enlisted as an Air Mechanic in the in the 27th Kite Balloon Sector *(Kite Balloons were used for observation)* of the Royal Flying Corps (Service Number: 42446) on 3 August 1916, aged 26 years and 3 months. He was a Colliery Salesman, 5' 5 ¾" tall with a 37" chest. The RFC became the Royal Air Force on 1 April 1918 and Ernest was promoted to Air Mechanic Second Class from 1 June 1918 at 2 shillings per day pay. Ernest had been wounded while serving in Salonika. He died of pneumonia 'from malaria fever during period of demob furlough – he had only been discharged for eight days – at home at Monckton Grange on 22 February 1919, aged 28.

Ernest was buried on 26 February 1919 in St Peter's Churchyard, Felkirk, where his parents would join him later in one of three family graves close to the church building; his two unmarried sisters, Muriel and Frances Jane, and youngest unmarried brother, Richard Douglas, were buried in two adjacent graves.

IN AFFECTIONATE MEMORY OF ERNEST WILLIAM, THE BELOVED AND ELDEST SON OF JOHN EDWARD AND EDITH MARY LITHERLAND OF MONCKTON GRANGE WHO PASSED AWAY FEB 22ND 1919 AFTER SERVICE IN SALONICA WITH THE ROYAL AIR FORCE, AGED 29 YEARS
THY WILL BE DONE

ALSO THE AFORESAID JOHN EDWARD THE DEARLY BELOVED HUSBAND OF EDITH MARY LITHERLAND WHO DIED SEPT 2ND 1925, AGED 61 YEARS
ALSO EDITH MARY, THE DEARLY BELOVED WIFE OF THE ABOVE WHO DIED JULY 27TH 1932, AGED 61 YEARS
AT REST

Ernest was the last of the Old Boys to die and the only one to do so in 1919, three months after the war had ended.

Ernest should have been awarded two medals: Victory and British War, and his parents should have received the 'Dead Man's Penny' plaque and scroll from King George V.

Probate was granted in London on 9 December 1919 for Ernest to his brother Cyril. Effects: £579 5s 11d.

Ernest's name is on the Holgate Grammar School Memorial and the Lychgate Memorial at St Peter's Church, Felkirk, where inside the Church there is a Memorial Stained Glass Window on the east wall dedicated to him – this is next to a window dedicated to Maurice Bradley Parker Boyd.

The three window panels depict St George (the patron saint of England and a soldier), St Michael with the badge of the Royal Flying Corps and St Alban (the first Christian martyr). (My photograph of this window is in the Colour Section).

Underneath the stained glass window is a small brass plaque:

TO THE GLORY OF GOD AND IN LOVING
MEMORY OF ERNEST WM LITHERLAND
WHO DIED FEBRUARY 21ST 1919 UPON HIS RETURN
HOME AFTER SERVICE WITH THE ROYAL
FLYING CORPS IN SALONICA IN THE
GREAT WAR 1914–18, AGED 29 YEARS

The grave in Darton All Saints Churchyard of Ernest's grandparents, William and Jane Litherland, has an inscribed cross, which includes memorials to Ernest, his parents and two of his brothers: John, buried in Barnsley Cemetery, and Cyril, who was cremated.

Connections

Ernest was Baptised on the same day as **Cyril Burton Dixon** at Darton All Saints Church.

Ernest was in the same Form as **Albert Edward Armitage, John Bruce Atha, Frank Bakel,** and **John Thomas Claude Westby;** they all won Cooper Prizes in 1907 for passing the Oxford Local Junior Exam.

Ernest (who won a cricket bat prize for bowling) was Captain of the Second Eleven Cricket Team, which also comprised: **Edward Batley**, **George Braham** and (probably) **Herbert Harry Jagger Mason**. The First Eleven Team included **George Percival Cowburn** (who won a cricket bat prize for bowling), **Cyril Burton Dixon** (who won a cricket bat prize for batting), **Duncan Fairley** plus **Harold Willott** and his brother **Ernest Spencer Willott**.

Ernest sang a solo in the Speech Day Programme for July 1907, as did **Harold Quest** and **James Christopher Speight.**

Ernest is commemorated at St Peter's Church, Felkirk, along with **Maurice Bradley Parker Boyd** and **Norman Bradbury**.

Old Boys Football Club by E Litherland

The Footer Club in connection with this Association is not in an altogether flourishing condition as regards the number of players at its disposal. When this section was first mooted, it was thought that scores of Old Boys would welcome it, but, alas, some are sick and some are lame and others have previous engagements, so that it is only after much trouble and coaxing that the faithful few are able to secure promises from 11 players. The last two matches have been actually played with only ten men. We want a few good sportsmen, who will play the game for the love of it, and not fall away simply because they do not always happen to be on the winning side. We have a very good ground, a first rate changing room and a low subscription, so that if any of you Old Boys care for good football, under the best conditions, just let the Secretary have your names and you will be welcomed. The Committee must also remind Honorary Members that a little money helps more than heaps of sympathy in a case like this. The money affairs, however, can be left over for a while, but great is the want of two or three more players.

Alumnus – December 1913.

***Alumnus* – April 1919**

E W Litherland, RAF (1906) died at Monckton Grange, Feb 21st, soon after his return from Salonika, where he had been in Hospital. He was one of the founders of the OBA.

***Barnsley Chronicle* – 1 March 1919**

MONCKTON SOLDIER'S SAD DEATH
AFTER TWO YEARS IN SALONIKA

Profound sympathy has been expressed in the sad bereavement, which Mr and Mrs Litherland of Monckton Grange, near Barnsley, have just sustained by the sad death of their eldest son Mr Ernest William Litherland. The deceased had been out in Salonika over two years with the Royal Air Force and only returned home as recently as the 14th February. He took to his bed immediately and despite the best medical treatment and skilful nursing, he passed away eight days later from pneumonia following malarial fever.

In civil life, the deceased gentleman was an official at Monckton Collieries, where he was held in the highest esteem by the management and colleagues alike. He was a former respected member of St Mary's Church Choir, Barnsley, and was an old Grammar School boy.

The interment took place at Felkirk Church on Wednesday and the large attendance of mourners bore tribute to the high respect in which the deceased gentleman was held.

***Barnsley Chronicle* – 1 March 1919**

DEATHS

LITHERLAND On February 22nd 1919 at Monckton Grange, near Barnsley, Ernest William, aged 28 years, the dearly beloved son of John Edward and Edith Mary Litherland, after serving over two years in Salonica with the Royal Air Force.

Fold him, O Father, in Thine arms
And let him henceforth be
A messenger of love between
Our earthly love and Thee

Mr and Mrs Litherland and family wish to thank all kind friends for kind messages of sympathy in their sudden and sad bereavement – also for floral tributes.

CYRIL LITHERLAND (born 8 December 1893 in Darton) attended the Holgate Grammar School for four years, from 1906 to 1910. He became a Colliery Salesman.

He enlisted as an Air Mechanic in the Royal Flying Corps on 7 August 1916, just four days after his older brother Ernest, aged 22 years and 8 months (Service Number: 42447, the next one after Ernest's). Cyril was a Technical Clerk, 5' 7½" tall with a 32" chest. He embarked on 27 November 1916 (no other details provided) and was promoted to Air Mechanic First Class on 1 October 1917 at four shillings a day pay. After leave from 9 to 23 December 1918, he was transferred to the RAF Reserve on 31 January 1919.

Cyril married **Grace Helena Gaunt** late August 1923 at Felkirk St Peter's Church – this was about six weeks after his younger brother George's wedding. They had two children in Barnsley: **John G Litherland** born spring 1925 and **Barbara Litherland** born late 1926. Cyril died in 1960, aged 67, and he was cremated at Lawnswood in Leeds.

GEORGE THOMAS LITHERLAND (born on 20 July 1898, in Barnsley) served in the Royal Air Force. RAF Officers Records show that George (Service Number: 26644) was a Second Lieutenant 'A' from 1 April 1918 then 'A & S (?)' from 12 June 1918. He was '2LT 2GN 103rd TRB' (Second Lieutenant, Second Gunner 1032rd Training Reserve Brigade) from 12 April 1918 then 'Camel Pilot' from 11 September 1918. (The Sopwith Camel was a single seat biplane fighter introduced to the Western Front in June 1917. It was difficult to handle but to an experienced pilot it provided unmatched manoeuvrability). George was wounded and admitted to 62 General Hospital on 24 September 1918, transferred to Officers' Convalescent Home Port Fino on 12 October then returned to 62 Hospital on 24 November before being discharged on 29 November 1918.

George married **Ellen Lodge** on 6 June 1923 in Felkirk St Peter's Church. George (24) was a Coal Factor of Monckton and Ellen (23) was the daughter of **Joshua Cornelly Lodge**, Coal Owner of Ryhill. They had six Witnesses: Ellen's father, both of George's parents plus his siblings Cyril and Muriel plus a friend. They had one son **Peter E Litherland** born summer 1924 in Barnsley. George died December 1971, aged 73, in Claro, Yorkshire

44

Herbert H Marshall

Herbert H Marshall
1890–1917 (aged 27)

HERBERT MARSHALL was born on 15 January 1890 in Leeds to **Alfred Ward Marshall** (born c1860 in Wakefield) and **Ann Elizabeth nee Ainsworth** (born c1860 in Wakefield). Herbert was Baptised at Holy Trinity Church, Armley Hall, on 22 March 1891 along with his brother James Arthur (born 21 October 1885) and his sister Emma (born 21 February 1888); their father was a Mechanic of 18 Croton Place. Alfred was also described as a Textile Machine Maker and Foreman Textile Department as well as Mechanic.

Herbert was the fifth of six surviving children: **Florence** (Florry), **Sarah, James Arthur** (served in the First World War), **Emma** – Tailoress at a Wholesale Factory, and **Elsie Annie** – Blousemaker at a Wholesale Factory. A child had died by April 1911 (name unknown).

In April 1911, the Marshall family lived in six rooms at Leamington House, 13 Lower Wortley Road, Wortley, Leeds, having previously lived at different addresses in Leeds. Florence, Sarah and James Arthur were living elsewhere.

Florence Marshall (24), who had been an Electric Armature Winder, married **Joseph Green** (24) Teacher Manual Instruction from Saltley, Birmingham, on 1 August 1906 at Armley St Bartholomew's Church. In April 1911, they were living in six rooms in Birmingham and Florence's brother Arthur was with them. They had a son **Arthur E Green** late 1912 in Leeds and may have had other children.

Sarah Marshall (26), former Engineer's Tracer, married **Willie Goodall** (29) Lithographic Printer from Wortley, on 26 March 1910 at Wortley St John the Evangelist Church. In April 1911, they were living in four rooms in Leeds. They had one son **Edward M Goodall** early 1915 in Leeds.

Emma Marshall (28) Tailoress, married **Clifford Meftcalfe** (26) Plumber of New Wortley, on 22 July 1916 at Wortley St John the Evangelist Church. They had two children: **Norman W Metcalfe** in Spring 1917 and **Mabel Metcalfe** late 1918

Herbert went to Leeds Central High School from 1902 to 1910, where he taught without a Teaching Certificate. He then attended Leeds University from 1910 to 1913 to complete his BA degree in Art and his Elementary Teacher's Certificate. Herbert was appointed to the Holgate Grammar School, to replace George Edgar Joyce, on 13 January 1914 at a salary of £140 as 'Whole Time Teacher Preparatory Form, Geography with Lower'. He left on 28 July 1915 for a Commission in the Army.

Herbert contributed a number of articles to *Alumnus,* including 'The Antarctic Expedition', 'Western Signal Station', 'Among the Pennines' and 'Explosives and Grenades' (some extracts in Part 3. Chapter 8).

Herbert was Second Lieutenant in the 10th Battalion of the West Yorkshire Regiment (Prince of Wales' Own). He went to France on 20 July 1916 and was killed in action during the Battle of Arras on 13 April 1917, aged 27, after serving in France for 268 days. As Herbert's body was never found or identified his name is listed on the Arras Memorial, Pas de Calais, France (Bay 4).

Herbert was awarded two medals: Victory and British War, after his older brother Arthur of 56 Bayswater Mount, Harehills Road, Leeds, applied for them on 6

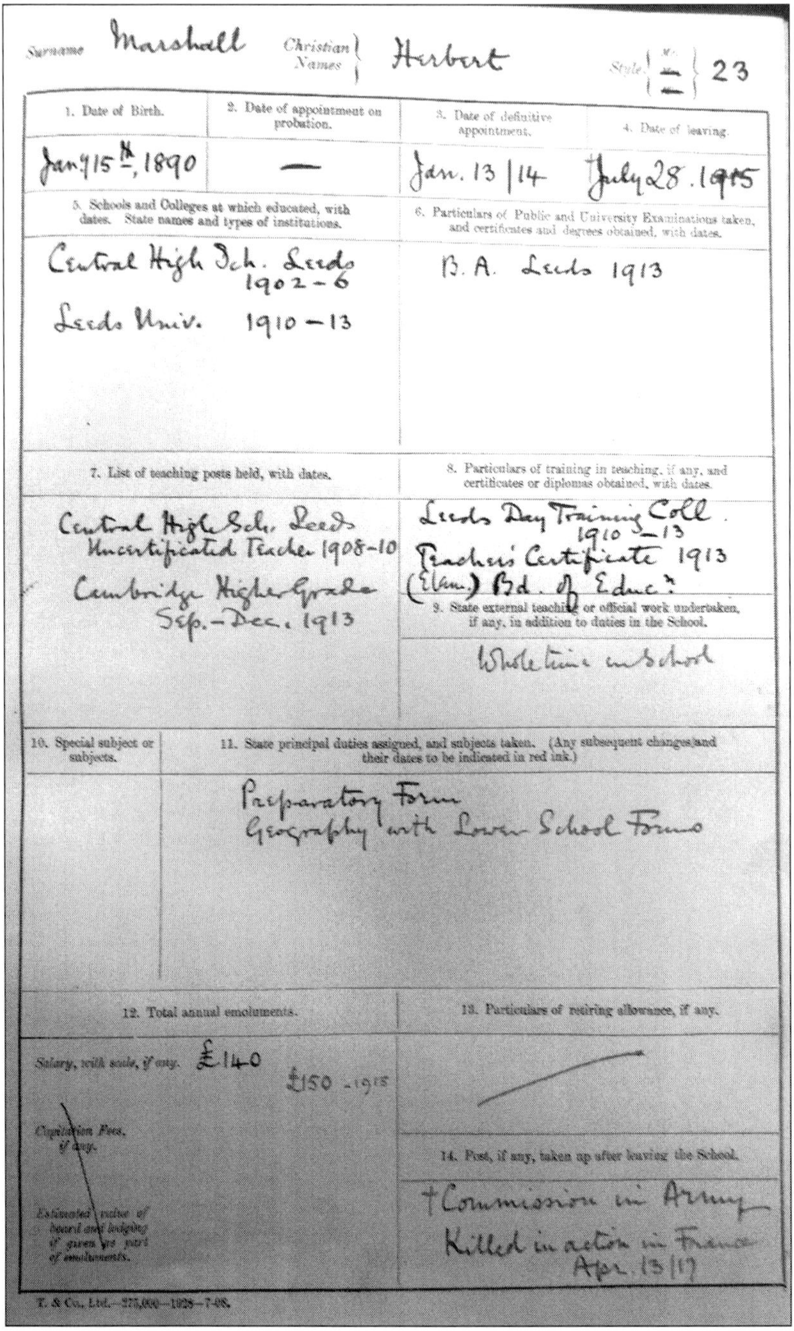

Surname Marshall Christian Names Herbert Style Mr. 23

1. Date of Birth.	2. Date of appointment on probation.	3. Date of definitive appointment.	4. Date of leaving.
Jan.y 15th, 1890	—	Jan. 13/14	July 28. 1915

5. Schools and Colleges at which educated, with dates. State names and types of institutions.	6. Particulars of Public and University Examinations taken, and certificates and degrees obtained, with dates.
Central High Sch. Leeds 1902–6 Leeds Univ. 1910–13	B.A. Leeds 1913

7. List of teaching posts held, with dates.	8. Particulars of training in teaching, if any, and certificates or diplomas obtained, with dates.
Central High Sch. Leeds Uncertificated Teacher 1908–10 Cambridge Higher Grade Sep.–Dec. 1913	Leeds Day Training Coll. 1910–13 Teacher's Certificate 1913 (Elem.) Bd. of Educ.n 9. State external teaching or official work undertaken, if any, in addition to duties in the School. Whole time in School

10. Special subject or subjects.	11. State principal duties assigned, and subjects taken. (Any subsequent changes and their dates to be indicated in red ink.)
	Preparatory Form Geography with Lower School Forms

12. Total annual emoluments.	13. Particulars of retiring allowance, if any.
Salary, with scale, if any. £140 £150 – 1915 Capitation Fees, if any. Estimated value of board and lodging if given as part of emoluments.	14. Post, if any, taken up after leaving the School. † Commission in Army Killed in action in France Apr. 13/17

T. & Co., Ltd.—275,000—1928—7-08.

Staff Register entry for Herbert, reproduced by kind permission of Barnsley Archives.

November 1922. His parents should also have received the 'Dead Man's Penny' plaque and scroll from King George V.

Herbert's name is on the Holgate Grammar School Memorial and on one of the 18 panels which flank the main entrance to the Brotherton Library at Leeds University.

Connection

Herbert was a Geography Teacher at the Holgate Grammar School as was **George Edgar Joyce**, whom he had been appointed to replace when he enlisted in 1914. Both were killed in action.

Alumnus – July 1917

2nd Lieut H Marshall (BA) was killed in action on April 13th 1917, aged 27 years. He was educated at Leeds Central High School and Leeds University, and was appointed a member of the School staff in January 1915. He had a natural aptitude for teaching and a sure instinct for the right management of boys. A loyal colleague, a true comrade and a cultured gentleman, he will be grievously missed by those who knew him.

The following extract from a letter sent by him to Mr C E Powell, Math. Master, only a few days before he was killed add to our feeling of pathos at his premature death.

Well, leave is out of the question at present. Who would be so base as to think of such a thing in these days of push? What I want is a spell of quiet – which I am having now – in bed, which I do not leave except for a bath. I've seen very little of the push – we had the dirty work to do. I have seen both Peronne and Bapaume. I know both only too well, especially Feb 7th. We got shelled very badly that night but having some Bosches' Red Lights – at that time a warning that they were shelling their own trenches – they got confused and gave up.

At present I've got the softest job and the idlest that I've ever had in my life. I am superintending road repairs! The only qualification necessary for this job was that the officer concerned should be able to speak French! So here I am on a main road, I am my own boss, have got quite a decent billet, and have regular hours – which is a thing almost unknown in the army. So I am happy. Half my day I am reading. Would you worry about leave? I forgot to tell you I've been interpretor for the battalion for some time and I had to go in advance getting billets. Some job if you've plenty of time. It's nice too to have the pick of the billets. Well, cheery ho! Remember me to all at BGS.

***Yorkshire Post* & *Leeds Intelligencer* – 20 April 1917**

THE ROLL OF HONOUR

> Second-Lieut Herbert Marshall, West Yorkshire Regiment, reported killed on April 13th, was the youngest son of Mr and Mrs Albert Marshall, Leamington House, Lower Wortley Road, Leeds. He was 27 years of age and before the war was a teacher at Barnsley Grammar School. He was formerly a pupil teacher at Leeds Central High School.

The Photograph of Herbert is from Alumnus, *reproduced by kind permission of Barnsley Archives.*

JAMES ARTHUR MARSHALL (born 21 October 1885 in Bramley, Leeds; died December 1934, aged 49, in Leeds North.). His Baptism was on 22 March 1891 at Holy Trinity Church, Armley Hall, at the same time as Elsie and Herbert. In April 1911, Arthur (25) Pattern Maker, was living with his oldest sister Florence and her husband Joseph Green in Birmingham. Arthur married **Agnes Howson Rawlin** on 31 July 1915 in St John the Baptist Church in New Wortley, Leeds. Arthur (29) was living at 13 Lower Road, Wortley, and Agnes (30), daughter of **Richard Rawlin**, Painter, was at 4 Skilbeck Street,. Elsie Annie Marshall and **Percy Rawlin** were Witnesses.

According to the RAF Records, Arthur enlisted in the Royal Flying Corps (Service Number: 37707) on 17 July 1916, when he was a Pattern Maker, 5' 3" tall with a 35" chest. Arthur was appointed '1/am' on 1 May 1917, then Acting Corporal on 1 September unpaid until 1 February 1918, RAF Corporal Mechanic on 1 April 1918, Acting Sergeant Mechanic unpaid from 2 April then promoted to Sergeant Mechanic on 1 August 1918, reclassified Sergeant (Carpenter) on 1 January 1919. Arthur was put onto the RAF Reserve list on 5 October 1919 and discharged on 30 April 1920.

Arthur and Agnes had three children: **Ronald Rawlin Marshall** was born on 13 October 1916 in Wortley but died on 18 January 1919 (RAF Record), **Alfred** was born summer 1918 and **Nellie** was born early 1920.

45

Herbert Harry Jagger Mason

Herbert Harry Jagger Mason
1890–1916 (aged 26)

HERBERT HARRY JAGGER MASON was born on 2 April 1890 in New Wortley, Leeds to **Joseph Mason** (born c1861 in Leeds) and **Laura nee Jagger** (born 1867 in Barnsley). Herbert's Baptism was at St Mary's Church, Tong Road, Leeds, on 9 July 1890 (St Mary of Bethany, New Wortley). Joseph was a Solicitor's Clerk and Laura had her own Furniture business.

Herbert was the oldest of four children: **Annie Genevieve, Laura** and **Edward Noel** (born 27 December 1901).

Joseph and Laura had married on 26 August 1889 at St George's Church, Barnsley, and their fathers were **John Mason**, Gentleman, and **John Jagger**, Furniture Dealer of Shambles Street, Barnsley. John and **Sarah Jagger** had five children

Herbert and his parents were living with his grandparents, John and Sarah Jagger, at 9 Market Hill, Barnsley, at April 1891, but moved to 25 Tong Road, Wortley, Leeds by April 1901. Joseph and Laura Mason were at 28 Ebor Place, Hyde Park, Leeds when the Commonwealth War Graves Commission record was compiled. (*I have been unable to locate any 1911 Censuses for any of the family).*

Laura's father John was one of seven children of **Joseph Jagger** and **Mary nee McLintock;** he married **Sarah Ann nee Chappel** at Silkstone Parish Church in 1847, when John and both fathers were Weavers. John and Sarah Ann had five children and the youngest of these was **John Edward Jagger**, the uncle referred to in *Barnsley Chronicle* at the time of Herbert's death (the surname was often spelt as Jaeger). After John Edward died in 1893, his widow Sarah Ann moved to 31 Roper Street; when she died in 1906 Probate was granted to her son, also called John Edward.

John Edward Jaeger (born c1864 in Barnsley) was an Auctioneer and Valuer, married to **Frances**, who was a Schoolmistress in her Private School in Sheffield Road until after their first child was born. They were at 33 Kensington Road by April 1901 then in nine rooms at 6 Cavendish Road on the 1911 Census, with two of their four children and a General Servant. John had attended Barnsley Grammar School – he is on a photograph of Locke Scholars taken in 1877 (Part 1. Chapter 1) – and he was a Governor at the Holgate, as the first representative of the Old Boys' Association from 1903 until at least 1927.

Laura Mason (27) married **Harry Jackson** (27) Civil Servant, both of 28 Ebor Place, Leeds, on 16 April 1927 at Leeds All Hallows Church.

Herbert went to Armley National School, Leeds, until the age of 12. He then attended the Holgate Grammar School in Church Street, Barnsley for two years, from 1902 to 1904. The Holgate Admission Register has 'Father Joseph Mason c/o Mrs Jaeger of 31 Roper Street, Barnsley, Solicitor' (ie his grandmother Sarah Ann Jagger) for Herbert's contact. Herbert went on to work for Leeds City Council's Treasurer's Office.

Herbert enlisted at Leeds as a Private (Service Number: 15/621) in the 15th Battalion (Leeds) of the West Yorkshire Regiment (Prince of Wales' Own). He was sent to Egypt on 22 December 1915 and was promoted to Lance Corporal. Herbert was killed in action on the first day of the Somme, 1 July 1916, aged 26, but as his body was never found of identified his name is listed on the Thiepval Memorial, Somme,

TOP: Pte. G. HARRISON (Barnsley, killed); Lce.-Cpl. H. H. J. MASON (an old Barnsley Grammar School boy, killed).

Photograph of Herbert in *Barnsley Chronicle*, used by their kind permission.

France (Pier and Face: 2A 2C & 2D).

Herbert was one of ten Old Boys who were killed in action on the first day of the Somme.

Herbert was awarded three medals: 1914–15 Star, Victory and British War. His parents should have received the 'Dead Man's Penny' plaque and scroll from King George V.

Herbert's name is on the Holgate Grammar School Memorial [incorrectly listed as 'H H Mason Jagger'].

Connection

Herbert probably played for the Second Eleven Cricket Team, which also comprised: **Ernest Litherland**, Captain (who won a cricket bat prize for bowling) and **George Braham.** The First Eleven Team included **George Percival Cowburn** (who won a cricket bat prize for bowling), **Cyril Burton Dixon** (who won a cricket bat prize for batting), **Duncan Fairley** plus **Harold Willott** and his brother **Ernest Spencer Willott**.

Herbert's uncle John Edward Jagger was living at 33 Kensington Road, Barnsley, at April 1901 next door but one to **Thomas Speight,** Newspaper Reporter, and his family, including **James Christopher Speight**, aged 8 at School; Herbert was 11 years old.

Alumnus – July 1917

Lance Corporal H J Mason (left 1904) had been reported missing since July 1st 1916, but is now officially presumed to have been killed. He joined Leeds Pals Battalion at the outbreak of the war, leaving his position as one of the staff of Leeds City Treasurer. He had been a member of the Old Boys Association for many years. A young man of noble character and promising career has been sacrificed by this cruel war.

***Barnsley Chronicle* – 26 MAY 1917 (PHOTO)**

Lance-Corporal H H J Mason, West Yorks Regiment, missing on the 1st July last is now officially presumed to be killed. He was the son of Mr and Mrs J Mason of Ebor Place, Hyde Park, Leeds, and the nephew of Mr J E Jaeger, of Barnsley, and before enlistment was on the staff of the Leeds City Treasurer. He was educated at the Barnsley Grammar School and joined the Leeds Pals in the early days of the war.

***Yorkshire Post* & *Leeds Intelligencer* – 30 April 1917**

Further Leeds men who have been notified as killed or to have died from wounds are as follows: Lance-Corporal H H J Mason (27) West Yorkshire Regiment, 28 Ebor Place, Hyde Park (formerly in the City Treasurer's Department.

The main photograph of Herbert is from Alumnus, *reproduced by kind permission of Barnsley Archives.*

Advert in *Barnsley Chronicle* under 'Sales by Auction'

J E JAEGER
(Fellow of the Auctioneer's Institute)

AUCTIONEER, VALUER, ESTATE AGENT
14 REGENT STREET, BARNSLEY TEL: 121

SALES conducted in Town or Country at moderate charges
Valuations made for all purposes

J E JAEGER undertakes the Management & Letting of Property and Estates & the Collection of Rents, References & Testimonials, on application

Sole agent for S Withers & Co Ltd Celebrated Bent Steel Sales
Price List on application

An early photograph of Barnsley Holgate Grammar School.
Postcard from Jane Ainsworth collection.

The Grammar School War Memorial. (© Jane Ainsworth)

Close ups of
decorative details on
the Grammar School
War Memorial.
(© Jane Ainsworth)

Memorial Stained Glass Window to Maurice Bradley Parker Boyd in the Parish Church of St Peter in Felkirk, used by kind permission of the Reverend Dr Matt Bullimore, Vicar, and the Churchwardens. (© Jane Ainsworth)

Memorial Stained Glass Window to Ernest William Litherland in the Parish Church of St Peter in Felkirk, used by kind permission of the Reverend Dr Matt Bullimore, Vicar, and the Churchwardens. (© Jane Ainsworth)

Plaque and Memorial Stained Glass Window to Cyril Burton Dixon in All Saints Church in Darton, used by kind permission of the Vicar, Father Jonathan Macgillivray. (© Jane Ainsworth)

Memorial Stained Glass Window and Plaque to John (Jack) Normansell in the Parish Church of St Mary in Barnsley, used by kind permission of the Reverend Canon Stephen Race, Parish Priest, and the Churchwardens. (© Jane Ainsworth)

Memorial Cross to Bernard Jaques Joyner (plus close up of inscription at base) in Cudworth St John the Baptist Church, used by kind permission of Father David Nicholson. (© Jane Ainsworth)

Archbishop Holgate's Coat of Arms as used on the School Badge from 1922, used by kind permission of Brian Sawyer.

Paintings by Albert Edward Armitage, reproduced by kind permission of the University of Gloucestershire Special Collections and Archives.

Presentation of my Memorial Book to Barnsley Archives on 2 December 2014, photograph kindly provided by *Barnsley Chronicle* (copyright).

The Name Calling Ceremony for Remembrance Day 2014, photograph kindly provided by *Barnsley Chronicle* (copyright).

46

Donald McNaughton

Donald McNaughton
1897–1918 (aged 20)

DONALD McNAUGHTON was born on 15 April 1897 in Barnsley to **Archibald McNaughton** (born c1868 in Dumfermline, Fife) and **Gertrude nee Wright** (born c1869 in Wragby). Donald's Baptism was on 3 October 1897 at St John the Evangelist Church, Carlton. Archibald was a Letterpress Printer.

Donald was the oldest of four children: **John, Jean Campbell** (also possibly known as Jane) and **Bessie Campbell.**

In April 1911, the McNaughton family lived in five rooms at 20 Greenwood Terrace, Barnsley, having previously lived at 4 Summer Street. The parents moved to Lancashire at some stage as Archibald died there in June 1943, aged 75, and Gertrude died in Blackpool in September 1943, aged 74. The two sisters may have married or emigrated to Canada but their names are too common to be certain.

John McNaughton (aged 25) was a Grocer living at 20 Greenwood Terrace in Barnsley, when he got married to **Margaret Robinson** on 24 June 1926 in St Mary's Church, Barnsley. John's sister Jean was one of the Witnesses. Margaret (aged 24) of 25 Pontefract Road was the daughter of **Richard Robinson**, who had also been a Grocer. Their only son called **Donald McNaughton** was born in Barnsley on 1 September 1929; he died in Blackpool aged only 47.

Donald went to Barnsley Elementary School until the age of 11. He then attended the Holgate Grammar School in Church Street, Barnsley for four years, from 1908 to 1912. When the Grammar School tried to update the Admissions Register they received no reply to their enquiries.

Donald enlisted at Barnsley as a Private (Service Number: 42983) in the 9th Battalion of the King's Own Yorkshire Light Infantry.* He was promoted to Lance Corporal then acting Sergeant and was killed in action on 22 March 1918, aged 20. As his body was never found or identified his name is listed on the Poziéres Memorial, near Albert, Somme, France (Panel 59 and 60).†

Donald was awarded two medals: Victory and British War. His parents should have received the 'Dead Man's Penny' plaque and scroll from King George V.

Donald's name is on the Holgate Grammar School Memorial.

* **9th (Service) Battalion of the King's Own Yorkshire Light Infantry**
This Battalion formed at Pontefract in September 1914 as part of K3, Kitchener's Third New Army, and came under command of 64th Brigade in 21st Division. They went to France in 1915 and participated in the Battle of Loos, the Somme Battles of 1916, the Arras Offensive and Third Battles of Ypres in 1917, then back to the Somme in 1918.

The Battle of St Quentin commenced on the morning of 21 March 1918, when the British Army attacked in the thick fog that had formed the previous evening. They wore gas masks for much of the day as poison gas was released from British cylinders facing St Quentin. As German infantry broke through gaps in the defences and attacked from behind, thousands of men were killed and more taken Prisoner of War.

† **The Pozières Memorial** commemorates over 14,000 casualties of the United Kingdom and 300 of the South African Forces, who have no known grave and who died on the Somme from 21 March to 7 August 1918.

47

Francis (Frank) Hirst Moore

Francis (Frank) Hirst Moore
1880–1916 (aged 36)

FRANCIS HIRST MOORE was born in 1880 in Barnsley to **Aaron Moore** (born c1842 in Denby) and **Sarah Ann nee Hirst** (born c1847 in Skelmanthorpe). His Baptism was on 28 November 1880 at St Augustine's Church, Scisset, York. Aaron was a General Builder Employer, having previously been a Stone Mason.

Frank was one of seven surviving children: **Clara Elizabeth** – Elementary School Teacher, Annie – Teacher's Assistant, **Flora** – Teacher's Assistant, **Walter Cecil** (attended the Holgate), **Kate Avonia** – Teacher's Assistant and **Ethel Grace.** Their brother **John** had died early 1887, aged 16. Their father died in summer 1909, aged 67.

In April 1911, the Moore family had lived in nine rooms at 12 Wharncliffe Road, Sheffield, for more than 10 years. Walter Cecil was not living at home. They had moved from 6 Victoria Street, Barnsley, having previously lived in Scisset. They later moved to 84 Brookhouse Hill, Fulwood, Sheffield. None of Francis' sisters appears to have got married but Moore is a common surname.

Frank went to St Mary's School, Barnsley, until the age of 12. He then attended the Holgate Grammar School in Church Street, Barnsley for three years, from 1892 to 1895. He was a Builder Employer by April 1911, having taken over his father's business.

Frank enlisted in 1914 and became a Sergeant (Service Number: 11835) in the 7th Battalion of the King's Own Yorkshire Light Infantry.* He went to France on 31 March 1915 and was promoted to Second Lieutenant in December 1915. Frank was killed in action while leading his Company over the parapet on 7 October 1916, aged 36, having served for 1 year and 191 days in France; his name was on the Daily Casualty List reported in *The Times* on 21 October 1916. Frank was buried in Bancourt British Cemetery, Pas de Calais, France (grave XII B 20), reburied from the original location, where he was identified by his disc.

Probate was granted in London for Francis on 21 November 1917 to his widowed mother, Sarah Ann Moore; Effects: £207 8s 3d.

* **7th (Service) Battalion KOYLI**
This Battalion formed at Pontefract on 12 September 1914 as part of K2 (Kitchener's Second Army) and came under command of 61st Brigade of the 20th (Light) Division. Initially poorly equipped and trained, they moved to Woking then Witley in February 1915, going on to Salisbury Plain in May before crossing to France on 24 July 1915.

In 1916, they participated in the Battle of Mount Sorrel, a Ypres sector counter-attack in which the Division recaptured the height with the Canadians, then Battles of the Somme at Delville Wood, Guillemont, Flers-Courcelette, Morval and Le Transloy.

The Battle of Le Transloy started on 1 October and the British Army faced severe difficulties because of the weather and terrain as well as the enemy. Despite being on higher ground, the heavy rains turned the battlefield into a muddy morass, difficult and exhausting to negotiate, and the increasing cold made conditions even more uncomfortable. The follow up attack was delayed because of the atrocious weather until 7 October, when there were heavy casualties with rain hampering their removal from the battlefield.

Frank was awarded three medals: 1914–15 Star, Victory and British War. His widowed mother should have received the 'Dead Man's Penny' plaque and scroll from King George V.

Frank's name is on the Holgate Grammar School Memorial. He is listed in the Sheffield Year Book and Record 1917, living at 84 Brookhouse Hill.

Connection

Frank was killed in the Battle of Le Transloy on the Somme, as was **Sidney Nicholson**.

***Barnsley Chronicle* – 28 October 1916**

DEATH OF LIEUT F H MOORE A FORMER RESIDENT OF BARNSLEY

Many Barnsley people will read with regret of the death of Second-Lieut Francis Hirst Moore, son of the late Mr Aaron Moore and Mrs S A Moore of 84, Brookhouse Hill, Fulwood, Sheffield. Mr Aaron Moore was a contractor and at one time resided in Victoria Avenue, Barnsley. Lieut Moore was educated at St Mary's Boys' School and the Barnsley Grammar School. He enlisted in the KOYLI at the outbreak of war, proceeded to France in May 1915, and received his commission in December of the same year. He was killed in action on October 7th. In a letter of condolence to the deceased officer's sister, his commanding officer wrote: 'He had been with us since December last, so that we had lived and gone through a great deal together in the last ten months and he was always one of the best. At the time of his death he was leading the company over the parapet, and he fell going across. One of the saddest things out here is the parting with the friends with whom you have lived so long. One of the first to join, and at it ever since, I don't think there is anyone who has shown a finer devotion to duty than your brother'.

DEATHS

MOORE – Killed in action on October 7th, Francis Hirst (Frank) Moore, Second-Lieut KOYLI, dearly beloved son of the late Aaron Moore and of Sarah A Moore, 84 Brookhouse Hill, Fulwood, Sheffield.

(Also in *Sheffield Evening Telegraph* – 16 October 1916)

WALTER CECIL MOORE (born in 1880 in Barnsley) was Baptised on 22 October 1882 at St John the Baptist Church, Barnsley; his father was a Builder of Buckley Street. Walter went to St Mary's School, Barnsley, then attended the Holgate for three years, from 1894 to 1897.

I have been unable to find any records to match him after the 1891 Census, but Walter had not died by 1911; he may have emigrated.

WAR SUPPLEMENT FOR WEEK ENDING, JUNE 8, 1918.

"SPURLOS VERSENKT."

"SUNK WITHOUT A TRACE."

[Early in 1917 the German Minister at Buenos Ayres recommended the Berlin authorities to sink neutral vessels on the high seas—*Spurlos Versenkt*, i.e., without leaving a trace, a black crime against neutrals and against humanity.

On May 11th, a British submarine encountered a large German cruiser-submarine off the Portuguese coast and torpedoed her. "A heavy sea was running at the time and there were no survivors." That was a real case of the evil practice of *Spurlos Versenkt* "coming home to roost." There is of course a difference—the German *Spurlos Versenkt* was against neutral trading vessels; the British against an ocean pirate seeking to destroy such vessels.

Our artist's picture illustrates the fact that we are gradually getting the mastery of the U-boat. It is, as Mr. Lloyd George says, still a ***nuisance***, but no longer a ***peril***, thanks to all that the Navy has done and is still doing.

48

Sidney Nicholson

Sidney Nicholson
1889–1916 (aged 26)

SIDNEY NICHOLSON was born on 8 November 1889 at 35 Lancaster Street, Barnsley, to **John William Nicholson** (born c1856 in Barnsley) and **Elizabeth nee Carroll** (born c1858 in Barnsley). John was a Timber Merchant's Clerk for Messrs Robinson & Son then Mill Manager.

Sidney was the seventh of 10 children: **Arthur** (attended the Holgate), **Edwin Stansfield, Emily, William James** (may have served in the First World War), **John Leonard**, **Elizabeth, Frank Cockcroft** (attended the Holgate and served in the First World War), **Laura** – a Finisher of Ready Made Clothes, and **Ernest Carroll** (attended the Holgate and served in the First World War). Their father died early 1906, aged 50.

In April 1911, the Nicholson family had lived in five rooms at 5 Lancaster Street (previously at 35), Barnsley, for over 20 years. Arthur, Edwin, Emily and William James had all left home.

Arthur (32) Certificated Schoolmaster, was a Boarder in Kettering with **Henry George King** and family. Emily and Laura may have got married but they have common names. Elizabeth died late 1918 in Barnsley, aged 30.

Edwin Stansfield Nicholson (aged 31), Iron Moulder, was living in Sheffield with his wife and their three young children: **Cecilia** (6), **Kathleen** (3) and **Arthur** (1); he had married **Florence Chambers** in Spring 1904 in Barnsley district.

John Leonard Nicholson, House Agent on his own account in 1911, married **Louise Mattie Lipscomb** early 1914 in Kingston, Surrey, and they had two children in Barnsley: **Rosemary** in 1915 and **Charles Noel Sidney (known as Sid)** in 1921.

Sidney went to St Mary's School, Barnsley, until the age of 10. He then attended the Holgate Grammar School in Church Street, Barnsley for three years, from 1900 to 1903. He won prizes for Divinity, Latin and English in July 1902 while in Form IV and, in the same year, won top prize in the Under 14 High Jump at the School Sports Day for clearing 3 feet 9 inches.

Sidney became a Glass Bottle Manufacturer's Clerk for Messrs Rylands' Glass and Engineering Company at Stairfoot, Barnsley, but went on to work for Messrs W Carr & Co Accountants of Regent Street, Barnsley. He was in the choir and taught at Sunday School at Ebenezer Church and was a good football player.

Photograph from the Yorkshire Rugby Football Union's *In Memoriam 1914 – 1919* via the Thiepval Memorial Project, used by their kind permission.

Sidney was engaged to **Hilda Taylor** (born 17 January 1890 in Darton), who was one of six surviving children out of eight on the 1911 Census, born to **John Henry Taylor**, Butcher, and **Martha Taylor** of 6 Western Street, Barnsley. Hilda was a Certificated Elementary School Teacher; she became the Godmother of Sidney's nephew Sid (NFW). Hilda died in Summer 1981, aged 91, in Barnsley.

Sidney, who was fluent in French and German according to one of his relations, enlisted at Leeds as a Private (C/12449) in the 21st Battalion of the King's Royal Rifle Corps. (This is the number just after his younger brother Ernest). The 21st Battalion were part of the 41st Division and participated in the Battles of the Somme in 1916; the Battle of Le Transloy took place from 1 to 18 October 1916 amidst persistent rain, fog and cold, which resulted in great difficulties for the men as the battlefield turned to mud.

Sidney, who had been promoted to Lance Corporal, was killed in action on 10 October 1916, aged 26. (This is the date provided by the Commonwealth War Graves Commission, although the article in *Barnsley Chronicle* states 7th). As his body was never found or identified his name is listed on the Thiepval Memorial, Somme, France (Pier and Face: 13A and 13B).

Sidney was awarded two medals: Victory and British War. His widowed mother should have received the 'Dead Man's Penny' plaque and scroll from King George V.

Sidney's name is on the Holgate Grammar School Memorial and the Memorial List of names for Ebenezer Methodist Chapel, Barnsley *(now demolished)*.

No 7 PLATOON "B" COY., 21st (SERVICE) BATTALION K.R.R. (YEOMAN RIFLES), ALDERSHOT 1916.

The Battalion photograph, reproduced by kind permission of Deborah Toft.

Connections

Sidney worked for Messrs W Carr & Co Accountants of Regent Street, Barnsley, as did **Harold Parkin**.

Sidney served in the 21st Battalion of the King's Royal Rifle Corps along with **Norman Bradbury**.

Sidney died in the Battle of Le Transloy on the Somme, as did **Francis Hirst Moore** (details in Part 2. Chapter 47).

Sidney's name is on the Memorial List for Ebenezer Methodist Chapel as well as **Frank Bakell** [sic] and **Harry Bambridge**.

***Ripon Gazette and Times* – 5 October 1916**

Tributes written by his comrades, including the Nicholson brothers, to the parents of Rifleman Tom Gains, who was Killed in Action on 15 or 17 September 1916

Dear Mr and Mrs Gains, – you will no doubt by this time have received the sad news of your son Tom's death in action, but the men who are left in the section to which he belonged felt they would like to write and express to your their sincere sympathy in your great loss. Tommy (as we called him) was always so cheerful and full of fun, and we all miss him very much indeed. It may be of some consolation to you to know that he suffered no pain, death being instantaneously. – Again expressing our sympathy, yours truly, **Ernest C Nicholson L/Cpl., S Nicholson Rfn.**, A G Day Rfn., H M C Young (3) Rfn., R Haywood Rfn.

***Barnsley Chronicle* – 21 October 1916**

DEATHS

NICHOLSON – In very affectionate memory of Corporal Sidney Nicholson, King's Royal Rifle Corps (Yeoman Rifles), dearly loved seventh child of Elizabeth and the late John William Nicholson, of Lancaster Street, Barnsley, who fell in action in France on October 7th [sic] 1916, in his 27th year. Mrs Nicholson and family and Miss Hilda Taylor desire to thank friends for their kind sympathy.

BARNSLEY GRAMMAR SCHOOL OLD BOY KILLED
"THE BRAVEST OF THE BRAVE"

The sad news arrived in Barnsley this week that Corporal Sidney Nicholson, Kings Royal Rifle Corps (Yeoman Rifles) was killed in action in France on October 7th [sic]. Corporal Nicholson was 26 years of age and was a son of

Mrs and the late Mr John Wm Nicholson of Lancaster Street, Barnsley. He was educated at St Mary's School and the Barnsley Grammar School, and was with Messrs Carr and Co., accountants. Also for a short time he was with Rylands Glass and Engineering Co. The deceased was associated with Ebenezer Church, being a member of the choir and a teacher in the Sunday School. His father, the late Mr J W Nicholson, was for many years in the employ of Messrs Robinson and Son, timber merchants.

Deceased's Platoon Commander, Second-Lieutenant Brooksbank writing to the dead hero's mother, said: 'It is a terrible blow to us all, both officers and men by whom he was greatly beloved. His poor heart broken brother's first thought was of you and the terrible grief it would cause you. He died instantly and without any pain. He was a good soldier – the bravest of the brave – and his loss has cast a great gloom over us for we were all so fond of him and fully appreciated his splendid qualities. Surely it must be some comfort to you to know that he died so nobly for his King and country, a hero's death, giving up all he had, even life itself'.

Company Sergeant-Major W Huddlestone in a letter to deceased's brother wrote: 'His high moral character, his cheerful willing spirit, his calm courage in face of danger had won for him the thorough love and respect of his companions'.

Sheffield Evening Telegraph – 20 October 1916

BARNSLEY CASUALTIES

Corporal Sidney Nicholson (26) of Lancaster Street, who has been killed in action whilst with the King's Royal Rifle Corps, was an old Barnsley Grammar School boy and for many years had been in the employ of Messrs W Carr and Co. accountants, Regent Street.

Yorkshire Evening Post – 20 October 1916

THE ROLL OF HONOUR

Barnsley's latest casualties include the death in action of Corporal Sidney NICHOLSON, King's Royal Rifles, who before enlisting was with Messrs W Carr & Co accountants, Regent Street, Barnsley. He was a well-known footballer and would have been 27 years of age next month.

The main photograph of Sidney is cropped from the Battalion photo, reproduced by kind permission of Deborah Toft.

ARTHUR NICHOLSON (born c1879 in Barnsley) attended the Holgate as a Locke Scholar from 1890 to 1892. By April 1901, Arthur (22) was a National School Teacher, boarding at 13 Mill Road, Kettering, with John Harvey (25) Shoe Heel Maker, and his family; **George Ford** (23) was also a Teacher Boarder. On the 1911 Census he is aged 32, Certificated Schoolmaster with Kettering UDC, boarding with **Harry George King** (31) Butcher and family at 'Buccleuch House', Avondale Road, Kettering.

ERNEST CARROLL NICHOLSON (born c1896 in Barnsley, died aged 97) was a Bank Clerk (Student part time) living at home at April 1911. Ernest enlisted at Leeds as a Private (Service Number: C/12448) in the King's Royal Rifle Corps then became a Sergeant; his number is the one before his older brother Sidney. Ernest was promoted to officer with the East Yorkshire Regiment and was awarded a Military Cross; he subsequently became Captain then Major on the General List in 1918. The Medal Card states: 'Commissioned 26 February 1918'.

Photograph of Ernest cropped from the Battalion photo, reproduced by kind permission of Deborah Toft.

Ernest became a Bank Manager after the war. He married **Gladys Irene Knee** in Summer 1921 and they had three children: **John Philip** in 1922, **Margaret C** in 1925 in Barnsley then **Michael B** in 1934 in Beverley. Gladys died just weeks before her 100th birthday.

The London Gazette – **15 October 1918: Supplement**

> Military Cross – Temporary 2nd Lieutenant Ernest Carroll Nicholson for conspicuous gallantry and devotion to duty while leading his platoon in an advance. He successfully rushed enemy posts, capturing prisoners and 2 machine guns, eventually gaining the final objective and consolidating. He maintained contact with the unit on his left, crossing and recrossing ground swept by intense machine gun fire, and reported clearly all developments to his company commander. His fearlessness and resource were beyond praise.

***Barnsley Chronicle* – 26 October 1918**

MC FOR BARNSLEY OFFICER SEC LT E C NICHOLSON

(Quotes from the London Gazette). Second-Lieutenant Nicholson, who is 23 years of age, enlisted in 1915. He went through the Somme battles of 1916 with the 21st King's Royal Rifles, Yeoman Rifles (now disbanded). His brother Sidney, who enlisted with him, was killed in October 1916 on the Somme. After being promoted Sergeant, Ernest came home in 1917 to train for a commission and was gazetted with the East Yorkshires. He returned to France in June and gained the MC for gallantry on July 13. An old St Mary's Boy, he is a member of the Ebenezer Church and was on the staff of the Yorkshire Penny Bank at Barnsley and Wombwell. He is the youngest of four soldier sons of Mrs and the late Mr J W Nicholson of Lancaster Street, Barnsley.

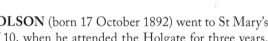

FRANK COCKROFT NICHOLSON (born 17 October 1892) went to St Mary's school, Barnsley, until the age of 10, when he attended the Holgate for three years, from 1902 to 1905; he was a Locke Scholar and passed the Oxford Local Senior exam. In April 1911 Frank (19) was a Bobbin Manufacturer's Clerk living at home.

Frank, a Conscientious Objector, was called up and attested in Barnsley on 8 May 1916, aged 24 years and 6 months. He was a Bobbin Maker's Clerk with Wilson & Co. Barnsley Limited and living at 5 Lancaster Street, Barnsley. Frank was a Private (Service Number: 889) in Number 2 Northern Company of the Non Combatant Corps* and served in the Forestry Division in Bayonne on the French/Spanish border from 29 May 1916. The Medical Form provides some personal details: 5' 6" tall, weight 112lbs, waist 34", slight hernia, vision in both eyes 6/6 and medical category A1. Frank was transferred to the Dispersal Camp in Ripon on 21 January 1919 and demobilized on 20 June 1919. Wilson & Co. wrote to the Army to confirm that they were keeping his post open and that he would return as Costings Order and Confidential Clerk on his return to civil life.

Frank married **Alice E Wood** in summer 1922 in Barnsley district and they had a son **Frank S** in summer 1925.

* **Non Combatant Corps** After the passing of the Military Service Act in early 1916 it was decided to form a Non-Combatant Corps (NCC) of conscientious objectors for work on roads, hutments, timber work, quarrying, sanitary duties and handling supplies. Eight NCC Companies existed by the middle of June 1916.

WILLIAM JAMES NICHOLSON (born c1884) was a Carpenter & Joiner Contractor on the 1911 Census, living in Barnsley, with his wife and their two young children: **John William** and **Mary;** he had married **Emily Wharam** in Summer 1907 in Barnsley district. William may have served in the Royal Air Force towards the end of the war. (I found records for several men with the same name but there was insufficient information to confirm if any were correct).

Deborah Toft, great great niece of Sidney Nicholson, generously shared family information and photographs.

The Thiepval Memorial Project kindly allowed me to use the photograph from Yorkshire Rugby Football Union's In Memoriam 1914–1919 *and the Tribute to Tom Gains.*

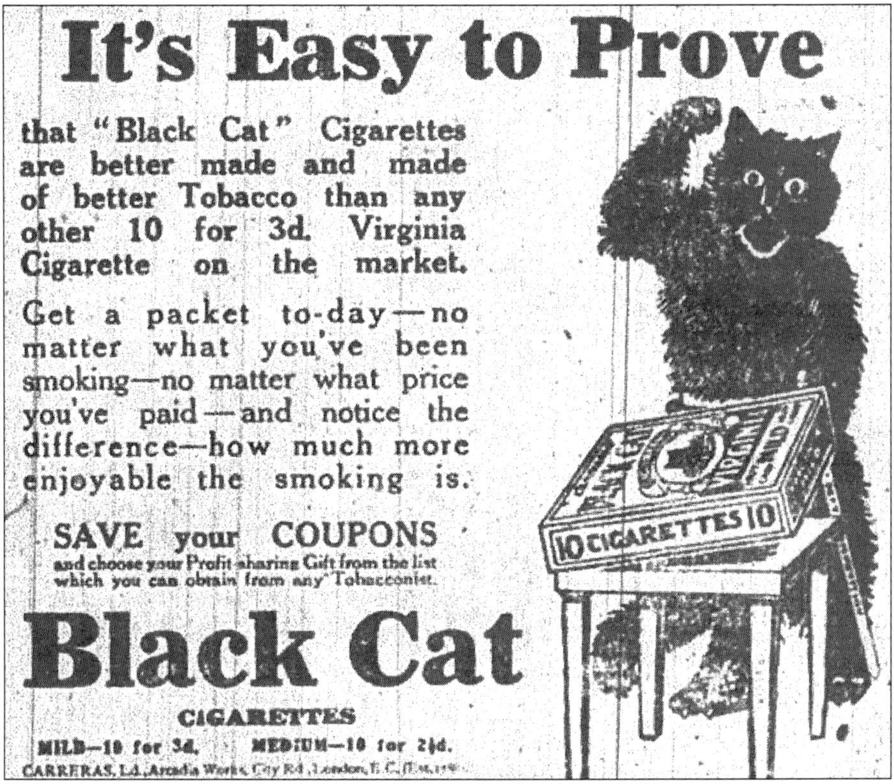

49

John (Jack) Normansell

John (Jack) Normansell
1889–1917 (aged 27)

JOHN NORMANSELL was born on 9 November 1889 in Barnsley to **Joseph Normansell** (born 1859 in Hoyland Common) and **Sarah Jane nee Hall** (born c1863 in Dukenfield, Cheshire). Joseph was a Glass Bottle Manufacturer's Representative, whose father John Normansell had been Secretary of the South Yorkshire Miners' Association.

John (Jack) had two younger sisters: **Dorothy Mary** and **Kate (Kitty)**. Another sister **Margaret Anne** had died on 27 March 1897, aged 7 months. **Dorothy Mary Normansell** married **William Arthur Lowrance** in August 1911 and they had one daughter **Margaret Anne Lowrance** born early 1913. **Kitty Normansell** married **Cyril Alfred Miers** in June 1921. Both marriages were at St Mary's Church in Barnsley.

In April 1911, the Normansell family lived in 11 rooms at 7 Cavendish Road, Barnsley, having previously lived in Hopwood Street for more than 10 years. They employed a Domestic Servant.

Jack went to St Mary's School, Barnsley, until the age of 10. He then attended the Holgate Grammar School in Church Street, Barnsley for six years, from 1900 to 1906. Jack worked for Qualter, Hall and Company Limited for two years learning the engineering trade then won a Mining Scholarship at Sheffield. (*Qualter Hall & Co Ltd, project engineers, are still based in Barnsley).* He joined Old Silkstone Colliery at Dodworth as a student and was preparing for his final certificate as Colliery Manager when war broke out.

Jack was engaged to be married to **Ruby Cook**, daughter of **Charles Richard Cook**, Dental Surgeon, and **Annie Cook** (both born c1862 in Grimsby). Ruby was born c1885 in Oxford and had two younger siblings: **Ida** and **Charlie Cook**. The family lived in 10 rooms at Havenhurst, Huddersfield Road, Barnsley, where Charles had his own dental business; they had moved from St Mary's Gate, Barnsley, and employed a domestic servant.

Photograph from Jon Cooksey's *Barnsley Pals*, reproduced by kind permission of the author and Pen & Sword Publishers.

Jack enlisted in September 1914 in the newly formed 13th Battalion (First Barnsley Pals) of the York and Lancaster Regiment. He was appointed as Temporary Second Lieutenant as listed in *Barnsley Chronicle* on 10 October 1914 and was promoted to Lieutenant in March 1915 then Captain on 1 August 1915, as reported in the *Birmingham Daily Post*. As many of the men in the First Barnsley Pals were Miners, they assisted the Royal Engineers with skilled and dangerous tunnelling work on the Somme under the leadership of Jack and his Lieutenants (Jon Cooksey).

In July 1916 Jack received wounds to the face from a rifle grenade, reported in the *Daily Casualty Lists* on 31 July 1916. He was treated in Chelsea Hospital, but his health deteriorated with septic poisoning, which almost proved fatal, and he was invalided home. On recovery he returned to France in January 1917 but was wounded again on the battlefield and died the next day, 10 March 1917, aged 27, after leaving the advanced dressing station at Beaumont Hamel. He was buried in Serre Road Cemetery No. 1, Pas de Calais, France (grave II C 30), reburied from the original location of Beaucourt Military Cemetery.

Photograph in De Ruvigny's *Roll of Honour 1914–1918.*

Jack was awarded two medals: Victory and British War. His parents should have received the 'Dead Man's Penny' plaque and scroll from King George V.

Probate was granted in Wakefield on 26 May 1917 to Jack's parents; Effects: £235 5s.

Jack's name is on the Holgate Grammar School Memorial, on the painted column in St Mary the Virgin's Church, Barnsley, where there is also a plaque dedicating a stained glass window to him, and a seat in St George's Chapel in Sheffield Cathedral with the dedication: 'CAPTAIN / J NORMANSELL / DIED 1917'.

The stained glass window in St Mary the Virgin's Church has three panels: Saint George, the Patron Saint of England, shown slaying the dragon; Saint Michael the Archangel, leader of God's army against forces of evil; St Martin of Tours, whose Feast Day is 11 November, shown cutting his cloak to share it with a beggar in winter. (My photograph of this window is in the Colour Section).

The plaque underneath reads:

TO THE GLORY OF GOD
and in proud & loving memory of
JACK NORMANSELL
Captain 13 (SB) Y & L Regt
aged 27 years, who fell in France for Freedom
Honour and Right on March 10th 1917
This window was erected
by his sorrowing parents

He is also remembered on his parents' headstone in Barnsley Cemetery, which has a cross above a tiered base and is adjacent to the grave of his grandparents:

In Loving Memory of …

ALSO JOHN NORMANSELL
CAPT 13TH BATT. Y & L REGT
WHO FELL IN FRANCE MARCH 10TH
1917, AGED 27 YEARS

Connection

Jack served with the 13th Battalion (First Barnsley Pals) along with **Cyril Burton Dixon**, who was also appointed Temporary Second Lieutenant in October 1914.

Jon Cooksey – *Barnsley Pals* (Published by Pen and Sword)

> Captain Normansell and two Lieutenants were responsible for ensuring that galleries were kept clear of dirt as tunnelling progressed. (As many of 13th Battalion were Miners, they assisted with tunnelling operations attached to Royal Engineers). …. Thunderstorms on 4 July hampered the walk back to the village by the exhausted men for a short period of rest. What was left of the 94th Brigade – the 13th Battalion had 15 officers and 469 men left – had just 4 days rest before being moved on to Vieille Chapelle. On 15 July both Barnsley Pals Battalions moved to the desolate and loathsome trenches of Neuve Chapelle to relieve 2nd /8th Royal Warwickshires. … Within 12 days the 13th Battalion had another 6 dead and 42 wounded including Jack Normansell with wounds to the face caused by rifle grenade.

Alumnus – April 1917

> On leaving the Grammar School, Captain J Normansell (1900–1906) was for two years in the works of Qualter, Hall and Co Ltd learning the engineering trade. Afterwards he became a mining student at the Old Silkstone Colliery, and was preparing for his final examination for qualification as mining engineer when war broke out. On the outbreak of war he obtained a commission in the First Barnsley Battalion. In September 1915 he was promoted to the rank of Captain. He was slightly wounded in July 1916 but later developed septic poisoning. On his recovery he returned to France in January 1917. He died of wounds received on the battlefield March 10th 1917.

***Barnsley Chronicle* – 17 March 1917**

A BARNSLEY OFFICER MORTALLY WOUNDED
CAPTAIN J NORMANSELL

Profound sorrow was expressed in Barnsley last weekend when by telegram, came the sad news that Captain John Normansell had died of wounds received in action in France. The deceased officer was exceedingly well known in Barnsley and districts and the deepest sympathy is universally felt with his parents, Mr and Mrs Joseph Normansell, of Cavendish Road, whose only son he was. Following the wire came a letter written by Captain Normansell so recently as the previous Tuesday on which date he was well, and this was followed by another cheery letter, penned on the Thursday. The telegram received on Saturday read as follows: 'HM War Office, London, to Joseph Normansell, of 7 Cavendish Road, Barnsley – Deeply regret to inform you that Captain John Normansell, York and Lancaster Regiment, died of wounds March 10th. The Army Council express their sympathy – Secretary War Office'.

The Captain was 27 years of age and, under his Commanding Officer Lieutenant-Colonel J Hewitt at the outbreak of war, he was one of the first to receive a commission on joining the 1st Barnsley Battalion. From the first the deceased soldier showed every promise, and with his superiors and men under his command he became exceedingly popular as a Lieutenant. He had not long to wait for a promotion, a Captaincy being offered and accepted by him in August of 1915. Going out to the front with the Barnsley lads at the close of the year named, he on many occasions displayed valour and at the end of July he received a rifle grenade wound on the face. This necessitated his being sent to the base and subsequently to the hospital at Chelsea. He soon was able to leave this institution however, but his bodily health gave way due in a measure to the septic poisoning which had resulted from the wounds, and for a short period whilst he was under treatment at home his life was despaired of. To the delight of everyone who knew him he recovered and in January last he returned to his duties in France.

'Jack', as he was so familiarly and affectionately known in Barnsley, was an old Barnsley Grammar School boy. Always of a cheery nature, he won the admiration of a host of friends, all of whom have received the news of his demise with deep regret. After leaving school, the deceased entered the engineering works of Messrs Qualter, Hall and Co. and went through every department of that concern with marked success. Very early did he give promise of a brilliant commercial career, and his engineering proclivities coming to the notice of Mr Larret C Parkin, general manager of the Old Silkstone Colliery Co. (whose father was a personal friend of Captain Normansell's grandfather, the late John Normansell, Secretary of the South Yorkshire Miners Association, who died December 24th 1875) this gentleman prevailed upon him to go in for mining studies under his direction. A mining scholarship was won at Sheffield by the deceased and at the time war was declared he was preparing for his final examination for the certificate of colliery manager. But he did not hesitate to put his country first when an appeal for fighting men was made. Personal considerations were set aside by 'Jack' Normansell; duty was his watchword and from the first day he joined the Barnsley Battalion he displayed marked ability in his new sphere of labours and thereby secured the confidence of his superiors. Of him Lieutenant-Colonel Hewitt was obviously proud, and his rise in the ranks was merely a matter of time. At Newhall Camp and at the other training grounds where the 1st Barnsley Battalion were pitched Captain Normansell was an officer beloved by all. He was a keen disciplinarian; his Company knew that to a man, but every one of them looked up to their leader with reverence and in him they found a trusted friend. While his death has cast a gloom in his native town, we can imagine the poignant grief which has been occasioned among the Pals out at the front. Many of the lads on their visits to Barnsley have mentioned with evident feelings of pride, the name of 'Jack' Normansell. By his death indeed the 1st Barnsley Battalion has been deprived of a gallant and fearless officer – a type of man whom it was a pleasure to know, and who has gallantly laid down his life in the service of his King and country.

With Mr and Mrs Normansell the sympathy of the people of Barnsley goes out unstintedly and since the sad news of their son's death reached the town on Saturday they have been inundated with letters of condolence – letters which express the fervent sorrow of the writers in the irreparable loss his esteemed parents have sustained. Sympathy too has been shown to Miss Ruby Cooke (daughter of Mr C R Cooke, Havenhurst, Huddersfield Road) to whom the deceased officer was engaged to be married.

Here are a few extracts from letters which Mr and Mrs Normansell have received: 'Jack was one of the sunniest hearted lads of the Battalion and his loss cannot be replaced. One's feelings cannot be expressed for our sorrow is so great. You have only one consolation – that you have raised a man who has gallantly laid down his life for the Motherland; one of whom the country is proud and whose memory will be an everlasting monument in our hearts'. 'He was always a most honourable lad who did his work well and was always respectful to those older than himself. For a young man he was a model officer and a true friend. If there is any consolation at all you know your boy did his duty; he was never a shirker; he died a hero's death'. 'Brave and fearless, the finest specimen of early manhood that this town has given'. 'There is no doubt "Jack" was a favourite of everyone in our town and he will be missed by all. Merciful Providence will reward him for his noble death. I have brothers in the fighting zone and we must look to them to avenge the loss of so gallant a hero as your beloved son'. 'I know that I have lost a dear friend, and I also know that the old country has lost another of its brave sons and also one its best officers'. 'War is a great leveller – we are all feeling the effects of the mighty upheaval and you have contributed your all in your son'. 'I cannot think that these boys, after willingly giving themselves for the greatest cause this country has ever fought for, can perish and I am certain we shall meet them again'. 'Jack was a good son to you, without an enemy in the town, respected by all and he has died the most honourable of deaths in defence of his country'. 'Jack was such a splendid young man and everybody loved him and looked for a great career'. 'At times like these, I know that words are but poor things to comfort those who like yourself and family are enduring the pangs of such a terrible bereavement. It must, however, be some solace to a father's heart to know how sincerely your gallant boy was loved and is lamented by all who knew him'. 'Having been closely associated in the earlier days of his soldiering I had every opportunity of judging and appreciating the high excellence of his character. He worked hard, was thorough and nothing was trouble to him. He always came up smiling however difficult the task and he was one of the very few to whom I could assign a duty knowing it would without fail be carried through'.

Barnsley Chronicle – 17 March 1917

PATRIOTIC PARS
LOSS TO THE PALS BATTALION

Since the 1st Battalion went to France and engaged in the mighty struggle with the Huns, they have suffered heavily. Officers and men, who to the public of Barnsley and district were so well-known, have in turn made the supreme surrender, and the report on Page 1 of this issue of the death from wounds received in action of Captain 'Jack' Normansell will be received with deep sorrow, a sorrow we respectfully and sincerely share. It would ill become us to add to the poignancy of the grief through which his esteemed parents are today passing. 'Jack' Normansell was a fine fellow whom to know was to admire. He has paid the supreme sacrifice like a gallant solder, but the life he led and the noble example he set both as a citizen and a solder of the King will never be eradicated from the minds of all who have been associated with him.

No details have been received up to our going to press describing how the Captain was wounded, but yesterday's post brought the following touching communication from Lieut-Col. Wilford, CO, 13th Y and L Regiment: – 'France, 10th March 1917 – My dear Mrs Normansell, I am writing to say your poor son died of wounds received last night. It has been a great blow to everybody. Your son was a brave and gallant officer, liked by all ranks, and in losing him the Battalion has indeed sustained a loss. Under all conditions he was an example of what a gallant officer should be. He was carried to Beaumont Hamel and died in the advanced dressing station there. His end, poor boy, was very peaceful. With every sympathy to you and your husband, Yours sincerely, E C Wilford'.

UK De Ruvigny's Roll of Honour 1914–1918

NORMANSELL JOHN

> ... Son of Joseph Normansell ... by his wife S J daughter of the late Edward Hall of Barnsley, Ironfounder. ... he won a Mining Scholarship at Sheffield and became a Student at the Old Silkstone Collieries at Dodworth. On the outbreak of war he was preparing for his final certificate as Colliery Manager. He obtained a Commission as 2nd Lieutenant in the York and Lancaster Regiment in September 1914, he was promoted Lieut. in March 1915 and Captain the following August. He served with the Expeditionary Force in Egypt and also in France & Flanders from 1 January 1916. He was wounded at Neuve Chapelle in July (31 July according to the Daily Casualty Lists) and invalided home ; he rejoined his Regt on recovery but was again wounded on 9 March 1917 while advancing a post at Puiseux-le-Mont and died the following day after leaving the advanced dressing station at Beaumont Hamel. He was Buried in Beaucourt Military Cemetery. ... Unmarried.

The main photograph of Jack is from Alumnus, *reproduced by kind permission of Barnsley Archives.*

Jack's Grandfather – JOHN NORMANSELL

JOHN NORMANSELL, born in 1832 in Norbury, Cheshire, was the oldest of four children of Joseph and Betty Normansell. His mother died in 1837, aged 25, followed by his baby sister Betty in 1838 then in October 1839 by his father, aged 35. The three orphaned children went to live with their grandfather William Normansell, a widower and retired Colliery Banksman, who was aged nearly 80, and at least one of the few survivors of William's nine children.

Although only 10 years old, John had to work in the local colliery to help to support the family, starting, as many children did at that time as a Hurrier, pushing corves or tubs for coal along the roadway underground for long shifts earning little pay. (Women and young children were routinely employed underground until 1842, when changes were implemented following public outrage at the Huskar Mining Disaster in Silkstone in 1838, which resulted in the Mines and Collieries Act 1842 prohibiting all females and boys under 10 from working below ground, although some unscrupulous colliery owners ignored this).

Premature death was to haunt John's life, as, after his grandfather died in December 1844, his brother Richard died in 1850, aged 17, then his sister Jane in 1853, aged 17. His maternal grandparents had also both died.

John married Susannah Greaves on 30 September 1852 in St Mary's Church, Stockport. Susannah's father was a widowed Farmer and she had been a Weaver along with most of her siblings. The only education John had received consisted of being taught the alphabet at Sunday School, encouraged by an aunt, so he was unable to sign his name on the marriage certificate whereas his wife could. John determined to learn to read and write by attending night school and his efforts benefited him greatly as his career in the mining industry progressed.

John moved to Derbyshire for about two years before relocating to the Barnsley area, where he was employed for several years at Wharncliffe Silkstone Colliery.

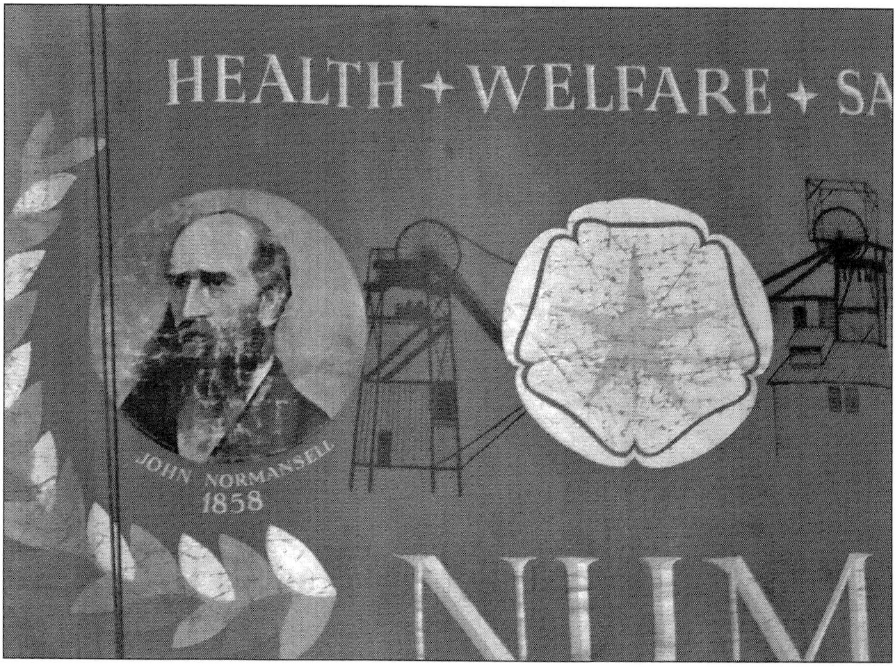

Photograph of John Normansell and image on Thrybergh Hall banner, used by kind permission of the National Union of Miners. (© Jane Ainsworth)

On the 1861 Census, he was living in Tinker Lane, Hoyland Common, with his wife and three young children, the two older ones being Scholars. John was a Coal Miner Weighman and he was the first Miner to hold such a position after being appointed in 1857. Until this time the Checkweighman was appointed by the colliery owner and he assessed how much the Miners should be paid for their output each shift. Miners, who had many grievances at this time, working long and hard in unpleasant conditions at the mercy of colliery owners keen to reduce their wages when coal prices dropped, succeeded in negotiating to appoint someone in this role, paid for by themselves, to check the assessment to ensure that they achieved a fairer reward for their efforts.

John Normansell was instrumental in the formation of the South Yorkshire Miners Association (SYMA) on 5 April 1858 and this resulted in further improvements for Miners as its role developed with John as its Secretary. John was involved in negotiating a pay increase for Miners in 1863 but Newton, Chambers and Company of Thorncliffe refused to pay the agreed 5% increase and this led to a lengthy lock out. The men were supported by SYMA during the months they were out of work, until a successful conclusion was eventually reached. Membership and funding continued to increase but did so dramatically after the explosion at Oaks Colliery in Stairfoot in 1866, when nearly 400 Miners and Rescuers were killed; SYMA extended relief to widows and children to prevent them having to go into the workhouse. The organisation expanded across the country with the National Association of Miners and became one of the most powerful Unions.

In October 1871, SYLA purchased a plot of land on the corner of Victoria Road and Huddersfield Road to build a 'handsome suite of offices with residences for the secretaries, in the Italian-Gothic style of architecture', designed by John Wade, and it was formally opened on 2 November 1874. The monument in front of the Miners' Headquarters was erected by members of the Yorkshire

Miners' Association in recognition of services provided by several important named officers. The inscription at the bottom reads:

TO THE MEMORY OF JOHN NORMANSELL 1830–1875
GENERAL SECRETARY FROM 1864 TO HIS DEATH.
HE WAS MAINLY RESPONSIBLE FOR THE BUILDING
OF THESE HEADQUARTERS.

John is also recognised on the Thrybergh Hall Miners banner: 'FROM OBSCURITY TO RESPECT', 'HEALTH & WELFARE & SAFETY'

In 1872, at the second attempt, John was elected as representative of South Ward on Barnsley Town Council for three years, the £1,000 deposit paid for by Miners. He was particularly interested in sanitary matters as an active member of the Sanitary and Smoke Committee. Although John 'overstepped the bounds of prudence in some of the things he said' … 'he was listened to with respect and frequently applauded'; 'He was born to command' and his name was familiar in every colliery district in England and Scotland.

Miners' Headquarters on the Barnsley Main banner, used by kind permission of the National Union of Miners. (© Jane Ainsworth)

John died at home in Victoria Road, Barnsley, on 24 December 1875, aged 45, as a result of pleurisy and brain inflammation. John had been subject to chest infections and this condition was exacerbated after he had visited Swaithe Main Colliery. He had descended the shaft with Her Majesty's Inspector of Mines for Yorkshire to try to ascertain the cause of the explosion on

6 December 1875, which killed 140 Miners, boys and men. John was affected deeply by this disaster and had attended the Inquest a few days before he died.

John left less than £450 to his widow Susannah, but representatives of SYMA set up a special fund to support his family in recognition of his endeavours on behalf of Miners. They also agreed that the £1,000 deposit collected from Miners so that John could become a Councillor should be awarded to his widow. Susannah moved to 126 Dodworth Road with their three youngest children as an 'Annuitant'. She had moved to Princess Street, when she died in 1887, aged 59, leaving a Personal Estate of over £700.

John was buried in Barnsley Cemetery and his Obituary was in *Barnsley Chronicle* on 1 January 1876, later reprinted as a pamphlet, as 'The Life and Labours of John Normansell'. John's funeral was well attended by representatives of collieries and notable people; the service was read by the Wesleyan Minister before John was buried in the Dissenting area of the cemetery. Mr MacDonald MP addressed the assembly, not to praise his friend as "his works would live long after all had passed away" but to say something of his history. "When he was first sent by the miners of the Barnsley district to represent them in a special meeting held for the amelioration of the conditions of the working miners of Great Britain, he saw at once that there were vigour and strength in all his actions that indicated for him a life of usefulness in connection with that work. Suddenly he came to the front and showed that the men of that district had made a happy and wise choice, as he proved himself to be not only their friend, but a true friend of the entire mining population. At that time they had no protection for either child or adult".

John and Susannah Normansell had five children: Mary Jane, Martha, Joseph, Annie and John William. They all went to school and enjoyed the advantages of a decent education.

MARY JANE NORMANSELL (1854–?) got married in February 1876 to Walter Walshaw Hutchinson, Gas Engineer and son of Barnsley's Gas Works Manager – a position Walter acquired later. They had moved from Old Mill Gas Works in Monk Bretton by 1901 to 10 Pontefract Road, Barnsley – a house with 10 rooms, where they employed a domestic servant. They had seven children, one of whom had died aged 6.

MARTHA NORMANSELL (1858–1945) got married in March 1880 to William Swindin, Station Master at Silkstone, whose father was a Farmer. They moved to Macclesfield but Martha returned to 14 Western Street, Barnsley with their three children after her husband died in 1893, at the age of 46.

JOSEPH NORMANSELL (1859–1930) got married in 1886 to Sarah Jane Hall, an Iron Founder's daughter. Jack Normansell was one of their children.

ANNIE NORMANSELL (1865–1890) had been a Pupil Teacher and was a Witness at the marriages of Martha and Joseph; she died aged 24 and was buried in the same grave as her parents.

JOHN WILLIAM NORMANSELL (1869–1919) was an Assistant Chemist when he got married in March 1893 to Edith Plews, daughter of an Accountant. They spent a period in County Mayo, Ireland, before returning to Cheshire. On the 1911 Census, John had no occupation and was living in four rooms with his wife and three children. John died in 1919, aged 50.

Graham Normansell, a distant relation, kindly sent me a copy of the Barnsley Chronicle pamphlet The Life and Labours of John Normansell *[senior]. I have also been in contact with Joan Hall, whose father was Jack's first cousin.*

50

Harold Parkin

Harold Parkin
1895–1916 (aged 21)

HAROLD PARKIN was born on 23 February 1895 in Barnsley to **George Mitchell Parkin** (born in 1867 in Dodworth) and **Catharine nee Walton** (born c1873 in Dodworth). George was a Colliery Engineman; his father George had been a Colliery Labourer then Horse Keeper in Dodworth as he got older.

Catharine, formerly a Woollen Weaver, was the only daughter by her father's second marriage; **John Walton**, Colliery Worker, had married **Fanny** after his first wife died, leaving him with three young daughters. John Walton, aged 46, died in spring 1881 when Catharine was only 8 and Fanny married again in 1883 to **Henry Gill,** Corn Miller.

Harold had two younger sisters: **Doris** and **Frances May**.

Doris Parkin (32) married **Winston Edwin Broadhead** (29) Colliery Onsetter (*responsible for the cage conveying Miners up and down the shaft)*, at Barnsley St Edward the Confessor Church on 4 November 1930; **James Broadhead** of Staincross was a Colliery Deputy. Doris' sister Frances May was one of the Witnesses. Doris and Winston had four children in the Barnsley area: **Rita W Broadhead** in late 1932, **Kathleen S** in late 1933, **Margaret J** in summer 1937 and **Maurice W** in early 1941.

In April 1911, the Parkin family lived in five rooms at 32 Sykes Street, Barnsley, having previously lived at 46 Keresforth Hill Road.

Harold went to Pitt Street School, Barnsley, until the age of 12. He then attended the Holgate Grammar School in Church Street, Barnsley for two years, from 1907 to 1909. Harold left to become a Railway Clerk and was an Accountant's Clerk by April 1911 for William Carr and Company in Regent Street, Barnsley.

Harold enlisted in 1914 at Birmingham as a Private (Service Number: 1327) in the 16th Battalion of the Royal Warwickshire Regiment, which was the Third Birmingham Pals. He went to France on 21 November 1915 and, after a period of being reported missing, Harold was confirmed killed in action on 3 September 1916, aged 21. This was the first day of the assault on Guillemont, near Trones Wood on the Somme, where thousands of men were killed by heavy German bombardment as they eventually succeeded in capturing the village with its maze of underground tunnels. Action had been delayed because of bad weather and the 5th Division advanced towards the protective strongpoint of Falfemont Farm, south-east of Guillemont, at 8.50am on Sunday 3 September. As Harold's body was never found or identified his name is listed on the Thiepval Memorial, Somme, France (Pier and Face: 9A 9B & 9C).

Harold was awarded three medals: 1914–15 Star, Victory and British War. His parents should have received the 'Dead Man's Penny' plaque and scroll from King George V.

Harold's name is on the Holgate Grammar School Memorial and on the War Memorial in St Edward's Church, Barnsley.

Connection

Harold worked for Messrs W Carr & Co Accountants of Regent Street, Barnsley, as did **Sidney Nicholson.**

Barnsley Chronicle – 14 April 1917

MISSING SINCE SEPTEMBER BARNSLEY
SOLDIER REPORTED KILLED

Mr and Mrs Parkin, of Kingstone Place, Barnsley, have received the sad news that their son Private Harold Parkin 16th Royal Warwickshires, has been killed in action in France. He has been missing since September last. Prior to enlisting Private Parkin was employed in the office of Messrs Wm Carr and Co, accountants, Regent Street, and was a former Grammar School boy. He was 22 years of ago.

The photograph of Harold is from Alumnus, *used by kind permission of Barnsley Archives.*

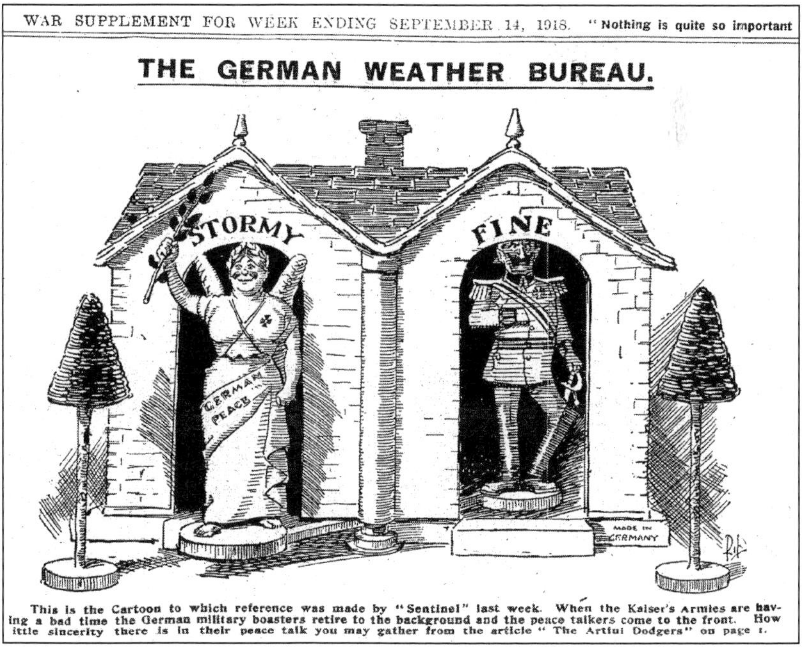
WAR SUPPLEMENT FOR WEEK ENDING SEPTEMBER 14, 1918. "Nothing is quite so important

THE GERMAN WEATHER BUREAU.

This is the Cartoon to which reference was made by "Sentinel" last week. When the Kaiser's Armies are having a bad time the German military boasters retire to the background and the peace talkers come to the front. How little sincerity there is in their peace talk you may gather from the article "The Artful Dodgers" on page 1.

51 and 52

Potter Brothers (Edwin Dalton and Francis (Frank) John)

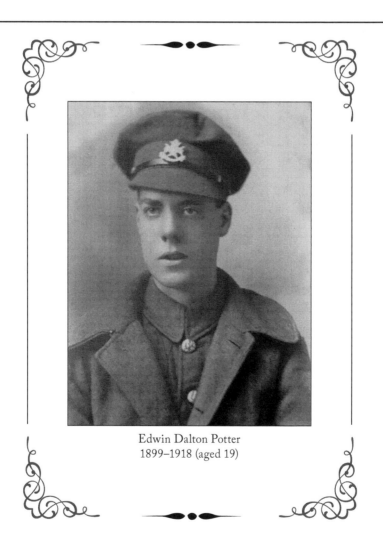

Edwin Dalton Potter
1899–1918 (aged 19)

Francis (Frank) John Potter
1893–1916 (aged 23)

POTTER BROTHERS

Charles Dalton Potter (born in 1858 in Fishlake, near Doncaster, to **Richard Potter** and **Jane Dalton**) got married on 9 August 1887 at St James' Church, Doncaster, to **Annie nee Reasbeck** (born in 1860 in Bentley, Yorkshire) and they had eight children: **Elsie, Harry** (served in the First World War), **FRANCIS JOHN, Alan Reasbeck** (Served in the First World War), **Dorothy Victoria, EDWIN DALTON, Richard Leslie** (attended the Holgate) and **Margaret Annie.**

All of the siblings of Francis John (Frank) and Edwin Dalton (Eddie) married in Barnsley and had children.

The headstone on the grave of Charles Dalton and Annie Potter in Barnsley Cemetery has memorials to their two sons who died in the First World War:

IN LOVING MEMORY OF

FRANCIS JOHN
2ND LIEUT 14TH Y & L
FELL IN ACTION NEAR SERRE WOOD
FRANCE, JULY 1ST 1916
AGED 23 YEARS

ALSO OF EDWIN DALTON, PTE
NOTTS & DERBY REGT
FELL IN ACTION NEAR ABEELE, FRANCE
JULY 17TH 1918, AGED 19 YEARS

FOR KING AND COUNTRY.
THE BELOVED SONS OF CHARLES DALTON
& ANNIE POTTER.

ALSO CHARLES DALTON POTTER,
THE BELOVED HUSBAND
OF ANNIE POTTER
DIED JULY 26TH 1939, AGED 80 YEARS.
'THY WILL BE DONE'.

ALSO THE ABOVE NAMED
ANNIE POTTER
WHO DIED JAN 11TH 1941, AGED 80 YEARS.

I hope to have a more detailed book about the family published in the future, after meeting relations at the end of 2015 and being allowed access to their family archives.

EDWIN DALTON POTTER was born on 29 May 1899 in Barnsley; his Baptism was on 2 July 1899 at Barnsley St John the Baptist Church.

Eddie went to St Mary's Elementary School, Barnsley, for four years until the age of 12. He then attended the Holgate Grammar School in Church Street then Shaw Lane, Barnsley, for three years, from 1911 to 1914; he won a Junior Locke Scholarship in 1911. Eddie passed the College of Preceptors' examination – this was the first professional body for Teachers – then 'he became an Apprentice to a Pharmacist'.*

Eddie enlisted at Barnsley on 19 March 1917, aged 17 years and 10 months, as a Private (Service Number: 106860, previously 6/14665) in the 14th Training Reserve Battalion, renamed '52nd Graduated Devonshire and Dorset Regiment'. He transferred on 2 April 1918 to the 15th Battalion of the Sherwood Foresters (Nottinghamshire and Derby Regiment). According to the Attestation form, he was a Chemist's Apprentice (to Mr Moorhouse of Market Hill, Barnsley) living at 119 Doncaster Road, Barnsley. Edwin may have worked for Wilson's in Market Hill (P*).

The Medical Form contains personal information: Height: 5' 7", Weight: 125 lbs, Chest: 35", Vision in right eye: 6/6, in left: 6/24, mole in centre of sternum.

Eddie went to France on 2 April 1918 and was killed in action on 17 July 1918, aged 19. He had served for one year and 121 days, 107 days of which were at the Western Front. Eddie's name is listed on the Tyne Cot Memorial, West Vlaanderen, Belgium (Panel 99 to 102 and 162 to 162A).

Eddie was one of the youngest of the Old Boys to die in the First World War – there were nine young men aged only 19 years of age.

Eddie was awarded two medals: Victory and British War. His parents should have received the 'Dead Man's Penny' plaque and scroll from King George V.

Eddie's name is on the Holgate Grammar School Memorial and he is remembered on his parents' headstone. His name was also on the War Memorial at St John's Church, Barebones in Barnsley, but this was lost when the church was demolished; at the end of 2015 a replacement oak plaque was created using a grant from Barnsley Central Ward and this will be displayed in St Peter the Apostle and St John the Baptist's Church in Brinckman Street, off Doncaster Road, Barnsley.

* Unfortunately the Holgate Admission Registers do not provide any information about whether Edwin Dalton Potter continued his education to become a Pharmacist, although this was cut short by his being called up. He did not study at the University of Manchester, the Manchester College of Pharmacy or the Manchester Municipal School of Technology (which later became UMIST).

Alumnus – December 1918

E D Potter (1911–14) son of Mr and Mrs Potter, Rhodes Villa, Doncaster Road, Barnsley, fell in action July 1918. His brother 2nd Lieut Potter, also an Old Boy, was killed during the Somme battles of July 1916.

Barnsley Chronicle – 27 July 1918

Private Edwin (Eddie) Potter, Sherwood Foresters … was killed in action on July 16th at the age of 19 years. He had been in the army just over a year. The deceased youth was educated at St Mary's School and the Holgate Grammar School. His two brothers are serving with the forces – Trooper A N Potter, Royal Hussars, and Lieutenant H Potter, York and Lancaster Regiment. His other brother (Mr Potter's second son) Lieutenant F J Potter, 14th York and Lancaster Regiment, was killed on the Somme on July 1st 1916.

DEATHS – POTTER Killed in action July 16th 1918. In loving memory of Private Edwin Dalton (Eddie) Potter, 15th Sherwood Foresters, the fourth and dearly loved son of Mr & Mrs C D Potter, Rhodes Villa, Barnsley.

Barnsley Independent – 3 August 1918

ROLL OF HONOUR
BROTHERS WHO HAVE FALLEN
BARNSLEY BUILDER'S SACRIFICE

Four sons of Mr C D Potter, builder, and Mrs Potter, Rhodes Villa, Doncaster Road, Barnsley, joined the Forces and two of them, whose photos we re-produce in this column, have made the great sacrifice. News of the second bereavement, the death in action of Private Edwin (Eddie) Potter, came to hand on Wednesday week and the other son, Lieutenant F J Potter, fell in the memorable 'push' on the Somme on July 1st 1916.

Private Eddie Potter was 19 years of age, having enlisted on attaining his eighteenth birthday, and only went to France with the Sherwood Foresters early this year. An old St Mary's scholar and afterwards at the Barnsley Grammar School, he passed the College of Preceptors' examination and was with Mr Moorhouse, chemist, Market Hill, when he joined the Colours.

The two other sons who are serving are Trooper A R Potter, Royal Hussars, in France, and Lieut H Potter, with the York and Lancasters, in training.

The main photograph of Eddie is reproduced by kind permission of Jean Copley.

FRANCIS JOHN POTTER was born on 11 February 1893; his Baptism was on 16 April 1893 at Barnsley St John the Baptist Church. Francis (Frank) went to St Mary's School, Barnsley, until the age of 14. He then attended the Holgate Grammar School in Church Street, Barnsley for one year, from 1907 to 1908.

Frank started work as an Apprentice in the United Counties Bank in Horbury, Wakefield, on 15 March 1909; he was promoted to their Head Office in Colmore Row, Birmingham in 1911, aged 18. The Bank continued to pay staff while they were serving in the Army.* (*The United Counties Bank was an amalgamation of three Birmingham banks and was taken over by Barclays Ltd in 1916 when their Head Office was set up in Birmingham).*

Frank enlisted as a Private (Service Number: 2668) in the 8th Battalion (Territorial Force) of the Royal Warwickshire Regiment in 4 August 1914. Frank was posted to 'A' Company and went out to France on 22 March 1915, sailing from Southampton to Le Havre. He was wounded in action on 15 May 1915 with a gunshot to his right groin; he was admitted to 3rd South Midland Field Ambulance but transferred the next day to 8 Casualty Clearing Station then to 10 General Hospital, Rouen. Frank was moved to Convalescent Camp by 2 June and was back on the front line four days later.†

Frank applied for a commission around this time and was subsequently promoted to Second Lieutenant in the 14th Battalion (Second Barnsley Pals) of the York and Lancaster Regiment. He went to Egypt with the Mediterranean Expeditionary Force before relocating to France. Frank later transferred to the Royal Artillery and, according to his Medal Card, he was on the General List attached to the 94th Light Trench Mortar Battery. Jon Cooksey lists him in *Barnsley Pals* as Reserve Scout Officer in 'A' Company of the 14th Battalion (Second Barnsley Pals).

Frank was killed in action on the first day of the Somme, 1 July 1916, aged 23, after one year and 102 days overseas; he received a fatal head wound during the opening stages of battle. As his body was never found or identified, his name is listed on the Thiepval Memorial, Somme, France (Pier and Face: 4C).

Frank was engaged to Ruth Noble.

Frank was awarded three medals: 1914–15 Star, Victory and British War. His parents should have received the 'Dead Man's Penny' plaque and scroll from King George V.

Frank was one of ten Old Boys to be killed in action on the first day of the Somme

Probate was granted for Frank on 22 November 1916 to his mother Annie (wife of Charles Dalton); Effects: £186 8s 8d.

Frank's name is on the Holgate Grammar School Memorial and he is remembered on his parents' headstone. His name was also on the War Memorial at St John's

* Andrea Waterhouse, Barclays Group Archivist, kindly confirmed details of Frank's and Harry Strong's employment.

† Pam and Ken Linge of the Thiepval Memorial Project allowed me to use the details of Frank's injury in May 1915 from the Service Records at the National Archives researched by Joe Devereux for the Project.

Church, Barebones in Barnsley, but this was lost when the church was demolished; at the end of 2015 a replacement oak plaque was created using a grant from Barnsley Central Ward and this will be displayed in St Peter the Apostle and St John the Baptist's Church in Brinckman Street, off Doncaster Road, Barnsley.

Connections

Frank served with the 14th Battalion (Second Barnsley Pals) along with **John Bruce Atha, Frank Bakel, Duncan Fairley** and **Harold Quest.**

***Barnsley Chronicle* – 28 August 1915**

PATRIOTIC PARS

From the *London Gazette* ... 14th York & Lancaster Regiment (2nd Barnsley) – to be temporary Second-Lieutenant: F J Potter.

***Barnsley Independent* – 5 July 1916**

SECOND-LIEUTENANT F J POTTER
PREVIOUSLY WOUNDED, NOW KILLED

Second-Lieutenant Francis John Potter, of the Second Battalion, fell in the advance on July 1st. He is the second son of Mr C D Potter, builder, and Mrs Potter, Rhodes Villa, Doncaster Road, Barnsley. Twenty three years of age, an old St Mary's and Barnsley Grammar School boy, he was in the services of the United Counties Bank, now Barclay's Bank, at Birmingham (and previously at Horbury) when war broke out, and in September 1914, along with a bank colleague, now Lieut Harry Strong, formerly in the company's bank at Barnsley, enlisted as a private in the Warwickshire Regiment. Both went out with that regiment, saw several months' active service, and the deceased soldier was badly wounded. He recovered and subsequently both he and Mr Strong received a commission in the Second Barnsley Battalion. They both went with the local lads when they set out on active service. At the time of his death Lieutenant Potter was with the trench mortar battery, and letters home from fellow officers pay a high tribute to his work and worth. Lieutenant Strong was also wounded in the same battle.

In a sympathetic letter to his parents his comrade Lieutenant Strong says: 'I cannot express in words how I feel for you all at this time. For myself, I have lost my best pal. We have been through a lot together, and I shall miss him greatly. Frank, of course, was with his guns, so I did not see him. The corporal in the section told me the sad news, and it will be some consolation for you to know that he suffered no pain. His men were all very sorry for they all loved him. His work with the guns on the morning of the assault was splendid. He was very keen on his work and I cannot say more than he died bravely doing his duty. He gave his life for his country and no-one could do more. I was wounded the same morning in the head, hip and shoulder, but am glad to say I am going on well'.

There are two other brothers of Lieutenant Potter with the Forces – one Trooper Allan Potter with the Yorkshire Dragoons in France, and Lance Corporal Harry Potter with the Dragoons on the East Coast.

***Barnsley Independent* – 15 July 1916**

IN MEMORIAM: POTTER – On July 1st, killed in action in France, Sec-Lieut Francis John Potter ... Mr and Mrs Potter and Family wishes to convey their thanks to the numerous friends for their kind letters of condolence in their loss.

***Barnsley Chronicle* – 15 July 1916**

ANOTHER BARNSLEY OFFICER KILLED
SECOND LIEUT F J POTTER

The sad news was received from the War Office last Friday of the death in action of Second-Lieutenant F J Potter, 94th 2nd French Mortar Battery. .... His loss will be much regretted by a large circle of friends in Barnsley and Birmingham. He was an old boy of St Mary's and the Barnsley Grammar School, leaving there to join the Staff of the United Counties Bank Ltd, at Horbury. From there he was transferred to the Head Office in Birmingham. Soon after the outbreak of war he enlisted as a private in the Royal Warwickshire Regiment and went with them to France. In May 1915 he was severely wounded and sent to hospital in Rouen. Soon after re-joining his regiment he received a Commission in the Second Barnsley Battalion going with them to Egypt and afterwards to France. While in France he was transferred to the 94th 2nd French Mortar Battery still remaining in connection with his old battalion.

***Barnsley Independent* – 3 August 1918**

ROLL of HONOUR (PHOTO)
Brothers who have fallen
BARNSLEY BUILDER'S SACRIFICE

... Lieutenant Potter was with the Trench Mortar Battery attached to the Barnsley Battalion when he fell in action. He was 23 years of age and was also

> an old St Mary's and Barnsley Grammar School boy. He enlisted soon after war broke out as a private in the Warwickshire Regt, being at that time in the Barclays Bank at Birmingham. He saw active service with the Warwickshires, was badly wounded, and on recovering received a commission in the Second Barnsley Battalion. …

The main photograph of Frank is reproduced by kind permission of Ian Potter.

Jean Copley and Ian Dalton Potter, relations of the Potters, generously provided information about the family; they each lent me photographs and other records.

WAR SUPPLEMENT, FOR WEEK ENDING OCTOBER 19, 1918.
THE VOICE OF THE CHARMER.
GERMAN
HIGH COMMAND
WESTERN FRONT
WILHELM (with the wind up):—"Hold on! I am trying the 'democratic trick!'

53

Edwin Poxon

Edwin Poxon
1899–1918 (aged 19)

EDWIN POXON was born on 25 January 1899 in Carlton to **William Poxon** (born c1866 in Whitwick, Leicestershire) and **Ada nee Senior** (born c1872 in Bretton West). William was a Coal Miner at Woolley Colliery.

Edwin was the youngest of three surviving children: **Elsie** and **George William** – Screen Hand at Woolley Colliery above ground. Three children had died in infancy before April 1911 (names unknown).

In April 1911, the Poxon family lived in three rooms at School Street, Darton, having previously lived in Carlton. Edwin's parents subsequently moved to 4 Beaumont Buildings, Darton.

Elsie Poxon married **Harry Jackson** in Spring 1921 in Barnsley and they had a son **Frank Jackson** late 1927 in Huddersfield. **George William Poxon** married **Mary A Parkin** in Summer 1923 in Barnsley and they had a daughter **Margaret Poxon** in Spring 1925 in Barnsley.

Edwin went to Canklow School for one year and nine months before Darton Elementary School for nine months, until the age of 12. He then attended the Holgate Grammar School in Church Street and later Shaw Lane, Barnsley, for five years, from 1911 to 1916. Edwin had a County Minor Scholarship, was a Bursar and a Student Teacher; he passed the Oxford Local Senior exam.

He taught at the Holgate for three days a week before he was called up.

Edwin enlisted as a Private at Barnsley on 3 October 1916, aged 17 years and 8 months; he was a Student Teacher living at 4 Beaumont Buildings according to the Attestation form. Edwin joined the York and Lancaster Regiment (Service Number: 47953) then transferred to the 2nd Training Reserve (5/6207 and 5/39428). On 1 December 1917, he transferred to the 51st Graduate Battalion of the Leicester Regiment (TR/6/30861). Edwin went to France on 8 March 1918 and three days later was transferred as a Private (Service Number: 102131) to the 2nd Battalion of the Sherwood Foresters (Nottinghamshire and Derby Regiment).

The Medical Form contains personal information: Height: 5' 5½", Weight: 118 lbs, Chest: 34", Vision in right eye: 6/36 (eye specialist 'optically fit') in left: 6/9.

Edwin had an operation to correct his astigmatism in Leeds General Infirmary on 31 January 1917 (result 6/18). His vision continued to be problematical as on 2 February 1918 his right eye was 6/60 and 'glasses advised'. Despite this he was sent to France, where he was assessed on 15 March 1918 as 'vision not fit for Action', but was killed in action eight days later.

Edwin had spent six days in 205 S M Field Ambulance at Foxhall Heath Camp early October 1917 because of tonsillitis; he was discharged with a recommendation of '2 days' light duties'.

After serving just two weeks in France, Edwin was killed in action on 23 March 1918, aged 19. As his body was never found or identified his name is listed on the Arras Memorial, Faubourg-d'Amiens Cemetery, Arras, France (Bay 7). Edwin had been reported missing for a long time before his death was confirmed. A form sent to his father on 22 December 1919 about returning any personal possessions was over-written 'No Effects'.

Edwin was one of the youngest of the Old Boys to die in the First World War; there were nine young men aged only 19 years.

Edwin was engaged to **Alice Maude Mary Doughty** (born 30 November 1891 in Nottingham), who was the daughter of **Frederick Doughty,** Colliery Banksman, and **Sarah Doughty**. At April 1911, Alice (19) 'Springbending for Lace Machine', was living at home with her parents and six siblings in Kimberley. **Joan Evelyn Poxon Doughty** was born on 29 August 1918, after her father had been killed in action; she married and had a son. Alice died late 1982 (aged 91) in Nottingham.

Edwin was awarded two medals: Victory and British War. His parents should have received the 'Dead Man's Penny' plaque and scroll from King George V.

Edwin's name is on the Holgate Grammar School Memorial.

NOT CAUGHT YET.

A FABLE BROUGHT UP TO DATE.

Once upon a time a Hunter went into a Forest to catch Birds. He fastened a decoy bird to a small peg in the ground and hung his net from the branch of a neighbouring tree. Then he climbed into the tree, and when the birds came along to inspect the decoy he dropped the net and caught them.

Now certain Dwellers in the Forest watched the Hunter, and thought they might profit by his example. So they made a net of the vines that climb about the trees in the Forest, and hung it on a branch, and caught a Dove and fastened it to a peg beneath. "If only the Lion will come and smell at the Dove," they said, "we shall catch him in the net, and he will be King of the Forest no longer."

But the Lion had seen a tethered Dove before, and all that he did was to lift his head higher and stiffen his mane.

IF THE KAISER GOVERNED BRITAIN—

THE PRESCRIPTION—

"In England the workmen are idle and capricious, but under a strong *regime* they would work well, and disciplined as they would be with us they would recognise their own place and become contented with it."

Prof. ERNST TROELTSCH, Pro-Rector of Heidleberg University.

AND THE INGREDIENTS.

"All men, all women, and all children over the age of 15 will work in the fields from 4 a.m. to 8 p.m. every day, Sundays included.

"Lazy men will receive twenty lashes a day; when the harvest is over they will be imprisoned for six months, and every third day will be fed on bread and water only.

"Lazy women will also be imprisoned.

"Lazy children will be beaten."

German Proclamation in Italy.

54

Harold Quest

Harold Quest
1894–1916 (aged 22)

HAROLD QUEST was born on 22 February 1894 in Pontefract to **Arthur Charles Quest** (born c1859 in Riby, Lincolnshire) and **Jane Hannah nee Dales** (born 1857 in Bridlington). Harold's Baptism was on 25 February 1894 at Pontefract St Giles' Church. Arthur was Chief Constable for the West Riding of Yorkshire Police Force, having progressed from Sergeant then Deputy.

Harold was the youngest of six children: **William** – Civil Engineer, **Jane, Mary, Arthur Charles** (attended the Holgate) and **Thomas Percival** (attended the Holgate and served in the First World War).

In April 1911, the Quest family lived in 12 rooms at 3 Burton Street, Wakefield. They had previously lived in the Superintendent's house at 1 Westgate, Barnsley, as well as in Bradford and Pontefract. They employed a General Domestic Servant. William (27) Surveyor to the Urban District Council, was a Boarder in two rooms in Wombwell with the Taylor family. Arthur Charles (23) Pawnbroker's Assistant, was living in Bath.

Mary Quest (31) married **Alexander Woodburn Thomson** (37) Brewer of Thetford, on 7 August 1918 at Wakefield Cathedral (All Saints Church). They had two daughters born in Thetford: **Mary W Thomson** in Spring 1920 and **Margaret E G Thomson** early 1924.

Harold went to St Mary's School, Barnsley, until the age of 12. He then attended the Holgate Grammar School in Church Street, Barnsley, for one year in 1907 until the family relocated to Wakefield, where he went to the Queen Elizabeth Grammar School from 1908 to April 1911 (aged 13 to 16) and was noted for his 'cheery optimism' and 'hearty robustness'.*

According to the Holgate records, Harold attended Bradford Technical College and became 'a Colour Wool Dyer's Apprentice'; Calendar records are available at Bradford College with more details of his education. (Bradford Technical College opened in 1882, building on the Mechanics Institute, which had been established in 1832 because of the growth of the wool industry, to provide education for the many people relocating to Bradford to work in the textile mills. The College had four departments: Textiles, Art & Design, Engineering, and Chemistry & Dyeing. As private funding ceased, Bradford City Council took over management of the College in 1904 and more vocational subjects were added).†

Harold was a member of the Wakefield Rugby Club and a keen player.

Harold enlisted on 21 September 1914 at Bradford as a Private in 8 Company of the 16th Battalion of the West Yorkshire Regiment (First Bradford Pals). He was given

* Elaine Merckx, Archivist at Wakefield Queen Elizabeth Grammar School, kindly provided information about Harold's attendance, the description of his character and details of their War Memorial.

† I appreciate information sent to me by Sarah Powell at Bradford Archives at West Yorkshire Archive Service (images of the Bradford Roll of Honour), Alison Cullingford, Special Collections Librarian at Bradford University, (detailed history of the College) and Helen Farrar at Bradford College (details of their Roll of Honour).

a Commission on 11 May 1915, while based at Skipton, and was transferred, as he had requested, to temporary Second Lieutenant (Service Number: 14/65) in 'A' Company of the 14th Battalion (Second Barnsley Pals) in the York and Lancaster Regiment. The Major certified that Harold was of good moral character for the last 15 years. Harold was subsequently promoted to Lieutenant in 1916 then Captain.

Photograph from *Yorkshire Evening Post.*

According to the Officer Records, Harold underwent his medical examination in Bradford on 21 September 1914, and the personal description states that he was a Dyer aged 20 years and 210 days: Height: 5' 9½", Weight: 171 lbs, Chest: 38½", Physical Development: Good. He had been vaccinated in his left forearm in infancy.

Telegrams from the War Office to Harold's father, Arthur Quest of 3 Burton Street Wakefield, reported that he received 'slight gunshot wounds right leg' on 4 June 1916 and was admitted to 8 General Hospital in Rouen on 6 June until his discharge on 24 June.

Harold was awarded a Military Cross for conspicuous gallantry when he proceeded with a raid despite being wounded early on (*London Gazette* on 27 July 1916).

Harold was killed in action on 3 November 1916, aged 22, and was buried in Hebuterne Communal Cemetery, Pas de Calais, France (grave I D 2). He had originally been buried under the name of another officer called Guest. A Telegram dated 7 November from the War Office to his father read: 'Deeply regret to inform you that Lieut Harold Quest, York & Lancaster Regiment was killed in action November 3rd. The Army Council express their sympathy'.

Arthur Quest wrote to the War Office on a number of occasions asking for his son's Death Certificate, whether there was a Will and for payment of all outstanding amounts due to his son. Harold's Officer Records comprise mainly forms about what payments are due, including a Gratuity and less Income Tax. Amounts vary but he seems to have been owed the following:

Gratuity	£96 12s 5d or £116 5s
Outfit Allowance	£50
Other *	£9 11s 11d

* Field, Lodging, Fuel, Light & Groom Allowance for the period 1–31 October 1916.

Harold had not made a Will so Letters of Administration were granted to his father in Wakefield on 26 January 1917. Effects: £682 11s 1d. The only personal effect to be returned to his father was a 'Two Centime Piece'.

Harold was awarded two medals: Victory and British War, and his parents received the 'Dead Man's Penny' plaque and scroll from King George V.

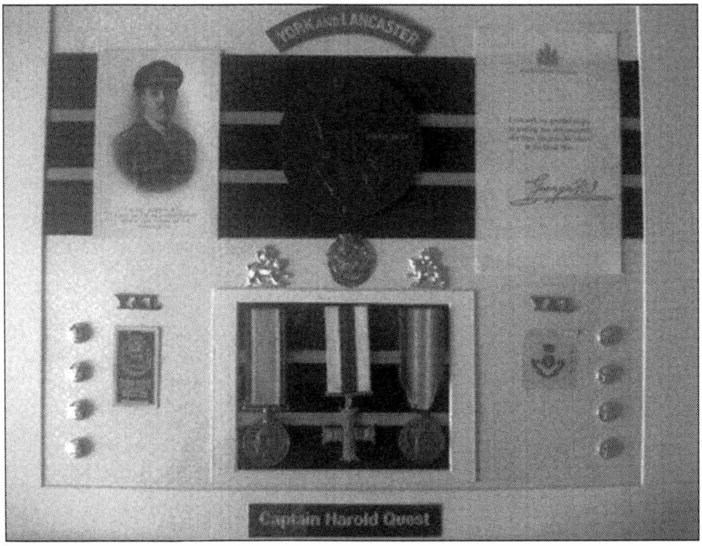

Photograph of Harold's Display, used by kind permission of Paul Quest.

Harold's name is on the Holgate Grammar School Memorial and the Wakefield Grammar School Old Savilians War Memorial, along with 81 other old boys who died in the First World War. He is on Bradford College's Roll of Honour for serving students produced in 1915, but he is not included on the handwritten City of Bradford Roll of Honour 1914–1918, which is also online.

Connections

Harold sang a solo in the Speech Day Programme for July 1907, as did **Ernest William Litherland** and **James Christopher Speight.**

Harold served with the 14th Battalion (Second Barnsley Pals) along with **John Bruce Atha, Frank Bakel, Duncan Fairley** and **Frank Potter.** Harold was promoted to temporary Second Lieutenant in the Second Barnsley Pals a week before **Duncan Fairley** and their names appeared together in the *London Gazette* on 4 June 1915.

***Barnsley Chronicle* – 8 May 1915**

PATRIOTIC PARS
OFFICERS FOOTBALL MATCH

This article explained how teams were selected from the Commissioned Officers in the First and Second Barnsley Pals to play at Oakwell; the First won 1–0 (Lieutenant Dixon was captain). Second Lieutenant Quest was captain of the Second, which included Second Lieutenant Fitton (Part 3. Chapter 18).

***Barnsley Chronicle* – 30 September 1916**

LETTER FROM HAROLD QUEST TO THE PARENTS OF
PRIVATE J WALKER, BARNSLEY PAL

Following the announcement of the death of the 20 year old son of Mr and Mrs Walker of 25 Rock Road, Barnsley, the letter from his Captain Harold Quest is quoted: 'Please allow me to offer you my most heartfelt sympathy in your great bereavement. I knew your son very well and I can assure you that having lost him the Company have been deprived of the services of a very good and steady fellow. He was always obedient and if there was any special work to be done he was always willing to undertake it. When he met his death he was just returning from a struggle at close quarters with some of the enemy, and whilst taking cover he was hit by a rifle bullet in the head and died an hour later at the dressing room. On behalf of the officers and men I again offer you my most heartfelt sympathy'.

Jon Cooksey – *The Barnsley Pals*

Lt Harold Quest undertook a raid on the Germans, planned originally for overnight 5/6 May 1915 with 70 men in seven parties under Captain Alphonse Wood, it was postponed to overnight 5/6 June. Things went wrong when higher authorities at Division didn't agree for the 10th East Yorks (Hull) Regiment to vacate their trench for the raiding party. Lt Quest and several others were injured by a shell bursting prematurely. The party found 14' of uncut German wire they'd expected to be able to get through after firing a torpedo but one man went out and cut it by hand. Germans retaliated and there were casualties in the Hull Regiment. Lt Quest and a couple of others got through but they had to retreat; 14 of the party were injured and 3 killed but no Germans were killed. Captain Wood's report commended a number of men including Lt Quest: 'excellent work done by Lt Quest and 2nd Lt Best. Lt Quest was wounded in two places in five minutes and he carried out his work thoroughly and actually shot one German himself in their trenches … I did not know until after Lt Quest's return that he had been wounded'.

Report by W B Hulke, Lt Colonel 14th Battalion – 'Lt Harold Quest – although wounded in two places during the first 5 minutes of the bombardment, this officer did not hesitate to go forward, but entered the enemy's trenches and assisted in controlling those who had entered with him'.

In September they moved on to Festubert for a short period before moving to Bethune in early October. The Pals got reinforcements and moved to the front line swamps of Hebuterne. The 14th suffered 30 more casualties there including 2nd Lieut Harold Quest, youngest son of the Deputy Chief Constable for the West Riding … He was killed on 3 November.

***Yorkshire Evening Post* – 10 July 1916 (PHOTO)**

WAKEFIELD OFFICER'S DISTINCTION

Lieutenant Harold Quest, York & Lancaster Regiment, son of Mr A C Quest of Burton Street, Wakefield, the Deputy Chief Constable of the West Riding, has been awarded the Military Cross for gallant work in connection with a raid on German trenches. Lieutenant Quest, who is 22 years of age, was educated at the Wakefield Grammar School and the Bradford Technical College. Joining the Bradford Pals as a private, he quickly rose to the position of Sergeant-major and was shortly after given a commission. He was a very prominent member of the Wakefield Rugby Football Club. The photograph was taken whilst he was Sergeant-major with the Bradford Pals.

(Similar articles were in *Liverpool Daily Post* – 28 July 1916, *Aberdeen Journal* – 28 July 1916 and *Newcastle Journal* – 29 July 1916).

***Barnsley Chronicle* – 11 November 1916**

DEPUTY CHIEF CONSTABLE'S SON
CAPT. HAROLD QUEST KILLED

Mr A C Quest, Deputy Chief Constable of the West Riding, has received a telegram from the War Office stating that his youngest son, Captain Harold Quest, of the York and Lancaster Regiment, has been killed in action. The deceased officer was 22 years of age and was educated at the Wakefield Grammar School and the Bradford Technical College. He joined one of the local battalions as a private, rose to be sergt-major, and shortly after received a commission. His many friends in Barnsley and Wakefield have received the news with feelings of great sorrow.

With the Wakefield Rugby Football Club he was a prominent player, and a very popular member. In July of this year Captain Quest was awarded the Military Cross for conspicuous gallantry during a raid on the enemy trenches.

> Though wounded at the outset he stuck to his post and led his party on. During the withdrawal he remained with two other officers till all the party had left the trenches and later assisted in bringing in the wounded. His brother Captain T P Quest is also in the York and Lancaster Regiment, but is at present in hospital suffering from shell shock.

(Also in *Yorkshire Evening Post* – 8 & 9 November 1916, with photograph in the latter, and similar article in *Yorkshire Post & Leeds Intelligencer* – 9 November 1916).

Wakefield Grammar School – *The Savilian Magazine* (Lent Term 1917) and *The Commemorative Issue* (December 1921)

Obituary possibly written by Charles Head, Deputy Headmaster.

> Harold Quest as a boy was chiefly remarkable for his cheery optimism and for his hearty robustness in all features of school life. His powerful frame and character stood him in good stead in the Army and he soon passed through the ranks to a commission. In France, although severely wounded, he held his ground in a dangerous position, and was awarded the Military Cross. We hoped he would have been spared to have gained even greater honours. When on leave a very short time ago he visited us and we were delighted to hear his hearty laugh once again and to submit to a grip from his strong right hand. (HQ).

The main photograph of Harold is a family one, used by kind permission of Paul Quest.

ARTHUR CHARLES QUEST (born on 21 March 1888 in Bradford, Baptism at Manningham St Jude on 13 January 1889; died in Bridlington in 1924, aged 65) went to Rotherham Parish Church school until the age of 12, when he attended the Holgate for three years, from 1900 to 1903. In 1908, he was a Pawnbroker's Assistant for John Guest and Sons in New Street, Barnsley. (Geoffrey Howse's Foul Deeds and Suspicious Deaths in and Around Barnsley has a photo of John Guest and Sons Pawnbrokers. It mentions that on 31 January 1908 Arthur C Quest, pawnbroker's assistant, put a pair of boots worth 6s 6d onto the display outside and these were stolen, but the thief was caught and sent to prison for a month). In April 1911, Arthur, Pawnbroker's Assistant for May Howard, was living in six rooms at 28 & 29 Westgate Street, Bath, along with another Assistant, two Apprentices and a Domestic Servant.

THOMAS PERCIVAL QUEST (born 29 November 1890 in Pontefract, died 30 June 1966, aged 75, in Bognor Regis, Sussex) also attended the Holgate from the age of 9; he was admitted in 1900 for one year then readmitted in 1904 for three years. He became a Bank Clerk with the Union of London and Smiths (eventually absorbed into RBS Bank).

Photograph of Thomas, used by kind permission of Paul Quest.

Thomas enlisted in the 14th Battalion (Second Barnsley Pals) of the York and Lancaster Regiment; he served in Egypt from December 1915 before going to the Western Front, where he spent a period in hospital in 1916 as a result of shell shock. Thomas was gazetted temporary 2nd Lieutenant on 13 January 1915 then had a series of promotions to Lieutenant then Captain.

Thomas (33) Bank Cashier of 12 Bond Road, Barnsley, married **Dorothy Charlesworth** (29) of 43 Huddersfield Road, Barnsley, on 10 April 1924 in St Mary's Church, Barnsley; **Charles Henry Charlesworth** was a Retired Merchant. Thomas and Dorothy had one son: **Hugh A L Quest** in 1925 in Barnsley.

ARTHUR CHARLES QUEST SENIOR (born c1859 in Riby, Lincolnshire) joined the West Riding Police Force in 1878 and was promoted up to Chief Constable. He moved to Barnsley as Deputy in 1900 and appeared in a number of newspaper articles across a wide area on a variety of subjects. Arthur was awarded an OBE and King's Police Medal on 29 December 1921, reported in the *Edinburgh Gazette* on 2 January 1922. He retired to Bridlington in March 1923 and died there on 30 September 1924, aged 66. According to an Obituary in *The Yorkshire Post* on 2 October 1924, Arthur was a well known Freemason, being a past master of the Barnsley Friendly Lodge.

Photograph of Arthur Charles, used by kind permission of Paul Quest.

***Yorkshire Post* & *Leeds Intelligencer* – 29 July 1912**

> An interesting function took place on Saturday morning at Leeds Town Hall, when Mr Justice Scrutton, one of the Assize Judges present in Leeds, presented [King George's] Coronation medals to 73 members of the West Riding Constabulary. The recipients included Deputy Chief Constable A C Quest…

***Yorkshire Evening Post* – 5 November 1915**

> WEST RIDING CONSTABULARY UNIMPAIRED
>
> (190 enlist out of 1,453) Acting CCWR A C Quest is interviewed by the Wakefield correspondent and adds "it had not been necessary to enlist the services of special constables to undertake the work of the absent men".

***Newcastle Journal* – 21 December 1916**

> At a meeting of the West Riding Standing Joint Committee at Wakefield yesterday, the salary of the Deputy Chief Constable Mr A C Quest was increased from £500 to £600.

Paul Quest, a distant relation of Harold's, generously shared his research into the Quest family, including Harold Quest's Officer Records, plus family photographs.

I am grateful to Jon Cooksey and Pen and Sword Publishers for allowing me to use the quotation from Barnsley Pals.

55

Reginald Royston

Reginald Royston
1888–1918 (aged 30)

REGINALD ROYSTON was born on 7 February 1888 in West Melton to **Ezra Royston** (born c1843 in Brampton Bierlow) and **Eliza nee Stenton** (born c1842 in Hemingfield). Ezra Royston was a Colliery Deputy, having previously worked as a Coal Miner and Beerhouse Keeper in the Crown Inn, Brampton Bierlow, then Publican in the Woodman, Masbrough. Eliza had managed her own Confectionery business.

Reggie was the youngest of 11 children: **Elizabeth Alice, Lewis**, **Vincent, Florence, Albina**, **Mabel**, **Amy**, **Olga** and **Lawrence Irving**; **Vernon**, who had been a Miner, died in 1908, aged 37, and another child had died before April 1911 (name unknown). Their father died at the end of 1910, aged 68.

In April 1911, Eliza was living in six rooms at 26 Corporation Street, Barnsley, with Albina – Milliner, Olga and Reginald; the family had previously lived in Barnsley Road, Ardsley, Brampton Bierlow and Masbrough.

Elizabeth Alice Royston married **Larrett John Mangham**, Coal Miner, in 1883 and they were living in Brampton Bierlow in 1911 with their three surviving: **Robert Irving Mangham, Amy** and **Elizabeth**. Three children had died (names unknown).

Lewis Royston (44) Coal Miner Hewer, was boarding with the Pells family in South Elmshall in 1911. **Mabel Royston**, a School Teacher on the 1901 Census, was elsewhere; she died in 1944, aged 65. **Amy Royston**, Art Needleworker, was admitted to the South Yorkshire Asylum (renamed Middlewood Hospital), Sheffield, on 5 October 1903, aged 20, because of 'Shock'; she died there on 24 February 1923, aged 40.

Vincent Royston,Colliery Deputy, married **Emily Dyson** in 1906 and they were living in Darfield in 1911 with their two surviving children but only **Reginald** (3) was at home. One child had died (name unknown).

Florence Royston married **John William Richardson**, Gardener, in 1910 and they were living in Arksey, Doncaster, in 1911. They had a son **William Richardson** in Doncaster in 1911 and may have had others.

Lawrence Irving Royston, Timber Merchant's Clerk having previously been a Post Office worker, married **Ethel Mary Beard** in 1908 and they were living in Sheffield in 1911. They had two children but only **Donald** born in 1910 in Barnsley was at home; Alan was born in 1912 in Eccleshall Bierlow.

Olga Royston, formerly a School Teacher, married **William Fletcher** late 1924 in Rotherham district; they had four children: **James Fletcher** in 1925, **Betsy** in 1927, **Mary** in 1928 and **Olga** in 1931.

Reggie attended the Holgate Grammar School in Church Street, Barnsley, from the age of 16 for three years, from 1904 to 1907. He was an Intending Pupil Teacher at Worsbrough Common Council School.

As a Teacher, aged 25, 'Reginald' sailed from Liverpool on 8 August 1913 on the Canadian Pacific Railway Atlantic Steamship Line. *Alumnus* December 1913 noted that 'Royston (1904–7) left for Canada last August, is now the headmaster of a school, attended solely by Russians, near Vermilion. He writes home to say that teaching is the worst paid in the country, and he is seriously planning to change his occupation'.

Reggie enlisted as a Private (Service Number: 2021) in the 46th Battalion of the Canadian Infantry (Saskatchewan Regiment); he was a Teacher at Marne near Winnepeg. 'He took part as a Machine Gunner in the successful attack made by his Battalion through Famars and captured Aulnoy. When the objective had been reached, he was hit in the head by a machine gun bullet and killed'. Reggie was killed in action on 1 November 1918, aged 30, only 10 days before the war ended, and was buried in Aulnoy Communal Cemetery, Nord, France (grave C 1 16).

Reggie ought to have been awarded two medals: Victory and British War, and his widowed mother should have received the 'Dead Man's Penny' plaque and scroll from King George V.

Reggie's name is on the Holgate Grammar School Memorial and the War Memorial in St Peter the Apostle & St John the Baptist Church in Barnsley.

Connection

Reginald was doing his second year as a Pupil Teacher at Worsbrough Common Council School at the same time as **Edward Sydney Haigh.**

Barnsley Chronicle – 14 December 1918

LATEST LOCAL CASUALTIES

News has been received of the death in action of Private Reginald (Reggie) Royston, 46th Battalion Saskatchewan Regiment, in France on November 1st. The Lieutenant-Colonel writing to his mother, Mrs Royston, Corporation Street, Barnsley, says: 'He went forward in the attack with his Platoon as a machine gunner and had reached his objective. Whilst this was being consolidated, the enemy opened up with heavy gunfire and a bullet struck him in the head, causing instantaneous death. He was a very efficient soldier and very popular in his Platoon, and his loss was keenly felt by one and all in the Battalion'. Mrs Royston received other letters from the Chaplain and deceased's pals, all showing how popular he was with all the Battalion. Private Royston was educated at Barnsley Grammar School and served under the Barnsley Education Committee for eight years. Before joining the forces he was a schoolmaster at Marne near Winnepeg. When in Barnsley the deceased was a worshipper at St Peter's Church. He was 30 years of age.

56

Charles Edward Savage

Charles Edward Savage
1893–1916 (aged 23)

CHARLES EDWARD SAVAGE was born on 10 February 1893 in Barnsley to **Thomas Savage** (born c1855 in Nottinghamshire) and **Martha nee Gill** (born c1858 in Pickering). Thomas was a Railway Signalman.

Charles was the third of four surviving children: **William Henry** (served and died in the First World War), **Clara Ellen** and **Beatrice Maud**. A child had died before April 1911 (name unknown).

In April 1911, the Savage family lived in five rooms at 2 Wigfield Cottages, Kendal Green, Worsbrough Bridge, having previously lived in Sheffield and Lancashire. They later moved to St Thomas House, Worsbrough Dale.

Clara Ellen Savage, Assistant Teacher, married **William N Addey** in Summer 1918 in Barnsley; they had three children in Barnsley: **Charles Addey** in 1924, **Margaret E** in 1926 and **Geoffrey** in 1927. They lived with Clara's invalid mother in Worsbrough; she was widowed when Thomas died early 1919, aged 64.

Beatrice Maud Savage, Apprentice Dressmaker, married **Herbert Garnett** in Spring 1918 in Barnsley; they had two sons in Barnsley: **Douglas S Garnett** in 1920 and **Edward** in 1926. They lived at 115 Wolseley Road, Abbeydale, Sheffield.

Charles went to Worsbrough Dale Elementary School until the age of 14. He then attended the Holgate Grammar School in Church Street, Barnsley for three years, from 1907 to 1910. He was an intending Pupil Teacher, Student Teacher and Bursar; he passed the Oxford Senior Local exam with 3rd Class Honours.

Charles attended York St John's College, from 1911 to 1913, and went on to become Assistant Master in Worsbrough Dale, where he 'also took a useful and an active part in the life and work of the Parish' at the Church Sunday School, Church Lads' Brigade and as Headmaster at the Worsbrough Dale Evening Continuation School.

Charles enlisted at Barnsley on 8 December 1915, aged 22 years and 10 months, as a Private (Service Number: 21838) in the 10th Battalion of the York and Lancaster Regiment; he was a School Teacher living at 2 Wigfield Cottages, Kendall Green, Worsbrough Bridge. Charles was posted Bomber in the 3rd Battalion while at Sunderland, but he went to France on 25 February 1916 in the 10th Battalion, where he was promoted to Lance Corporal on 24 July 1916.

Charles was killed in action on 16 November 1916, aged 23, having served for 344 days, 265 of which were in France. As his body was never found or identified his name is listed on the Thiepval Memorial, Somme, France (Tier and Face: 14A and 14B).

The Medical Form contains some personal information: Height: 5' 9", Weight: 124 lbs, Chest: 34", Vision both eyes: 6/6. The thorough inspection identified 'Varicocele (L)' *(varicose veins next to the testis, which usually causes no symptoms but may cause discomfort in a small number of cases).*

Charles' mother was sent a form to complete c1920 with details of his relatives; this mentions his two married sisters but states 'none' against 'Brothers' as William Henry had died in service. This form was countersigned by the Vicar of Worsbrough Dale who added: 'The above Mrs Savage is an invalid and unable to get up to the Vicarage – I know the family, you may depend upon it being correctly signed'. A form regarding Charles' personal possessions dated 17 April 1917 was stamped 'No Effects'.

Charles was awarded two medals: Victory and British War. His widowed mother should have received the 'Dead Man's Penny' plaque and scroll from King George V. Martha Savage died in Barnsley district early 1933, aged 74.

Charles' name is on the Holgate Grammar School Memorial, the St Thomas' & St James' War Memorial in Worsbrough and the Roll of Honour at St John's College in York.

He is remembered on the headstone in St Thomas' & St James' Churchyard in Worsbrough for the family grave, where his brother William, both parents, his sister Clara and her husband William Addey were buried.

LANCE-CORPL
WILLIAM HENRY SAVAGE
13TH YORK & LANCS
ELDER BELOVED SON OF
THOMAS & MARTHA SAVAGE
OF KENDAL GREEN
BORN JAN. 27TH 1887, DIED MAY 6TH 1917.

ALSO LANCE-CORPL CHARLES EDWARD SAVAGE
10TH YORK & LANCS, THEIR YOUNGER SON
BORN FEB 10TH 1893, FELL IN ACTION
IN FRANCE NOV 16TH 1916

GREATER LOVE HATH NO MAN THAN THIS

Connections

Seven of the Old Boys qualified as Teachers after attending St John's College in York: **Crossland Barraclough** (B 1894), **Edward Batley** (B 1893), **Norman Bradley** (B 1891), **John Middleton Downend** (B 1888), **Arthur Heathcote** (B 1890), **Charles Edward Savage** (B 1893) and **Charles Waldegrave Wood** (B 1883). Several of them would have attended during the same period.

Charles served in the 10th Battalion of the York and Lancaster Regiment along with **Paul Timson.**

Alumnus – April 1917

> Lance-Corporal Savage (1907–1910) went for his two years training for the teaching profession to York College, afterwards becoming Assistant Master at Worsbrough Dale. In addition to his professional duties he took a useful and an active part in the life and work of the parish.

***Barnsley Chronicle* – 16 December 1916**

A WORSBRO' DALE LOSS
ASSISTANT SCHOOLMASTER PAYS SUPREME SACRIFICE

News of the death in action of Lance Corporal C E Savage of the 3rd Y and L has caused great sorrow to his many friends in Worsbro' Dale, where he has been a well known and popular figure for many years. Before joining the forces, Mr Savage was an assistant master in Worsbrough Dale National School. He was an earnest, vigorous and able teacher, devoted heart and soul to his work, and his loss is keenly felt by the school which has already lost three teachers in the war.

Lance Corporal Savage was an indefatigable worker and took an active part in almost everything that went on in the parish. In addition to his work in the day school, he was headmaster of the Worsbrough Dale Evening Continuation School, Superintendent of the Church Sunday School and a most enthusiastic officer of the Church Lads Brigade, which has now lost all its four officers in the war. Much sympathy is felt for his parents, Mr and Mrs Savage of Kendall Green, Barnsley, in their sad bereavement.

***Barnsley Independent* – 23 December 1916**

WAR BRIEFLETS
A POPULAR TEACHER

The news of the death in action of Lance Corporal Charles Edward Savage, York & Lancaster Regiment, of Kendal Green, assistant master at the Worsbrough Dale Council School, was received with profound regret, deceased being a very popular and devoted Church Worker in that parish. He was superintendent of the Church Sunday School, headmaster at the Worsbrough Dale Evening Continuation School and an enthusiastic officer in the Church Lads Brigade.

The photograph of Charles is from Alumnus, *reproduced by kind permission of Barnsley Archives.*

WILLIAM HENRY SAVAGE (born early 1887 Barnsley – died 6 May 1917, aged 29) was an Office Boy Colliery, living at home, in April 1901. By April 1911, William (24) Tramway Clerk on the Llandudno – Colwyn Bay Light Railway, was one of three Boarders with Mrs Davies in Colwyn Bay, Wales.

William enlisted at Silkstone on 19 January 1915, aged 27, as a Private (Service Number: 1296) in the 13th Battalion (First Barnsley Pals) of the York and Lancaster Regiment. He was a Clerk living in Worsbrough Dale on the Attestation form.

William went to the Mediterranean on 28 December 1915 before being sent to France as a Lance Corporal on 11 March 1916. The Medical Form contains a personal description: Height: 5' 9½", Weight: 140 lbs, Chest: 34", Vision right eye: 6/6, left eye: 6/12, slight varicose vein in right leg.

William was admitted to hospital No. 5 on 23 March 1917 with 'ICT leg' and he died six weeks later of 'ICT leg & arm', after being transferred to 'UEH Northam'. (ICT is Inflammation of the Connective Tissue and was a general term used in the First World War for suppurating skin disease, ulcers or gangrene. Injury was caused by wearing hard soled boots and carrying heavy loads over uneven ground with infection the result of living in filthy conditions).

William's name is on the Commonwealth War Graves Commission database and he should have been awarded two medals: Victory and British War, in addition to the 'Dead Man's Penny' plaque and scroll.

William was buried privately in St Thomas' Churchyard in Worsbrough Dale in what became the family grave. His name is on the St Thomas' and St James' War Memorial in Worsbrough.

***Barnsley Chronicle* – 19 May 1917**

MILITARY FUNERAL AT WORSBRO' –
TWO BROTHERS GIVE THEIR LIVES

An impressive service was witnessed at St Thomas' Church, Worsbro' Dale, last Thursday, when the remains of the late Lance-Corporal W H Savage, of Kendal Green, were laid to rest.

Deceased joined the Barnsley Pals' Battalion (13th Y & L) in January 1915, and was with them until March this year, when he was invalided home with septic poisoning in the arm. Hopes of his ultimate recovery were held both by his parents and the authorities at the hospital at Exeter, but unfortunately he collapsed while being moved to another hospital.

Military bearers and a firing party were supplied from Pontefract.

Much sympathy is felt in the district for Mr and Mrs Savage, who have now lost both their sons in the war (the youngest Charlie, having been killed in action in France last November). Many floral tributes were sent and a large number of people from the parish attended the church, the deceased, until his business career took him to Colwyn Bay, being connected with the Sunday School, Men's Guild, and the Church Football Club. He was cashier at the Barnsley and District Electric Tramways for the first 4½ years after its opening, leaving there for a similar position at Colwyn Bay on the opening of the Llandudno – Colwyn Bay Tramways, with which company he remained until the date of his enlistment.

William Henry Savage was not included in the casualty list reproduced in Jon Cooksey's Barnsley Pals, *which comprised those who joined in 1914, but who died on or before 1 July 1916.*

57

Ronald John (Jack) Saville

Ronald John (Jack) Saville
1896–1916 (aged 20)

RONALD JOHN SAVILLE was born on 28 September 1896 in Worsbrough to **Edward Saville** (born c1861 in Worsbrough) and **Helen Muriel nee Bycraft** (born c1866 in Leeds). Edward was an Assistant Sanitary Inspector.

Jack was the third of four surviving children: **Hilda Mary**, **Doris Anna** and **Bernard Walter** (attended the Holgate and served in the First World War). **Edward Bycroft [sic] Saville** died in infancy in 1887.

Hilda Mary Saville, Teacher, died in Barnsley in December 1989, aged 101.

Doris Anna Saville (31) Teacher, of Acle House, Park Grove, Barnsley, married **Stanley Warr** (30) Salesman of 22 Bond Road, Barnsley, on 5 June 1922 at Edward the Confessor Church, Barnsley; his father **George Moss Warr** was a Salesman. Witnesses were both fathers plus Hilda Mary Saville and Stanley's mother Ann Beaumont Warr. (Stanley was the brother of Old Boy **George Harrington Gerald Warr** (Part 2. Chapter 69).

In April 1911, the Saville family had lived in eight rooms at 209 Park Road, Barnsley, for over ten years since moving from Worsbrough. **Edward S Bycraft**, widower and Retired Joiner, aged 71, was living with his daughter Helen and her family.

Jack went to Barnsley Central Elementary School for three and a half years until the age of 14. He then attended the Holgate Grammar School in Church Street, Barnsley for one year in 1911. When he left school at the end of 1911, the Holgate Management Committee wrote to confirm that they would accept payment of the fee for the term in lieu of notice; the amount payable for both sons was £5 12s. Jack became a Bank Clerk at London and Smith's Bank, Barnsley branch. (*The Union of London & Smiths Bank Ltd (1839–1918), established in London, was a past constituent of The Royal Bank of Scotland Group).*

Jack was involved with St John's Church, Barnsley, and he was Assistant-Scoutmaster of the 15th Barnsley (St John's) Troop.

Jack, still at the Bank in Barnsley, enlisted at Woolwich in November 1915 as a Private (Service Number; 20261) in the 26th Battalion (Bankers Battalion) of the Royal Fusiliers; he joined along with his friend and colleague **Albert Gordon Cooper**.

Jack was in the Signalling Section of the Battalion and survived two engagements without injury. However, he was hit by a shell when he accompanied a Lance-Corporal to repair some wires at midnight on 9 October. Jack was killed in action on 10 October 1916, aged 20, but as his body was not recovered Jack's name is listed on the Thiepval Memorial, Somme, France (Pier & Face: 8C 9A & 16A).

Jack was awarded two medals: Victory and British War. His parents should have received the 'Dead Man's Penny' plaque and scroll from King George V.

Jack's name is on the Holgate Grammar School Memorial, War Memorials for Gibson Hall National Provincial and Union of London and Smiths Banks, the National Provincial Roll of Honour and he is on the RBS (Royal Bank of Scotland) Remembers 1914–1918 website. His name was also on the War Memorial at St John's Church, Barebones in Barnsley, but this was lost when the church was demolished; at the end of 2015 a replacement oak plaque was created using a grant from Barnsley

Central Ward and this will be displayed in St Peter the Apostle and St John the Baptist's Church in Brinckman Street, off Doncaster Road, Barnsley.

Connections

Jack's father Edward Saville, Assistant Sanitary Inspector, was the same age as and would have worked with **William Savage**, Sanitary Inspector, who was the uncle of **John William Kilner**.

Jack started as a Bank Clerk at the Union of London and Smiths Bank Ltd at about the same time as **Thomas Westby** and **Harry Liddall Bambridge** – a few years before **Frank Bakel.**

Jack served in the 26th Battalion (City of London Regiment) of the Royal Fusiliers along with **Benjamin Holroyd Rymer Laycock.**

Jack's younger sister Doris Anna married Stanley Warr, the younger brother of **George Harrington Gerald Warr.**

Alumnus – April 1917

> From letters received from Mrs Saville from her son we learn that R J Saville, who was a signaller, had volunteered to assist in patrolling a telephone line which had been broken by shell fire. After repairing the line he was returning when within 10 yards of his dug-out, a shell from the enemy killed him instantly. His CO spoke highly of the very excellent way he always carried out his work as a signaller.

Barnsley Chronicle – 11 November 1916

> ASSISTANT SCOUTMASTER KILLED
>
> News has been received that Private Ronald J Saville, Royal Fusiliers, elder son of Mr & Mrs E Saville of 209 Park Road, Barnsley, has fallen in action. Pte Saville enlisted in November of last year at which time he was on the staff of the London & Smith's Bank. Barnsley, and he went out to France in May of this year. The deceased soldier was assistant scoutmaster in the Barnsley St John's Troop.

***Barnsley Independent* – 11 November 1916**

BARNSLEY BANK CLERK FALLS
COLLEAGUE FOLLOWS COLLEAGUE
PRIVATE R J SAVILLE

The death in action is officially announced of Private Ronald John (Jack) Saville, Royal Fusiliers, eldest son of Mr E Saville, formerly assistant sanitary inspector for Barnsley, and Mrs Saville of 209 Park Road, Barnsley. The deceased soldier ... was a close colleague of the late Private A Cooper, Solicitor with Mr C McNaughton, Regent Street, and both joined the same battalion (Bankers) of the Royal Fusiliers last November as privates. They went out to France together and they were killed within a month of each other. Private Cooper fell on the 15th September and the death in action of Private Saville occurred on the 9th October.

Details of the death of Private Saville were forthcoming in a letter to his parents, from a comrade who said he hardly knew how to break the terrible news. 'We went over the top on the 15th of September and again on the 7th October (two o' clock Saturday afternoon)', writes this colleague. 'Jack went through the two engagements without being scratched. At midnight on the 9th Jack went out with a lance-corporal to repair some wires, and a shell came, killed Jack instantly, and buried the lance-corporal'. The writer also refers to the death of Private Cooper, and in a tribute to them, said: 'They were two of the finest men I have ever met, full of pluck'.

Private Saville belonged to the Signalling (Headquarters) Section of the Battalion. He was closely associated with the work of St John's Church, keenly interested in the Boys' Scout movement and was Assistant-Scoutmaster of the 15th Barnsley (St John's) Troop.

Ruth Reed, Archives Manager for the Royal Bank of Scotland, confirmed Jack's employment at the bank.

The photograph of Jack is from Alumnus, *reproduced by kind permission of Barnsley Archives.*

BERNARD WALTER SAVILLE (born 28 October 1898 in Barnsley) went to Park Road Elementary School for six years until the age of 13, when he attended the Holgate for five years, from 1911 to 1916. Walter was awarded a Continuation Scholarship and Bursar.

Alumnus stated that he was called up for Military Service in January 1917. There is a Medal Card for Bernard W Saville, Private (Service Number: 42673) in the Leicester Regiment; he was awarded two medals: Victory and British War. (I could not find any other records with more details)

Walter was an early Honorary Secretary of the Old Boys Association and, in March 1925, he wrote a letter, printed in *Alumnus* April 1925, expressing concern that a permanent special War Memorial to the Old Boys had not yet been provided. He became the President of the OBA in 1927, and was present at the dedication ceremony of the War Memorial on 28 October 1928, almost ten years after the end of the First World War (Part 1. Chapter 18).

Walter became a Headmaster in an Elementary School in Barnsley. He died on 9 February 1979, aged 80, at 209 Park Road, Barnsley, and left an estate worth about £21,000.

Jack's Friend and Colleague

ALBERT GORDON COOPER (born about 1887 in Barnsley) was one of six children of **John Cooper** and **Zillah nee Buckley**. A sibling had died before 1901, his father, Restaurant Proprietor, died in 1902, aged 54, and his older brother **John William Cooper** died in 1909, aged 31. By April 1911, the family were living in eight rooms at 8 Cavendish Road, Barnsley, where widowed Zillah was looking after two grandchildren: **Marjorie Beatrice Cooper** (9) and **Donald Cooper** (7). Albert (23) was a Solicitor's Articled Clerk (with Mr C McNaughton, Regent Street, Barnsley) and his younger brother **Reginald Frank Cooper** (17) was a Butter Dealer's Shop Assistant. They had two Boarders: **Edward William Metcalfe** (39) Bank Accountant, and **Charles Henry French** (41) Bank Manager. Two siblings, **Adeline Beatrice Cooper** and **Harry Buckley Cooper,** were living elsewhere.

Albert enlisted at Woolwich as Private (Service Number: 20262, which was the number after his friend Jack Saville) in the 26th Battalion of the Royal Fusiliers. Albert was wounded in an engagement on 15th September and died on 18 September 1916, aged 29. His name is on the Thiepval Memorial in Somme, France.

58

Arthur Hammond Butler Shipley

Arthur Hammond Butler Shipley
1895–1916 (aged 21)

ARTHUR HAMMOND BUTLER SHIPLEY was born on 26 August 1895 in Ledbury, Herefordshire, to **Reverend Arthur Granville Shipley** (born c1858 in Nottinghamshire) and **Caroline Mary Ellen nee Butler** (born c1858 in Buckinghamshire). Rev Arthur Shipley was a Clergyman in the Established Church; he was Curate at Markfield while Rev Charles Stokes Butler was incumbent and spent the last nearly 30 years of his tenure as Vicar of All Saints Church in Pontefract.

Arthur was their only child. He was the nephew of **Rev Charles Stokes Butler**, Headmaster of the Holgate Grammar School, who was the oldest brother of Arthur's mother Caroline (Part 1. Chapter 16). Arthur's second name of Hammond was after his grandfather **Hammond Shipley** (c1835–1919) Hosiery Manufacturer, and his uncle **Hammond Smith Shipley** (1858–1930) who was appointed her Majesty's Consul in Angora in 1896 and became Companion of the Order of St Michael and St George (CMG); he lived with his brother in All Saints Vicarage from retiring until his death.

In April 1911, the Shipley family lived in seven rooms in West Street, Wath upon Dearne, having previously lived in Sheffield; they had a General Domestic Servant. Arthur was a Student Boarder at Haileybury College, a boarding school at Heighford House, Hailey, near Hertford. Rev and Mrs Shipley subsequently moved to Pontefract.

Arthur went to a Private School until the age of 9. He then attended the Holgate Grammar School in Church Street, Barnsley for one year, from 1905 to 1906. Arthur moved on to Haileybury College, where he was at Hailey House from 1909 to 1914.* He was awarded a scholarship of £40 and passed other necessary qualifications in 1914 to attend Peterhouse College, Cambridge University, to read History, but he did not take up residence.†

Arthur joined the Public Schools Brigade‡ in November 1914 and he became Second Lieutenant of the 'A' Company of the 6th Battalion of the Yorkshire Regiment. He served in Gallipoli from August 1915 and suffered a period as an invalid because of septic poisoning; he subsequently returned to the front in Egypt then France. Arthur wrote an account of being on board a destroyer, included in *Alumnus* (Part 3. Chapter 9).

* The Archivist at Haileybury College provided details of their Memorials and the Obituary in The Haileyburian, copied from The Times.

† Dr Philip Pattenden at Peterhouse College, Cambridge University, clarified the position about Arthur being accepted to attend but not actually starting his course plus details of Memorials, including photographs of that in Peterhouse Chapel.

‡ **Public Schools Battalion**
The Royal Fusiliers or City of London Regiment raised 47 battalions for the First World War. Four Public Schools Battalions (18th to 21st Service) formed on 11 September 1914 at Epsom from Public Schools and Universities. They came under command of 98th Brigade, 33rd Division on 26 June 1915 and crossed to France in November 1915, transferring to 19th Brigade, 33rd Division on the 27th. They disbanded on 24 April 1916 as many of the men had become commissioned as officers.

Arthur was killed in action while leading his Company in a successful attack on 27 September 1916, aged 21, after more than a year serving overseas. As his body was never found or identified his name is listed on the Thiepval Memorial, Somme, France (Pier and Face: 3A and 3D).

Arthur was awarded three medals: 1914–15 Star, Victory and British War; his father applied for the 1914–15 Star on 30 July 1919. His parents ought to have received the 'Dead Man's Penny' plaque and scroll from King George V.

According to the Army Registers of Soldiers' Effects, Arthur appears to have been owed about £85 when he died. There is no stamp on the register to indicate the award of the usual War Gratuity.

Arthur's name is on the Holgate Grammar School Memorial, the Memorial Roll of the Officers of Alexandria Princess of Wales Own Yorkshire Regiment, on the cloister wall at Haileybury College, where there is also a War Memorial Cross to all Old Haileyburians who lost their lives in service to their country, on the Haileybury & Imperial Service Register and Haileybury College Roll of Honour website. Arthur's name is also on the War Memorial in Peterhouse Chapel under the year 1916 and he is also listed among the war dead in *The War List of the University of Cambridge 1914–1918* edited by G.V. Carey (also on their website).

He is remembered on his parents' family headstone in All Saints Churchyard, Pontefract:

IN LOVING MEMORY OF
CAROLINE MARY HELEN SHIPLEY
DIED MARCH 7TH 1924
ALSO ARTHUR GRANVILLE SHIPLEY, MA,
HUSBAND OF THE ABOVE
VICAR OF ALL SAINTS, PONTEFRACT, 1911–1959 [*26 January*]

ALSO ARTHUR HAMMOND BUTLER SHIPLEY, 2ND LIEUTENANT
6TH YORKSHIRE REGT
KILLED IN ACTION NEAR THE SOMME SEPTEMBER 27TH 1916

AND OF HAMMOND SMITH SHIPLEY
DIED 16TH MARCH 1930 (CMG)

Alumnus Magazine

A B Shipley was educated at the Barnsley Grammar School and Haileybury College. In 1914 he took an open History Scholarship at Peterhouse, Cambridge, but immediately the war broke out offered his services. He became 2nd Lieutenant and went out to the Dardanelles. He was invalided suffering from septic poisoning. After serving in Egypt he was moved to France where he fell on Sept 27th while gallantly leading his Company in a successful attack. His CO describes him as one of the best subalterns he had. 2nd Lieut Shipley was nephew of the Headmaster of this School. (Rev Charles Stokes Butler).

***Yorkshire Evening Post* – 9 October 1916**

TODAY'S YORKSHIRE CASUALTIES

This morning the Rev A G Shipley, Vicar of All Saints Pontefract, received official intimation that his only son Second-Lieut Arthur Hammond Butler Shipley had met a like fate [killed in action].

On the outbreak of war, Lieutenant Shipley, fresh from College, joined the Army as a private, but received a commission and went to Egypt. He was only 21 years of age. He joined the Public Schools Battalion and served with the Yorkshire Regiment in the Dardanelles and was invalided home suffering from septic poisoning. He returned to the front in July and he was killed on September 27th.

(Mentioned again in ***Yorkshire Evening Post*** – 10 October 1916 with a photograph).

***The Times* – 12 October 1916**

FALLEN OFFICERS
'THE TIMES' LIST OF CASUALTIES
BIOGRAPHIES AND SERVICES

SECOND LIEUTENANT ARTHUR HAMMOND BUTLER SHIPLEY was the only son and child of the Rev A G and Mrs Shipley of All Saints' Vicarage, Pontefract. He was educated at Haileybury College, and after being in the V1th Form and college prefect, he gained an open history scholarship at Peterhouse, Cambridge. At the outbreak of war he enlisted in the Public Schools Brigade, receiving a commission in the Yorkshire Regiment in November. In August 1915, he went out to the Dardanelles, where he was invalided to Alexandria, suffering from septic poisoning. Rejoining later he served with his battalion in Egypt and being transferred to another theatre of war fell in action on September 27.

(This article was copied into *The Haileyburian* – 26 October 1916).

***Barnsley Chronicle* – 14 October 1916**

PONTEFRACT VICAR'S ONLY SON
NEPHEW OF BARNSLEY GRAMMAR SCHOOL
HEADMASTER KILLED

Second-Lieut Arthur Hammond Butler Shipley, only child of the Rev A G Shipley, Vicar of All Saints, Pontefract, was on Monday officially announced by telegram to have been killed in action. He was educated at Haileybury College, where in 1914 he took an open history scholarship at St Peter's Cambridge, but immediately war broke out, and before his first term opened, he joined the Public Schools Battalion. In November he received a commission in the 7th Yorkshire Regiment and after nine months' training went out to the Dardanelles with another battalion, and here he was invalided suffering from septic poisoning. After the evacuation he served in Egypt, but in July last moved to another theatre of war, where he fell on September 27. He was a nephew of the Rev C S Butler, headmaster of Barnsley Grammar School, and only attained his 21st birthday on August 25th last.

Mary Wortley, a distant relation of the Shipley and Butler families, kindly provided more family information for Arthur Hammond Butler Shipley and Rev Charles Stokes Butler.

The main photograph of Arthur is from Alumnus, *reproduced by kind permission of Barnsley Archives.*

59

Cecil Skues

Cecil Skues
1897–1917 (aged 19)

CECIL SKUES was born on 14 July 1897 in Nottingham to **Ernest Skues** (born c1870 in Halifax) and **Clara nee Roberts** (born c1875 in Nottingham). Ernest was a Warehouse Manager.

Cecil was the oldest of five children: **Vincent** (served in the First World War), **Richard, Florence Muriel** and **Jack**.

In April 1911, the Skues family lived in seven rooms at 49 Gawber Road, Barnsley, having previously lived in Nottingham; Richard was born in Hanwell, Middlesex in 1904 and Florence Muriel in Halifax in 1905 (her grandparents lived in Salterhobble). They subsequently moved to 70 Sackville Street, Barnsley, then 9 Eldon Road, Blackburn.

The Skues Family c1912 – left to right: Clara, Cecil, Jack, Vincent, Florence Muriel, Ernest and Richard; family photograph used by their kind permission.

Richard Skues married **Doris E Hughes** early 1938 in Runcorn and they had three children: **Richard K Skues** in 1939 in Bucklow, **Margaret E** in 1947 in Stockport and **Christopher R** in 1949 in Manchester.

Florence Muriel Skues married **Harry L Coulthurst** in Spring 1938 in Stockport and had one daughter, **Anne Coulthurst**, born there in 1939.

Jack Skues married **Lily Bruckshaw** on Boxing Day 1935 in Stockport and had three daughters there: **Joy C Skues** in 1937, **Jennifer** in 1939 and **Patricia M** in 1943. The family emigrated to Canada in 1967.

Cecil went to St Mary's Elementary School, Barnsley, for three years until the age of 13 and he attended the Holgate Grammar School in Church Street then Shaw Lane, Barnsley for three years, from 1910 to 1913. Cecil was awarded a County Minor Scholarship 'tenable for school life'. He went on to become a Clerk in an Accountant's Office.

Cecil was resident in Blackpool when he enlisted as a Rifleman (Service Number: R/37015 formerly TR/13/26043) in the 109th Training Reserve Battalion then the

16th Battalion of the King's Royal Rifle Corps, where he had also been a Signaller. He was killed in action on 20 May 1917, aged 19, but as his body was never found or identified Cecil's name is listed on the Arras Memorial, Faubourg-d'Amiens Cemetery, Arras, France (Bay 7).

Cecil is listed in the Army Registers of Soldiers Effects, which show that he was owed £3 12s 6d when he was killed and this was paid to his father several months afterwards. He was also awarded a War Gratuity of £3 10s, which was paid to his father in 1919.

Cecil was one of the youngest of the Old Boys to die in the First World War – there were nine young men aged only 19.

Cecil was awarded two medals: Victory and British War. His parents should have received the 'Dead Man's Penny' plaque and scroll from King George V.

Cecil's name is on the Holgate Grammar School Memorial.

His name is included in Winchester Cathedral's Book of Remembrance and as a memorial on his grandparents' (Richard and Lucy Skues) headstone, a stone cross on tiered plinths, at All Saints Cemetery in Salterhobble, Halifax:*

ALSO CECIL SKUES, SIGNALLER, KRR
ELDEST SON OF ERNEST SKUES

Alumnus – **July 1917**

> Private Cecil Skues (left 1913) Signaller, was only 19 years of age when he made the supreme sacrifice. He was killed by a sniper while signalling. C Skues will be remembered by his school friends for his untiring efforts in the production of a Form Magazine, of which he was, I believe, the owner, printer, chief editor and principal contributor.

Barnsley Chronicle – **16 June 1917**

DEATHS

> Killed in action on May 27th (Whit Sunday) in France, Signaller Cecil Skues, King's Royal Rifle Corps, dearly loved and eldest son of Ernest & Clara Skues, Eldon Road, Blackburn, late of 70 Sackville Street, Barnsley, aged 19 years. RIP

* Caroline and Cecil Skues kindly provided some family details and allowed me to use the family photograph.

Ann Cameron at Blackpool Local History Centre checked their index to newspapers (unfortunately nothing was found) and sent me the Ancestry record of Soldiers' Effects, mistranscribed as Shrives.

The main photograph of Cecil is from Alumnus, *reproduced by kind permission of Barnsley Archives.*

VINCENT SKUES (born 7 May 1899 in Nottingham) enlisted at Warrington on 15 April 1915, aged 15 years and 11 months, as a Band Boy (Service Number: 16490) in the South Lancashire Regiment. He had previously been a Band Member and a Turner; his father was next of kin at 70 Sackville Street, Barnsley. Vincent was discharged on 10 December 1915 after 240 days' service, during which period he had been deprived of pay for misconduct. The Conduct Form lists offences on six different occasions between 18 August and 5 November 1915, with more than one offence on each occasion and punishment ranging from loss of between three and eight days' pay. The list includes: destroying personal clothing, gambling in the Barracks, reporting sick without cause, 'highly irregular conduct', being absent from Parade & Roll Call, losing his great coat and being deficient of his kit.

The Medical Form provides a personal description: Height: 5' 0½", Weight: 87 lbs, Chest: 30", Vision both eyes 6/6, Complexion Fresh, Eyes Blue, Hair Light Brown, Considered Fit for duty as Band Boy.

Vincent seems to have re-enlisted on 5 January 1917, aged 17 years and 8 months, in Blackburn, after the family moved there. He was a Private in different regiments. One record has 2/5th Battalion of the Cheshire Regiment, Number 6 Labour Company of the K L Regiment, King's Own Loyal Lancashire Regiment and the Royal Army Service Corps (Service Numbers: 65415, 42366 and 324842). Vincent went to France on 2 March 1917, but when the Battalion realized that he was under-aged at Boulogne, he was transferred back to the Home Establishment at Oswestry on 6 July. On 2 August 1917 he was posted to the 3/5th Battalion of the Cheshire Regiment at Oswestry then transferred on 23 November to MT Army Service Corps at Grove Park. On 5 January 1918 he passed the Learner's Test at Isleworth and was granted 4th Rate Corps pay; after three days leave on 25 January 1918, he transferred to 613 M Company Army Service Corps at Liverpool.

Vincent was discharged from the Army on medical grounds on 1 November 1918, aged 19. The old Tuberculosis disease of his right ankle, originally diagnosed in 1911 when living in Barnsley, had begun to cause 'pain in the ankle on walking too much' in 1918. An X-Ray report from the Royal Herbert Hospital on 25 September 1918 revealed 'evidence of active disease and some fullness round the ankle joint'. Discharge was recommended as permanently unfit, although the Board decided that Vincent had not suffered any impairment to his health since entry to the service as the disease was prior to enlistment. Vincent was awarded 8/3* per week for 38 weeks. (* A Private's basic pay was 1/– per day plus 1d per day when in a war zone).

Vincent married **Evelyn Rowland** on 23 December 1922 in Blackburn and they had three children in different areas: **Vera J Skues** in 1924 in Blackburn, **Muriel M Skues** in 1926 in Liverpool and **Donald Skues** in 1929 in Leeds.

Butterfields SALE.
The greatest occasion of the year to save money.
Butterfields (The Drapers), Ltd., 1, Church Street, BARNSLEY.

The Barnsle[y]
AND PENISTONE MEXBRO' WAT[H]

VOL. LVIII. NO. 4013 SATURDAY

LOCAL HEROES FALL IN ACTION.

BARNSLEY BATTALIONS CHARGE THE HUNS

THROUGH SHOT AND SHELL.

OFFICERS & MEN MAKE GREAT SACRIFICES.

Hundreds of troops from Barnsley and district took part in the great British offensive on Saturday, July 1st, in the region of Albert, France, and though they succeeded in carrying out their plans this was done at a great sacrifice of life and limb.

It was about seven o'clock on the morning of the 1st inst. that the order was given for the men of the two Barnsley Battalions, the Territorials, and other regiments to fix bayonets preparatory to leaving their shielded quarters for the move forward. The Germans, it was known, were only about 100 yards away, and no sooner had the Britishers mounted the parapets than they were faced with terrific machine-gun and shrapnel fire. Many officers and men were struck down and the casualty list is sorrowful reading.

Grief-stricken parents, relatives, and friends can take consolation from the reading of the observations made by the General leading the Division and which appears in this issue.

Taking a rough calculation, it may safely be said that fully 6,000 men from Barnsley and the immediate district took part in the great attack. Special mention should be of made our brave Territorials who have been in the thick of it so long; once again they acquitted themselves splendidly.

Lieut.-Colonel Hewitt has this week received letters from many of the officers of the 13th Y & L (1st Barnsley Battalion), six of whom it is thought were killed and at least as many wounded. These wounded officers vividly describe the attack and say that the Battalion lads performed as coolly as though on parade at Silkstone—a fact which Colonel Hewitt is delighted with, but by no means surprised to hear.

Major T. Guest is reported missing, and Colonel Wilford writes of him: "He was l st seen leading a Company into a German trench; he was shot in the right leg just as he reached the trench; there is still hope."

Major Kennard, Captain de Ville Smith, and Lieuts. Dart and Hirst were killed; Capt. Maleham believed to be killed; Lieut. Sharp reported missing (believed to be killed).

Amongst the wounded officers are Lieuts. Heppinstall, Hunter, Cooke, and Knowles.

Captain Hewitt, of the Barnsley Territorials, was wounded and is suffering from shell shock. From the firing line he was transferred to Rouen Hospital and thence to the Whitworth Hospital, Manchester. It is only a week or two short of a year since Captain Hewitt was wounded before. Last night we were pleased to learn that he is making satisfactory progress towards recovery.

Details concerning many of the victims will be found appended.

THE STRICKEN BRAVE.

CAPTAIN DE VILLE SMITH.

boys, and when I left he was busy sending and receiving reports. I sent back two runners reporting my arrival, and on their return I was informed of his death. He was struck by shrapnel and died instantly. I

munity of South Yorkshire. He held the bronze medal of the City and Guilds of London Institute in surveying. His death has undoubtedly cut short what promised to be a brilliant career in the mining world. He devoted a great deal of time and interest to the Wombwell Church Lads' Brigade, of which he was Captain for several years.

Lieut. Hirst was married as recently as August, 1915, to Miss Bertha Lockwood, daughter of Mr. and Mrs. S. Lockwood, of Wath-on-Dearne. He was 30 years of age, and the elder son of the late Mr. John Hirst, for many years curator of the Wombwell Cemetery. His only brother, Mr. John Hirst, is now serving as a writer in the Royal Navy.

LIEUTENANT D. FAIRLEY.

Lieut. Duncan Fairley, of the 14th Battalion York and Lancaster Regiment, was the youngest son of Mr. Barker Fairley, Park Grove, Barnsley, and headmaster of St. John's School, Barnsley. Although no official intimation has been received, letters from comrades have conveyed the sad news to Barnsley, and there is no doubt that Lieut. Fairley has made the highest of all sacrifices. He was 26 years old and had had a distinguished and promising scholastic career. After receiving his early education at St. John's School, he gained the Locke Scholarship and a County Minor Scholarship, and proceeding to the Barnsley Grammar School he was successful in matriculating and securing a County Major Scholarship. Lieut. Fairley took his B.A. degree with first class honours at the Leeds University, and subsequently became English master at the Scarborough Municipal Secondary School.

He was in Scarboro' at the time the town was bombarded and had a narrow escape, a piece of shell striking his bed whilst he was in the room.

Early last year Colonel Raley asked Lieut. Fairley to accept a commission in the 14th Battalion York and Lancaster Regiment, and this he accepted, joining on May 18th, 1915. When the Battalion left for Egypt Lieut. Fairley remained behind on Salisbury Plain in charge of a draft of men, and after a period of suspense, when he three times received orders to embark, to be cancelled at the last moment, he left for Egypt. After being only six days in Alexandria Lieut. Fairley went with the Battalion straight to France, where he has been ever since. He had been looking forward to getting leave at Whitsuntide, but this was stopped and the parents of the gallant officer have not seen him since Christmas Day.

The greatest sympathy is felt with Mr. and Mrs. Fairley in their irreparable loss, for their son was known to a very wide circle of friends, and he was held by all in the highest esteem. An able scholar, he gave promise of having a distinguished career as a schoolmaster, and he proved himself during his short military life to be a capable and gallant officer. Mr. and Mrs. Fairley's eldest son is a Quartermaster-Sergeant with the Canadians and he has been with them in the trenches for many months.

LIEUT. H. CLARKE.

News reached Hoyland on Friday that Lieutenant Harry Clarke, the son of Mr. C. Clarke, of West Bank, Hoyland, was killed in action whilst leading a charge in the offensive on Saturday, July 1st. At the time he enlisted he was studying at the Edinburgh University with a view to entering the medical profession, having previously been a prominent member of the Officers' Training Corps at Worksop College. He was 22 years of age, an only son, and was most popular with his men.

SERGEANT R. DUNK.

60

George Smith

George Smith
1899–1918 (aged 19)

GEORGE SMITH was born on 29 May 1899 in Barnsley to **Tom Smith** (born July 1869 in Ecclesfield) and **Mary Margaret nee Peel** (born c1877 in Barnsley). Tom was Grocery Warehouseman for Barnsley Co-operative Society – he had also played for Barnsley Football Club.

George had a younger brother **Leslie. Leslie Smith** (aged 28) married **Gladys Hepworth** in summer 1933 in Barnsley and they had two sons called **George**: George B was born in summer 1936 and George G late 1940.

In April 1911, the Smith family lived in five rooms at 39 Derby Street, Barnsley, having previously lived at 57 Farrar Street. They later moved to 37 Limesway, Gawber.

George went to Barnsley Elementary School for three years until the age of 10. He then attended the Holgate Grammar School in Church Street, Barnsley for seven years, from 1909 to 1916. He was awarded a County Minor Scholarship for four years and a Bursar for one year; he passed the Oxford Local Senior exam with 2nd Class Honours and the Higher Alternative Papers Sheffield Matriculation. George was then awarded a Borough Major Scholarship for further education for four years.

George attended Sheffield University and matriculated in March 1916 to study Arts. In June 1917 he is recorded as Failed in Latin, English and Pure Mathematics, although Passed in French and Military Science; a note was made that he was to be credited with his pass in French and Military Science and subsequently with a pass in English.*

According to the RAF Officer Records, George enlisted in the Royal Air Force (Service Number: 26354) on 18 September 1917, aged 18 years. He was based as Farnborough, Folton Park, St Leonards and then Reading by 3 December 1917. He was attached to the 68th Flying Squad on 16 March 1918, transferred to the 72nd on 14 May 1918 until 3 August, when he was promoted to Second Lieutenant despite being so young. The entry in the *London Gazette* has his first name as Gerald. Extracts from a letter from George were included in *Alumnus* (Part 3. Chapter 10).

George joined the British Expeditionary Force in the 80th Squadron on 10 August 1918 and was killed in a flying accident, when he crashed into an AW FK8 over the airfield, just five days later on 15 August 1918, aged 19. George was buried in Vignacourt British Cemetery, Somme, France (grave V C 5). His father had the words OF BARNSLEY WORTHY OF EVERLASTING LOVE FROM THOSE HE LEFT BEHIND added to the War Grave headstone.

George was one of the youngest of the Old Boys to die in the First World War – there were nine young men aged only 19.

George should have been awarded two medals: Victory and British War and his parents ought to have received the 'Dead Man's Penny' plaque & scroll from King George V.

* Matthew Zawadzki, Records Manager at Sheffield University, provided information about George's education there. This information is used by the kind permission of Sheffield University Records.

George's name is on the Holgate Grammar School Memorial and the name 'Geo Smith' was on the list of names read out at the old St George's Church, Barnsley. His name is on the Sheffield Roll of Honour on the internet with little other information. Barnsley Pace Street Swimming Club had a G Smith listed on its Memorial according to an article in *Barnsley Chronicle*.

***Alumnus* – December 1918**

> 2nd Lieut G Smith RAF (1909–1916) was killed in action on August 15th 1918. At the end of his school career he was awarded the Borough Major Scholarship tenable at Sheffield University. A letter from the deceased officer to the Editor appeared in the July number. A fellow officer writes to his father: 'I cannot express the deep feeling of sympathy which is felt for you by every member of the squadron. He was engaged in firing practice at the time, and was flying above the aerodrome. As he dived to the target, he collided with another machine, which was similarly engaged. He must have died instantly without suffering the slightest pain. He was buried in Vignacourt Cemetery yesterday'.

***Barnsley Chronicle* – 31 August 1918**

> LATEST LOCAL CASUALTIES: Lieutenant George Smith RAF, son of Mr T Smith, Derby Street off Dodworth Road, Barnsley, has been accidentally killed whilst flying in France. Lieut Smith, who was 19 years of age, had only been overseas a few days. He was an old Barnsley Grammar School boy and winning a scholarship he qualified for Sheffield University and joining the OTC he gained his commission in February last. His officer states: 'The whole thing was simply pure bad luck as a collision in the air is the rarest of accidents'. Lieut Smith's father was a former well-known member of the Barnsley football team and with the family the deepest sympathy has been expressed.

(A copy of this article is in *Holgate Ephemera* in Barnsley Archives).

The photograph of George is from Alumnus, *reproduced by kind permission of Barnsley Archives.*

TOM SMITH (Born early 1869 in Ecclesfield; Baptism at Ecclesfield St Mary's Church on 25 July 1869) was the youngest of ten children of Sampson and Mary Smith, from Ecclesfield, where they lived next door to the Independent Chapel in 1861 and at Walletts End in 1891. Sampson's father was called Thomas and they both worked in the File industry in Ecclesfield, as (Horse Rasp) Cutter and Hardener respectively.

Photograph of Tom in *Topical Times*, used by kind permission of David Wood and Grenville Firth.

Tom left school aged 12 and became a File Cutter. Although he enjoyed playing football from an early age, he joined his first team when he was 16; Tom played outside right for the Ecclesfield Church Juniors, who were in the Sheffield Sunday School League. After five seasons with Ecclesfield, Tom transferred to Sheffield United Reserve, known as Sheffield Strollers, for one season before signing with Barnsley St Peter's, who subsequently became Barnsley Football Club, in summer 1892, when he relocated to Barnsley.

During his nine seasons at Oakwell, Tom played in all of the forward positions and regularly scored goals; in his early years he made more than 120 appearances and scored at least 60 goals. Tom played in Barnsley Football Club's first League season of 1898/9 and his debut was in a home game at Oakwell against Luton Town.

In 1900/1, Barnsley Football Club's Committee decided to award Tom (then aged 31) a Benefit Match as a tribute to one of the Club's 'most loyal and respected players' – the net Benefit to Tom was £13 12s 8d. Tom went on to act as a Referee and he officiated at some big English Cup-ties.

Tom married **Mary Margaret Peel** in Barnsley in summer 1897; he worked for the Barnsley British Co-operative Society in their grocery warehouse in Summer Lane for 46 years until his retirement.

Tom (aged 77) was interviewed by *Barnsley Chronicle* in 1946 about his football history and this 'dapper little outside right' was described as the most gentlemanly player. No longer able to attend matches because of failing health, Tom still took a keen interest. In his day professional players had not received huge salaries – he had not made more than 12s for any match; 6–7,000 attendance was considered a good crowd and it cost 6d at the gate or 1/– on the stand.

When Tom died on 6 January 1947, he left everything to his son Leslie, who was a Technical College Lecturer; his effects were valued at £226 14s 2d.

Topical Times – 22 December 1928

THE MAN IN THE CROWD (PHOTO)

> Tom Smith is an institution in (Barnsley); reverently they point him out to visitors as one of the sights of the town. No one has a more comprehensive knowledge of the Barnsley club than this unassuming little man. In his younger days a player and later a referee, Tom began to associate himself with the fortunes of the Tykes some 40 years ago …

The subsequent interview with Tom Smith provides a detailed history of Barnsley Football Club, from the setting up of a football team in association with the Bible Class at St Peter's Church by Rev Tiverton Preedy, to joining the Sheffield & District League to winning the Football Association cup. Amongst the famous players mentioned, Tom recalled that 'in 1909 came the famous intermediate line, Glendinning, Boyle and Utley, certainly one of the greatest trio of half-backs the game has known. All three developed amazingly with other clubs: **Glendinning** with Bolton Wanderers, **Tommy Boyle** with Burnley and **George Utley** with Sheffield United'.

In that year, Barnsley reached the finals of the FA Cup at Crystal Palace, where they equalised with Newcastle United then lost in the replay in Liverpool. They were at the bottom of the League in 1910 with the same line up but won the cup in 1911, beating West Bromwich Albion in a replay of the finals – their first and last victory.

After further reminiscences, Tom explained that the present side was 'not too happy'. 'For one thing, support is poor, and a club needs good support nowadays to do anything. The falling off in attendance is, of course, due to the bad industrial conditions prevailing around the town'. … However, Tom felt that Barnsley Football Club had some good players, whose potential could develop well: 'I have few worries for the future'.

David Wood, 'The Official Historian to Barnsley Football Club', and Grenville Firth kindly allowed me to use the extract from their book, published in 2011: A Who's Who of Barnsley Football Club *in addition to the photograph, the article in* Topical Times *from 1928 and other newspapers circa 1900 and 1946.*

61

James Christopher Speight

James Christopher Speight
1893–1916 (aged 23)

JAMES CHRISTOPHER SPEIGHT was born on 1 March 1893 in Barnsley to **Thomas Speight** (born 1 April 1852 in Kendal, Westmoreland) and **Alice nee Casson** (born c1859 in Wombwell). James' Baptism was on 2 April 1893 at St George's Church, Barnsley. Thomas was a Newspaper Reporter in Westmoreland before moving to Barnsley to join the *Barnsley Chronicle* as a Journalist in 1879.

Thomas had married **Kezia Dawson** early 1877 in Kendal. They had two children before Kezia died in Barnsley on 20 October 1881, aged 25: a son **Thomas Dean** (attended the Holgate) and a daughter **Kezia Beatrice**, who was born less than two months before her mother died. Kezia's Baptism was at St George's Church, Barnsley, on 18 September 1881 and she died aged only nine months. Thomas got married again in Barnsley in Spring 1884 to Alice Casson and they had three children: **Alice May, Dorothy Casson** and **James Christopher**.

James was the youngest of four surviving children.

In April 1911, James was living in nine rooms at 112 Park Grove, Barnsley, with his widowed mother and sister Dorothy, Elementary School Teacher. They had previously lived at 13 and 23 Dodworth Road and 48 Kensington Road, Barnsley.

Alice May Speight married **Henry Sagar**, a Chemist, in Barnsley in Spring 1907 and in 1911 they were living in four rooms at 174 Main Road, Darnall, with their two children: **Dorothy Sagar** (2) and **Henry Sagar** (7 months) plus Henry's mother.

James went to St Mary's Elementary School, Barnsley, until the age of 12. He then attended the Holgate Grammar School in Church Street, Barnsley for four years, from 1905 to 1909. He passed the Oxford Local Junior and Senior exams. 'He left to take up Journalism – Newspaper Reporter' and was on the Staff of the *Barnsley Independent* and *Leeds Mercury*.

Photograph from *Barnsley Independent*, reproduced by kind permission of Barnsley Archives.

James enlisted on 30 November 1914, aged 21 years and 8 months, with the newly formed 15th (Bantam) Battalion of the Cheshire Regiment, after being rejected three times because of his height. He was promoted to Sergeant (Service Number: 19096) in the 16th Battalion of the Cheshire Regiment and went out to France in January 1916. James was killed along with many others, while asleep in the headquarters, during a heavy bombardment at Trones Wood on 19 July 1916, aged 23. James had served for one year and 231 days, of which a maximum of 200 days were in France.

According to Major Worthington's letter to James' sister, he was unconscious when found but died soon afterwards and was buried in Haricourt. The Commonwealth War Graves

Commission list James as 'killed in action' with his name listed on the Thiepval Memorial, Somme, France (Pier and Face: 3C and 4A). *(Subsequent action on the battle-field must have resulted in the grave and grave marker being destroyed).*

James was awarded two medals: Victory and British War. His widowed mother should have received the 'Dead Man's Penny' plaque and scroll from King George V.

James' name is on the Holgate Grammar School Memorial and on the list of names read out at the old St George's Church, Barnsley.

Photograph of James in De Ruvigny's *Roll of Honour 1914–1918.*

Connections

James sang a solo in the Speech Day Programme for July 1907, as did **Ernest William Litherland, Harold Quest** and **James Christopher Speight.**

Arthur Charles Quest, father of **Harold Quest**, attended James' father Thomas' funeral.

***Alumnus* – December 1916**

> James Christopher Speight was a Journalist. After several unsuccessful attempts to join the army he was accepted for services in a battalion of the Cheshire Regiment. Here he quickly rose to the rank of Sergeant. His affability, unfailing courtesy and uprightness of character won him a large number of friends who held him in high esteem.

***Sheffield Evening Telegraph*– 14 August 1916**

BARNSLEY JOURNALIST KILLED IN ACTION

> Regret was spread in a large circle of friends and acquaintances today when it became known that Sergeant Thomas Christopher Speight (22) Cheshire Regiment, had fallen for his country's cause. His mother, Mrs Speight, of 23 Dodworth Road, Barnsley, received the sad news through an official source today that her son was killed in action on July 19th. The intimation confirmed the fears caused by the absence of communication from the deceased for the past month.

Sergeant Speight was a well-known and promising young local journalist, the youngest son of the late Mr Thomas Speight and brother of Mr T D Speight, both of whom were journalists and were in turn formerly associated with the *Yorkshire Telegraph and Star* in the capacity of Barnsley and district correspondent. Sergeant Speight was educated at the Barnsley Grammar School and was on the staff of the *Barnsley Independent* when war broke out.

Barnsley Independent – 19 August 1916

OUR BEREAVEMENT (PHOTO)
A POPULAR AND PROMISING JOURNALIST
SERGEANT JAMES CHRISTOPHER SPEIGHT

The tragedy of war has already come home to almost all of us. Gallant sons, brave brothers, and close colleagues, true to tradition have taken their stand as heroes, and as heroes have fought and died. We have this week to record the loss of one of our own circle, a member of the literary staff of this journal, a young, faithful and promising journalist, and one popular with all. We refer to the death in action of Sergeant James Christopher Speight, which sad news came to hand on Monday morning and was received with widespread regret. The absence of news of him for close upon a month had naturally begun to to cause a feeling of suspense and anxiety amongst his relatives and friends, but having regard to the strenuous hostilities of late, the hope was cherished that all was well with him. Sad to record, however, that was not so. He had paid the big sacrifice, having fallen during the big advance, and the official notification received by his mother, Mrs Speight, of 23 Dodworth Road, Barnsley, came as a pitiful shock to all. He was killed in action on the 19th July.

The younger son of the late Mr Thomas Speight, a well known and highly respected Barnsley journalist, Sergeant Speight was 23 years of age last March. After leaving Barnsley Grammar School he joined the reportorial staff of this paper some six years ago, and had made great progress in the profession, being marked as a journalist of rich promise. When war broke out, he was amongst the first to hearken to the country's call for men. He promptly offered himself for enlistment, but was rejected three times, his shortness in height being the chief barrier. With the opening of the Bantams Regiment at Birkenhead he quickly seized his opportunity and was one of the first members of the Battalion. Entering into his military duties with characteristic whole-heartedness he speedily won promotion and held the position of orderly-room sergeant. He was home on last leave at Christmas and went out to France with his regiment (the 15th Cheshires) in the early part of January. About three months ago he was transferred to the 16th Cheshires.

Of cheerful disposition, big hearted and a most loveable lad, Sergeant Speight's death is keenly felt in many quarters and particularly by the staff and employees of this journal, to whom he had very closely endeared himself. His brother, Mr T D Speight, who was also formerly on the *Independent* staff, is a journalist in Australia, where he went some years ago for the benefit of his health.

Barnsley Chronicle – 19 August 1916

BARNSLEY JOURNALIST KILLED

It is with very sincere regret that we have to announce the death in action in France of Sergt James Christopher Speight, of 23 Dodworth Road, Barnsley, who was formerly a well-known journalist in this town. Sergeant Speight was 23 years of age and upon the outbreak of war showed a very keen desire to join the Army. In November 1914, he was accepted for the 15th Battalion Cheshire Regiment, which gained great popularity as the first 'Bantam' Battalion to be raised, but prior to this he had several times tried unsuccessfully to join the army. He was in fact one of the earliest recruits for this Battalion of the Cheshire Regiment. Sgt Speight quickly gained promotion to non-commissioned rank and readily adapting himself to his new surroundings did splendid work on the orderly room staff. Recently he was transferred to the 16th Battalion of the same regiment. After being home on leave for the last time at Christmas, Sgt Speight went to France in January and according to the official notification which was received at his home on Monday he was killed in action on July 19th. No news of him had been received for some weeks but the sad tidings came as a great shock to his relatives and friends.

Educated at Barnsley Grammar School, Sgt Speight, when about 16 years of age joined the editorial staff of the *Barnsley Independent* with which he remained until he entered the army. During the time he was associated with our company Sgt Speight showed exceptional promise as a journalist. His ability, his kindly nature and his cheerful disposition made him a great favourite amongst the Pressmen of Barnsley, who deeply deplore his untimely end. In the many circles of life in Barnsley and district with which Sgt Speight became associated in a professional capacity he was held in high esteem, and the news of his death has been received with sincere regret.

Sergeant Speight was the younger son of the late Mr Thomas Speight, journalist, of Barnsley (who was associated with the "Chronicle" for many years) and his brother, Mr T D Speight, was also at one time connected with the journalistic profession in Barnsley.

***Barnsley Independent* – 2 September 1916**

HEADQUARTERS SHELLED THE LATE SERGEANT J C SPEIGHT

A fortnight ago we recorded with regret the death in action of Sergt James Christopher Speight … The family sought further information regarding Sergt Speight's death and on Sunday last Miss Speight received a letter from Major R Worthington:

Your brother was killed [in Trones Wood] on July 19th during a very heavy bombardment. He was at headquarters asleep when I passed through going up to a further trench. The shelling was terrible and fearing something had happened two of us retraced our steps and found all the headquarters men dead or dying. Your brother was unconscious when we bandaged him and he slept peacefully away. He had no suffering and his end was quite restful.

We are all very sad to lose your brother. He was a good soldier, an excellent fellow, and very popular with both officers and men alike. He died the best possible death in laying down his life for others in the cause of right, and I am certain he has earned an eternal reward. May God enable you to bear up under this very sad affliction, and may you find Him very close to you at this time.

The writer also mentioned where Sergt Speight was killed and where he was buried.

***Barnsley Chronicle* – 2 September 1916**

KILLED IN HIS SLEEP

Particulars are to hand showing how Sergt J C Speight, 16th Cheshire Regiment (Bantams), met his death at the Front. The sergeant will be remembered as a Barnsley journalist, being on the reporting staff of the Barnsley "Independent" at the time of his enlistment.

Major R Worthington [wrote]: '… He is buried in Haricourt. I shall endeavour to obtain from our Chaplain a photograph of his grave if at all possible. …'.

Writing to the Editor from France, Signaller Fred Brown, 16th Cheshires, says: 'I would like to express my deepest sympathy with the parents and relatives of one of our own townsmen, a promising journalist – Sergt Speight. I was only about 15 yards away from him when he received the fatal blow. I am a Barnsley man, my home being at 16 Allison Terrace, Grace Street. All the Barnsley boys here are in the best of health. I wish the Barnsley Pals, the Territorials & the Royal Engineers good luck. I receive the *Chronicle* every week'.

UK De Ruvigny's Roll of Honour 1914–1918

SPEIGHT JAMES CHRISTOPHER

Sergeant No. 19096 in the 16th (Service) Battalion (2nd Birkenhead) of The Cheshire Regiment. Younger son of the late Thomas Speight, Journalist, by his wife Alice (23 Dodworth Road, Barnsley) daughter of Christopher Casson of Wombwell. … Served with the Expeditionary Force in France and Flanders from January 1916; he transferred to the 16th Battalion of The Cheshire Regiment in March and was killed in action at Trones Wood on 19 July following. Buried at Haricourt; unmarried.

***Sheffield Evening Telegraph*– 19 July 1917**

IN MEMORIAM SPEIGHT

In memory of Sergeant J C Speight, formerly a journalist of Barnsley, who was killed in action July 19th 1916.
From Mr and Mrs Henry Sagar. [James' sister and husband].

The main photograph of James is from Alumnus, reproduced by kind permission of Barnsley Archives.

THOMAS DEAN SPEIGHT (born in 1879 in Kendal) attended the Holgate for four years from the age of 12, from 1891 to 1895; he was a Locke Scholar and passed the Cambridge Local and Oxford Local Senior exams. Thomas became a Reporter with *Barnsley Independent* and played in the Old Boys Eleven team before he emigrated c1900 for health reasons to Australia, where he worked as a Reporter in Melbourne. He married out there and had one son (details unknown). Thomas died in 1916, about nine months after a throat operation, aged only 37.

***Yorkshire Post* & *Leeds Intelligencer* – 28 December 1916**

OBITUARY

News has been received in Barnsley of the death at Melbourne, Australia, of Mr T D Speight, a journalist well known in the Barnsley and Sheffield districts. He was the son of a journalist and was associated with Barnsley's papers until he succeeded his father on the staff of the *Sheffield Daily Telegraph*. Considerations of health led to his going to Australia about six years ago. There he was on the staff of the *Sydney Telegraph* and latterly the *Federal Hansard Melbourne*. About nine months ago he underwent an operation for an affection of the throat and never really recovered. He was only 37 years of age and leaves a widow and a son. His only brother Sergt J C Speight, Cheshire Regiment, fell in action a few months ago.

THOMAS SPEIGHT (SENIOR) (1 April 1852 Westmoreland – 16 January 1902, aged 49, Barnsley) was a newspaper reporter in Westmoreland before moving to Barnsley to work for *Barnsley Chronicle* from January 1879. Thomas remained at the *Chronicle* for some years but was also appointed the local reporter of *Sheffield Daily Telegraph* plus other daily and weekly journals. He represented Barnsley then Sheffield on the Institute of Journalists and he was a member of the choir and a church warden at St George's Church, Barnsley. Thomas continued to work while suffering from ill health, which led to his premature death of consumption in 1902, aged 49. Thomas was buried with his first wife in Barnsley Cemetery; his funeral had been held at St George's Church and 'a large number of beautiful floral tributes were sent, amongst these being wreaths from the staffs of the *Barnsley Chronicle* and *Barnsley Independent*. Thomas' Obituary was in *Sheffield Daily Telegraph* on 17 January 1902.

EVERY SHOULDER TO THE WHEEL!

62

Charles Stuart

Charles Stuart
1895–1918 (aged 23)

CHARLES STUART was born on 18 January 1895 in Barnsley to **William Norton Stuart** (born c1868 in Manchester) and **Mary Jane nee Lockwood** (born c1873 in Barnsley). William was a Manager of a Textile Factory.

Charles was the oldest of three surviving children: **William Litherland** and **Mary**. One child had died in infancy before April 1911 (name unknown).

In April 1911, the Stuart family lived in seven rooms at 39 Peel Street, Barnsley, having previously lived at 18 Greenwood Terrace, Barnsley.

William L Stuart married **Elsie Richardson** in spring 1926 in Barnsley; they may have had children if they moved from the West Riding of Yorkshire.

Charles went to Barnsley Elementary School until the age of 13. He then attended the Holgate Grammar School in Church Street, Barnsley for four years, from 1908 to 1912. Charles was awarded a County Minor Scholarship for three years. 'He worked in the Linen Factory after leaving' and became Assistant Works Manager at Messrs Taylor and Sons Ltd. (*Thomas Edward Taylor opened the first linen factory in Barnsley in 1844, using James Locker's power loom. The factory no longer exists but Taylor Row is off Sheffield Road in Barnsley).*

Charles served as a Driver (Service Number: 200653) in the 'K' Battery of the 4th Brigade of the Royal Horse Artillery.* He died of Influenza Pneumonia in hospital in France on 7 November 1918, aged 23, just a few days before the war ended. (The First World War claimed about 16 million lives but the 'flu' pandemic that raged late 1918 killed 50 million people across the world, mostly previously healthy young adults. The movement of troops helped to spread the virus and soldiers were more susceptible because their immune systems were weakened by malnourishment, the stress of combat and chemical attacks).

Charles was engaged to be married to Sally (no other details known).

Charles was buried in Etaples Military Cemetery, Pas de Calais, France (grave XLIX D 8). His father had the words THE BELOVED SON OF WILLIAM AND MARY J STUART BARNSLEY ENGLAND added to the War Graves headstone.

Charles was awarded two medals: Victory and British War. His parents should have received the 'Dead Man's Penny' plaque and scroll from King George V.

Charles' name is on the Holgate Grammar School Memorial.

* **The 4th Brigade of The Royal Horse Artillery**
This was part of the 3rd Cavalry Division, which formed in September 1914 and went to France in October 1914. They participated in various battles up to the Battle of Loos in September 1915 but were not involved in any major engagements in 1916. In April 1917, they took part in the First Battle of the Scarpe and the attack on Monchy le Preux (Arras Offensive). In 1918, they participated in various Battles of the Somme: St Quentin, actions at the Somme crossings and Avre in Spring then Amiens (8–11 August), Cambrai (8–9 October, a phase of the Battles of the Hindenburg Line) and the Pursuit to the Selle (9–12 October). Charles died before the Final Advance in Flanders (9–11 November).

Three Drivers would manage a team of six horses to pull a gun on a two wheeled wagon or limber.

Alumnus – December 1918

C Stuart, Driver RHA (1908–11) son of Mr and Mrs Stuart, Peel Street, Barnsley, has died in France of Influenzal Pneumonia. Before enlisting he was Assistant Works Manager at Messrs Taylor and Sons Ltd.

Barnsley Chronicle – 16 November 1918

DEATHS

STUART November 7th at the 4th General Hospital, France, from pneumonia, Charles Stuart, RHA, aged 23 years, the dearly loved son of William N & Mary Stuart and beloved brother of William D (in hospital) and Mary Stuart, 39 Peel Street, Barnsley: also fiancee Sally.

The photograph of Charles is from Alumnus, *reproduced by kind permission of Barnsley Archives.*

Y 29, 1915.

PUBLIC NOTICES.

TERRITORIALS WANTED.

5th Batt. York & Lan. Regt.

300 MEN WANTED

to complete the Territorial Battalion of the above splendid Regiment.

Apply Drill Halls, Barnsley, Wath & Rotherham.

You saw the first draft ready to go abroad, which is being trained by me at Strensall, on their Recruiting March last week. They did you credit as neighbours, and are worth following as Pals.

Come early and be made as fit as they are to help those now fighting your battle abroad.

T. W. H. MITCHELL,
Colonel.
Commanding 2/5th Battalion, York and Lancaster Regiment.

996

63

James Stuart Swift

James Stuart Swift
1885–1916 (aged 30)

JAMES STUART SWIFT was born on 15 September 1885 in Barnsley to **James Swift** (born c1855 in Wombwell) and **Sarah nee Morton** (born c1851 in Sheffield). Stuart's Baptism was on 10 October 1885 at Barnsley St Mary's Church; his father was then a Bank Cashier. James became Bank Manager at the Midland Bank, formerly the London Joint Stock Bank, formerly the York City and County Banking Company Limited, in Market Hill, Barnsley, where he was well known and respected. According to his obituary in *Barnsley Chronicle* in 1931, James was a 'staunch churchman' being a warden for a number of years at St George's Church, where his funeral was held.

Stuart's older sister **Muriel Morton** was aged 30 when she got married on 7 December 1911 at St Mary's Church, Barnsley, to **Percy Guest Wadsworth** (35) Ironmonger (as was his father Thomas) of 16 Victoria Road, Barnsley. Witnesses were 'J Stuart Swift' and Percy's sister **S E [Sarah Elizabeth] Wadsworth**. They lived at Bella Vista in Penistone and did not have any children.

In April 1911, the Swift family lived in nine rooms at 2 Beech Grove, Barnsley, having previously lived at 13 Victoria Crescent, Barnsley, where Stuart was born, then Neath House, High Street, Silkstone. They had always employed a General Domestic Servant but in April 1911 there were also two Sick Nurses for their mother, who died soon after, aged 60.

Stuart went to a Private School until the age of 9, before attending the Holgate Grammar School in Church Street, Barnsley, for about three years, from 1895 until the end of 1898. He was admitted to Ackworth School of the Society of Friends, near Hemsworth, on 19 January 1899, aged 13, and left on 20 December 1901. As the family were not Quakers the annual boarding and tuition fee for Stuart was £45.*

According to the Ackworth School magazine, Stuart played a full and active role during his three years there, as one of 'the family'. At the age of 15, he wrote about Courtly Manners in the 15th Century and his scholarly, neat and stylishly handwritten essay is

Photograph of James Swift, senior, from Benjamin Turner's St George's Church, Barnsley - Retrospect 1821 to 1912

* The Honorary Archivist at Ackworth School generously checked their various records and allowed me to photograph information and their photographs of Stuart. She also sent me photographs of students laying poppy wreaths on Stuart's grave in remembrance of an Old Boy.

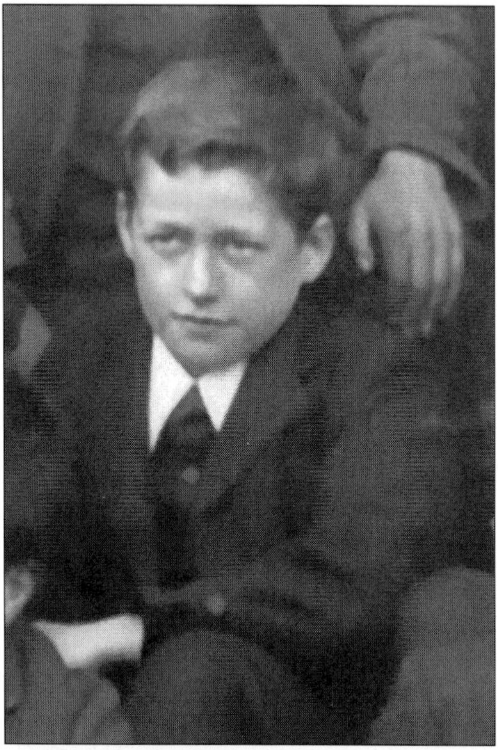

Stuart in official photographs of class groups in 1899 and 1901 (Ackworth School Archives). Frederick William Robinson's 3rd Class 25 April 1899. William Fletcher Nicholson Ba Boys 1st Class 22 April 1901 (middle of back row).

preserved in the bound volumes of the Essay Society which are kept in the main school library (extracts at the end of this Chapter). In October 1901, Stuart was on the executive committee of the Essay Society, which was a prestigious organisation within school, membership being by invitation and reserved for the brightest boys and girls; he also became Vice-President of the Debating Society, having led a debate 'Ought Competitive Examinations to be Continued?' in April 1900, and he was in the 2nd XI Football Team.

Stuart worked for the York City and County Banking Company Limited at their Wath on Dearne branch on leaving school until 1907, when he transferred to Barnsley branch, where his father was Bank Manager. (This bank, connected with the London Joint Stock and Midland Banks, subsequently became part of HSBC, but no records have survived there.* A letter dated 22 October 1907 from the Wath Manager to Stuart's father provides an unsolicited testimony for Stuart, who had needed little instruction to perform his duties since joining from school: 'He has been punctual & diligent – neat, tidy and methodical. Modest, respectful, considerate and thoughtful and observant… He has had excellent Reports and not a whit better than he deserves.'†

Stuart enlisted at the Corn Exchange in Sheffield on 11 September 1914 as a Private (Service Number: 1064) in the 12th Battalion (Sheffield Pals) of the York and Lancaster Regiment. He was a Bank Cashier, aged 28 years and 361 days, according to the Attestation form. The Medical Form contains a personal description of Stuart: Height: 5' 7 ¼", Weight: 123 lbs, Eyes: blue, Complexion: dark, Hair: light brown, Vision in both eyes: 6/6, Physical Development: good. His *Soldiers' Small Book* dated 5 February 1915 states: height: 5' 7½", Complexion: fair.

Stuart was promoted to Lance Corporal but reverted to Private at his own request some time after leaving England in December 1915. On 22 July 1915 he committed the offence of 'allowing a light in hut at 10.55pm' and was reprimanded. Stuart served in the Mediterranean from 10 December 1915, having sailed from Devonport to Alexandria, until 9 March 1916, when he was transferred to the British Expeditionary Force in France, serving in the 'D' Company of the 12th Sheffield City Battalion.

Stuart married **Alice Maude Watkinson** on 22 April 1915 by Licence at the British Church in Handsworth, Woodhouse, Sheffield district. Stuart (29) Soldier, was at Fulwood, Sheffield and Maude (22), the daughter of George Henry Watkinson, Engineer, was living in Woodhouse.

I only became aware early January 2016 of the large quantity of uncatalogued material in two boxes in Barnsley Archives relating to Stuart and his family. This includes one box of private letters, mainly written by Stuart to Maude from before they were married until June 1916; there is also an envelope filled with blonde hair but nothing

* Gertrude Zimmerman at HSBC Archives informed me that James S Swift was on the War Memorial to the 717 employees of the London Joint City & Midland Bank who lost their lives in the First World War. Unfortunately, no other records have survived.

† Swift collection in Barnsley Archives.

Wedding photograph from negative in Barnsley Archives.

Photograph of Stuart, his wife and baby son, used by kind permission of Barnsley Archives.

to identify whose it was. Another box contains memorabilia, such as Stuart's death plaque (but not medals), Birth and Marriage Certificates, photographs and various items belonging to his son. I obtained copies of the photographs, including some from negatives of Stuart and Maud's wedding day, and have used a few of these.

I was unable to read all of the letters but found one that must be the last letter that Stuart wrote; the letters are very personal love letters in which Stuart, solicitous of his wife's condition and circumstances, avoids writing about anything that might worry her. I have included some extracts, being sensitive to their intimacy.

Extracts from Stuart's Letters to his wife Maude

My Own Darling, I suppose you will have got my letters by now, saying that we are in France & I hope you are not worrying your dear self as I am quite safe here. … I can hardly realise that I shall be able to take you in my arms again & tell you how much I love you. We are, I believe, getting leave from here in turn and I think that if I explain my case I might get permission to come home very soon. … I got another letter from you last night but written a week ago & it is a beauty it is full of love & it did make me feel proud to know what a star of love there is waiting for me when I get back. I can't tell you how much I worship and adore you & shall never know any happiness again till I can be with you; you are all the world to me. … I have not quite got used to the thought of being a daddy. I shall not be able to realise it till I have seen our little babbie. It should be here in about a fortnight now. I wonder how old it will be when I see it … I still have a feeling sweetheart that we shall all soon be home again for good & that the war will be over very shortly.

All my great love to you my own wife, Your adoring hubby, Stuart xxxxx

Their son **James Stuart Morton Swift** was born on 27 March 1916 in Handsworth but tragically Stuart was not granted leave to visit his wife and son. Maude had the photograph taken of herself with their baby son to send to Stuart, but it seems that it did not arrive in time to give any comfort to Stuart in the trenches.

Saturday 1 April 1916

Poor little girl it is a shame to make you go through all you have suffered, it shows how much you love me to be willing to do it. I shall spend the rest of my life trying to make it up to you pet. How happy we shall be in the glorious days to come which I hope & believe will be before very long.

4 April 1916

I so long to see the little chap myself, everyone seems to think he is a fine specimen…. I am hoping to get my leave as you suggest early next month … I am glad you feel so much happier now I know you must have been very depressed just before baby was born, but he will make up for all that won't he?

18 April 1916

I am glad you are up & about again darling & I hope you are gaining strength every day, you must not let 'little Jim' take it all from you. …

I hope I shall be home for the christening, I am glad you are going to call him James but I don't know what other name to suggest, you have a favourite surely so I shall leave it to you & Father to decide. Moody* suggests Kitchener. What about Douglas & Kenneth?

It will be a year on Saturday since we were married pet!!! Muriel's birthday so she will remember it.

Give our little man a kiss for daddy…

6 June 1916

I am apt to lose sight of the fact that I am a father, you see I can't quite realise it yet till I have seen him.

And now darling you are not to worry your dear little head about me. I am all right & safe. We are at present in a very pretty village having quite a good time. We have band performances every evening …

13 June 1916

I am waiting for your account of the christening. I am glad you have not delayed it any longer – 'young Jim,' as he is called out here, seems to have taken Beech Grove by storm.

22 June 1916

It is nice to think of our little love being of such a happy disposition & I am glad he has such winning ways. I can see he takes after his little mother in those respects.

27 June 1916 – Stuart's last letter to Maude

My Own Darling, I am eagerly looking forwards to getting your next letter as I expect to get the promised photo you are sending of your dear self & our little darling. Of course I have tried to picture him to myself but have no idea what he is like. I also want to see what you yourself are like & whether you have altered during all these months. …

I do long for the time darling when I can come home & join you & I feel that we shall not have long to wait now so keep bright & cheerful sweetheart; we shall soon have our long delayed honeymoon.

I may be home on leave in a week or two & if not I don't suppose it will be long before the war is over.

* Stuart's pal Frank Moody died 31 October 1918, aged 30, in Italy serving as Lance Corporal (12/996) with 9th (Service) Battalion York & Lancaster Regiment.

I do so love you my own wifie. I think of you every minute of the day & night & it makes me thrill when I think of the time when I can fold you in my arms again & tell you how much I do love you. I shall want you to tell me all that has happened whilst I have been away & I shall never tire of listening to your dear sweet voice. I shall want petting & making a fuss of & I am afraid you will spoil me.

I wonder if you realise darling what you are to me how I worship you & what the thought of your being mine has meant to me all these months. You have been my guiding star all the time & the thought of what is in store for us has cheered me up many a time & made me feel much happier but at the same time very impatient at being kept so long waiting. …

No more this time Darling. Give my love to Muriel & Percy. Thank you for the note received all right.

All my fondest adoring love to you my own precious darling. Always your own hubby & lover Stuart

⊗* (A Kiss for you pet)

Stuart had taken part in an overnight patrol or raid on 26/27 June, during which several men were severely wounded. When he wrote to Maude he knew of the imminent assault on Serre as part of the Big Push and, while there was a general feeling of confidence about the outcome, Stuart must have been fully aware of the risks.

Stuart was initially reported missing before it was confirmed that he had been killed in action on the first day of the Somme, 1 July 1916, aged 30. He had served for one year and 295 days, of which 194 days were overseas. He was buried in Luke Copse British Cemetery, Puiseux, Pas de Calais, France (grave 18) with a simple wooden cross to mark his grave. His widow had the words REST IN PEACE added to the War Graves headstone. Maude had received a Separation Allowance while her husband was in the Army and, after he died, she was awarded 15/– per week Pension for herself and their son from 3 March 1917. (*The basic pay of a Private in WW1 was 1/– per day plus 1d per day when in a war zone*).

The Honorary Archivist at Ackworth School has taken groups of A' Level students out to the Somme each year and they visit Luke Copse Cemetery to pay tribute to Stuart, leaving a poppy posy and observing silent remembrance; on one occasion, three students, who were excellent singers, sang impromptu some of Jenkins' *Armed Man* at the graveside. 'The cemetery is very small and just about on the line of the front line trenches of the Sheffield Pals'.

Stuart was one of ten Old Boys who were killed in action on the first day of the Somme.

Stuart was awarded two medals: Victory and British War. His widow received the 'Dead Man's Penny' plaque and scroll from King George V; she received a letter on

* Stuart often kissed the paper and drew crosses around where his lips would have been.

14 November 1919 confirming that there were no personal effects to be forwarded to her; the medals were sent to her in 1921.

Alice Maude Swift got married again late 1918 in Sheffield to Arthur Vincent Bradbury (born c1890 Low Moor, Bradford), son of James Albert and Maud Elizabeth Bradbury. Arthur was a Fruit Merchant in Sheffield as his father had been; he served as a Private in the RAMC during the First World War, until discharged in March 1918 because of Exostosis, a condition since childhood where bone grows on bone causing chronic pain and weakness. Maude and Arthur had two children: **Joyce M Bradbury** in 1919 and **James A Bradbury** in 1921.

Photograph of Stuart junior, used by kind permission of Barnsley Archives.

Stuart Swift junior served as a Lieutenant in the Royal Navy in the Second World War. He married Rhoda Amelia Parker on 10 June 1950 in Torquay; she was a Hairdresser who later owned a Ladies' Gown Shop in Torquay, while Stuart was an Estate Agent; they died in Torquay in 1978 and 1983 respectively with no issue.

Stuart's name is on the Holgate Grammar School Memorial, Ackworth School Memorial, Sheffield Council Official Roll of Honour, Sheffield City Battalion Roll of Honour and the War Memorial in front of HSBC Group Head Office at 8 Canada Square, Canary Wharf.

Ackworth School was founded by John Fothergill in 1779 for The Religious Society of Friends – Quakers – boys and girls; the premises in Ackworth had originally been built in 1757 as a branch of Thomas Coram's Foundling Hospitals. There are 75 names on the carved oak War Memorial in Ackworth School hall, headed: 'TO ALL OLD SCHOLARS WHO FOLLOWED / THE CALL OF DUTY AND WHOSE EXAMPLE / WILL BE AN ABIDING INSPIRATION'. Many of the men became Conscientious Objectors, with about 200 serving in the Friends' Ambulance Unit and others working with refugees or going to prison for their beliefs. However, about 500 Old Boys joined the armed forces, including the navy, and they certainly lived up to their school motto: 'Non Sibi, Sed Omnibus' (Not for oneself, but for all).

The HSBC Memorial, which lists the names of the 717 employees of the London Joint City & Midland Bank who lost their lives in the First World War, was originally unveiled on Armistice Day in 1921 at the bank's Threadneedle Street branch, before moving to Leadenhall branch and then Canary Wharf in 2002, when a re-dedication service took place.

Connections

Stuart probably knew **George Gregory**, who was four years older, as they both worked for the same bank prior to enlistment.

Stuart served in the 12th Battalion (Sheffield Pals) of the York and Lancaster Regiment along with, **Edward Batley, Laurence Baylis, George Braham, Sidney Gill** and **Arthur Henry Thompson**. They were all killed in action on 1 July 1916.

Some Courtly Customs of the 15th Century by J S Swift, Aged 15 (Extracts)

The middle of the 15th Century saw the close of the old fashioned chivalry & many strange old world customs. ... The laws & regulations pertaining to the entertaining of people at that period gave many opportunities for distinguishing in minute particulars between persons of high & low ranks; in the position at table, the forms of speaking to one another, the decorations of a room or the length of a lady's train & the manner of carrying it. .... A nobleman was even known to wait bare-headed at table on his own daughter who had married a man of higher rank than himself & falling on his knee when he presented the basin & napkin to her before the meal. .... I am sure it would seem ridiculous now to see two people arguing in the street for three quarters of an hour as to whether they should ride or walk exactly side by side or whether one should walk two spaces behind the other. ...

Perhaps the queerest of these customs was the manner of showing grief for any near relative. In this province as in every country the chief mourning was done by the women probably because they had nothing better to do. On the death of a husband, father, brother or any other relative, a lady of the 15th Century was expected to take to her bed for a certain number of days or weeks, the length of the time being in proportion to the rank of the person & the relationship to the deceased.

Isabel of Bourbon, the first wife of Charles the Bold, after the death of her father, attended the funeral ceremonies & then retired to her bedroom, where she remained for 6 weeks, lying most of the time on her bed completely dressed, wearing a tall head dress & a large mantle trimmed with fur. The bed was covered with a white cloth, the walls were draped with black &, instead of a carpet, black cloth was spread on the floor. The queen of France after the death of her husband had to remain in her room for a year ...

> … when it came to fighting the men had their turn. Nowadays wars are managed badly enough, but in the 15th Century they weren't managed at all. Let us take for example a war that Philip of Burgundy entered into against Louis XI of France & see how it was carried on. … [The men] came without any weapons, baggage or food, these being more or less provided by the Duke … On the way [to France] the knights rode to the walls of various towns & challenged the people to come out & fight, not because they were at war but just for fun. … As nobody would oblige them, the ardent knights determined to hold a tournament amongst themselves … when the French army suddenly turned up. The Burgundians asked them f they would mind not fighting just then as it would spoil the fun of the tournament …. After the tournament was over they said they wanted to fight … the Frenchmen saw that they were greatly outnumbered & so they said they would not fight just then after all. …. The Burgundians marched to Paris, summoned the town to surrender, it refused … They held a debate as to whether they should return or not. Many said that they had done quite enough, as they had crossed two big rivers & had challenged everyone they had met. ….

The main photograph of Stuart is from Barnsley Archives, reproduced by their kind permission.

I am grateful to Julia Armstrong Reporter for Sheffield Star, *for devoting a page in the Retro section on 23 January 2016 to promoting my book and using Stuart's tragic story. This led to my meeting a relation of Stuart's, Peter Swift. He kindly lent me Benjamin Turner's book about St George's Church and Ralph Gibson & Paul Oldfield's* Sheffield City Battalion.

I was delighted to learn from Peter that his children were paying for him to visit the Somme for the centenary commemoration of 1 July for his 70th birthday; he will now be able to take Stuart a print of the photograph of Maude with their baby son.

64 and 65

Thompson Brothers (Arthur Henry and Cecil Cuthbert)

Arthur Henry Thompson
1894–1916 (aged 22)

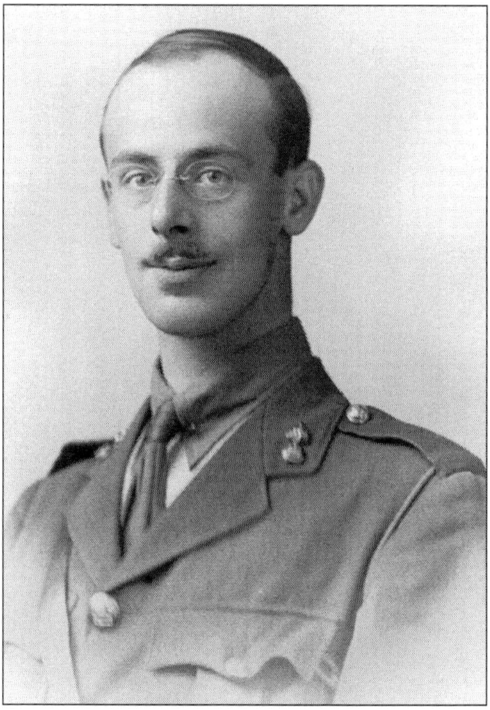

Cecil Cuthbert Thompson
1890–1916 (aged 25)

THOMPSON BROTHERS

Samuel Thompson (born c1866 in Carlton) and **Fanny Elizabeth nee Poppleton** (born c1866 in Worsbrough Dale) had three children: **CECIL CUTHBERT**, **Constance Priscilla** and **ARTHUR HENRY**. Samuel was an Assistant Superintendent of the Prudential Assurance Company, having formerly worked in various roles in a colliery.

In April 1911, the family lived in five rooms at 156 Hough Lane, Wombwell, having previously lived in Monk Bretton. They subsequently moved to 'Oakleigh' Westville Road, Barnsley. Fanny Elizabeth, died early 1924, aged 58.

Constance Priscilla Thompson (born in 1892, Baptism on 12 June 1892 at St Paul's Church in Monk Bretton, when her father was a Pit Corporal) was a Teaching Assistant at St Mary's Girls' School until she resigned in 1914. She married **Frank Bakel** on 27 April 1916 in St Mary's Parish Church, Barnsley. Frank was a friend of the Thompson brothers with whom he had attended the Holgate. Her father Samuel, Insurance Superintendent, was one of the Witnesses. *Barnsley Chronicle* had a description of the wedding (details in Part 2. Chapter 4). Constance lost both of her brothers soon afterwards and then her husband about a year later on 20 May 1917.

ARTHUR HENRY THOMPSON was born on 1 May 1894 in Monk Bretton; his Baptism was at St Paul's Church in Monk Bretton on 22 July 1894, when his father was a Colliery Hoodman. He went to Barnsley Elementary School until the age of 13. He then attended the Holgate Grammar School in Church Street, Barnsley for five years, from 1907 to 1912. Arthur was a Senior Locke Scholar for three years and passed the Oxford Local Senior exam with 3rd Class Honours.

'He became a Bank Clerk after leaving' and was working at the Doncaster branch of the Union of London and Smiths Bank when he enlisted.* *(The Union of London and Smiths Bank was a past constituent of The Royal Bank of Scotland Group).*

Arthur enlisted at Sheffield on 8 March 1915 as a Private (Service Number: 12/1363) in the 12th Battalion (Sheffield City) of the York and Lancaster Regiment. He was a Bank Clerk, aged 20 years and 10 months, living at West View, Outwood, Wakefield, according to the Attestation form. Arthur went to France on 10 March 1916, after serving in Egypt. He was reported missing for a period until it was confirmed he had been killed in action on the first day of the Somme, 1 July 1916, aged 22, after serving for one year and 116 days, of which 195 days were overseas. As his body was never found or identified Arthur's name is listed on the Thiepval Memorial, Somme, France (Pier and Face: 14A and 14B).

* Ruth Reed, Archives Manager for the Royal Bank of Scotland, who is responsible for the RBS Remembers website, confirmed that Arthur worked for the bank.

Arthur was one of ten Old Boys who were killed in action on the first day of the Somme.

The Medical Form contains a personal description of Arthur: Height: 5' 6½", Chest: 35", Scar on the left of his forehead.

Arthur was awarded two medals: Victory and British War. His parents should have received the 'Dead Man's Penny' plaque and scroll from King George V.

Arthur's name is on the Holgate Grammar School Memorial, Sheffield City Battalion Roll of Honour, the Institute of Bankers Roll of Honour Sheffield, for Gibson Hall National Provincial Bank War Memorial, the National Provincial Roll of Honour and RBS Remembers 1914–1918 website.

Cecil's widow Mary had the words: ALSO IN MEMORY OF HIS BROTHER 'JYM' AGE 20, MISSING 1ST JULY 1916 added to Cecil's War Graves headstone.

Connections

Arthur served in the 12th Battalion (Sheffield City) of the York and Lancaster Regiment along with, **Edward Batley, Laurence Baylis, George Braham, Sidney Gill** and **James Stuart Swift**. They were all killed in action on 1 July 1916.

***Barnsley Chronicle* – 9 September 1916**

MISSING

> Official intimation has been received by Mr and Mrs Thompson of West View, Outwood, near Wakefield, that their son, Pte Arthur H Thompson 1363 12th York and Lancaster Regiment (Sheffield Pals) has been missing since July 1st, and they would welcome any news concerning him. Mr and Mrs Thompson and family take this opportunity of thanking friends for their sympathetic letters regarding their son, Captain C C Thompson, who, as already announced in these columns, was killed in action.

The photograph of Arthur is from Alumnus, *reproduced by kind permission of Barnsley Archives.*

CECIL CUTHBERT THOMPSON was born on 16 October 1890 in Monk Bretton; his Baptism was at St Paul's Church in Monk Bretton on 28 December 1890, when his father was an Engine Plane Man. He went to St Mary's School, Barnsley, until the age of 13, then attended the Holgate Grammar School in Church Street,

Barnsley for four years, from 1904 to 1908, where he had been an Intending Pupil Teacher and a Bursar.

Cecil went to Reading University College from 1909 to 1912, where he joined the RUC Officers' Training Corps; he was a Students Union Council Member 1911–12, Athletic Club Football Captain and Cricket Deputy Captain 1911–12 and Shells Marshall 1911–12. ('Shells' was the name of the principal social club for men; the 'Marshalls' had to maintain order during the various activities, which seem to have involved smoking, drinking, dining and singing – there was a fairly light-hearted initiation ceremony). Cecil took a commission in the 4th Battalion of the Inniskilling Fusiliers in July 1912 and was admitted as Associate of the University of Reading in the same year.*

Cecil was appointed Geography Master at Handsworth Grammar School, Birmingham, by 1913, but I have been unable to obtain any information from Handsworth School Alumni to confirm details.

Cecil was elected a Fellow of the Geographical Society on 8 December 1913 and remained so until his death in 1916. The information on his certificate stated that he was Assistant Master at The Grammar School, Handsworth, Birmingham, where he was resident. He took a special course of instruction in geography for one year at University College, Reading and carried out some research work.†

Cecil contributed from the start to the new *Alumnus* magazine that began in April 1913, writing an article 'Weather Proverbs' then letters about his war experiences (Part 3. Chapter 11).

Cecil joined the Officer Training Corps Reserve before August 1914 and gained the War Office Certificates A and B. The London Gazette dated 12 July 1912 states: 'The under mentioned to be Second Lieutenant (on probation): Cadet Sergeant

Photograph of Cecil from *Alumnus*, reproduced by kind permission of Barnsley Archives.

* Guy Baxter, Archivist at the University of Reading Special Collections, checked records for me and Caroline Benson generously allowed me to use their photograph of Cecil, which is better quality than the one in *Alumnus*.

† Joy Wheeler, Assistant Picture Librarian at the Royal Geographical Society, sent me information from their records.

Cecil Cuthbert Thompson from the Reading University College Contingent Officers Training Corps'. When the war started, he joined as Lieutenant in the 2nd Battalion attached to the 4th Battalion of the Royal Inniskilling Fusiliers. Cecil went to France in October 1914 and served in the first battle of Ypres. He was wounded around 18 May 1915 – 'a graze along the shoulder by a piece of shell' – and this was reported in the *Daily Casualty Lists* on 25 May. Cecil was promoted to Captain in 1915 and, at the time of his death, was second in command of the battalion as acting Major.

Cecil married **Mary Ward** on 9 July 1915 in Oxford. 'Lieutenant Thompson, who has on many occasions contributed to the magazine, was wounded at the great battle of Festubert but is back again in the trenches fighting as bravely as ever. We heartily congratulate him on his recent marriage'.

In 1915 Cecil made an appeal to his old school for cigarettes for his men: 'The boys collected £3 10s 10d for Captain Thompson's Company Fund'. He sent thanks for the cigarettes: 'I'm sure that it will be of interest to the boys to know that many cigarettes were smoked while 2,000 howitzer shells passed over our heads, into a little village a few yards behind and that many were being smoked whilst the Germans made an unsuccessful attack on the regiment adjoining us on our left'.

Cecil was killed in action on 14 July 1916, aged 25, after serving in France for one year and nine months. He was buried in Ovillers Military Cemetery, Somme, France (grave VI F 5), reburied from the original location. According to the Commonwealth War Graves Commission website, his parents were still living in Wakefield and his widow Mary was at 18 Monmouth Road, Bayswater, London. Mary was at 9 Corsington Road, Westcliffe on Sea, Essex, when she requested that the words: ALSO IN MEMORY OF HIS BROTHER 'JYM' AGE 20, MISSING 1ST JULY 1916 added to her husband's War Graves headstone.

Probate was granted for Cecil in Wakefield on 10 November 1916 to his widow Mary: Effects: £316 9s 3d.

Cecil was awarded three medals: 1914–15 Star, Victory and British War. His widow, Mary Thompson of 18 Monmouth Road, Bayswater, London W2, ought to have received the 'Dead Man's Penny' plaque and scroll from King George V.

Cecil's name is on the Holgate Grammar School Memorial, the painted column in St Mary's Church, Barnsley, the ornate bronze War Memorial Plaque in the Memorial Clock Tower at Reading University College and their Memorial Book, which has more details and a photograph (both are also on the internet). He is also included in the Books of Remembrance in Birmingham's Hall of Memory and in Ireland's Memorial Records 1914–1918.

The Royal Geographical Society did not have a Roll of Honour or War Memorial for its members, although many discussions took place and some names were recorded for the first two years of the War in their Journal in December 1915 but it was not comprehensive (RGS).

Alumnus – April 1915

Lieut C Thompson, who returned on a four days leave after months in the firing line, visited the School one day in February. The story of his experience in the trenches brought home to our minds with greater force than ever the horrors of this cruel and pitiless war.

Barnsley Chronicle – 22 May 1915

PATRIOTIC PARS: News has reached Barnsley that Lieut C C Thompson of the Royal Inniskilling Fusiliers has been reported wounded. Lt Cecil Cuthbert Thompson was educated at St Mary's and the Barnsley Grammar School. He was a student teacher at St Mary's before proceeding to Reading University College where he spent three years. While at College he joined the Officer Training Corps Reserve and on the completion of his military training was attached to the 2nd Battalion of the Inniskilling Fusiliers. His regiment was sent to France soon after the outbreak of war and Lt Thompson saw much service in mid winter in the trenches. He was granted a home leave of absence in February last when he visited Barnsley. He then looked very fit and expressed himself as much pleased with his life. His many friends hope that he is not severely wounded.

Alumnus – December 1916 (PHOTO)

Cecil Cuthbert Thompson FRGS held the rank of Captain in the Royal Inniskilling Fusilers. He first went to France in October 1914 and was in the firing line practically without intermission from that date until July 12th 1916, when he was last seen jumping over the German parapet. He had after joining thrown himself with characteristic energy and enthusiasm into his military duties, showing such quickness and readiness of resources, fearlessness and resoluteness in action that his progress was very rapid. Just three weeks before his death he had been made second in command of his battalion. Captain Thompson was a frequent contributor to the Magazine and readers will remember his many interesting letters from the Front.

Evening Despatch, West Midlands – 27 July 1916

HANDSWORTH OFFICER KILLED

Captain C C Thompson of the Inniskilling Fusiliers, who was a member of staff at Handsworth Grammar School, was killed in action on 14 July.

Captain Thompson was educated at Wakefield (sic) Grammar School and afterwards at Reading University College, where he was in the OTC and gained the War Office certificates, A & B, a distinction not easily earned. He was a fellow of the Royal Geographical Society and joined the staff of Handsworth Grammar School about four years ago.

At the time of the outbreak of war he was in the special reserve of officers and was called up to join his regiment, being drafted to France in October 1914, in time for the first battle of Ypres. After one of the advances last May he was made a Captain and at the time of his death was second in command of the battalion, holding the acting rank of Major.

***Barnsley Chronicle* – 29 July 1916**

THE TERRIBLE TOLL OF THE WAR
CAPTAIN C C THOMPSON FORMERLY A BARNSLEY SCHOLAR

Many Barnsley people hear with feelings of sorrow of the death in action on the 14th inst, of Captain C C Thompson, whose parents reside at West View, Outwood. The gallant captain, who was only 25 years of age, was gazetted as Second-Lieutenant from the Reading University O T C, in which he held the rank of sergeant, and he was made full Lieutenant in December 1914 in which month he was admitted as a member of the Royal Geographical Society. He was wounded in the battle of Festubert on May 15th 1915, and in June of the same year he was promoted to the rank of captain, whilst three weeks ago he was appointed second in command of his battalion. He was wounded in May last by a trench mortar, and was in hospital for a fortnight. Deceased was a young man of considerable promise. .... He was married on July 9th 1915, on his second leave home, and was home on his last leave for his only sister's wedding. Deceased's only brother, who is in the Sheffield Pals, has not been heard of since July 1st.

***Sheffield Evening Telegraph* – 28 July 1916**

AMONG THE FALLEN

Captain Cecil Cuthbert Thompson (25) formerly a Barnsley scholar, was educated at St Mary's School, the Barnsley Grammar School and subsequently at the University College, Reading. He was a master at a Birmingham Grammar School and was married a year ago. He died in action on July 14th.

***Birmingham Daily Post* – 28 July 1916**

MORE MIDLAND CASUALTIES
HANDSWORTH SCHOOLMASTER KILLED

> Captain Cecil Cuthbert Thompson of the Royal Inniskilling Fusiliers, who has been killed in action, was one of the masters at the Handsworth Grammar School. Before coming to Birmingham 5 or 6 years ago, he was a member of the Officers Training Corps at Reading and, when the war broke out, was in the special reserve of officers. He went out to the front early in the war and saw a good deal of fighting. In May last he was the senior officer of the battalion and shortly afterwards he received his captaincy. At the time of his death he was second in command and acting major.

The main photograph of Cecil was kindly provided by the University of Reading Special Collections, who generously agreed to waive their fee for use in this book.

66

James Edward Thompson

James Edward Thompson
1888–1917 (aged 29)

JAMES EDWARD THOMPSON was born on 30 June 1888 in Ardsley to **Henry Thompson** (born c1858 in Ardsley) and **Sarah Ann nee Brooke** (born c1862 in Ardsley). Henry was a Mechanical Engineer and Organist at the United Methodist Church in Stairfoot for many years.

James was the youngest of three surviving children: **Charles Henry** – Mechanical Engineer, and **Ada Mary**. One child had died before April 1911 (name unknown). Their father died at the end of 1899, aged 41.

By April 1911, the Thompson family had lived in four rooms at 5 Bridge Street, Stairfoot, Ardsley, for more than ten years. They had previously lived in Church Street, Ardsley, when their father was alive, with Sarah Ann's widowed grandfather, Joseph Wilkinson, Retired Shoe Maker, and her unmarried sister Annie, School Mistress.

Ada Mary Thompson got married in spring 1909 in Barnsley to **Benjamin Nicholls** or **Leonard Beardshall.**

Charles Henry Thompson, Mechanical Draughtsman, married **Betsie nee Brittain** in 1909 and they had one son **Cecil Brittain Thompson** in 1910; they lived in five rooms at 115 Summer Lane, Barnsley.

James attended the Holgate Grammar School in Church Street, Barnsley for two years from the age of 16, from 1904 to 1906. He was an Intending Pupil Teacher and went on to become a Teacher at Low Valley School then Assistant Master at the Senior Council Mixed School in Stairfoot. James was Scoutmaster for the local troop plus trustee and secretary for Ardsley United Methodist Church's Sunday School.

James enlisted on 19 March 1916 as a Private (Service Number: 242099) in the 1/5th Battalion of the York and Lancaster Regiment. He was killed in action by a sniper on 9 October 1917, aged 29, shortly before he was due to take some leave after a long period at the front. As his body was never found or identified James' name is listed on the Tyne Cot Memorial, West Vlaanderen, Belgium (Panel 125–128).

James was awarded two medals: Victory and British War. His widowed mother should have received the 'Dead Man's Penny' plaque and scroll from King George V.

James' name is on the Holgate Grammar School Memorial and the Ardsley United Methodist Church Roll of Honour and plaque, now in Christ Church, Ardsley.

He is remembered on the kerbstones around his parents' grave in Ardsley Cemetery:

HENRY THOMPSON
WHO DIED NOVEMBER 21ST 1899
AGED 41 YEARS
ALSO SARAH ANN THOMPSON
THE BELOVED WIFE OF THE AFOREMENTIONED
WHO DIED MARCH 27TH 1920
AGED 59 YEARS

ALSO THEIR DEARLY BELOVED SON
JAMES EDWARD THOMPSON
WHO WAS KILLED IN ACTION IN FRANCE
OCTR 9TH 1917 AGED 30 YEARS

WITH CHRIST WHICH IS FAR BETTER

Connections

James served in the 1/5th Battalion of the York and Lancaster Regiment along with **Harold Feasby** and **Arthur Heathcote.** James and Arthur were killed a fortnight apart.

James was a teacher at Ardsley Council School along with **Arthur Heathcote** and their deaths are included together in the article in *Barnsley Independent.*

Alumnus – December 1917

> J E Thompson, Y & L Regiment, of Stairfoot (1904–06) was a teacher at Ardsley. He was killed in October 1917, just when he had obtained leave to come home after a long period at the front.

Barnsley Independent – 10 November 1917

> ROLL OF HONOUR
> STAIRFOOT'S TOLL
> TWO TEACHERS FALL
>
> More Stairfoot men are amongst the latest list of those who have fallen. Private James E Thompson, 1/5 Y and L, who was a certificated assistant master at the Senior Mixed Council School, Stairfoot, and previous to which was at Low Valley School, was killed in action on October 9th. He was single, 26 years of age and the youngest son of Mrs Thompson and the late Mr Henry Thompson, Bridge Street, Stairfoot. He joined up on March 19th 1916 and was held in high esteem by both parents and scholars and by all with whom he came into contact. He was for some time scoutmaster for the local troop and also acted as secretary for the United Methodist Church, where his father was organist for many years.

***Barnsley Chronicle* – 24 November 1917**

STAIRFOOT TEACHER'S SACRIFICE
SHOT BY SNIPER

Lance-Corporal James Edward Thompson, Y and L (Territorials), youngest son of Mrs Thompson and the late Mr Henry Thompson, of Bridge Street, Stairfoot, has paid the supreme sacrifice, being killed by a sniper in France on October 9th,where he had served for 16 months and was expected home the same week, having gained his commission on the Field. Previous to joining H M Forces, the deceased soldier was an assistant master at the Ardsley Council Schools, also Scoutmaster to the 1st Troop of Stairfoot Boy Scouts of which he took a keen interest. From a boy he attended the Ardsley United Methodist Church, being a trustee and secretary of the Sunday School.

From the Officer Commanding C Co., York and Lancs. Regt., the following letter has been received: 'Dear Mrs Thompson, I am writing on behalf of the officers and men to offer to you and the relatives of Lance-Corporal Thompson our deepest sympathy in your loss, occasioned by his death. Your son, who was killed on the 9th inst., was shot by a sniper whilst carrying out his duties in the advance. His death was instantaneous and he suffered no pain. He was one of my oldest lads and was especially marked for his intelligence and tact in dealing with anything which came his way. He was a very capable, most reliable and conscientious NCO. He was buried on the battlefield by our own fellows. He always worked as a soldier and died as one. He will be missed by all for he was a general favourite amongst officers and men. I regret that I am unable to give you any further information as to where he fell'. Yours very sincerely, Francis E Allen, Second-Lieutenant.

The photograph of James is from Alumnus, *reproduced by kind permission of Barnsley Archives.*

67

Paul Edmund Timson

Paul Edmund Timson
1892–1917 (aged 25)

PAUL EDMUND TIMSON was born on 3 July 1892 in Bury St Edmunds, Suffolk, to **John Robert Timson** (born c1857 in Berkhamstead) and **Susanna nee Barker** (born c1851 in Hatfield). John was Head Teacher (BA) of the Royston Council Boys' School, and Susannah was an Assistant Teacher.

Paul was the youngest of four children: **John Barker, Noel Violet** and **Lilian Mary**.

In April 1911, the Timson family had lived in six rooms in School House, Midland Road, Royston, for over ten years since moving from Bury St Edmunds.

John Barker Timson (30) Managing Brewer, had got married about 1910 to **Annie Bessie** (24, born in Douglas) and they were living in seven rooms at 'Roystone', York Road, Douglas, Isle of Man, where they had a Domestic Servant.

Noel Violet Thompson died in 1941, aged 59, and was buried in Onchan, Isle of Man.

Lilian Mary Thompson (23) School Mistress, living at the School House, Royston, got married on 29 March 1910 at Royston Parish Church to **Frederick Henry Webster** (26) Grocer, of Midland Road, Royston; his father Joseph Webster was an Off Licence Grocer. There were four Witnesses including both of Lilian's parents. Lilian and Frederick had five children between 1911 and 1919: **Freda, Frederick, Joan, Joseph** and **Rosemary Webster**.

Paul went to Royston Elementary School until the age of 13. He then attended the Holgate Grammar School in Church Street, Barnsley for two years, from 1906 to 1908. He became a Colliery Officer and on the 1911 Census was 'Hanger-on Colliery Cage Underground'.

Paul enlisted on 12 September 1914 as a Private (Service Number: 17338) at Wakefield for the Yorkshire Light Infantry then transferred to the 'C' Company of the 10th Battalion of the York and Lancaster Regiment,* where he was promoted to Lance Sergeant (Service Number: 19711) then temporary Corporal. Paul went out to France on 10 September 1915 and he 'belonged to the machine gun section'; his rank was 'reduced misconduct' to Lance Sergeant, but there are no other details.

Paul was killed in action on 1 August 1917, aged 25, after serving at the Western Front for one year and 324 days. His name was on the *War Office Weekly Casualty List* on 3 September 1917. Paul was buried in Derry House Cemetery No. 2, West

* **10th (Service) Battalion of the York and Lancaster Regiment**
This formed at Pontefract in September 1914 as part of K3 (Kitchener's Third Army) and came under orders of 63rd Brigade in 21st Division. They went to France on 11 September 1915 and from 8 July 1916 transferred with Brigade to 37th Division.

They participated in the Battles of the Somme in 1916 at Albert in July then Ancre in November. In 1917, they took part in the Arras Offensive at the Battles of the Scarpe and Arleux in April then relocated to Ypres area for the Battle of Pilckem Ridge (Third Battle of Ypres) from 31 July to 2 August. The artillery bombardment started by 3.50am on 31 July in mist and semi-darkness; progress was slow as the weather deteriorated with heavy rain as well as determined counter attacks by the Germans. They held on to advanced positions over the next two days despite appalling conditions and ferocious fighting. Paul was killed in action on the second day at Pilckem Ridge.

Vlaanderen, Belgium (grave I C 3). His mother of The Bridge, Royston, had the words PEACE PERFECT PEACE added to the War Graves headstone.

Paul had made a Soldier's Will on 3 March 1917 and left 'the whole of my property and effects to my mother'.

Paul was awarded three medals: 1914–15 Star, Victory and British War. His parents should have received the 'Dead Man's Penny' plaque and scroll from King George V. His father died in 1920, aged 64, and his mother died in 1925, aged 74.

Paul's name is on the Holgate Grammar School Memorial and the Memorial in St John the Baptist churchyard in Royston.

Connection

Paul served in the 10th Battalion of the York and Lancaster Regiment along with **Charles Edward Savage.**

Alumnus – December 1917

> Sergeant P E Timson (1906–08) was the son of Mr J Timson, Headmaster of the Royston Council Boys' School. He belonged to the Machine Gun Section and was killed in August 1917.

Barnsley Chronicle – 19 September 1914 PATRIOTIC PARS

> Royston is well represented at the war. Mr Paul E Timson, youngest son of Mr John R Timson, BA, on Saturday last joined the forces of the KOYLI.

Barnsley Chronicle – 17 August 1917

> ROYSTON HEADMASTER'S LOSS
>
> Last weekend Mr John Timson, BA, Headmaster Royston Council Boys' School, received the sad news that his youngest son Sgt Paul E Timson had been killed in France. He belonged to the Machine Gun section and joined the colours at the commencement of war. He received his early education at the Royston Council Boys' School and afterwards attended the Barnsley Grammar School.

68

Alfred Utley

Alfred Utley
1899–1918 (aged 19)

ALFRED UTLEY was born on 22 March 1899 in Elsecar to **Harry Cecil Utley** (born c1869 in Elsecar) and **Mary Hannah nee Ashley** (born c1873 in Low Haugh, Rotherham). Harry was a Colliery Clerk/Cashier.

Alfred was the older of two sons. His brother **Harry** (born on 23 December 1914; died January 1992, aged 77, in the Barnsley area) got married in June 1938 in Barnsley to **Mary E Pullan**. They had two children in Wharfedale: **Molly C Utley** in Spring 1938 and **Kenneth Utley** in Summer 1942.

In April 1911, the Utley family lived in four rooms at 13 Skiers Hall, Elsecar, having previously being split between both parents' homes: Harry senior was with his parents, **David & Rose Utley**, at 2 Forge Lane, Elsecar; Mary & her son Alfred were with her parents, **Sam & Lucy Ashley**, at Cortworth Lane, Wentworth. They subsequently moved to Highfield House, Hoyland.

Alfred went to Elsecar Elementary School for five years until the age of 12. He then attended the Holgate Grammar School in Church Street, Barnsley for four years, from 1911 to 1915. Alfred was awarded a County Minor Scholarship for his school life.

Alfred left school to become a Bank Clerk and by the First World War he was working for the Sheffield Banking Company at its Sheffield branch.* [*This was a small bank that joined National Provincial in 1919 and subsequently became part of the Royal Bank of Scotland*].

Alfred enlisted at Barnsley as a Private in the West Yorkshire Regiment (Service Numbers: 107371 and 23717); he then transferred to Private (Service Number: 29455) in the 8th Battalion of the Border Regiment. He died as a result of 'concussion of a shell' while on duty in a trench on the front line on 10 April 1918, aged 19, but it seems that his body was either not recovered for burial or identification was subsequently lost as his name is listed on the Ploegsteert Memorial, near Ieper, Hainault, Belgium (Panel 6).

Alfred was one of the youngest of the Old Boys to die in the First World War; there were nine young men aged only 19.

Alfred was awarded two medals: Victory and British War. His parents should have received the 'Dead Man's Penny' plaque and scroll from King George V.

Alfred's name is on the Holgate Grammar School Memorial, the Hoyland War Memorial as 'A Uttley' and on the RBS Remembers 1914–1918 website.

He is remembered on his parents' unusual headstone in Hoyland Kirk Balk Cemetery:

* Ruth Reed, Archives Manager for the Royal Bank of Scotland, kindly confirmed which bank Alfred worked for. She is responsible for the RBS Remembers website providing details of 1 582 men, who worked for various banks amalgamated within RBS and died in the First World War. I was able to provide correct details for Alfred's inclusion on this website.

TREASURED
MEMORIES OF
MARY HANNAH
THE DEARLY LOVED WIFE OF
HARRY CECIL UTLEY
WHO DIED JANUARY 20TH 1936
AGED 63 YEARS

ALSO ALFRED UTLEY, SON OF THE ABOVE
KILLED IN ACTION IN FRANCE APRIL 10TH 1918, AGED 19 YEARS

MILTON'S PARADISE LOST
"GRACE WAS IN ALL THEIR STEPS, HEAVEN IN THEIR EYES!
IN EVERY GESTURE DIGNITY AND LOVE"

SPOHR'S LAST JUDGEMENT *(with the bars from the music)*
"BLEST ARE THE DEPARTED WHO IN THE LORD ARE SLEEPING"

MENDELSSOHN'S ELIJAH *(with the bars from the music)*
"O REST IN THE LORD"

ALSO THE ABOVE NAMED
HARRY CECIL UTLEY
WHO FELL ASLEEP
SEPTEMBER 24TH 1948
AGED 79 YEARS

RE-UNITED

Alumnus – December 1918

A Uttley [sic] (1911–15) Border Regiment, son of Mr and Mrs Utley of Highfield House, Hoyland, was killed on April 11th 1918 by a concussion of a shell. Before the war he was on the staff of Sheffield Banking Company, Barnsley. I quote from a letter written by a companion to his parents: 'On the morning of April 10th the Germans made their offensive and Alfred & I were on gas sentry together. We retired several times that day and at night slept in a ditch full of water. Next morning we were shelled out of it. We took another position and were then informed that the Germans were almost round us. Then we seemed to run for miles through streams etc with bullets flying between our legs and over our heads and from every direction. We at last reached a trench where we could take cover from the bullets and where we had a nice rest and enjoyed a smoke, although wet to the skin at the time. Then the Captain posted us in different places along the trench in groups of four or five, when suddenly the Germans put on a barrage all round us and all the while we were laughing and saying how lucky we were and the Captain telling us we were being relieved that night. We were only a few left but it put new life into us. I was in a group four or five yards lower down in the trench than Alfred, when suddenly there was a crash and I was knocked on my back. On getting up I saw all the trench knocked in on both sides where Alfred's group was, but Alfred was sitting in exactly the same position as before but he never spoke when I shouted to him. So I went up to him. He was quite dead but with not a wound to be found anywhere'.

***Sheffield Evening Telegraph*– 10 April 1919**

IN MEMORIAM

UTLEY – In loving memory of Pte Alfred Utley, 8th Border Regiment, reported missing April 10th 1918 and now presumed to have been killed on that date, aged 19 years, the dearly loved elder son of Mr and Mrs Harry C Utley of Highfield House, Hoyland.

Peter Marsden shared limited information from his Hoyland Memorial Book, available on his website, in Barnsley Archives or in Hoyland Library.

Brian Yarham sent me a photograph of the family headstone.

The photograph of Alfred is from Alumnus, *reproduced by kind permission of Barnsley Archives.*

69

George Harrington Gerald Warr

George Harrington Gerald Warr
1895–1918 (aged 23)

GEORGE HARRINGTON GERALD WARR was born on 29 July 1895 in Andover, Hampshire, to **George Moss Warr** (born c1861 in Crewkerne, Somerset) and **Mary Ann Beaumont nee Harrington** (born c1861 in Honiton, Devon). George (senior) was a Commercial Traveller, having previously owned a Drapery business.

Gerald had an older brother **Stanley** (served in the First World War).

In April 1911, the Warr family lived in eight rooms at 74 Sackville Street, Barnsley, having moved from 7 Longcar Lane. They had left Grantham in Lincolnshire between 1901–1907 and subsequently moved to 22 Bond Street, Barnsley.

Gerald went to a Private School in Southampton until the age of 11. He then attended the Holgate Grammar School in Church Street, Barnsley for four years, from 1907 to 1911. Gerald was a Locke Scholar and passed the Oxford Local Senior exam. 'He left to become apprenticed to a Colour Printer in Leeds'.

He enlisted at Leeds on 15 August 1914, aged 19, as a Private (Service Number: 407040) in the Royal Army Medical Corps and he went out to France on 30 October 1914 to work in No. 7 Casualty Clearing Station. He was a Designer (Adverts) for Alf Cook Limited of Leeds and lived at 3 Kingston Terrace, Leeds, according to the Attestation form. (*Alf Cooke Crown Point Printing Works in Hunslet Road, Leeds, were the largest printing works in the world in 1895; they went on to produce high quality playing cards and games in the 1920s).*

Gerald had two periods of leave: one week in September 1915 and one month from 20 August 1916; he was admitted to the Casualty Clearing Station for a fortnight in December 1915 with German Measles. On 25 August 1916 Gerald was registered as a qualified Operating Room Attendant, which led to a pay increase.

He died of Labar Pneumonia on 7 November 1918, aged 23, and it was 'Certified that the disease was contracted while on Active Service, and was aggravated by the conditions under which he was working at the time'. This was only a few days before the war ended. Gerald was buried in Ligny-St Flochel British Cemetery, Averdoingt, Pas de Calais, France (grave IV E 4). His father had the word CREDENCE added to the War Grave headstone.

Gerald was the first of the 76 Old Boys to enlist. He served for the longest period – a total of 4 years and 85 days – and spent the longest time in France – 4 years and 9 days. *Alumnus* magazine printed one of Gerald's letters (Part 3. Chapter 12).

The Medical Form contains personal information about Gerald: Height: 5' 6 ¾", Weight: 132 lbs, Chest: 35", Vision in both eyes: normal, Physical Development: fair.

Gerald was awarded three medals: 1914–15 Star, Victory and British War – but only after his father had written twice to the War Office to chase them up; on 8 February 1920 he wrote: 'I am again making an application for the 1914 medal and other medals due to my son (deceased) who joined the RAMC in August 1914 and went to France in 1914 – remaining at the front till Nov 7th 1918 when he died... I have written for the above before but have had no reply – why? Please give this attention – surely a man who gave his life for his country is worth the medals due. Yours truly George Warr'. His parents should have received the 'Dead Man's Penny' plaque and scroll from King George V.

On 11 April 1919 Gerald's father was sent his personal possessions, which included: letters, photos, pipe, soapbox, wristwatch, knife, scissors, shaving brush, hair brush, two razors, nail clippers, pencil case, cap badge, pocket case, money case, case & photos, purse, pouch, cigarette case, lighter, war savings book, packet of books (3). George had to chase up his son's War Savings Book, which contained '4 receipts value £15 6d each'.

Gerald's name is on the Holgate Grammar School Memorial and on the painted column in St Mary's Church, Barnsley.

Connection

Gerald's brother Stanley married Doris, the younger sister of **Ronald John Saville**.

Alumnus – December 1918

> Gerald Warr (1907–11) RAMC died in France of Influenzal Pneumonia on Nov 7th 1918. The Major of the Casualty Station writes: 'It has all come as a shock to us all. We can hardly realise it yet. He was one of the most popular boys in the unit, and I don't think he can ever have had a single enemy. He was my chief Theatre Orderly ever since I joined the unit 2½ years ago and during all that time I never had anything but loyal support and assistance from him, and we were equal friends rather than officer and man. I know I shall miss him most terribly. He was such a fine character that things always ran smoothly and discipline in the Theatre kept itself rather than my having to keep it'.
>
> From the Chaplain: 'I have only been with the unit six months but during that time I had got to know your son well and to know his value and how much all the men thought of him. It is indeed tragic that we should be carrying to his rest one who had been out the whole time just at the moment when emissaries were crossing to sign the armistice'. The place of burial is Leginy St Flockel

The photograph of Gerald is from Alumnus, *reproduced by kind permission of Barnsley Archives.*

STANLEY WARR (born 4 January 1891 in Andover, Hampshire) was an Engineer's Fitter, at April 1911, and one of three Boarders in Hunslet, Leeds.

Stanley enlisted on 21 June 1916, aged 25 years and six months, for the Canadian Overseas Expeditionary Force. He was Lieutenant (Service Number: 505453) and had previously served for four years as a Sergeant with the Yorkshire Dragoons Yeomanry.

His father, George Moss Warr, of 74 Sackville Street, Barnsley, was his Next of Kin. Personal information on the Attestation form: he was a Mechanic living at Lakelse Lake, British Columbia, Height: 5' 10½ ", Chest: 38", Complexion: Fair, Eyes: Brown, Hair: Brown, Distinguishing Marks: brown mark on each shin.

Stanley (30) Salesman of 22 Bond Road, Barnsley, got married at Edward the Confessor Church, Barnsley, on 5 June 1922 to **Doris Anna Saville** (31) of Acle House, Park Grove, Barnsley. George Moss Warr was a Salesman; Edward Saville was a Clerk. Witnesses were both fathers plus Stanley's mother Ann Beaumont Warr and Doris' older sister Hilda Mary Saville. (Doris was the sister of Old Boy **Ronald John Saville** (Part 2. Chapter 57)).

70

James Alec Wemyss

James Alec Wemyss
1897–1917 (aged 19)

JAMES ALEC WEMYSS was born on 19 November 1897 in Cawthorne to **James Charles Wemyss** (born in 1863 in Cawthorne) and **Florence Ann nee Moxon** (born c1868 in Cawthorne). The Baptism of James Aleck [sic] was on Christmas Day, 25 December 1897 at Cawthorne All Saints Church. James Charles Wemyss, whose Baptism had also been on Christmas Day in 1863 at Cawthorne All Saints Church, was a Private Secretary and Land Agent for the Cannon Hall estate. Alec's grandfather, Charles Wemyss, had also been Steward for the Spencer Stanhopes at Cannon Hall.

Alec had two older sisters: **Mabel Mary** and **Kathleen Isobel**. Their brother **Charles Walter** had died on 6 August 1894, aged seven months.

In April 1911, the Wemyss family lived in nine rooms at Tivy Dale in Cawthorne, where they had a Domestic Servant.

Mabel Mary Wemyss married **John Herbert Hinchcliffe**, Building Contractor/ Stone Merchant, in 1910 at Cawthorne All Saints Church; they lived in four rooms at The Quarry, Skelmanthorpe, in 1911 with their baby son **George H Hinchcliffe**.

Kathleen Isobel Wemyss married **William Tyne Barker** in 1923 at St Mary's Church, Barnsley; they had two sons: **William A W Barker** in 1923 and **James Wemyss Barker** in 1925. James became Land Agent of Fitzwilliam & Strickland Estates.

Alec went to Cawthorne Elementary School for six years until the age of 11. He then attended the Holgate Grammar School in Church Street then Shaw Lane, Barnsley for four years, from 1910 to 1914. 'He left for Wireless Telegraphy (School) Liverpool'.

Alec was a 'Marconi Operator in the Admiralty Transport Service', as was another Old Boy, A Hardcastle, and 'Wireless Operator on Transport Ship / Merchant Service'* according to *Alumnus*.

Charles Wemyss, Alec's Grandfather, reproduced by kind permission of Barry Jackson from his *History Of Cawthorne*.

* **Marconi, Wireless & Radio Operators**
Guglielmo Marconi, 1st Marquis of Marconi (1874 to 1937) was an Italian Inventor and Electrical Engineer, who was renowned for his pioneering work on long distance radio transmission, Marconi's Law and Radio or Wireless Telegraphy (eg. Morse Code).

The Senior Archivist at the Bodleian Library checked their Marconi Records and found some details for Alec in Staff Salary books but the Record Cards no longer exist: 'Name: Wemyss James Alec, Date joined: 5 Oct 1915, Died 10 July 1917'. The magazine *Wireless World* recorded the loss of Wireless Operators due to enemy action but Alec's death was not included as he died at home.*

There are some photographs of Marconi Schools, including an exterior and an interior view of the Liverpool School, on the Marconicalling website; these show what these schools would have looked like around the time that Alec attended. The Liverpool School is described as being in Seaforth and Waterloo, which are adjacent, so must be the same school.

Alec was suddenly taken ill in June 1917 and he died on 10 July 1917, aged 19, in the Royal Infirmary, Sheffield, of kidney problems ('Ureteral Calculus and Uraemia'). According to his Death Certificate, Alec was a Wireless Operator and his father was in attendance at his death. Alec was buried on 13 July 1917 in Cawthorne All Saints Churchyard, in the same grave as his grandparents – Charles Wemyss, who had died on 13 January 1891, aged 66, and Jane Wemyss, who died on 2 April 1898, aged 70 – and with his older brother, Charles Walter. The memorial inscriptions are on a red granite base with stone cross.

Alec was one of the youngest of the Old Boys to die in the First World War – there were nine young men aged only 19 years of age.

Alec's name is not included on the Commonwealth War Graves Commission database because he served in the Merchant Marines but did not die as a direct result of enemy action. Their rules for the Merchant Service are different from the Royal Navy or Army, where names are included whatever the cause of death provided that the person is still employed in the service at the time. I have been unable to find any detailed records at the National Archives to clarify Alec's role and service.

In 1901, Marconi's Wireless Telegraph Company opened the first wireless school in the world at Frinton in Essex. The school supplemented students' knowledge of engineering with the principles and practice of Marconi wireless. This school subsequently moved to Chelmsford to become Marconi College. A college at Liverpool also opened in 1901 that proved to be the main gateway for many years for Marconi operators serving on the Oceans of the world.

Wireless or Radio Operators were employed in the Royal Navy (Admiralty) and Merchant Navy from 1900; they also served in the Royal Engineers in the trenches. They performed an essential role of ensuring the safety of life at sea by providing the means by which ships could maintain emergency communications with each other and land based stations. Many of these Operators lost their lives in the First World War as they stayed in post in the Radio Room until the last moment before their ship went down.

* Michael Hughes, Archivist at the Bodleian Library, kindly provided me with background information and found records confirming Alec's service, reproduced here by kind permission of Oxford, Bodleian Library, MS. Marconi 2042.

Barry Jackson, President of Cawthorne Museum and an Old Boy of Barnsley Grammar School told me that Cynthia Hindley, related to the Wemyss family, still lived in Cawthorne. I am grateful to her for purchasing Alec's Death Certificate.

Alec does not appear to have been eligible for any war medals.

Alec's name is on the Holgate Grammar School Memorial but it was not included on the Cawthorne War Memorial and his grave was not designated as a war grave.

I wrote to Cawthorne Parish Council in January 2015, providing all the information I had found out, with a request for them to consider adding Alec's name to this Memorial. Unfortunately, they decided at their meeting on 12 March that they could not support having his name added to the Cawthorne War Memorial because he was not killed in action. I was pleased, however, that Barry Jackson used my research to include Alec in Cawthorne Jubilee Museum's special exhibition on the First and Second World Wars in 2015.

Connection

James Alec Wemyss was Baptised at All Saints Church, Cawthorne, 11 days after **Donald Stanley Laycock.**

Alumnus – December 1917

> J A Wemyss (1910–14) son of Mr J Wemyss of Cawthorne, was a wireless operator in the Merchant Service. He was in, June 1917, suddenly taken ill and died in hospital.

I have found no mention of Alec's death in Barnsley Chronicle, *but the next month a Public Notice was put in by James Charles Wemyss, Honorary Secretary.*

Barnsley Chronicle – 18 August 1917

> CAWTHORNE COTTAGERS' FLORAL, HORTICULTURAL AND AGRICULTURAL SOCIETY
>
> Owing to the continuance of the War, the Committee of the above Society have again decided to abandon the Annual Exhibition, which has usually been held in Cannon Hall Park on the first Saturday in September.

71

Thomas Westby

Thomas Westby
1895–1917 (aged 22)

THOMAS WESTBY was born on 24 August 1895 in Wath on Dearne to **Francis Waring Westby** (born c1869 in Thurlstone, Sheffield) and **Mary Jane nee Hellewell** (born c1866 in Ardsley). Thomas' Baptism was on 1 March 1896 at Wath upon Dearne Church. Francis was Colliery Manager at Old Silkstone Colliery and Church Lane Colliery.

Thomas was the oldest of three children: **Frank Hellewell** (attended the Holgate and served in the First World War) and **Katherine Josephine**.

In April 1911, the Westby family lived in nine rooms at White House in Dodworth, having moved from Methley. They employed a Domestic Servant. **Katherine Westby** married **Clifford H Lant** late 1924 in Birkenhead; they had one son **David Lant** in 1928.

Thomas went to Rothwell Church School until the age of 11. He then attended the Holgate Grammar School in Church Street, Barnsley for three years, from 1907 to 1910. He was a Bank Clerk at the Union of London and Smith's Bank. *(The Union of London & Smiths Bank Ltd. 1839–1918, established in London, was a past constituent of The Royal Bank of Scotland Group).*

In December 1914, Thomas was part of a pierrot troupe fundraising for Belgian refugees, along with his brother and Old Boy **Harry Bambridge** (Part 2. Chapter 5).

Thomas, still working at the Bank in Barnsley and aged almost 20 years, enlisted at Lincoln's Inn, London, on 5 August 1915 as a Private (Service Number: 5397) in the Inns of Court Officer Training Corps. He was discharged to a temporary commission as Second Lieutenant in the Royal Marines on 10 November 1915. Thomas was admitted to the Royal Navy hospital in Plymouth on 15 March 1916 for a month with an injury to his ankle. He completed a Musketry Course in Hayling on 31 July 1916 and was then transferred to the Machine Gun Corps on 7 September 1916, being promoted to Lieutenant on 10 November 1916. He was at the Base Depot in Camiers, France, on 31 January 1917, from where he was posted to the 190th Brigade of the Machine Gun Corps on 5 February 1917. He completed a Gas Course on 13 May 1917.

The Medical Form included some personal information about Thomas: Height: 5' 5", Weight: 128 lbs, Chest: 35", Vision in both eyes: 6/6, Physical Development: fair.

Thomas was awarded a Military Cross on 30 November 1917 in Belgium and it was reported in the *London Gazette* on 18 January 1918: 'Military Cross awarded for gallantry at Passchendaele on 26.10.1917 whilst in charge of four mobile machine guns, after making a reconnaissance under heavy fire, disposed them with such skill that he achieved his task with negligible casualties'. He was mentioned in Despatch of Field Marshall, Commander in Chief, the British Armies in France for gallant service and devotion to duty (*London Gazette* on 7 December 1917).

Thomas, a Lieutenant in the 190th Brigade Machine Gun Company of the Royal Marine Light Infantry, was killed in action on 30 December 1917, aged 22, after serving for 2 years and 148 days, almost two years of which were in France. He was buried in Metz-en-Couture Communal Cemetery British Extension, Pas de Calais, France (grave II E 2).

Probate was awarded for Thomas at Wakefield on 29 July 1918 to his father of Dodworth. Effects: £265 8s 1d.

Thomas was awarded two medals: Victory and British War, and his parents ought to have received the 'Dead Man's Penny' plaque and scroll from King George V. They had moved to 46 Elgin Drive, Wallasey, Cheshire.

Thomas' name is on the Holgate Grammar School Memorial and he is on the RBS (Royal Bank of Scotland) Remembers 1914–1918 website.

Connection

Thomas was a Bank Clerk at the Union of London and Smiths Bank Ltd at about the same time as **Ronald John Saville** and **Harry Liddall Bambridge** – a few years before **Frank Bakel**.

Barnsley Chronicle – 26 December 1914

DODWORTH BELGIAN FUNDS

If Dodworth, as described in the Council, is a disgrace so far as recruiting is concerned, it cannot be said it is otherwise than most enthusiastic as well as sympathetic so far as assistance for those who do join the colours and the suffering Belgians goes. This was clearly demonstrated last Thursday night by the hundreds who assembled in the Council School, Keresforth Road. The object was to augment the local distress fund as well as to arrange for the maintenance of the Belgian refugees in the two homes provided by the Rev. T T and Mrs Taylor. The programme was of a high class character. The pierrot troupe were highly successful, these comprising Mrs Peddle, Miss Amy Norton, Miss Ownsworth, Messrs H Bainbridge, T Westby, Peddle, F H Westby, J Holland and W Norton.

Alumnus – April 1918

Lieut T Westby, MC, (1907–10) Royal Naval Division, the eldest son of Mr and Mrs F W Westby, White House, Dodworth, was killed in action on Dec 30th 1917. He joined the Inns of Court OTC early in 1915. On receiving his commission in the MGC, RN, he proceeded to France in Jan 1916. He won the Military Cross for conspicuous gallantry in the battlefield, and was mentioned again in Sir Douglas Haig's Despatches. ...

***Barnsley Chronicle* – 12 January 1918**

A DODWORTH OFFICER KILLED

LIEUT T WESTBY MC: We deeply regret to announce the death in action of Lieutenant Thomas Westby .... the sad intelligence by a melancholy coincidence, following upon the official announcement that the dead officer had been awarded the Military Cross for bravery in the field. In the Barnsley and Dodworth districts where the family are so well known and highly esteemed, the profoundest sorrow has been expressed and the late officer's father, who is manager of the Old Silkstone Colliery (Church Lane pit) has received innumerable letters of sympathy from all parts. Lt Westby was in charge of a Machine Gun Corps attached to the Royal Naval Division, and, as appended communications from the front show, he died a hero at his post.

Lieutenant Westby before the war was on the staff of the Union of London and Smith's Bank, Church Street, Barnsley, but prior to that was in the service of the same Company at their Batley branch, and at both banks he had won the esteem of all his colleagues. He joined the Inns of Court Officers Training Corps in the early part of 1915 – when 20 years of age – and after quickly gaining a Commission he went to various training centres in England being finally drafted to the Machine Gun Corps at Grantham, departing to France just a year ago, where he was attached to the Royal Naval Division. Since then he has been in the thickest of the fighting on the Western Front, his last leave being in September last. On November 27th, on the occasion of a great advance, he was 'mentioned' in Sir Douglas Haig's dispatches, this being preceded by the winning of the Military Cross. This pleasing intelligence had barely become circulated amongst his friends at home when the sad news came along that the gallant officer had been killed on December 30th. Lt Westby was born at Wath-on-Dearne and had received his education at Rothwell (Leeds) and the Barnsley Grammar School.

Writing to the bereaved parents on December 31st, Lieutenant Lightbody said: 'Dear Mrs Westby – It is with the very greatest regret that I have to tell you of the death of your son Thomas. Yesterday morning (30th) at about 6.30 your son was standing by his guns directing their fire on an enemy attack when he was hit. I was at once informed and as soon as I heard I hurried to the spot but to my great regret on arriving at his gun positions I found that he had died shortly before. Everything possible had been done for him before I arrived, medical aid sent for, but it appears that he succumbed to his wounds shortly after being hit. His body has been removed behind the lines and will be quietly interred. I should wish to be present but owing to the present exigencies I do not think I shall be able. At any rate rest assured that all that can be done is being done. I may say that your son was loved by all officers, Non Commissioned Officers and men with whom he came into contact. It is a sad blow for Major McCreedy his OC, of whom you have doubtless heard, and it is a still greater loss to the

Company as a whole, which will miss his cheerful disposition and his frank and open manner. I may say that personally, although I have known your son for a comparatively short time, I have always regarded him as a personal friend and a splendid soldier. I cannot express how deeply I feel this terrible loss and my deepest sympathy goes out to you and your family'.

Major E R McCreedy wrote: "Dear Mr Westby – I cannot tell you how it grieves me to write to inform you of the death of your son Lieutenant T Westby, Royal Navy, who was killed in action on the morning of December 30th and was buried at ----- Cemetery at 2.45pm on the 1st inst by the Rev. H G South, Chaplain of the Bedfords, in the presence of us all. I cannot tell you my feelings towards your son. I have known him for a very long time – first at Plymouth then Tavistock and for nearly 12 months out here. A few weeks ago he won the Military Cross at Passchendaele, more recently he was 'mentioned' and there is no doubt that, if he had survived, he would have obtained many more honours. Your son was the bravest, most fearless and loveable fellow I have ever met, and I can assure you that is the opinion of every officer, NCO and man of the Company. We shall miss him terribly. To me he was a very dear friend. I cannot hope to console you or those he leaves behind, but I trust that it may be some consolation for you to know that he died a death any soldier would choose and for the great cause, which he and I believe to be just. Again I offer you my deepest and heartfelt sympathy'.

(Similar article, with photo, in *Barnsley Independent* – 12 January 1918; mentioned in *Yorkshire Evening Post* – 12 January 1918).

The main photograph of Thomas is from Alumnus, *reproduced by kind permission of Barnsley Archives.*

FRANK HELLEWELL WESTBY_(born 31 October 1896 in Wath on Dearne) went to Rothwell Church School until the age of 10, when he attended the Holgate for four years from 1907 to 1911. After this he was 'stated to be travelling abroad'. *Alumnus* printed a letter from Frank (Part 3. Chapter 13).

Frank enlisted in the 12th Battalion (Sheffield City) of the York and Lancaster Regiment and was promoted to Second Lieutenant. He was taken Prisoner of War on 26 March 1918 and was repatriated on 10 December 1919. Frank's Medal Card states 'Exonerated Officers List/29' with no explanation. Frank died in Kent in 1970, aged 73.

***Barnsley Chronicle* – 13 April 1918**

Lieutenant F W Westby of Dodworth is officially posted as missing from March 26th last. He is a son of Mr F W Westby, manager of the Church Lane Colliery, and of Mrs Westby, White House, Dodworth,who have already lost one son in the war. Hope is expressed that the missing officer may have been made a prisoner in the enemy's hands.

***Barnsley Chronicle* – 20 April 1918**

THE TOLL OF THE WAR
DODWORTH OFFICER A PRISONER

In last week's 'Chronicle' the announcement was made that Lieut Frank H Westby, Y and L, was missing. Later information to hand shows that he is unwounded and a prisoner of war. …

***Barnsley Independent* – 13 April 1918**

DODWORTH LIEUTENANT CAPTURED

Lieutenant Frank H Westby, York & Lancs, son of Mr & Mrs F W Westby of White House, Dodworth, reported missing from March 26th is now reported a prisoner and unwounded. His elder brother Lieutenant Thomas Westby MC fell in action last December.

(Similar article in *Yorkshire Post* & *Leeds Intelligencer* – 15 April 1918)

72

Charles Railton Whitelock

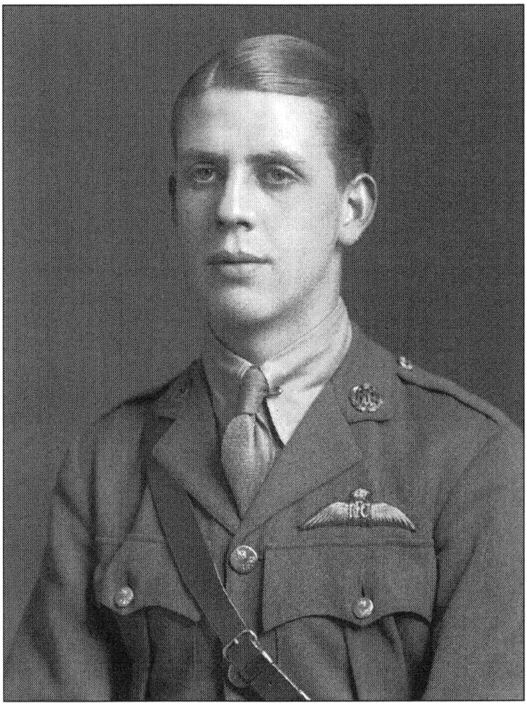

Charles Railton Whitelock
1898–1918 (aged 20)

CHARLES RAILTON WHITELOCK was born on 14 March 1898 in Barnsley to **Thomas Railton Whitelock** (born c1859 in Stokesley) and **Mary nee Kay** (born c1859 in Heslington). Thomas was a Head Teacher.

Charles was the youngest of three children: **Arthur Thomas** (attended the Holgate and served in the First World War) and **Agnes Mary**.

In April 1911, the Whitelock family lived in seven rooms at Oakdene, Mount Vernon Road, Barnsley, having previously lived in Sheffield Road. They employed a Domestic Servant.

Agnes Mary Whitelock (born 10 August 1889; died late 1989, aged 90, in York) was an Assistant Teacher in 1911.

Charles had private tuition until the age of 9. He then attended the Holgate Grammar School in Church Street then Shaw Lane, Barnsley for eight years, from 1907 to 1915. Charles was a Locke Scholar for three years and County Minor Scholar 'for school life'; he passed the Northern Universities Matriculation exam in 1915. Charles was awarded a Cooper Scholarship for Further Education of £80 for three years and a Governors' Exhibition of £250 for three years.

Charles went to Worcester College, Oxford University, in October 1916, matriculating on 19 October 1916 (subject unknown); he attended for Michaelmas term 1916 and Hilary term 1917.*

Charles enlisted on 25 May 1917, aged 19 years and 10 months, in the 55th Squadron of the Officers' Cadets Battalion of the Royal Flying Corps, and was promoted to Second Lieutenant in the Royal Air Force on 15 August 1917 then to Lieutenant in June 1918. He was killed when his

The photograph of Charles is from *Alumnus,* reproduced by kind permission of Barnsley Archives.

* Emma Goodrum, Archivist at Worcester College, University of Oxford, generously provided confirmation of the period that Charles attended Worcester College, the copies of letters from his father, details and photographs of the War Memorials plus a better photograph of Charles than that in *Alumnus.*

aeroplane overturned and crashed to earth while he was on a long distance raid on 16 July 1918, aged 20; he had served for one year and 44 days, of which 165 days were in France. He was buried in Charmes Military Cemetery, Essegney, Vosges, France (grave 1 A 9). His father had the words YEA HE DID FLY UPON THE WINGS OF THE WIND added to the War Graves headstone.

Alumnus printed extracts from some of Charles' letters (Part 3. Chapter 14). Charles' father wrote to Worcester College to inform them of his son's death and extracts from these are transcribed in this Chapter (CRW*).

Probate was granted for Charles of Oakdene at Wakefield on 3 January 1919 to his father, Schoolmaster. Effects: £88 8s 3d.

Charles should have been awarded two medals: Victory and British War, and his parents ought to have received the 'Dead Man's Penny' plaque and scroll from King George V.

Charles' name is on the Holgate Grammar School Memorial, the St Thomas' & St James' War Memorial in Worsbrough, the Oxford University Roll of Service for Worcester College and the Worcester College War Memorial, which is situated in the Main Quad to the right of the Chapel door with names listed by date of matriculation.

Extracts from two letters written by Thomas Railton Whitelock to Reverend Francis John Lys, Bursar of Worcester College, Oxford, in 1918 Regarding his son's death

> **28 July 1918** – I deeply regret having to inform you that my son, Charles Railton Whitelock, … was killed in action on July 16th 1918.
>
> He went out to France on Feb. 2nd as a member of the Independent Air Force, whose particular duty it is to carry out log distance bombing raids on the Rhine district of Germany. He has taken part in all the big daylight bombing operations since that date, & visited most of the towns in that district: Mainz, Coblentz, Saarbrucken, Offenburg, Karlsruhe, Metz, Thionville etc. His letters have always been bright & breezy and though the work was so exacting and dangerous, he treated the most difficult expeditions simply as a matter of course. ….
>
> His death is a heavy blow to us, for we had hoped he might survive the war and be able to resume his studies at Oxford but fate has decided otherwise. … We have the consolation of knowing that he had no prolonged suffering for his death was instantaneous ….
>
> **10 August 1918** – … we thank you most sincerely for your expression of sympathy in our sorrow and for your generous appreciation of his character. Had he survived the chances of war, I trust that he would have fully justified your good opinion. …

He obtained a Commission in the Royal Air Force in August 1917, and after a period of training at Tadcaster, Cramlington, Turnberry and Catterick, he went out to eastern France on Feb. 2nd 1918 … and from that date to his death on July 16th 1918 he was engaged almost daily in carrying out important raids over the German towns and munition areas in the Rhine district. …

I also enclose his photograph for printing in the supplement and shall be anxious to have a copy when it is completed. We feel particularly interested in Oxford's contribution to the forces for both our sons are Oxford men. ….

In the midst of our grief at the loss of the younger boy, we feel devoutly thankful that the elder has so far been spared to us and is at the present time in England.

Reproduced by kind permission of the Provost and Fellows of Worcester College, Oxford.

Alumnus – December 1918

Lieut C R Whitelock RAF (1907–16) was killed in action on July 16th 1918. On the morning of that day, two large formations were starting on a long distance raid into Germany with Lieut Whitelock as a deputy leader of the raid, when another machine crashed to earth in front of him. His observer says they appeared to be clearing it safely: but, suddenly their machine swung downwards, as if caught by the descending air current, and their under-carriage struck the top of the wrecked machine. Lieut Whitelock immediately regained control and continued his flight; but the collision had displaced one of the bombs, which exploded, blowing off all the left side and tail of his machine, and causing it to turn over and crash to the earth. He was killed instantaneously. Many letters of sympathy and appreciation have been received from his fellow officers.

His CO speaks of him as a fine young officer, and one of the best pilots in the Squadron. A fellow pilot who has since then been awarded the Distinguished Flying Cross and the Croix de Guerre writes: 'Charlie and I have been in many a tight corner together. On one occasion we were the only two to get back out of the whole formation, and several times our machines were absolutely riddled although we ourselves were untouched'. Lieut Whitelock took part in 31 long distance raids over German towns, factories and munition areas, including such places as Mainz, Coblenz, Mannheim, Thionville, Stuttgart, Offenburg etc. He is buried in the Military Cemetery at Charmes, about 15 miles south of Nancy, on the edge of a pine forest.

***Barnsley Chronicle* – 3 August 1918**

DEATH OF A BARNSLEY FLYING OFFICER
LT C R WHITELOCK

We regret to announce the death in action of Lieutenant Charles R Whitelock, Royal Air Force, the younger son of Mr and Mrs T R Whitelock of Mount Vernon Road, Barnsley. Lt Whitelock was 20 years of age and was educated at the Barnsley Grammar School, from which he took the Cooper Scholarship and Governors' Exhibition. He entered Worcester College, Oxford, in October 1916 and, after residing there for two terms, he joined the Officers' Cadet Battalion of the Royal Flying Corps and received his commission in August 1917. After a course of training on various types of aeroplanes, he was attached to the Independent Force of the RAF, which is engaged in long distance bombing raids over Germany. He proceeded to eastern France at the beginning of February 1918 and from that time he has taken part in many raids, bombing important areas and engaging in frequent air combat with the Hun machines. His death took place owing to the overturning and crashing to earth of his machine and his death must have been instantaneous, though his observer escaped serious injury. His Commanding Officer describes him as a fine young officer and one of the best pilots in the squadron. It is a consolation to know that he fell on our side of the lines and is laid to rest in a British cemetery.

***Barnsley Independent* – 3 August 1918**

BARNSLEY FLYING OFFICER
KILLED THROUGH MACHINE OVERTURNING

Lieut Charles Railton Whitelock, Royal Air Force, … has met with his death through his machine overturning whilst flying on the Western Front. Much regret is felt for the bereaved family.

… After a course of training on various types of aeroplanes he was attached to the Independent Force of the RAF, which is engaged in long distance bombing raids over Germany. He proceeded to Eastern France at the beginning of February 1918 and from that time he has taken part in many raids, bombing important areas and engaging in frequent air combats with the Hun machines. His death took place owing to the overturning and crashing to earth of his machine, and must have been instantaneous, though his observer escaped serious injury. …

De Ruvigny's Roll of Honour 1914–1924

CHARLES RAILTON WHITELOCK

Lieutenant Royal Air Force younger son of Thomas Railton Whitelock of Oakdene, Mount Vernon Road, Barnsley, BA, by his wife Mary daughter of Robert Kay of Heslington; .... Served with the Expeditionary Force in France from 2 February 1918 being appointed Pilot in the Independent Air Force engaged in carrying out long distance bombing raids in Germany and was killed in aerial action in Eastern France 16 July following. .... Lieutenant Whitelock took part in 31 long distance raids into Germany, including Maintz, Coblentz, Mannheim, Offenburg etc. Unmarried

The main photograph of Charles is reproduced here by the kind permission of the Provost and Fellows of Worcester College, Oxford. (Copyright)

ARTHUR THOMAS WHITELOCK (born 25 March 1888 in Barnsley) had private tuition until the age of 9, when he attended the Holgate for nine years from 1898 to 1907. Arthur won a Senior Locke Scholarship in July 1901 and passed the Oxford Local exam in Honours 1st Class (plus 'Responsions Pass') in July 1902, when he also won a Cooper Prize; he was awarded a County Major Scholarship and Governors' Exhibition of £50 for four years to support him at Jesus College, Oxford, where he obtained a BA Honours Degree in Classics and 'Lit Hum' (Literae Humaniores). He became a Classical Master.

Arthur was successful in many areas: 'prize winner in 'The King's' and 'St George's' competitions at Bisley in 1910, he was winner of the King's Cup at Oxford University Officers' Training Corps in 1911 and was Captain of the College Boat in 1911'. His 'success with the rifle is becoming phenomenal' and he won several prizes.

Arthur contributed several articles to *Alumnus*, including 'The Trough Of Bowland', 'Rudyard Kipling', 'Impressions Of Brooklands', 'Aerodrome No. 2' and 'A Visit to the Trenches' (Part 3. Chapter 14). He continued to write about his experiences in the RAF and Major Whitelock's detailed account 'A Voyage to India on a Troopship' begins in *Alumnus* July 1920.

***Alumnus* – Various**

A T Whitelock's success with the rifle is becoming phenomenal, as is shown by the following record of his accomplishments in the competitions promoted by the Yorkshire Rifle Association at Strenshall, May 12th and 13th 1913:

(1) Winner of the First Prize inYorkshire Territorial Forces Competition
(2) Winner of the First Prize Yorks. Rifle Club's Championship Cup and Badge
(3) Prize Winner in Marquis of Ripon's Competition
(4) Prize Winner Zetland Aggregate
(5) Prize Winner Ebor Competition

Arthur joined the C Company of the University and Public Schools Day Battalion of the Royal Fusiliers and became Sergeant. He joined the 5th Squadron of the Royal Flying Corps and was sent to France on 4 July 1915. Arthur was promoted to Second Lieutenant early 1915 then Major in December 1916. Aviator's Certificate 1263 dated 22 May 1915 was taken on a Maurice Farman Biplane at the Military School, Brooklands.

Lieut. A T Whitelock ... was then sent to Dartford to gain experience on the Vickers Armoured Aeroplane, which carries the latest type of machine gun with engines of 100 hp and which attains a speed of over 100 miles an hour. A few days before leaving Dartford Lieut. Whitelock was sent after the hostile seaplanes which attempted a raid on Harwich. On July 5th he was awarded his 'wings' – the higher military qualification – and directed to report himself at the War Office, where he received orders to proceed at once to France. He has contributed to this number a very striking article on his experiences.

Captain Whitelock (1900–6) is now in charge of large aerodrome in England for instruction and training of pilots and observers ... he recently 'had a miraculous escape from being killed. His machine fell to the ground from height of 150 feet but although injuries were such as to necessitate his removal to hospital he has now so far recovered as to be able to resume duties at the aerodrome'.

HONOUR FOR AN OLD BOY – In the New Year's List of Honours and Promotions for 1922, A T Whitelock (1898–1907) was gazetted Wing Commander in the Royal Air Force (a rank equivalent to Lieutenant Colonel in the Army). Colonel Whitelock is still attached to the staff at the Headquarters of the RAF in Ambala, India.

Old Boys will be pleased to hear of this advancement and the School feel proud that BGS boys can achieve success in all professions. The Editor is happy in being able to voice the general congratulations of Past and Present.

73

John Thomas Claude Wilby

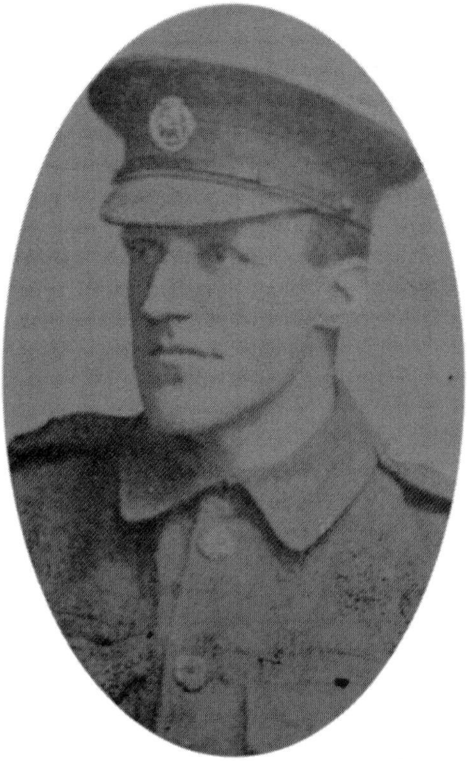

John Thomas Claude Wilby
1891–1918 (aged 26)

JOHN THOMAS CLAUDE WILBY was born on 5 November 1891 in Barnsley to **Joshua Wilby** (born c1856 in Barnsley) and **Charlotte Elizabeth nee Shaw** (born c1857 in Barnsley). John's Baptism was on 1 January 1892 at Barnsley St Mary's Church. Joshua was a Tailor, Hatter and Hosier Employer.

John was an only child.

After Joshua died on 28 May 1909, aged 53, Charlotte became Hosiery Dealer and Fancy Draper. Administration was granted for Joshua to his widow at Wakefield on 21 July 1922, more than 13 years after his death. Effects: £350.

In April 1911, John and his widowed mother lived in five rooms at 12 Wesley Street, Barnsley. The family had previously lived at 56 Doncaster Road, 18 Church Field and 14 St George's Road, Barnsley.

John went to Barnsley Wesleyan School until the age of 11. He then attended the Holgate Grammar School in Church Street, Barnsley for six years, from 1903 to 1909. John was a Senior Locke Scholar, Bursar and Student Teacher; he passed both the Oxford Local Junior and Senior exams with 3rd Class honours and became a Teacher.

John enlisted at Barnsley as a Private (Service Number: 21923) in the 1/4th (Hallamshire) Battalion of the York and Lancaster Regiment (JWYLR). John was wounded in the Battle of Pozieres, which took place between 23 July and 3 September 1916, and it was reported in the *Daily Casualty List* on 13 September 1916 and in *Barnsley Chronicle* on 23 September 1916. He was killed in action on 17 April 1918, aged 26, but as his body was never found or identified John's name is listed on the Tyne Cot Memorial, West Vlaanderen, Belgium (Panel 125 to 128).

John completed an Informal Will form on 26 May 1916:

> In the event of my death, I give the whole of my property and effects, including the lock up shop situate and being No. 6 Primrose Hill, Sheffield Road, Barnsley, and the house and shop situate and being in Market Place, Penistone, to my mother Mrs Charlotte Elizabeth Wilby, 12 Wesley Street, Barnsley, Yorkshire.

Probate was granted for John on 22 July 1922 at Wakefield to his mother. Effects: £399. This took over four years and was granted the day following the Administration of his long deceased father's estate.

John was awarded two medals: Victory and British War. His widowed mother should have received the 'Dead Man's Penny' plaque and scroll from King George V.

John's name is on the Holgate Grammar School Memorial and the Sheffield Road Baptist Church Memorial.

Connections

John was in the same Form as **Albert Edward Armitage**, **John Bruce Atha, Frank Bakel**, and **Ernest William Litherland**; they all won Cooper Prizes in 1907 for passing the Oxford Local Junior Exam.

. served in the 1st/4th Battalion of the York and Lancaster Regiment along . **Stewart Green**.

Alumnus – **July 1918**

J T C Wilby, York and Lancaster Regiment, fell in action May 1918. At the end of his school career he passed in Honours at the Oxford Senior Local Exam and later the Certificate Exam of the Board of Education and was appointed Assistant Master under the Barnsley Education Committee.

The 1/4th (Hallamshire) Battalion of the York and Lancaster Regiment

This formed in August 1914 in Sheffield and they went to France in April 1915, becoming part of 148th Brigade in 49th (West Riding) Division on 15 May 1915. They were involved in defence against the first Phosgene attack on 19 December 1915. In 1916 they participated in Battles of the Somme at Albert, Bazentin Ridge, Pozieres Ridge and Flers-Courcelette. In 1917 they took part in Operations on the Flanders Coast (Hush) and The Battle of Poelcapelle (Ypres). In 1918 they participated in the Battles of the Lys at Estaires, Messines, Bailleul and Kemmel Ridge, where John was killed in action on the first day.

The German high command had planned *Kaiserschlacht*, the 'Emperor's Battle', as a huge offensive against the British Army in two phases in 1918: Operation Michael on the Somme from 21 March then Operation Georgette, also called the Battles of the Lys, in French Flanders from 9 April. They took Bailleul but were halted at Kemmel Hill, failing to take Bethune, the centre of which they destroyed by incendiary bombs.

The photograph of John is from Alumnus, *reproduced by kind permission of Barnsley Archives.*

74

Melvin Clement Williamson

Melvin Clement Williamson
1897–1918 (aged 20)

MELVIN CLEMENT WILLIAMSON was born on 13 October 1897 in Stairfoot to **Arthur Carr Williamson** (born c1872 in Swinton) and **Martha nee Bird** (born c1873 in Darfield). Arthur was a Commission Agent for a Clothing Supply Company.

Melvin was the oldest of three sons: **Cyril Carr** (attended the Holgate and served in the First World War) and **Eric Victor.**

In April 1911, the Williamson family lived in six rooms at 13 Shaw Street, Barnsley, having previously lived in Grange Lane, Ardsley.

Eric Victor Williamson (30) married **Charlotte Beecroft** in 1931 and they had four children in Barnsley between 1932 and 1946: **Edna, Alan, Myra J** and **Edwin Williamson**.

Melvin attended the Holgate Grammar School in Church Street then Shaw Lane, Barnsley for five years from the age of 12, from 1910 to 1915. Details of his previous school are unknown. He was a Keresforth Scholar for three years, a Borough Continuation Scholar, Bursar and Student Teacher. Melvin passed the Oxford Local Senior exam (except Geography). He was then called up for Military Service.

Melvin enlisted at Barnsley and became a Gunner (Service Number: 185790) in the 'D' Battery of the 162nd Brigade of the Royal Field Artillery. He was killed in action on 2 May 1918, aged 20, and buried in Nine Elms British Cemetery, Poperinge, West Vlaanderen, Belgium (grave XI C 7).

His father had the words GREATER LOVE HATH NO MAN THAN THIS WHO LAYS DOWN HIS LIFE FOR HIS FRIENDS added to the War Graves headstone.

Melvin was awarded two medals: Victory and British War. His parents should have received the 'Dead Man's Penny' plaque and scroll from King George V.

Melvin's name is on the Holgate Grammar School Memorial and the Pitt Street Wesleyan Methodist Church Roll of Honour.

Melvin is also remembered on the 'kerbstones' around his parents' grave in Ardsley Cemetery:

MARTHA WIFE OF ARTHUR C WILLIAMSON
DIED 27TH NOV 1943, AGED 71 YEARS
ALSO THE AFOREMENTIONED
ARTHUR C WILLIAMSON
DIED JANY 19TH 1946, AGED 74 YEARS

ALSO MELVIN C WILLIAMSON
SON OF THE AFORESAID
KILLED IN ACTION IN FRANCE

Connections

Melvin's death was reported to the same Education Sub-Committee meeting, as reported in *Barnsley Chronicle*, as **Crossland Barraclough**.

Melvin's name is on the Pitt Street Wesleyan Methodist Church Roll of Honour along with his brother Cyril plus the three brothers **Harold Willott, Frank Willott** and **Ernest Willott**.

***Alumnus* – July 1918**

M C Williamson (1910–15) 1st Class Signaller RFA, the son of Mr A C Williamson of 33 Shaw Street, Barnsley, was killed in action on May 2nd 1918. Just two years ago he was a student at the school and, after he had passed the Oxford Senior Local Exam, with the ultimate view of entering a College for Teachers, he joined the forces. I quote from a letter received by Mrs Williamson: 'The only consolation I can offer is that his death was instantaneous. He was standing under a tin shelter just behind the battery. A German shrapnel shell burst low and the fuse tore through the protection and hit him on the head killing him instantly. I was his section officer and had more to do with him than any other officers in the battery and I feel his loss very keenly. He was a capable and willing worker and, for his share in this great battle, I had recommended him for a commission since I knew that was what he most desired'. (2nd Lieut R G G).

***Barnsley Chronicle* – 1 June 1918**

BARNSLEY EDUCATION MATTERS

At a meeting of the Teachers' Salaries and School Staffing Sub-Committee ... The Secretary reported the death in action of the following teachers: Mr Crossland Barraclough and Mr Melvin C Williamson, and was instructed to convey to the parents the Committee's deep sympathy with them in the sad loss they have sustained.

***Barnsley Chronicle* – 8 June 1918**

BARNSLEY & DISTRICT CASUALTIES
LOCAL HEROES OF THE WAR

Great sympathy is felt with Mr and Mrs A C Williamson of 33 Shaw Street, Barnsley, in the sad loss they have sustained by the death in action of their son Melvin C Williamson, 1st Class Signaller, Royal Field Artillery, on May 2nd. Mr and Mrs Williamson during the past week received the official notice. The deceased soldier was first educated at St Mary's School, Barnsley. On being awarded a Keresforth Scholarship, he became a student at the Barnsley

Grammar School from September 1910 to December 1916. At the end of his school career he passed the Oxford Senior Local Examination with a view ultimately of entering a college for the training of teachers.

The following is an extract of a letter received by Mrs Williamson … 'All the officers join with me in offering you our sympathies for your having lost so good a son and our having lost so good a soldier'.

Mr and Mrs Williamson's second son, Cyril Carr Williamson, is a Second-Lieutenant in the Royal Air Force.

The main photograph of Melvin is from Alumnus, *reproduced by kind permission of Barnsley Archives.*

CYRIL CARR WILLIAMSON_(born 22 September 1899 in Stairfoot) went to St Mary's School, Barnsley, for four years until the age of 13. He then attended the Holgate for five years in the Shaw Lane buildings from 1912 to 1917; he was awarded a County Minor Scholarship for his school life and passed the Oxford Local Senior exam. Cyril was called up into Military Service from school.

Cyril attested on 9 October 1917, aged 18 years and two months; he was a Student. He joined the Royal Air Force (Service Number: 100065) and graduated as Flight Cadet on 25 May 1918. Cyril was Commissioned as Temporary Second Lieutenant on 31 August 1918, in the London Gazette on 17 September 1918 (11096). The RAF Officer Record states his PI Number as 46231 with his father's address at 33 Shaw Street. Cyril was admitted to Queen Alexandria's Hospital, Dunkirk, on 18 October 1918, with no explanation, and discharged to rejoin the 217 Squadron on 28 October. On 2 November 1918, his plane was hit during a raid and crashed to the ground, throwing Cyril clear but killing his Observer; he describes his experiences that day in *Alumnus* (Part 3. Chapter 16). On 4 November, he was back in the Queen Alexandria Hospital with 'Pleurisy Severe', then transferred to the Central Military Hospital on 9 November 1918. An entry dated 28 February 1919 states 'for disposal ground duties only'. Cyril was demobilised on 7 March 1919 and transferred to the unemployed list the next day.

Cyril's name is on the Pitt Street Wesleyan Methodist Church Roll of Honour for serving in the war.

In 1935 Cyril was living at 10 Woodcock Dell Avenue, Harrow (Wembley-Kenton Polling District). He married **Mary G Austin**, who was 15 years younger, in summer 1937 in Hull. They had one daughter **Sheila Williamson** in 1942. Cyril died in 1946, aged 47, in Hendon, Middlesex.

PLEURISY is a condition in which the layer covering the lungs, called the pleura, becomes inflamed. It is sometimes called pleuritis. The most common symptom of pleurisy is a sharp chest pain that feels worse with breathing. Other symptoms include shortness of breath and a dry cough. Pleurisy is usually caused by another condition. In most cases it is the result of a viral infection (such as the flu) or a bacterial infection (such as pneumonia). In rarer cases, pleurisy can be caused by conditions such as a blood clot that blocks the flow of blood into the lungs (a pulmonary embolism) and lung cancer.

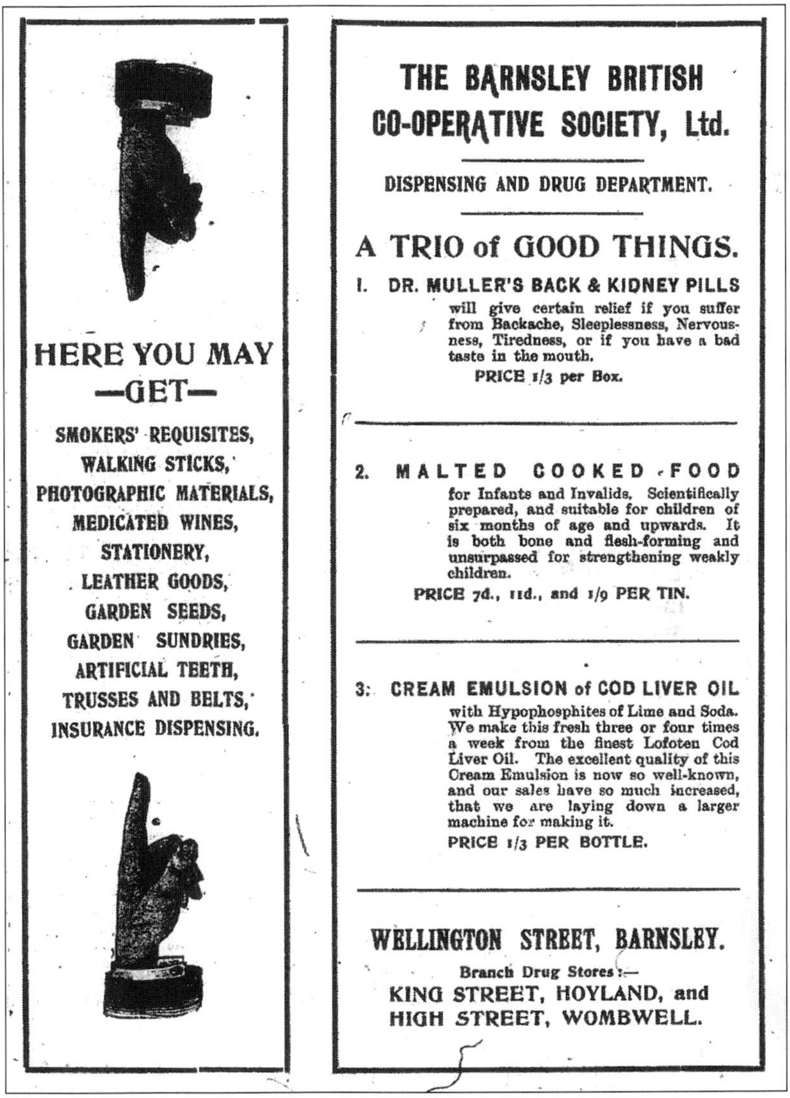
HERE YOU MAY
—GET—
SMOKERS' REQUISITES,
WALKING STICKS,
PHOTOGRAPHIC MATERIALS,
MEDICATED WINES,
STATIONERY,
LEATHER GOODS,
GARDEN SEEDS,
GARDEN SUNDRIES,
ARTIFICIAL TEETH,
TRUSSES AND BELTS,
INSURANCE DISPENSING.
THE BARNSLEY BRITISH
CO-OPERATIVE SOCIETY, Ltd.
DISPENSING AND DRUG DEPARTMENT.
A TRIO of GOOD THINGS.
1. DR. MULLER'S BACK & KIDNEY PILLS
will give certain relief if you suffer from Backache, Sleeplessness, Nervousness, Tiredness, or if you have a bad taste in the mouth.
PRICE 1/3 per Box.
2. MALTED COOKED FOOD
for Infants and Invalids. Scientifically prepared, and suitable for children of six months of age and upwards. It is both bone and flesh-forming and unsurpassed for strengthening weakly children.
PRICE 7d., 11d., and 1/9 PER TIN.
3. CREAM EMULSION of COD LIVER OIL
with Hypophosphites of Lime and Soda. We make this fresh three or four times a week from the finest Lofoten Cod Liver Oil. The excellent quality of this Cream Emulsion is now so well-known, and our sales have so much increased, that we are laying down a larger machine for making it.
PRICE 1/3 PER BOTTLE.
WELLINGTON STREET, BARNSLEY.
Branch Drug Stores:—
KING STREET, HOYLAND, and
HIGH STREET, WOMBWELL.

75

Harold Willott

Harold Willott
1890–1917 (aged 26)

HAROLD WILLOTT was born in 1890 in Macclesfield, Cheshire, to **John Willott** (born c1859 in Manchester) and **Emilia Mary Macbeth nee Tomlinson** (born c1859 in Wirksworth, Derbyshire). John Willott (BA London) was a Head Teacher at Barnsley Wesleyan School.

Emilia and John Willott, family photograph used by their kind permission.

Harold was the fourth of five surviving children: **Frank** (attended the Holgate and served in the First World War), **Edith, Ernest Spencer** (attended the Holgate and served in the First World War) and **Marion**. Their sister **Dora** had died in infancy in 1891. Marion died in Spring 1915, aged 21.

Edith Willott married **Percival Floyd** and emigrated to Tyabb, south of Melbourne, Victoria, Australia, where they owned a fruit farm; they had two children: **Charles** (who joined the Air Force and was killed in 1941 while training in the Second World War) and **Marion**.*

In April 1911, the Willott family had lived in eight rooms at 10 Hopwood Street, Barnsley, for at least ten years. They employed a Domestic Servant. By 1911, Harold was a Schoolmaster boarding with **Abel Roberts**, Schoolmaster, and his family in six rooms at 27 Norbury Street, Higher Broughton, Macclesfield.

Harold went to the Wesleyan School in Barnsley until the age of 12. He then attended the Holgate Grammar School in Church Street, Barnsley for six years, from 1902 to 1908, having won one of two Sykes Memorial Prizes for 'the highest unsuccessful candidates in the Junior Locke Scholarship examination' in July 1901, while at the Wesleyan School. Harold was awarded a County Minor Scholarship and passed

* Mary and Dominic Willott, Frank Willott's grandchildren, who live in Canada, were able to provide more information about the other members of Harold's family from research carried out by their uncle Harold and their father Geoffrey's reminiscences. Mary emailed me quite a few old family photos, some of which had handwriting on the back by Ernest and Frank.

Ernest, Harold and Frank c1912, family photograph used by their kind permission.

the Oxford Local Junior exam and Senior exam with 1st Class Honour, for which he won a Cooper prize in 1907. He did an Intermediate BA at London University then his teacher training at Westminster College, 1908–1910.

Harold made several contributions to *Alumnus* (Part 3. Chapter 17).

Harold had been a teacher at Southall Street Municipal School, Manchester, for four years, when he enlisted at the outbreak of war in Manchester. (This school closed some time ago and there are no records in Manchester Archives for the period that Harold was a teacher there; it is unlikely that there was a War Memorial at the school).

After being initially rejected, he underwent an eye operation and enlisted again as a Private (Service Number: 5966) in the 20th (Public Schools) Battalion of the Royal Fusiliers, before joining the 23rd Battalion of the Royal Fusiliers. He went to France on 14 November 1915 and was wounded twice late 1916; there is one report in the *Daily Casualty List* on 26 August 1916 with no details. Harold was killed in action, hit by a 'whizz bang' shell, on 28 January 1917, aged 27, after serving for one year and 67 days in France. He was buried in Courcelette British Cemetery, Somme, France (grave I D 16).

Harold's father had the words *VITAE PORTAM MORTE FORTI OCCUPAVIT* added to the War Graves headstone. The words are no doubt influenced by the Holgate motto: *Fortiter Occupa Portam* (bravely hold the gate), and I am grateful to Brooke Westcott for translating them for me: 'With a brave death he held the door to (eternal) life'.

Harold was awarded three medals: 1914–15 Star, Victory and British War. His parents should have received the 'Dead Man's Penny' plaque and scroll from King George V.

Harold's name is on the Holgate Grammar School Memorial, the painted column in St Mary's Church, Barnsley, the Pitt Street Wesleyan Methodist Church Roll of Honour for Supreme Sacrifice, the University of London War List and the Manchester Roll of Honour for Employers: Manchester Education Committee.

Connections

Harold was in the same form as **Arthur George Batley, Duncan Fairley** and **Henry Ryland Knowles.** They all won Cooper Prizes in 1907 for passing the Oxford Local Senior exam.

Harold played for the The First Eleven Cricket Team, which included **George Percival Cowburn** (who won a cricket bat prize for bowling), **Cyril Burton Dixon** (who won a cricket bat prize for batting), **Duncan Fairley** and his brother **Ernest Spencer Willott**. **Ernest Litherland** (who won a cricket bat prize for bowling) was Captain of the Second Eleven Cricket Team, which also comprised: **Edward Batley**, **George Braham** and (probably) **Herbert Harry Jagger Mason**.

Harold's name is on the Pitt Street Wesleyan Methodist Church Roll of Honour along with his brothers Frank and Ernest plus brothers **Melvin Williamson** and **Cyril Williamson**.

Barnsley Chronicle – 12 August 1916

LOCAL WESLEYANS WHO HAVE FALLEN

In current issue of the Barnsley Wesleyan Circuit Magazine appropriate reference is made to the local heroes who have played their part in the war and who formerly took an active part in church life ... wounded ... Harold, the youngest son of Mr and Mrs Willott.

Alumnus – April 1917

Harold Willott (1902 -8) Intermediate BA (London) on passing the Oxford Senior Local Examination, in First Class Honours, at the Grammar School, proceeded to Westminster College for his training as teacher, afterwards becoming a certificated teacher in Manchester. On the outbreak of war he immediately offered his services and though at first rejected he voluntarily underwent an eye operation to remove the slight impediment in the way of his facing the strain. For 16 months he had seen much active service at the front where he was twice wounded several months ago. He was killed when struck by 'whizz bang' shell while taking his machine gun into action and died almost immediately.

H Willott contributed to the pages of the Magazine some vividly descriptive accounts of war conditions prevailing on the Western Front.

Manchester Evening News – 13 February 1917

LATEST CASUALTIES
FALLEN FIGHTERS
MANCHESTER TEACHER KILLED

Pte HAROLD WILLOTT, Royal Fusiliers, was killed by a whizz bang shell on January 28. Pte Willott volunteered for service in September 1914, was rejected, but after undergoing a private operation was accepted for service in January 1915. After training he proceeded to France, where during the past sixteen months he saw much service, being twice wounded.

Prior to enlistment, he had been a teacher at Southall-street Municipal School, Manchester, for four years, under Manchester Education Committee. He was an Inter BA of London University and was trained at Westminster College, 1908–1910.

Mr Willott was extremely popular among the teachers and boys, by whom he will be greatly missed. He is the son of Mr and Mrs John Willott, BA, of Barnsley, both of whom were at one time well-known Manchester residents.

Barnsley Chronicle – 24 February 1917

KILLED AFTER BEING TWICE WOUNDED
PROMISING CAREER CUT SHORT
PRIVATE H WILLOTT, OF BARNSLEY, FALLS IN ACTION

We regret to record the death in action of Private Harold Willott, a son of Mr and Mrs Willott of 10 Hopwood Street, Barnsley. The sad news has been officially notified as having occurred in France on January 28th.

The deceased soldier was educated at the Barnsley Wesleyan School, of which his father was headmaster, and later, as the holder of County Scholarships at the Barnsley Grammar School. After passing through a course of training in a West Riding County Council School and at the Wesleyan Training College, Westminster, he served several years as certificated teacher in the Southall Street Council School, Manchester.

Under an overwhelming sense of duty to his country he offered himself for service soon after the outbreak of the war, and, though at first rejected, he voluntarily underwent an operation which it was considered might remove the slight impediment in the way of his facing the strain of active service. This being quite satisfactorily done, he joined the Public Schools Brigade, which was attached to the Royal Fusiliers.

During the past 16 months, Private Willott has seen much active work at the front, where he was twice wounded several months ago. While taking into action the machine gun of which he was in charge, he was struck by a 'whizz-bang' shell, and died almost instantaneously.

The deceased was very highly spoken of by his teachers and college tutors, who appreciated his upright and honourable character, as well as his brilliant intellectual gifts. At college he stood out as far beyond the general average of students in his knowledge of classics and of general literature and when he entered the army he was eagerly looking forward towards passing two months later final examination of the London University for an exceptionally good degree – the BA Honours in modern languages.

***Barnsley Independent* – 24 February 1917**

THE ROLL OF HONOUR BARNSLEY STUDENT'S SACRIFICE
KILLED BY A 'WHIZZ BANG'
BROTHER TEACHER'S PATRIOTISM
PRIVATE HAROLD WILLOTT

(*The same information is provided as in Barnsley Chronicle for the first 3 paragraphs*)
The deceased was very highly spoken of by his teachers and college tutors, who appreciated his upright and honourable character, as well as his intellectual gifts. At college he stood out as far beyond the general average of students in his knowledge of classics and general literature, and he had passed with distinction all the examinations for a good degree at the University of London (BA honours in modern languages) with the exception of the final which he intended to take in Oct. 1914 but unfortunately the outbreak of war interfered with his plans. [*Continued with news of his brother Ernest*].

The main photograph of Harold is from Alumnus, *reproduced by kind permission of Barnsley Archives.*

FRANK WILLOTT (born on 6 December 1884 in Macclesfield, died in 1966, aged 82) went to Barnsley Wesleyan school until the age of 12. He then attended the Holgate for five years, from 1897 to 1902; he passed the Oxford Local Senior exam in Honours 2nd Class in July 1902. Frank was awarded a County Major Scholarship and Governors' Exhibition to support him at Owens College, Manchester University. At the Distribution of Prizes on 30 July 1900, Frank (Form VI-V, Cooper Scholarship) won prizes for Latin, French, English, Maths and Drawing; in 1902 he won a Cooper Prize.

After obtaining his BSc, he taught for a short while at a Methodist School near Leeds, where he met **Marguerite Bishop** and married her in 1912. According to a postcard sent by Frank to Miss M Willott at Wakefield Girls' High School, he played in a football team around 1909–1910 and a photograph of the team is on the front.

Frank taught at Rutherford College in Newcastle upon Tyne, became Vice Principal at Whitley Bay in 1912 and was promoted to Principal at Monkseaton Grammar School, where he remained until retirement in 1950, when they moved to Heswall, in the Wirral Peninsula, Cheshire. (HW*)

Frank c1905, family photo used by their kind permission.

Frank served for three years (mostly around the Firth of Forth and at Scapa Flow) in the Royal Naval Volunteer Reserve (RNVR) as an Instructor promoted to Lieutenant. F Willott is listed on the Pitt Street Wesleyan Methodist Church Roll of Honour for Serving his Country.

Frank had two sons, who both served in the Second World War; **Geoffrey** served as a Lieutenant in the RNVR and **Harold** served in the Fleet Air Arm.

ERNEST SPENCER WILLOTT (born in July 1888, died in 1958, aged 70) went to Barnsley Wesleyan school until the age of 10. He then attended the Holgate for eight years, from 1898 to 1906; he was a Keresforth Scholar and a Locke Scholar and passed the Oxford Local Senior exam in Honours 3rd Class in July 1902 and the London Matriculation; he played in the First Eleven Cricket Team along with his brother Harold. Ernest was granted a County Free Studentship and Governors' Exhibition of £50 for three years to support him at Leeds University. At the Distribution of Prizes on 30 July 1900, Ernest (Form IV) won for Latin, French and Maths; in 1902, he won a Cooper Prize.

Ernest 'has had a wide and varied experience since he left Leeds University. He has taught in schools of all sorts and sizes in Westmoreland, Bedfordshire, Sussex, Belgium, New Zealand and

New South Wales and during an interval from teaching has tried his hand at sheep farming, bush-falling, road mending, acting as mounted constable, 'wharf-lumping' and even as a ship's stoker'. Ernest contributed a number of articles and letters to *Alumnus* (Part 3. Chapter 17).

Ernest's family have several photographs of him with his writing on the back and these are reproduced to illustrate his articles.

Ernest, family photo used by their kind permission.

Ernest enlisted on 19 August 1914 at Toowoomba, Queensland, for the Australian Imperial Force (AIF). On 16 May 1917, he was given a Commission as Lieutenant with the 11th Field Artillery Brigade (4th Division); he had previously served for one year with the 7th Reg. Infantry and for two years as Second Lieutenant with the Territorials in New Zealand. His father, John Willott of 59 Hopwood Street, Barnsley, was his Next of Kin. Personal information on the Attestation form: he was a Schoolmaster, Height: 5' 11", Weight: 12 stones, Chest: 36½", Complexion: Fair, Eyes: Blue, Hair: Fair. Ernest served in Gallipoli, where he spent time in hospital in Malta because of dysentery, before being sent to France. Late 1917, he was invalided home with Trench Fever. After being wounded by shell and gas in June 1918, he was invalided to England for two months before returning to his Regiment. Ernest received a Distinguished Service Order. E S Willott is listed on the Pitt Street Wesleyan Methodist Church Roll of Honour for Serving his Country.

Ernest was granted leave of absence with pay, subsistence allowance plus £20, from 25 January to 30 September 1919 to complete his BA degree at Leeds University. During this time he got married to **Fanny Hoyland** and *Alumnus* provided more details. After Fanny died, Ernest married **Kathleen Duff** in 1939.

***Barnsley Chronicle* – 24 February 1917**

A BROTHER SECURES A COMMISSION

While the sad news of Private Willott was on its way, news reached his family of the well-earned promotion to the rank of Lieutenant of his elder brother, Sergeant Ernest S Willott, of the Australian Artillery, now in France. He had held a commission in New Zealand soon after his emigrating there, but on his removing to Queensland shortly before the outbreak of the war, it was found that, not having lived for 6 months in the last-named colony, he was not eligible to hold a commission in the Australian Forces. However, determined not to be left behind when the first batches of volunteers started, he left his post, travelled hundreds of miles to intercept the transport vessels, and enlisted as a private in the Australian Light Horse. After serving some months in Egypt, he went through practically the whole of the Dardanelles Expedition and was invalided to Malta (suffering from enteritis) only a few days before the evacuation. Since joining the Australian Contingents training in this country he has been transferred to the Artillery, and it was not until he reached the final destination of his section in France, that he learned that he had been gazetted lieutenant ever since November last, without knowing it until a few days ago. Like his brother, Lieutenant Willott was also educated at the Barnsley Grammar School and subsequently passed through an advanced course at the Leeds University (BSc Honours Course in Chemistry). When the war broke out he was engaged in teaching in a Grammar School in Queensland.

(*Barnsley Independent* – 24 February 1917 provided almost the same details as above)

Alumnus – April 1917

E S Willott (left 1906) the elder brother of the late H Willott, has been promoted to the rank of Lieutenant of the Australian RFA. We heartily congratulate him on this highly deserved honour. The Magazine is greatly indebted to Lieut Willott for the exceedingly interesting articles he has on numerous occasions contributed to its pages on the ill-fated Gallipoli Expedition. Lieut Willott is now in France.

Alumnus – December 1917

Lieut E S Willott (left 1915) who was invalided home from the Western Front suffering with Trench Fever, has now recovered and has re-joined his unit.

Alumnus – 1919

An interesting wedding was celebrated on Saturday June 7th, at the Parish Church of Felkirk, near Barnsley, between Lieut Ernest S Willott, Australian Field Artillery, and Miss Fanny Hoyland, only daughter of Mr Ernest H Hoyland and Mrs Hoyland of South Heindley. The bridegroom, who is a son of Mr John Willott, BA, a well-known schoolmaster of Barnsley, was educated at The Holgate Grammar School, Barnsley (1898–1906) and at the University of Leeds where he took a prominent part in the social and athletic sides of University life.

The University of London's Special Collections Department kindly sent me links to the digitized War List for 'Appointed and Recognized Teachers, Graduates and Matriculated Students who have served or are serving in His Majesty's Forces 1914–1918' and the Roll of War Service for the University of London's Officer Training Corps published in 1921, which did not apply to Harold but provides a fascinating detailed history of an OTC from its establishment in 1909.

76

Charles Waldegrave Wood

Charles Waldegrave Wood
1883–1915 (aged 32)

CHARLES WALDEGRAVE WOOD was born on 2 March 1883 in Barnsley to **Joseph Matthias Wood** (born c1849 in Barnsley) and **Sarah Ann nee Horner** (born c1853 in Barnsley). Charles' Baptism was on 4 May 1883 at Barnsley St Mary's Parish Church. Joseph was a Bookkeeper for a Painter and Decorator, having previously been an Ironmonger then Colliery Clerk.

Charles was the fourth of seven children: **Robert John Fletcher** – Printer & Stationer, **William Alfred**, **Ethelwyn Mary Elizabeth**, **George Reginald** (attended the Holgate), **Helen Gertrude** and **Winifred Alice**.

In April 1911, the Wood family lived in six rooms at 70 Gawber Road, Barnsley, having previously been at 9 Hopwood Street and 14 Nelson Street, Barnsley – Charles, William and Ethelwyn were residing elsewhere. **Winifred Alice Hawke** (25) Widow, was there with her two young children: **Reginald Hawke** and **John Hawke;** Winifred Wood had married **John Hawke,** Butcher, on 15 June 1908 in Edward the Confessor Church, Barnsley, but John died in Spring 1910, aged 28.

William Alfred Wood, Groom / Coachman, married **Eliza nee Dixon** in 1903 at Darton All Saints Church. By 1911 he was 'Man Domestic Servant' (31) living in four rooms at 26 Palm Street, Barnsley, and they had three children: **Joseph Alfred** (6), **Charles William** (4) and **Elsie Gwendoline** (1).

Ethelwyn Wood (29) Hospital Nurse, who had previously worked as a Restaurant Waitress, was visiting **Henry and Hephzebah Lingard** in Theddlethorpe, Lincolnshire on the 1911 Census.

Helen Gertrude Wood (29), previously a Hospital Nurse, married on 21 April 1919 at St Mary's Church, Barnsley, **Frederick Henry Woodcock** (26) 'Optional Barowster Attendant' of Eccleshall; they had a daughter **Helen Woodstock** late 1920.

Charles went to the Wesleyan School in Barnsley until the age of 11. He then attended the Holgate Grammar School in Church Street, Barnsley for three years, from 1894 to 1897. Charles was a Keresforth Scholar. He went on to attend York St John's College, from 1903 to 1905.

In April 1911, 'Waldegrave Wood', Elementary Schoolmaster (Assistant) aged 28, was one of two Boarders at 131 High Street, Marske-by-Sea, between Redcar and Saltburn in North Yorkshire, with **Frances Mills** and her son; the 1911 Census form was signed by 'Chas W Wood'.

Charles enlisted at Durham as a Private (Service number; 2920) in the 1/8th (Territorial Force) Battalion of the Durham Light Infantry, which became part of the 50th (Northumbrian) Division. He was a teacher in Middlesborough. Charles went to France on 20 April 1915 and the Division had concentrated in the area of Steenvoorde, near Ypres, by 23 April, the day after the German Army had first used poison gas (chlorine) successfully at the Second Battle of Ypres. Charles was reported missing for about 11 months before it was confirmed that he had been killed in action on 26 April 1915, aged 32, just six days after arriving in France. As his body was never found or identified Charles' name is listed on the Ypres (Menin Gate) Memorial, West Vlaanderen, Belgium (Panel 36 and 38).

Charles was the first Old Boy to die and one of only three who died in 1915.

RCH 18, 1916. PRICE ONE PENNY

LOCAL SOLDIERS WHO HAVE FALLEN.

SAPPER L. WAKELIN (DARTON.)

PTE. V. SANDERSON (BARNSLEY.)

PTE. S. PRITCHARD (CUDWORTH.)

A BARNSLEY RECHABITE'S DEATH

ENGINEMAN AT PLATTS COMMON COLLIERY BEFORE THE WAR.

Official news is to hand of the death in action of Private Walter Emmott, 1st West Yorks Regiment, whose home was at 42, Longcar Street, Barnsley, where his wife and children reside.

The deceased soldier, whose photo appears in this issue, worked as an engineman at Platts Common Colliery prior to the war and he was a member of the Firemen's Union. Private Emmott was also an enthusiastic member of the Rechabites' Order. He was over on leave last October when his friends carried him shoulder high.

DODWORTH CORPORAL'S ADVENTURES.

A FALL INTO A SHELL HOLE.

Mr. and Mrs. W. Cosford, of Dodworth, have received an interesting letter from their son, Corporal W. G. Cosford, 9th N. Fusiliers, who is in a Convalescent Camp "Somewhere in France." Matters having been so lively in his region he had not been able to write earlier. "I counted over 600 dead whilst out getting in the wounded. In getting in rations after being without for 48 hours we had four knocked out. We had to run for our lives. It was then that I fell and hurt myself tripping and falling into a

PTE. C. W. WOOD (BARNSLEY.)

PTE. W. EMMOTT (BARNSLEY.)

Front page of *Barnsley Chronicle*, used by their kind permission.

Charles was awarded three medals: 1914–15 Star, Victory and British War. His parents should have received the 'Dead Man's Penny' plaque and scroll from King George V.

Charles' name is on the Holgate Grammar School Memorial, the painted column in St Mary's Church, Barnsley, and the Roll of Honour at St John's College in York. (The name Charles Wood was on the Oak Tablet that used to be in St John's Church, Barnsley).

Connections

Seven of the Old Boys qualified as Teachers after attending St John's College in York: **Crossland Barraclough** (B 1894), **Edward Batley** (B 1893), **Norman Bradley** (B 1891), **John Middleton Downend** (B 1888), **Arthur Heathcote** (B 1890), **Charles Edward Savage** (B 1893) and **Charles Waldegrave Wood** (B 1883). Several of them would have attended during the same period.

***Barnsley Chronicle* – 5 June 1915**

PATRIOTIC PARS

Private W Wood, son of Mr Wood of One Heights, Barnsley, is missing. Private Wood was attached to the Durham Light Infantry and prior to enlistment was a teacher in Middlesborough.

***Barnsley Chronicle* – 11 March 1916**

DEATHS

WOOD – In loving memory of Charles Waldegrave Wood, 1/8th Durham Light Infantry, son of Mr and Mrs J M Wood of Gawber Road, Barnsley, who was killed in Flanders April 26th 1915, aged 32 years. R I P.

***Barnsley Chronicle* – 18 March 1916**

LOCAL SOLDIERS WHO HAVE FALLEN PHOTOGRAPH OF PTE C W WOOD ON THE FRONT PAGE

Teeside Archives in Middlesborough checked their records but Charles' name is not listed on any Roll of Honour or Memorial there, ie the bronze panels at the back of the Middlesborough War Memorial Cenotaph, the Teesside War Graves Lists or the Teesside Service Deaths of the First World War.

The main photograph of Charles is from the front page of Barnsley Chronicle, *used by their kind permission.*

GEORGE REGINALD WOOD (born 12 August 1887 in Barnsley; Baptism on 28 October 1887 at St Mary's Parish Church, Barnsley, when his father was an Ironmonger of Sackville Street) attended the Holgate from 1898 to 1903 on a Cooper Scholarship. On the 1911 Census, he was Stockbroker's Clerk, Stock & Shaw Broking (aged 23) living with his parents at 70 Gawber Road, Barnsley. George Wood is a common name and I have been unable to find other records.

Part 3

Contributions to *Alumnus*

1

Poems by C S Butler, Headmaster

Some Folks Say That Barnsley's Black – Song 1889

Some Folks say that Barnsley's black,
Some folks do, Some folks do,
And of sunshine has great lack,
But that's not me nor you!

Chorus: Long live the merry Barnsley heart,
That tries by night and day
To do what he ought, and to care for nought
Except what the wise folks say.

Some Folks say that Barnsley's bleak,
Some folks do, Some folks do,
Perhaps poor things! Their lungs are weak,
But that's not me nor you!

Chorus

Some folks say the coal's worked out,
Some folks do, Some folks do,
Loss of trade they talk about,
But that's not me nor you!

Chorus

Some folks rail against the town,
Some folks do, Some folks do,
Seem to like to run it down,
But that's not me nor you!

Chorus

Some folks go to Grammar School,
Some folks do, Some folks do,
There they learn a nicer rule,
That's just like me and you!

Chorus

Some folks say it is not fit,
Some folks do, Some folks do,
Yorkshire's right eye so to hit,
That's just like me and you!

Chorus

Some folks say in prose or verse,
Some folks do, Some folks do,
They've seen many towns far worse,
That's just like me and you!

Chorus

Some folks say that folks who fret,
Some folks do, some folks do,
Never did the world good yet,
That's just like me and you!

Chorus

Some folks say the thoughtful mind,
Some folks do, some folks do,
Everywhere some good will find,
That's just like me and you!

Chorus

Some folk's say that Duty's Call,
Some folks do, some folks do,
Shews the best place for us all,
That's just like me and you!

Chorus

Football Song 1891

Come ye Holgate football-kickers,
All arrayed in snowy knickers,
And in gay and airy rayment, sashes yellow, jerseys blue!
Three times five the men of mettle
Matched with five times three to settle,
Which team shall travel homeward crowing – 'Cock-a-doodle-do!

Chorus: There you go – thud!
Sprawl in the mud!
Up again! Don't care a couple of pins!
Quick! At it! Kick at it! Oh!! My shins!
At it again! And the best team wins.

They've kicked off – the fun's beginning;
Towards your goal the ball is spinning,
The Non-descripts are after it – now spoil their little game!
Don't they wish that they may get it!
For the prompt half back has met it,
And punted it serenely to the place from which it came.

Chorus

Here is dribbling and here's passing,
Here is tackling too and grassing!
Here like a whirlwind o'er the field a charging champion goes!
Now they're squashing all together,
Now they're touching down the leather,
Or touching one another up with misdirected toes.

Chorus

Here is collaring and tugging,
There you see a runner hugging,
As if he loved it tenderly, that earth-bespattered ball;
Then with inconsistent ardour,
Takes and kicks it from him harder
Than his fickle heart embraced it as the dearest thing of all.

Chorus

Oh! The mauling and the grunting,
And the lively leather-hunting,
And the dodges of the wily and the bungles of the slow!
And the jeers that greet a blunder,
And the cheers that roar as thunder
When the battle rages fiercest, and the play is full of go!

Chorus

Oh! The tussles and the justles,
And the glow of limbs and muscles,
Though the wind is blowing chilly, and the clouds are dropping rain!
Better physics for the pupils
Of the Grammar School than blue pills,
For to make them eat their dinners, and to clear the muddled brain.

Chorus

Now this mimic toil and scrimmage
Is the very type and image
Of the field where men in earnest in life's battle meet and mix,
Strive to win, but help their neighbours,
Fewer triumphs find than labours,
And never find that halfpence are as numerous as kicks.

Chorus

Shall the Right be unprotected?
Shall the wrong go uncorrected?
Honour's goals are worth the winning, Duty calls to do and dare,
Till the Captain's voice commending,
Shall reward you at the ending:
'You have played it well and wisely, you have played it straight and fair'.

Chorus

*Mens Sana in Corpore Sano**
A Song of Cricket 1891

Enough of Grammar and of Exam.,
And books and sums and all:
Leave Learning's damps and study your stumps,
And work at bat and ball
It's well to train your power of brain
For manhood, while you can;
Yet what's your corpus given you for
But to complete the man?

Said our Great Duke: 'It was not a fluke
That won us Waterloo;
We'd learned the way in our Eton play
As men to dare and do.
We faced the shot, for we never forgot
Those lessons out of School
That gave us nerve from no ball to swerve
And heads in danger cool.

'We gained small store of the classics yore
Of Greek and Roman gods,
But learned to fight for our Home and Right,
Nor reckon up the odds;
To prove our pluck and to take our luck
In any sort of game,
To back our side with a British pride,
And leave to cowards, shame'.

Old boys too fat to bowl or to bat,
Old boys too slow to run
Will come to cheer young players, no fear,
And still enjoy the fun,
When Time their score shall increase no more,
Life's innings closed at last,
Remorse no sting to their Souls shall bring
From blameless playdays past,

* A healthy mind in a healthy body

But memories fair of the free fresh air,
Green field and sapphire sky,
Of comrades gone, of victories won
In happy rivalry,
Their hearts shall fill with a tender thrill
Of joys as pure as keen,
With after-glow from youth long ago
To light Life's evening scene.

The Quest of Wonderland 1907

So here we go through Blunderland!
Through Blunderland!
Through Blunderland!
With faltering feet and many a slip
On many paths we stray and trip,
Yet daily plant with firmer grip
Our footsteps on the rugged way
That leads through twilight to the day
Which grows not dark in Wonderland.

So here we go!
Heigh ho! Heigh ho!
We go plodding along through Blunderland
As we follow the Quest of Wonderland.

Young travellers through Blunderland
Through Blunderland!
Through Blunderland!
With magic spell does some fair isle
Mid purple seas your hearts beguile,
Where everlasting summers smile
And scenes more lovely to the view
Than once the golden ages knew,
Make far away a Wonderland?
So here we go! etc

Not so: but now in Blunderland,
In Blunderland!
In Blunderland!
Unfolding buds from hour to hour
Give promise of the perfect flower

Of Knowledge, bearing fruit in power
To find, not far beyond our ken,
But here amidst the lives of men
In England's realm, our Wonderland.
So here we go! etc

Oh! not in vain through Blunderland,
Through Blunderland!
Through Blunderland!
To seekers opes Life's deeper lore
And nobler thoughts take wings and soar
And Light and Truth dawn evermore;
Till the Mind's vision, clearest grown,
Sees Wisdom on her starry throne
Reveal the wide world's Wonderland.
So here we go! etc

The Old Boy Who Never Grew Old

Term by term, for work and play
Here he lived in Schoolboy way
Till to manhood's threshold brought
Wider visions winged his thought
Far through fancy's gates of gold
Wondering what the years might hold
For the boy I used to know
Just a year or two ago.

When the German war-cloud broke
When the voice of England spoke
Straight he answered 'Here am I!'
Scorned to whine the craven cry
'They must fetch me, if they can'
No, he chose to play the man!
That's the boy I used to know
Just a year or two ago.

As the billows sweep the main,
Surged our ranks across the plain
Where the bullets poured like hail,
And the boldest hearts might quail -
Foremost, as his comrades tell,

Cheering, fighting, till he fell,
Charged the man I used to know
Just a year or two ago.

Proudly for the son she gave
Lying in his unknown grave,
Proudly falls a mother's tear
For the young, the brave, the dear -
Dead that England might be great
In the crisis of her fate –
Dead the boy I used to know
Just a year or two ago.

Yet I deem there is a prize
Won by life's last sacrifice
Somewhere in a deathless clime
Sphered above the ills of time -
Light upon his pathway gleaming
Bright beyond his early dreaming
Lives the boy I used to know
Just a year or two ago.

Alumnus December 1915

The Man Who Wouldn't Fight

True valour claims not for her own
The deeds of warrior men alone,
But numbers with the brave
Unwarlike souls, in calmness strong,
That nobly roused to strife with wrong
Flame forth to dare or save.
Now let the praise of such be told,
The lamb who waxed a lion bold.

It was a Quaker, peaceful, prim,
Broad in the shoulders, stout of limb,
Who for his business or his ease
Was sailing through the Southern Seas.
A pirate-galley hove in sight,
The wind had failed, no hope of flight:
The Captain called upon his crew

To do or die: to arms they flew.
'Quaker, shew fight', the Skipper cried.
'I guess you'ld best throw fads aside;
Here take a cutlass or a gun,
Unless below you'ld rather run!'
'Friend Captain', quoth he, grave of face,
'Thy words do savour not of grace:
Here still upon the deck I'll stand,
Nor carnal weapon take in hand;
Methinks I may endure most freely all
Assaults of yonder sons of Belial'.

Close rowed the cut-throat band atrocious,
Up climbed the pirate chief ferocious -
Just as he stepped upon the ship
The Quaker caught him in his grip,
Told him in accents soft and clear:
'Friend thief, thou art not wanted here!'
Hurled him right back with swing terrific,
Then did that most astonished pirate
Spin round in empty air and gyrate
Till he plunged deep in the Pacific.
Four more alike he seized and flung
With gentle chidings of his tongue:
'Friend pirate, see thy pirate chief!
Thou art not wanted here, friend thief!'
Until the rogues, baulked of their prey,
Sheered off, and scuttled in dismay.

Up spoke the Captain (he was Yankee)
'Shake! Quaker, shake! For this I thank 'ee!
You are an innocent, you are!
I'd sooner face a grizzly bear!
You giv 'em fits, you wakened snakes!
And on this ship the cake you takes!'

Loud shouted all the sailor men:
'Ay! Ay! sir, that's the talk!' and then
They cheered that Quaker, peaceful, prim,
Broad in the shoulders, stout of limb,
Whose speech was soft, whose ways were slim,
Whose heart was mild, whose grip was grim!

Alumnus July 1916

After the War – The Old Boys Retrospect

There is no book so hard to read as boyhood's inmost heart,
And those who learn its secrets best know but a little part,
For only boy to boyish ears reveals in moments rare
What dearest thought in silence wrought, what young desires, are there.

Fond memory! Recall the hours, as Schooldays neared their end,
When we would talk, a merry group, or question, friend with friend;
What should we be, what should we see – in gay or graver tone -
In the great world all before us, in the great world all unknown.

As Time's new landscape opening out with wistful eyes we scanned,
This choice or that of manhood's work, of weal and worth, we planned,
Unlocked the guarded treasure house and for a comrade true,
Flashed forth to light like jewels bright our hopes for years in view.

But whether bold and venturesome we felt Ambition's goads,
Or well content to shun the heights we chose the lowlier roads,
Our path should be (so fancied we) till our allotted span,
By ordered ways in peaceful days, the homeland lot of man.

Thus did we dream in Academe what drama on the stage
Of this familiar English life should all our powers engage,
Nor thought amid more tragic scenes a sterner part to play
Than any of our fathers had, the boys of yesterday.

To arms! To arms! War's wild alarms! Hear ye the beaten drum?
Not dreams but deeds Old England needs! Come, sons of Freedom, come!
Away, the Day brooks no delay! Hear ye your Country's call?
Behold your post amid the host of Warriors one and all!

O you shall fight in Picardy and give a deathless name
To many a hamlet, many a stream and hill unknown to fame;
And you shall march where deserts parch beyond Euphrates' flow,
And you shall find Gallipoli a glory and a woe.

And you shall fly athwart the sky to battle in the air;
And you whatever Nelson's men have dared again shall dare,
Where perils Nelson never knew our guardian Fleets shall brave,
The death that crashes from aloft, or lurks beneath the wave.
On Afric shore where lions roar you gallantly shall go,
Through forest dense and fevered swamps to seek a ruthless foe;

And you where Israel dwelt of old, from Egypt's Eastern strand
Shall rout the Turk and bring new hope to Israel's hallowed land.

Ranged at your side in freemen's pride comes Canada to war,
From far Vancouver's forest glades to snows of Labrador:
And those young nations on whose isles the Southern Cross shines down
Shall rival in heroic deeds Britannia's old renown.

From Belgic strand to Switzerland the battle-line shall wind,
And Russia's ranks in patriot France their field of honour find:
And princely Chiefs of martial race their swarthy warriors bring,
True to their India's Emperor as Britain's to their King.

On Europe's hills allied with you the Stars and Stripes shall spread,
For Washington is not forgot, nor Lincoln's spirit dead -
Their flag unfurled from that New World, home of our kindred stock,
Who dwell between the Golden Gate and Plymouth's Pilgrim Rock.

Must Freedom yield when tyrants wield an ever-threatening sword?
Shall peaceful nations stand in awe of one ambitious lord?
And daily dread where next he springs to plunder and to slay,
What victim next is marked to be the tiger's hapless prey?

Nay! Rather, War! the mightiest war against the deadliest foe
That ever yet mankind has met or evermore shall know:
Four Continents shall clash in arms on every sea and shore,
And myriads fall where millions fight and a hundred battles roar.

Had thus some Seer with vision clear arisen to unroll
That page of youth's high destiny, our future's fateful scroll,
With what light heart, incredulous as all whom prophets warn,
We should have heard his boding word, what mirth and mingled scorn!

Yet haply might our brooding souls in meditative hour
Have yielded to the prophet's spell, and owned his mystic power,
And wondered with misgivings deep if we should prove our worth
In that grim strife with terrors rife, nor shame our British birth.

Old Boys! Old comrades in the War! we fought, we live to tell
How we were there where Freedom marched her recreant foes to quell:
No heroes' bays we claim, nor praise, but this we prize the most -
With hand and heart a Briton's part we bore – our manhood's boast.

Yet oh! not here those Schoolfriends dear, the fallen in the fray!
Peace be their rest, and with the Blest their Home, Eternal Day!
Never their memory grow dim! nor our affection cool
For the olden days, the golden days, when we were boys at School!

Alumnus July 1917

Waiting

Our hearts a-glow with gratitude are yearning
To greet you, victor-brethren, warriors staunch,
When, heralding the joys of your returning,
Blest Peace lifts o'er the world her olive-branch.

We wait, yet not those dear brave souls forgetting
Who in your ranks the ways of warfare trod, -
Not here! but where their Sun shall know no setting,
They wait for us, they wait for you, with God.

Alumnus December 1918

2

Maurice Bradley Parker Boyd

Royal Garrison Artillery in British East Africa – Extracts from Letters Home 1916 (*Alumnus* December 1916)

3 June 1916 – We were very disappointed on landing to find that we were not to proceed immediately to the scene of operations. We were still more disappointed when the seventh week found us within half a mile of the spot of disembarkation. By this time fully fifty per cent had paid a visit to the hospital with either malaria or dysentery, principally the latter. When at last we made a move it was to a much healthier spot within view of Kilimanjaro but still a considerable distance from the actual fighting.

9 August 1916 – Since writing the above I have spent the whole time in hospital. The left section of our battalion have had some really serious fighting. The principal hardship they had to undergo was shortage of supplies, a daily ration of mealie meal being the principal article of diet. Tobacco too was very scarce, as much as eight rupees (10/8 = *10 shillings and 8 pence*) being charged for a 2-oz bag of Boer tobacco, which in civilised parts cost 6d. One of the most noteworthy features of the company is the universal popularity of General Smuts. Other generals may be criticized and their methods condemned by the camp fires authorities but one and all have nothing but praise for General Smuts.

Impressions of German East Africa

It has occurred to me that perhaps a few impressions of the country, into which my duty took me during 1916, may be of some interest to the readers of *Alumnus* for the following two reasons: firstly that, as far as I am aware, no other ex Barnsley Grammar School men have been up there and, at any rate, if they were, none of them has so far written anything for the school magazine on that subject; and secondly because the country is so remote and so little known to the 'man in the street' that no doubt it has been hard for the majority to appreciate the difficulties, under which this minor campaign has been carried on. It is well nigh impossible for one, who has not been brought into contact with the conditions there, to realize the vastness of the country and its adaptability to prolonged guerilla warfare. One may go for mile after mile through bush so dense that it is impossible for the eye to penetrate more than a few feet and always there is the possibility of a lurking enemy every foot of the way. Thus the whole campaign varies so greatly from any other at present being fought, that perhaps a few notes about it and the country generally may arouse some little interest?

Perhaps the most trying factor in the whole affair was the climate – and here to a certain extent the enemy had an advantage over our forces. In the first place, the major portion of their force was composed of native soldiers (Askaris) officered by whites in the proportion, apparently, of one to fifteen or twenty. In the second place, during our long advance from Moshi and the borders of British and German East Africa down to the coast at Tanga and Dar-es-salaam and past the Central Railway, they were always falling back on supply depots – destroyed before they left you may be sure – whilst our forces were totally dependent on our own transport and on what could be got out of the natives: and as the latter had been told by the Germans that we should kill them on sight, this source of supply was almost negligible. Thus the advancing forces were in a perpetual low condition of health owing to hard trekking and insufficient nourishment, and easily fell prey to malaria and dysentery, the chief of our foes in the disease line.

One can well realize why East Africa has long been known as the 'sportsman's paradise'. Of course, the game is not so plentiful in the dense bush – that is chiefly inhabited by wild beasts of a more or less ferocious nature. It is on the great plains – principally the Magadi and Athi Plains near Nairobi, British East Africa – where they are found in such huge numbers. From the railway line between Magadi Junction and Nairobi – about fifty miles – countless herds of game can be seen across the rolling plains, some being well within a hundred yards of the line. All varieties of buck and gazelle are there with ostriches, buffalo and an occasional giraffe. It is, of course, an unusual thing to see (though not to hear) a lion as their principal hunting hours are dawn and dusk. Jackals, however, are plentiful while a short distance from Nairobi are several rivers, which like those in less frequented parts of the country, are the haunt of crocodiles, rhinoceri and hippopotami innumerable, as well, of course, as the ubiquitous monkey. All game is, however, strictly preserved as far as possible and, without a licence, there are heavy penalties for anyone caught shooting.

There are, of course, many objects of exceedingly profound interest for the newcomer to such a country. Everything he sees is transmuted by its environment: and thus the most commonplace things become far more attractive than if beheld under different and more usual circumstances. Naturally one of the principal things worth seeing is the lofty mountain Kilim 'Njaro, whose twin snow-capped peaks soar some twenty thousand feet heavenwards. And that within a few degrees of the Equator! The effect is felt after sundown when the wind is from the quarter of the mountain, exceedingly cold nights ensuing, to such an extent that whilst during the hours of daylight the thinnest and scantiest of clothing seems superfluous, by night a great-coat and blanket are little enough protection from the piercing cold. Then again, all the native customs hold the interest of novelty. It was certainly a most interesting experience to watch the brewing of *tembo* the native beer, which is made from roasted mealies or maize. The stench was rather overpowering, though many Europeans drink it with apparent gusto – possibly on the same principle as we smokers consumed the vile Kafir tobacco, viz, that the worst is better than none. The 'Can-Can' dance, though bestial and essentially of an uncivilized and abandoned character, was, nevertheless, not without a certain fascination. The usual modes of conveyance, too, evoked a good deal of comment. In Mombassa, a sort of hand car was used, running on two rails of about 18 inch gauge and pushed by two natives. These cars carried two or four passengers. In Nairobi – the only other town of any importance in BEA with which I formed even a nodding acquaintance – rickshaws are the principal means employed for getting about. I was unable to form any opinion on this side of life as applied to German East Africa as I was not in any town of importance there.

Naturally the natives form an eternally engrossing study of human nature in its infancy. What strikes one very forcibly is their keen talent for enjoyment of little things. Whilst my unit was in the Rest (?) Camp at Kilindini, the YMCA there imported a drawing room cinematograph instrument, throwing a picture of about three to four inches feet diameter, which was shown in the open air after sun-down. I well remember the unrestrained enjoyment of some natives at a film which was shown, depicting the wonderful adventures of some hero, who, chased by a crowd, knocked over barrows, ladders, house walls and so on, on his headlong flight – the type of thing we were accustomed to in the early days of the bioscope. To their unsophisticated minds it was the height of humour and they treated it accordingly.

I think I have said enough to convey to my readers some of the interest I experienced during my stay in East Africa. I have, of course, glossed over the worst features of the campaign – for the days when, newsless, smokeless, foodless and sleepless, we tramped after an ever-elusive enemy hold but little pleasure either vicariously or in personal retrospect. From that point of view, perhaps the best summary is the somewhat ribald parody on Browning's *Home Thoughts from the Sea* the last three lines of which run:

If they take me back tomorrow, I shall never say them 'Nay',
Here, we're rank with fell diseases and – we get no bally pay!
So three cheers when this yer chicken sees the last of Africa

December 1916 – The Chief Consolation I can extract from the situation is that it has afforded me a splendid chance of seeing South Africa. I am sure I will never forget my sojourn here. Of course its jolly hard lines being tied here when there's a man's work going on elsewhere, but as the Doctors still pronounce me unfit and incapable of tackling either East Africa or Europe awhile, there is really nothing else to do but to pocket one's personal feelings in the matter and slog away at the work which falls to me.

East African Campaign by Brian McArthur

General Paul Emil von Lettow-Vorbeck, Commander-in-Chief of German Forces in East Africa during the First World War is, by military standards, a legendary character. For over four years, he kept a large allied army chasing him, but always succeeded in repulsing attacks and threatening further guerilla action. The action took place over a stretch of East Africa then known as Kenya, Tanganyika and Uganda. At one time the Germans were operating south of the present Mozambique border. Von Lettow finally surrendered on 25 November 1918, days after the official armistice of 11 November, at Abercorn in present day Zambia. At most, the German forces numbered approximately 3,000 white troops and 11,000 Askari.

The topography of the country, the climate and the heavy rain were an onerous handicap to the allied forces which were drawn from South Africa, Great Britain, Belgium, India and Portugal. Malaria, dysentery and other tropical diseases took their toll of unacclimatised troops. By the end of 1916, it is recorded, 12 000 white troops had succumbed and been repatriated. If the objective of war is to nullify the fighting ability of the opposition, disease was certainly a factor which assisted von Lettow-Vorbeck.

Barnsley Chronicle – 2 September 1916

THE SWITZERLAND OF AFRICA

> German East Africa whose fall is momentarily expected, is the largest and in some respects, the finest of all the possessions our enemy held. Some 384,000 square miles in extent it is little more than three times the size of the United Kingdom. … In the Chagga district on the southern slopes scores of flourishing coffee, tobacco, banana and other plantations show capital results. Here there is complete immunity from the dreaded malaria, while the adjoining Usambara highlands, which has been the scene of some stiff fighting between the Germans and the columns operating under General Smuts, are also a beautiful healthy region. Indeed when in 1885 a personage from Whitehall told an official of one of our great missionary societies that this district had just been ceded to the Germans, the official exclaimed: 'Heavens! You've given them the Switzerland of Africa!'. H J Shepstone in the *Millgate Monthly*.

Barnsley Chronicle – 2 February 1918

BARNSLEY BOYS IN EAST AFRICA

Private Robert Peel from Bradford wrote to the Editor of *Barnsley Chronicle* on 20 November 1917 from East Africa, where he knew several lads from Barnsley and had enjoyed reading *Barnsley Chronicle* while in hospital.

Famous for glassworks we know it is because we have drunk ginger beer out of Barnsley made bottles even in this far off land'. Many of them were in Morogoro 'a town of decent size and much importance and its geographical position is magnificent.' [After a detailed description] 'of great official importance in the days of German rule'.

But even here our joy is touched with all kinds of difficulties and pests. The sun is unbearable, dysentery is terrible and malaria caused by the mosquito bites is even worse. The ground is covered with every specie of biting and stinging insect or reptile: snakes, lizards, tarantelle spiders, teetee flies, mosquitoes, "thousand feet" and ants by the million.

3

John Middleton Downend

The Big Push – Extract from a Letter (*Alumnus* December 1916)

18 July 1916 – At last I have a moment to spare and so I will try to tell you a few more or less interesting things relating to my experiences out here. 'Fragments from France' they'll be and no mistake for my whole life has been made up of fragments since June 15th, the day on which I left England for 'somewhere'.

We had a very pleasant and uneventful sea voyage which lasted less than two hours. I don't suppose for one minute I should be allowed to say where we landed and again rather than betraying trust reposed in me, I prefer to mention the place as merely A--- There we spent some four hours before we entrained for B--- Travelling in France at the present time is by no means speedy and we were something like three hours before we arrived in the sidings at B---, although it was distant only about eighteen miles from A-- Perhaps you will remember that when I said *Au Revoir* to you I mentioned that we were coming out to some 'base camp' (I purposely use a small 'b') and that we expected to remain there some five or six weeks. Well, so it seemed when we arrived for we settled down to courses of instruction and began to write home from our new address, which was as follows: – 32nd NF, 34th IDB, APO (S) 17, BEF France. (The easiest way is just to put down all the letters of the alphabet together with the number you first thought of). Two days later we were given instructions to report to the Railway Transport Officer and entrain for a destination unknown. After a period of twenty four hours in the train we found ourselves at a rail-head, from whence we proceeded by motor lorries a further distance of six or seven miles, eventually finding ourselves at a little village some eight or nine miles west of a place, which has become famous during the great 'push'. In passing I would say that our journey by rail took us through some of the most peaceful scenes of Peasant Life in France that one might wish to meet with. It was impossible, quite impossible, to realize that we were in a country shattered, torn and bleeding at the hands of a treacherous foe.

We had now arrived at our journey's end and, having reported to Headquarters, we joined the companies to which we had been posted in the 26th Northumberland

Fusiliers, better known as the 3rd Tyneside Irish. The Battalion was at that time in rest billets, but was supplying working parties to the trenches. There is no place in the whole world where things develop so quickly as in the Army and within 24 hours of our joining the battalion we were listening to the details of the scheme for the great advance. The new officers were, of course, simply to be held in reserve to fill up any gaps that might occur as a result of the forward move.

But again there was a rapid development and in the course of a very few days we lost our company commander (killed) and another officer (wounded) with the result that on the ever to be remembered July 1st, I found myself in charge of a platoon, taking part in the greatest move the war has seen. What a day! What memories! Our battalion moved forward with 20 officers and of these 8 were killed, 10 were wounded and another was hit by a glancing bullet but his pocket-book bore the brunt and he received only a bruise, and I, the remaining officer, came out untouched. When I moved forward with my platoon, we were 38 strong, carrying barbed wire and all the materials necessary for the building of a strong post, when we reached the first stage (400 to 600 yards from our starting point) I had 5 men left with me. True there were a few others unhurt, but they had lost connection with us and when the roll was called there were 11 of the 38 who had come through safely. Three others who had shell-shock have now returned.

I wonder if people at home can appreciate the situation. I had 37 men with me, all carrying a heavy load, simply moving forward through a living hell of machine gun and shell fire. These brave fellows had no opportunity of coming into contact with the Bosche – their bayonets were fixed but their rifles were slung across their shoulders and there was nothing of the madness of the battle rush or the natural instinct of self preservation to help them forward – they simply moved slowly forward and answered the command of my whistle so long as they were able to hear it. I could never wish for braver fellows under my control – bluff, blunt, undisciplined in some ways they are, but they are of the real stuff and so long as the Empire has such sons she will ever remain a power for good in the world. The scene we passed through absolutely baffles description, and the most terrible pictures that a morbid mind could paint are no exaggeration of the actual happenings of that morning.

Any further account of what happened on that dreadful day would be tedious reading to you so I will say no more about it.

I was over in the German front line before the end of the day, where a party of some 200 men were holding the line against all attack. I was through a sap choked with wounded and dying, I was over No Man's Land enfiladed by German snipers and hidden machine guns. The next day I was over again with a platoon, carrying rations and water to the brave fellows who were holding the German line and the crater of the mine which we had exploded in the first stage of the advance. At five thirty on the morning of July 1st I had breakfast, my next meal was at 2pm on July 2nd. Just about this time I received authority to leave the trenches and rejoin the remnant of the battalion, which was now collecting at a farm some two or three miles behind our front line. There had been heavy rains and the trenches were miniature rivers, progress was slow and heavy and by the time I reached my destination I was well-nigh exhausted.

Since that time we have been constantly moving – resting a day here and there – marching at night or in the early morning and changes have been many. For a short space of time I was Company Commander – at another stage I was on a course which would qualify me for the position of machine gun officer for the battalion. Today we are billeted in a little village almost thirty miles from the scene of our activities and tomorrow we move forward again in a north easterly direction.

4

Duncan Fairley

Forward

There are hills to climb and valleys to cross
Before you reach the height;
And it all takes time, and may mean loss,
In many an uphill fight:
But once you're there, and can breathe fresh air,
You feel that the race is run,
Not for glory or fame, but a sense of shame
If you'd left your work undone.

Oh! It's forward and upward and onward and through,
Till your strength gives out as the day draws in.
Let the night ever find you staunch and true
To the hope that you'll conquer, the faith that you'll win.

There's the sea of knowledge for all to sail
Where you'll meet with storms and calms.
To win to the port you must pump and bale
And row with blistered palms.
In the shock of the winds and waves take heart:
Strain nerves that were slack before:
For think – even shipwreck helps to chart
The course to the distant shore.

There's a mountain steep, as a barrier set
On whatever road you tread;
You must square your shoulders and cry 'Well met!'
And make for the very head.

You'll slide on shingles and fall in streams,
Face chasms and cliffs uncouth,
But every stride leads man from dreams
To the perfect vision of Truth.

There's the river of Faith and its broad and strong
Without a bridge or ford;
But though the passage is fierce and long
You must plunge of your own accord.
It's no use shivering on the brink
To wait till the waters fall;
What matters it whether you sink or swim
If you answer the inward call.

There's a wide morass that's hard to pass
For loathsome pools abound;
Deceit and Sloth make the sodden grass
And Envy slimes the ground.
The fogs and mists of Vice obscure
The track that leads ahead;
It's for you to see that their feet are sure
Who are following where you tread.

The path of your life may lead through strife,
Bring peace or anxious doubt;
And a friend may stand on either hand
Or alone you step it out.
Still follow your soul to the distant goal,
It's a lamp to guide your feet;
For it's in that light you'll be judged at night
When the map of your life's complete.

Oh! It's forward and upward and onward and through,
Till your strength gives out as the day draws in.
Let the night ever find you staunch and true
To the hope that you'll conquer, the faith that you'll win.

Sunset: A Sonnet

We paced our Shadows on the Derwent's breast
Through the slow ageing of a quiet day,
When April coins a richer gold than May:
Kingfishers darted, brilliant, sun-caressed
Past Mowthorpe, where the water-ousels nest,
And where we saw rare goldfinch, to repay
A toiling scramble round each river bay.
The world wooed Peace to take eternal rest
And languish on the slopes of vernal grass,
Valanced with primrose, sorrel, violet,
Falling to where the thirsting sedges met
The silent eddies in a cool morass.
Suddenly fell the sun: we saw a cold,
Comfortless valley, unfamiliar, old.

To A Migrant

Have [you seen] the wastes of the spacious East?
Have you crossed the Tartar wall
Which the great Khan built, that his soul might feast
Secure in a Shang-tu hall?
Have you perched on the cedars that never ceased
To nod their heads or shiver at least
To Orpheus' madrigal?

Have you flown from the seas of the fleecy West?
Have you traversed rare Peru?
By the forest stream, where the pirate pest,
John Oxenham led his crew?
Have your flagging pinions taken rest
On a whaler's mast that swelled on the crest
Of Atlantic combers blue?

You have flown, I know, from a land more rare:
You'll return to a stranger sea;
And my spirit will strain to follow you there,
Till the leash is slipped, and unaware,
The body sets it free.

5

James Hirst

The Battle of Loos – 25–28 September 1915 (*Alumnus* December 1915)

After weeks of preparation – digging advanced trenches, making store houses for ammunition and food, sandbagging partially demolished houses for safety of wounded, rehearsing the coming attack on ground marked out to represent the land we should have to go over etc – the eventful day came when it was ordained that we were to make the attack which had absorbed our interest for weeks.

Friday was the day when we received our final instructions. On the morning of this day our Battalion was ordered to parade and our Colonel gave, as it were, a final send-off. He gave us an outline of the titanic struggle that was going to take place on the morrow – a struggle involving no less than three million men, and attacks taking place from the North Sea to the Swiss frontier. To bring home to us more readily the tremendous preparations that had been made, he told us of the preparations for our own division. I forget how many guns we had behind us but each one had an abundant supply of rounds per day. These guns had been 'pounding' away at the Huns for four days, and I think we calculated that about 60,000 shells were sent over each day for four days preceding the day of attack. The rest of the day was spent in fitting us up with anything necessary and the discussing of the plans for attack, using for reference large scale maps, which, thanks to the aviators, showed the various lines of trenches occupied by the Bosches, and the relative strength of the various parts.

The hour of 8pm had been fixed for the Battalion to parade, to march off to the trenches, for we had been billeted for a few days at a small French town about six miles from the firing line.

Amid cheers, singing, shouting *Bonne Chance*! etc we marched out of the town. Gradually as we moved to the firing line, the raucous strains of music began to die away and one could feel that a different kind of spirit – a spirit of determination and resignation – pervaded the atmosphere due partly to the fact that discretion forbade noise or we might be shelled if the Germans heard us. We had marched about three miles seeing unmistakeable signs of increased activity – large motor wagons full of shells of all kinds and sizes being rapidly emptied, when of a sudden out of the darkness a blinding flash greeted one's eyes and simultaneously a deafening roar reached one's ears, followed by a dull moan of a missile passing through the air sounding in all probability, the knell of some poor German. A gun only a few yards from the dark column of men had just sent a souvenir to the Bosches.

We reached the place where we were to 'dine' – a pot of tea and little 'shackles' – the Army term for a stew of bully beef and vegetables etc. This was less than a mile from the firing line.

By 3.00 am we were in the assembly trenches, each man of the Brigade knowing what he had to do, when the time came. It was a long time until 6.30 am. About 5.30 am the guns became more active – hushed messengers – 'Put smoke helmets on at 6.15', 'No. 3 Platoon will lead out at 6.27', etc – were passed from man to man as each crouched as near as possible to the trench, for lead and iron were flying fast and thick.

At last the words came 'Lead out!' What moments! Suspense was cruel. One knew not what the next five minutes had in store for him.

A minute after the word to lead out had passed along I found myself in the open. Running as hard as I could with rifle and bayonet firmly clenched I could see men dropping down, others trying to bandage their wounds, many who had already paid the full penalty. It was a sight never to be forgotten.

After running about 150 yards my breathing became very hard, our smoke helmets not facilitating breathing. Grim determination or rather resignation set in. I jumped into a shell hole for security from the hail of bullets issuing from machine guns and German rifles, took off my helmet, risking being gassed, got my wind – and then set off on my journey to the German second trench. All around earth was flying about, caused by bursting shells. The noise was terrible, bangs of shells, the spluttering of the rifles and machine guns, mingled with the shouting of men and the groans of wounded men.

All this which seemed hours occupied only a few minutes.

On reaching the German second trench I found some of our own men already reversing the firing side and I immediately began to assist. Looking over the parapet a few minutes later I saw some of the men of my platoon – the first I had seen of them since we left our trenches, for with smoke helmets on everyone looked the same.

It had been planned that three of our companies had to consolidate the second German line and a part of Loos named the Garden City. Our company had not to stop but go up the hill about 300 or 400 yards further, two platoons bearing to the left to take a chalk pit, in which the aviators thought there was a German battery of guns, and the other two platoons to work to the left to try to take a house on the road, in which were three or four machine guns. It was with the former I had to go, so on seeing my platoon officer (a fine fellow) with a few men making for the chalk pit, I immediately finished digging and, jumping out of the trench, went with them, bringing with me about ten 'Jocks' who had lost their direction in the attack and became mixed up with us.

Reaching the chalk pit I came to close quarters with a very young Bosch who quickly held up his hands shouting '*Kamerad*'. He was very nearly killed by a friend of mine only a few yards off him, who raised his rifle at him, but I could not see a man shot down in cold blood – the thought seemed to freeze my blood, so I made a mad clutch at my friend's rifle and then took the Hun prisoner.

It was at the chalk pit that we captured our brace of 85 mm, the two largest on show at the Horse Guards Parade, but at that time we had no time to worry about them for the Germans might counter attack us, so 'Dig in lads' was the word and we did it with such alacrity that we had in three hours got decent cover.

It is all very well taking trenches but having got them the work is to keep them.

For four days we were there and some sights I saw I never wish to see again, but some made me feel proud to be a Britisher.

Imagine a line of kilted men of fine physique over a quarter of a mile long line up and in one line charge up a slope. Yet I saw this done five times, each time after the poor men were forced to retire. I even saw a large boned 'Scotty' carrying a wounded man forward in a charge.

Again I saw late in the afternoon the attack by the Guards Division to retake the ground which a Division had had to retire from – magnificent is a mild term for it. I first became aware of dark specks on the skyline in our rear. Then it became known the Guards were attacking – in artillery formation – on our left. It was sublime! The men in compact order advanced – although the Germans were furiously sending shells over. Thick clouds of smoke could be seen everywhere, earth, stones, etc. going up in the air caused by the explosion of shells named by the 'Tommies' Coal-boxes'!

On they came and on and I heard that the Division had comparatively speaking few casualties – due to their fine morale for it is no comfort to know that if a shell dropped on them in the formation in which they were about 40 men would be laid low.

I can assure you we had plenty of thrilling incidents during our four days' occupation. For three days we were no more than forty yards away from the Germans, we being on one side of a country road and they a few yards the other side.

At last the relief came, to our infinite joy!

It had been raining all day and the conditions were deplorable, but on nearing our allotted billets, although wet through, covered from head to foot with sludge, we could not refrain from singing.

6

Henry Rylands Knowles

Letters to his Parents from France (RAMC)* – 4 February to 18 March 1915 (*Alumnus* April 1915)

February 4 1915 – If you send any papers will you send – say the *Weekly Times*. We get quite a number of daily papers but nobody reads them much; we look at the pictures in the *Mirror* and use the rest for shaving paper. … We have now moved to fresh billets and I am in the smallest and dirtiest room of the dirtiest farm I ever saw. We are 4–5 miles behind the trenches and expect to go up for our turn any time. We do not go up for long – about 2 to 4 days – and then come back for 6 days' rest … I am writing this by the light of 1½" of candle stuck onto a *Daily Mirror* – the rest of the room is 'pitch' dark. I cannot send my clothes home to be washed – it is forbidden. I sometimes get my servant to wash something, but it is precarious. On the march here we passed a string of 150 London buses and then several dozen motor lorries. You never saw such a collection. The first belonged to a jam firm with its highly coloured advertisement painted on its sides. One had belonged to some 'patent medicine' people; one the L & Y Railway; then Harrod's Stores and dozens of lorries. These go in strings of from 20 to 300 on narrow roads about half the width of Pitt Street, so you will see we have a little excitement when we march out even if we are not fired upon.

February 19 – For the last 12 days we have been in the firing line. At one time I was as much as 72 hours without sleep. We had rather a bad time in the trenches. I was located at headquarters about 600 yards behind the firing trenches. The wounded could only be collected at night and so, for me, night became day and day night. I got my full share of the excitement. In the first place a 'sniper' used to hover in our vicinity; and one night he scored three men in an hour and within a hundred yards of 'headquarters'. Again we were shelled two days running and had great difficulty

* Royal Army Medical Corps

in preventing the wounded from getting up and running into the open, where they would have been shot by rifle fire. Fortunately, beyond taking one wall of a barn away the shells did not do much harm. I was lucky on one occasion – I went to help a stretcher in by daylight and, unfortunately, we had lots of shells quite near us. One wounded a man who was walking by my side, and so saved me.

I believe our particular 'sniper' whom we christened 'Percy the Popper', because his rifle made a peculiar noise, has been accounted for, at any rate for three days he has given no sign, nor bullet, and previously he was most regular in his daily habits. We believe we are now going to have six days rest, but we are not sure, as we have twice started out for the resting billet and been fetched back again. Whilst in the firing line our 'commissariat' is most ridiculous.

At 'headquarters' we lived in comparative luxury and at times boiled tea over a candle; in fact we manage to have about four tablespoonfuls of tea most days, and then I unearthed a spirit lamp, which was a perfect 'godsend', especially when I obtained spirit, which, by the way, was half-a-crown a pint.

February 27 – I have just come back from another turn in the trenches, and we have had a very easy time – two nights no casualties at all and on the other two nights very few. At present we do 4 days in and then 4 days out of the trenches. I live at Headquarters which is a house and we no longer feel like rats in a cellar as we are able to go out safely in daylight if we take care not to be seen by aeroplanes. We were wonderfully lucky in leaving our old trenches as they were mined shortly after our regiment left. Of course I should not have been in them, except later if necessary.

We have to censor the men's letters before they are posted and almost without exception they commence: 'I hope you are well as this leaves me at present' and after that they have few ideas except to ask for parcels.

March 9 – I shall not be inspired to write much tonight as I am sitting in a sack. I strolled up a ditch about 3' deep in water and it seems to have damped my nether garments, hence the sack. Yesterday we went on to a hill to watch artillery fire. We were directly under the line of fire of one of the guns and could see the shells go over and then burst a mile away in about two seconds. They do not look anything like the livid pictures one sees in the picture papers; they just look like cricket balls going at an incredible speed through the clouds.

March 13 – We are having an extra long spell down here and I am 'bored stiff'. I am strictly forbidden to go into the trenches and I have to hang around Headquarters until we get shelled. Les Bosches generally put in a few for luck in the afternoon between three and four. Thereupon we hastily collect what belongings we can carry and adjourn to the bank of a flowing river, alias a dirty ditch. We sit on bits of wood and keep our feet cold in the ditch.

The other day I went down to another regiment's Headquarters, where Colonel Du Maurier was killed. They were being shelled out and we went to see if we could do anything. Finally I strolled back up a ditch about three feet deep in water as this was the only cover. My nether garments got quite wet and I spent the evening in a sack which was wonderfully warm considering. If the authorities do not give me leave, they will have to send me home for being insufficiently clothed as my uniform is decidedly the worse for wear.

My great coat will last a long time as it is strongly 'reinforced' with Belgian mud. My 'Burberry' no longer looks new, as my intelligent servant took it into his head to wash it whilst coated with wet mud. The result is a delicate mud colour somewhere between mouse-gray and 'washed-out' green. We have got some fine going officers in the regiment now – we have lost nearly all those who came out with us from wounds and half from frost bite. One of the new youngsters enquired if he and his trench party were to assault the enemy. As his trench party consisted of only ten men you can imagine the 'assault'. A man in another regiment got as far as the German barbed wire and found that all his command had fallen, so he stood up three yards in front of the German trenches and waved for others to come on. We have another just joined. He is 21 and got a DSO in October. I have to stick here to eat, sleep and dodge occasional shells.

March 18 1915 – We have struck a very fine billet this time and have a dining room and a bedroom. We also found some very nice glass tumblers and some plates and so had a very 'civilised' dinner last night. Today there is the most infernal row created by the owner of the crockery. We are now raising a band and tomorrow are giving our first concert to the brigade.

The bathing arrangements for the men are most amusing – they are in connection with a brewery; the brewer brews beer, and at intervals pumps hot water into a large tank; that is the bath. The men then bathe until 'all is blue' or rather black. Officers can go to an asylum to bathe. I hope to go tomorrow.

Ernest Arthur Knowles
Letter to his Parents from Cairo – 16 February 1915 (*Alumnus* April 1915)

We were sent down to Ishmalia a fortnight ago as the Turks had begun to put in an appearance and were expected to attack in force, but changed their minds later. There was a good deal of fighting the day we left here and the next day, but we did not get into the trenches until about a week later, when we were in them for about three days, and, as the Turks were still going back, we were withdrawn back to the camp at Mera, Cairo.

Ishmalia is a lovely little town and is much prettier than Cairo. It is very quiet at present as most of the people have left to go to safer places. We were camped once more on sand, only while we were there we were without tents, as it was expected that we might have to move any time, and tents take up too much room on the transport.

The notice we got to move was rather short. The first I knew of it was about half past three in the morning when I was wakened up by hearing the rest in the tent talking about it, somebody having gone round the lines late the night before. We got up a good time before daylight to pack our kit-bags and get our ammunition. We were ready by breakfast but did not march into Cairo until about ten. The 7th Battalion and we were the only Australian Battalions to go, much to the disgust of the rest. C and D Companies of the 8th were the only Companies who got in the trenches but some of the New Zealanders (who were down there before us) were in the trenches first. A good many prisoners were caught and some gave themselves up, but they were mostly Bedouins whom the Turks had driven on before them and forced to fight.

Cyril Reginald Knowles
Mesopotamia Expeditionary Force (RAMC) – Letter dated 9 October 1918
(*Alumnus* December 1918)

I've been intending to write to you for a very long time, and am afraid my only excuse for delaying so long is an innate dislike of putting pen to paper, coupled with the fatal policy of 'tomorrow will do' which is a progressive disease in this climate. I hope that you and all the school are well and progressing steadily in the new buildings, will you remember me to the Head and all who know me. I was sorry to see the name of the younger Whitelock on a recent casualty list, and often wonder what has happened to my contemporaries Taglis, Fitton, Everall and others.

I suppose you would like to have a few first hand impressions of conditions out here, but please remember that censorship regulations still exist, and lead to somewhat stilted descriptions. When I got out here in May 1917 I was sent straight up river to join this regiment above Baghdad, so that I have actually seen only a very little portion of the country. What I have seen of the Tigris etc is flat, deadly, monotonously flat, the only relief to the expanse of flatness being occasional groups of palm trees, which mark out Arab villages. Cultivation is limited to the vicinity of the rivers and to the banks of the few existing ancient irrigation canals, and methods used probably date back to Biblical times. The soil is remarkably productive even so. The Arab varies tremendously in different parts, but roughly there are two kinds: those who stay in their villages from year's end to year's end and engage in agricultural pursuits, and those who live in tents and move their flocks about from one grazing patch to another; all are almost Semitic in their love of driving a hard bargain when selling you local produce, in the shape of eggs, dates, tomatoes, vegetable marrows, apricots, plums, grapes, figs, pomegranates, sweet limes, melons etc etc of which there is an abundance in their season.

There has not been a great deal of war in our part – we have had three or four bouts with the Turk but now it does not take a very intense argument to persuade him to take to his heels. When he does this he takes more than enough catching and frequently we have done day and night marches for 3 or 4 days and then been disappointed. Conditions have improved beyond all realization since 1916 and now supplies of all sorts are more than adequate to meet any demand. Our rations are excellent and there are luxuries of all sorts to all ranks; I've no doubt that I have fed better than most people in England over the last few months.

The months of latter half of June, July, August and first half September are hot – as far as possible all work is over by 7.30am. A burning sun and blasts of scorching wind then make the day a time when always perspiration is flowing in profuse streams; anything up to two gallons of liquid are consumed, it is too hot to read, too hot to sleep and, strangely enough, never too hot to eat; it is remarkable what a zest one gets up in the middle of the day, when the thermometer is nearly boiling, in order to get down to 'tiffin'. At last the sun disappears in the west and sighs of relief go up all round, chairs etc taken outside and a blissful hour of recovery with the aid of "pegs" begins that first cold chuta feg and soda in the evening. How many hymns have been sung in your praise! During the hot weather we have rations of soda water and ice and live in marquee tents, with double roofs, in which the temperature rises to its maximum of anything from 115–129 degrees F at about 3pm. A cloud in the sky is a great rarity.

From middle of November to end of March, it is the most delightful climate. Cool (comparatively), sunny days, cold nights – last December on a few mornings we had to break the ice in our buckets before being able to perform our ablutions – never too hot, as a cool breeze always tempers the sun's heat at its zenith and makes one feel most invigorated. Flies, mosquitoes and other insect pests disappear, gazelle, wild pig, geese, teal, partridge and sandgrouse are plentiful and the man with a gun has a happy time. Rain occurs about once every three weeks, it comes on suddenly and very heavily, lasts at most a few hours and then out comes the sun again, for two days after we flounder about in the stickiest and most slippery mud I've come across, but after that the sun has dried everything up again. Grass of the greenest springs up in no time and lasts till well into May. The remaining months are transition periods from heat to cold and cold to heat and are remarkable for their petty inflictions. By day dust storms not only cover every thing with layer after layer of fine dust, but they are inclined to scatter the lighter portions of one's kit to the four corners of heaven.

Myriads of horse-flies make the hours of light a perpetual torment and as one man said: 'If you kill one, something like a couple of hundred turn up for its funeral.' At night sand-flies and mosquitoes abound to take toil of your blood and sleep and make the time one perpetual scratch.

It is not really a very unhealthy country, even in the summer, while in the winter it is the finest climate in the world. Even during the 17 months I've been out here the sick-rate has decreased enormously and would be even less if the men would be persuaded to take the slightest care, While I've been out here I've never had a single day off with sickness and only seven days of change in Baghdad.

I expect this will arrive about Xmas and take this opportunity of wishing you, and all my friends at school, every happiness then and in 1919.

7

Donald Stanley Laycock

Work in the Army Veterinarian Corps (*Alumnus* July 1917)

As I have spent rather more than 12 months in the Army Veterinarian Corps, I think that an outline of the work done by the Corps may prove of some interest to readers and particularly so as this branch of the Service is not known to the public and, consequently, lacks the appreciation and encouragement which it undoubtedly deserves.

Even the very existence of the Corps is not known to all as is well proved by loud whispered speculations by many on seeing the letters AVC on a man's shoulder straps. I have frequently heard, on these occasions, such irritating suggestions as Army Volunteer Corps and even Army Veterans' Corps. Ignorance of the Corps is however not so surprising after all when one learns that the strength of the AVC in pre-war days was almost a negligible quantity. It is no exaggeration to say that the Corps has been increased proportionately with the army since 1914.

As the number of horses actually engaged in warfare in France is comparatively small and many of the wounds inflicted on the horses when in action are such as to render the immediate killing of the poor beasts the most humane treatment, it follows that the greater part of the work in this theatre of war is the treatment of horses which become unfit for transport and other work owing to the severe conditions under which they have to work. Food is often more or less deficient in quantity or quality, water the same, adequate shelter for the horses is lacking in the more severe weather and the work is at all times hard.

Most Veterinary Hospitals are now equipped with adequate shelter for the patients in the form of long well ventilated sheds holding from 30 to 50 horses and, in addition to the above, with loose boxes for the more serious cases which require more comfortable quarters. In the early days of the war many horses had to stand outdoors picqueted to lines owing to lack of this accommodation, so that it is not surprising that the results of careful treatment then were not as good as they are today.

Many cases come into the hospital almost, if not quite, as serious as those resulting from shell fire in France. These animals, which have been hurt by accidents are often terrible sights. We had one poor beast, which had run away at a railway siding, and, coming in contact with a wagon, had produced a terrible wound in its side from front to rear, many stitches being required to close it. The horse was doing well under treatment and would in all probability have recovered, if it had not afterwards reopened the wound when in an excited state whilst still in slings. … The most wonderful case I ever saw was a beautiful mare which had been operated on as an experiment for a nasal complaint. Two holes had been bored through the bone into the nostrils, between the eyes, and through these she used to breathe regularly.

There are many pitiable sights to be seen in most Veterinary Hospitals and I am sure if people could see the patients entering the hospital, the skilled and careful treatment which they receive and see them afterwards leaving the hospital amongst a batch of well groomed, fit looking horses, unrecognisable except to the practised eye, they would realise what splendid work the AVC is really doing.

8

Harold Marshall

The Antarctic Expedition (*Alumnus* December 1914) (extract)

Harold expatiated upon the expedition by Captain Robert Falcon Scott (1868–1912) and his team, to the South Pole in 1912.

What is the use of these expeditions? Are the results worth the labour and the risks attached to these terrific contests with Nature? These and a host of other questions flash across the mind, and they are difficult to answer. Scott did not regret the sacrifice. To men such as these there lies the Unknown: here is the spirit to conquer and tempt all dangers. It is that same spirit which has characterised the most glorious achievements of our past history. And if Nature sometimes exacts the price, who shall say that such sacrifices are all in vain?

Among the Pennines (*Alumnus* July 1915) (extract)

Clapham is a picturesque village nestling under the south-eastern slopes of Ingleborough. The church stands in the middle, whilst the houses straggle alongside the mountain stream which comes babbling over the moss-clad boulders. It was quite early morning, the chimneys were beginning to show signs that another day had arrived with its accompanying round of domestic duties; the birds in the blossoming trees were supplementing the music of the running water, when, rucksack on the back and stout ash plant in hand, we, Becky [a friend] and I, set out to mount Ingleborough. A narrow lane, typical of all the lanes of this country, with 'dry' walls of limestone in place of the more usual hedges, leads from the northern limits of the village winding in its tortuous ascent towards Ingleborough Cave. En route, we passed the erratics at Norber, 'erratics' because they are rocks which have 'wandered'! from their true position. In this case they are old dark grey Silurians resting on the top of the newer limestone and they mark the track of glaciers from the north in the days when a large part of Europe lay under ice.

Explosives and Grenades (*Alumnus* April 1916)

There are few subjects more vitally important than that dealing with grenades and their use, and at the same time so exceedingly interesting. Consequently, when reading once more that lucid article on Shells by Mr Peddle in *Alumnus* for July 1915, I thought that an article on Bombs would prove welcome to many readers and supplement much of the information he gave. I shall endeavour to make my remarks as non-technical as possible so that those still at School will follow me without difficulty.

Grenades are no new thing in warfare though they have not been used for a very long period. Nevertheless, we are having to rediscover much at the same time as we make considerable progress upon the achievements of the past. The duties of the grenadier remain the same, however, ie to precede the attack. It will be remembered that the range of the rifle was very small even up to Waterloo, a hundred years ago, when the effective range was probably not more than 50 yards. Subsequently to that date the range was increased to one thousand yards, thus driving the opposing sides apart, with the result that the services of the grenadiers were no longer of use and 'Grenadiers' and 'Fusiliers' became names only. How comes it that grenadiers are so conspicuous once more? Modern artillery is so deadly that the opposing forces must be out of range or so close in to the enemy that they dare not shell. This is precisely the state of affairs in France and Flanders and hence the grenade comes into use again. Again, the protection which the parapets afford to those within the trenches is so great that the rifle is becoming less important and bombs, with their higher trajectory or line of flight, are becoming more important, in that struggle for superiority of fire which invariably precedes the attack. It will be understood without difficulty that the grenadier must be an infantry man, and I leave it to the reader to imagine the qualities required in a good grenadier.

As regards throwing, while the man who plays cricket may make a good thrower, it must not be taken as a foregone conclusion that such is the case, for the manner of throwing is quite different, as the swing of the arm and body is utilised. Any cricketer would tell you how fatiguing it is to throw a cricket ball from a long field, say, for ten minutes continually. A bomber's services may be demanded for hours at a stretch. Nor is it the man who can throw the greatest distance who makes the best bomber, though distance is an important factor. The most important item is to hit the target – generally a trench of course – and the reader must bear in mind that *no thrower is out of the danger zone of his own bomb unless it falls inside the enemy's trenches.* I have seen a fragment of a bomb which fell more than a hundred yards away and could have killed anyone so unfortunate as to be in the line of flight.

Explosives

An explosive consists of units temporarily bound together but which are liable to disunite when certain forms of persuasion are applied. To be effective, an explosive must assume a new form exceedingly rapidly so as to supply the propulsive force. A low explosive, unless *tamped*, causes a number of small explosions instead of one large one. Tamping blocks up the line of least resistance and so produces the accumulative effect of the whole series of small explosions that would otherwise take place. Gunpowder is the only low explosive generally used. On the other hand, a high explosive develops the whole effect simultaneously and, therefore, tamping is unnecessary and the force is felt equally in all directions. All high explosives are ignited by means of a detonator which may be said to give a small explosion to induce a larger one.

Little need be said about gunpowder as I believe its use and properties are well known. It was known to the Chinese in very early times and it was first used in Europe at the battle of Crecy in 1346, with the purpose, note, of frightening the horses of the opposing forces. Its composition is generally: Saltpetre 75%, Sulphur 10%, Charcoal 15%; and the gas requires 280 times the bulk of the mixture.

Among the high explosives I have space for a few important ones only. First and foremost comes gun-cotton, which will be familiar to most readers. It consists of cotton waste treated with nitric acid (1 part) and sulphuric acid (3 parts) and has twice the effect of gunpowder when tamped. It can be used either wet or dry, but the larger pieces, weighing almost one pound, are kept in a moist condition as it is then much safer to handle, and, in addition, is much more powerful in that state. So safe is it that a bullet can be fired into it without result. To explode the wet gun-cotton, a small primer of dry gun-cotton is used, fitted with a detonator. The explosive in the detonator is fulminate of mercury, a very powerful but very unstable compound. The very small quantity in the detonator would blow off the hand; in one case, the detonator, carelessly allowed to slip from the fingers, fell down the shirt front of the operator with the result that wounds terrible and mortal were inflicted on the abdomen. To return to our subject, gun-cotton is an admirable explosive because it is so safe and so reliable. It is used chiefly for demolitions.

Apart from these, the explosives generally used can be classified as follows:

I. NITRO-GLYCERINE GROUP – Dynamite, Cordite perhaps the best known
II. CHLORATE EXPLOSIVES – chiefly found in Percussion Caps
III. AMMONIUM NITRATE GROUP – of which ammonal is very important, as it is the one most used in grenades
IV. PICRIC ACID GROUPS – Lyddite (very much like French Melinite), Trinitrotoluene ('TNT')

CORDITE is made of nitro-glycerine, gun-cotton and a small proportion of some mineral jelly such as vaseline. It is used as a propellant for bombs, shells and bullets.

DYNAMITE consists of nitro-glycerine and a kind of clay, which, in peace times, came from our friend the enemy. We obtain a substitute now from the land of thistles. It freezes at 40 degrees Fahrenheit, and thaws at 50 degrees, and is very dangerous in this condition. Dynamite is chiefly used for blasting purposes, but the old notion that the great advantage to be derived from its use was that its force was downwards, should be as dead as the proverbial dodo. The reason that such a belief ever came into existence was that people could see the hole in the ground while the '*hole in the air', if I may use such a term, remained invisible.*

AMMONAL, consisting of ammonium nitrate, aluminium powder and charcoal is very important as it is so largely used in our grenades. It is safe in transport and very powerful.

The PICRIC ACID group is very important and those who have an opportunity of visiting the Silkstone works will have made acquaintance with the base of this group of explosives. TNT is especially safe; we use it for shells and some bombs; the Germans use it for torpedo heads; while the French make a very extensive use of it. It is so stable that a hard blow will not explode it.

The following table of relative strengths may be interesting to some:

Gunpowder (tamped)	5
Cordite	8
Dynamite	9
Gun-cotton	10
TNT	12
Lyddite	13
Ammonal	14

As far as the bombs themselves are concerned I am not allowed to give any details. An interesting feature is the similarity of one of our enemy's rifle grenades to ours. This is explained in that their origin was in the same fertile mind, but the British Government declined to purchase the first one, while the German Government saw some merit in it. Ours is a slightly improved form of the German pattern. There are constant changes in detail in the types of grenades owing to the improving on old patterns.

Nearly all bombs are charged with high explosives and therefore a detonator is required. A detonator may be exploded by a blow from some pointed instrument (remember that Fulminate of Mercury is a very powerful and *very sensitive* explosive), or by means of a fuse. In the former case the explosion takes place immediately on impact and so receives the name 'Percussion Bomb'. These, of course, require careful handling and many serious accidents have happened from very slight indiscretions in this respect, in spite of many safety devices that have been adopted. The latter take a short time to explode – the length depending on the estimated time of flight and the length of fuse depending thereon. There must not be sufficient time for picking up the bomb and throwing it back. Thus we can put bombs into two classes, 'percussion' and 'time'.

They might be divided into two classes under other headings. Some bombs are thrown by hand, others by one of several mechanical devices such as the trench mortars. With the former method, a good thrower can reach nearly fifty yards; with the latter two hundred yards is an average range, but four hundred and fifty can be attained with certain trench appliances. The advantages of the latter are that covering fire can be obtained during a grenade attack and trenches are within range which cannot be reached with hand grenades; in short, the trench engines take the place of artillery which cannot be employed owing to the danger to its own trenches.

In the matter of grenades and grenade appliances, I think we are superior to the enemy and, incidentally, to the French. Such was the opinion of a German I met some time ago. In the early days of the war however, they had enormous supplies of bombs and that gave them the advantage. I believe this is largely remedied now. I am of the opinion, too, that where hand grenades are concerned we are decidedly superior in throwing. Perhaps our sports again have here helped us and another light is shed on Wellington's dictum:

Waterloo was won in the playing fields of Eton.

Letter to the Headmaster October 1916 – British Expeditionary Force (*Alumnus* December 1916)

My first introduction to the war was in the Somme area, very shortly after the first push and, as a breaking in, I think nothing could be more thorough. Words fail! In spite of the *Daily Mail* and Beach Thomas, it is impossible to describe such scenes of desolation with hell itself raging on top. I remember one night there, when we were digging a communication trench up to the front lines, which then ran through two famous woods. The German front line and ours were on opposite sides of the same valley, our support line over the brow of the hill to the south. The position had not been consolidated sufficiently to be secure, and so everybody was highly strung, for this was the men's first baptism too. When we had dug to an even depth of a foot a party came out of the front line, using our route. The tail end began to run, to make up their distance, I presume, and they could be seen by the enemy, who were keeping a good supply of Blue Lights going. Their advance batteries opened up and reduced the party to hopeless confusion. Then we experienced a full bombardment of three hours' duration, every type of projectile being hurled over. The men were lying down in their one foot trench, shells falling to the right, to the left, in front and behind. I never expected to take back more than a platoon out of that company. When we resumed digging, we had not had a single casualty. An RE [*Royal Engineers*] officer came up to me and marvelled how we had pulled through. Two minutes later a stray bullet got him.

The whole district was almost unendurable. The excessive heat, the clouds of dust, the stench of dead bodies and the plague of flies made an awful combination.

Many villages in France have acquired a fantastic picturesqueness from their battered ruins; but in some villages, like Fricourt, I doubt whether one brick is left joined to another. Although they have suffered infinitely more than the other villages, they do not call up half so many pangs; they are not half as terrible!

We had a few days' march for the purposes of tightening up our nerves again, then back to the line further North, but still within sound of the 'Pushing'. These were in the real thing in trenches – our previous ones had been shell holes solely – dug in chalk, well drained, well built. The two lines were four or five hundred yards apart; rarely a shot was fired during the day. It seemed as though there were no war going on. But from day to day the situation became warmer and warmer, this was more noticeable still from relief to relief, until at the end of about twenty days the position looked as if it was going to rival that on the Somme. Our trenches could be observed directly from the German slopes and they could register every hit. Certain corners became notoriously unsafe but they had to be used just the same. With the fall of Thiepval and the rendering more acute of the salient, I suppose we shall not hold them much longer. We are ready – and eager! One has a glorious mad rush – and fears nothing! It is all very grim – but very exciting.

9

Arthur Hammond Butler Shipley

Introduction by Charles Stokes Butler

A DESTROYER, otherwise torpedo-boat destroyer or TBD, is a small warship rarely exceeding 900 to 1,000 tons, very fast, carrying a few quick firing guns of about 4 inch calibre, and fitted with torpedo tubes. The British Navy has a very large number of them and every squadron of battleships and cruisers has some attached to it.

Their duties are so numerous that they have been called the 'maids-of-all-work' of the Navy. As their name implies they were originally designed to defend the larger vessels against the insidious attacks of an enemy's torpedo-boats: to do this effectually they must be speedy, handy and provided with sufficient gun-power to overwhelm and sink such boats. Then they are not only destroyers of similar small craft in a hostile fleet but are themselves torpedo-boats intended to attack with their torpedoes the enemy's large ships wherever and whenever an opportunity offers: and when an opportunity does offer they make one – 'It's a way they have in the Navy'.

The speed attained by the best of these TBDs, with driven engines, is anything up to 35 knots, or even more (one knot is approximately 2,020 yards). This is only possible by sacrificing almost everything else below deck for the installation of the highest possible engine power. Her accommodation for officers and crew is comparatively cramped and none too comfortable especially in rough weather, when they are reported to be particularly lively vessels.

Besides the functions already mentioned the destroyers form an escort to transport crossing; fleets cruising or a screen around vessels disabled in action; they are scouts doing reconnaissance and patrol work, dispatch carriers, skirmishers and tireless hunters of submarines.

The following account of his experiences in the battle off the West Coast of Jutland (AHBS[1]) was written in private letters by a nephew of the Headmaster, who, after serving as a midshipman for some time on a battleship, transferred to a new destroyer of the latest type, in which he was so fortunate as to be in 'the thick of it' and to come safe out of it. Modern battles, whether by sea or on land, are fought over so wide an area that the observer can see only what occurs in one limited part of it and not all of that; for he is not there as a mere spectator but as a combatant, whose active duties on board necessarily demand his attention first, last and all the time.

On Board A Destroyer at Horns Reef – May 31 to June 1 1916 (*Alumnus* July 1916)

We were in the big action the other day in the North Sea. The --- was one of the destroyers attached to the battle fleet. About 4pm on May 31st we got a signal from Admiral Beatty that he was heavily engaged with the German battle fleet and that he had cut off a portion from their base. About an hour later we sighted the battle cruisers and four fast battleships on our starboard bow firing, though as yet we could not see the Germans because there was a low kind of mist on. We could see the flashes of their guns and soon we saw the ships themselves. Our battleships got into line ahead and followed astern of the battle cruisers. The German battle fleet were in the same formation and both sides were firing away at each other as hard as they could go. The destroyers were inside the British line towards the Germans, ready to rush out and attack enemy torpedo craft that came over to attack our battle fleet. As none came we simply had to wait there and watch.

Of course all the German 'short' shots were falling among us. This went on for over two hours and not one of us was hit. We got a piece of shell weighing about 2½ lbs on board and a small hole in the side of our boat that you could insert a match through with ease.

When our battleships came up I never saw one of our ships hit the whole time, but I saw lots of hits and fires breaking out in the enemy's lines.

A good many of our 'short' and 'over' shots hit their destroyers and of course sank them immediately. We came across one of their destroyers disabled; the destroyers fired on it and sank it. Later on one of the German Dreadnoughts hauled out of their line totally disabled. I don't know what she was, she had no runners and only one mast standing and was on fire fore and aft: a cruiser went for her and sank her. About this time the 'Defence' (AHBS[2]), steaming between the lines, was receiving a good deal of the German fire, blew up and as soon as the smoke had disappeared she had sunk.

The Germans were getting a rotten time of it: many of their ships had been sunk, including some of their leading battleships, so they sent a flotilla of destroyers to attack our battle fleet and theirs turned and fled, making a smoke screen to prevent our getting a 'point of aim' to fire at them. They had the disadvantage of not being able to fire at us, but they considered it paid them best to make the smoke screen. Of their battleships two escaped back, one was left afloat, but damaged, which we sunk by gunfire, and the remainder we sunk by a terrific fire from battleships.

It was now about 10pm and getting dark. Our destroyers were sent in chase of the German battleships to make an attack with torpedoes. During the night firing broke out in different places but of course we could not tell who was firing. Once we got the searchlight on us and were fired on; we set off at full speed and were not hit.

At about 2am we came across the whole of the German battle fleet steaming in line ahead of us. We could see them quite plainly, every gun they had in fact, while we were rather too small to be seen by them in that light. The order was given to attack, which we did. Ourselves and three other destroyers steamed down their line, firing our torpedoes. After 2 or 3 minutes there was a terrific explosion in one of their Dreadnoughts, flames reaching twice as high as the top of the masts, about 400 feet. The torpedo had apparently struck and ignited one of their magazines. We were lit up by the explosion and furiously fired at by the remainder of their fleet. One salvo of shells fell and exploded in the water just short of us. We altered course towards them: the next salvo fell the other side of us just where we should have been, had we not altered. Owing to the rain of bursting shells and gunfire, we could not make out whether any more torpedoes exploded, and it was very improbable that we should unless the magazine had gone up as in the first case. We got clear all right and only one of us was hit, that was the one astern of us in which the Captain was badly wounded and the First Lieutenant and a few men were killed.

We did not see any more that night. The following day we joined up with three battleships. About 9am a Zeppelin was sighted. One of the battleships fired at it and their Captain reports that it was destroyed, although I did not see it drop. Later on we passed some wreckage. Men were hanging onto it and waved to us. We were sent back with orders to pick them up; they turned out to be Germans.

Finally we got back to our base, oiled, ammunitioned and were ready again.

Notes

1 The Battle of Jutland
This battle was fought by the Royal Navy's Grand Fleet, commanded by Admiral Sir John Jellicoe, against the Imperial German Navy's High Seas Fleet, under Vice-Admiral Reinhard Scheer, on 31 May and 1 June 1916 in the North Sea, near Jutland, Denmark. It was the largest and last full scale naval battle of the First World War.

As the German Navy was too small to engage the entire British fleet, their strategy was to lure out, trap and destroy some of it; they also hoped that this would break the British blockade and allow German merchant ships to operate. However, the Royal Navy learned from signal intercepts that a major operation was being prepared and Jellicoe moved the Grand Fleet to support Vice-Admiral Sir David Beatty's battleship squadron.

The British lost 14 of its 151 ships and about 6,000 men were killed, whereas 11 out of 99 German ships were sunk and many ships suffered serious damage, with the loss of 2,500 men. While the British sustained the greater loss, the outcome was that Germany recognised Britain's superior naval power and that it would be unable to take control of the North Sea.

2 *HMS Defence*
This ship was launched in 1907 and was the last of three Minotaur-class armoured cruisers. She played an important role before the First World War, when she became part of the Royal Navy's Grand Fleet. During the Battle of Jutland she was the flagship of the First Cruiser Squadron, ahead of the main body of the Grand Fleet, and she came under heavy fire from German ships. Fire spread to the ammunition causing the ship to explode with the loss of all 900 men on board.

10

George Smith

Extract from a Letter – Royal Air Force, France (August 1918)

As you know, I left the OTC* at Sheffield and went to a fearful hole, well-known to all members of the now defunct RFC.† After five days, I was packed off with 600 other Embryo officers to ---- Here various diseases broke out, which necessitated our being isolated for the greatest part of my five weeks' stay. Then to – At length the examiners having decided that I was proficient in machine guns etc I moved once more – to --- this time. When we were just nearing the end of the course an extra fortnight was tacked on in order that we might learn the elements of Aerial Navigation. Here I might say that navigation was an absolute walkover so far as I was concerned. It was merely your Physiography put to a practical use and I never realised how much you had taught me until then. Cyclones and anti-cyclones etc, it seemed child's play.

I satisfied the Air Board that I could fly so I was gazetted and instructed to report for duty at --- We fly first of all a machine called the DH6 fitted with a 90 hp RAF** engine. Its top speed on level is about 60 mph, which is very slow. Still it can be looped and stalled, which, after all, is something to gladden the heart of the conceited young aviator, who rather fancies himself as a stunt pilot. The ---- squadron fly Maurice Farman Shorthorns (GS‡), unofficially dubbed Mechanical Cows, Birdcages etc. Of a total number of Category A1 cadets, who enter cadet schools, about 20% become fully fledged pilots. At the Air Board Medical Exam, some are turned down as unfit for flying; some are made observers and others Kite Balloon Officers. More are turned down on account of failing to pass exams in the schools, and still more break down or crash whilst in training at the squadrons.

* Officers' Training Corps

† Royal Flying Corps merged with the Royal Naval Air Service on 1 April 1918 to become the Royal Air Force in 1918.

‡ This two-seater biplane was developed before the First World War by the Farman Freres, aviation pioneers in France. It was used initially for reconnaissance and as a light bomber, but was later being used for training.

11

Cecil Cuthbert Thompson

An Old Boy at the Front – Letter to the Headmaster (*Alumnus* December 1914)

26 November 1914 – I have just received your letter dated October 24th. The next day after I had written to you I was ordered to the front to join our 2nd Battalion. After some little stay at the Base Camp at Havre I travelled in a troop train up to the front. My only impressions of the journey are the cold, the uncomfortable diet of bully-beef and biscuit and a cheering population. We had a sixteen mile walk from the railhead to my Battalion. I could not realise that I was so near the front. One could hear the dull rumbling of the distant guns but it might only have been a thunderstorm. One could see here a deserted trench left by the Germans and occasional cottages that had lost bits of their walls. I slept that night in a billet most comfortably, in a village less than a mile from the Germans, but it was impossible to realise their nearness. I realised their nearness more the following day. I joined my Company in the reserve trenches, about 800 yards from the Germans. Bullets which missed our forward trenches whizzed over us there. With some men I was cutting trees in front of the trenches to make barbed wire obstacles of. One of the huge shells, nicknamed by the men 'Jack Johnsons' from their excessive black smoke, burst in a field on my left; one could have buried several horses in the hole that it made. Returning at night to the billet – we had been relieved by another company – one heard the somewhat uncomfortable whistling of stray bullets over one's head.

But it was left to my first appearance in the forward trenches to enlighten me as to the fact that I was really at the front. When I tell you that the trench I had to take my platoon to was only 50 to 80 yards from the Hun, you will realise that it was a somewhat risky business getting there. Of course we can only get there at night time. I had a guide to show me the way as I had never been before. The Germans were particularly active that night. One part of our way lay parallel to a hedge through which the bullets whizzed like angry wasps. We came ultimately to a road parallel to the enemy's trenches and only 100 to 150 yards from them. The guide took us along this road single file. I learned afterwards that we should have crawled along a ditch filled with water. The firing became very heavy and looking to the left I could see the German rifles flashing. The guide who was walking alongside me was hit, so I at once ordered all my men into the ditch to take cover. Most of them needed no command. I then carried the guide into the ditch myself and, incidentally, got two neat button holes bored by a German in the opening of the tail of my great coat. I propose putting two buttons on the opposite side and so turning their remembrance to some use. I found the trench alright, after wading up to my knees in water for up to 50 yards in the ditch. The trench was my home for two days and nights. You cannot realise how cold it is in a trench when it snows and you are wet through up to the knees. I never slept a second all the time, for responsibility plus cold left me without the desire. In addition bullets would hit the top of the trench and send a shower of earth on one. I had only one casualty – a poor Lance-corporal shot through the head. That made me feel sick for an hour or more, for I saw his hat fly up and his body fall to the ground. The queer part is the poor fellow felt he was going to be killed and had written a letter to his wife to be posted in the event of it happening. We got out of the trench without further casualty, two bullets in a man's pack being the extent of the damage. I was so cramped and benumbed with cold that I could scarcely walk. Our regiment is having a rest to recover from the effects of the campaign, for we have suffered heavily in Officers and NCOs. We expect to be back again in a day or two.

I am sorry this letter is rather personal to myself. All of our Officers have had of course miraculous escapes. One poor Second Lieutenant had to lie the greater part of the day so near a German trench that a German reached over and knocked the brains out of a Highlander next to him who would talk. Our bullets too hit all round him but never touched him; he crawled back at dusk.

Please do not expect us to move from our present position. I dare not write more. Please send a Magazine. Thanks so much for letter and your kind wishes. So glad the School is doing well. Give my kind remembrances to those of the Staff who know me.

Letters to the Editor from France – 16 March to 2 July 1915 (*Alumnus* April and July 1915)

16 March 1915 – Thanks so much for your letter, which reached me last night and which I read in the modest glow of my candle in my clay home. I think I cannot do better in this letter than tell you something of what has happened since my leave ended.

Safely escorted by torpedo boats (and incidentally by means of a somewhat zig-zag course) we crossed the Channel. At the end of the succeeding railway journey, I found my regiment had left – and was moving that day to a part of the line farther to the right. Before dusk I was in the forward trenches again. I should imagine that they are the most comfortable trenches in the whole of the British line. They are very deep and very dry. One walks up very long communication trenches to others, which are labelled with such familiar names as Harley Street, Old Kent Road and so on. You pass on the way – in some cases actually through – empty shells of houses. And the village Church, which one passes by, is battered into a ruin like some ancient English monastery stripped of its signs of age.

The Germans are very close. In places 50 yards is all that separates. This very closeness brings into prominence other weapons of offence besides what were thought the usual ones. You look up and see what looks like a policeman's baton hurtling towards you. The wise – and all are now wise – very quickly get out of the line of flight; it is a bomb from a German trench mortar. It hits the parapet, it knocks it in and the amount of earth you receive over you depends on your proximity to the burst. Hand bombs, too, are ready to be used for attack or defence. They vary from a very harmless looking ex jam pot to quite elaborate cane handle ones. The Germans have, too, some light gun very close up and it has been named 'whizz bang', for all you hear is just a faint 'whizz' and 'bang' and the shell bursts. Yesterday I was quite staggered by the displaced air in front of one and immediately covered with earth. They are rather annoying as they can blow quite a large parapet in.

When we have done our tour of duty in the trenches we go back to very comfortable billets nearly three miles. I have a clean nice bed in a typical French home. In the morning a steaming bowl of *cafe au lait* is brought up to me. It is the height of luxury and the little discomforts of the trenches are completely forgotten. The first touch of clean sheets on the first night is an inconceivable joy and one is thankful for the discomforts, which have made it such a pleasure. Then there are the joys of the little walks into a French town and heavy raids on the *patisseries.* Of course, we do a little work when we are back in billets. We get rid of the trench mud and try to get the trench stiffness out of the men's bones by Swedish Drill and short route marches.

May – I am so sorry that I have not replied to your awfully nice letter before, but times have been quite busy with us. Ostensibly we have been out for a little rest. In reality we have been working hard charging over breastworks at imaginary Germans. Shortly we shall do the same in reality so I thought I would write to you first.

I added another new experience a few days ago. The Germans blew a mine up in front of our trenches. It was a magnificent sight, but awful. There was a huge column of smoke and earth, more than a hundred feet high, and the falling debris caused a few casualties. The ground trembled violently before the sound of the explosion. The Hun immediately shelled us with huge shells afterwards. We quite expected an attack, but nothing happened. In one way I was glad the mine was not directly in front of us for we should have had to occupy the crater. The weather is frightfully hot here and I am as brown as a berry – awfully fit though.

I was so pleased to read about Knowles in the magazine. I can place him pretty well, for I was in that locality before Christmas. I should just love to meet some of the old Boys. When Kitchener's Army reaches us I expect I shall.

28 May – Yes, I got my slight wound – a graze along the shoulder by a piece of shell – in the fighting you mention.

You would like to hear 'impressions and feelings'. You must know from *Eye Witness* that an attack was made on May 9th by other troops on the same position, which failed. We were in reserve behind, waiting to carry on the advance should it have succeeded. The same afternoon I had to go up to the front to help to reconnoitre the position for an attack we were going to make. I shall never forget the reserve trenches there full of the wounded and dead. I went up to an Artillery observation post and from there saw the dead out in front lying thickly in front of the German trenches. Two attacks had been made that day with the utmost gallantry, taking the German trenches but at such a loss that is was impossible to hold them. The Black Watch actually walked as on parade under the most awful fire of machine guns.

Until the night of our attack, except for one night in a house, we were in our front trenches or reserve ones. I remember it as a time of most awful shell fire, one long day and night of deafening noise and flying splinters of shell. As you know we attacked at night, for another failure would have resulted in the day time.

I went over the parapet with my platoon amid the deafening noise of machine guns and rifle fire. Many were hit getting over. As soon as I was over, until the fight finished, I never had the thought that I should be hit I am sure. I forgot all in the mad desire to get to the Germans as quickly as I could. I think I went mad, for I know I yelled to inspire my men. Not that they needed any, for one and all ran until they were shot and only six reached the Germans with me. You see we were enfiladed badly owing to the failure of the regiment on our left to advance, and as we came under the fire of a machine gun a whole line would melt away.

I ought to have said that a ditch ran across our front and I had the misfortune to miss my footing going over and got wet up to my middle. This made my weight a few stones heavier and I stumbled and fell all the way across. I did not lose my sense of humour for I shook with laughter when a man of mine bellowed out 'Och, Mr Thompson, shtop I'se shot through the heart'.

All next day I shivered with cold in the captured trenches in a state of coma, devoid of any fear or any sentiment. The Germans shelled us heavily and I watched without any feeling scarcely, the shells dropping on dead and wounded and throwing up legs, heads etc. I was not unnerved for I felt no fear but I was tired out. We were relieved that night and staggered back. Went to base hospital and on to Boulogne. A few days in bed put me right so I asked to re-join the regiment and tomorrow for the trenches again.

2 July 1915 – For many months there has been running through my brain a phrase in a letter of a very respected friend of mine. It commenced 'We, at home, thoroughly realise' and went on to say that they realised what we are doing out here and what we had to put up with. Funnily enough your last letter had just the opposite 'It is hard to realise or even imagine'. Of course, you are right. But I feel that your ideas on our average ordinary trench life exaggerated considerably its discomforts and dangers, or to be more exact, how those discomforts and dangers appear to us. This fine weather trench life, except in the active parts of the line, is sheer boredom. Its dangers, except again in certain parts of the line, are not pronounced. A new subaltern taking the part of the line I was in charge of was in mortal terror because I peered over the top of the parapet to show him things. Another had his 'imaginings' of trench dangers rudely upset when, taking over from me at night, he saw me walking along the top of the parapet showing them in. The Germans were 600 yards away in these two cases, except for a wandering patrol and I knew from experience that I was in just about as much danger as crossing a road in front of a certain amount of traffic.

In fact, I think generally that what people at home think must approximate closely to what the new fellow here thinks. When one has more or less got hardened one can tell where a shell is coming and so avoid the 'duck' characteristic of the new comer.

But one's experience here is continually enlarging. I thought I had seen the last thing in villages almost levelled but Vennelles altered my previous opinion. French and Germans in this small town fought from house to house and every house has been battered by shells.

You write I did not say how I was wounded. It was not got in any interesting way. I had just stopped to get a breather for we had more than 300 yards to go. Luckily I stopped a few yards behind where their shells were bursting. It was rather awful, expecting anyone to come a few yards farther and blow one to bits. However, a flying splinter from one hit me, made me very angry, and so I got up, rushed on to arrive safely in the German trenches. There I essayed the somewhat difficult task of clearing out Germans who were throwing bombs whilst we had none. After being nearly blown to bits, the half dozen men I had and myself gave it up until reinforcements arrived, when we cleared them out.

I come home on leave for eight days on the 8th of this month that is of course if I am still alive and kicking. I shall come over to Barnsley to see you all.

Extract from the Sprig of Shillelagh *the monthly journal of the Royal Inniskilling Fusiliers, on the battle of Festubert, where the Second Battalion won fame and glory by its brilliant attack on the German position. It was in this battle that Lieut Thompson was wounded.*

The strength of the Battalion going into action on the night of May 15th was well over 1,000 not including many men left with the transport. Captain J P Crawford was in command and it was Captain C C Hewitt of 'D' Company that first succeeded in storming and taking the German trenches. The Battalion did very well and 'D' Company exploit was magnificent.

The attack along the whole division line was timed for 11.30pm and shortly after that hour the crack of the German rifles and hammering of machine guns began, and rose till it reached a roar. At the same time the ground was lit up by white, green and red flare lights, the latter being the German call for artillery action, which was not long in coming for soon the whole of the breastworks seemed to be deluged in a rain of bursting shells. Our attack was divided into two parts by a cinder road and a deep ditch running at right angles to the breastworks. The order of attack was – on the left of the road 'A' Company, supported by 'B' Company, and on the right of the road 'D' Company, supported by 'C' Company.

Although our artillery had bombarded the German breastworks for days and had laid them flat, yet they had neither dissipated the Germans nor their courage as their lines were full of men when we arrived up to them. 'D' Company however, overcame all obstacles and managed to hold on until the arrival of reinforcements, when the captured lines were consolidated. Some hours after the remains of the Battalion were withdrawn on being relieved.

Total losses were 20 officers and about 700 men.

12

Gerald Warr

Letter to the Editor from No 7 Casualty Clearing Station, BEF* – 18 March 1915 (*Alumnus* April 1915)

You know, of course, we are running a Clearing Hospital† here, about seven miles or so from the firing line. In the ordinary run of events we are kept busy with sick and wounded, which we sort into three classes: those who are serious who go down to the base, those less serious who are sent to various convalescence camps further down the country and the third class minor cases are patched up here and sent back to duty.

In the event of a rush, such as we had last week, we evacuate the hospital as often as the Ambulance trains come up to the rail head, of all cases except those who are too serious to be moved. Sometimes we evacuate so many as 5 and 6 times in 24 hours.

Last week, when the advance was made in front of us, we worked day and night.

In 72 hours I had six hours off duty, which in other words meant sleep, snatched anytime and anywhere, for the most part on the floor, fully clad, in the middle of a ward.

In normal times we have *reveille* at 6.00, parade for duty at 6.30. We are off duty at 7pm and lights out at 9.30pm. One day is much the same as another so much so that we find it difficult to keep account of the date.

At present we are quartered in a rambling building that was once a Jesuit College.

Soon after landing in November a party of 20 of us was sent into Belgium. There we had a time very similar to that last week except that we were shockingly understaffed and lacking in all necessary equipment. It was an experience of a lifetime. Although up to now we have not been under fire yet I feel that we are doing our little bit for the good of the cause.

* British Expeditionary Force.

† The Casualty Clearing Station.

The Casualty Clearing Station

The CCS was part of the structure for dealing with casualties from the front; it was in between the Aid Posts and Field Ambulances close to the front line and the Base Hospital. It was staffed by the Royal Army Medical Corps, with support from the Royal Engineers and men of the Army Service Corps, and was intended for short stays only. The CCS treated injured men sufficiently for them to return to duty on the battlefield or, in most cases, to enable them to be taken to a Base Hospital and so were usually located close to railway lines.

The CCS were large but moved often to deal with casualties from the different battles; they followed the victorious Allied advance during 1918 and some went into Germany with the army of occupation in 1919. Their locations can often be identified today from the military cemeteries that surrounded them.

CCS 7 was at Merville, between Bethune and Armentieres, from December 1914 to April 1917.

War Surgery 1914–1918 by Thomas Scotland, Retired Orthopaedic Surgeon

In an assessment of nearly a quarter of a million casualties admitted to the casualty clearing stations in France and Flanders the majority were caused by high explosives or shrapnel. When men went over the top, then rifle and particularly machine-gun bullets took their toll.

Hand-to-hand fighting within the trenches, moving from one segment of a trench to another, resulted in wounds caused by hand held bombs and grenades. Bayonet wounds were conspicuous by their absence, either because they didn't occur at all or because when inflicted they were almost invariably fatal. Gas in its various manifestations was responsible for 18 per cent of admissions to casualty clearing stations by 1918.

The most important thing about war wounds on the Western Front was that they were absolutely filthy. And the heavy bacterial contamination of the soil, with organisms responsible for tetanus and gas gangrene, meant that these were particularly serious problems in 1914. So much so that consulting surgeon to the Expeditionary Force, Sir Anthony Bowlby, said: 'It is absolutely essential for success that wound excision should be done as soon as possible after the infliction of an extensive wound because in such cases gas gangrene may become widely spread within 24 hours. It is therefore necessary to operate on such cases before the patient is sent by train to the base.'

Wound excision meant removal of all dead, devitalised tissue. It meant removal of all foreign material – shell fragments, clothing driven into the wound at the time the wound was inflicted, and all the filth and debris from the battlefield that goes deep into the body tissues. Only healthy, bleeding tissue is left behind and only then, only when you've got healthy, bleeding tissue will the organisms responsible for gangrene be deprived of the opportunity to grow because they only grow in the absence of oxygen.

In 1914 a clearing station was supposed to be just that. It was to clear the casualties back to the base hospitals at Calais, Boulogne. But it took too long. The clearing stations were far enough away from the front line to be generally out of range of shell fire and yet close enough that ambulance wagon convoys could get there reasonably quickly. So it was at the casualty clearing stations, as the war went on, that most of the major limb and life saving surgery was carried out before the patient was sent by train to the base.

The First World War led to the development of orthopaedic surgery. Compound fractures of the thigh bone were extremely common and led to 80% mortality in 1914 and 1915, most deaths being preventable with the right treatment. Sir Robert Jones from Liverpool, and Sir Henry Gray from Aberdeen carried out pioneering work, which not only saved lives but improved the quality of life of those wounded.

Extract from *War Surgery 1914-18* edited by Thomas Scotland & Steven Heys published by Helion & Company 2012, used with permission.

13

Frank Hellewall Westby

Letters to the Editor (*Alumnus* December 1917)

I will try to tell you briefly of two of my most exciting experiences.

OVER THE TOP
At last we had got our chance to make up for some of our old scores with the Hun. We were going over the top and in about five minutes …

A GAS ATTACK
Just picture this. It is 1.30 am a moon shining and it is misty, a gentle breeze but very cold. Everything was quiet, no shells, just a few machine guns firing and a stray bullet, here and there.

All at once a Hun barrage falls on us with surprising rapidity. High explosive shells, shrapnel, trench mortars, machine-guns and rifles come into action. Every man who is asleep jumps to his rifle and gets his bayonet fixed and feels whether his ammunition is alright. Everybody is eagerly questioning 'What is it?'. We all get on the parapet and wait. Our machine guns have opened out: men are firing rapidly and all of us are unconscious of our danger. Then something happens. Men begin to cough and fall down, and a great shout goes up 'GAS'. Everybody adjusts his helmet and keeps on firing, whilst the stretcher-bearers get the poor fellows away as quickly as possible. Then all is quiet again and I walk to the dressing station to see how the fellows are. There one of the worst sights you can imagine is to be seen. Poor fellows are lying on the floor in agony groaning and vomiting; and one suddenly realises the horror, the hideousness and pitifulness of this devastating war.

However most nights we have our 'own back'. We give the Boche about five times as much as he gave out. We have the pleasure of seeing about 20 white crosses spring up in the night behind the enemy's line …

I hope I have not bored you with this long letter. I only wish I were at the old school again. I could stand the routine quite easily now. One gets a bit tired of war sometimes and it is 13 months since I first came to this country.

Wilfred Owen – ***Dulce et Decorum Est*** 1917

Gas! GAS! Quick, boys! — An ecstasy of fumbling,
Fitting the clumsy helmets just in time;
But someone still was yelling out and stumbling,
And flound'ring like a man in fire or lime ...
Dim, through the misty panes and thick green light,
As under a green sea, I saw him drowning.
In all my dreams, before my helpless sight,
He plunges at me, guttering, choking, drowning

Chemical Weapons in the First World War

Poison gas was used to demoralize, injure and kill men in trenches. All sides used disabling and lethal chemicals, which included:

Tear gas – an irritant that could cause blindness, first used by the French in 1914
Chlorine – an irritant first used by the Germans in 1915 at the Second Battle of Ypres; its visible clouds acted as a psychological weapon causing fear
Phosgene – the most deadly gas was odourless and caused suffocation; it was first used by the French in 1915
Mustard gas – caused blindness and lethal blistering of both skin and lungs; it was first used by the Germans in 1917 at the Third Battle of Ypres.

Gas masks were developed to protect men, but often they were ineffective, and more than one million were killed by gases in the armed forces plus many civilians in nearby villages; an unknown number of people suffered long term health problems.

The use of poison gas by all parties throughout the First World War constituted war crimes as it violated the 1899 Hague Declaration Concerning Asphyxiating Gases and the 1907 Hague Convention on Land Warfare, which prohibited the use of 'poison or poisoned weapons' in warfare.

14

Charles Railton Whitelock

Extracts from Letters – 9 March to 31 May 1918 (*Alumnus* July 1918)

9 March 1918 – Here I am lying in bed feeling as if somebody had been hitting me all over the body. However, I am not the only one. The rest in this day's raid are just the same. I have always put off giving you an account of my experiences till this raid, which we accomplished most successfully, and created a record for the Royal Flying Corps, beating any Hun bombing raid on England.

This morning we were turned out at 7 o' clock by the usual call '*Raid on*'. There was a scurry to put on electrical clothing, flying boots with three pairs of stockings, etc. After that there was a procession of pilots and observers, dressed as if for a Polar expedition, up to the aerodrome. I got my engine started, whilst B-- fetched his gun with 1,000 rounds of ammunition. Meanwhile, I tested my own gun which is synchronised through the propeller.

At last everybody got going, and we lined up in two fan-shaped formations, each consisting of six machines, and all carrying bombs. We circled round above our little district to gain height and then dashed across the lines at 12,000 feet, occasionally hearing the customary '*whoop*' and seeing the cloud of black smoke. However, Archie was not accurate enough this morning to be a nuisance and we kept on without anything unusual happening, and no Hun machines in sight. At various other places Archie had a go at us, but was far enough away. Still we kept in an easterly direction till we reached the Rhine. Here we turned north and finally arrived at ----- Of course you will know all about it in the *Daily Mail* tomorrow morning. The two formations went straight over the town. I saw our leader fire his light and then everybody just pulled their plugs. The little clouds of smoke rising from various quarters of the town looked very pretty, and then round went our noses for home as quick as lightening. By this time the barrage had got going, angrily attempting revenge, but it was of no use.

I occasionally glanced in my mirror at B--- he looked a most forlorn sight once, when we were at 16,000 feet and going at ninety miles an hour. He just pointed to his face and when we landed I found he had got frost bitten like most of the others. He told me that his compass and all his other instruments had frozen stiff when we were up there. At another time he had his eyes closed so I just rocked him about, because I really couldn't stand the idea of his being comfortable when I was not. However, we all landed safely after just under five hours in the air. That was quite good and I sincerely hope the effect on the Huns' morale was considerable. The total journey, I should imagine was just over 400 miles.

This raid has been on the cards for some time but the weather only allowed us to do short shows. However we were as pleased as could be to get on it – in fact it is quite an honour. I have a little souvenir of that raid which I hope to get sent home some time.

Coming back over the lines I kept getting slight periods of 'wind up'. My engine kept popping and spitting and cut out dead four times. It wasn't such a big worry though because I was over French territory and did not mind a forced landing. Then she suddenly picked up with a real good roar and got home with ten minutes' petrol left. That is the secret of the whole business – being able to run at the most economic rate. One man, unfortunately, got within a mile of home when his petrol was exhausted but he crashed safely to earth 200 yards away.

12 March – Today nine of us went on another raid and created a fresh record for distance, beating Saturday's by quite a bit so you may imagine we were getting rather tired and cold. We got to our objective without much trouble. A few Archies went puffing up near the line but that was all. When we got over the town, however, and started pulling the plugs, a most terrific barrage got up. The Boche gunners had a very blue sky as a background and so were not very accurate in their shooting. Naturally we did not stay long enough to give them a chance, but I circled once round the town to give B-- a chance of spotting the bursts, which happened to be quite good, and then made for home with the engine full out.

Half way back, however, we got the real thing. Evidently the Hun had seen us going on our outward journey and had sent up his scouts to catch us coming back. I suddenly saw three red-nosed beggars, presumably Albatross scouts, flash out of the sun, where they had been sitting, straight across the front of us and curl round behind our tails. Then came the ominous pop-pop-pop in our rear. I was quite busy managing my job, but just caught a glimpse of B-- planking ammunition at them. The other eight observers were doing the same so the Huns must have got it somewhere. At any rate I saw one topple over and go earthwards with a trail of smoke from his fuselage.

17 March – We had only a tiny raid arranged for the 13th – one that would take about two and a half hours but it turned out to be a more serious affair than we anticipated. Only eight of us got away on the raid and on the way out got the worst Archie we have ever experienced – just whacking all over the place. We got our objective, did good business and then the Huns arrived. Unfortunately three of ours did not have enough respect for them and lagged behind. Consequently they got cut off and what happened to them I do not know – they are missing. Then came the fun. One of ours had slight engine trouble and got below us, thus leaving four of us together. We stuck together like leeches with sixteen Albatross scouts on our tails. For once in a way, I discovered that trick-flying was of use. We had a running fight for half an hour. B-- scrapped away like a Trojan and so did the other observers. In such circumstances it is a pleasure to hear the rattle of an observer's gun. We got three Huns that day, and one is credited to me.

Today we went off and did exceedingly good business from the reprisal point of view. I am sure it was the best I have ever been on. On the way back the usual thing happened, some of their scouts appeared but did not come up close. Apparently they do not relish attacking our type of machine unless they outnumber us by about five to one. I got one which was making itself a nuisance. It was the only one brought down, but that makes two on my list during a week.

28 March – We have been working rather hard this week, for the weather will persist in keeping good and when the weather conditions are favourable there is no rest. You will have seen that we did good work on Sunday – the column of smoke caused by a direct hit on an oil dump could be seen a hundred miles away. It is the biggest we have ever seen. However we got it very hot on our way back and had three distinct scraps. The total number of machines that attacked us would be about fifty of which we got seven.

5 April – Since I last wrote we have been doing small raids but this morning had to turn out for work of importance. It was a perfect morning with the wood pigeons cooing in our wood and scarcely any wind. We got off eventually after the buttoning up of flying suits. In fact that is the most alarming part of the whole business. When we got up into the air small cumulus clouds were beginning to gather and the wind was quite strong at 12,000 feet. Then away we raced into Hunland, reached the town which we bombed about a week ago, swerved about for position and then let them go. The results were quite good from what I could see – a big explosion in railway sidings with various minor bursts – and then turned our faces homewards. By this time the clouds had got thicker and the open patches were becoming smaller and fewer. We could just manage to recognise country half-way back and after than there was nothing but a fleecy cotton wool floor. There were all sorts of fantastic shapes and really I have never seen a prettier cloud scene. Still I am afraid none of us were artistic enough to linger.

We knew our course by compass and kept on. To relieve the monotony I fired about a hundred rounds from my front gun to see if it was working properly. Then the leader thought we were on the right side of the line so we started gliding down. I entered the clouds at just under 9,000 feet and then got a most awful bumping. I watched my altimeter register 8, 7, 6, 5,000 feet and then began to wonder if it was raining down below and the clouds almost on the ground. However, at 4,000 feet the earth appeared but the country was absolutely strange. So I wandered round aimlessly for half an hour trying in vain to pick up familiar landmarks. Then I caught sight of some trenches from which I fled precipitately. Shortly afterwards I saw an aerodrome and landed. After some trouble I managed to find out the name of the place from some Italians, who were much interested, so off I went again and with the wind behind me did the forty miles home in fifteen minutes.

17 May – Yesterday morning we were called at 4.30 for an early visit to Hunland. It was a most gorgeous morning – everything still asleep. At the same time there was a thick ground mist, but we could just discern the blue sky directly above. We had breakfast and then went on to the aerodrome where the twelve buses were glistening in the sun, drawn up in four rows of three. The ground mist was very bad then and we could not see more than thirty yards ahead. We knew however that the sun would soon clear it.

The first formation, of which I was one, took up its position on the ground with the mist still very thick. The leader disappeared into it and one by one we followed a hundred yards behind each other. What a queer experience it was to dash into the stuff at eighty miles an hour, knowing that somebody was just in front! Then with startling suddenness came the brilliant sunshine and we found ourselves floating along above the cotton-wool floor – the mist was approximately 200 feet thick. Still more wonderful were the tops of pines and firs on higher ground just peeping through their blanket and the picturesque steeples of the village churches.

Then in about half an hour the mist cleared and we were able to discover our whereabouts. Here started the journey, heralded by the black puffs of Archie at the line. Just before reaching the objective, the leader gave the signal '*Huns about*' and a half mile behind us came a dozen enemy scouts. We managed to drop our bombs all right, with good effect and without interference. Then came the signal again and right in front of us loomed a hornet's nest of about twenty more hostile scouts. It was at this moment that pilots began to think it was time they got busy. I opened my engine all out and closed in to the fifty foot distance of the formation. The way we all bunched up together made the finest formation I have ever seen.

Pop, pop-pop – and I knew B-- was busy. I looked round for an instant and saw his tracer spraying round a Hun, who was driving on T--. Then on we went slithering about the sky, every now and then hearing the machine guns of the Huns. Suddenly B-- shook his joystick vigorously to attract my attention. A big two-seater was slyly edging in under my tail and I started 'S' turning as hard as I could go and after about ten minutes B-- signalled his departure. The scrap lasted 35 minutes as far as I could estimate, almost as far as the line, and then came peace. In all we had five Huns shot down out of control. Incidentally I got another one, so really it was quite nice.

20 May – On Friday night orders came for six machines to do the biggest raid yet attempted. Then followed the dispute about the six pilots, as there were eight of us specially keen to go on the job. After an hour and a half of argument with the C O he decided to draw lots and by bad luck I drew number seven and so was first reserve. The next morning I was up at 4.30 and set off with the rest. I accompanied them ten miles over the line but everybody was going all right so I had to return. After a second breakfast I set off again with three others loaded up with ammunition on a fighting patrol. We roamed round and round forty miles over the line at 16,000 feet looking for trouble and to distract the Huns' attention from the returning formation. We had one or two scraps at long distance but nothing really serious. In the afternoon we had an invitation from an American flying squadron forty miles away so ten of us went in the car and had a great time.

31 May – Still lovely weather and consequently raids. I have been on continuously for the last week, every day, and now I feel just a wee bit tired and a nasty head. This morning I was called at 2.45 and went off as soon as we could see. An impressive sight, I should imagine, from a spectator's point of view to watch all of us roar off the ground in the semi darkness with two-feet flame belching from the exhausts on each side. Off we went on another visit to the dear old district. As usual I held the place of honour but at the same time unenviable position in the rear. B---- was the cameraman today so he had plenty to do. We went over with visions of fat old Fritz running at full speed in his nightie for the nearest shelter. The shooting was really great today. Eleven direct hits on the principal railway and eight plank into the town. With great good luck one of mine got a munition factory right in the centre. Meanwhile B-- was busy snapping away like a professional until I drew his attention to sundry black specks in the sky. Still he kept on with his camera just jumping up now and then to let off a burst at a Hun who was getting troublesome, and then down in his cock-pit again. Thus we went on for about ten minutes; then peace again and home. B--'s pictures, I find, are very good and he has been congratulated. Tomorrow work again, I suppose, so good-night.

Arthur Thomas Whitelock
The Trough of Bowland – *Alumnus* April 1913 (extracts)

A glorious afternoon saw us motoring forth with the Trough of Bowland – or Bolland in local pronunciation and spelling – as our objective. Through the Hundred of Amounderness we sped, that ancient land of oaks, whilst in the distance the slopes of Beacon Fell and Parlick Pike and Fairsnape stood out in growing relief; past villages where trim low-thatched cottages came boldly close up to the road in their rampart of roses and honey-suckle; between steep banks with their lavish store of campion and harebell and foxglove; till at last St Michael's appeared, with its picturesque old church, once unique in the Fylde.

The level country was with us still, a peaceful, pastoral scene. In no long time we were in Garstang, whose charter granted in 1314 conferred upon the town the curious privileges of a 'court of pie-poudre (ATW*), stallage, lastage and portage'. The car swung on past purling streams that flashed bright to the sun, through solemn vistas of mysterious woods. Along winding country lanes, round abrupt corners never shaped for the motor era; past quaint, moss covered churches and country halls buried deep in clustering trees; we had a godly prospect of hills and dales and woods and lawns and spires.

Arthur wrote a great deal more of his lively and poetic description of their continued journey.

The scene had a subtle charm – the grandeur of far flung outlines,and the atmosphere of quiet and solitude. A bleat from a frightened mountain sheep; a rippling murmur from the stream below, as it bickered down its bed over pebbles tumbled and rounded and scored by many a winter torrent; or a whistle from a curlew, hovering and gliding with inimitable grace till a swift swoop buried it in the waving fern brake; these were the only sounds that broke the stillness of the moor. …

Our run was almost ended. Slowly the evening haze gathered, first in faint wisps across the fields, then ever thicker and thicker, till it wreathed the fells in a magic purple, giving them depth and mystery; slowly the sun sank downwards, a circle of glowing orange in a sombre sea of grey cloud. The Trough had lived up to its reputation; its scenes and splendours will linger long in the memory.

Rudyard Kipling – *Alumnus* April 1914 (extracts)

We can in part imagine the feelings of an anxious mother when a nurse introduces to a drawing room of irreproachable callers that phenomenon of the present day known as the enfant terrible. We can picture the silence and expectation with which visitors look for some new exhibition of precocity. In introducing Kipling, we confess to a similar shrinking of heart, for Kipling is a man with a reputation – of a kind; how far deserved it is not yet time to discuss; and it is hard to live down, or in rarer cases, to live up to a reputation once gained. Our author has a double burden to bear. …

Most Public Schools have their own particular code of language, outside whose bounds it is rank heresy to stray without incurring the charge of 'bounderism'. So Literature has an atmosphere peculiarly its own, in application myriad-fold, yet in essence the same, a recognised sort of good manners, a system of etiquette. Its devotees look with suspicion on an apostle of the unconventional, who burst unceremoniously

* Court pie-poudre or Pie Powder Court dates back to Medieval Times when a special tribunal took place in connection with a fair or market to deal with disputes, thefts and violence. The origin of the name is in the dusty feet (French = pieds poudres) of travellers and vagabonds, which then got used for the courts to deal with them.

in, flouting the unwritten law and violating the canons of breeding with a devil-may-care nonchalance.

Granting for the moment that Kipling is all this, we ought before cleaving our critical half brick, to consider him apart from his oddities. We ought to regard, if we can, his whole scope and range, and to form some estimate of his general purpose and effect. We must catechise ourselves as follows: Are we the better for reading him? Does he appeal to our higher feelings? Does he seek to purify whatever is base? Do we regard him as a philosopher and guide? Do we turn to him for consolation, inspiration, for relief in distress of body, mind or estate? If a writer has said anything which leads us to do any of these things, his work has not been in vain, and to charge him with mediocrity is both folly and ingratitude. …

Arthur continued to write a very long critique of Kipling's work.

Kipling's patriotism, moreover, is confined to no limited circle. Whether you love him or loathe him, you must admit he is Vox Imperii; the only poet who knows how the liberties of England have been enlarged in these latter days, the only poet who has praised aright the works and days of the pioneers of Empire-building. …

… none there is to compare with Kipling for passionate loyalty and devoted faithfulness to his native land, to that England whose symbol is the Rose

… crimson sweet,
Rose of the world yet unrequited,
Dewy-fresh with the souls of lovers,
Golden-hearted with golden deeds;
Unfolding in undying sunsets,
Baring her breast in the breath of Time,
Changing Time to a gale of sweetness,
A crimson tide thro' Eternity.

Impressions of Brooklands – *Alumnus* July 1915

At first glance Brooklands strikes the visitor as extremely picturesque. Set as it is in Surrey, it could hardly be otherwise. The air is heavy with the fragrance of pines and lilac and hawthorn. Round the aerodrome runs the curving white ribbon of its three mile track, taking the form of an oval or more correctly of an egg, the narrow end forms the paddock and stands at race meetings. These are now few and far between; and the droning exhaust of a high powered car is rarely heard; for as it stands at present the track has been practically taken over by the government and rows of workshops and transport sheds occupy part of the spare ground in the centre.

The long axis of the aerodrome runs about due North and South and it is generally along this axis that machines take off on their flight. A portion of the track is skirted by the railway. Elsewhere you get a background of green woods, inviting enough to the casual eye, but for the purposes of flight leaving much to be desired, as they tend to set up air eddies, known technically as 'bumbs' due to the refracting action of the foliage. Practice, however, teaches one to avoid these dangerous spots.

Imagine us then, at 4.30 one Tuesday morning, collected into a group near the Atlantic shed, the home of the 'School buses' as they are disrespectfully called. Antiquated they may seem to the practised flyer, but for the beginner they are fraught with numerous possibilities. An instructor comes up, climbs into the nacelle, or car, and proceeds to test the controls, rudder, warp and elevating planes. The fitter in attendance on the machine, after enquiring whether the petrol is on, and the switch off, swings the propeller over several times, to fill up the cylinders with explosive vapour; then, at his question 'contact?' 'contact' replies the pilot, who turns up the switch on his left hand side, and with another swing of the propeller, the 70hp eight cylinder Renault starts up. For several minutes the engine is kept running at a comparatively slow revolution rate. The object of this is to warm up the oil by degrees, so as to avoid undue pressure in the oil ways; when it has had time to thin, the throttle is opened wider and wider, until the hum of the engine develops into a loud throated roar. Behind the propeller a furious blast of air levels the grass and the whole machine rocks and quivers as the chocks under the wheels prevent it from running forward. A few minutes of this and the throttle is closed again, the roar dies away and the pilot switches off for a brief space to don his flying gear and cast a comprehensive glance round. Then 'contact' he echoes once more: the Renault is started up again; a wave of the hands gives the signal for the chocks to be hauled away and, as the propeller turns round on quarter throttle, two mechanics hold onto the wing tips until, with another wave, the pilot signals that he is straight. Away he 'taxies' across the ground, in order to get the head of his machine up wind. A brief run along the aerodrome and without a falter up come the wheels. You hardly realise that the machine has left the earth so gradually does she mount. A circuit of the track suffices to show that engine and controls are correct and that the air is fit for the pupil's trial flight. The pilot makes his landing with graceful ease and ends his run almost at your feet.

Meanwhile you have wrapped yourself up, for a white frost still lies thick on the ground: donning a safety helmet you dodge in amongst the stays, very much as if making your way through a wire entanglement and, with cautious steps, climb up into your seat. As the beginner you sit behind the instructor, but this school 'bus' is so designed that you can operate a duplicate rudder bar and, by passing your hands under the pilot's arms, get a grip on the elevating and warping mechanism. 'Go easy on the controls', says the pilot: 'let them move about freely and feel what I am doing with them'.

Once more the Renault is started up and, on partial throttle, we 'taxi' up to the narrow end of the aerodrome, slewing round gradually, to come up head to wind.

Suddenly you are conscious of a different note in the engine, from a hum it rises to a boom and your seat digs you in the back as the machine gets into its stride. The ground skims past at an ever growing rate until at last the speed seems to reach a maximum and fade away. No, you are not slowing down, it is the ground that is leaving you, and making it more difficult for you to estimate your pace. The elevator moves back, not with a jerk but with a steady even draw; and all you are conscious of is a gradual swoop upward. The broad end of the track, quite far away a few seconds ago, is now almost due below: down comes the left hand control, the machine heels over, precisely like a cycle on a curve and simultaneously you feel the left hand rudder bar slide forward. On this inward bank the aeroplane swings round until it picks up the line of the track once more, off goes the rudder and over goes the warp, with the result that the machine comes up on an even keel, and in response to a touch on the elevator proceeds to climb another hundred feet. Thus, with alternate turns and rises, we are soon at 400 feet; and after several circuits at this height it is time to come down. Like the ascent this must also be into the wind. The pilot skilfully jockeys his machine into position for a downward flight, closes the throttle and firmly pushes the elevator forward. The boom of the engine fades to a muffled hum, you can hear the swish of the wind in the wires and the planes as you settle down nose foremost on a rapid glide; and all the sensation you experience is that of free wheeling downhill in a powerful car with all the road bumps smoothed out. Up comes the earth at a surprising rate, back comes the elevator and you flatten out some four feet above the ground in horizontal flight. As the way dies off the machine settles down and you make your landing with an imperceptible contact.

'Next please', says the pilot in a matter of fact tone, as you alight; another takes your place and the evolutions are repeated till everyone in the squad has had his preliminary trip. This over, M ---- prepares to give pupils a demonstration of how to do it. Once more you mount to the rear seat and in a few moments are up again.

You are conscious on this flight that you are exercising a more active control than before and feel that your tentative touches on the controls are not altogether repressed. In fact on landing, M--- remarks over his shoulder: 'You'll take front seat next trip'. In due time this comes to pass. Having strapped yourself in, you proceed to set the throttle lever and operate the switch under his direction. Off slides the machine, and, turning up wind, the engine begins its by now familiar roar and you are speedily on your third flight.

There is no pilot's back now to obstruct the view and, like the mechanic in Steam Tactics, you find a whole lot of gauges and instruments on the dashboard in front. At these you have time to steal a surreptitious glance while the instructor takes responsibility for the first hundred feet of ascent. A compass is suspended low down, its prism adjustable to render it visible from the pilot's seat. Next to it comes a revolution counter, which at the moment is registering 1,800 revolutions; and so long as it continues to do so, you have no cause to worry about the behaviour of the engine. Straight before you is a spirit level. On some machines this is supplemented by a clinometer, but it does not appear on the instruction 'bus'. Near to the level is a vertical gauge, fed by two copper tubes, leading, as you follow them, to a species of funnel placed narrow end forwards on one of the distant struts. An index is marked on this gauge and a column of reddish fluid in it stands as 52. This represents, approximately, the force of the wind, miles per hour, in the funnel nozzle; and from it you can in some measure calculate your speed. One more indicator remains, the altimeter, and while you have been scanning the dash, the needle of this has climbed up to 400 feet level.

Still blindly following the instructor's hold on the controls, you venture a look round at the landscape. On this third trip it begins to assume some degree of familiarity and you find yourself looking out for prominent landmarks. The line of the railway is easy to follow. Away in the distance are the reservoirs. A river stretches its winding, molten silver-like surface parallel to your course. Right below lies a sewage farm, in the confines of which some pilots have been known to land with dire results.

While you have been taking stock of all of these, the machine has been persistently climbing and your height is now in the neighbourhood of a thousand feet. Reconciled to some extent to the novelty of the front seat, you once more attempt a more personal influence on the controls; and presently it comes with somewhat of a surprise, first, to see the instructor's hands slipped away from the dual grips and then to feel his arms withdrawn from your sides. Soon a tap comes on your left shoulder and, divining its meaning, you attempt a left hand turn. To your gratification the machine obeys. On completing the turn, a hand is laid on your right shoulder; another guess; you straighten out, and are relieved to find that you have guessed right.

It is not easy at first to fly at a steady height. The elevator is powerful and one can easily overdo a movement. The tendency, consequently, is to steer a miniature switchback course and make continual corrections; but the pilot's guiding hand keeps coming to your aid. It gives you a great feeling of comfort, this, especially when the time arrives for a descent. Down you glide in a wide spiral, with engine throttled; M--- easily jockeys you into position for the final downward swoop; and once more the earth rushes up to greet you. The machine lands like a feather, but instead of being headed up to the waiting mechanics, the propeller speeds up again and you rise for another flight. A circuit at 200 feet is completed and the nose is turned earthwards. This time the landing is not so smooth; you wonder why and the reason is soon vouchsafed. 'Not so bad for the first time', says M-- over your shoulder, 'you did most of that yourself, you know'. As a matter of fact, you didn't know; but that is a detail.

In the Shops

The foregoing description is not intended to convey the impression that the Brooklands course of instruction consists of flights only. The mechanical side is equally important, for once in the air you must have implicit confidence in the engine behind you; and there is no chance of attending to it up there.

After breakfast then, on our first morning, we novices muster at one of the aeroplane sheds. Several others, whose training is more advanced, are already there, studying text books or stooping over instructional engines. Full length on the floor is a main plane, lying on its side; perched up against the walls are spars and other things,the significance of which is not at once evident. Festoons of wire hang from the struts in apparent confusion. The fabric of the planes, like the character of the nursery rhyme, is all tattered and torn; it has seen better days; but 'tis enough, 'twill serve.

A taciturn sergeant indicates with a gesture that the main plane is to be hoisted, right way up, onto a pair of trestles. This done, 'nacelle, tail booms and tail', he mumbles, pointing out each with a descriptive finger and then disappears elsewhere. Here is something new, with plenty of scope for the working of our inner consciousness. The nacelle, or car, comes first. After sundry pushings and pullings, we contrive to squeeze it into place between the two centre struts. Then, casting our eyes about, we find four sockets wherein the tail booms must surely fit. A step ladder is necessary, in order to knock out the securing bolts; and with much manoeuvring the tail booms quiver and waggle into position.

At this stage the sergeant reappears, casts a glance round the tattered machine, so far as we have got it erected, and signifies that we are to fasten up all the loose wires. These seem to run in every conceivable direction, up and down, backwards and forwards and diagonally across the framework. A turnbuckle at the end of each wire connects up the ends by simultaneous right and left hand threads. We feel that here, at all events, is something we can do and scurry round, fastening up all the wires we can grasp. Apparently we are going too fast for our taciturn instructor, who, by way of choking us off for a while, demonstrates with a pair of round-nose pliers how to make connecting loops in a piece of wire. In his hands it obeys docilely enough; so, arming ourselves with similar instruments from a mechanic's box we set about this new operation. Somehow it is not as easy as it looks. Either the round-nosed pliers aforesaid won't grip the wire or the wire itself is suddenly gripped with a demon of obstinacy. One genius is seized with the brilliant idea of using smaller gauge wire, slavishly we copy his example and soon produce a colourable imitation of the sergeant's handiwork. We show our loops to him with pride; but with a sniff he waves them away and grimly suggests a wire several sizes thicker. It is no good, our dodge; he is an old bird: and we are perforce compelled to wrestle and struggle, what time he watches us with a surly chuckle. In the end, by way of a change, he consents to point out how the tail planes are attached to the tail booms.

This done we survey our handiwork with a curious eye. Poor thing, it has seen better days. Strips of fabric hang down in many places, mute evidence of someone's careless handling in the past. The car would hardly be windproof, could it be taken aloft, so many are its rips and rents; whilst in the absence of controlling wires, the twin rudders flap disconsolately in the breeze. Still, it has taught us something and we feel it deserves our gratitude. A parting word from the sergeant and we are free until 4.30pm, when, weather permitting, we shall once more go on instructional flights.

As a matter of fact the weather does permit, though the conditions are not exactly ideal for instructing a pupil in his early stages. The heat of the day, playing upon the tree tops and sheets of water near the aerodrome have helped to create local air-drafts of 'bumps', both up and down, the presence of which is only too evident at certain points. You are not yet sensitive enough to their proximity to anticipate them, but

M--- says that the knack will come in time. He has got it developed to a positively uncanny degree. As you sail along on a level keel, you suddenly and for no apparent reason feel the controls pushed over to the right or left, and the machine begins to bank accordingly. Sure enough, within a fraction of a second, there comes a gust under the lower wing tip, restoring you once more to a state of equilibrium: and on a bad day this juggling is practically continuous until you land. M---'s theory is that each puff is heralded by a gentle, almost imperceptible one: this, he says, is enough to make the machine quiver slightly, and to put the watchful pilot on his guard.

It would seem that fore and aft bumps are less to be feared than side bumps, that is assuming you are fairly high up. A falling column of air hits the nose of the machine and forces it down, the aeroplane then pointing earthwards; but within a fraction of a second that same falling column hits the tail, forces it down too and so restores you to flying level. A side gust, on the contrary, may hit one wing tip and heel you over: but it does not necessarily follow that a compensating gust will immediately strike the other tip and put you straight again. My second pilot insists on this with much emphasis. 'There is no need', he screams in my ear, 'to be afraid of a slight list one way or the other, only don't let it get dangerous'. And with this warning he pushes the warping levers forcibly up and down, while the old 'bus' tilts from side to side and rocks and wallows as if in a stormy sea. 'So long as she doesn't sway more than that, you can go ahead'.

It is so simple, really, the whole control of an aeroplane, for the movements are quite instinctive. Suppose you are heeled over to the left, all you have to do is to press the right hand warping lever downwards and the machine responds to the touch, exactly as if you had put out a giant hand to the distant tip of the right plane now perched high above you, and pressed it firmly downwards. Similarly with rising and falling. A stumbling horse you would rein in; with a bucking horse you would do no such thing, for you might pull it over on its back. You rein in an aeroplane that wants to get its nose down in just the same fashion …

Extracts from Letters – *Alumnus* December 1915

21 July 1915 No. 5 Squadron, 2nd Wing RFC, British Expeditionary Force

As soon as you arrive in France now you can't help scenting a different atmosphere from anywhere in England except in the neighbourhood of Garrison towns. I think it must be the sight of English soldiers on French soil, cheerfully accommodating themselves to French ways; of the great piles of stores by the side of the quay and long lines of transport lorries ready packed to go up to the Front.

Such of the French towns as I actually passed through by motor had quaint, winding, cobbled streets with notice boards in duplicate – au pas, dead slow – and sentries at almost every turn, to regulate the almost constant stream of carts and despatch carriers and motor buses and ambulances and staff cars. These are practically the only outward and visible signs of war. Except in the areas actually shelled, there is barely anything to show the grim struggle which is being waged so close at hand. The countryside is calm and peaceful enough. It scarcely matters which way you look; in all directions nothing strikes the eye but acres of rapidly yellowing corn, or crops of beans or roots or potatoes, or hop gardens with their leafy forests of hop poles. True, the farmsteads wear a deserted appearance, for all their young men are long since called away; and as you drive along the pave roads, you may see a battery sheltered under a belt of trees, or bodies of troops marching along, or large houses and farms with large notices outside to mark them as the headquarters of some unit.

Perchance too you may meet some lumbering vehicles that tower above their fellows on the road. They are now a dingy hue; their advertisements are gone and their windows are shuttered with dust-stained, dark green boards, but you can no more conceal their identity than you can transform a Ford into a Rolls-Royce. They are old familiar friends who have long done their duty at Barnes, or Liverpool Street, and now by some trick of transport have come to look for fresh fares across the Channel. Supply columns stand patiently waiting by the road side. Night is their day, and day their night, for from above their movements are quickly discerned and it is from them that the observer can infer the concentration of troops.

Our billet is out in the quiet countryside a mile or so from the squadron aerodrome. The single line railway runs quite close, and until a few days ago, a perfect stillness reigned. Now, the roads past the house resound to the jangling of harness and the rumbling of wagons and the patient tramp of a freshly arrived infantry brigade. We are told much of the wit and humour, the grit, the splendid courage and the endurance of the British soldier. He needs it all too. I feel almost ashamed of my comparatively soft job as I watch those sections of fours pegging cheerily away, despite aching feet and sagging equipment, and the grilling sun overhead and the clouds of dust below. They do need every ounce of encouragement they can get, and you should have seen the magical effect a gramaphone had when we set it by the open window and it wheezed out some rollicking chorus. And when I saw the men a night or two back cheerfully preparing to bivouac in a wind swept field, all hot and weary after a full day's footslogging, I felt more than ever ashamed to compare their lot with my own comfortable bed, and our piano furnished drawing room and our elaborately equipped bathroom.

Perhaps you would like a brief outline of a typical day out here. To begin with my 'flight' is a fighting flight: that is to say it goes out with the intention of having a scrap if there are any Huns to scrap with. Other flights are sent out to do photographic work or range battery fire or make reconnaissances of various kinds; and on such occasions we are supposed to go on patrol work, that is cruise round in their vicinity and act the policeman, if and when necessary. In the event of there being no early flying, we breakfast at 8 o' clock. About 8.30 a motor calls to run us down to the aerodrome. The country road is deep in dust when the weather is fine, a sea of mud if it rains. It is so narrow in parts that you have to lean inwards to avoid being lashed in the face by overhanging branches. Peasants thrust themselves into the hedgerows and screw up their faces into weird grimaces at the dust storm in our train. Occasionally, in the narrowest part, one meets a typical French three-wheeled cart. Then confusion reigns for a while until the team of horses can be persuaded to stop plunging and draw their load into the nearest farm gate. A quarter of a mile of pave is all we have of the main road. As a rule this stretch is very slow, because there is either a stream of waggons plodding along or else gangs of men are employed in patches on corvee duty. Here you come across the old style of French uniform – a tattered shako, red or blue, brass buttoned blue tunic and baggy blue and red pantaloons.

Arrived at the aerodrome, the first thing is to wait hopefully for the arrival of the post. It is disappointing to sort over envelopes when they appear, anxiously scanning addresses for one's own, and then, finding nothing, resign oneself to wait until the same time next day – for we enjoy one delivery per diem here. If there is no patrol work there is the previous day's Times, which I get regularly, to read; Morse code to rub up, machine guns to clean and test at the range, engines to look over and maps to learn. With these pursuits and letter writing, time soon passes until lunch. In the afternoon should there be no real business on, we improvise a scratch game of cricket. What a subject for the Mail! 'England's national game within sound of the guns'. 'Eton's playing fields at the Front', 'Intrepid aviators at play!' Then tea at 4.30; and more work or novel reading or searching the sky with telescopes until 7.30 when the tender takes us off to dinner and we round up the evening with a gramaphone.

Patrol work is quite amusing. You get away a few minutes before the machine you are escorting, hang about waiting for it and then start off towards the lines. The cruise lasts, as a rule, about an hour and a half, at an average height of 6,000 feet.

If the day is clear the yellow line of trenches can easily be picked out in all sorts of fantastic designs and zigzags. Oval tracks, hoof trodden in pasture land, mark an exercising ground for horses. Sometimes you may see a string of transport moving along the roads, but this is rare and generally at some way back from the lines. The other day, a long trail of smoke from a burning chateau testified to shell fire from the other side, flames were streaming out of all the windows and next day the building was a mere shell, completely gutted. Elsewhere the ground is literally plastered with craters, the result of incessant big gun activity. At length the patrol is over. The engine subsides into silence and you start on a six mile glide over the chess board and hop gardens and corn squares and pasture, in delightful calm.

It was a perfect summer night last night, just such a one as the many I have spent in Oxford on a college roof, watching for the dawn to come up over Magdalen Tower and the twin turrets of All Souls. Down below my window, the narrow winding street, with the village nestling round – rows of small, red-tiled, uninteresting houses, not picturesque at all. Above, the black purple dome of the sky, spangled with innumerable stars. A windmill showed its gaunt bare arms in sombre profile to the left; while away on the right a range of tree-clad hills was capped by a monastery, standing out in vague outline against the starlight. It was hard to realise that only a few miles away stretched the valley dividing the two great armies; and for a few moments at a time, one could almost fancy oneself out here for a rest cure. But signs both near and far soon dispelled that dream

The silence of the village street was broken by the regular tramp-tramp of the sentry, varied by his crisp challenge to occasional passers by. Its narrowness was intensified by row upon row of motor vehicles packed as closely as they could be. Here were a hundred lorries, or more perhaps, covering the best part of a mile, ready to start off at a moment's notice, with their stores, under the friendly shadow of the darkness. The tiny railway Halte, usually so placid and undisturbed, was a centre of activity, from which came the frequent clink of metal upon stone, and an interlude of the West Riding tongue, while dim figures of men hastened about in the gloom, their shadows grotesquely distorted in the light of the lanterns they carried. Almost without intermission the purple blackness of the sky was lit up by weird flares and star shells, sent from the German trenches. For a moment hills, monastery and windmill would stand out in sharper relief, to relapse once more into sombre shadow. Searchlights swung their restless beams hither and thither in constant scruting; and ever and anon, across the intervening distance, came the long rumble and roll of heavy guns. Thankfully we turned in, grateful to be spared these latest exhibitions of German frightfulness.

Sept 1915 – R and I were working in cooperation with artillery, signalling their shots to the battery by wireless from above. It wasn't an ideal day, however, our target was well over the lines and we were just under the clouds at 3,500 ft, not a healthy height in that district. The cloud bank was practically solid. We had to get clear of it by some means, so climbed and climbed and climbed through the thick, damp, clinging whiteness, passing through an occasional welcome rift, till at last we swam out into the upper daylight at 6,500 feet. It was a wonderful sight. As far as we could see there was nothing but a billowing, fleecy floor, like the rippling surface of the sea, apparently so firm and stable that one might almost have stepped out upon it. Still, we could not make much headway in conditions like that. My observer kept tapping out messages to the gunners below, to say where we were and what the weather conditions were like. Finally, we nosed down very, very gingerly through the mistiness once more, steering by compass to get our bearings, picked out our battery on the ground and got a signal from them to go home.

You are quite right when you say there are plenty of things to keep two of us occupied. On ordinary reconnaissance trips the pilot has his hands fairly full. There's an eye to keep on the revolution counter, on the compass, the speed indicator and altimeter. There is the petrol gauge to watch and a hand pump to work at when the level begins to fall. There is the map to watch and the direction to pick up on the ground. Incidentally there is also the business of flying the machine, whilst keeping an ear open to detect faulty engine running. When one gets some special show, such as bomb-dropping or photography or wireless there are a few more oddments thrown in: such as timing one's passage over the ground by stop watch, elaborate sighting devices and compensating dodges, unrolling a long aerial of copper wire and painfully rolling it up again. In fact the actual business of flying the machine comes to be almost as automatic as riding a cycle.

R and I had a long reconnaissance last Tuesday, just about 200 miles, across the lines and back again. Before we started out, though, we had a sort of early morning exercise canter. I was pilot on guard duty, that is my job was to chase off any Hun machine that came sniffing round; and I had to sleep at the aerodrome all night. Sure enough at 5.30 am I was waked up with the news that a German machine was in the neighbourhood. It was very misty but we went out and cruised round at 3,000 feet to no purpose however. Our reconnaissance proper began at 8.20. We carried it out at a height of 8,700 feet and had practically observed all the positions necessary when we spotted a Hun machine cruising away below to our left. We watched it for some time but our petrol was low, so we could not risk chasing it. Then, with watching it, we lost our direction and R's compass went wrong. I just struck west, steering by the sun, until we crossed the lines again, plugged along for some time, but neither of us could pick up our whereabouts: and at last, to save trouble, we came down in the countryside. Some people who were reaping near came up and to begin with regarded us with suspicious reserve. Murmurs of 'espion, espion allemand' [spy, German spy] passed round; but I cut that libel short with a hasty 'non, non, aviateur anglais' [No, no, English pilot] pointing at the same time to the red, white and blue circles on the wings and fuselage. Then they grew quite friendly and we soon had a whole village population gathered round. We discovered out exact spot on the map but then the engine got obstinate, though we wrested with it for an hour and a half. There were three boys, brothers, among the crowd each with a cycle. I borrowed one and, under the guidance of one of the brothers, rode off some five miles to the nearest telephone office and arranged for mechanics to be sent over. At last the mechanics appeared. The engine was still troublesome and it was not until 5.30 that we were able to make a start. Before we got off there was another interesting ceremony, the presentation of an enormous bouquet of flowers, with an inscription attached: 'Un souvenir des jeunes filles de la Herelle' [a souvenir from the young girls of Herelle]. We made no mistake about the way on our return trip. The B E went along at a steady 68 miles per hour for mile after mile, with never a finger or touch on the controls. Its wires are of rather peculiar make, not circular in section but a long, narrow oval so as to cut into the wind and not offer so much resistance. As soon as you get over 60 miles an hour all the wires take up a note of their own and it is just like being inside a gigantic organ as they blend so beautifully. I can imagine that wireless cooperation with artillery from an aeroplane does sound mysterious at first. It is all worked by code though; so if the Germans do pick up our messages, as they no doubt do, the signals mean nothing to them. In just the same way our wireless receiving station picks up German code messages but of course can make nothing of them. Where the Germans do attempt to mislead us is this. One of our observers, say, orders a battery to open fire on a given target. Then he watches the target to spot the accuracy of the fire by looking for the shell-burst and the consequent puff of smoke. Finding a certain position bombarded and knowing that an aeroplane is ranging above, the wily Germans will simulate shell bursts by artificially producing white smoke puffs somewhere quite away from the fall of the shells, and so try to confuse the observer. Thus it develops into a contest of wits. It sounds wonderful I know, but it is not one of the most wonderful things of this war. It's sliminess that's all and in sliminess we have a lot to learn.

October 1915 – Since I last wrote my main job has been photography. R and I were given a sealed reconnaissance last Saturday morning: he to take notes and myself to work the camera. I made eight snaps from 8,500 feet. It is not quite the easy job it sounds to press the trigger release while bending over the aeroplane side and squinting down the camera sights. The last of all was remarkable in one or two respects. To begin with it was an extra. We had finished what we had been told to do and I had turned our nose homewards. We were jogging steadily along when a Hun appeared away on our left coming for us at right angles, a shade higher than ourselves. R unstrapped himself and got up in his seat to manoeuvre our machine gun into position being thus precluded from watching the ground. Just at that moment I caught sight of something below which I thought might proved interesting ; so steered for position over it and snapped it for future reference. The Hun meanwhile – a monoplane – having approached us from the left, suddenly sheered off and came along behind, probably thinking he was in for a good thing and expecting doubtless that we could not lay on him where he was behind us. This was just where he made his mistake. It was our very best fighting position and he realised it after a bit: for we just pushed on quietly and in the end he cleared off. By and by a biplane came up and did just the same performance with similar results. So we carried on over the lines and then had a peaceful twenty miles cruise home. The extra photograph did turn out to be interesting in two ways. One is that it contains some rather useful information. The other is that it shows a German machine rising from the ground in pursuit of us – a fairly hopeless quest as we had over 8,000 feet advantage in height…

After more than a week of east winds and consequently fine bracing weather, conditions have changed. The wind is now from the west and has brought clouds and rain with it, in place of the gorgeous unbroken expanse of blue sky to which we have been accustomed. So, flying conditions have altered somewhat. Last week I was taking photographs at 9,000 feet; and they came out beautifully clear and distinct; and what was more I managed to hit the places I wanted. Monday and Tuesday I was piloting on artillery shows while my observer did the wireless work. There is a growing tendency, however, to put this branch in the hands of the pilot as well. They say it keeps him from worrying whether his engine is all right and from being disturbed from the shelling he gets. It may be so, perhaps! The battery is completely under the direction of the aeroplane operator. It is the operator who selects targets, describes them, orders the guns to load, gives them the command to fire, spots from the smoke puffs the position of the shell bursts and sends down the necessary correction for succeeding shots. The battery we were co-operating with on Monday worked fairly well. As you can imagine there are no end of things that can go wrong. The wireless may break down or develop some defect which renders its signals indistinct. Or two aeroplanes operating simultaneously in different areas may jam each other's signals, with the result that the battery below may receive no message at all or perhaps a mutilated one which is worse than useless. Or the ammunition may give trouble. Shells may refuse to explode and thus make it impossible for the observer, who has sent down the signal to fire, to mark where the shot has gone.

On Monday, however, there was no hitch. We were working round and round in a small salient for a couple of hours; and the shots reached quite a good standard of accuracy. They were two absolutely dead hits on one place sent down as a target, smashing it to smithereens. It's quite consoling to see a thing like that... Photography work has not been so much in evidence since I last wrote. Artillery work has, though, and reconnaissances of other kinds. Yesterday, Thursday, I was up on artillery for an hour and a half, in pelting rain that stung like hail and clouds that make observation a bit difficult. On Tuesday, I had the longest reconnaissance in a two-seater that has ever been given to this squadron to do. We had a fifteen minutes' scrap with a Hun on the way back. I think he had been wired for on our way out and was lying in wait for us. His gunner was beastly accurate too; but my gunner, B, a canny Scot, was splendid and even when things went worst for us and our gun jammed, he just gave me a slow grin and went on methodically letting off single shots.

You remember the last letter I wrote saying I expected to be sent out in the early morning on a special mission. As a matter of fact, it did not come off until afternoon, when two machines were hustled out at 3.30pm with pilots only, and under instruction to keep close to each other. Within the first five minutes we managed to lose each other most successfully on account of the clouds. I chased diligently along corridors in them, trying all heights up to 9,500 feet to get a clearer view, but even there great white masses towered mountains high above me and there was nothing for it but to get through them. After some time, I got to a gap and fortunately recognised where I was; and so set myself on a compass course for my objective, where presently I laid an egg (dropped a bomb) and speedily hid myself in the welcome embrace of a cloud, as my attentions did not seem to be appreciated. Then some more guess work, after which I laid a second egg through the carpet of cloud as near as I could judge to the right spot. At this place they threw up at me the most comic thing I have seen yet – a bunch of glowing white balls, apparently strung together in some peculiar way. They came whirling up in a cluster, and at about 7,000 feet, stopped there suspended in a long wavy line. I watched them for a bit, but in the end clouds hid them, and I set about getting home, which I did with the friendly assistance of a winding river which gave me the key to my position. They were sending up rockets for me at the aerodrome when I got in sight of it. It was so funny. There were two rivers to cross and between them there was a regular curtain of fog, black and forbidding. I had had enough of clouds for one day and didn't fancy pushing through it, so I dived and dived and dived until I crawled under its fringe. It was very low too. I had to come to 600 feet to get below it. It was from there I saw the red signal flares – a welcome sight. The other pilot had landed twenty minutes before me.

A Visit to the Trenches

Yesterday was impossible from a flying point of view, and greatly daring, I went on a visit to see L-- in the trenches. After looking down at them so often from above, it is a curious experience to survey them at close quarters. As you go along there is an occasional ping from a rifle, like the sound of a shotgun after pheasants, varied by the rat tat tat of a machine gun, the sharp smack of shrapnel discharge or the red glare of a bursting shell. But everyone moved about unconcerned. From a clearing in the wood comes the blast of a whistle, where a football match is in progress. Alongside a farm building a gang of men is busy sawing up and methodically piling into heaps great piles of tree trunks and branches. Only their rows of rifles, the bolts stocking-cased to exclude dust and dirt, remind you that it is war. Elsewhere a platoon is streaming out through a cobwebby, mud-daubed archway, their billy cans and bread ration in their hands. This they supplement from a shop close by, its tiny paned window faintly revealing a show of fruit and pastry and chocolate within.

At Brigade Headquarters an orderly leads you down an extemporised earth stairway into a dug-out, faintly lit by a single guttering candle, which reveals clusters of wires, that stretch like nerves right up to the front line trenches and three operators sitting at their desks, the blue and white riband on their arms marking the Signal Service.

The walk back to the town makes one think very hard. Here within a mile of the lines are peasant people, watching their cattle or tilling the fields. For the most part, the cattle are tethered for grazing and the regular semi-circles into the patches of clover, like the edging on lace, mark the thrifty economy of the French.

The telegraph wires that border the road are everywhere hanging in festoons and the tiny railway track has long been wearing its coat of rust. Pretty country houses by the roadside, with once dainty gardens and well filled conservatories, now stand disconsolately empty, their windows close shuttered and the gardens abandoned to the ravages of weeds. A stray dog, perhaps, still barks defiance at the passer-by through the creeper-clad railings. It is a strange feature of France that the dog is rarely a friend of man as he is with us. He always regards you with suspicion and obvious mistrust, and an advance at friendship is an uncommon event in his kick-marked career.

The town itself is a curious spectacle. Before the war it had a population of 6,000. You would scarcely find a tenth of that number in the place now. The streets wear a melancholy look, dirty and deserted. Everything is standing idle. The railway station is empty. The shops are all shuttered up. So too are most private houses. Those whose fronts have been closed with planking and the like, have their windows blown in by shell concussion. Broken tiles and slates and fragments of brick lie across the pavement in untidy masses just where they fell. A peep through a shattered doorway reveals a living room whose ceiling is half torn down, and lathe and plaster are piled high on the floor. Some furniture still remains; but stained patched on wallpaper and wide-open drawers in cabinets and cupboards are mute evidence of a last hurried ransacking before the occupants quitted their home. The church itself is perhaps the saddest sight of all, originally it was built of decorative brick with ornamental designs in colour on the outside. But now little remains but its gaunt, shell scarred tower. Most wonderful is the gilt figuring which crowned it – a figure of the Virgin with the Child in her arms. Now it is poised like a Gargoyle of old, overhanging the street in perilous fashion, but hanging there none the less, gazing piteously, as it were, over the waste of shell holes and splintered roofs and tottering houses all around.

15

Cyril Carr Williamson

Bombs for the Hun (*Alumnus* December 1918)

'Car 'ere Sir'. These were the words that interrupted my dreams of home early in the morning of November 2nd 1918 and cries of 'Hold that car' came from two or three apartments of the long dilapidated hut forming our sleeping quarters, which, so as to lessen the risk of being shelled, had been built in a wood far away from the aerodrome, hence a car to take us to work. After a hasty toilet we were aboard the car and rushed through the village to the 'drome.

The day was not exceptionally bright and a slight mist was hanging over the ground.

Arriving at the 'drome everybody rushed to see the orders. Here was a great surprise for all: a neighbouring squadron had, on the previous day, been attacked by 30 Huns and had suffered terribly, five machines lost out of eleven. This was rather a rude awakening for everything had gone smoothly for two or three days and I think a little 'wind-up' was experienced by all. 'What if we run into this circus?' was the common talk.

At 9am the observers were fixing their Lewis Guns, while the pilots just looked over their machines to see if everything was 'OK', despite the reassuring remarks given by the flight sergeant. The CO with rather a jovial smile on his face, came along and was free with his advice for all: 'Now boys, show them what we can do, no funking', 'You have the best machines so let 'em have it'. We jumped into the machines, which were all loaded with two 230 lb bombs besides ammunition for their three guns; and opened out the throttle to see if the necessary revolutions for flying were given; with a roar the engine answered and the revolution indicator showed the required number. We then taxied out and took up formation behind the leader, and in V shape formation, and I had the position of fourth on the right hand side.

One by one with a tremendous roar took the air, circled round the aerodrome and automatically fell into position, The whole formation circled round until a decent height was obtained and then followed the coast to Nieuport. At a height of about 12,000 feet we crossed the lines. It is rather a quaint sight to look down upon the lines to see the zig zag trenches, little puffs of smoke and the numerous small holes on all sides.

About five minutes after we had crossed, I felt a little pressure on the 'joystick': my observer wished to speak to me. On looking round he pointed away to the right. There was a little formation but whether enemy or not could not be ascertained for the moment. Then small puffs of black smoke began to appear on all sides, we were in an 'archy barrage', the leader began to throw his machine in all directions so as to bluff the ground gunners. In this way we reached our objective and all eyes were on the leader to see when his load was dropped. As soon as we saw the two cigar shaped bombs drop from their carriers all the 'toddles' in the machines were pulled. The formation went straight on and the records of hits were observed.

We then returned unmolested having been in the air two and a half hours.

At two o' clock we started out on another raid with lightened hearts owing to the success of the morning's raid. We hadn't gone far before we were 'strafed' on all sides, there was an enemy formation above and below, this kept the observers' guns busy for some time, but still they kept in perfect formation awaiting their chance. Their chance did come. On dropping our bombs and turning round our formation was not quite as strong as it should have been and down the Huns came and the 'pop pop' of their guns rattled through the air. We answered and soon were in formation again but my observer had been hit and lay in the fuselage. This was rather bad – suppose we should get into another scrap, without a back gun I should be 'in the soup'. Black puffs of smoke were visible on all sides, 'archy' indeed was getting rather troublesome. All at once my machine shuddered a little then her nose dropped and she began to spin. At about 4,000 feet I regained control but my head was buzzing and I seemed to have lost all sense of bearings, then the machine gave a terrible lurch forward and went nose down towards the ground. After this I remember no more until I awoke in hospital.

The machine had been hit by 'archy', breaking completely one side of the empennage; my observer had been killed during the scrap and I crashed just behind our lines being thrown out of the machine 50 or 60 yards away on impact with the ground. The machine was on fire and was totally destroyed.

16

Harold Willott

Letters from France – November 1915 To January 1916

15 November 1915 *(first day in France)* – We did not reach the expected port for some mysterious reason and, consequently, reached our camp several hours later, after the aforesaid journey. We had an amusing experience after disembarking, finishing our journey in commodious trucks designed for '*hommes 40 ou chevaux 10 (en long)*'. We found a camp for the English Expeditionary Force, where we slept eleven in one tent, my first experience of sleeping under canvas. It was cold but fairly comfortable after the journey. We were not given permission to go into the town but found a most accommodating YMCA place and I heartily agree with all the eulogisms of solders at home and abroad regarding that most admirable institution. There one can procure most excellent tea, coffee, or cocoa, most delightful rolls and butter, chocolate, tobacco and cigarettes at prices lower than at home.

Next day was an easy day including a route march round and through the town where the inhabitants appeared most friendly. We are not permitted too much intimacy with the people. I suppose the average English Tommy is not at his best when allowed to run loose among foreign people and we have to pay the penalty.

The route marches are now more exacting with a fuller and heavier kit than we have ever carried before but they are shorter fortunately and we are as cheerful and enthusiastic as ever, now that we are on the point of realising one ambition.

Quite six or seven inches of snow fell in the night but it was fine during the day when we moved off and had another cattle-truck journey to our present quarters. On arriving here, it was raining heavily and we were overjoyed eventually to find ourselves billeted in barns just outside a small village, of which I shall have more to tell you when rules and restrictions become laxer.

With ground-sheet, overcoat, blanket, helmet and air-pillow, I spent by far the most comfortable night I have had since reaching foreign soil and woke quite refreshed. Thirty of us in one barn represents crowding but not discomfort, and the sheet and pillow convert it into downright luxury. It is really quite a pic-nic at present thought this happy-go-lucky wandering sort of life is likely only to be a short one. We are well out of range of artillery fire, but near enough to hear the explosion of shells at times, and at night see a flame in the sky and perhaps in the course of the next few days or weeks may even take one turn in the trenches for a brief time to receive our baptism of fire. Not till then shall I really consider myself a trained solder and, curiously enough, I am quite looking forward to my first experience in that line.

21 November 1915 – We are still moving about and left our comfortable barn, where Madame proved so hospitable, two days ago. We divided the distance, rather less than 20 miles, into two days' marches, each being quite sufficiently long in view of the heavier packs we now carry and the uncomfortably rough cobble-stones with which many of the roads are paved. Our first halt was another barn where Monsieur et Madame were not so well-favoured as in the first place I stayed. Yesterday we arrived here and are billeted in a regular French barracks. English soldiers may thank Providence that we are not French conscripts if this is a sample of barracks in France. A plentiful sprinkling of chloride of lime everywhere lends a feeling of safety and as yet I have discovered no intruders, somewhat to my surprise.

Two of our companies have gone into the trenches, a distance, I believe, of about six miles. The sector of trenches we expect to take over is a particularly quiet one and one can be quite comfortable and reasonably safe if we are to stay there. I will let you know more of the town and the trenches when I write again. Time is short now; my next letter will tell you how I like the trenches. The noise of the guns is for all the world like an old woman shaking blankets, at this distance, and though the batteries of either combatants shell the other regularly there have been no hand-to-hand combats between the men in months.

28 November 1915 – I think I am permitted now to tell you the names of places I visited a fortnight ago so long as I do not mention where on the front we actually are or have been for a week or so. If I err at all the censor will easily put the matter right. (*I am sorry but this is a mistake – Censor*). We left … and sailed for … but owing to some mysterious reason I will not mention partly because I do not know and partly for fear of the censor, we disembarked at … instead. We were not allowed any liberty and were rushed off at once in cattle trucks (closed) for …. It is a largish town and our billet was a regular French barracks – very bleak and bare certainly but roomed off, 25 of us occupying a place intended for 12. The townspeople are quite ready to accept English money and we can buy every kind of thing we want. Most of my money went on eatables. French coffee and confectionery are delightful and we are as ever underfed and my food is as unpalatable as in English barracks.

I had my first day and night in the trenches and on … my second. The experience was a new one certainly and it was with vast relief and not a little surprise I found it possible to keep perfectly cool under fire. Of course it is possible at most times to keep one's head down and the trenches are perfect cover from snipers' fire on ordinary occasions. The noise of exploding shells (of which I have learned to distinguish the coal-box from the whizz-bang, and that of the trench mortar, an implement designed to throw a sort of bomb further than is possible by hand) is loud enough certainly but is for all the world like a glorified Nov 5th and it is even possible to derive entertainment and amusement out of it all.

Our first day was a sort of trial day. The trenches were held by another body of men – I will give the amiable Censor a chance (*Thanks)* and say that they were a ... and we were there for instruction purposes, not undertaking really difficult work on our own initiative. It was a quiet day though the artillery fire passing over us between the guns of the respective armies was very heavy and our own men sending by far the greatest number of shells. Whenever they get a little obstreperous our artillery has word and shells them heavily and they gradually die down into comparative quiet. The second day was in another part of the trenches less comfortable than the first and we had it more or less to ourselves, though the particular bombing party, to which I was attached, was in the hands of three old regulars of an English line regiment. The trenches are very dirty though, where the ground is too wet and apt to give way, they have floors of wood and even bricks laid down, and the parapets are now mainly composed of sandbags filled with earth quite bullet-proof and more permanent than were earthworks.

16 December 1915 – We were sent to take charge of a part of the line and spent the first few days in reserve near the town and I lived in a very comfortable barn, of which I think I wrote as the best thing we had as yet struck in the billeting line. Curiously enough, the very night after I wrote that my sleep was disturbed by rats, which insisted, to my great discomfort, in walking over my body and head. I was in a cold sweat and far more funked than I have been in the trenches, but I have made further subsequent acquaintance with the rodents and can see the time coming when I shall grow to care for them.

Our last spell in the trenches was by far the most exacting we have yet had. It is absolutely impossible for me to make you realise the conditions we work under. I will, however, make an attempt.

Our first day was spent in reserve, ie second line, trenches to which on this occasion it was necessary to march at night, ending our march in single file along a road full of deep holes and all filled during this rainy season with pools of water. We had a weary time of waiting while our men in turn divested themselves of packs and boots in order to replace the latter by long gum-boots reaching half way up the thighs and strapped under the sole, round the calf and to the braces. This took about 3½ hours, what time we waited outside in the aforementioned road near and on which occasionally exploded an enemy shell. We took no harm in our company and we continued the journey into the trenches during an incessant downfall of rain. The communication trench from the village to the reserves had wooden planks laid down but in many instances they were covered with as much as a foot and a half of water, whence the need of gum-boots.

Mud, mud everywhere – no dry dug-outs. Sleep we had to get wherever possible, mostly without shelter from the rain. It was the mud everywhere that covered everything, boots, clothes, greatcoats, even food if we did not exercise the greatest care, that made things so insupportable. However we kept up our spirits and waited for the morning, even contriving to sleep in snatches.

I had a period of guard and was entertained by the swimming exercises of numerous rats and mice in pools which abounded. As far as warfare went, we had a very quiet time and left at night for the front line or fire trenches. Here we had a journey that I shall always remember. In actual distance not more than 500 yards had to be traversed but the journey had to be done at night where we could not see in front of us and had to keep in close touch with the man in front. There is no real pathway and the mud even reached the top of our great boots making necessary a big effort at times to withdraw them from the clutches of the mud, the whole being a terrific marsh whose like I have never seen or dreamed of. Men whose boots were not securely strapped on had to abandon them and leave them in the mud, finishing in stocking feet (fortunately this was rare). Some other new troops had previously done the same journey and lost heart, abandoning rifles and equipment, but I am glad to say this happened to none of us. I was able, especially on the return journey, to give a helping hand to a man, who experienced greater difficulty than I did, and this occupied my mind to the exclusion of my own little troubles. We got there and, after a stay of a day, made the return journey, which in that section must always be done at night as it is across the open and we still kept up our spirits to the satisfaction of our colonel.

I cannot describe the mud. It is not ordinary dirt, but an inferno of slime and filth, hideous in truth, even to men used to the ordinary mud that one expects in the trenches. There could be no trenches proper in ground like this, – I had forgotten to tell you but the barricades were constructed by sandbags filled with earth above the level of the ground.

The mud on our greatcoats, impossible to remove, to the depth of½ inch made their weight intolerable and we marched back to the French town, which by now we knew so well, utterly exhausted even thought the distance was only 6 or 7 miles. Our billet this time was for a couple of days in an orphanage room, with numerous holes through the ceiling admirably adapted to let the rain in.

Cold and wet through with no blankets, nothing but wet clothes and hard dirty floor and rain coming in we were yet so tired, not having had a couple of hours consecutive sleep for several days, that we slept where we lay, like logs, waking up yet none the worse as we were marched to a public bath for a hot bath and a complete change of clean (in fact new) underwear supplied. Now we are in Elysium, having come for a real rest to a village further away from the firing line, of which I shall have much to tell you in my next letter.

17 January 1916 – Somewhere in France. As regards names and places you can tell anyone where you know or think I am. That is quite allowable and, if you ask me if I were at Kirjathjearim on Jan 35th, I am quite at liberty to say 'Yes' or 'No' in my reply as long as I do not repeat the question.

I am writing in a cosy (?) dug-out while there is a rather hot artillery bombardment going on. A lovely piece of shrapnel, or rather a part of a high explosive shell, struck my valise a few inches away just now, but it was only a stray fragment the real force of the bombardment being directed on a village in the rear. This time of trench occupation I am rather in luck's way being a bomber in reserve and doing nothing much except fatigue works and sentry duty – plenty of it, but quite safe apart from the rather remote chance of a shell dropping near.

25 January 1916 – I am back again at the old game and am having quite a busy time as mess orderly, which involves my carrying – with three others – food for about 50 men, all of whom are stationed, for the present at any rate, in a kind of 'keep' and not in the firing line. Our dug-out is a cellar with concrete roof and there is room to stretch our legs which is quite a treat, I can assure you.

March 27th 1916 – I have been promising myself the pleasure of writing to you for some considerable time and the fact that I have not done so is due largely to sheer indolence, but I think more to a feeling of diffidence. Others of your correspondents have written letters, copies of which I have been delighted to read in the *Alumnus* telling of experiences so varied and interesting that I felt that anything I could say would make dull reading by contrast. Feeling, however, more in letter-writing vein than is usually the case, I am rather inclined to attempt some small atonement for my remissness in the past.

How to begin is a matter of no small difficulty as there are so many things I might speak of, each of which would provide me with material for several hours writing. There is no one outstanding event, such as a general advance, the repulse of a desperate enemy assault or a brilliant counter attack on our part, which would suggest itself at once as an obvious subject for an essay, and, as I must confine myself within certain limits, I think I will choose one little 'scrap' we had quite recently, which added to the reputation of our battalion and increased our popularity with older units out here. The little affair was the outcome of the explosion of a German mine, an event of by no means infrequent occurrence on this part of the front, in the early hours of the morning. It was too near broad daylight for any attempt at occupying the crater during the daytime, and beyond an inevitable interchange of machine-gun fire on the part of the combatants and sapping out from either line in the direction of the crater, nothing of note transpired until after nightfall.

Parties of our men and the Germans patrolling encountered each other and there was a brisk little bombing engagement, in which both sides lost a number of men, the enemy losses, once our reinforcements came up, far exceeding our own, though at the commencement of the action the Bosches were numerically superior.

There were four or five saps to be held in our little sector, and as a bomber I had the task of holding one of these every night for several nights, being on duty from 6 o' clock in the evening until 7 next morning on each occasion. It was rather trying, though personally I had good luck in not being in any one sap at the precise moment when caterpult-hurled bombs and rifle grenades happened to burst directly inside, though friends of mine who came in on subsequent or preceding nights were less fortunate.

On one of the nights when the enemy's grenades made some effort to regain lost ground, I was fortunate enough to be able to watch from my own sap-head the whole of the strafeing that took place between our men in another sap to the left and the Germans at the opposite side of the crater.

I had omitted to mention that there were four or five huge craters in front of our line, and I wonder whether anyone at home can quite realize what these are like without first having seen one. Picture an immense basin-shaped cavity perhaps forty or fifty yards in width, seventy or eighty in length and possibly sixty feet in depth, sometimes fairly regular in shape, at others with jagged boulders jutting out assuming weird shapes in the moonlight and the flares from the star-shells projected by the enemy in much profusion. Running out from either front line trench is a narrow trench or sap and at the end of this sap there may be a trench branching out to the right or left in a direction roughly parallel to the nearer lip of the crater. On one side, whether in the sap or lying out as a fringe, are bombers, whose objective is the prevention of a flanking attack round the crater, while sappers are at work completing, improving or repairing the trenches.

Similar conditions probably obtain on the other side. If strict watch were not kept, enemy parties might creep round and lob bombs into and then along the sap. A superior force may come and attempt to take the trench, regardless of loss of life, but after two or three attempts, the whole business resolves itself into the interchange of bombs and rifle-grenades, supported by trench-mortar batteries and occasionally by the artillery considerably in the rear.

On the occasion of which I speak, I became fascinated by the sight of bombs, English and German, exploding sometimes in mid air, sometimes on impact with the ground, while most of those which were thrown anywhere near to me fell down the precipitous sides of my particular crater, or fell directly into its depths, exploding there quite harmlessly.

After all I find it impossible to convey any idea of the effect of the varying explosions, easily distinguished, of our own and that of the enemy's grenades, of the whiz-bangs from the rival guns and one especially heavy shell which we put over at a time when emotion was very tense and we were wearied with physical exertion. The outcome was the driving out of the Germans from their principal position gained, the establishment of trenches, saps and bombing-posts to assist in preventing any repetition of an early success – losses on our side far outweighed by those of the enemy, and the feeling of satisfaction that we could do what we were called upon to do, and on our own initiative.

Forgive me for having let myself drift so aimlessly but it is exceedingly difficult to preserve any sequence in a letter written in odd moments, and in odd phrases. For instance, during the writing of these notes we have been in three different villages, once in the trenches, once in reserve billets and once a little further back in a small town six or seven miles behind the firing line. I felt however that I should like to write, partly because you have asked me to do so on several occasions and partly because I am beginning to regret not having kept in touch with the old school in recent years.

Ernest Spencer Willott

A Day's Work on a New Zealand Sheep Farm (*Alumnus* July 1914)

I. MUSTERING (extracts)

Sheep-work perhaps appears tame by comparison with cattle-work. Certainly it lacks the spice of danger, the thrill of the gallop to head a wild steer or to dodge the charge of a maddened bull or of a cow defending her calf, and there is not the excitement of bellowing beasts and cracking stock-whips which invariably accompanies work among cattle. But, as I hope to show, sheep-work is not altogether as slow and devoid of interest as might be expected.

The Boss is away ill in hospital. Three of the men have suddenly 'packed their swags' and left the place and two of us, Bill, the head shepherd, and myself are left to run the farm as best we can.

Ernest provided a lengthy, detailed description of work on the farm with a typical day's work.

Our horses know their way fairly well and, following the best beaten sheep tracks, we wind along through gullies, up spurs and along ridges for a couple of hours until we reach the far corner of '400 acres'. As it is still too dark to see where the sheep are, we dismount, dance a hornpipe to restore circulation to our frozen toes and pass the time till daybreak with smoke and yarn. My mate, like many a man in the colonies, has had a varied and eventful career. …

We are on the highest point for many miles and command a magnificent view in all directions. [east to the Rushines, north to Ruapehu] … But there is no time to rhapsodise over the beauty of the view and the 20th Century shepherd, at any rate in the Colonies, is not like his medieval ancestor, particularly aesthetical. …

Extracts from Letters to his Parents August 1914 to November 1915 (*Alumnus* April and December 1915)

Toowoomba, Queensland, 9 August 1914 – Since I last wrote the war has begun and – needless to say – it has occupied our attention almost to the utter exclusion of everything else. The news we get here is much censored, very fragmentary, not altogether reliable, but even so – and although we seem to have heard nothing for several days – we have heard of a tremendous lot since last Monday. Rumours of fights and chases in the Baltic, North Sea, 'Thames Estuary', St Lawrence, China Sea, Mediterranean and even off the Australian coast.

I have been going to the station to meet the Brisbane train (10.15pm) with the latest papers, hanging about in front of the local paper office, and thinking that I would give every thing I possess to be in England again… Numbers of regiments have already mobilised to defend points of strategic importance here in Australia, and I, even I alone, seem to be the sole man in Toowoomba, who cannot be called out save by a special Act of Parliament. Every man from 14 to 60 is liable, but not emigrants till they have been in the country six months. I trust no war will come on to English soil. If it does we Australians will be there.

August 16 – Still nothing but war. War, war occupies our thoughts and if that is so with us here in Antipodean Australia it must be much worse with you at home. Censoring news here is, or course, much easier than in England, as our channels of communication are so much fewer.

More than a week ago we heard news of a terrific battle in the North Sea. The most cautious reports claimed that at least 30 German boats were sunk; and the Metropolitan papers each rancorously claimed to have been the first to print the news. Next day the report was officially contradicted and the squabble suddenly ceased. Since then the papers have been most cautious, printing nothing except unimportant fragments of news such as that 'a certain Belgian soldier killed four Germans and returned safe to his own ranks' – no doubt a most praiseworthy act, and yet, though we are delighted to hear it, we think the money spent on cabling such an account might have been better employed.

The wonder to me is that, considering the paucity of news, the public interest remains so intense. The other night Hewitt and I, sitting up here about 10 o' clock, heard strains of God save and vigorous cheering in the town a mile away. We went to see what was 'up' and read in capital letters on the notice board: AUSTRALIAN FLEET HAS CAPTURED NEW GUINEA. OFFICIAL. BRITTANIA RULES THE WAVES.

Toowoomba had gone mad. Half the male population processed behind a Union Jack and an Australian Ensign to a sung accompaniment. A little man was standing on the kerb, an expression of awe in the face. It was the editor of the paper whose notice board bore the announcement. 'Is it true?' I asked him. 'Divil a word' he replied, so we retired sadly to bed.

Now we strain at the gnats, even if we do, perhaps, swallow a canard. Yesterday one T'mba paper bore an account of the North Sea fight, while the other said in block capitals: NOTHING HAS BEEN HEARD IN MELBOURNE ABOUT THE NAVAL ENGAGEMENT WE REPORTED LAST WEEK.

Yet I heard (in confidence!) from a military authority yesterday that it was quite true and also the rumour of the Australian capture of German New Guinea and of the Bismark Archipelago. Occasionally fragments of news filter through by devious routes. The Sydney man I mentioned told us that two Germans had been arrested in the attempt to blow up the Hawkesbury Bridge – a feat which would have cut off Sydney from the north – and that they had been shot at dawn. Also that he had seen the HMAS Parametta return into Syd Harbour with the Seydlitz, which we knew she had been chasing.

I also heard to day that among the English losses were HRH the Prince of Wales and Admiral Jellicoe and that was why no news was published!

I don't know whether I mentioned the great number of Germans living in Toowoomba. Their attitude is somewhat amusing; though many of them would, I believe, love to see England smashed, many are, and more pretend to be, now Australian citizens. I was amused to hear one old gent, with the very Australian name of Rosenstaengel, exclaiming before the notice board which announced a German reverse, 'Dat is gut. I vud like to see all ter ----- Charemanse viped off ter face of te airtse'!

Some shops having signs bearing Teutonic names have done little or no business since war was declared and now bear large notices: 'WE ARE NOT GERMANS. WE WERE FORMERLY RUSSIANS. NOW WE ARE AUSTRALIANS. SEE OUR NATURALISATION PAPERS', which are shewn therewith, beautifully framed and surmounted with the crossed flags of England and Australia.

Enoggera Camp, Brisbane, August 26 – They have called for volunteers in case of emergency, so behold me I am a trooper in the Australian Light Horse. The trustees of the Grammar School are keeping my place open.

August 29 – No appointments have yet been made to the NC [Non Commissioned] ranks, but I have been temporarily put in charge of a troop consisting of about 30 Toowoomba volunteers, two or three of them South Africa veterans, several old Home Army men and nearly all them men with bush experience and hard as nails.

... In this camp out of three squadrons of 154 men each, I have heard that half are Englishmen – this, remember, in the Australian Light Horse! In the infantry camp about a mile away, out of over 1,000 men, it has been calculated that 90% are Englishmen and the variety of accents would astonish the builders of the Tower of Babel; Kentish men and Cockneys rubbing shoulders with 'Yorkies' and 'Scotties' and Ulster men fraternising with Nationalists.

September 14 – We have had one or two more or less exciting episodes to relieve the monotony. One day I spotted some confusion in the middle of my troop on parade, and, on going up to see what caused it, found half a dozen men killing a carpet snake. Another day a 'dust-shout' whirled through the camp. Luckily it missed the horselines and so failed to stampede the horses, but it upset a few men sitting on wheelbarrows, got under a marquee and lifted it sky-high, and demolished an officer's tent, greatly to our amusement. The last traces we saw of it being oilskins and shirts carried miles away over the bush. A couple of days ago I was inoculated for typhoid but beyond feeling tremendously tired and as if a horse had kicked my arm, I suffered no ill effects. The mounted parades yesterday and today were rather amusing. A number of the horses are 'rogues' and 'outlaws' which the stations have been glad to get rid of at any price. The new saddles are beautifully polished and slippery, and have been nick-named by our bushmen, accustomed to the large knee– and thigh–pads of the buckjumping saddle, 'self-emptying'. The military bits are cruel things to which any self-respecting horse would object on first acquaintance.

Melbourne October 19 – Latest rumours have it that we are to call at every possible port for the sake of exercising the horses. We had some camp sports the other day. I was chosen to represent our squadron on the committee and the position entailed a lot of work in arranging the programme and organising the affair. We had the usual events: tent pegging, lemon cutting, hurdle jumping, tug of war on horseback etc etc and I think the day provided – as was intended – a pleasant break in the monotony.

Troopship 'Star of England', October 25 – We have had very calm weather, an unusual thing in the Australian Bight, which out-Biscays Biscay as a rule .... We have on board parallel bars, a German vaulting horse and one or two other things, so I am in my element (though just at present terribly stiff) ... Reveille goes at 6, Parade at 6.30. This usually takes the form of Physical Training of some sort or another. Breakfast about 7.30 ... At 10 o' clock parade again. There are all sorts of things that can be taught on board ship and I am thankful that I have been through them before, signalling, musketry, bayonet fighting and many others too numerous to mention. Dinner 12.30, Parade 2.0, Tea about 5.30 and then the evening is free, unless there is a lecture or unless one is on duty.

Port Said, December 4 – Arrived here yesterday. We stayed at Suez a day, as also at Aden, but there was no mail at either place. We may (probably shall) stay at Cairo.

Maadi, Cairo, December 14 – We disembarked the other day at Alexandria and were allowed a few hours ashore – the first time we had set foot on terra firma since leaving Melbourne, though we called at Albany, Colombo, Aden, Port Said and Suez. We reached Cairo about 8pm and without any delay marched straight on here – a distance of 8 miles – each man leading two horses. Considering that we had done no walking for months, that most of us had not worn boots for 6 weeks and that the night was dark and the roads in some places were ankle deep under water, it wasn't too pleasant a performance. After picketing our horses we fell asleep anywhere and anyhow.

We are camped within sight of the Pyramids. By 'we' I mean the Australian Cavalry Brigade. There are a number of other Regiments – some 15,000 men all told – I believe, camped right at the foot of the Pyramids. Altogether I hear there are 160,000 British Troops in Egypt, including, besides the Army of occupation, English

Territorials, Australian and New Zealand, Ceylonese and Ghurka and other Indian Contingents. The Eastern bank of the Suez Canal was guarded by troops mostly Ghurkas, a company or so every mile and along the railway line from Alexandria to Cairo we noticed a number of camps containing native Egyptian solders.

Maadi, Cairo, December 20 – The camp is within a mile of the Nile, on whose capacious bosom (isn't that the proper phrase?) are innumerable feluccas with their peculiar single sail, and numbers of sluggishly floating crocodiles. At the other side of the Nile are the Pyramids to which, by the way, I promise myself a visit on Sunday; and to the north, on this side of the river, is a typical oriental town, beautiful domed and minaretted mosques in the centre and a conglomeration of mud and huts on the outskirts. On the opposite side of the camp to the river is a low range of hills with old forts at intervals – relics of Napoleon we are told – but I want to learn more about that before stating too much.

Our camp is pitched on a sandy flat between these hills and the river. Sand, sand and again sand is the prevailing feature, loose shifting sand interstrewn with pebbles and shells which leave no doubt as to its origin. Sand serves instead of salt in our tucker and is an excellent substitute for water in the wash basin.

In contradistinction to the almost universal yellow is the verdure along the actual banks of the river. There are no fences between the fields, their places being taken by irrigation channels, from which in turn smaller channels criss-cross all over the field. Maize, cotton, lucerne and clover appear to be the staple products so far as I have noticed hitherto. There are power stations (English and American) along the banks of the river at intervals for pumping, and cheek by jowl with them are the native wells familiar from pictures. This mixture of incongruities appears to be the characteristic of the country, the dress of the natives is a weird mixture of turbans, fezzes, caps, ex-sporting jackets, shawls, blankets and linen cloaks, stockings, shoes, red slippers and sandals.

Cairo, Egypt, January 12 1915 – Life is going on here pretty much the same; in fact I often feel guilty when I think how we, who enlisted – many of us with the best intentions – are enjoying ourselves eating and drinking and making merry, sightseeing like the veriest Cook's tourists and having almost the time of our lives under a sunny sky, while thousands of our fellow solders are fighting in the trenches amid snow and slush and incidentally receiving less than one quarter of the screw that we get. Well, as I was saying, I went to the pyramids on Sunday. It was a real American rush, but I decided not to lose the opportunity. We took car from Cairo and even so didn't reach there till about 3.30pm. There is a beautiful macadamised road all the way from the city to Mena House, the up to date Hotel within a stone's throw of the Pyramids, now alas!, within the bounds of the Infantry Camp and transformed into a military hospital. We took a dragoman, or rather he took us, as he pounced on us as soon as we alighted from the car and refused to be shaken off. He presented us to the Sheikh of the Pyramids and left us. The latter, a dodder lipped specimen of senile decay, took our boots, leggings and spurs and handed us over in stockinged feet to one of his myrmidons, who, armed with three inches of wax candles, with the grease of which he attempted to annoint us at every possible opportunity, was to act as our Hermes in these infernal regions.

After our guide's injunction 'mind your head' we ducked under an iron wicket-gate and found ourselves in the biggest mausoleum in the world, Cheops' burying place. We wandered along over polished alabaster slopes of 30 or 40 degrees with footholes worn every yard or so until we came to the King's Chamber in the centre of the Pyramid. The journey reminded me of the Jenolan caves and of a coal mine. There was the same re-iterated 'mind your head', the same bump of the cranium if you neglected to do so, and the same clawing for finger and toe-holds as in the caves. The heat was intense and we sweated some before we got out. Our guide showed us several ventilating shafts but the candle didn't splutter when held in the aperture and they seemed rather curios and receptacles for aerated water bottles than any utility. Then we visited the Queen's Chamber. The guide burnt a piece of magnesium ribbon, which revealed little or nothing and for which he charged two piastres (5d). My chief feeling was one of wonder how the immense sarcophogi could be taken in and out the winding passage.

January 15 1915 – This is a poly-glot place. To be able to read all the papers, menus, shop-signs, and so on it is necessary to know English, French, Italian, Greek, Arabic, Armenian and the wonder is that one is constantly meeting people (some youngsters of 10 or 12), who speak all these in addition to one or two others – German, Turkish or Russian. My Arabic studies have not yet proceeded very far. My vocabulary comprises three or four very useful words, in particular 'Inishi' or 'Zallah' (Go away, get out) and 'Mafish feloosi' (No more money) but it is surprising how far a few suitable words will carry you. The words oftenest used by the natives are 'Bagshish' (which we heard before leaving the boat), 'ma' aleyah' (never mind) used whenever they can't supply what you want and 'mafish' (there is none or no more) where any article is out of stock. The natives have also two English words 'Alright Gibit' which they use when you beat down their price from £E1 (£1–0–6) to PTI (2½ d).

January 25 – I don't know whether I mentioned it before but we have great extremes of temperature here. Today for instance it has been uncomfortably hot, yet the nights are extremely cold. There are heavy dews and every morning there is a fog. If there is not one at Reveille (we rise at 6am in the dark) one is sure to come rolling along before breakfast at 8am. During stables – 6.30–8 – it is bitterly cold and I, by virtue of my three stripes (by the way I am a fully fledged sergeant, the chrysalis period of lance sergeantship only being about five days), am denied the possibility of warming myself by manual labour with rake, shovel or barrow. Instead I have to walk up and down the lines seeing that the men do their work and cursing the cold.

I had a most interesting day yesterday, I got leave for the whole day and went into Cairo, intending to 'do' the mosques … I was introduced to an Egyptian gentleman

– a minister of something or other – agriculture I think ... He spoke very little English, though, he had a large English library and was highly delighted when he found I could speak French. He lived a number of years in France and of course speaks like a native. It was quite a pleasure to be in a decent house again, books, pictures and photos about, and a fire in the grate. He showed me one curio which he thought would interest me. To get it he removed from one of the shelves of a locked glass- doored bookcase about 12 volumes of Encyclopedia Britannica. Then after groping about at the back produced in a leather case a copy of the Koran. It was just like the pictures one sees and very similar to the old Illustrated Bible; all hand-done on parchment, beautifully coloured and gilded and a different pattern on each page. In the centre of the page was the chapter of the Koran. In one margin was the 'interpretation' in Arabic and in another margin outside this again an interpretation in Persian.

The book has a history too. It was prepared by some Caliph between 800 and 1,000 years ago to present to the Caliph of Samarkand, came into the possession of an ancestor of my host and has been handed down as an heirloom. Now it is worth thousands of pounds and devout Mohammedans come to consult it. I asked Hamid whether he was afraid of it being stolen and he told me that he changed its hiding place every two or three weeks. Even his brother never knows its whereabouts.

Hamid's brother Mustapha (formerly a lieutenant in the Egyptian army and who has served in the Sudan) took me round the native bazaars in the Moucki quarter, we visited the coppersmith's bazaar, the shoemaker's, jeweller's and others. Chiefly, I am afraid, through lack of funds, I resisted all the blandishments of the merchants, even when they cooed 'Austrahlia come here, varry goooood, vairy cheap, no need to buy, just to look'. All the same I hope to go back there just after pay day! We went into one mosque – no longer used for worship so I didn't need to cover my boots. By the way visitors now-a-days don't take off their boots. They are supplied at the door with large sandals, which are worn on top of, or rather underneath, the ordinary boots. The wearing of western dress has interfered sadly with a great deal of Mohammedan ritual. The up-to-date Moslem won't take off his patent leather boots and silk socks every time he wants to – and ought to – pray, so the command 'thou shalt wash thy feet as far as the ankle' has become a dead letter. Similarly the majority of Cairenes, when dining in a restaurant or hotel, don't go to the trouble of enquiring whether the food has been cooked in porcine lard or not. This applies equally to many who would never dream of eating bacon or ham.

... our future movements are still shrouded in uncertainty. We have no idea whether we are to go to fight the 'unspeakable Turk' in Syria or to hang on here till K of K wants us to proceed against the equally unspeakable Prussians. I only trust that we are not doomed to stay on here in inglorious inactivity – euphemistically termed readiness – until there is no further use for us. It is surprising how little time one seems to have in 'Mounted' Camp. Sometimes I almost envy the Infantry who are 'off' at 2pm. We spend 2 or 3 hours every day looking after our horses.

Here is one time-table (Inverted commas – trumpet calls):

6am	'Reveille', Dress and get a cup of tea
6.30	'Stables' 'Water', First unrug. Then one party takes horses to water while remainder clean the horse lines and fill horse bags. When horses return all turn in and groom (I always groom my own horse and he is beginning to look well under it). 'Feed' when all horses are reported groomed, we feed up and fall in to hear army orders read. 'Dismiss'
8am	'Breakfast', Feed, shave and don drill dress, possibly clean our rifles!
8.45	Sergeant-Major calls out 'get ready to parade'. We saddle up and file out into the parade ground.
9.15	'Fall in', march off and have possibly half an hour's squadron or regimental drill. Then practice 'advance guard' or 'rear guard', perhaps attack imaginary positions.
11.30	'Stables' 'Water' 'Feed up' and 'Dismiss'.
12.45	'Dinner'. Only break in the day, half an hour's rest
2pm	'Fall-in'. Usually foot work, musketry and so on.
3.30	'Stables' etc
5–0	'Tea'

It is dark by 5.30 and we are usually too tired to do anything except necessary cleaning.

Detention Barracks, Abbazzia, Cairo, Feb 5th – Did the address at the head of this letter frighten you? It certainly ought to. Let me make a clean breast of it. I am in gaol, or at least a military prison to be exact. But the truth is not so bad as it perhaps appears. Each brigade in turn sends a guard to look after the gaol. This week it fell to the turn of ours, so behold me in charge of a corporal, 18 men, a trumpeter, a bicycle orderly, a cook and five horses to keep some couple of hundred gaol-birds from getting out, and their friends from getting in.

We quitted the cap at Maadi last Saturday, leaving the tents standing for our 2nd contingent to occupy. We had a most interesting ride, passing through the 'City of the Dead', a mile or more of graves, Jewish, Coptic and Mohammedan. We marched right past the Citadel and between the finest mosques of Cairo, then through the densest part of the native bazaars to the east of the town, and along through Abbasia and Heliopolis – fashionable residential suburbs, and into our new camp at Zeitun, 10 or 12 miles north of Cairo, Maadi being an equal distance south.

I have a guard of four men, under the corporal, stationed in a little guard house at the gate. They are 'on' in 2 hour relief from reveille 6am until 8pm and their duty is to examine passes, to register all persons coming in and to prevent, of course, all prisoners going out, ie until their sentence expires.

Zeitira, Cairo, February 18 – I don't think I have written since I left 'gaol'. We have been going pretty solid ever since with regimental brigade and divisional training and field firing. Many thanks for the *Alumnus*. When I saw the list of the Old Boys on active service it made me wish I was with them ... and I envied Lloyd Jones and Jack Normansell. I am, as you may see from the address, writing this in the YMCA tent, or rather hut. It is a rectangular flat topped box made of rush mats fixed on a wooden frame.

We had a fairly heavy day today. The Division attacked a position held by a Brigade of Artillery, a Regiment of Light Horse and a Brigade of Infantry – represented by flags of various colours and shapes. The N Z Mounted Rifles formed of our vanguard: we, the Aust LH Brigade, the main guard section. We were feeding our horses then our Brigadier told our Colonel: 'I want you to be on such and such a ridge at 3.45'. It was then about 3.30 and we were two miles from the ridge; but we took off our nose-bags, tied them to the saddles, put the bits in the horses' mouths and galloped ventre a terre [at full speed] and we were actually in position by 3.46. It was a gallop! We were in column of troops, ie each troop in line and a few yards from the one in front, and we raised such a dust that I couldn't see the ground under my horse's hoofs much less the troop in front that I was supposed to be following. (I was in command of A troop); and the stones kicked up by the horses of the troop in front hit us in the face. The ground was very rough and stony, with desert bushes scattered all over, but we could only tell whether we were going up or down hill by the feel of the horse under us, and we guessed the presence of the bushes by the horses' swerving to right or left as they dodged them.

Feb 20th – I visited the N Z Regiment the other night. My old Regiment (the 7th Inf Wellington West Coast Rifles) is at the Canal, where they had, I believe, some of the fun; but most of my personal friends are in the 6th (Manawatu Mountain Rifles). I found Clutha Mackenzie, my old Hinau colleague, son of the High Commissioner for N Z, and Darcy McGregor and Bill East all from the 'Clearing' and a whole crowd of old Huntley and Wanganui Boys that I used to meet at every dance I went to. One other old friend I struck – but her memory being as short as most of her sex – I don't think she recognised me. That was 'Peggy' a mare I used to ride at Hanau. She came with Clutha and is now assisting him in his duty as galloper to the Colonel.

March 3 – In all probability we shall be moved from here within the next fortnight, but as to where we are as ignorant as we were 6 months ago. I don't think anybody will be sorry to leave Egypt. The Sirocco has started. The table, on which I am writing, is covered with sand, which blows through the rush-mat walls, covers this paper and clogs my pen. In the tent there is a layer of an inch thick of fine sand on everything – shirts, towels, tunics and all! I believe this state of affairs lasts 7 or 8 weeks only it gets frightfully hot towards the end of April.

June 25 Somewhere in Gallipoli – We have been here six weeks as infantry, and though it went against the grain to say farewell to our steeds, we are rubbing along comfortably enough. Our brigade, the (...) is holding a line of trenches along the top of a spur of hills, each regiment being actually in the trenches for one week, and in the reserve below for a fortnight. Needless to say, this doesn't appeal to us so much as dashing about the country on our mettlesome mounts, but we still hope to rejoin them some day, and to feel once more immeasurably superior to the 'gravel-crushers' though now we are learning to regard them with more sympathy and admiration than heretofore.

'I wish my mother could see me now' as I sit in truncated pants writing this on a shovel. In company with our Trumpeter Walker, I am occupying a dug-out some 6 feet by 3 foot 6 inches. Our roof is a blanket supported on sticks. Our furniture consists of three biscuit tins. One of them is let into the wall and acts as a meat safe, pantry and cellar, one suitably punctured with a bayonet forms a stove and kitchen range; and the third makes a water-tank and reservoir.

We are all becoming great culinary experts; the dishes we can contrive from an issue of bully beef and biscuits, bacon, cheese and jam are legion. Here is a typical day's menu:

Breakfast	(1) Porridge and jam	(2) Bacon and Welsh rabbit
Lunch	(1) Cold beer and ham (good mixture)	(2) Biscuits and jam of cheese
Tea, Dinner or Supper (your social status being judged on the name you give it)	(1) Hash, ragout, stew, 'hashmagundi' or Rissoles, meat-pies or dry hash	(2) Queen cake, jam tart or Swiss roll.

If the diet gets monotonous change the name and you can eat it with renewed zest. The chief trouble is water. We have to go about a mile to fetch it; the supply is limited and the road back is all uphill. So naturally it is precious and washing is verboten [forbidden]. I haven't had a wash for six weeks, but I must hasten to allay your horror by explaining that we occasionally get down to the beach and bathe. There is quite a sporting element about a sea-bathe too. Just as you are getting used to the water and beginning to enjoy it there is a 'boom'. A filmy, cotton-wool like cloud appears over your head, innumerable 'zips' patter along the surface of the water, where a triangle 200 yards by 25 is struck by the shrapnel bullets and one gets a splendid exposition of the Australian Crawl Stroke as dozens of white or sun-tanned forms race the the beach, a few of the bolder staying out and prolonging their swim by ducking whenever a shell comes along.

The beach presents an animated scene in pleasant contrast to the drab – or rather khaki – monotony of the trenches. Amid the multitude of Australians and New Zealanders are numbers of sailors clad in dirty white ducks and leggings, and often surrounded by Tommies, trying, not always in vain, to bribe them for baccy, cigarette papers and other coveted dainties.

We are having quite a concentrated multum in parvo [a great deal in a small space] little war here. We have artillery duels and aeroplane reconnaissances and attacks:

trench warfare with its fire fights, mining and counter-mining, bomb-throwing, sorties and counter attacks; and sea fights between men-of-war, torpedo boats and submarines on one side and submarines and forts on theirs. Then, when we are not in the trenches, we have pickets and fatigues, widening and levelling roads or deepening trenches or perhaps cutting fresh saps closer to the enemy, with their bullets pinging and whining and moaning unpleasantly near our ears, while the 'star shells',with which they endeavour to turn night into a Brock's Benefit, make us attempt to duck out of sight behind the nearest grain of sand.

But apart from the drawbacks that I won't deny this sort of life has, it undoubtedly possesses a charm of its own and I for one, at any rate, have struck many jobs I like less.

16 August 1915 Mediterranean Expeditionary Force – You would be amused if you could see the column of the paper that I devour with the greatest avidity. I don't think you'd every guess what it was – the Cookery Column! I'm becoming a wonderful cook – theoretically – and pass long hours in the night watches making marvellous jellies, custards and fruit puddings, pies and salads (in my head). I could tell you 1,001 ways of making an appetizing dish of old meat scraps and dozens of 'war recipes' for making cakes with bread crumbs and without butter or sugar. But 'Who can hold a fire in his hand, By thinking on the frosty Caucasus?'. Morning comes round and we return, not alas 'to our muttons' but to canned dog and salt pig (alias bully beef and bacon)...

One of the men on my tanks, a Scotch New Zealander, by the way, was a splendid cook, had cooked for seven years on board ship, in fact, and we fared sumptuously till one of the officers discovered and commandeered him.

Since writing the above I have been shifted. I was called to rejoin the regiment but as I was still a bit out of order [Ernest had enteritis or dysentery, which are both inflammation of the intestine accompanied by diarrhoea. They are caused by bacteria in contaminated food or water and were common in Egypt during the First World War], the doctor sent me down to the Field Hospital, where I might get proper tucker and a rest. Then the brigade got their marching orders, the hospital was cleared and I was packed off – with the result that I am now en route for Malta at the present moment, being somewhere to the south of the Grecian Archipelago.

A whole crowd of us, wounded, sick, left the beach on lighters, which were towed to one of the Hospital Ships lying a mile or two out. (Let me say here that our Red Cross Ships lie well within artillery range, but I have never seen the Turks fire on them yet. I have actually seen them shelling one warship over the top of the Hospital Boats, but as far as I personally have seen, or anybody I have actually spoken to, Johnny Turk has been fighting with scrupulous fairness and his observance of the Red Cross would put the Christian Germans to shame.) ...

14 September 1915 St John's Hospital, Valetta, Malta – Most of us have been suffering from dysentery in some form or other for some time. The doctors in Gallipoli are unable to cope with it as it requires complete rest and change of diet and scenery,

'The King of the Castle, Ghain Tuffieha, Malta, Mar 1916,' message by Ernest on the back of a family photograph, reproduced by their kind permission.

'A Boy from the Bush, Malta, Mar '16,' message by Ernest on the back of a family photograph, reproduced by their kind permission.

which are just the things they can't supply us with in the trenches. I stuck out as long as I could – I wanted to finish my whole year's active service without 'parading sick' – but at last I went to the doctor for the first time since I had appendicitis!

Each unit in the firing line (a Regiment in one case) has a dressing station a few yards in the rear of the trenches. Here the MO (Medical Officer) hangs out with a few cases of bottles of tabloids. 'Quinine Jack' as our MO is irreverently called, gave me a few pills and a little advice and put me on a milk diet – the latter being a work of supererogation, as he had no milk, rice or arrowroot to issue, and I was unable to get down to the beach to buy any. 'QJ' went away sick and his locum continued his treatment, increasing the doses. He usually gave about 13 pills at a time, white, pink, brown, chocolate and black, evidently trusting that one or other would meet the case; he was equally lavish with advice, which it was impossible to follow under our circumstances, and he put all and sundry on the hypothetical 'milk diet'...

(Hospital Ships) are unmistakeable. They are painted in three huge horizontal stripes, red, white and green, with two large red crosses at intervals; and, at night, a row of green lights the length of the ship gives them quite a gala appearance.

We had lunch on board (stew! and bread!) and I'm afraid I passed up my bowl for a second and a third helping and then some of us were taken on to the Neuralia, which took us first to Mudros and then to Malta.

We all came to the same hospital. 'Dysenteries' were kept on milk diet but I wagged my red label in the orderly's face and persuaded him by specious argument that I didn't come under that category and got into the 2nd class mess. Imagine, five course meals, soup, fish, and the rest of it; clean cutlery and napery and crockery; attentive Hindoo waiters; and, by no means least, the pleasure of putting one's knees under a table.

We landed at Valetta in a pouring rain, after staying in the harbour a day or so. The Red Cross people are most hospitable. As we filed from the landing stage to the cars that were to take us to our respective hospitals, one lady gave us a couple of biscuits (not Army Biscuits) and a cake of chocolate, a second gave us a glass of delicious, cool, lemon syrup and a third crowned the gift with three cigarettes.

On reaching the hospital we received another gift from the Red Cross and St John Societies, a neat parcel containing this note-paper, envelopes, tobacco, cigarettes and matches and a pack of playing cards, with which I have beguiled tedious hours by innumerable games of 'Patience'.

We were assigned to our wards, all the 'Dysenteries' being put together – no distinction being made between gastritis, enteritis, gastro-enteritis, entero-colitis and the other names which the young MO on Gallipoli delighted to bestow.

We drew a suit of hospital clothes, eating utensils etc, had a hot bath and changed into clean clothes sending all our dirty ones to be washed and also sending all our kit, except what we need here, to the pack-room. By the way, we 'drew' clean shirts and socks on the boat and can say with what joy I heaved my old shirt overboard. It was as I consigned it to the watery deep, I murmured 'Saul may have slain his thousands and David his ten thousands' but on you old brute, I could have knocked the two together into a cocked hat.

So we are now clad in suits suggestive of convicts, but very comfortable; rough blue outside and white swansdown inside…

The sisters have worked a change. We have a cloth on the table now, our beds are better made, everything is cleaner, more orderly and brighter, and they take a greater, more personal interest in the patients' comfort than the RAMC [Royal Army Medical Corps] orderlies.

September 20 1915 – This is probably the last letter I shall write from here as we are going this afternoon, or so we are told, to the Convalescent Camp at Ghain Tuffieha. … In the Barracca Gardens are a number of memorial stones erected by the men of the Mediterranean Command to their comrades killed in various parts of the inland sea. It afforded me an interesting little sidelight on the ceaseless and ubiquitous activity of our Navy – and even our 'contemptible little Army' – two or three men killed here, a dozen there, here an explosion, there a capsized cutter, and everywhere little 'scrap' that never get into the history books but are all the time making British history. It brought to my mind Kipling's lines (and he always seems to hit the point better than any other):

Never the lotus closes; never the wild fowl wakes,
But a soul goes forth on the East wind, that died for old England's sake;
Man or woman or suckling, mother or wife or maid,
Because on the bones of the English, the English Flag is stayed.

17 November No. 1 Convalescence Camp, Malta – I have got a job on the Staff here (merit recognized at last!) as Section Sergeant. The duties are not particularly onerous but they are enough to occupy one's mind and one's time and that is a great consideration. The section of which I am in charge contains 12 tents each containing 10 beds...

29 November – I have been appointed Pay Sergeant which means that I rank as Squadron Quarter-master Sergeant, draw an extra 1/6 or so per day, am entitled to wear a crown above my 3 chevrons and have a permanent pass, which enables me to be absent from camp whenever I am not on duty. This is a much better job than my last – where I was on duty from reveille to tattoo (or 'last post' 9.30pm) and where a large part of my duties consisted of reporting absentees and giving evidence against them at subsequent Orderly Room, or Court Martial – a job that I abhor ...

When I left Anzac after 4 months there, there were hardly half a dozen left out of my original troop of nearly 40, while at one time even with reinforcements one Regiment had dwindled from 500 to 200. As to the cold weather – conditions are now awful there. Hundreds of cases of frost-bite come into the Hospitals here weekly. There are daily amputations and deaths from haemorrhage. In some cases, according to recent arrivals, hostilities are suspended, Turks and our fellows sleeping on the parapets as the trenches are half full of water. No shots for weeks perhaps because the bolts of the rifles are frozen. I must confess I'm not keen on going back there yet.

And now you'll want to know how I spent my Christmas. I was one of 3 chosen to form a committee for arranging the dinner, and as the other 3 men were nonentities, most of the work fell on me... We Australians received from the Aus Branch of the British Red Cross a neat tin of 50 cigarettes, 2g of tobacco, a piece of Christmas cake, a pack of cards, a handkerchief, and notepaper and envelopes.

With the Anzacs – Humour at the Front (*Alumnus* 1916)

It is surprising how circumstances affect one's appreciation of humour and on active service one laughs at unusual incidents in a way that would appear extremely callous to anyone living under peaceful conditions.

One of the more striking instances of a perverted sense of humour I overheard in a dressing station on Brighton Beach. One of our chaps had lost his hand through trying to return a Turkish hand grenade. While the stump was being dressed he was smoking the inevitable cigarette and chuckling intensely as if at the recollection of some excruciatingly funny joke. The Padre, who was standing close by in conversation

'In my celebrated pose of "Wounded Warrior" - Streatham, while at Wandsworth, Apr 1916,' message by Ernest on the back of a family photograph, reproduced by their kind permission.

with the Colonel, asked him the cause of his mirth and he explained: – 'I've just seen the funniest thing I ever saw. Bill Jones was trying to light a bomb with the hot end of his cigarette. The blamed thing wouldn't light and Bill began to get shirty. He kept on saying 'I will get the blanky thing to light!' and he kept on puffing and puffing away at his cigarette to keep it burning. Just then Tom Smith sang out something to Bill, Bill turned his head and' – he almost choked with laughter as he reached the cream of the joke – 'the blamed thing went off in his hand and blew his head clean off. Crikey I did laugh!'.

The psychology of this case I leave to others. The fact that Bill was his mate seemed to make no difference to his appreciation of the comical side of the incident and, strangely enough, his humour was so infectious that the Padre, Doctor, orderlies and even the wounded, lying about on stretchers awaiting their turn, joined in the laugh.

A shell that lobbed in the soup or the tea never failed to produce roars of laughter from everyone except the unfortunate, who owned the soup or tea and who had had all the risk and all the trouble of collecting the firewood, carrying the water and bringing the billy to boil, and I shall never forget the shout that went up from the whole regiment when a shell burst right under a box that was being used as a seat in a snug little corner and upset and completely buried the cook sergeant and a QMS who had sought and annexed the safest spot on Pope's Hill. Volunteers promptly rushed up with picks and shovels and the laugh was renewed when the cook, who was old and very fat, was dragged out by the feet and stood blinking in the light of day.

Cooped up as we were with nothing to see but trenches in front and the sea behind, tempers suffered and, as we seldom had the chance of venting our ill-feelings on the Turk, fights sometimes occurred in our own lines. One dark night, within ten yards of the enemy's lines, the tense stillness of my own troop's trench was broken by a furious fight between two of the troop, one of them a barrister in civil life, now a commissioned officer in the British Army. But I think the most amusing fight took place between two of our squadron on the steep slopes of Pope's Hill. The assailant was a little English immigrant who, for some trivial grievance, real or imaginary, attacked a man twice his size, a former runner-up for the heavy-weight championship of Australia, and the fight was watched by half a mile of Australian trenches and nearly a mile of New Zealanders in rear. The ground was hardly suitable for an exhibition of scientific boxing and it was not long before, in a clinch, one of them slipped, and the two rolled together some dozens of yards down the cliff. Then the officers were startled out of their dugouts by a hundred voices calling 'One, Two, Three!' as every colonist within sight solemnly counted out both combatants, and when the vast amphitheatre re-echoed to a vast 'Eight, Nine, OUT!' a furious volley came from the Turks, who must have thought we were practising our battle cry for a charge.

These incidents may not appear so amusing to anybody, who can sit in an armchair before a cosy fire while he reads or hears them, but I verily believe that, if a beneficent Providence had not granted us the power to laugh at them, we should have gone mad. Some of us did!

With the Anzacs in France – Trench Mortars – Letter to Mr Davies Dated 30 March 1917 (*Alumnus* July 1917)

Yes, I'm with the Trench Mortars. To be precise I'm in charge of a whole battery of them and after my signature on official documents I append the letters O C X 3 A M T M B.

'Yours Ernest, France, Apr '17,' message by Ernest on the back of a family photograph, reproduced by their kind permission.

To the uninitiated I suppose the words Trench-mortar conveys little or nothing. To my mind only a few weeks ago it called up two visions, one that of the TMO in Ian Haigh's First Hundred Thousand, slinking, pariah like, along the trenches, with what angry field officers opprobriously termed his 'infernal stink-pots' ; the other Bairnfather's libellous picture of Bert and Alf, slinking amidst showers of wreckage and anxiously enquiring 'Ours or theirs?'

Now I hardly know whether I like the weapons or not. The 'piece', a weird contrivance of stove-pipes and odds and ends of discarded rifle-mechanisms and which, if not actually invented by

Heath Robinson, must have been suggested by one of his sketches, certainly fails to arouse the personal enthusiasm that its relatives, the 18–pounder and the 4–5 howitzer, evoke in every artillery man's heart, but one is so much nearer to one's target and the effects of the TM shells is so much greater than in the case of the field guns, that one is almost compensated for the ludicrousness of the mortar by the results it achieves.

Trench-mortarmen are called by the Infantry the 'shoot and scoot brigade',which is unkind, if perhaps not untrue, and by the artillery the 'suicide brigade', which is unduly flattering. I have known a whole week to pass without a single casualty and we have one officer who has been here nearly 3 months with no ill effect, save on his nerves.

Of Trench Mortars, TMs (Toc-emmas) as they are usually called, we have 3 chief varieties: Heavy, Medium and Light. The Heavies fire the 'Flying Pigs', the Mediums the 'Plum Puddings' while the Lights are generally known as Stokers' Guns. My battery is one of the 'Plum pudding guns' though the War Office calls them 'Howitzer, Trench, 2-inch'.

It is 8am and my batman reminds me that it is time to get up. I don't want to but duty triumphs over inclination. I went to bed late last night, tired after a long day's tramping over greasy duck-boards, and in places where there are no duck-boards, thigh deep in mud of varying consistencies. I blessed the men who invented bootjacks and the lucky chance that gave me a carpenter to attend to my creature comforts ....

It was something after midnight that I awakened, a revolver in one hand, an electric torch in the other, 'All right, sir, runner from Col X'. I tore open the envelope (from the Colonel) which was labelled 'Secret', glanced through it and signed a receipt for it, allowing the perspiring runner to return to HQ much to his relief as he doesn't like the trenches at night and there is not a glimmer of light from moon or stars.

'XSAMTM Bty will bombard enemy's wire and machine gun emplacement at xxxxx guns xxxx rounds'. The map 'co-ordinates' enabled me to locate the exact position within a few yards. Out from under my pillow came map and protractor and, while an orderly went to chase out of bed the long suffering sergeant, whose dug out was some yards away, I measured a few angles and distances and made a few calculations. Then when the sergeant came, shivering as one does when turned out into the snow from one's first sleep, we made the arrangements for today's shoot.

'We'll use A and C and D guns, A will fire from .... and C and D from .... Make Cpl M No 1 of A, Bdr N of C and K of D. (By the way we shall have to train more Nos 1. I think K will be all right but we are still short since V and L have gone and until Cpl P comes out of hospital). I want you to observe for A, I'll observe for C and D. We've got enough shells up at ... position but you'd better get some from Warwick Dump for ... position. Infantry carrying party? No, I think not. Those poor beggars have quite enough to do. I don't like asking for them unless it is absolutely necessary. Have we plenty of cordite? Component parts? Mechanisms? Clinometers? Confound Capt Q. I've indented every day for the last fortnight for another to replace that cracked one. We shall have to manage somehow. Anything else, sargeant? Right, get 'em on to those emplacements first thing in the morning. I'll be round at 9 o' clock. Good night, sergeant'.

Once more to sleep, though the rats effectively prevented that for some time. Just as I was falling asleep, 'B r r r !' gently but insistently, 'B r r r!' Drat Mr Bell or Mr Edison, or whoever invented telephones! 'Hello! Yes, X speaking, Your message? Yes, runner left three quarters of an hour ago. Should be back by this unless he stopped one at Suicide Corner. Fritz is on to that tonight. Was I asleep? Oh, no! We never sleep! So long old thing! Bon soir!'

Sleep at last when 'Cr- rash!'. Blow that rat; he's broken my new china tea pot! Then, as I lay awake another sound like the falling of a piece of wood on metal. 'Fred, wake up! I believe you've won that franc'. 'I thought this trap would catch him', 'Here, I'll hold the bag, you shake him in. Right I've got him. Where's that shell case? That'll make a good sinker. Now that bucket of water'. Splash! 'Now, see if the blighter can swim! Better set the trap again. What! No cheese. Put a bit of that Everton Toffee in. That'll stick to his teeth, good-oh!'

Three times did this happen during the night. One rat we lost, but two were drowned and this morning my batman is richer by two francs.

This is how it happens that at 8am I'm still disinclined to exchange my comfortable blankets for the snowy rigours of a French wintry morning.

Ugh! These boots are still wet inside. That's the worst of rubber-boots. Once slip up to your waist in water and it is weeks before your boots get properly dry. Still, c'est la guerre! Cold feet are a detail. And this water, how cold it is to wash in! Still, I philosophically recall the times when I would have sold my shirt for such a bucket of water. Better cold water than none at all! At last the painful operation of shaving is over, and then comes breakfast – bacon, again! The Australian's attitude towards bacon has rather amused me. At first they regarded it as a delicacy (so it is where beef and mutton are so plentiful) and thought they were being extremely well treated, but army bacon, morning after morning begins to pall and one hankers after the fruit-pots of Australia.

Our mess room is – or rather was – an estaminet. The windows are innocent of glass and there is a gaping hole in the floor, but we are under shelter and that's something. The mess arrangements are not very elaborate. At present I'm alone, so I feed with the battery and we all 'put something in' to eke out the issue of bully-beef and maconochie.

At nine o'clock I'm in the trenches, inspecting the emplacements, seeing that all is ready and that preparations are made for every eventuality. Just before the time fixed for the shoot, a runner comes up with my watch which I sent down to HQ to be synchronised. With the watch he brings a note from the adjutant, 'Hour-hand correct, minute-hand correct, second-hand 7–6 seconds slow'. What silly asses adjutants can be at times, I reflect.

The time is approaching and after a last look round I send away all the men who will not be actually needed on the guns and take up my station in the O Pip (observation post) that I have selected. The guns have been laid at the correct elevation and pointing in the desired direction and the Nos 1 know what charges and fuses I want to use. So I wait with my eye on the minute hand until it reaches the appointed time. 'Fire!' Three tremendous explosions sound quite close to me. I watch the comical flight of the plum-puddings, following them with the eye as they soar up in the culminating point and downwards until there is an ear-splitting crash and fountains of loose soil and lumps of more solid material spout up into the air. Simultaneously there are other explosions and we hear over our heads frightfully near it seems – the whistle of shells from our field guns, while the air seems full of howitzer shells, H E shells, shrapnel, flying pigs, Stoker bombs, rifle-grenades and many other weird instruments of destruction. However, I must rivet my attention on my own pieces. 'C-gun, 3 degrees more right; D-gun drop 50 yards!' The first round didn't hit the target, though one shell blew down a portion of the parapet, while fragments of duck-board in the air prove that the other fell in a communication trench, neither being wasted. The next round is better, both shots hitting the emplacement, one blowing the side in, while the other lands square on the top, twisting steel girders and corrugated iron into a shapeless mass, and flinging sandbags and fragments of concrete into the air.

For five or ten minutes there is silence from the German lines as though we had taken Fritz by surprise. Then he 'gets busy' and his retaliation starts. 'Minnies' and 'pine-apples' start falling perilously close, 'whiz-bangs' seem to go off all round us and surely that was a 'coal-box' evidently trying to find our 'flying-pig' but luckily landing in quite the wrong spot.

Our guns continue to fire, so presumably none of the Hun shells have affected us. 'There!', I think 'that M G emplacement is finished' – there appears to be nothing but a gaping hole where it once stood and there is no parapet for yards on either side. I drop the range and get onto the 'wire', 'Oh, a beauty! Right into the middle of his wire!' 'Knife-rests' fly up and the burst wire flies back in both directions like a steel cable that breaks under a strain. I fire the next rounds into practically the same place. Good work! I shall hear from our scouts tonight how clean a cut we have made and at any rate our Lewis Gunners will have some fun when Fritz comes out to repair it.

There is nothing more to do now but to wait until Fritz's display of temper – natural enough, perhaps – is over. We light up pipes and cigarettes and possess our souls in patience. A lull in the tempest! No, we are too old to be caught. In a few minutes he starts "strafing" the communication trenches where we might have been if we had 'scooted' as soon as the shoot was finished. The Nos 1 report to me, we compare notes and enjoy ourselves until it is time to get back. While I am washing, changing my wet clothes – for it has alternately rained and hailed during the afternoon – and writing my report, the sergeant comes to inform me that all men have reported back at their dug-outs. With a feeling of relief I add 'Casualties – nil', when a runner comes in with a note. It is from an irate and timorous infantry colonel who has found in a locality occupied by some of his men 'two of your projectiles, fully detonated' ('Liar', ejaculates the sergeant under his breath.) 'As these constitute a serious danger to the garrison', he requests me to have them removed as soon as possible. 'That's all right, sir' says the invaluable sergeant, 'they were brought down half an hour ago'. I send a reply to this effect and then go to report to my own 'old man', who asks:

'Good shoot?'

'Yes, sir'

'Do any damage?'

'Some, sir'
'Get that machine gun emplacement you told me of?'
'Finished it, sir'
'Cut any wire?'
'A bit, sir'
'Break any parapet?'
'A few yards, sir'
'That's right, give 'em hell. Every time!'

With the DAC (Divisional Ammunition Column) (*Alumnus* 1917)

Do the letters DAC require any explanation? Three years ago undoubtedly they would, but now even the girl-in-the-street has such an uncanny knowledge of things military that possibly no explanation is necessary.

For the benefit of any that do not know, I may state that DAC stands for Divisional Ammunition Column. Before the war the DAC was regarded by the gunner almost as the ASC is by the soldier, but in addition to its duty of taking up ammunition to the guns, the DAC fulfils another function, that of providing a sort of reservoir for personnel. New gunners usually put in a certain amount of time with the DAC before being attached to batteries, and gunner officers and men in need of rest after a period of strenuous activity, take it by being attached temporarily to the DAC.

I won't attempt in any way to describe in detail the work of the DAC, but here are one or two typical days from my own experience with it in rain, in snow and in sunshine. ....

Our Division are having a fairly slack time in the line and as the batteries are carting a lot of their own ammunition, we can do pretty much as we please. This gives us a glorious and much-needed opportunity for straightening up and getting clean. The last few months have been utterly miserable. No cover for the horses; mud up to their bellies; horses actually drowned during the night on their own lines; men constantly going sick with 'trench feet'. It has been practically impossible to keep harness and accoutrements clean but now all is changed. It is freezing fit 'to split a stone' as the French say. The ground is hard and dry; everyone is feeling better in health and more cheerful in spirit and we are starting to get things ship-shape.

We have already built a roof over the horse lines; the men's huts have each got a stove – seek not to know whence they came! – and now we are putting down brick floors in all the stables. In a town just behind the trenches, not many miles from here, there are thousands of houses in utter ruin. Millions of bricks are to be had for the asking and we have got permission to utilise some of them for our purpose. It is rather too dangerous to go during daylight. In fact, mounted traffic is strictly forbidden there, so we have to wait till night to commit our depredations...

While the grooms are getting our horses ready, just come round the lines and have a look at our animals. Why do I call them animals? Well, we chiefly use mules for this game of ours. The once despised mule has come into his own here. You know of course that he is a more expensive animal to buy than the horse and most of us who have had much to do with him would say that he is far more useful. A little harder to manage, perhaps, but that only adds to the excitement.

Look out for that big black fellow! That is Satan our champion kicker. He can stand on one leg and kick in three different directions with the other three. One of the pet amusements of our drivers is to roll an oil drum along the line behind him. He watches it out of the corner of that wicked eye and almost invariably without a miss kicks it at the exact moment it passes him. What a fine cricketer he would make! The boys say he could kick the eye out of a mosquito – but I've never seen him do it. You see those 6 greys? That is my favourite team, not one of them under 14 hands and I'd back them against any team in the division. Other people admire them too and I always warn the stable-picket to keep a special eye on them. …

You can get a rough idea of the shape and direction of our front line by looking at the observation balloons. Those on the right and left, I can count 26 in all, are ours. The sausages you can just see over the crest are Fritz's. There are only 6 visible at present. There were 9 this morning but our bird-men dropped 3 of them an hour or two ago.

That ridge in front is the old German position. We can hardly yet realise why they let us get it. Look what a command it has of all our position. They could see everything. If we had been there, ten times our own number of Boches would not have driven us out. There is only one possible explanation as far as any of us can see. Fritz is beaten! That hill to the right is where the King was last week. From there, on a fine day and with a good telescope you can see on your left the Belgian coast from Dunkirk to Ostend and on your right even as far as Brussels – so they say! …

Put your horse straight at the trench. Follow me. I'll give you a lead. Hup! Over we go. We shall have a lot of those to cross before we reach the batteries. Come on, I'll give you a race. Look out for the shell-holes and you're alright. We're off! It is good to be alive, good to breathe the fresh air, best of all, perhaps, to be on a good horse and to forget for a few minutes the horrors of war. But we are rudely reminded of them. Pull up and let this stretcher party get past. What is that sewn up in the blanket? Well, think a minute. Didn't you notice that Padre a few hundred yards back, and the rows of silent, bare-headed men? Think and be thankful it is not you! It might be your turn tomorrow – it might, perhaps, even today.

We'll go on at a walk. Keep a tight rein on your horse. He is new and is still a little gun-shy. He'll soon get used to the sound of the guns. At present he starts and flings his head up every time a gun goes off near him – which is every two or three seconds, for we are now right amongst the guns… Have you remarked that peculiar smell, rather like stale potato-peelings. That's Fritz's gas. We are getting quite used to it now, and can sleep in our gas-helmets quite comfortably. His new gas is rather worse than that – but I believe ours is worse still, so we don't mind.

… Um! … That is rather ghastly isn't it? I was hoping you hadn't noticed it. You are not as used to such sights as we are. Now you have seen it, have a good look at it, if you think you can stand it, and go home and tell your shirkers and your strikers about it. Where is the rest of it? Well, I saw a boot – not an empty one – a hundred yards back, a pipe about 50 yards away and you must have seen those heaps of flies all around for yards in every direction. Dead three or four hours, I should say. Padre will bury it tonight. Death must have been instantaneous and he died in a good cause…

Hello, here are a dead horse and a couple of mules, fully muddied. An officer's charger too, not long dead by the looks of it. Fritz must have got on to an ammunition team. This is the way we have to bring the shells up. Cheerful, isn't it? The other day I finished with two mules left out of six in one team – one of those so badly wounded that I had to shoot it as soon as we had handed over the ammunition. You see, life in the DAC isn't always a bed of roses.

Well, here we are back at the wagon-lines. Just in time for a bath before dinner. Sorry you missed your afternoon tea! What's on for dinner tonight? Soup, tinned herrings, bully-beef rissoles, peaches and blancmange – and a glorious appetite to season them all. War has its compensations after all.

Carrying On (*Alumnus* July 1918)

Very soon we have our first casualty. An ugly fragment of shell strikes a bombardier on the shoulder inflicting a ghastly wound. He gives a grunt, then a grin, claps his right hand to the wound and says 'Ugh, that's the beggar I've been waiting for for three and half years'. Willing comrades bandage the wound and carry him to the nearest dressing-station, but the firing never ceases for an instant.

Another shell lands near one of the guns. A corporal, the Number One of the gun, gets a piece through his left ear, entirely destroying the ear-drum. He never even reports the occurrence until the officer on one of his periodical trips notices the blood and orders him away. He indignantly refuses to be carried and insists on walking to the dressing-station.

Now the enemy gets a direct hit on the telephone pit. The unfortunate signallers inside, along with all their gear, their telephones, switch-boards and lamps, are blown to pieces and the officer who was standing at the entrance is mortally wounded, dying a few hours later.

We cannot afford to lose many more officers. Our captain went out yesterday to hunt for a Hun machine-gun-sniper, whom I had reported to have dug in behind the front line. He was sceptical at first but we decided to blow him out. Fritz spotted the captain first and he was brought home on a stretcher, with two neat holes in the front of his steel helmet and a horrible gash in the back of it…

At present we are oppressed with grief, even the most callous of us, for the loss of so many fine comrades, perhaps we never realised till now how fine they were – but we know that their lives were not given in vain. They died the noblest, the most glorious death that any man can die, 'facing fearful odds' for all that we all hold dear – and not even cornered in a dug-out, but manning their guns and fighting bravely till the last. Inarticulate though most of us are, there is hardly a man who does not pray, and pray fervently, that 'his latter end may be like theirs'.

This was not merely a 'soldiers' battle'. The higher ranks proved themselves no less than the gunners and the N C Os. Our own colonel watching from an O P and seeing parties of infantry straggling, leaderless, back over the near crest, rushed out with the Observation Officer, then ordered the latter back with the words 'No! You'd better stay at your post. You're on duty. That's an order. Compree?' and went on alone through the enemy barrage, collected and organised the stragglers and led them back to man the trenches.

17

Captain Charles V Fitton, MC

Letter to the Editor dated 29 December 1917 (*Alumnus* April 1918)

You have asked me to write some reminiscences for *Alumnus*, but, though glad to do my bit, I hardly know where to start. The common incidents of the War, with their extremes of pathos and humour, have been so thoroughly portrayed: while personal adventures crowd my memory to forgetfulness. It is quite impossible to attempt any account of experiences under fire. Some day, perhaps, when the memories are not so fresh, I may. I think, however, it will be of some interest if I describe the manner of my spending the last four Xmases.

During the Xmas season of 1914, as a full private in the DLI, I was one of a number engaged in coast defence at Hartlepool. I remember several things about those days. I was very new and keen. Even my 'guards' were a pleasure to me, though the East winds had a bitter sting. Xmas Eve and Boxing Day were both passed on 'guard' – the sentry beats being on deserted cliffs – but there was no suspicion of complaint in my occasional challenges. Feasts and holidays were put away until 'the job' was finished. Nevertheless we made merry on Xmas Day. We were a jolly crowd so that the few turkeys we had lacked both youth and trimmings who cared? The beer arrived in buckets and we drank in turns; but we made a great noise and were happy. There were four hundred of us there, of whom not four are now left with the Regiment, but all the survivors will remember how we cheered the Sergeant-Major when he came to read some nasty order which confined us to the barracks for most of the day. It shows the power of Xmas for the Sergeant-Major only smiled.

It is interesting that Charles Fitton makes no reference to the Princess Mary gift tin, which was issued to 'every sailor afloat and every soldier at the front' for Christmas 1914, in accordance with her wishes and paid for by public donations. Princess Mary had made an appeal via newspapers for donations to a £100,000 fund to buy a 'little token of love and sympathy on Christmas morning – something that would be useful and of permanent value, and the making of which may be the means of providing employment in trades adversely affected by the war'. 'The gift will take the form of a bossed brass tobacco or cigarette box, pipe and tinder lighter. In the case of Indian troops sweets will be supplied instead of tobacco or cigarettes'. Many of these tins have survived although very few contain their original contents.

Xmas 1915 saw a change in my fortunes. I was then a Subaltern in the Y & L R and after several weeks of wearying delay, our embarkation orders came through for Boxing Day. The Regiment was granted final leave at Xmas time and I was one of the Officers who paraded with it on May Day Green, Barnsley at 10.0 o'clock on Xmas night. My own leave had been very short as I did not get home until Xmas Eve. I remember it was very enjoyable but the outstanding memory is the scene on May Day Green. We stood from 10.0 pm until 1.0 am and the surging crowd was suspiciously jolly. I had charge of two platoons but as fast as I had assembled them they disappeared. Sweethearts and wives were the only recognized authority. The comedy of the situation there was a strain of pathos, which saved it from being farcical.

Xmas Eve 1916 was very wet. We were quartered for the night in huts with floors below the mud level. I had been in command of a company for some months and though our festive celebration was arranged for a day in January, I did all I could to create a Xmas feeling. My greatest accomplishment was to subsidise the rum ration, mainly of course by robbing other Companies. On Xmas morning we moved up into the front line trenches. Our cheeriness was not enhanced but we made the best of things. Our gunners had arranged to strafe all known enemy cookhouses when meals were about due. This seemed to be a rare good jape and made a wonderful improvement in our outlook on life. So long as 'Fritz' was having a worse time than ourselves Xmas was still a thing of joy. In spite of the hard work and a few casualties our thoughts harked back to other times. The things for which we fight seemed very near and it is my belief that we never were in a better fighting mood.

(1917) This year Xmas has found me at home and I have had a rare good time. Preparatory to going to India I am getting together that mysterious conglomeration known as a tropical kit. Today as I write I am snuggling close to the fire and it is queer to think that in a few weeks I shall be simmering. At times I wonder where I shall be next Xmas. The last four stand out like milestones in my career. Perhaps – and I hope for it – next Xmas will see a victorious peace: and the World going about its usual business. In any case I have no doubt the year will be an exciting one for me and I hope it will be a successful one for the school. It was a great pleasure to me to pay you a visit a few days ago. I often think of you and I will make it in my way to send news of myself from time to time.

Sir Charles Vernon Fitton OBE MC (Born 13 November 1894 in Barnsley; Died 10 April 1967, aged 72, in Cleveland) was the youngest of four children of Charles Fitton and Sarah Ann Hall. His father, born in Kirkburton, was a Grocer, Director of Wallace's Ltd of Huddersfield, and the family were living in eight rooms at 3 Kensington Road, Barnsley, on the 1911 Census. Charles went to St Mary's Elementary School then attended the Holgate from 1906 to 1913, where he passed the Northern Matriculation in 1911. He went to Barnsley Technical College and School of Art in 1914, where he passed the Pure Mathematics external exam.

Charles enlisted early in the First World War, being gazetted in March 1915 as temporary Second Lieutenant in the 14th Battalion (Second Barnsley Pals) of the York and Lancaster Regiment. Charles' duties were varied and his responsibilities great but he proved himself to be very capable, whatever he had to do. One of Charles' duties as Commander of 'C' Company was to write letters of sympathy to relatives, when men were killed in action, and several of these were printed in *Barnsley Chronicle*, when their deaths were announced.

On 22 September 1917, *Barnsley Chronicle* reported:

> the Military Cross has been awarded to Temporary Captain C V Fitton, York & Lancaster. After having successfully captured and consolidated his objective, he held a very important position for two days under an intense bombardment which obliterated a large portion of his front line trenches. But for his skilful dispositions the casualties would have been very much heavier.

Charles' father also played a public civilian role during the war and was reported in *Barnsley Chronicle* as a Mason with the Regent Lodge Brothers, an early subscriber to the Barnsley Patriotic Fund, Honorary Treasurer of the Committee for Old Folk's Christmas Tea & Entertainment and he was named as one of the local businessmen, who were to be co-opted onto a new Advisory Committee for training disabled soldiers and sailors, as agreed by the Education Committee in September 1918.

Charles married Kathleen May Rushforth in 1920 in Ealing and they had two children: Kathleen D Fitton in summer 1921 and Philip V Fitton in summer 1923.

Charles received an Order of the British Empire in 1942, when Lieutenant Colonel of the North Riding Home Guard, and he was knighted as Colonel on 11 February 1955 'for political and public services in the North Riding of Yorkshire'.

18

November 11th 1918 by B Greaves, VIB

The news of the signing of the armistice spread through the town like wild-fire. By eleven o'clock, Barnsley had undergone a remarkable transformation in aspect and customary habits. Flags unfurled, colours flying and smiling faces, all bespoke one word – PEACE. Union Jacks and the various flags of the Allies came out with surprising prodigality and were suspended from windows and other points of vantage. Bells that had been silent for the greater part of the war clanged in measured refrain as they do on royal occasions. Then the hooters sounded, this time the piercing siren seemed to carry a note of Jubilation. Even the anti-aircraft guns which are found about the town joined in the deafening chorus. Even nature seemed in sympathy with us and the sunshine painted the buildings in radiant colours, which found a fitting response in the hearts of the people.

Labourers and artisans, immediately the news came through, ceased work with common accord. There was no waiting for word of dismissal from foremen, for it was realised that there was no longer need for making implements of human destruction, to which brain and muscle had been unceasingly applied for 4 years. They could take a holiday without incurring the reproach of conscience or master. The schools were overjoyed. They gathered in the Assembly Halls and sang hymns and gave thanks that they were given a peace, which they could enjoy. These people were all the more overjoyed because we were able to impose upon this savage and barbarous nation, which we have vanquished on such drastic terms. These are roughly:

1) Surrender in good condition 35,000 guns
2) Surrender 2,000 aeroplanes and 5,000 locomotives and 150,000 wagons
3) To deliver to the Allies, Belgium, Luxembourg, Alsace & Lorraine & any other territory they occupied during the war
4) 14 cruisers, 10 battleships and 50 destroyers
5) Allied prisoners to be handed over for repatriation

They have given the Huns 31 days to complete these terms.

The sights in the streets were such as hadn't been seen since the commencement of war. In the evening bonfires and fireworks were displayed everywhere and the light restrictions being cancelled all went to make the streets a pre-war sight. The lights in the shop windows were again shedding their pale yellow rays of light on to the footpaths now thronged with happy people.

Meanwhile whilst we were holding revel in the Motherland, the soldiers were doing likewise out in France. As soon as the Tommies heard, there began the most wonderful collective demonstration of joy the world has ever witnessed. The bells started pealing and motor cyclists tore along the roads shouting 'It's all over, boys!' Myriads of caps went up in the air and a true British cheer echoed far and wide across France. Innumerable locomotive whistles and horns shrieked the great news with such violence as though they were determined that the tidings should reach the prodigiously distant stars. There will never be such a day again in the history of our planet.

BERNARD GREAVES (born 22 August 1903 in Barnsley) was one of five children of George Broadbent Greaves, Boiler Smith, and Sarah Ann Greaves, who lived in six rooms in Charlton Brook, Chapeltown, Sheffield. Bernard went to Burn Cross Elementary School for seven years then attended the Holgate for eight years from 1914 to 1922 on various Council Scholarships. He passed the Oxford Senior Local Exam and the Higher School Certificate (Northern Universities) before going to Selwyn College, Cambridge.

***Barnsley Chronicle* – 16 November 1918**

END OF THE WORLD WAR
ARMISTICE SIGNED BY GERMANY
GREAT REJOICING THROUGHOUT ENGLAND

At 11am last Monday came to an end the cruellest and most terrible war that has ever scourged mankind … *(terms of the Armistice were printed in full)*

HOW BARNSLEY RECEIVED THE JOYFUL NEWS

… In Barnsley as in other towns, the news was awaited anxiously. From early morning the people about the streets discussed the situation eagerly and, shortly after eleven o' clock, when the joyous tidings came through that Germany had signed the Armistice, these same people gave vent to pent-up feelings in no uncertain way. Market Hill and Peel Square soon became thronged with an enthusiastic concourse of townspeople and when the official declaration was

> made by printed poster in the *Chronicle* windows, all doubts – if any existed – were set at rest. It was really astonishing how quickly the glad news spread and it was equally surprising to find that nearly the whole of the mills and workshops closed as if by prearrangement to do so. The workers were too excited to finish their tasks; they swarmed into the streets and vigorously shook the hands of their friends. Flags, banners and bannerettes were hoisted from all manner of buildings and the children, as they dashed from the schools, sang with gusto. It was a memorable scene unequalled in the history of man. The bells of the Parish Church rang a merry peel and the entire town was given up to holiday …

At the Parish Church a thanksgiving service was held in the evening, the sacred edifice being crowded. Simultaneously, the holiday throngs filed to the various places of amusement and they had almost 'record' houses.

Appendix I

Personal Details

---

1 Birthplace

The boundaries for local government were different in the First World War from what they are today. The main changes took place under local government reorganisation in 1974. For this summary, I have used the current Barnsley District area, which includes the former urban districts of Cudworth, Darfield, Darton, Dearne, Dodworth, Hoyland Nether, Penistone, Royston, Wombwell, Worsbrough, Wortley.

The catchment area for Barnsley (& District) Holgate Grammar School is significant in determining which pupils attended; Felkirk was included in this.

Barnsley Town	31	
Barnsley District	26	(none in Darfield, Penistone or Wortley)
Elsewhere in Yorkshire	11	
Bedfordshire	1	
Cheshire	1	
Gloucestershire	1	
Hampshire	1	
Herefordshire	1	
Leicestershire	1	
Nottinghamshire	1	
Suffolk	1	

2 Residence on 1911 Census, Service Records or Education

Barnsley Town	31	
Barnsley District	22	(none in Darfield, Penistone or Wortley)
Felkirk	2	
Elsewhere in Yorkshire	8	
Cambridge	1	
Cheltenham	1	
Manchester/Salford	2	
Oxford	1	
Dublin, IRELAND	1	

3 Scholarships at Barnsley Holgate Grammar School

The youngest Old Boy was admitted at the age of 8 years but most were aged 11 years. 44 obtained one or more types of funding.

Keresforth Scholar (3)	Choyce, Williamson, Wood
Locke Scholar (9)	Bakel, Bambridge, Banks, Carter JR, Lindley F, Thompson AH, Warr, Whitelock, Wilby
Cooper Scholarship and Trustees Exhibition for Further Education (1)	Whitelock
County Minor (9)	Batley AG, Fairley, Laycock DS, Poxon, Skues, Smith, Stuart, Whitelock, Willott
County Major (2)	Fairley, Smith
Governor's Exhibition (1)	Boyd (awarded £50 but unable to use it)
Agricultural Exhibition of £40 for 3 years (WRCC) (1)	Laycock DS
Borough Continuation Scholarship (1)	Williamson
Intending Pupil Teacher (12)	Armitage, Atha, Barraclough, Batley E, Baylis, Hirst, Laycock BJR, Potter FJ, Royston, Savage, Thompson CC, Thompson JE
Pupil or Student Teacher (10)	Bradbury, Braham, Downend, Haigh, Hall, Heathcote, Hirst, Savage, Wilby, Williamson
Bursar (11)	Armitage, Atha, Barraclough, Batley (E), Baylis, Laycock BJR, Poxon, Savage, Thompson CC, Wilby, Williamson

4 Most Recent Occcupation

School Master (Head, Assistant or Student) (25)	Armitage A, Atha, Barraclough, Batley E, Baylis, Bradbury, Braham A, Downend (Head), Fairley, Haigh, Hall, Heathcote, Hirst, Joyce, Kellett, Laycock BJR, Marhsall, Poxon (Student), Royston, Savage, Thompson CC, Thompson JE, Wilby, Willott, Wood
Doctor of Medicine	Knowles
Architect	Dixon
Chartered Accountant	Green
Coal Mining Engineer	Normansell
Solicitor's Clerk	Allott
Accountant's Clerk	Parkin
Clerk Estate Office	Feasby
Bank Clerk (9)	Bakel, Bambridge, Gregory, Potter FJ, Saville, Swift, Thompson AH, Utley, Westby
Colliery Clerk	Litherland
Accountant's Clerk	Cowburn, Kilner, Skues
Glass Bottle Manufacturer's Clerk	Nicholson
Council Treasurer's Office	Mason
Civil Servant	Batley AG (Dublin)
Processman TWD	Doughty
Agriculture	Laycock DS
Pharmaceutical Chemist	Lindley F
Chemist's Apprentice	Potter ED
Colour Wool Dyer's Apprentice	Quest
Newspaper Reporter	Speight
Designer (Adverts)	Warr
Wireless Telegraphy	Wemyss
Joined father: (6)	
Hairdresser	Banks
Confectioner/Baker	Booker
Draper's Assistant	Carter JR
Builder/Employer	Clarke, Moore
Plasterer	Lindley FM
Linen Factory	Stuart
Groom	Choyce
Colliery Cashier/Clerk	Boyd, Joyner

Mining & Surveying	Gill
Colliery Engineman	Parkin
Colliery Underground	Jones, Timson
Electric Engineer	Carter H
called up, enlisted from study	Kelsey, McNaughton, Shipley, Smith, Whitelock, Williamson

5 Relationships

Married

1912	Allott TR	Olive Charlesworth
1913	Downend JM	Jane Hiles
1915	Swift JS	Alice Maude Watkinson
1915	Thompson CC	Mary Ward
1916	Atha JB	Ena Hawley
1916	Bakel F	Constance P Thompson
1916	Bambridge HL	Amy Norton
1916	Choyce WH	Florence Smith
1916/7	Hirst J	Ethel Powell OR Jane Lee
1917	Batley AG	Winifred Anne Welch

Engaged

Haigh ES	Clara Edith Carter
Kellett GW	name unknown
Potter FJ	Ruth Noble
Poxon E	Alice Maud Mary Doughty
Stuart C	Sally Surname?

Children

27.3.1916	SWIFT James Stuart Morton	(not seen by his father)
late 1916	ALLOTT Julia K	
11.1.1917	ATHA John Philip	(born after his father had died)
29.8.1918	POXON DOUGHTY Joan Evelyn	(born after his father had died)

Appendix II

Family Background

---

1 Father's most recent occupation

The occupations of the majority of fathers were professional or managerial with a number owning their own business; a minority were employed in administration or manual work.

They included:
Headmaster, GP, Solicitor, Bank Manager, Architect, Chief Constable, Minister, owners of shops, building contractor or other businesses, colliery manager, head gardener, innkeeper, clerks, newspaper reporter, sales representative, miner, railway signalman, footballer

2 Families where a parent died before 1911

NB based on 71 families as there are five pairs of brothers.

Father	9
Mother	6
TOTAL	14 (20%)

(One Old Boy was brought up by his mother only as father unknown)

3 Parents had children who died

(NB not usually noted on 1911 Census if one of parents had died before 1911)

1 child	21
2 children	6
3 children	4
4 children	1
5 children	1
TOTAL	33 (< 46%) 54 children died

4 Households with servants

1 Servant	12
2 Servants	3
4 Servants	1
TOTAL	16 (23%)

Appendix III

Information About Service in Forces

---

1 Age enlisted or called up

18–19	9*
20–30	25 plus those where records not found
31–40	3 plus those where records not found
42	1

*5 were called up from being a student: McNaughton, Shipley, Smith, Whitelock, Williamson

2 Service details from various sources

Service Records found	33 out of total of 49 men
Officer Records seen	3 out of total of 27 Officers
TOTAL	36

Name	Age Enlisted	Total Service	France (Other Theatres)	Age Died
Allott	28	2 years	24 days ?	29
Armitage	23	268 days	106 days	24
Atha	24	1 year 157 days	186 days (Mediterranean & France)	25
Batley AG	24	4 years	2 years 270 days (Med & France)	28
Batley E	21	1 year 295 days	Unknown (Med & France)	23
Booker	18	1 year 253 days	77 days	20
Boyd	19	2 year 138 days	1 year 330 days (Africa)	21
Bradbury	24	289 days	Unknown	25

Name	Age Enlisted	Total Service	France (Other Theatres)	Age Died
Braham	27	1 year 288 days	Unknown	29
Carter H	19	1 years 253 days	Unknown	20
Cowburn	24	3 years 117 days	2 years 21 days	29
Dixon	24	4 years +	3 years + (Med & France)	28
Doughty	21	102 days	50 days	21
Downend	26	2 years 85 days +	1 year 162 days	29
Green	32	3 years 56 days	2 years 250 days	35
Haigh	26	2 years 139 days	173 days	29
Hall	21	1 year 57 days	Unknown	22
Hirst	24	3 years +	3 years 189 days	28
Jones	20	2 years 227 days	14 days	23
Marshall	25	2 years ?	268 days	27
Moore	34	2 years +	1 year 191 days	37
Potter ED	17	1 year 121 days	107 days	19
Potter FJ	21	1 year 300 days ?	1 year 102 days	23
Poxon	17	1 year 172 days	16 days	19
Savage	22	344 days	176 days	23
Shipley	c20	1 year 330 days ?	1 year 30 days ?	21
Speight	21	1 year 231 days	200 days ?	23
Swift	28	1 year 295 days	194 days (Med & France)	30
Thompson AH	20	1 year 116 days	194 days (Med & France)	22
Thomson CC	24	2 years	1 year 240 days ?	25
Timson	23	2 years ?	1 year 324 days	25
Warr	19	4 years 85 days	4 years 9 days	23
Westby	19	2 years 148 days	1 year 363 days	22
Whitelock	19	1 year 44 days	165 days	20
Willott	25	2 years +	1 year 67 days	27
Wood	31	140 days ?	6 days	32

Special efforts made to enlist
These men made several attempts to enlist before being accepted:
Fairley because of his defective vision
Green discharged after 42 days as unfit but accepted six weeks later
Speight because of his height
Willott had an eye operation to meet the required vision standard to enlist
(Poxon had an eye operation after enlisting but should not have served on the front)

Summary of total length of service (36 Old Boys)

less than 1 year	5 (Armitage, Bradbury, Doughty, Savage, Wood)
1 to 2 years	14
2 to 3 years	11
3 to 4 years	3
more than 4 years	3 (Batley AG, Dixon, Warr)

Service overseas

Warr	RAMC	4 years 9 days	longest service overseas
Dixon & Hirst	Army	3 + years overseas	longest service in action
Green	Army	2 years 250 days	longest service at the front
Jones, Poxon & Wood	Army	less than 16 days	shortest service

Theatres of war

Europe – Western Front
Europe – Greece, Italy
Africa – Egypt, Namibia, East & South
Israel & Palestine – Jerusalem

3 Regiments (at death)

Many men enlisted in one Regiment but were later transferred to another; I have used the latest details. They served in 35 different Regiments or other services, with 55 different Battalions etc.

Regiment etc	Battalion etc	
Canadian Infantry	46th	Royston
Black Watch (Royal Highlanders)	6th	Joyner
Border Regiment	8th	Utley
Cheshire Regiment	2nd	Speight
Coldstream Guards	1st	Kellett
Duke of Wellington (West Riding)	1st/2nd attached 9th	Jones
Durham Light Infantry	1st/8th	Wood
East Yorkshire Regiment	7th	Bambridge, Lindley,
–"–	?	Hall
General List (CWGC)	Att'd 94th Light TM Bty	Potter (FJ) – see 14th YLR

Regiment etc	Battalion etc	
King's Own Yorkshire Light Infantry	1st	Allott
	7th	Moore
	9th	McNaughton
King's Royal Rifle Corps	16th	Skues
	21st	Bradbury, Nicholson
Lancashire Fusiliers	3rd/5th	Lindley (FM)
Leicestershire Regiment	8th	Haigh
	10th Bn att'd 7th	Joyce
Lincolnshire Regiment	10th	Carter (H), Cowburn
London Regiment	(London Scottish)	Barraclough
	2nd/14th 20th	Hirst
Manchester Regiment	4th Bn att'd 11th	Batley (AG)
Northumberland Fusiliers	26th (Tyneside Irish)	Downend
Oxford & Bucks Light Infantry	2nd	Kilner
Royal Engineers	"M" Coy No. 3 Spec Rly Bn	Doughty
Royal Field Artillery	?	Kelsey
	70th Bty 34th Bde	Laycock (DS)
	D Bty 162nd Bde	Williamson
Royal Fusiliers	23rd	Willott
	26th City of London	Laycock (BHR), Saville
Royal Garrison Artillery	293rd Siege Bty	Booker
	11th Hull Heavy Bty	Boyd
Royal Horse Artillery	"K" Bty 4th Bde	Stuart
Royal Inniskilling Fusiliers	2nd Bn att'd 4th	Thompson (CC)
Royal Warwickshire Regiment	16th Bn ?	Parkin
Sherwood Foresters (Notts & Derby Regt)	1st/8th	Armitage
	2nd	Poxon
	15th	Potter (ED)
South Lancashire Regiment	4th att'd 12th Somerset L I	Clarke
West Yorkshire Regt (Prince of Wales' Own)	1st/5th	Carter (JR)
	10th	Marshall
	15th	Mason

Regiment etc	Battalion etc	
York & Lancaster Regiment	1st/4th	Wilby, Green,
	1st/5th	Thompson JE, Feasby, Heathcote
	2nd/4th	Dixon
	7th	Gregory
	10th	Timson, Savage
	12th (Sheffield)	Batley (E), Baylis, Braham, Gill, Swift, Thompson (AH) Normansell,
	13th (1st Barnsley)	Atha, Bakel, Fairley,
	14th (2nd Barnsley)	Potter FJ, Quest
Yorkshire Regiment	6th	Shipley
Other Services		
Army Service Corps	74th Mechanical Transport Co	Choyce
Royal Army Medical Corps (RAMC)	7th Casualty Clearing Station	Warr
	att'd 7th Bn King's Own (Royal Lancaster)	Knowles
Royal Air Force	27th Kite Balloon Sect (support service)	Litherland
		Banks
	55th Sqdrn	Whitelock
	80th Sqdrn	Smith (George)
Royal Marine Light Infantry RN Div	190th Bde MG Coy	Westby
Merchant Navy	Wireless Operator	Wemyss

York & Lancaster Regiment

At least 27 out of 76 men served with different Battalions of this Regiment at some time (36%).

Sheffield City	(12th Battalion)	6
Barnsley Pals	(13th and 14th)	7
	13th (First)	Cyril Burton Dixon*, Jack Normansell
	14th (Second)	John Bruce Atha, Frank Bakel, Duncan Fairley, Francis John Potter, Harold Quest

* Dixon transferred Battalion before his death

4 Ranks other than Private (at death)

27 Officers (36%)
14 higher rank than Private (18%)
Total = 41 (54%)

Officers (Commissioned)			**Non Commissioned**	
Captain	Lieutenant	2nd Lieutenant	Lance Corporal Sergeant	Other
Dixon	Fairley	Allott	**Corporal**	**Gunner**
Downend	Joyce	Bakel	Atha	Booker
Knowles	Kelsey	Bambridge	Braham	Boyd
Normansell	Lindley	Batley A G	Wemyss	Moore
Quest	Westby	Clarke		Williamson
Thompson C C	Whitelock	Feasby	**Lance Corporal**	
		Gregory	Bradbury	**Pioneer**
		Hirst J	Hall	Doughty
		Jones R	Heathcote	
		Laycock D S	Mason	**Air Mechanic**
		Marshall	McNaughton	**2nd Class**
		Moore	Nicholson	Litherland
		Potter F J	Savage	
		Shipley		**Rifleman**
		Smith	**Regimental/Company**	Skues
			Quartermaster Sergeant	
			Cowburn	**Driver**
			Green	Stuart
			Sergeant	
			Speight	
			Lance Sergeant	
			Timson	
6	**6**	**15**	**14**	

5 Awarded Distinguised Conduct Medal, Military Cross or Medal

The Distinguished Conduct Medal (DCM) was introduced in 1854 for Other Ranks for 'gallantry in the field'.

The Military Cross (MC) was introduced on 1 January 1915 for Officers for 'distinguished and meritorious service in time of war'. The Military Medal (MM) was introduced for Other Ranks on 25 March 1916. The Royal Warrants instituting both awards appeared in *The London Gazette*, and by 1920, over 120,000 MMs and 40,000 MCs had been gazetted.

Harry Liddall Bambridge	DSO
Cyril Burton Dixon	MC
James Hirst	MM
Henry Rylands Knowles	DCM and MC
Harold Quest	MC
Thomas Westby	MC

Appendix IV

Deaths and Cemeteries or Memorials

---

1 Deaths

1915	3	Charles Waldegrave Wood was the first to die (26 April 1915)
1916	30	
1917	18	
1918	24	
1919	1	Ernest William Litherland was the last to die (22 February 1919)

Deaths were mostly fairly spread out but there are some concentrations reflecting involvement in key battles, eg Somme and Arras.

1 July 1916, the first day of the Battle of the Somme
10 men were killed with 2 others dying soon afterwards; an unknown number were wounded. At least 20 other Old Boys survived action on 1 July and died later, more than 15 on the Somme in 1916.

John Bruce Atha	YLR 14th	(Barnsley Pal)
Edward Batley	YLR 12th	(Sheffield City)
Laurence Baylis	YLR 12th	(Sheffield City)
George Braham	YLR 12th	(Sheffield City)
Duncan Fairley	YLR 14th	(Barnsley Pal)
Sidney Gill	YLR 12th	(Sheffield City)
Herbert HJ Mason	West Yorks 15th (Prince of Wales' Own)	
Francis J Potter	YLR 14th	(B Pal / Brigade TMB)
James S Swift	YLR 12th	(Sheffield City)
Arthur H Thompson	YLR 12th	(Sheffield City)

Edward Haigh	Leicestershire Regiment	15 July 1916
James C Speight	Cheshire Regiment	19 July 1916

Cause of death

55 Killed in Action	(direct consequence of battle, includes missing presumed dead)
16 Died of Wounds	(as direct consequence but after receiving medical attention, includes illness)
4 Died Other Reasons	(non military causes eg disease or accident) Banks – suicide at Blandford Camp Boyd – bicycle accident while at home on leave Hall – TB at home after discharge (not recognised by CWGC) Wemyss – in hospital after an operation (not recognised by CWGC)

2 Cemeteries and Memorials

76 men's bodies lay in 52 different locations:
44 Cemeteries
8 Memorials

Name	Area	Casualty
Belgium		
Bleuet Farm Cemetery	West Vlaanderen	Gregory
Coxyde Military Cemetery, Koksijde	West Vlaanderen	Lindley (FM)
Derry House Cemetery No. 2	West Vlaanderen	Timson
Kemmel Chateau Military Cemetery	West Vlaanderen	Armitage
Lijssenthoek Military Cemetery, Poperinge	West Vlaanderen	Green
Nine Elms British Cemetery, Poperinge	West Vlaanderen	Williamson
Ploegsteert Memorial	Hainaut	Utley
Ridge Wood Military Cemetery	West Vlaanderen	Laycock (BHR)
Tyne Cot Memorial, Zonnebeke	West Vlaanderen	Feasby, Heathcote, Potter (ED), Thompson (JE) Wilby
Ypres (Menin Gate) Memorial	West Vlaanderen	Wood

Name	Area	Casualty
England		
Barnsley Cemetery	Yorkshire	Kelsey
Cawthorne Churchyard	Yorkshire	Wemyss
St Peter's Cemetery, Hoyland	Yorkshire	Hall
St Peter's Churchyard, Felkirk	Yorkshire	Boyd, Litherland
Blandford Cemetery	Dorset	Banks
Greece		
Lahana Military Cemetery, Lachanas Village	Thessaloniki	Choyce
Israel & Palestine		
Jerusalem War Cemetery	North of walled city	Barraclough
Italy		
Magnaboschi British Cemetery, Cesuna Village	Vicenza	Booker
France		
Achiet-le-Grand Communal Cemetery Extension	Pas de Calais	Cowburn
A. I. F. Burial Ground, Flers	Somme	Batley (E)
Arras Memorial, Faubourg	Pas de Calais	Bambridge, Marshall, Poxon, Skues
Aulnoy Communal Cemetery	Nord	Royston
Awoingt British Cemetery	Nord	Dixon
Bailleul Road East Cemetery, St Laurent-Blangy	Pas de Calais	Bakel,
Bancourt British Cemetery	Pas de Calais	Moore
Beaulencourt British Cemetery, Ligny-Thilloy	Pas de Calais	Laycock (DS)
Becourt Military Cemetery, Becordel-Becourt	Somme	Carter (H)
Charmes Military Cemetery, Essegney	Vosges	Whitelock
Connaught Cemetery, Thiepval	Somme	Carter (JR)
Courcelette British Cemetery	Somme	Willott
Ecoivres Military Cemetery, Mont-St-Eloi	Pas de Calais	Doughty
Etaples Military Cemetery	Pas de Calais	Stuart
Euston Road Cemetery, Colincamps	Somme	Fairley

Name	Area	Casualty
Flatiron Copse Cemetery, Mametz	Somme	Haigh
Guard's Cemetery, Lesboeufs	Somme	Bradbury
Hebuterne Communal Cemetery	Pas de Calais	Quest
Ligny St Flochel British Cemetery, Averdoignt	Pas de Calais	Warr
Loos Memorial	Pas de Calais	Kilner
Luke Copse British Cemetery, Puiseux	Pas de Calais	Swift
Metz-en-Couture Communal Cemetery British Extension	Pas de Calais	Westby
Ovillers Military Cemetery	Somme	Thompson (CC)
Peronne Communal Cemetery Extension	Somme	Clarke
Pozieres Memorial	Somme	McNaughton
Quarry Cemetery, Marquion	Pas de Calais	Batley (AG)
Rocquigny – Equancourt Road British Cemetery	Somme	Jones
Romeries Communal Cemetery Extension	Nord	Allott
Serre Road Cemetery No. 1	Pas de Calais	Normansell
St Martin Calvaire British Cemetery, St Martin-sur-Cojeul	Pas de Calais	Downend
Thiepval Memorial	Somme	Atha, Baylis, Braham, Gill, Joyce, Joyner, Kellett, Knowles, Mason, Nicholson, Parkin, Potter (FJ), Savage, Saville, Shipley, Speight Thompson (AH),
Varennes Military Cemetery	Somme	Lindley (F)
Vignacourt British Cemetery	Somme	Smith
Vis en Artois Memorial	Pas de Calais	Hirst

Summary:	**Men (Cemeteries)**		**Men (Memorials)**	
Belgium	7	(7)	7	(3)
England	6	(5)		
France	29	(29)	24	(5)
Greece	1	(1)		
Israel & Palestine	1	(1)		
Italy	1	(1)		
Total	45	(44)	31	(8)

In addition to the Commonwealth War Graves Commission Cemeteries and Memorials, the Old Boys are listed on a large number of War Memorials in Barnsley District and elsewhere in England; this includes being remembered on family headstones.

Appendix V

Other Brothers and Brothers-in-Law of the 76 Old Boys who Attended the Holgate

32 brothers attended the Grammar School (BHGS), 20 of whom also served in the First World War (FWW)
42 brothers served in FWW, 5 of whom died
4 brothers-in-law served, 2 of whom died
Some of these men also contributed articles or letters to *Alumnus*

Brothers			**Article**
Reginald Smith ALLOTT	BHGS		178
Walter BAKEL	BHGS	FWW	195
Bertram Arthur BAMBRIDGE	BHGS	FWW	202
Arnold Walker BANKS	FWW		209
James BATLEY	BHGS	FWW	225
John William BATLEY	BHGS	FWW	226
Raymond BAYLIS	FWW	DIED	229
William Stanley BAYLIS	FWW		230
Arthur BOOKER	FWW		235
Ernest Goodall BRAHAM	BHGS	FWW	249
Arthur Goodall BRAHAM	BHGS	FWW	250
Andrew Fletcher DOUGHTY	BHGS	FWW	280
Joseph Neatby DOUGHTY	BHGS	FWW	281
George William DOWNEND	BHGS		289
Joseph FAIRLEY	BHGS	FWW	297
Cyril FEASBY	FWW		302
Clifford FEASBY	FWW		302
Douglas John FEASBY	FWW		302

Brothers			Article
Maurice GREEN	BHGS	FWW	310
Douglas GREEN	BHGS	FWW	310
Henry GREGORY	BHGS		315
Walter Bertram HAIGH	FWW	KILLED	318
Joseph Reginald HAIGH	FWW	DIED	318
William Henry JOYNER	BHGS	FWW	353
Raymond KELLETT	FWW	POW	362
Cyril Reginald KNOWLES	BHGS	FWW	381 *Alumnus* p.612
Ernest Arthur KNOWLES	BHGS	FWW	382 *Alumnus* p.611
Cyril LITHERLAND	BHGS	FWW	407
George Thomas LITHERLAND	FWW		407
James Arthur MARSHALL	FWW		412
Walter Cecil MOORE	BHGS		422
Arthur NICHOLSON	BHGS		428
Ernest Carroll NICHOLSON	FWW		428
Frank Cockroft NICHOLSON	BHGS	FWW	429
William James NICHOLSON	FWW		430
Harry POTTER	FWW		448
Alan Reasbeck POTTER	FWW		448
Richard Leslie POTTER	BHGS		448
Arthur Charles QUEST	BHGS		464
Thomas Percival QUEST	BHGS	FWW	465
William Henry SAVAGE	FWW	DIED	473
Bernard Walter SAVILLE	BHGS	FWW	478
Vincent SKUES	FWW		488
Thomas Dean SPEIGHT	BHGS		501
Stanley WARR	FWW		539
Frank Hellewell WESTBY	BHGS	FWW	549 *Alumnus* p.635
Arthur Thomas WHITELOCK	BHGS	FWW	556 *Alumnus* p.641
Cyril Carr WILLIAMSON	BHGS	FWW	564 *Alumnus* p.657
Frank WILLOTT	BHGS	FWW	571
Ernest Spencer WILLOTT	BHGS	FWW	572 *Alumnus* p.665
George Reginald WOOD	BHGS		580
Brothers-in-law			
Francis Pimblett INSLEY (Bambridge)	FWW		203
Bernard Washington KILNER (Booker)	FWW	KILLED	235
Harold Cecil LATHAM (Boyd)	FWW		242
Claude SCOTT (Lindleys)	FWW	KILLED	401

Appendix VI

School Staff Appointed from 1888 to 1918

Information from the Staff Register, started by Rev Butler when he became the first Headmaster of the Barnsley Holgate Grammar School in 1888.

The 76 Old Boys would have been taught by some of these Teachers. I have not distinguished between permanent and visiting or temporary Teachers, especially during the war. I have not indicated those who were Form Masters. Those with their Staff Register Number underlined served in the First World War (Part 1. Chapter 19).

SR	Name	Started	Left	Comments
1	Rev Charles Stokes Butler	1/1/1888	29/7/1919	Headmaster
2	Thomas Parks	16/9/1891	28/7/1927	Chemistry, Physics
3	Reginald Trenchard de Pittard	16/9/1903	31/7/1919	Geography, History
4	Samuel Horace Miller	17/9/1904	12/3/1936	English, Maths, French, Latin
5	Charles Edmund Gaze Walker	15/9/1904	20/12/1912	French, General Subjects
6	Evan Davies	11/10/1904	18/12/1918	English, Various, Editor of *Alumnus*
7	Samuel Rendell Tomlinson	25/7/1905	29/7/1909	Chemistry, Physics, Maths
8	William John Berryman	15/9/1905	1930	Latin, English, History, RI, Algebra
9	Charles Edwin Powell	?/9/1906	31/8/1944	Maths, Scripture
10	Herbert Champion	17/9/1907	12/12/1907	French, Various
11	Bernard Charles de Wiederhold Siffken	14/4/1907	30/3/1908	English, Latin, French
12	George Henry Rees	14/1/1908	31/8/1944	French
<u>13</u>	Captain John Broderick	15/9/1896	?/7/1914	Physical Exercises

SR	Name	Started	Left	Comments
14	Edwin Haigh	30/4/1899	?	Art, Designer of *Alumnus* cover etc
15	Joseph Soar	1/5/1904	4/2/1915	Music, Singing
16	Arthur Whittaker	16/9/1905	29/1/1943	Art, Modelling
17	Leonard Atkinson	28/1/1907	29/1/1943	Woodwork
18	James Westbury	16/9/1908	29/7/1909	English, Maths, Latin
19	Cyril James Peddle	16/9/1909	14/4/1916	Chemistry, Physics
20	George Edgar Joyce (Died in WW1)	16/9/1909	19/12/1913	Geography
21	John Whitehead Cheshire	12/1/1911	11/4/1911	English
22	William Edward Evans	14/1/1913	31/7/1942	French, History
23	Herbert Marshall (Died in WW1)	13/1/1914	28/7/1915	Geography
24	William Edward Ashworth	12/1/1915	29/10/1917	Swedish Drill
25	Henry Nelson Horton	11/2/1915	27/7/1918	Music, Singing
26	Thomas Shaw	15/9/1915	23/3/1916	Geography
27	William Broad	15/9/1915	29/7/1919	Art (Head of Barnsley School of Art)
28	Arthur Bernard Williams	2/5/1916	25/7/1916	Science, Maths
29	Arthur Stephen Matthews	2/5/1916	?	Geography
30	Harry Casmay Rands	14/9/1916	4/4/1917	Science, Maths
31	Cyril Edward McGuire	14/9/1916	30/7/1920	French
32	Ethel Rees	21/9/1916	29/7/1919	Various
33	Thomas Edward Wilson	7/5/1917	1938	Science, Maths
34	Henry Edward Allen	18/9/1917	19/12/1919	English
35	John Archibald Graham Greenhalgh	?/5/1918	18/12/1918	Unknown
36	Frank Thomas Barton	17/9/1918	18/12/1918	Languages
37	Dorothy Phyllis Roberts	17/9/1918	17/12/1924	Various, Maths
38	William Granger	17/9/1918	30/7/1929	Music, Singing

Salary

1904	£140 to £200
1912	£120 to 175
1918	£220 to £378

Bibliography

Barnsley Archives and Local Studies

The Holgate Collection:
Admission Registers from 1888 (A/3428/E/1/1/1–3)
Staff Register from 1888 (A/3428/E/2/1)
Alumnus magazines from 1913 to 1930 (A/3428/E/9/2/1–4)
Programmes and Ephemera 1888 to 1919 (A/3418/E/6/1/1–3)
Manager's Letter Books 1887 to 1912 (A/3428/E/3/1/1 & 6)
Trustee Records (A/2086/T)

The Cooper Collection:
Letter dated 7 February 1926 from John Clegg of Newman & Bond Solicitors to the Trustees "Inspection of Keresforth House" (Ref: SY/386/B)
Anon, *Bishop Holgate Grammar School – A Short History of the School and the Foundation* (373.24)
Burland, John Hugh, *The Annals of Barnsley 1744 to 1864* (microfilm)
Clay (ed.), John William, *Yorkshire Royalist Composition Papers* (942.74)
Greenland, Reginald Harry, *Barnsley & District Grammar School (Its Origins and History)* (373.24)
Hargreave, John, *A Manual for the Use of Barnsley Grammar School* (373.24)
White, William, *1837 Directory of the West Riding of Yorkshire* (942.746)
Uncatalogued collection of archives for James Stuart Swift.

Books

Anon., *The History of the Archbishop Holgate Hospital in Hemsworth 1555–2005 and the Life of its Founder Robert Holgate* (Hemsworth: Holgate Trustees, 2005)
Bridger, Geoff, *The Great War Handbook* (Barnsley: Pen & Sword, 2009)
Cooksey, Jon, *Barnsley Pals* (Barnsley: Pen & Sword, 2008)
De Ruvigny, Marquis of, *Roll of Honour 1914 to 1918* (Uckfield: Naval & Military Press, reprint of 1922 edition)
Elliott, Brian, *The Making of Barnsley* (Barnsley: Wharncliffe Books, 2004)

Gibson Ralph & Oldfield Paul *Sheffield City Battalion* (Pen and Sword 2006)
Howse, Geoffrey, *Foul Deeds and Suspicious Deaths in and Around Barnsley* (Barnsley: Wharncliffe Books, 2007)
Hoyle, Eli, *A History of Barnsley* (Barnsley: Barnsley Family History Society, n.d.)
Hoyle, Eli, *Barnsley Streets and Byways* (Barnsley: Barnsley Family History Society, n.d.)
Hunter, Rev. Joseph, *South Yorkshire Vol II The History and Topography of the Deanery of Doncaster* (London: Printed for the author by J.B. Nichols, 1831)
Jackson, Barry, *Cawthorne 1790–1990* (Cawthorne: Cawthorne Jubilee Museum and Taylor Hill, 1991)
Prince, Rev. J.F., *History of the Parish of Silkstone* (Penistone: J.H. Wood, The Don Press, 1922)
Tasker, E.G., *Barnsley Streets Volume 1* (Barnsley: Pen & Sword, 2010)
Turner Benjamin *St George's Church, Barnsley Retrospect 1821 to 1912* (R E Griffiths Ltd 1915)
Warr, Peter, *Sheffield's Great War and Beyond* (Barnsley: Pen & Sword, 2015)
Warrington, Peter, *For Distinguished & Meritorious Services in Time of War* (Uckfield: The Naval & Military Press, 2015)
Wilkinson, Joseph, *Worthies, Families and Celebrities of Barnsley and the District* (London: Bemrose & Sons, 1883)

Electronic Sources

Dugdale, Sir William, The Visitation of the County of Yorke begun in anno Domini MDCLXV (1665) and finished in anno Domini MDCLXV1 (1666) (edited by Robert Davies for the Surtees Society, 1859, Durham Publishers) online at <https://archive.org/stream/visitationyorke00dugdrich/visitationyorke00dugdrich_djvu.txt > (utilised in 2013, checked 4 September 2015)
Lawton, George 1842 [from old catalog]; Ducarel, Andrew Coltree 1842, *Collectio Rerum Ecclesiasticarum de Dioecesi Eboracensi (London, J G and F Rivington [etc]; York, H Bellerby, 1842*) (translation: "Collections Relative to Churches and Chapels Within the Diocese of York") online at <https://archive.org/stream/collectiorerum00ducagoog#page/n7> (utilised in 2013, checked 4 September 2015)